Francis H. Dunwell

A Commentary on the Authorized English Version of the Gospel According to St. John

compared with the Sinaitic, Vatican, and Alexandrine manuscripts, and also with

Dean Alford's revised translation

Francis H. Dunwell

A Commentary on the Authorized English Version of the Gospel According to St. John
compared with the Sinaitic, Vatican, and Alexandrine manuscripts, and also with Dean Alford's revised translation

ISBN/EAN: 9783337227654

Printed in Europe, USA, Canada, Australia, Japan

Cover: Foto ©Lupo / pixelio.de

More available books at **www.hansebooks.com**

A COMMENTARY

ON THE

AUTHORIZED ENGLISH VERSION

OF THE

GOSPEL ACCORDING TO ST. JOHN;

COMPARED WITH THE

SINAITIC, VATICAN, AND ALEXANDRINE MANUSCRIPTS,

AND ALSO WITH

DEAN ALFORD'S REVISED TRANSLATION.

BY

THE REV. FRANCIS HENRY DUNWELL, B.A.,

VICAR OF HENSALL WITH HECK,
(LATE HASTINGS EXHIBITIONER, QUEEN'S COLLEGE, OXFORD).

LONDON:
J. T. HAYES, LYALL PLACE, EATON SQUARE; AND
4, HENRIETTA STREET, COVENT GARDEN.
1872.

TO

THE HONOURABLE CHARLES L. WOOD,

THIS VOLUME

IS

RESPECTFULLY DEDICATED,

AS A REPRESENTATIVE OF THE LAYMEN OF ENGLAND,

WHO ARE STRIVING TO SECURE,

FOR THE ENGLISH CHURCH,

THE OLD ENGLISH DOGMATIC TEACHING.

PREFACE.

During the thirty years that I have been in Holy Orders, I have watched with eager interest the various Commentaries that have been published in England on different portions of the Scriptures. To many of these too much praise cannot be given, especially for the careful attention which has been paid of late years to the teaching of the Scriptures on the Incarnation, and on the effects of the Incarnation on man's present life, not merely on his future state, but on his present life, as preparatory for his future. But there is still required, as it appears to me, a Commentary on the New Testament for English readers and others, more critical in its character, and at the same time more Catholic in its doctrinal tone, as well as more continuous and connected in its explanations, than is usually the case with Commentaries intended for general use.

The present volume is submitted to the public, with a view to ascertain how far a Commentary of this kind, and by the same hand, would be acceptable to members of the English Church. The object aimed at throughout has been, to combine the ancient Faith of the Church with the results of modern investigation. A few words about its leading characteristics will not be deemed out of place.

In preparing the following pages I have especially endeavoured to meet the case of that large and increasing class of intelligent readers, who feel a warm interest in every thing that tends to the elucidation of the Scriptures, but who lack either the opportunity or the inclination to consult numerous books of reference. Considerable advantage has been taken of the immense accessions, which the last half century has added to our stores for the illustration of the Old and New Testament, and in a no less degree of our English Authorised Translation of them. Among these it will be sufficient to refer to the important addition made within the last few years to our Manuscripts of the text, to the more critical examination of the historical documents relating to the Jews, and to the various nations that were contemporary with them, and to the more accurate knowledge which we possess of the topography of Palestine.

The three principal objects, which I have kept in view, are:—

1. To lay before the reader St. John's Gospel in a form so correct, that no exception could possibly be made against it, either as a text or as a translation. This has been accomplished chiefly through the labours of Professor Tischendorf, and the late Dean Alford and his four coadjutors.

Each verse is given from the Authorised Version, and under that whatever various readings there are, in either the Sinaitic, Vatican, or Alexandrine Manuscripts, and then any difference of translation as revised by the late Dean Alford and his friends.

2. To give the sense of St. John's words as interpreted by the best Commentators from the earliest times. After several unsuccessful trials to appropriate to each author his own, as far as possible, I relinquished the attempt, and have contented myself with endeavouring to weave into one connected whole, and within reasonable limits, interpretations ranging from the third century to the nineteenth. No age or school has been exclusively regarded, but what appeared best in each has been selected. In this Commentary no claim is made to originality. My object has not been to invent new interpretations, or new ways of expressing old interpretations, but to make use of other men's successful labours, and to throw these into a popular form for the common good.

3. By means of an introductory note to each chapter, as well as by foot-notes, to show the exact meaning of the original text or of the English translation; to illustrate the history, geography, and customs referred to, and by means of extracts from travellers, chiefly modern, to bring before the mind of the reader a living picture of the various localities and scenes that are named. I have preferred, where possible, to give the glowing description of the travellers themselves, rather than a more concise but necessarily more dry summary of their words by myself. In this part each statement is attested by the name of the writer. I am answerable only for the selection.

In the foot-notes will also be found all the most important improvements in translation, and illustrations of the grammatical construction, that have been suggested by Bishop Middleton in his *Treatise on the Greek Article*, by Archbishop Trench in his *Synonyms of the New Testament*, by Winer in his *Grammar of the New Testament diction,* and by Dr. J. B. Lightfoot in his *Revision of the New Testament,* as well as by others.

It is acknowledged on all hands, that the best key to unlock the meaning and spirit of any ancient document is contemporary literature. To see the full force of this as applied to the New Testament, we have only to call to mind, how minute and numerous the religious observances of the Jews were in the days of our Saviour, and how intimately these were interwoven with all their public, social, and domestic life. To such a degree was this the case, that the life of a truly devout Jew, according to their meaning of the term, must have been, so to speak, an endless ritual. But the great mass of these rites and ceremonies were not prescribed in the Law of Moses, but in that body of traditionary interpretations, that had been accumulating for ages, and which in the time of our Saviour had become both burdensome to the people, and destructive of the very spirit and intention of the Law. These traditionary rules had succeeded in rendering the Law not only nugatory, as to any moral effect on the Jewish mind, but positively injurious to it. Our Saviour's denunciations are not directed against the Law, but against their observance of it, and against those who insisted on such observance. "Woe unto you Scribes and Pharisees, woe unto you Lawyers," were His usual words; and to enter into the full meaning of His words, a knowledge of the received interpretation of the Law is scarcely less necessary than a knowledge of the Law itself. For we miss the point in a rebuke, when we know not the nature of the abuse, which calls forth the rebuke. Among the most successful students in this branch of literature, Dr. John Lightfoot, Master of Catherine Hall, Cambridge, and who died 1675, has always stood in the foremost rank. Few greater services, as I conceive, can be rendered to the English Church, than to make Dr. Lightfoot's learning more accessible to the general reader. Probably no man ever possessed the same amount of Rabbinical learning, with the same accurate scholarship, that he did. But this, imbedded as it is in two thick folio, or in thirteen octavo volumes, is little known except to students. Copious illustrations of the meaning of St. John's words have been given from Lightfoot, based on the Rabbinical traditions.

It will thus be seen that an attempt has here been made to bring the information, furnished to the public in the shape of a popular Commentary, up to a level with the knowledge and the scholarship of the present day, and that without any faltering as regards the

b

Faith once delivered. The Christian Religion has nothing to fear from real learning. For past experience shows, that whatever new discoveries are made in any branch of science or literature, so far as they bear on Holy Scripture or on the Christian Religion, they help to confirm and illustrate them. All, that is required, is a full and fair investigation, that the science be sufficiently understood, and fairly applied. For Christians can scarcely be expected to surrender their Faith to crude theories, or to deductions drawn from imperfect information.

It has been rather the fashion of late years to believe, that the Greek Text, from which the English Authorised Translation was made, was in a state of almost hopeless corruption, and that the Translation itself was, to say the least, full of inaccuracies, if not of actual mistranslations. The labours and publications of Professor Tischendorf and of the late Dean Alford, have therefore a peculiar interest for English Churchmen. For the one may be said to have been investigating the genuineness of our text of the New Testament, and the other the accuracy of our Translation. No one will question their competency for the task which they undertook. They have laboured for years, each in his own department, as men only labour, who have a love for their work. The results of Professor Tischendorf's labours not only prove, but put it into the power of every man to verify this statement for himself, that the Greek Text of the English Authorised Translation is singularly correct, and that the emendations introduced from the Sinaitic, Vatican, and Alexandrine Manuscripts, the three oldest and most valuable, are, with few exceptions, of the most trifling nature. The labours of Dean Alford and of his four coadjutors are also valuable in many points of view, and not the least, as proving the general accuracy of the Authorised Translation. The Church of England owes a large debt of gratitude to these men for their respective publications, as showing the hollowness of objections, which from their very nature many could make, but few were able to answer.

One other result of their labours is exceedingly satisfactory. Neither the emendations made in the Text nor the alterations in the Translation have in any way affected, even in the slightest degree, any one single doctrine of the Christian Religion. Improvements many they have doubtless introduced, both in the way of a more genuine correctness of the Text, and also of a more scholarly accuracy in the Translation. But the Christian Faith stands exactly what it was, and as it was, before their publications.

From what has been effected by the labours of individuals in a private capacity, we may fairly infer what will be the result of the labours of men, when united together for the common object of revising our Translation of Holy Scripture. If their purpose be a thoroughly honest one, namely, to make our Venerable Translation a better representative of our improved knowledge of ancient Manuscripts, as well as of our more delicate and correct rendering of the Greek, with the ample materials which we have at command, the gain will be immense. A judicious reproduction, for instance, of Trench, Alford, and Tischendorf, would be a blessing acknowledged by all. Our Translation would be a more exact and faithful representation of the original, and that original would be more like what it was, when it left the hands of the Evangelists and Apostles; but there would be no alteration in the doctrines of the Church, not one, and scarcely a single text would be withdrawn from its office of proving what it was thought to prove before. But if with this there be also allied the sinister object of altering our ecclesiastical expressions of Christian Truth, in order to introduce into them unostentatiously, it may be, a greater degree of laxity, by rendering them into more colourless terms, the blessing will prove a curse, and the Revisers will succeed, not in producing a Bible for the English Church, but in leaving a legacy for the various English Sects to wrangle over. To attempt to effect a theological revolution, under the cover of a purely scientific revision, would be a mistake, and would certainly entail failure on the whole scheme.

In order to represent, as far as possible, the knowledge and the acquirements of the present day, the notes in this Commentary have been taken in a great measure from the works of living authors. The following is a rough classification of the writers quoted, many of whom will be recognised as eminent authorities in their own department.

VARIOUS READINGS OF THE GREEK TEXT.—Professor Tischendorf. Mr. Scrivener, Mr. Burgon.

CRITICAL SCHOLARSHIP.—Dr. John Lightfoot, (17th century), Bishop Middleton, Dean Alford, Archbishop Trench, Dr. J. B. Lightfoot, Dr. Winer, &c.

TOPOGRAPHY AND CUSTOMS OF PALESTINE.—Bishop Pococke, (18th century), Dr. Robinson, Dean Stanley, Dr. Williams, Thomson, Lady Strangford, (Miss Beaufort,) Miss Rogers, Lord

Lindsay, Carnarvon, Mr. Porter, Hepworth Dixon, Captain Lynch, Macgregor, Wilson and Warren, and other members of the Palestine Exploration Society, &c.

HISTORICAL ANALYSIS.—The Right Hon. W. E. Gladstone, Canon Norris, Mr. Sanday, &c.

It only remains to add, that if this volume should meet with sufficient favour to justify me in having incurred the risk of its publication, it will shortly be followed by a similar Commentary on the other three Gospels, treated separately and synoptically, and eventually by a Commentary on the Epistles.

HENSALL VICARAGE,
    June 4th, 1872.

INTRODUCTORY CHAPTER.

THE FOURTH GOSPEL.

DID St. John the Apostle write the Fourth Gospel? The Primitive Church, which had the best means of knowing, said that he did, and affirmed this with singular fulness and unanimity. Within the last few years this question has been again raised, and with the purpose of giving to it a different answer.

The late Dean Alford, a cautious writer, and one who could not be accused of giving undue weight to the claim of divine Inspiration, which the Church makes for this Gospel, has thus summed up the evidence for and against the genuineness of St. John's Gospel, which is again but the summary of the arguments used by German writers, who have gone more minutely into this question than himself. Referring to Lücke's *Einlertung*, he says, "The result of his researches on this subject is, that down to the end of the second century the Gospel was by all recognised and attributed to the Apostle whose name it bears, with the sole exception of the Alogi, an unimportant sect in Asia Minor, who from excessive opposition to the heresy of Montanus, rejected both the Apocalypse and Gospel of John, as favouring (according to them) some of the views of that heretic. Such an exception rather strengthens than weakens the general evidence of ancient Christendom in its favour.

"Equally satisfactory is the testimony of the Fathers after the close of the second century. The citations by Irenæus from this Gospel are very frequent and express, both as to its canonicity and the name of its author. And his testimony is peculiarly valuable, because (1) he was an anti-Gnostic; (2) his acquaintance with the whole Church, Eastern and Western, was greater than that of any other ecclesiastical writer; and (3) in his youth he had conversed with Polycarp, himself a disciple of the Apostle John. Theophilus of Antioch, Tertullian, Clement of Alexandria, Hippolytus, Origen, Dionysius of Alexandria, Eusebius,—the ancient Syriac Version, the Peshito,—the adversaries of Christianity, Porphyry and Julian,—all these refer to the Gospel as without doubt the work of the Apostle John.

"We may then, *as far as antiquity is concerned*, regard its genuineness as established. But there is one circumstance which has furnished many modern writers with a ground for doubting this. Neither Papias, who carefully sought all that Apostles and apostolic men had related regarding the life of Christ,—nor Polycarp, who was himself a disciple of the Apostle John,—nor Barnabas, nor Clement of Rome, in their Epistles,—nor, lastly, Ignatius (in his genuine writings), makes any mention of, or allusion to, this Gospel. So that in the most ancient circle of ecclesiastical testimony, it appears to be unknown or not recognised.

"But this circumstance, when fairly considered in connection with *its universal recognition by writers following on these*, rather serves for a *confirmation of the genuineness* of the Gospel. It confessedly was written *late in the apostolic age*. As far, then, as silence (or apparent silence) can be valid as an argument, it seems to show that the recognition of this Gospel, as might have been expected, was *later than that of the others*. And it is some confirmation also of this view, that Papias, if Eusebius (iii. 39) gives his testimony entire, appears *not to recognise Luke's* Gospel, but only those of Matthew and Mark. It is remarkable, however, on the other hand, that Papias (Eusebius *ibid.*) recognises the First Epistle of John, which, as already remarked, was probably written after the Gospel. This would seem to make it probable that we have not in Eusebius the whole testimony of Papias given: for it would certainly seem from internal grounds that the First Epistle and the Gospel must stand or fall together.

"It is evident that too much stress must not be laid on the silence of Polycarp, from whom we have one short Epistle only. He also (apparently) was acquainted with the First Epistle of John. But he wrote with no purpose of giving testimony to the sacred books, and what reason therefore have we to expect in his Epistle quotations from, or allusions to, any particular book which did not happen to come within his design, and the subject of which he was treating?

"The same may be said of the silence of Barnabas, Hermas, and Ignatius. Had any intention existed on the part of the primitive Christian writers of informing posterity about books which were counted canonical in their days, their silence would be a strong argument against any particular book: but they had no such intention: their citations are fortuitous, and most of them loose and allusory only. So that we cannot argue from such silence to the recognition or otherwise of any book, unless it be universal and continuous, which is not the case with regard to the Gospel.

"Again, the *kind of testimony* furnished by Irenæus is peculiarly valuable. He does not relate *from whom* he had heard that John wrote a Gospel, but he treats and quotes it as a well-known and long-used book in the Christian Church. What could have induced Irenæus to do this, except *the fact of its being thus known and used?* So that this character of his testimony virtually carries it back farther than its actual date. Besides, when one who has had the means which Irenæus had of ascertaining the truth in a matter, asserts things respecting that matter, the ordinary and just method is to suppose that he *draws his information from his superior opportunities of gaining it*, even though he may not expressly say so: so that when Irenæus, who had conversed with Polycarp himself, the friend of the Apostle John, quotes this Gospel as the work of that Apostle, we may fairly presume that he had assured himself of this by the testimony of one so well capable of informing him."—Alford's Greek Testament, *Prolegomena*, p. 66.

In the face of such unanswerable reasoning as the above, the old objections have been again brought forward within the last few years, and in such a form as to catch the eye not of the student but of the general reader, who could not be prepared with an answer to them. It is asserted in a tone of confident boldness and pertinacity, "that no genuine testimony to the authenticity of this Gospel is of an earlier date than the year of Christ 180:" and "as far as regards external evidence—that there is not the same full and satisfactory amount of it in the case of the Fourth Gospel, as in that of the other three."

To see the force, or rather the want of force, in these objections, it will be necessary to call to mind who were the Christian writers which flourished within the first 180 years after the Birth of Christ, what was the nature of their writings, and in what state those writings have come down to us.

We shall not be far wrong in saying that the following list includes all the Christian writers of any note within the first 180 years after Christ, with the probable date at which they each flourished. St. Barnabas, A.D. 71; Clement, A.D. 96; Hermas, A.D. 100; St. Ignatius, A.D. 107; St. Polycarp, A.D. 108; Papias, A.D. 116; Justin Martyr, A.D. 140; Dionysius of Corinth, A.D. 170; Tatian, A.D. 172; Hegesippus, A.D. 173; Melito, A.D. 177; Irenæus, A.D. 178.

These writers may be conveniently divided into two classes:—
1. Those who are commonly spoken of as ancient Christian writers, because the names of some of their writings, or a few fragments of their writings, have been preserved by some later author, such as Eusebius and Jerome. 2. Those to whom have been generally attributed some of the treatises that are still extant. Under the first head five of these twelve writers must be ranked—Papias, Dionysius of Corinth, Tatian, Hegesippus, and Melito. No argument against the authenticity of St. John's Gospel can be drawn from the want of their evidence. For all that they wrote, with the exception of a few lines, is lost. The other seven—Barnabas, Clement, Hermas, Ignatius, Polycarp, Justin Martyr, Irenæus—will come under the second class, as being credited with having written some of the letters or early treatises that are still received as genuine. Of the first five no more need be said. Of the remaining seven, one, Barnabas, may have written his one work, Catholic Epistle, even before St. John wrote his

Gospel: four, Clement, Hermas, Ignatius, Polycarp, wrote so near the time that is usually assigned as the date of St. John's Gospel, A.D. 93, that we cannot reasonably expect to find in them any reference to it.

It would therefore appear that of the twelve Christian writers, who, as we know, flourished within the first 180 years after the Birth of Christ, there are only two, Justin Martyr and Irenæus, that are not precluded, either by the loss of their writings or by the lateness in the publication of St. John's Gospel, from handing down to us any testimony in favour of its genuineness and authenticity.

Lardner has shown that, there are not only proofs that Justin Martyr had read St. John's Gospel, but there are also unmistakeable references to it, even in those writings which are acknowledged by all to be by him. For instance:—

JUSTIN.	ST. JOHN.
Ὁ χριστὸς εἶπεν, ἂν μὴ ἀναγεννηθῆτε οὐ μὴ εἰσέλθητε εἰς τὴν βασιλείαν τῶν οὐρανῶν.	Ὁ Ἰησοῦς εἶπεν, Ἐὰν μή, τις γεννηθῇ ἄνωθεν οὐ δύναται ἰδεῖν τὴν βασιλείαν τοῦ Θεοῦ.
Christ said, Except ye be born again ye may not enter into the kingdom of heaven.	Jesus said, Except a man be born again he cannot see the kingdom of heaven. (iii. 3.)
Ὅτι, δὲ καὶ ἀδύνατον εἰς τὰς μήτρας τῶν τεκουσῶν τοὺς ἅπαξ γεννωμένους ἐμβῆναι, φανερὸν πᾶσίν ἐστι.	Πῶς δύναται ἄνθρωπος γεννηθῆναι γέρων ὤν; μὴ δύναται εἰς τὴν κοιλίαν τῆς μητρὸς αὐτοῦ δεύτερον εἰσελθεῖν καὶ γεννηθῆναι;
But, that it is impossible for those who have once been born to enter into their mothers' wombs, is plain to all.—*Apolog.* i. p. 89. Thirlby's ed.	How can a man be born when he is old? Can he enter the second time into his mother's womb, and be born? (iii. 4.)

It would seem impossible to deny that Justin is here quoting not only the sentiment of St. John but the very words. None of the other Evangelists record our Saviour's conversation with Nicodemus, or contain the doctrine of regeneration expressed in this precise form.

Again, St. John quotes the prophecy of Zechariah, "They shall look on Him whom they pierced." (xix. 37.) If we compare St. John with Zechariah we shall see that the Evangelist does not quote the words of the Prophet quite literally, that he alters a single word "Me" into "Him," but without destroying the reference of the prophecy to Christ. Justin Martyr also quotes this prophecy of Zechariah. Either he must have quoted from the Septuagint translation of Zechariah, or he must have translated it direct from the Hebrew, or he must have quoted it from St. John. It is all but impossible that Justin should have quoted the prophecy from the Septuagint. For they have not a single word in common.

JUSTIN.	SEPTUAGINT.
Ὄψονται εἰς ὃν ἐξεκέντησαν.	Ἐπιβλέψονται πρὸς μὲ, ἀνθ ὧν κατωρχήσαντο.

It is also extremely improbable that Justin translated the prophecy direct from the Hebrew. For in that case we must believe that he translated by exactly the same four Greek words that St. John had used, and that he translated three of these words, and the same three words literally, while he altered one and the same one as St. John had done: a performance which those who are accustomed to translation from one language into another will not easily credit. A comparison of Zechariah's prophecy in Justin with the same prophecy in St. John will scarcely fail to produce the conviction that Justin was quoting from St. John's Gospel.

JUSTIN.   ST. JOHN.

Ὄψονται εἰς ὃν ἐξεκέντησαν.—*Apolog.* i.   Ὄψονται εἰς ὃν ἐξεκέντησαν. xix. 37.
p. 77. Thirlby's ed.

These two instances may serve as examples of the way in which Justin Martyr refers to St. John's Gospel. Others are given by Lardner in his *Credibility of the Gospel History* (ii. p. 125, ed. 1838), and more recently by Mr. Kentish Bache, in a letter to Dr. Davidson (Kitto, London, 1871).

As to the evidence, which Irenæus gives to St. John's Gospel, it is impossible to state this in a clearer form than has been done by Dean Alford, and which has been already quoted from his works.

Tertullian, who wrote at the end of the second century, when there had been sufficient time for the Fourth Gospel to become generally known to the Church, makes numerous quotations from it as the work of the Apostle St. John,—Professor Tischendorf says, not less than two hundred quotations. Thirty or forty years later Origen published a formal and very full Commentary on St. John's Gospel, a work which had occupied many of the best years of his life. Though St. Matthew's Gospel was written forty years before St. John's, there is no author who has written a commentary on St. Matthew earlier than Origen— at least, there is none whose works have come down to us.

To estimate fairly the value of the testimony, which the early Fathers have given to the various writings of the New Testament by their incidental quotations from them, we must take into account several collateral considerations. Among others we must not forget the great scarcity of copies, which there must always have been, before the days of printing, in the case of any document immediately after its first publication: and that to quote any document would imply that this document was known not only to the person who quotes it, but also to those for whose edification and confirmation it is quoted. If, for instance, a Bishop in his Epistle to any particular Church, quoted the Gospel of St. John in confirmation of his words, it would imply that this Gospel was known not only to the Bishop who quotes it, but also to those to whom he was writing, and that it was acknowledged by them as a work of authority.

It has been objected against St. John's Gospel that it was not quoted by the earliest writers, or by the earliest extant writers as fully as St. Matthew's was. A little reflection will show that, so far from being an objection to it, this is the very proof of its genuineness and authenticity. At the time Clement wrote his Epistle to the Corinthians, about A.D. 96, St. Matthew's Gospel had been published and probably read in some of the Churches for forty years, while St. John's Gospel had not been published more than three years. There is the same interval between the first publication of St. Matthew's Gospel and the time that Clement wrote his Epistle, as there is between the first publication of St. John's Gospel and the time that Justin Martyr wrote. We should not therefore expect to find that Clement quotes St. John as often as he does St. Matthew, but that Justin Martyr quotes St. John as often as Clement quotes St. Matthew.

Again, there is the same interval between the first publication of St. John's Gospel and the time that Tertullian wrote, as there is between the first publication of St. Matthew's Gospel and the time that Justin Martyr wrote. But there are twice as many quotations from St. John in Tertullian's writings, as there are in Justin Martyr from all the various books of the New Testament together.

Mr. Sanday, the latest writer on this subject, and whose elaborate and exhaustive treatise has been published, while the sheets of this Commentary were passing through the press, does not rate the *external evidence* in favour of St. John the Apostle being the author of the Fourth Gospel so high as Dean Alford does. But he maintains as strongly as Dean Alford, that the *external* and the *internal* evidence for it taken together is perfectly conclusive.

He says: "the subject of the external evidence has been pretty well fought out. The opposing parties are probably as near to an agreement as they ever will be. It will hardly be an unfair statement of the case for those who reject the Johannean authorship of the Gospel, to say, that the external evidence is compatible with that supposition. And, on the other hand, we may equally say for those who accept the Johannean authorship, that the external evidence would not be sufficient alone to prove it. As it at present stands, the controversy may be regarded as drawn: and it is not likely that the position of parties will be materially affected.

"Thus we are thrown back upon the internal evidence: and I have the less hesitation in confining myself to this, because I believe it to be capable of leading to a quite definite conclusion."—p. 4.

Mr. Sanday then takes St. John's Gospel chapter by chapter, and submits it to a rigid examination, not as an inspired production, but as a document that commends itself to the reason on grounds purely theological, literary, and historical. Nothing can be more fair and able than the way in which Mr. Sanday handles his subject, on the low grounds that he takes. There may be, as it is said, a necessity in these days to take such grounds, but the necessity for this certainly indicates a not very healthy state of Christian society.

After Mr. Sanday's preparatory investigation, which extends over 280 pages of his work, he approaches the following questions "Was the author of the fourth Gospel a Jew? Was he a Jew of Palestine?

Was he a member of the original Christian circle? Was he an eye-witness? Was he the son of Zebedee?" All these questions he answers in the affirmative, and concludes his work with these words, "The Gospel is the work of the Apostle, the son of Zebedee: it is the record of an eye-witness of the life of our Lord Jesus Christ: and its historical character is such as under the circumstances might be expected—it needs no adventitious commendation to make it higher."—p. 304.

St. John is generally supposed to have written his Gospel at Ephesus. The traditionary date is somewhere about A.D. 90, which is much the same as modern scholars have assigned to it on independent grounds.

MANUSCRIPTS OF THE NEW TESTAMENT.

It is not proposed here to enter on the subject of the Manuscripts of the New Testament, further than to explain the references made to them in this Commentary. The particulars contained in these pages are taken chiefly from Mr. Scrivener's volume on the Introduction to the Criticism of the New Testament, and from Prof. Tischendorf's Introduction to his edition of the English New Testament.

To Prof. Tischendorf belongs the credit of having reduced the subject of various readings of the New Testament within convenient and definite limits. By his publication of the English New Testament with the readings of the Sinaitic, Vatican, and Alexandrine MSS., he has so far simplified a very intricate subject, that any intelligent reader can now understand at a glance, what is the weight of authority by which each reading is supported. It is sincerely to be hoped that this has not been done at the expense of truth or accuracy. But Mr. Scrivener, who has made a full collation of the Sinaitic Manuscript, has already raised the question, whether judging from internal evidence the character of the Sinaitic Manuscript is such, as to justify Prof. Tischendorf in attributing to it alone, or to it in conjunction with the Vatican and Alexandrine MSS., an authority against all other manuscripts. (Scrivener's Preface to Coll. of Sinaitic MS., p. v*, vii*.)

Copies of the New Testament yet existing in manuscript, and dating from the fourth century downward, such as have been discovered and set down in catalogues, are hardly fewer than two thousand. There are little short of one thousand manuscripts proper or Lectionaries of the Gospels, and about another thousand of all the other books put together.

Manuscripts of the New Testament have been divided into **Uncial** and **Cursive**.

I. The former called Uncial from uncia (an inch), referring to the size of the characters, are those manuscripts that are written in what are now called capital letters, formed separately, having no connection with each other, and (in the earlier specimens) without any space between the words, the marks of punctuation being few. Uncial letters prevailed in Greek manuscripts of the New Testament from the fourth to the tenth century, and in the case of liturgical books to the eleventh century.

II. Cursive, or running-hand, manuscripts are those written in letters more easily and rapidly made, those in the same word being usually joined together, with a complete system of punctuation, not widely removed from that of printed books. Cursive letters were employed as early as the ninth or tenth century, and continued in use until the invention of printing.

The Uncial Manuscripts are few : in the Gospels about 34, but the greater part of these are fragments ; in the Acts 10 ; in the Catholic Epistles 6, and in the Pauline Epistles 14 (many of these fragments) ; and in the Apocalypse 4.

The following are the principal Uncial Manuscripts :—

    א. Codex Sinaiticus, discovered in the Convent of St. Catherine, on Mount Sinai, by Prof. Tischendorf, in 1844 and 1859. Middle of fourth century.

    B. Codex Vaticanus, in the Vatican Library at Rome. Middle of fourth century.

    A. Codex Alexandrinus, in the British Museum, presented to Charles I. by Cyril Lucar, Patriarch of Constantinople, 1628. Fifth century.

    C. Codex Ephræmi. No. 9 in the Imperial Library of Paris. Fifth century.

    D. Codex Bezæ—Græco-Latino ; University Library, Cambridge ; presented in 1581 by Theodore Beza.

The following more particular information respecting the Vatican, Alexandrine, and Sinaitic MSS., and the Greek Text of the English Authorised Version, is taken from the Introduction to Prof. Tischendorf's English New Testament, 1869.

"*The Vatican, Alexandrine, and Sinaitic Manuscripts.*—Providence has ordered it so that the New Testament can appeal to a far larger number of all kinds of original sources than the whole of the rest of ancient Greek literature. Before all others which it possesses, Christian scholars have for a long time highly valued two manuscripts, which to great antiquity add the distinction that they contain, not merely more or fewer portions of the sacred text, but the greater part of the entire New Testament as well as the Old. One of these manuscripts is deposited in the Vatican at Rome, and the other in the British Museum. To these, within the last ten years, a third has been added, brought from Mount Sinai, and now at St. Petersburg. These three hold undoubtedly the first place among the many copies of the New Testament of a thousand years old : and by their authority will have to be judged and rectified, both the earlier Greek editions of the New Testament, and all existing modern translations of it. It should not be forgotten, however, that the three manuscripts of which we speak, differ among themselves both in age and importance, and that not one of them stands so high as to exclude all gainsaying of its bare authority.

"The *Codex Vaticanus* came first into the possession of learned Europe. From what place it came into the Vatican Library is not known, but it is entered in the very first catalogue of the collection, dating from 1475. It contains the Old and New Testaments. Of the New it at present contains the four Gospels, the Acts, the seven General Epistles, nine of St. Paul's Epistles, and that to the Hebrews as far as Chap. ix. 14: but all that followed this place is lost, namely, the last chapters of the Hebrews, the two Epistles to Timothy, the Epistles to Titus and Philemon, and the Revelation. The text is written in three volumes to a page. The peculiarity of the handwriting, the arrangement of the manuscript, and the character of the text itself, more especially certain remarkable readings, induce the opinion that the *Codex* is to be referred to the fourth century, and probably to about the middle of that century.

"The *Codex Alexandrinus* was, in 1628, sent as a present to King Charles I. of England, from Cyril Lucar, Patriarch of Constantinople. Cyril Lucar, who had formerly been Patriarch of Alexandria, brought it with him to Constantinople: and this explains why it is called the Alexandrian Codex. It is written in two columns to a page, and contains the Old and New Testaments. It is imperfect in the New Testament, having lost Matt. i. to xxv. 6: John vi. 50, to viii. 52, and 2 Cor. iv. 13, to xii. 6. It contains, however, the two Epistles by Clement of Rome, which in it alone have descended to posterity: also an Epistle of Athanasius, and a production by Eusebius on the Psalter. On Palæographic and other grounds it is believed to have been written in the middle of the fifth century.

"The *Codex Sinaiticus* I (Tischendorf) was so happy as to discover in 1844 and 1859 in the monastery of St. Catherine on Mount Sinai. In the year last named I was travelling in the East under the patronage of the Emperor Alexander the Second of Russia, and to him it was my good fortune to transmit the manuscript. It contains the Old and New Testament, and is written with four columns to a page. The New Testament is perfect, not having been deprived of a single leaf. To the twenty-seven books of the New Testament are appended the Epistle of Barnabas complete, and part of the Shepherd of Hermas, which books even at the beginning of the fourth century were reckoned for Holy Scripture by a good many. We are led, by all the data upon which we calculate the antiquity of manuscripts, to assign the Codex Sinaiticus to the middle of the fourth century. The evidence in favour of so great an age is more certain in the case of the Sinaitic Codex, than in that of the Vatican manuscript. It is even not impossible that the Sinaitic Codex—we cannot say as much of the Vatican MS. —formed one of the fifty copies of the Bible which in the year 331 the Emperor Constantine ordered to be executed for Constantinople under the direction of Eusebius, the bishop of Cæsarea, best known as a Church historian. In this case it must be understood that the Emperor Justinian, the founder of the Sinaitic monastery, sent it as a present from Constantinople to the monks at Sinai.

"From what has been said it follows, that the first place, for antiquity and extent, among the three chief manuscripts, belongs to the Sinaitic Codex, the second place belongs to the Vatican, and the third to the Alexandrian. This arrangement is altogether confirmed by the condition of the text of the manuscripts. The text is not only in accordance with the writing of manuscripts in the fourth and fifth centuries, the same which was read in the East is precisely those centuries: but rather, for the most part it truly represents the text which was then copied from much earlier documents by Alexandrian scribes who knew very little of Greek, and therefore did not intentionally make the least alteration:—that is to say the very text which, in the third and second centuries, was spread over a great part of Christendom."

Greek Text of the English Authorised Version.—" The English Authorised Version, equally with the Lutheran translation, is based upon the editions of the Greek text which Erasmus in 1516, and Robert Stephens in 1550, had founded upon manuscripts written after the tenth century. Whether those Greek copies out of which Erasmus and Stephens prepared their editions, were altogether reliable, that is, whether they exhibited as far as possible the Apostolic text, has long been matter of earnest discussion with the learned. Since the sixteenth century, Greek manuscripts have become known far older than those of Erasmus and Robert Stephens, and besides the Greek, also Syriac, Egyptian, Latin and Gothic, into which languages the original text was translated in the second, third, and fourth centuries. Moreover, in the works of the Christian Fathers who wrote in the second and following centuries, many citations from texts of the New Testament have been found and compared. What was the result? The learned saw on the one hand, that the text of Erasmus and Stephens, had been for the most part in use in the Byzantine national Church long before the tenth century: but on the other hand, they learned the existence of thousands of readings which had not been edited by Erasmus and Stephens. Now the problem came to be, what reading in each instance most correctly represented that which the Apostles had written. This problem is by no means an easy one: for variations in the documents are very ancient: Jerome already notices them. Even in the fourth century there were diversities in very many places of the New Testament. The learned have been and are very much divided in opinion as to which readings represent the word of God most exactly, but one thing has been admitted by most who understand the matter, and it is that the oldest documents must come nearer to the original text, than those that are later."
—Tischendorf's Introduction.

It is only fair to state that Mr. Scrivener, a very great authority, has formed a much higher estimate of the character of the Textus Receptus. He says : " It is no less true to fact than paradoxical in sound, that the worst corruptions to which the New Testament has ever been subjected, originated within a hundred years, after it was composed ; that Irenæus, and the African Fathers, and the whole Western with a portion of the Syrian Church, used far inferior manuscripts to those employed by Stunica, (Complutensian Editor) or Erasmus, or Stephens thirteen centuries later, when moulding the Textus Receptus."—Introduction to *Criticism on New Testament*, p. 386.

The letter **S.** means the Sinaitic Manuscript.
,, **V.** ,, the Vatican.
,, **A.** ,, the Alexandrine.

S* V* A* point out any reading of S. V. A. which has been altered by some later hand ; though we give the original, and not the altered reading, in such cases. When we give an altered reading, it is marked **S¹. V¹. A¹.**

Alf. means Dean Alford's revised Translation (1870).

INTRODUCTORY NOTE.

"**Palestine** stands alone; alone in its boundaries of seas and sandy deserts, and snow-clad mountains; and alone in the variety of its soil, climate, and productions. I do not claim for it either beauty or grandeur—which may be found in almost every region of the globe—but I claim for it peculiarities and contrasts to which no other region can afford a parallel. . . . . . Is there no poetry, nothing affecting to the imagination, in the physical structure of a country which is without a parallel on earth? For within a space so small that the eye can take it in from more than one point, there are heights, like Hermon, covered with eternal snow, and depths, like the Jordan valley, with a heat exceeding that of the tropics; there is on one side the sea, and on the other a lake whose surface is 1300 feet lower down, with soundings as deep again. Where is there such a river as the Jordan, whose turbulent waters never gladdened a human habitation, nor ever irrigated a green field—which pursues its continuous course for two hundred miles within a space easily visible, and ends at last in the sea of death never to reappear? Where on earth is there such a variety of vegetation, from the palm on the sultry plain to the lichen beside the glacier? Where such howling wildernesses, such dreary and utterly desolate wastes, with such luxuriant plains, fertile valleys, pasture lands, vineyards, and corn-fields? Where such a climate varying through every degree of temperature and of moisture?"—*Eastward*, by Macleod, p. 176.

"In Palestine, as in Greece, every traveller is struck with the smallness of the territory. He is surprised, even after all that he has heard, at passing, in one long day, from the capital of Judæa to that of Samaria; or at seeing within eight hours, three such spots as Hebron, Bethlehem, and Jerusalem. The breadth of the country, from the Jordan to the sea, is rarely more than fifty miles. Its length, from Dan to Beersheba, is about a hundred and eighty miles. The time is now gone by when the grandeur of a country is measured by its size, or the diminutive extent of an illustrious people can otherwise than enhance the magnitude of what they have done."—Stanley's *Sinai and Palestine*, p. 113.

"The length of the Holy Land from Dan to Beersheba is only one hundred and forty miles, and its breadth sixty miles; and yet this small area, the theatre of the most engrossing portion of the world's history from the earliest times, still remains only partially explored."—*Recovery of Jerusalem*, p. 471.

"Of Palestine we are shamefully ignorant, though the whole area of the country is not larger than Lancashire and Yorkshire together."—MacGregor's *Jordan*, p. 212.

"The great elevation of this country above the level of the sea is most forcibly brought out by the journey we have made. From the moment of leaving the Arabah has been almost a continual ascent. We mounted the great Pass of Sâfeh, and having mounted, hardly descended at all, crossed the great table-land of Beersheba, and then mounted the barrier of the hills of Judah, and thence have been mounting ever since. Hebron is, in fact, only four hundred feet lower than Helvellyn, (three thousand and fifty-five feet). How well one understands the expression, 'They went down into Egypt.'"—Stanley's *Sinai and Palestine*, p. 102.

"The atmosphere of Palestine is very clear; and there are many points from which Mount Hermon at one extremity of the Holy Land, and the Dead Sea at the other, can be distinctly seen, the view thus extending over a distance of one hundred and fifty miles. The hill tops also are all bare, and large trees are rarely seen."—*Recovery of Jerusalem*, p. 441.

"I am struck by what is also noticed by Miss Martineau—the Western, almost the English character of the scenery. Those wild uplands of Carmel and Ziph are hardly distinguishable (except by their ruined cities and red anemones) from the Lowlands of Scotland or of Wales; these cultivated valleys of Hebron (except by their olives) from the general features of a rich valley in Yorkshire or Derbyshire."—Stanley's *Syria and Palestine*, p. 101.

In the time of our Saviour all Palestine was divided into three provinces—Galilee, Samaria, and Judæa. These were the territorial divisions, which succeeded to the overthrow of the ancient landmarks of the tribes of Israel and Judah, caused by their respective captivities.

I. **Galilee**, which in the Roman age was applied to a large province, seems to have been originally confined to a little circuit (the word Galil signifies a circle or circuit) of country round Kedesh Naphtali, in which were situated the twenty towns given by Solomon to Hiram, King of Tyre, as payment for his work in conveying timber from Lebanon to Jerusalem. (Josh. xx. 7; 1 Kings ix. 11.) They were then, or subsequently, occupied by strangers, and for this reason Isaiah gives to the district the name "Galilee of the Gentiles." (Isa. ix. 1.) It is probable that the strangers increased in number, and became during the Captivity the great body of the inhabitants; extending themselves also over the surrounding country, they gave to their new territories the old name, until at length Galilee became one of the largest provinces of Palestine. In the Maccabæan period, Galilee contained only a few Jews, living in the midst of a large heathen population. (1 Macc. v. 20-23.)

The name Galilee was applied to the whole northern section of Palestine, including the ancient territories of Issachar, Zebulun,

Asher, and Napthali. It was divided into two sections, "Lower" and "Upper." Lower Galilee included the great plain of Esdraelon, with its offshoots, which run down to the Jordan, and the Lake of Tiberias, and the whole of the hill-country adjoining it on the north, to the foot of the mountain range. It was one of the richest and most beautiful sections of Palestine. The chief towns of Lower Galilee were Tiberias, Tarichæa, at the southern end of the Sea of Galilee, and Sepphoris. The towns most celebrated in New Testament history are Nazareth, Cana, and Tiberias.

Upper Galilee embraced the whole mountain range lying between the Upper Jordan and Phœnicia. To this region the name "Galilee of the Gentiles" is given in the Old and New Testament. (Isa. ix. 1; Matt. iv. 15.)

Galilee was the scene of the greater part of our Lord's private life and public acts. His early years were spent at Nazareth: and when He entered on His great work He made Capernaum His home. (Matt. iv. 13; ix. 1.) It is a remarkable fact that the first three Gospels are chiefly taken up with our Saviour's ministrations in this province, while the Gospel of St. John dwells more upon those in Judæa. The Apostles were all Galilæans by birth or residence. (Acts i. 11.)

"Galilee, always the garden of Syria, might become that of the world. Everything grows here, from the Caspian walnut to the Egyptian palm; while the hills of Judah are stern and bare, and the meadows of Sharon burnt and dry. These wadies of Galilee are almost everywhere laughing with herbs and flowers. A forest of oak clothes the sides of Mount Carmel; cedar clumps nestle in the clefts of Mount Hermon; myrtles enlarge into trees, and myriads of orange-blossoms throw their scent into the air. Every hill is a vineyard, every bottom a corn-field. The delta of the Nile is not more sunny; the vega of Granada is not more picturesque; the ghota of Damascus is not more green and bright. For here the fierce sun and the refreshing rain come together, and water flows through Galilee not in tanks and pools, but poured out royally towards the sea in streams."—Dixon's *Holy Land*, I., p. 187.

II. **Samaria.**—This province took its name from the city of Samaria, the capital city of the kings of Israel. It included the tract of country originally occupied by the tribes of Ephraim and Manasseh, west of the Jordan, and was enclosed by Lower Galilee on the north, and Judæa on the south; so that persons taking the direct route from Judæa to Galilee must needs go through Samaria. (John iv. 4.) The chief places of this district, noticed in Scripture, are Samaria, Salem, Saron, Sichem, or Shechem, and Antipatris.

III. **Judæa.**—This was the most southern, and the most distinguished district in Palestine, embracing the territories assigned to the tribes of Judah, Benjamin, Simeon, and part of the tribe of Dan; being nearly co-extensive with the ancient kingdom of Judah. Its metropolis was Jerusalem. Its general breadth was from the Jordan to Joppa.

It was made a portion of the Roman province of Syria upon the deposition of Archelaus, the Tetrarch of Judæa, A.D. 6, and was governed by a Procurator, who was subject to the Governor of Syria. During the whole time of our Saviour's ministry, Pontius Pilate was the Procurator of Judæa. He was appointed, A.D. 26, in the twelfth year of Tiberius Cæsar.

"**The Mountains of Judæa.**—Their features are not those of a regular mountain chain like Lebanon; but rather a cluster of rounded rocky hills, sloping down into dry tortuous valleys. They are scantily clothed with greyish and brown shrubs, intermixed with aromatic plants and gay flowers; they are encircled besides by concentric rings of white rock, and studded with huge cairns of white stones, which give them a desolate and sometimes even forbidding aspect. Here and there we meet with deep picturesque glens where the winter-torrent beds are bordered with belts of olives, and the steep banks above glisten with the foliage of the prickly oak. Such are the features of the western declivities and broad summits of the Judæan hills; but the eastern slopes are wilder and far more desolate. From the top of Olivet or the Frank Mountain, the eye wanders over a wilderness of white hills, jagged cliffs, and yawning chasms, without tree, or shrub, or green grass tuft, until at length it rests on the leaden waters of the Dead Sea, lying in their deep mysterious bed, far away below.

"A superficial observer from some western land of sunshine and showers may wonder at it, and write of the barrenness of Southern Palestine; and with semi-sceptical surprise ask, 'Is this that Land of Promise which flowed with milk and honey?' It may be well to remind such an one of the power of a Syrian sun, of the character of an eastern clime, and of the effect of centuries of neglect and desolation. The destruction of the woods which once covered the mountains, and the loss of the vegetation consequent on the want of tillage, have entailed upon the whole country a greater degree of drought than in early times; and then again, the neglect of the terraces that supported the soil on the hill-sides, has given full play to the winter rains, leaving tracts of naked rock where belts of corn once flourished, and vines spread out their long branches. To see what the hills of Judæa might be under proper care and culture, one has only to look at the western slopes of Lebanon. There is another proof of the ancient fertility and great resources of the country which no accurate observer can overlook —the vast number of ruined towns and villages which everywhere stud the landscape. In Judæa we may wander for miles and miles without seeing a vestige of *present* habitation, save the little goat-pen on the hill-side, and the flocks round the fountains; but there is scarcely a fountain where fragments of walls and scattered heaps of stones do not indicate the sites of former dwellings."—*Handbook of Palestine*, p. 175.

INTRODUCTORY NOTE TO CHAPTER I.

Jerusalem, as being the place which God had chosen in which to record His Name, was the chief city in Palestine. On the revolt of the ten tribes it became the capital of the Kingdom of Judah. Its ancient name was probably Jebusi, or Jebus, after the name of its occupiers, the Jebusites. (Joshua xv. 8; Judges xix. 10.) Jerusalem is thirty-two miles distant from the sea, and eighteen miles from the Jordan; twenty from Hebron, and thirty-six from Samaria. One of the earliest notices of it is that the Children of Judah fought against Jerusalem and took it; (Judges i. 8;) and almost the last notice of it in the New Testament is contained in the solemn warning, in which our Saviour foretold that Jerusalem should be compassed with armies, (Luke xxi. 20,) and the abomination of desolation standing in the Holy Place. (Matt. xxiv. 15.) In the fifteen centuries that elapsed between these two points, Jerusalem was besieged no fewer than seventeen times; twice it was razed to the ground, and on two other occasions its walls were levelled.

Judah and Simeon captured only the lower city; the upper city remained in the hands of the Jebusites until David took it, about 1046 B.C. (1 Chron. xi. 4-7.) It remained the capital of the Kingdom of Judah until it was captured and sacked by Nebuchadnezzar, 586 B.C., and its inhabitants carried in captivity to Babylon. The decree of Cyrus, King of Persia, authorising the rebuilding of the Temple was issued 536 B.C. On this an immense number of the Jews returned to Jerusalem; the Temple and the walls of the city were rebuilt.

After centuries of misrule and misery, Judæa was reduced to a Roman province, the procurator of which did not reside at Jerusalem, but at Cæsarea on the coast, A.D. 6. In A.D. 26, Pontius Pilate was made Procurator of Judæa. After the Crucifixion of our Saviour Jerusalem was captured and burnt by Titus, A.D. 70. Hadrian, A.D. 135, endeavoured to obliterate the very existence of Jerusalem as a city. The ruins which Titus had left were razed to the ground, and the plough passed over the foundations of the Temple. Its name was changed to Œlia Capitolina, and for many years the Jews were forbidden to enter it on pain of death. In process of time its very name was forgotten.

The Empress Helena, mother of Constantine the Great, visited Palestine, A.D. 326, and erected magnificent churches at Bethlehem and on the Mount of Olives. In the reign of Julian the Apostate

(A.D. 362) an unsuccessful attempt was made to lay the foundations of a temple. The work, as it is said, was interrupted by supernatural agencies, balls of fire from time to time bursting from the foundations. In the fourth and fifth centuries Jerusalem became the centre of attraction for Christian pilgrims. It was captured by Khalif Omar, A.D. 637 ; by the Crusaders, 15th July, 1099 ; in 1187 by Saladin. After various fortunes Jerusalem was restored to the Sultan, A.D. 1840.—Williams' *Holy City;* Gibbon's *Decline,* ch. xxiii; Smith's *Bib. Dict.*

The following are a few of its principal features :—" Jerusalem is emphatically a mountain city. The Bible teems with allusion to this peculiarity in its situation. Built on the very backbone of the country, the summit of that long ridge which traverses Palestine from north to south, and only approached by wild mountain roads, the position of the city was one of great natural strength, and this gave the inhabitants that feeling of security from hostile attack which seems to be implied by the Psalmist in the well-known verse, " As the mountains are round about Jerusalem, so is the Lord round about His people." (Ps. cxxv. 2.) The modern city stands, as the ancient one did before it, on the southern extremity of a spur, or plateau, enclosed by two ravines, which bear the familiar names of Kedron and Hinnom. The ravines rise at the watershed within a short distance of each other, at an altitude of 2650 feet above the Mediterranean ; the easternmost, the Valley of Kedron, or Jehoshaphat, runs eastward for a mile and a half, and then makes a sharp bend to the south ; the westernmost, the Valley of Hinnom, after following a direction nearly south for one mile and a quarter, turns to the east, and passing through a deep gorge, joins the Kedron at Bir Eyûl, a deep well south of the city. Both ravines are at first mere depressions of the ground ; but after the change in their respective courses they fall more rapidly, and at Bir Eyûl are 670 feet below the original starting-point. A third ravine, the Tyropœon—Valley of the Cheesemongers, or perhaps Tyrians,—rises well up in the plateau, and after passing through the city and dividing it into two unequal halves, joins the Kedron at Siloam. On the eastern spur, Mount Moriah, once stood the temples of Solomon, Zerubbabel, and Herod ; and on the western, which is 120 feet higher than Mount Moriah, were situated the Palace of Herod, the three great towers of Hippicus, Phaselus, and Mariamne, and the upper city of Josephus."—*Recovery of Jerusalem,* p. 6.

" The plateau on which the city stands slopes uniformly to the south-east, and contains about 1000 acres ; it is of tertiary limestone, and the upper beds provide an extremely hard, compact stone, called by the Arabs " Mezzeh ;" while the lower, in which most of the ancient tombs and cisterns have been cut, consists of a soft, white stone, called Melekeh."—*Recovery of Jerusalem,* p. 8.

" Jerusalem, in a sense the metropolis of the world, has still many nooks not even visited by men who can use their eyes and their pens, and yet all that is left of that city would easily be contained in Hyde Park."—MacGregor's *Jordan*, p. 202.

"Jerusalem is surrounded by walls, high and imposing in appearance, but far from strong. . . . They were erected as they now stand by Sultan Suleiman, in the year 1542, and they appear to occupy the site of the walls of the Middle Ages, from the ruins of which they are mostly constructed. The circuit of the walls is 4326 yards, or nearly two and an eighth geographical miles. The form of the city is irregular, the walls having many projections and indentations."—*Handbook to Palestine*, p. 75.

St. John's Gospel may be conveniently divided into four parts :—

I. The Acts of Jesus before His solemn manifestation, while John was still baptizing, including chapters i., ii., iii., iv.—First Passover of his Ministry. (ii. 13.)

II. His Acts in Judæa.—Second Passover. (v. 1.)

III. His Acts in Galilee and Judæa, including chapters vi., vii., viii. ix., x., xi.—Third Passover. (vi. 4.)

IV. His Passion in Jerusalem during the week of the Fourth Passover, His Resurrection, etc., including xii.-xxi.

THE GOSPEL ACCORDING TO ST. JOHN.
[S.V. After John. A. The Gospel after, or according to John.]

I.

THE ACTS OF JESUS BEFORE HIS SOLEMN MANIFESTATION OF HIMSELF WHILE JOHN WAS STILL BAPTIZING, INCLUDING CHAPTERS I. II. III. IV. FIRST PASSOVER OF HIS MINISTRY. (II. 13.)

CHAPTER I.

1 *The Divinity, Humanity, and Office of Jesus Christ;* 15 *The testimony of John;* 39 *The calling of Andrew, Peter, &c.*

THE Incarnation may justly be called the basis of the Christian religion. A flaw here would bring down the whole superstructure. Even an error in apprehending it would materially affect a man's whole moral system. Hence St. John in his writings endeavours, first of all, and above all, to establish this fact, and to correct the various false views which were growing up around him. He had already done this in his Epistles, and he pursues the same course in the opening verses of his Gospel.

The Incarnation, the fact itself, and the way in which it was to be understood, was the first battle-field in the early Church. In St. John's own day, Anti-Christs, men who either denied the truth and reality of the Incarnation, or who explained it away, had already begun to give the Church cause for trouble and anxiety.

It is not with Jesus Christ as it is with mere man. Our existence dates from our conception, or at least, from our birth. He did not begin to exist for the first time when He was born of the Blessed Virgin. He had been from all eternity. In order that there might be no possibility of mistake on this head, the Evangelist, before he relates the birth of Jesus Christ, proceeds to state His Eternal Generation:

1 In the beginning was the Word, and the Word was with God, and the Word was God.[1]
2 The same was in the beginning with God.

The Word, the Second Person in the Godhead, was in the beginning, before all time, before all creation.

It is plain that in the first verse the word God is used essentially, of the Godhead, and personally in the second verse, of God the Father. It is probable that the Evangelist quotes the words "In the beginning" from the first chapter of Genesis, and uses them in the same sense in which they are used there, namely, in the beginning of the Creation. He does not by these words assign any date or limit to the existence of the Word, but simply states that He was in, or at the beginning of the Creation. The natural inference from this is that He, who was at the beginning of the Creation, before all time, was, as we with our finite capacities express it, from everlasting, from all eternity.

The threefold form in which this is declared: the Word was with God—the Word was God—the same was in the beginning with God—expresses (1) That the Word is a distinct Person from the Father. (2) That He is One with the Father—of the same nature as the Father. (3) That He is from all eternity. Being with the Father He is a different Person from the Father; being God, He is co-equal with the Father. Such is the relation of the Word to God. He is

---

[1] "The Word, not pronounced, but substantial, not the voice of an articulate speech, but the begotten substance of the Divine efficacy.

"From the places of the Old Testament, where the Son of God is called the Word, it became most familiar and ordinary among the Jews to use this title personally for Him. And this may be a second reason deduced from that that was named before, why the Evangelist here useth it, namely, as a name most familiarly and commonly known among His own people. Examples hereof might be alleged out of the Chaldee Paraphrast, even by hundreds. It will suffice to allege some few: Gen. xxviii. 20, 21, 'If the Word of the Lord be my help,' and, 'The Word of the Lord shall be my God;' Exod. xix. 17, 'Moses brought forth the people to meet the Word of the Lord;' Isa. i. 14, 'Your appointed feasts My Word abominateth;' and verse 16, 'Put away the evil of your doings from before My Word;' and chap. xlv. 2, 'My Word shall go before thee,' etc. etc.; and in hundreds of other places. And so likewise in some of the writings of the Talmudists, and Philo Judæus, in lib. 'De Mundi Opificio,' explaineth this title."—Lightfoot, i. 302 and 303.

The Word was God (Θεὸς ἦν ὁ λόγος.) —"With respect to Θεὸς, there is, I believe, no instance in the New Testament, though the word occurs more than thirteen hundred times, in which it does not conform to that law of Regimen which forbids an anarthous appellative to be governed by one having the article prefixed, and hence such a phrase as ὁ υἱος Θεοῦ is not to be found. In some other respects also its follows the common rule of appellatives, e.g., in rejecting the article where it (Θεὸς) is the Predicate of a proposition which does not reciprocate, as in John i., for as to Θεὸς being sometimes used in an inferior or qualified sense, there is not a single instance of such an use in the whole New Testament. Θεὸς is God, or a God, either true or false, real or imaginary; but never *superior* or *inferior*."—Middleton on *Greek Article*, p. 206; see also, p. 240.

See note on verse 23.

Himself God, He is from all eternity, He is of the same nature as the Father. His relation to created things is contained in the following verse :—

3 All things were made by Him ; and without Him was not anything made (that was made).[1]

(Alf. That hath been made.)

The Word was the Creator of all things. All things were made by Him : but not by Him as a mere instrument; but by Him as a willing, intelligent co-operator in the work of Creation.

As the Creator, the Word is the author of all natural life. He is also the author of all moral life.

4 [In Him was life]: and the life was the light of men.

[S. In Him is life.][2]

5 And the light shineth (in darkness) : and the darkness comprehended it not.

(Alf. In the darkness.)

Moral darkness, the darkness of the soul, is indicated by ignorance of God, by sin, vice, wickedness. In like manner, the tokens of light in the soul are fear of God, holiness, virtue, goodness. Whatever of these existed in the world before the Incarnation, the power to perform them was derived from the Word.

The way in which He diffused the knowledge of God and of right and wrong among men before His coming, was by reason, by manifest indications of God and of His goodness in the works of creation, and by conscience. By these, in many and various ways in the individual and in the nation, the preparation of the world for greater blessings

---

[1] Without Him was not anything made that was made. "Some end the sentence here, and some but begin it, and some neither, but bring it a step further. Some point thus, ' All things were made by Him, and without Him was nothing made. That which was made in Him was life.' A reading which Chrysostom (Hom. 5 in John) saith was used by heretics, whereby to prove the Holy Ghost to be a creature...... Others read it thus : 'All things were made by Him, and without Him was nothing made which was made by Him.' And then they begin a new sentence : ' He was life,' etc., a reading conceived to have been used by the Manichees, whereby to prove *duo principia*, a good and a bad. "Ignatius Martyr, Epist. ad Antioch, Tatianus, in Harmon, Chrysostom, in loc., and others of the ancients, and the Arabic, Syriac, Italian, Spanish, French, Dutch read as we do ; and so the very sense of the place requireth to read."—Lightfoot, i. 392 and 394.

[2] In Him was Life.—ἦν is the reading of all the MSS. in the world, except the Sinaitic and Codex Bezæ.—Burgon *On the last Twelve Verses of St. Mark*, p. 110.

when the fulness of time should come, was constantly going on.[1] In addition to these, His chosen people, Israel, had a special teaching; by direct revelation from Himself, by the Law of Moses moral and ceremonial, and by His servants the prophets.

Notwithstanding all this, men loved darkness rather than light; they lived lives of sin rather than of holiness. The light shineth in the darkness, and the darkness did not receive nor understand it. In the Epistle to the Romans (chapter i.) St. Paul draws a fearful picture of the state of the heathen world before the Incarnation—of its ignorance and depravity.[2]

In verses 4th and 5th, the word "light" is used virtually of Christ, for the light that was diffused from Him, the light that was in Him; in the 7th and following verses it is used personally of Christ, Who is Himself the Light.

There is a difference between a light and the true Light; between a light that shineth among men, and the Light which is the source and fount of light to all other lights. John Baptist was a shining light among men; but the Word was the true Light, the source from which John and all other saintly men derived their power to give light to others. John, by his holy, self-denying life, and by his fearless reproof of the sins of all around him, was so far raised above the men of that time, that they mistook him for the true Light. Holy as he was, he was not the true Light. His mission was to bear witness to the true Light, that through his testimony men might be induced to believe that He, Whom they knew as the son of Joseph and Mary, was the true Light, the Word, the Second Person in the Godhead.

6 There was a man sent from God whose name was John.

---

[1] **Preparation for the Advent.**—"The history of the race of Adam before the Advent is the history of a long and varied, but incessant preparation for the Advent. It is commonly perceived that Greece contributed a language and an intellectual discipline, Rome a political organization, to the apparatus which was put in readiness to assist the propagation of the Gospel; and that each of these, in its kind, was the most perfect that the world had produced."—*Gladstone's Juventus Mundi*, p. 374.

[2] **Man's Downward Course.**— The poems of Homer never can be put in competition with the sacred writings of the Old Testament as regards the one invaluable code of Truth and Hope that was contained in them. But while the Jewish records exhibit to us the link between man and the other world in the earliest times, the poems of Homer show us the being, of whom God was pleased to be thus mindful, in the free unsuspecting play of his actual nature. The patriarchal and Jewish dispensations created and sustained, through Divine interposition, a state of things essentially special and exceptional; but here, first we see our kind set to work out for itself, under the lights which common life and experience supplied, the deep problem of his destiny. Nor is there, perhaps, any more solemn or melancholy lesson than that which is to be learned from its *continual downward course*.—Gladstone's *Studies on Homer*, i. p. 7.

7 The same came (for a witness) to bear witness of the Light, that all men through Him might believe.
(Alf. For witness.)

8 He was not (that Light), but (was sent) to bear witness of (that Light.)
(Alf. The Light—came—the Light.)

9 (That was the true Light which lighteth every man that cometh) into the world.[1]
(Alf. The true Light which lighteneth every man came.)

By reason, by the works of creation, and by conscience men failed to recognise, and to pay the honour, which was due to God. Even when God came and dwelt among men, how few believed in Him, not to say, how few of those who were His own by creation, how few of those who were His own peculiar people! So far were they from worshipping Him as God, that they put Him to death, the death which they themselves deemed accursed. The Romans were merely the instruments in His death; the Jews were His accusers and the authors of His crucifixion. Of His twelve Apostles, of His seventy disciples, whom He had sent to teach and to work miracles, all forsook Him and fled.

10 He was in the world, and the world [was made by Him,] and the world knew Him not.[2]
[S.* Was made because of Him.]

11 He came unto (His own) and (His own) received Him not.[3]
(Alf. His own possessions—His own people.)

---

[1] "This verse may be either read, 'which coming into the world, lighteth every man,' or as our English hath it; which latter is approved the true. 1. By the very place where the word *coming*, or ἐρχόμενον lieth, for it followeth not immediately the word Φῶς, but ἄνθρωπον, and so being joined with it, reason and the custom of grammar tell that it should be construed with it. 2. It is ordinary among the Jews to call men by this periphrasis, 'such as come into the world,' which idiom of the Hebrews the Evangelist followeth here. The Syriac readeth as we do."—Lightfoot, i. 392.

[2] The World. From the signification of κόσμος as the material world, which is not uncommon in Scripture, (Matt. xiii. 39; John xxi. 25; Rom. i. 20,) followed that of κόσμος as the sum total of the men living in the world (John i. 29, iv. 42; 2 Cor. v. 19), and then upon this, and ethically, those not of the ἐκκλησία, the alienated from the life of God (John i. 10; 1 Cor. i. 20, 21; James iv. 4; 1 John iii. 13.)—Archbishop Trench on the *Synonyms of the New Test.* p. 206.

[3] Received.—"In verse 11 it is παρέλαβον, in verse 12 it is ἔλαβον, which though they signify the same thing, yet might some distinction of sense be observed in the distinction of words. For Christ came among the Jews bodily, yet they would not so much as receive Him bodily, nor acknowledge Him for Messias at all; but coming among the Gentiles by His Word and Spirit, they received Him spiritually."—Lightfoot, i. p. 393.

God came unto mankind through the Economy of the Incarnation. The Jewish nation was "His own," by choice (Deut. vii. 6): by purchase (Exod. xix. 4, 5): by covenant (Deut. xxvi. 18): and by kindred (Heb. ii. 16.)

To the few who did receive Him He gave the privilege of becoming sons of God. He Himself, the Word, was the Son of God by Eternal Generation; they were to become sons of God by birth. But this birth was not, like their human birth, by the will of man, by the will of their parents, but by the will of God. Their human or natural birth had taken place independently of themselves. A condition was required prior to this birth; namely, they must believe in the Son of God the Word, who had come into the world.

12 But as many as received Him, to them gave He (power) to become (the sons of God), even to them that believe (on) His Name.¹

(Margin, the right or privilege.)
(Alf. Children of God—in.)

13 [Which were born], not of blood, nor of the will of the flesh, nor of the will of man, but of God.²

[V.* A. Which were made.]

By three separate forms of expression the Evangelist shows that the privilege of becoming sons of God was not an inheritance, to which they succeeded as a matter of course, because they were sons of Adam, but that it was a supernatural gift, over and above their natural endowments, and that it was given to whom He would and in the way in which He would. (1.) "Not of blood;" it was not a birthright, nor in any way connected with natural descent. Their descent from Abraham, on which they prided themselves so much, could not give them this privilege of becoming sons of God; (2) "Nor of the will of the flesh;" (3) "Nor of the will of man." It could not be acquired by any power inherent either in the body or in the mind of man.

This birth is by the will, by the operation, of God. The effect of this birth on the soul cannot, like the natural birth, be recognised by

---

¹ On His Name.—"That is, in or on Him. For the Name of God in Scripture doth often stand for God Himself, as Ps. lxxvi; Micah vi. 9; Acts iii. 16, etc. 'For God is without any mixture or composition, but a most pure and simple essence, and therefore His Name and Himself are not two several things, as they be in the creatures, but one and the same.'—R. Menahem on Exod. 60."—Lightfoot i. 396.

² Of blood, literally of bloods (ἐξ αἱμάτων). "Not a few nouns, which, in most modern languages, are used only in the singular, are in Greek authors and the New Testament employed, for the most part in the plural. This is owing to their having, from a general, or Grecian, or Biblical point of view, a manifold or comprehensive signification.

"Of the plural αἵματα, as source of descent, a direct parallel occurs only in Eurip. 'Ion' 693, in the poetic style."—Winer's *Grammar of New Testament*, p. 189.

the senses. But nevertheless this birth is no fiction, no accommodation of language. It is more real than the natural birth, more lasting, more important to the soul, as much more so as the will of God excels the will of man.

This birth of man by the will of God is a great mystery. But the Birth of God of a woman is a greater, a more wonderful mystery even than this.

14 And the Word (was made) Flesh, and dwelt among us, and we beheld His glory, (the glory) as of the only begotten (of the Father) full of grace and truth.[1]

(Alf. Became—glory—from the Father.)

The Incarnation is revealed to us by Holy Scripture, and it must be explained consistently with the language of Scripture. This is no subject for unbelieving, speculative reason to define. The teaching of the Catholic Church, directed by the Holy Spirit, and limited by the language of Scripture and by the analogy of the faith, is to the following effect:

"The Word was made Flesh," not in the sense in which water is made wine by being mixed with it; not in the sense in which food is made flesh by being taken into it and assimilated to it; not in the sense in which gold is made into a statue by the skilful hands of the workman, but rather in the way in which the soul and body being united together make one man.

The term "flesh" is here used for the whole man. It is used in this sense in many places in Holy Scripture. The following are instances : "By the deeds of the Law there shall no flesh be justified in His sight." (Rom. iii. 20.) "Except that the Lord had shortened those days, no flesh should be saved." (Mark xiii. 20.) "That no flesh should glory in His presence." (1 Cor. i. 29.)

By this union the nature of God was not changed into man, nor the nature of man into God. Each remained perfect, with its own power, its own weakness, so to speak, its own will. The union was in the Person. God and Man became One Person, Christ Jesus. In the One Person there were two natures, two wills.

"And dwelt among us." Of old God had dwelt among His chosen people Israel, and had given visible tokens of His presence among them in the Tabernacle, and in the Temple. For thirty-three years the Word made Flesh sojourns or tabernacles among men. His glory as of the only begotten of the Father, though veiled by His

---

[1] The glory as of, etc., (δόξαν ὡς μονογενοῦς παρὰ πατρὸς). "The meaning is simply, *as* of the only begotten, etc. Even in this instance the particle, of itself, does not indicate what exists *re vera*, though, if we regard the sense, this notion is implied in the comparison (*exactly as*, i.e. *the true, perfect* glory of the Son of God, etc.)."—*Winer's Grammar of New Testament*, p. 639.

Human nature, He manifests among them, in His Life, in His miracles, in His Transfiguration on the Mount, in His glorious Resurrection and Ascension.

By the term "us," the Evangelist probably means himself and the rest of the disciples, who had been His intimate companions, and had witnessed His daily life and miracles, and who could most truly say, "We beheld His glory."

As one of the three who had been chosen to behold His glory in the Transfiguration, St. John may make special reference to that event. St. Peter had already said: "We have not followed cunningly devised fables, when we make known unto you the power and coming of our Lord Jesus Christ, but were eye-witnesses of His majesty. For He received from God the Father honour and glory, when there came such a voice to Him from the excellent glory, This is My Beloved Son, in Whom I am well pleased. And this voice which came from heaven we heard, when we were with Him in the holy mount." (2 Peter i. 16.) St. John here adds his testimony to this fact: "We beheld His glory, the glory as of the only-begotten of the Father."

There could be no question that the Word, the Second Person in the Godhead, was full of grace and truth. Though the Divine nature was veiled from the eyes of men by the Incarnation, It was not thereby diminished, or affected. The Word made Flesh, God Incarnate, was full of grace and truth. "In Him dwelleth all the fulness of the Godhead bodily." (Coloss. ii. 9.)

The Evangelist supports his own testimony by that of John the Baptist. Even before Jesus had begun His ministerial life the Baptist had spoken of Him to his disciples, and when He did come, he cried, saying, This was He of whom I spake.

In verse 15 the Baptist when speaking of Jesus, said : "'This was He" (οὗτος ἦν); and in verse 27 and 30, he said, "This is He" (οὗτός ἐστι). Some have explained this difference of tense in this way: When John delivered his first testimony and said: "This was He," it was immediately after Jesus had been baptized, and when the Spirit, in some manner visible to the bystanders had caught Him up from the very midst of the company and carried Him to the wilderness. It was on this, when Jesus had been just carried out of their sight, that John exclaimed to the people who stood there: "This was He, of whom I spake." On the other two occasions when John said, "This is He," Jesus Himself was present.

15 John (bare witness)¹ of Him, (and cried,) [saying,

---

¹ John beareth witness and cried (μαρτυρεῖ καὶ κέκραγε).—" The word μαρτυρεῖ of the present tense is properly to be understood of John's whole ministry, function, and office, as verse 7 explaineth it, He came for a witness; not to be restrained to this or that particular, vocal and verbal testimony that John gave of Christ, nor even to all the vocal testimonies that he gave of Christ, but to be dilated to John's whole course and ministry that he beareth witness to Christ, in

This was He of Whom (I spake.) He that cometh after me (is preferred) before me]: (for) He was before me.

[S. Omits, saying: S.* This was He who cometh after me. Who is preferred before me.]
(Alf. Beareth witness—and crieth—I said—taketh place—because.)

Jesus came after the Baptist. His Conception was announced to the Blessed Virgin Mary six months after Elizabeth had conceived John. His Birth was after John's. He began His Ministry after John. But He was preferred before him, He was placed before him in honour, in dignity, and glory, because He was before him. He was God, while John was a mere man; He was from all eternity, while John Baptist began his existence with his birth of Elizabeth.

After he had introduced the testimony of John the Baptist the Evangelist resumes the subject of His fulness.

16 [And of His fulness] have all we received, and grace for grace.[1]

[S. V. Because of His fulness.]
(Alf. And out of His fulness all we received.)

Many explanations have been offered of the words "grace for grace," ($\chi\acute{a}\rho\iota\varsigma$ $\mathring{a}\nu\tau\grave{\iota}$ $\chi\acute{a}\rho\iota\tau o\varsigma$). It may be that he intended to say, that through Jesus we receive continual accessions of grace; that where one grace is improved, another is given. The Evangelist may

---

that God raised up such an one to be his forerunner. And the word κέκραγε, in the præter tense is to be applied to the particular testimony that John gave of Christ in that his ministry; so that the former word referreth to John's person, and his whole function, and the latter only to the manner of his executing of one particular of that function."—Lightfoot, i. 517.

"Is preferred before me.—ἔμπροσθέν μου γέγονεν, which the Vulgar Latin hath dangerously translated, ante me factus est, He was made before me: and accordingly the Arians in ancient time made use of this phrase in this sense, against the eternity of the Son. Whereas the word ἔμπροσθεν (as Beza well observeth it) in the New Testament, doth constantly refer to place, and not to time, as Mark i. 2; Matt. xvii. 2; Luke xii. 8; and xix. 27, 28, and divers other places, and therefore our English hath well expressed it with an intimation of such a thing, is preferred before me. For ἔμπροσθέν μου and πρῶτός μου, in this speech of the Baptist, must needs have a distinct and different sense, because the word ὅτι between them doth show that the one is made the reason of the other; He was before me in place and pre-eminence, because He was before me in time and being. Now the word γέγονε which seemeth to refer to the time past, (and which hath occasioned ἔμπροσθεν by some to be understood concerning priority of time) is to be construed in such a construction, as the word ἐγενήθη is in Matt. xxi. 42, and γενόμενος, Acts iv. 11, words not of the present tense, and yet necessarily to be rendered in the present time, is become the head of the corner."—Lightfoot, i. 518.

[1] Grace for grace ($\chi a \rho \iota \nu$ $a \nu \tau \grave{\iota}$ $\chi a \rho \iota \tau o \varsigma$), $\mathring{a}\nu\tau\grave{\iota}$ "has here a peculiar signification, which, however, is easily traced to its primary import:—grace over-against, in equal measure with grace; a subsequent portion of grace in the place of that which preceded,—and thus grace uninterrupted, unceasingly renewed."—Winer's Grammar of New Testament, p. 382.

18   COMMENTARY ON ST. JOHN'S GOSPEL.

also mean that the grace, which we receive through the Word made Flesh, corresponds with His fulness of grace; that as He is the Son of God, so He gave them also, who believed in Him, power to become sons of God; He by Eternal Generation, they by the birth which he has just described.

He next compares the old system under which the Jews had been trained, "the Law," with the new system, "the Kingdom of Heaven." Moses, by God's direction, had inaugurated a system of special preparation for the Incarnation by positive commands, and by ceremonial acts, of which the chief force lay in their being types and shadows of something to come: all comprehended under the term "the Law." But this system, as being prophetic of the Incarnation, was in itself imperfect, and could only be completed by the coming of God in the Flesh. Jesus was God in the Flesh, He was the Word made Flesh.

Moses had, it is true, given them "the Law," but he could not give them grace or power to keep the Law. Moses gave men the knowledge of what was right; Jesus Christ, as being God, could alone give them the power to do it.

17 (For) the Law was given (by Moses), (but) grace and truth came (by) Jesus [Christ.]¹

[S. Omits Christ.]
(Alf. Because—through Moses—omits, but—through.)

Jesus Christ alone could give them grace to become sons of God. He alone could give them remission of their sins, peace with God, and power to fulfil the Law.

The temporal blessings, and the temporal punishments, which Moses promised them, on their keeping or on their neglecting the Law,

---

¹ Truth.—When it is said, the Law was given by Moses, but grace and *truth* came by Jesus Christ (John i. 17), it is plain that the antithesis cannot be between the false and the true, but only between the imperfect and the perfect, the shadowy and the substantial. So, too, the Eternal Word is declared to be τὸ φῶς τὸ ἀληθινόν (John i. 9), not denying thereby that the Baptist was also "a burning and a shining light" (John v. 35), or that the faithful are "lights in the world" (Phil. ii. 15; Matt. v. 14); but only claiming for a greater than all to be "the Light which lighteth every man that cometh into the world." Christ declares Himself ὁ ἄρτος ὁ ἀληθινός (John vi. 32), not that the bread which Moses gave was not also "bread of heaven" (Ps. cv. 40), but it was such only in a secondary inferior degree: it was not food in the highest sense, inasmuch as it did not nourish up unto eternal life those that ate it. (John vi. 49.) He is ἡ ἄμπελος ἡ ἀληθινή (John xv. 1), not thereby denying that Israel also was God's vine, which we know it was (Ps. lxxx. 8; Jer. ii. 21), but affirming that none except Himself realized this name, and all which this name implied, to the full. (Hos. x. 1; Deut. xxxii. 32.) It would be easy to follow this up further; but these examples, which the thoughtful student will observe are drawn chiefly from St. John, may suffice. The fact, that in his writings the word ἀληθινός is used two and twenty times as against five times in all the rest of the New Testament, is one which he will scarcely dismiss as accidental. See also note on III. 18.—Archbishop Trench on *Synonyms of New Testament*, p. 25. See also note on V. 35.

were but shadows of those which Jesus announced. Prosperity in this life was but a shadow of the life everlasting. Punishment in this world was but a foreshadowing of everlasting punishment with the devil and his angels. The rites, the ceremonies, the sacrifices under the Law were not perfect in themselves. They all foreshadowed One to come, One from Whom they derived whatever significance, whatever efficacy, they possessed. They all foreshadowed, and they were all fulfilled in, the Word made Flesh.

The reason here given why Jesus declared the will and the knowledge of God perfectly, and why Moses did not, is that no one but He had seen God. The Patriarchs did not see God. They saw an angel or representative of God. No one had seen God but He Who was the Word, Who was One with God, of the same nature, and Who shared the most intimate relation with God, that language can express. Neither had the Incarnation diminished His Oneness with the Father. The Word made Flesh is perfect God and perfect Man.

18 No man hath seen God at any time: [the only begotten Son which is in the] bosom of the Father, (He hath declared Him).[1]

[S. V. The only begotten God which is (S. omits, which is) in the.]
(Alf. He declared Him.)

It is plain from the other Evangelists that St. John does not record all the testimonies which the Baptist bears to Jesus as the Christ. He probably selects the following as the most public and official, as that given in direct answer to the authoritative inquiries of the Priests and Levites as to the nature of the office which John was sent to fill.

19 And this is (the record) of John, when the Jews[2]

---

[1] The Only Begotten God.—The minute but weighty variation θs (i. e. θεοs) for ὖs (i. e. υιos) is supported by Codd. Sinaitic and Vatican; by the codex Ephræmi, in the Paris Library, (p. m.), by L. 33, the Peshito and margin of the Philoxenian, the Memphitic, Roman, Æthiopic, and a host of Fathers.—Scrivener's *Collation of Sinaitic MS.*, p. xlviii. See also his Introduction to *Criticisms of the New Testament*, p. 436.

[2] The Jews.—" The scrutiny and judging of a prophet belonged only to the Sanhedrin or great Council at Jerusalem; and so is the Talmudic tradition, in the treatise Sanhedrin Perek I.: " They judge not a tribe, nor a false prophet, nor the high priest, but in the judicatory of Seventy and One; And to this law and practice of theirs those words of Christ relate in Luke xiii. 33: 'It cannot be that a prophet perish out of Jerusalem,' because a prophet could not be judged upon life and death in any place but there. " This Court and Council sent these messengers to John to make inquiry after him, and after his authority; and so is the word, *the Jews*, to be understood in this verse, for the representative body of the Jews in the great Judicatory. And they sent Priests and Levites to examine him, as men of the greatest knowledge and learning in the Law, and men of the likeliest abilities to try him, and to dispute and discourse with him according to that in Matt. ii. 7, 'The Priest's lips should keep knowledge, and they should see the Law at his mouth.' "—Lightfoot, i. 521.

sent Priests and Levites [from Jerusalem] to ask him, Who art thou?

[V. A. Unto him from Jerusalem.]
(Alf. The testimony.)

There were many reasons to induce the priests and scribes to turn their eyes towards John the Baptist. By his priestly descent he was one of their own order. The miracle which had attended his birth would be well known in Jerusalem; for it had happened when his father, Zacharias, was engaged in the public ministration of the service of the Temple. The sanctity of John's life, his baptism, the novelty of his preaching, of his dress and mode of living, and his success among the people, all combined to draw the attention of the authorities at Jerusalem to him.

The signs of the times, too, were ominous of some great event. The sceptre had departed from Judah, and was now in the hands of Herod, the Edomite. The seventy weeks foretold by Daniel (ix. 24) for the coming of the Messiah were completed. As the national interpreters of the Scriptures they would be well acquainted with all this. Their contempt for the claims of the carpenter's son, if rumours respecting Him had as yet reached them, might lead them readily to acquiesce, in case John should declare himself the Messiah, the Christ. John's reply seems to indicate that their question was put in such a form as to require a direct answer whether he were the Christ or not; and if not, as some think, to lead him to make such a claim.

20 And he confessed, and denied not; [but confessed] I am not the Christ.

[S. Omits, but confessed.]
(Alf. And he confessed.)

21 [And they asked him], What then? (Art thou Elias?) [And] he saith, I am not. [Art thou (that prophet?)][1] And he answered, No.

[S. And they asked again; S. omits And; S. art thou a prophet?]
(Margin, a prophet.)
(Alf. Art thou Elijah?—the prophet.)

---

[1] Art thou a Prophet? (ὁ προφήτης εἶ σύ.) "There is some question whether to read it in the force of the Article, or no; there are some that do read it so, and some that do not. The Syriac and the Vulgar Latin take no notice of the Article at all, but read it as if it were without, 'Art thou a prophet?' And so doth the margin of our English Bible; and others, with our English text, do interpret the words as speaking of some peculiar pro- phet, which was neither Christ, nor Elias, but some other pointed at and intended by that prediction. Deut. xviii. 15, vid. Cyril, and Chrys., &c.

"I cannot but apprehend that their questioning of the Baptist in these words, ὁ προφήτης εἶ σύ, is indefinitely meant, Art thou a prophet? Not this or that prophet, but art thou a prophet at all? For prophecy had been long decayed amongst them, and when they saw one

22 (Then said they) unto him, Who art thou? that we may give an answer to them that sent us. What sayest thou of thyself?

(Alf. They said therefore.)

23 He said, I am the voice of one crying in the wilderness, Make straight the way of the Lord, as said (the prophet Esaias.)¹

(Alf. Isaiah the prophet.)

appear now of so prophetical a character, as the Baptist was, and when he had resolved them he was neither Christ nor Elias, their properest question then was, Art thou then any other prophet come after so long a time, as there have been no prophets among us? And he answers, No; that is, not in their sense, not a prophet of the same ministry with those in the Old Testament, but of another nature, or not one of those prophets of the Old Testament revived, as Matt. xvi. 14, but a Minister foretold of by one of those prophets, as Isa. xl. 3.

"The reason that I refuse the strict interpretation of this question, Art thou that prophet, as if they spake of some particular man, is partly because the article ὁ is not always to be construed in such a strictness, as pointing out a particular thing or person, but is very commonly, nay, most commonly, of a more large and general signification. But chiefly because I find not in the Jewish writers any particular prophet mentioned, whom they expected to come as they did Christ and Elias; and for aught I find, they do not interpret that place in Deut. xviii. 15 of any such a particular person, but of the succession of prophets in general." &c.—Lightfoot, i. 525.

¹ Voice, word.—φωνή from φάω, rendered in our version "voice," (Matt. ii. 18,) " sound," (John iii. 8,) " noise," (Rev. vi. 1,) is distinguished from ψόφος, in that it is the cry *of a living creature*, being sometimes ascribed to God, (Matt. iii. 17,) to men, (Matt. iii. 3,) to animals (Matt. xxvi. 34,) and, though improperly, to inanimate objects as well, (1 Cor. xiv. 7,) as to the trumpet, (Matt. xxiv. 31,) the wind, (John iii. 8,) the thunder (Rev. vi. 1). But λόγος, a word, saying, or rational utterance of the νοῦς, whether spoken or unspoken, being, as it is, the correlative of reason, can only be predicated of men, of angels, or of God.

... The great theologians of the early Church—above all, Origen in the Greek, and Augustine in the Latin—loved to transfer the antithesis of the φωνή and the λόγος to John the Baptist and his Lord; the first claiming for himself no more than to be "the voice of one crying in the wilderness," (John i. 23,) the other emphatically declared to be the Word which was with God, and was God. (John i. 1.)

In drawing out the relations between John and his Lord, as expressed by these titles, the Voice and the Word, Vox and Verbum, φωνή and λόγος, Augustine traces with a singular subtlety the manifold and profound fitnesses which lie in them for the setting forth of these relations. A word, he observes, is something even without a voice; for a word in the heart is as truly a word as after it is spoken; while a voice is nothing,—a mere unmeaning sound, an empty cry,—unless it be also the vehicle of a word. But when they are thus united, the voice in a manner goes before the word, for the sound strikes the ear before the sense is conveyed to the mind; yet while it thus *goes* before it in this act of communication, it *is not* really before it, but the contrary. Thus, when we speak, the word in our hearts must precede the voice on our lips, which voice is yet the vehicle by which the word in us is transferred to, and becomes also a word in, another; but this being accomplished, or rather in the very accomplishment of this, the voice has passed away, exists no more; but the word which is planted now in the other's heart, as well as in ours, remains. All this Augustine transfers to the Lord and to His forerunner. John is nothing without Jesus; Jesus just

The Baptist answered their question in the sense in which they asked it. Both our Saviour Himself (Matt. xi. 14) and the Angel (Luke i. 17) declared that John was the Elias, or Elijah of the New Testament dispensation; but he was not Elias in the sense in which the Jews were looking for the coming of Elias, he was not Elijah the Tishbite reappearing among them.

The prophet Malachi (iv. 5) had declared that Elijah the prophet— or as the Septuagint renders it, Elijah the Tishbite—should come before the great and terrible day of the Lord. The Jews who did not believe in two Advents of Christ,—the first in humility, the second in glorious majesty,—were now anxiously looking for the coming of Elijah the Tishbite in person. When, then, the Baptist declared in the strongest possible form that he was not the Christ, they ask him,

---

what He was before without John: however, to men the knowledge of Him may have come through John. John the first in time, and yet He Who *came* after, most truly having *been* before him. John, so soon as he had accomplished his mission, passing away, having no abiding significance for the Church of God; but Jesus, of Whom he had told, and to Whom he had witnessed, abiding for ever. (Sermon 293.)—Archbishop Trench, *Synonyms of New Testament*, 318.

"The Wilderness in which John the Baptist dwelt until his thirtieth year, and into which Jesus, when His time arrived, passed for His forty days of prayer and watching, begins at the gates of Hebron and Jerusalem, spreads beyond and below these cities to the south and west, and covers the mountain slopes of Judah from the crest of the high table-land of Ramah and Olivet down to the Fountain of Elisha and the shores of the Dead Sea. It is a tract of country about the size and shape of Sussex, not being a mere waste of scorching sands, herbless and waterless all the year, like the deserts of El Arish and Giseh, but only a dry, unpeopled region, in which the wells are few, the trees low and stunted, the wadies full of stones instead of water, and the caves tenanted by leopards and wolves. It contains no town, not even a village. It has no road, no khan. The fox, the vulture, the hyæna prowl about its solitude. But even in the wilderness nature is not so stern as man. Here and there, in clefts and basins, and on the hill-sides, grade on grade, you observe a patch of corn, a clump of olives, a single palm; but the men who sow the grain, who shake down the fruit, are nowhere to be seen. They dare not stay upon the grounds which they rip with their rude ploughs, or on which with careless husbandry they watch the olive-trees grow: they hie away for protection to the hamlets, and watch-towers on the hill-tops: to Maon, Tekoa, Bethlehem, and Bethany; for the Taâmra Bedaween claim to be lords of the soil, and the spring grass and wild herbage tempt the Adouan from El Belta, the ancient Ammon, into these stony parts. No Syrian peasant dares to build his hut on land over which a Bedaween spreads his tent. In the wilderness of Judah the children of Esau are still what they were of old, the only abiding sheikhs and kings."—Dixon's *Holy Land*, i. 244.

"We were in a most dreary country: calcined hills and barren valleys, furrowed by torrent beds, all without a tree or shrub, or sign of vegetation. The stillness of death reigned on one side, the sea of death, calm and curtained in mist, lay upon the other; and yet this is the most interesting country in the world. This is the Wilderness of Judæa; near this God conversed with Abraham, and here came John the Baptist preaching the glad tidings of salvation. These verdureless hills and arid valleys have echoed the words of the Great Precursor; and at the head of the west ravine lies Bethlehem, the birthplace of the meek Redeemer,—in full sight of the Holy City, the theatre of the most wondrous events recorded on the page of history, — where that Self-Sacrifice was offered, which became thenceforth the seal of a perpetual covenant between God and man!"—Lynch's *Expedition to the Dead Sea*, p. 383.

Art thou Elijah? When he saith, I am not: they ask him, Art thou the prophet? they may mean either the prophet of whom Moses spake, (Deut. xviii. 15-18,) or some distinguished prophet, who would immediately precede the coming of the Messiah.

John Baptist's mission was not to prophesy, but to arrest the attention of the people, and direct it to Jesus as the Christ; to preach repentance, and to prepare the way for Christ's approach ; and to bear witness to Him, and to point Him out to the people. John was not a prophet who foretells the distant coming of his King; he was the herald who announces His arrival, His actual presence among them.

Ezekiel (xxxvi. 25) had prophesied that the Christ should cleanse His people from all their filthiness by baptism, and that He would give them a new heart, and a new spirit. Zechariah (xiii. 1) had also declared that he would open for the house of David, and for all the inhabitants of Jerusalem, a fountain for the remission of sin and uncleanness. The priests and scribes who were sent from Jerusalem to examine John would be well versed in such passages as these. The Pharisees had the reputation of being skilled in the words of Scripture, and in all the questions of the day. Whether those who were sent were Pharisees themselves, or, as some translate the passage, had been sent by the Pharisees, they were sure to represent the intelligence and acuteness of that sect. They therefore retort upon John with a charge of inconsistency in baptizing, if he were not "the Christ," nor Elijah, nor the prophet.

24 (And they which were sent were of the Pharisees.)[1]

[S. V. A.* And they were sent of the Pharisees.]
(Alf. And they had been sent by the Pharisees.)

25 [And they asked him, and said unto him,] Why

---

[1] "The Pharisees in this Evangelist are generally to be understood the Sanhedrin; nor indeed do we find in St. John any mention of the Sadducees at all."—Consult John i. 24, iv. 1, viii. 3, and xi. 46, &c.

"Josephus (Antiq. xiii. 10, 5) says the Pharisees have such a sway amongst the people, that, if they should say anything against the king or high priest, they would be believed.

"And a little after, the Pharisees have given out many rules to the people from the traditions of the Fathers, which are not written in the laws of Moses : and for that very reason the Sadducees rejected them, saying they ought to account nothing as law or obligatory, but what is delivered by Moses, and what hath no other authority but tradition only ought not to be observed. And hence here arises questions and mighty controversies, the Sadducees drawing after them the richer sort only, while the multitude followed and adhered to the Pharisees."—(Antiq. xiii. 10-6.)

"Hence we may apprehend the reason why the whole Sanhedrin is sometimes comprehended under the name of the Pharisees, because the common people, and the main body of that nation, were wholly at the management of the Pharisees, governed by their decrees and laws."—Lightfoot, ii. 571.

baptizest thou then, if thou (be not that Christ, nor Elias, neither that prophet ?)

[S. And they said unto him (omits, asked him and.)]
(Alf. Art not the Christ, nor Elijah, neither the prophet.)

The Baptist answers this question by pointing out to them the difference between his baptism and that of the Messiah. His baptism was not that foretold by the prophet. It did not confer a new heart and a new spirit. It was in no sense a fount to wash away sin and uncleanness. His baptism was merely the badge of those who undertook to repent of their sins, and to look forward to the Christ. His baptism was no outward rite conveying grace to the soul; it was a washing of the body only, and did not affect the soul.

My baptism, he would say, is only a preparation for the Messiah's. By inducing men to repent of their sins, I put them into a state to receive the forgiveness and the Holy Spirit, which the Christ will shortly bestow on them by Baptism. He is already in the very midst of you, but ye know Him only as the carpenter's son. It is He, of whom I have already spoken, who coming after me is preferred before me, and for whom I am not worthy to perform the most menial acts.

26 John answered them, saying, I baptize with water; (but there standeth[1] one among you), whom ye know not:

(Alf. But in the midst of you there standeth one.)

27 (He it is, [who coming] after me [is preferred before me], whose shoe's latchet) I am not worthy to unloose.

[S. V. Who cometh (omit, he it is); S. V. omit, is preferred before me.]
(Alf. This is He that cometh after me, who taketh place before me, the thong of whose shoe.)

28 These things were done [in Bethabara] beyond Jordan, where John was baptizing.

[S. V. A. In Bethany; S. beyond the river of Jordan.]
(Alf. In Bethany.)

Three of the oldest MSS., the Sinaitic, the Vatican, and the Alexandrine, as well as others of less note, read in Bethany beyond

---

[1] There standeth (ἕστηκεν).—" The Syriac readeth it in the present tense, as doth also our English, and so doth Beza and divers others, and so indeed might the Greek word very well bear it; but since it is said, John saw Jesus coming the next day, it is an argument that He was not present there now, and therefore it is most properly to be read in the time past, *there hath stood* one among you."—Lightfoot's Works, i. 513.

Jordan. The Bethany there referred to could not be the Bethany, the town where Lazarus and his sisters lived. That was on the west side of Jordan; this beyond Jordan, or on the east side of it. Bethabara and Bethany have much the same meaning: the one being the house of the ferry or ford, and the other the house of the ship or ferry-boat. It is not, therefore, improbable that these are two names for the same place, or for adjoining places.[1]

The following appears to be the order of events. After Jesus had been baptized by John, which this Evangelist does not relate, He retires into the wilderness for forty days to be tempted by the devil. In the meantime a deputation of priests and Levites had arrived from Jerusalem to examine the Baptist on the nature of his office, when he delivers the foregoing testimony to Jesus in His absence. Then on the next day John seeth Jesus, who was returning from the Temptation, coming to him, when he again bears witness to Him in His presence, apparently before his own disciples. Then on the next day John again bears witness to Jesus who was again present before two of his disciples.

The only objection to this is on the ground that the expression "there standeth one among you" ($\mu\acute{\epsilon}\sigma\sigma\varsigma$ $\delta\grave{\epsilon}$ $\acute{\upsilon}\mu\hat{\omega}\nu$ $\acute{\epsilon}\sigma\tau\eta\kappa\epsilon\nu$), is to be understood literally as implying that Jesus was actually then and there standing in the midst of them. It may, perhaps, be more correctly interpreted as meaning that the Christ was dwelling in the very midst of them, going in and out daily amongst them, but that they did not recognise Him, that they knew Him only as the son of Joseph and Mary, or it may be explained as in the note.

Thus the Baptist delivers three testimonies to Jesus on three consecutive days; (1) in His absence to the deputation from the Jewish Sanhedrin at Jerusalem; (2) in His presence to the general body of John's own disciples; (3) in His presence to two of John's disciples.

29 The next day [John[2] seeth] Jesus coming unto him,

---

[1] **Bethany or Bethabara.** — Origen seems to have read "in Bethany" in various MSS., and also in Heracleon (whom Cave places A.D. 126), but was persuaded that Bethabara was meant, because on making inquiry he found there was a place called Bethabara, but not a Bethany, in the neighbourhood where he supposed this spot must lie. The only Bethany which he knew being, as he says, near Jerusalem, and not on the other side of the Jordan. Origen has the unfortunate reputation of having introduced Bethabara into the text instead of Bethany; he says, $\sigma\chi\epsilon\delta\grave{o}\nu$ $\acute{\epsilon}\nu$ $\pi\hat{a}\sigma\iota$ $\tau o\hat{\iota}\varsigma$ $\grave{a}\nu\tau\iota\gamma\rho\acute{a}\phi o\iota\varsigma$ $\kappa\epsilon\hat{\iota}\tau a\iota$ $\tau a\hat{\upsilon}\tau a$ $\acute{\epsilon}\nu$ $B\eta\theta a\nu\acute{\iota}a$ $\acute{\epsilon}\gamma\acute{\epsilon}\nu\epsilon\tau\rho$. (Origen *in loco*, vol. iv. p. 270; Migne.)

[2] **Interpolations.**—Mr. Burgon observes that the word John, here, and the word Jesus, in John i. 43; vi. 14; xiii. 3; xxi. 1, are confessedly interpolations, their presence being accounted for by the fact that in these places *an ecclesiastical lection begins*, that therefore some word more definite than "He" was required to indicate the person speaking or acting.—Burgon on *St. Mark's Gospel*, p. 221; see also note on i. 43.

Christ's Place of Baptism.—"On the twenty-eighth (Easter-Tuesday, March, 1738) we set out, from near Jericho, about two o'clock in the morning to go to the river Jordan; we went north-east, and the Greeks soon left us to go south-east;

and saith, Behold the Lamb of God, which taketh away the sin of the world.
[S. V. A. He seeth.]
(Margin beareth.)
(Alf. He seeth.)

30 This is He of whom I said, After me cometh a man which (is preferred) before me: (for) He was before me.
(Alf. Taketh place—because.)

Those by whom the Baptist was surrounded were Jews, men who from their earliest years had been so accustomed to the sacrifice of a lamb at the Passover, and to the daily sacrifice of a lamb morning and evening; they were so accustomed to this, that the very mention of a lamb without any further addition whould naturally suggest to their minds a victim, a sacrifice, and atonement for sin. When then the Baptist points out Jesus, and cries, "Behold the Lamb, of God, which taketh away or beareth the sin of the world," they would at once know what he meant, and they would see in Jesus the Victim to be offered in sacrifice, by His death to make atonement for the sin of the world. The Baptist, too, would be well aware that such would be the sense which his words would convey to the Jewish mind. Yet he lays no restriction on his meaning, no limit to the efficacy of this Sacrifice, no limit either in time or in amount of guilt. The reason is this: God Himself is the Victim, which is offered, God Himself is the Priest which offers. The Baptist then goes on to say that he had learnt this by special revelation from heaven.

31 And I knew Him not: but that He should be made manifest to Israel, (therefore am I come) baptizing with water.
(Alf. For this cause came I.)

32 And John (bare record), [saying,] (I saw) the Spirit descending (from heaven like a dove), [and It (abode)] upon Him.
[S. Omits saying: S. And abiding.]
(Alf. Bare witness—I have beheld—as a dove from heaven—remained.)

for those of both religion propose to go to the place where Christ was baptized, but happen to differ in their opinions, and are three or four miles wide of each other ... The river Jordan is deep and very rapid; it is wider than the Tiber at Rome, and may be about as wide as the Thames at Windsor."—Pococke's *Travels*, ii. 32.

"When the Children of Israel passed over Jordan, they went six miles and a quarter to Gilgal, where they set up an altar of twelve stones, in memory of that passage, at the distance of a mile and a half from Jericho (Joseph. Antiq. v. 1; Josh. iv. 20.) So that it is probable they passed over the river Jordan about this place, which seems to be the nearest part of the river to Jericho, and is said to be about seven miles from it."—Pococke's *Travels*, ii. 33.

33 And I knew Him not: but He that sent me to baptize with water, the same said unto me, (upon whom) thou shalt see the Spirit descending, and remaining on Him, the same is He which baptizeth with the Holy Ghost.
[Alf. Upon whomsoever.]

34 (And I saw, and bare record) [that this is the Son of God.]¹
[A. That He is: S. That this is the chosen of God.]
(Alf. And I have seen, and have borne witness.)

When the Baptist says that he did not know Jesus until He was revealed to him by a special sign, he may not mean that he did not know Jesus at all, not even as his own kinsman, nor as the reputed son of Joseph and Mary. Though even this would not be very surprising, when we consider the retired life which John had led from his childhood upward, in the wilderness, apart from the haunts of men. What he undoubtedly does assert is, that he did not know Jesus as the Lamb of God, as the Word made Flesh, as the Christ, until God had by special revelation declared Him; that he did not know Him, at least with such fulness of knowledge as to manifest Him unto Israel. He came for that very purpose, but he must wait until he had the appointed sign given him.

Some knowledge of Jesus as the Christ John seems to have had before His Baptism. As such he had demurred to baptize Him. (Matt. iii. 13.) This knowledge, such as it was, may have been the result of his own inferences from what he had seen and heard of Jesus. John had come to manifest Jesus unto Israel, but before he was allowed to do this, his knowledge must be confirmed in the most unmistakeable manner, he must have a direct revelation from heaven, before he could point Him out as the Lamb of God that taketh away the sin of the world.

St. Matthew iii. 16.	St. Mark i. 10.	St. Luke iii. 21, 22.	St. John i. 32.
And, lo, the heavens were opened unto Him,	He saw the heavens opened,	The heaven was opened,	
and He saw the Spirit of God descending	and the Spirit descending	and the Holy Ghost descended in a bodily shape ($\sigma\omega\mu\alpha\tau\iota\kappa\tilde{\omega}$ $\epsilon\tilde{\iota}\delta\epsilon\iota$)	I saw the Spirit descending from heaven
like a dove ($\dot{\omega}\sigma\epsilon\dot{\iota}$ $\pi\epsilon\rho\iota\sigma\tau\epsilon\rho\dot{\alpha}\nu$) and lighting upon Him.	like a dove ($\dot{\omega}\sigma\epsilon\dot{\iota}$ $\pi\epsilon\rho\iota\sigma\tau\epsilon\rho\dot{\alpha}\nu$) descending upon Him.	like a dove ($\dot{\omega}\sigma\epsilon\dot{\iota}$ $\pi\epsilon\rho\iota\sigma\tau\epsilon\rho\dot{\alpha}\nu$) upon Him.	like a dove ($\dot{\omega}\sigma\epsilon\dot{\iota}$ $\pi\epsilon\rho\iota\sigma\tau\epsilon\rho\dot{\alpha}\nu$) and it abode upon Him.

---

¹ I saw and bare record ($\kappa\dot{\alpha}\gamma\dot{\omega}$ $\dot{\epsilon}\dot{\omega}\rho\alpha\kappa\alpha$ $\kappa\alpha\dot{\iota}$ $\mu\epsilon\mu\alpha\rho\tau\dot{\upsilon}\rho\eta\kappa\alpha$).—"The latter perfect appears to denote that the testimony borne by John at the Baptism of Christ remains firm and valid: *I have seen and I have testified.*"—Winer's *Grammar of New Testament*, p. 288.

By a comparison of the Evangelists we see that three, Matthew, Mark, and John, say that the Holy Spirit descended from heaven upon Jesus, "like a dove," and that Luke is even more definite still, and says that He descended "in a bodily shape like a dove." We can scarcely imagine it possible that these expressions were intended to mean no more, than that the Holy Spirit came down from heaven upon Jesus, and that the manner of His descent was like that of a dove flying down. It is far more in accordance with the genius of the Greek language, and with the traditionary belief of the Church in all ages, to conclude that the Holy Spirit made use of the form of a dove to descend visibly upon Jesus. At the Day of Pentecost He descended upon the Church in the form of tongues, and sat upon each of them. (Acts ii.) At the same time we must be careful not to suppose that the dove was more than an instrument for His visible descent. Here was no union between the Holy Spirit and the dove, as in the Hypostatic Union, when the Word was made Flesh. The dove may have been chosen for its symbolic use, as, by its gentleness and purity, indicative of the influences and of the fruits of the Holy Spirit.

Whether the Baptist was alone with Jesus when he baptized Him; and if not, whether others beside himself saw the descent of the Holy Spirit, or heard the voice, there is nothing in the narrative to determine. Different conjectures have been held with respect to these points.

The visible descent of the Holy Spirit upon Jesus was a proof to John that Jesus the Son of Mary was also the Son of God. This was his warrant henceforth to proclaim Him to Israel as the Lamb of God, which taketh away the sin of the world. It has also been considered as a pledge from God to the Church, that Baptism preceded by repentance, and celebrated as Jesus afterwards commanded, with water in the Name of the Father, and of the Son, and of the Holy Ghost, should always be accompanied by the Holy Spirit. For eighteen hundred years the Church has acted in the belief that as surely as the Holy Spirit, in the form of a dove, descended visibly upon Jesus, and remained upon Him, so surely, though not visibly, would the Holy Spirit descend upon every sincere penitent, who is baptized with the Baptism of Christ.

On the next day the Baptist again bears testimony to Jesus, before two of his disciples. Either these two disciples had not been present the day before, when he pointed Jesus out as "the Lamb of God, which taketh away the sin of the world," or John repeats his testimony before them, in order, by a kind of gentle pressure to induce them to withdraw themselves from him, and to attach themselves to Jesus as His disciples.

35 (Again the next day after John stood), and two of his disciples.

(Alf. Again the next day John was standing.)

36 And looking upon Jesus as He walked, he saith, Behold the Lamb of God!
37 [And] the two disciples heard him speak, and they followed Jesus.

[S. Omits, And.]

Neither St. Matthew, St. Mark, nor St. Luke says anything about our Saviour's actions from His Baptism, with the exception of the Temptation, until the imprisonment of John the Baptist, when He departs into Galilee. The Evangelist St. John is silent about the Temptation, but he alone fills up the interval and traces the steps of Jesus from the time when He returned from His Temptation until the imprisonment of the Baptist. The other three Evangelists relate only John's actions, and the testimony which he bore to Christ before His Baptism, while St. John relates both other acts and other testimonies of the Baptist to Christ besides those before His Baptism. It is in strict accordance with this that St. John here relates that Peter and Andrew follow Jesus before He calls them to be His disciples, while the other Evangelists make no mention of this; for this was while the Baptist was still at liberty. St. Matthew (iv.) relates that Jesus called Peter and Andrew, and that then they follow Him. But there is no contradiction here. These are relations of two different events, with an interval of probably twelve months between them, one before the Baptist's imprisonment, and the other after.

38 [(Then)] Jesus turned, (and saw) them following, and saith [unto them], What seek ye? They said unto Him, Rabbi which is to say, being interpreted, Master, (where dwellest Thou?)¹

[S. Omits Then : S. Omits, unto them.]
(Margin abidest.)
(Alf. But—and beheld—where abidest Thou?)

39 He saith unto them, [Come and see], [They came]

---

¹ Rabbi.—" This and other titles of their doctors, as Rab, and Rabban, and Ribbi, were but lately grown into use and request among them, and sprang up but very little before the birth of Christ. The prophets, and the men of the great synagogue, and all the generations till the times of Hillel, had been content with their bare proper names, as Sadoc, Baithus, Antigonus, Sammai, Hillel, Shemaya, Abtalion, and the like very frequent and common in mention in the Jewish authors. But Simeon the son of Hillel (he that took our Saviour in his arms, Luke ii.) was the first Doctor among them *cum titulo*, and he was called Rabban. From his times and forward, titles came exceedingly into request and fashion among them, and none more common than the title Rabbi, as appeareth frequently in the Gospel, and infinitely in their own writers," &c.—Lightfoot's Works, i. 514.

and saw where (He dwelt),[1] (And abode) with Him that day : [for] it was about [the tenth hour.]

[V. Come, and ye shall see: S. V. A. They came therefore: S.V.A. Omits, for A. The sixth hour.]
(Alf. He abode—and remained—omits, for.)

According to all the old commentators the tenth hour would be 4 P.M.; a few modern scholars make it 10 A.M. The latter maintain that St. John does not, like the other three Evangelists, use the Roman mode of calculating time, and begin from sunrise, about 6 A.M.; but that he uses, what they call, the Asiatic method, and reckons, like ourselves, from 12 at midnight to 12 at noon. This explanation has been introduced doubtless in order to explain the difficulties which exist in harmonizing the various accounts of the Crucifixion, but besides failing fully to remove all those difficulties, it adds one of its own. Is it probable that St. John, who confessedly wrote his Gospel after the others, and, as many think, to supply their omissions, is it probable that, in relating the same events, he would use a totally

---

[1] Where He dwelt (τοῦ μένει).—"It is questionable whether μένει here doth intimate His inn or His habitation, but I rather understand the latter, and that the place was Capernaum; where Christ had an habitation, and was a member or citizen of that city. For though he was a Nazarite in regard of His mother's house and residence, yet it is very probable He was a Capernaite by His father Joseph. For:

"1. Observe that Capernaum is called His own city, Matt. ix. 1 compared with Mark ii. 1.

"2. There He pays tribute, as the proper place where He should pay it, Matt. xvii. 24.

"3. When He is refused at Nazareth, His mother's town, He goeth down to Capernaum, His father's, Luke iv. 31.

"4. His resort to Capernaum was very frequent, and His abode there very much, John ii. 12; Luke iv. 31; John vi. 17; Luke x. 15.

"5. That His father and mother are very well known there, John vi. 42.

"6. That in regard of this frequency of Christ's being in this town, and its interest in Him as an inhabitant and member of it, Capernaum is said to be lifted up to Heaven.

"Now Capernaum, standing upon the banks of Jordan, and on the very point of the lake of Gennesaret, as Jordan began to spread itself into that lake, He and these disciples that go with Him, pass over the water before they come thither, for now they were on the other side Jordan where John baptized."—Lightfoot, i. 530.

Houses.—"Many of the dwelling-houses (at Keraseh, Chorazin) are in a tolerably perfect state, the walls being in some cases six feet high; and as they are probably the same class of houses as that in which our Saviour dwelt, a description of them may be interesting. They are generally square, of different sizes—the largest measured was nearly thirty feet—and have one or two columns down the centre to support the roof, which appears to have been flat, as in the modern Arab houses. The walls are about two feet thick, built of masonry or of loose blocks of basalt; there is a low doorway in the centre of one of the walls, and each house has windows twelve inches high, and six and a-half inches wide. In one or two cases the houses were divided into four chambers."—Recovery of Jerusalem, p. 347.

"Several lamps, weights, jars, and an iron bar were found in this canal, and also a stone roller for rolling flat roofs, precisely similar to those in use on the flat roofs of the Lebanon; so it is evident that at some period at least one house in Jerusalem was covered with a flat roof of wooden joists and mud: and I am inclined to the opinion that this was the general mode of construction of roofs until after the city was destroyed by Titus, when wood becoming scarce, the vaulted roof came into use."—Recovery of Jerusalem, p. 108.

different method of reckoning the times at which they happened, and not give some intimation of this, especially in a book which abounds with explanations of words as well as of customs? To many this is an insuperable objection.[1]

40 [One of the two] which heard John speak, and followed Him, was Andrew, Simon Peter's brother.
[A. Now one of the two.]

Some, by comparing this verse with chapter xxi. 2, have conjecture that Thomas was the other disciple; but the general opinion is that the other disciple was St. John himself. In relating the transactions in which he and others were concerned, this Evangelist's invariable custom is never to speak of himself by name. Throughout the whole of his Gospel he never once mentions his own name. John and his brother James were partners in the fishing trade with Andrew and his brother Simon. It would thus follow, very naturally, that they would be companions in other matters of common interest, especially if, as appears, they were both disciples of the Baptist.

Thus Andrew was first drawn to Jesus by the testimony of John the Baptist, and then by an internal conviction derived from his own conversation with Jesus. Full of love and zeal after this conversation he is not content to keep the discovery to himself. He hastens to communicate to his brother that they have found the Messias the object of their search.

41 He first findeth his own brother Simon, and saith unto him, We have found the Messias, which is, being interpreted [the] Christ.[2]
(Margin, the Anointed.)
[All MSS. omit the.]
(Alf. Omits, the.)

42 [And] he brought him to Jesus. ([And] when Jesus beheld him, He said,) Thou art Simon [the son of Jona] :[3]

---

[1] The tenth hour.—For arguments in favour of the former interpretation, or 4 P.M., see Dean Alford's Greek Testament; in favour of the latter, or 10 A.M., see Bishop Wordsworth's Greek Testament.

[2] Which is being interpreted, Christ. —" These are the words of the Evangelist the historian, and not the words of Andrew; for it was needless for him to tell Peter what was the meaning of Messias, and accordingly the Syriac translator hath omitted this clause; and that in verse 42, which is by interpretation, Peter; and that also, chap. iv. 25, which is by interpretation, Christ, as knowing it unnecessary to tell an Hebrew, or a Syrian, what is meant by Messias, or Cephas."—Lightfoot's Work, i. 515.

[3] The Son of Jona.—" There are that conceive a corruption to be in the writing of this word, for, they say, it should be Joanna. And of that mind is Jerome, the Vulgar Latin, Erasmus, at John xxi. 15; and of that writing is Erasmus, his Greek copy there, and some others here. But

thou shalt be called Cephas, which is by interpretation, (a stone.)

[S. V. omit, And: S. V. A. omit, And: S. V. The son of John.]
(Margin, Peter.)
(Alf. Jesus looked on him and said—which is by interpretation, Peter.

Jesus begins to teach Simon, on his very first introduction to Him, that He is more than man, that the past and the future are alike open to Him. He discovers to him his name and his origin, Simon, son of Jona. He changes his name from Simon to one that was more expressive of his future, either of his future faith, or of his future office in the Church. For both these have been held to be the point especially intended in the name Peter by different commentators, influenced chiefly by their different prepossessions.

Dr. Lightfoot (i. 531) has given an interpretation, which is founded on the etymology of the word, and is deserving of attention. He gives several weighty reasons to prove that Cephas is the adjective form of Cepha, and that as Cepha means Petra, a Rock, so Cephas means Petrus or Petrosus, Rocky, or belonging to the Rock.

The reason why our Saviour gives Peter the name of Cephas, or Rocky, as he thinks, was not so much because he was built upon the Rock, for so were all the rest of the Apostles except Judas, but because he had a special work to do about that building, which Christ was to found upon the Rock. In the Church, which Christ built upon the Rock, Peter had this special and singular work and privilege, that he was the first that preached the Gospel to the Gentiles. (Acts x. and xv. 17.)

Philip was the first whom Jesus expressly called to be His disciple. Being of the same city as Andrew and Peter, Bethsaida, it is possible that Philip had already been favourably impressed towards Jesus by their report of Him. Bethsaida was a city or town on the west side of the Sea of Galilee. A little to the south of Bethsaida was Cana, also in Galilee, the city of Nathanael, who appears to have been a friend of Philip's.

43 The day following, [Jesus[1] would go forth] into

---

upon what ground this facile and most general reading of Jona (for so the Syriac, Arabic, most and best Greek copies, and most translations utter it) should be forsaken, and one so far-fetched and strained as Joanna be embraced and taken for the right, I cannot yet understand or apprehend."—Lightfoot, i. 531.

"Jona was a name among the Jews very commonly used, and we meet with it frequently among the Talmudic authors, written Jonah; why therefore should not Peter's father be allowed the name of Jonah, as well as that of John."—Lightfoot, ii. 531.

[1] Interpolations.—Introductory clauses or proper names are frequently interpolated at the commencement of Church Lessons (περικοπαί), whether from the margin of ordinary manuscripts of the Greek Testament (where they were usually placed for the convenience of the reader), or from the Lectionaries or proper Service Books, especially those of the Gospels

Galilee, and findeth Philip, [and saith unto him,] Follow Me.

[S. V. A. He would go : S. V. A. and Jesus saith unto him.]
(Alf. Was minded to go.)

44 [Now] Philip was (of Bethsaida), (the city) of Andrew and Peter.

[S. Omits, Now.]
(Alf. From Bethsaida—of the city.)

Nathanael is only once besides mentioned in the Gospels (John xxi. 2)—at least, by this name. Many have thought that Nathanael and Bartholomew were only two names for one and the same person, and for the following reasons.
1. The other Evangelists (Matt. x. 3 ; Mark iii. 18 ; Luke vi. 14) join Philip and Bartholomew together, while St. John joins Philip and Nathanael. 2. If Nathanael and Bartholomew be not the same, we nowhere read of the call of Bartholomew by Jesus. 3. The other three Evangelists speak of Bartholomew but never of Nathanael ; and St. John names Nathanael, but not Bartholomew. The plain inference from which is that these two names denote the same person. 4. St. John (xxi. 2) associates Nathanael, Peter, Thomas, James, and John as fishing together, when Jesus appeared to them after His Resurrection, on the Lake of Tiberias. Four of these were apostles ; it is therefore probable, or at least not improbable, that the fifth, Nathanael, was also an Apostle, and if he were an Apostle, he must be the same as Bartholomew. 5. Bartholomew was not a proper name at all, but merely a description of his descent—son of Tolmai, while Nathanael was the proper name. A similar instance we have in the case of Simon Bar-jona (Matt. xvi. 17), Simon being the proper name, and Bar-jona, son of Jonas, a description of his origin. 6. Of no man's character did our Saviour express greater admiration, and to none did he promise greater things than to Nathanael. He might therefore, with great probability, have chosen him one of His twelve Apostles.[1]

45 Philip findeth Nathanael,[2] and saith unto him, We

(Evangelistaria). Thus in our English Book of Common Prayer the Name of Jesus is introduced into the Gospels for the 14th, 16th, 17th, and 18th Sundays after Trinity ; and whole clauses into those for the 3rd and 4th Sundays after Easter, and the 6th and 24th after Trinity. To this cause is due the prefix εἶπε δὲ ὁ κύριος Luke vii. 31 ; and καὶ στραφεὶς πρὸς τοὺς μαθητὰς εἶπε, Luke x. 22 ; and such appellations as ἀδελφοί or τέκνον Τιμόθεε (after σὺ δὲ in 2 Tim. iv. 5) in some copies of the Epistles. Hence the frequent interpolation (e.g., Matt. iv. 18 ; viii. 5 ; xiv. 22) or changed position (John i. 43) of Ἰησοῦς.—Scrivener's *Introd. to Criticism of New Testament*, p. 11. See also note on i. 29.

[1] See Cornelius à Lapide.
[2] Nathanael.—" We find the name Nathanael in the Old Testament also : as 1 Chron. xv. 24 ; Ezra x. 22, &c. But Philip and Andrew, and Nicodemus, &c., were names of a later edition, taken up

D

have found Him of whom Moses in the Law; and the
prophets did write, (Jesus of Nazareth, the son of Joseph.)

(Alf. Jesus, the son of Joseph, which is from Nazareth.)

Philip may be here describing Jesus to Nathanael, as he was
known by common rumour, Jesus of Nazareth, the son of Joseph. As
such Nathanael, who was of Cana, a city close to Nazareth, would
easily recognise Him. It may be that Philip in these words gives his
own opinion of Jesus, as the Messiah, as He who was foretold by Moses
and the Prophets, and yet as the son of Joseph. At a much later
period than this (John xiv. 9), Philip had a very imperfect opinion as
to who Jesus really was. Though He had been three years with His
disciples, Philip had scarcely then mastered the truth that Jesus,
whom men called the son of Joseph, was the Son of God, the Word
made Flesh, One with the Father and equal to the Father.

46 [And] Nathanael said unto him, (Can there any
good thing come) out of Nazareth?[1] Philip saith unto
him, Come and see.

[S. Omits, And.]
(Alf. Can any good thing come.)

---

into use since the Grecian power and
language had overspread Judæa, and those
Eastern countries. This Nathanael was
of Cana of Galilee, John xxi. 2, one of the
first disciples called, and that continued
with Jesus to the very last, as it appeareth by that place in John; now since
all these that are mentioned in this chapter by name, as Peter, and Andrew, and
Philip were made Apostles, it is somewhat strange if Nathanael missed the like
place."—Lightfoot's Works, i. 515.

[1] Nazareth.—"It is one peculiarity of
the Galilean hills, as distinct from those of
Ephraim or Judah, that they contain or
sustain green basins of table land just
below their topmost ridges..... Such,
above all, is Nazareth; fifteen gently
rounded hills seem as if they had met
to form an enclosure for this peaceful
basin—they rise round it like the edge of
a shell to guard it from intrusion. It is
a rich and beautiful field in the midst of
those green hills — abounding in gay
flowers, in fig-trees, small gardens, hedges
of the prickly pear; and the dense rich
grass affords an abundant pasture. The
expression of the old topographer, Quaresimus, was as happy as it is poetical:
'Nazareth is a rose, and, like a rose, has
the same rounded form, enclosed by

mountains as the flower by its leaves.'
The village stands on the steep slope of
the south-western side of the valley."—
Stanley's *Sinai and Palestine*, p. 365.

"There is a well, named after the Virgin,
to the east of the city, which we gazed at
with extreme interest; it still supplies
Nazareth with water, and thither, without
doubt, came the Virgin Mother and her
Saviour Son, day after day, to draw water
— as we saw the daughters of Nazareth
coming while we stopped our horses to
drink of it."—Lord Lindsay's *Letters from
the Holy Land*, ii. 84.

Galilee.—The geographical position of
Naphtali produced great effects upon its
history. The tribe occupied border-land.
It came into close contact with the Syrians
of Damascus, with the mountain tribes
of Lebanon, and especially with the great
commercial nation of Phœnicia. Separated from the body of the Jewish people,
forced into connection with strangers, the
Naphtalites became less exclusive than
their brethren. The Phœnicians traded
with them, and settled among them.
(1 Kings ix. 11-13.)

"That sharp line which separated Jew
and Gentile was in part at least obliterated. In worship, in manners, and even
in language, they accommodated them-

Nazareth was a small obscure town in Galilee, a district despised by the inhabitants of Judæa for the rudeness and want of cultivation of its inhabitants, and also perhaps for the great admixture of Gentiles or foreigners which it always contained.[1] Here Jesus was conceived (Luke i. 26), but He was not born here, but in Bethlehem of Judæa. The popular opinion at this time was that Jesus was born at Nazareth. From knowing only this popular rumour arose Nathanael's prejudice against Jesus as the Christ. But his objection was to Galilee, not to Nazareth in particular. He would have had a similar objection against any place in Galilee. This appears from John vii. 41, etc. How can this Jesus be the Christ, reasons Nathanael; He was born in Nazareth, and the prophets say that the Christ shall spring from Bethlehem. Nathanael's question to Philip, " Can there any good thing come out of Nazareth ? " was prompted partly by the reputation of Galilee, and partly by the prediction of the prophets. But Nathanael did not shut himself up in the belief of this, and close his heart to all explanation and examination on the subject. Here doubtless was one proof of the guilelessness of his character. Nathanael was an earnest and a sincere seeker after the truth.

47 Jesus saw Nathanael coming to Him, [and saith of him,] Behold an Israelite indeed, in whom is no guile!

[S. And saith of Nathanael.]

48 Nathanael saith unto Him, Whence knowest Thou me? Jesus answered and said unto him, (Before that Philip called thee,) when thou wast under the fig-tree,[2] I saw thee.

(Alf. Before Philip called thee.)

---

selves to their Gentile neighbours, and at length the whole land was called 'Galilee of the Gentiles,' and its people lost caste with the exclusive Jews of the South. These facts may help to explain the question of Nathanael : ' Can any good thing come out of Nazareth ? ' (John i. 46) ; and the remark of the woman regarding Peter, 'Thou art a Galilean, and thy speech agreeth thereto.' " (Mark xiv. 70.) —*Giant Cities of Bashan*, p. 260.

[1] See Note to Chap. vii. 52.

[2] The Fig-tree.—The advantages of the fig-tree as a shade are shown in the following : " As we approached, one of the camel-drivers, pointing to a cluster of six large fig-trees, cried out, ' Tacht et-teen,' —under the fig-tree ? And soon we felt the pleasantness of this shade ; for there is something peculiarly delightful in the shade of the fig-tree. It is far superior to the shade of a tent, and perhaps even to the shadow of a rock ; since not only does the mass of heavy foliage completely exclude the rays of the sun, but the traveller finds under it a peculiar coolness, arising from the air gently creeping through the branches. Hence the force of the Scripture expression, ' When thou wast under the fig-tree.' "—*Mission to the Jews from Scotland*, p. 108.

Some have explained this passage as follows :—The words, "the true and guileless Israelite" was a name by which Nathanael was known amongst his friends, and was descriptive of his singularly upright dealing towards others, in the same way that Aristides was called "the Just," among his fellow Athenians. As Jesus had given to Peter the first intimation that He knew more than mere man could know by telling him what was his name and who was his father, though He had never seen him before, so He acts towards Nathanael and addresses him by the appellation by which he was known among his intimate friends. When Nathanael expresses his surprise that Jesus knew him at all, and especially that He knew the name which his friends had given him, Jesus goes on to inform him that He knew not only his upright dealing towards men, and the name by which they described that, but that He knew also his righteous conduct towards God, that He knew even his most secret acts of devotion which, as he thought, could be known only to himself, as they were performed within the thick impenetrable shade of the fig-tree. It was by slight proofs at first and by slow degrees that He led on both Peter and Nathanael to acknowledge that He was God as well as Man. Thus Jesus both gave His sanction to the truth of the description, ["an Israelite indeed, in whom there is no guile," as applied to Nathanael, and also used it as a means to discover to him who He was.

49 Nathanael (answered) [(and saith unto Him), Rabbi], Thou art the Son of God : [Thou art the King] of Israel.

[S. Said, Rabbi : V. Omits, And saith unto Him : A. Thou art King.]
(Alf. Answered him. Omits, And said unto Him.)

50 Jesus answered and said unto him, Because I said unto thee, I saw thee under the fig-tree, believest thou ? Thou shalt see greater things than these.

51 And He saith unto him, Verily, verily,[1] I say

---

[1] Verily, verily, Greek, Amen, amen.—"Let the reader observe a peculiar use of the word Amen among the Jews. The judges adjured a man, saying, We adjure thee by the Lord God of Israel, or by Him whose name is Merciful, that thou hast nothing of this man's in thy hand; and he answered, Amen ; or they said, N. the son of N. is cursed of the Lord God of Israel, or of Him whose name is Merciful, if such a man's goods be in his hand, and he discover it not ; and he answered, Amen.'—Maimonides' tract Shevugnoth, ver. 11. And so he related concerning vows, that 'whosoever vowed any holy thing, and bound it up by Amen, he was tied.' &c.—Vid. Sam. Petit variarum Lect. i. 7, who concludeth hereupon thus,

unto you, [Hereafter]¹ ye shall see (heaven open,) and the angels of God ascending and descending upon the Son of Man.

[S. V. Omit, hereafter.]
(Alf. Omits, hereafter—the heaven opened.)

In His conversation with Nathanael, Jesus refers to two well-known events in the life of the Patriarch Jacob: (1) His wrestling with the Angel of God, in memory of which his name was changed to Israel; for as a prince he had power with God and with man, and had prevailed. (Gen. xxxii. 24.) (2) To the vision which appeared to him at Bethel: (Gen. xxviii. 12 :) "And he dreamed, and behold a ladder set up on the earth, and the top of it reached to heaven : and behold the angels of God ascending and descending on it."

Jesus addresses Nathanael by a term which indicated that he, like Jacob, had wrestled with God in prayer, and had prevailed with Him. In reply to Nathanael's question, how He could know anything of his character at all, Jesus alludes to certain of his secret acts of devotion and meditation, which Nathanael thought could be known only to God and to himself. But to reveal the secret thoughts of the heart was but a small thing for the Word made Flesh. He had much greater things than this to do. His work was to renew the intercourse between heaven and earth, which by man's sin had been so long interrupted, to reconcile man to God, to establish on earth the Economy which Jacob's dream had prefigured.

It is probable that in these words Jesus refers to the Church, and to her spiritual privileges, to the angels who should act as ministering spirits for them who should be heirs of salvation, to the unbroken communication which should henceforth be maintained between heaven and earth, quite as much as to any special appearance of angels, in the Agony in the Garden, or in the Ascension. Though these words were spoken to Nathanael, the promise was to all : " Ye shall see."

Nathanael calls Jesus " the Son of God." But it is more than probable that neither he nor Philip, nor any of them, except the Baptist, as yet understood the full meaning of these words. They believed Him to be the Messiah, who had been foretold by the prophets, and, in some sense, to be the Son of God ; but it is doubtful whether they understood that He was the Word made Flesh, the

---

¹ Cum dicit Christus, Αμὴν λέγω ὑμῖν, idem est ac diceret, Juratus vobis dico.' "— Lightfoot, i. 515.
¹ Hereafter.—" Our English and Erasmus render ἀπάρτι hereafter, and so have left the time at a very large and uncertain scantling. But the Syriac and the Vulgar render it, from this time, or henceforward, and so it most properly and naturally meaneth. For it signifieth not only a date of time, and some one action done after that date at a time uncertain, but a continuance of such actions or things from that date forward."—Lightfoot, i. 537.

Second Person in the Godhead, One with the Father, and equal to the Father. Jesus leads them on by degrees to a perfect knowledge of this great Mystery.

It was probably for this purpose, that after Nathanael had confessed Jesus to be the Son of God, He calls Himself the Son of Man. This is the name by which He is constantly styled in the Gospels, and always by Himself. It may be that He uses this expression here to recall Nathanael's thoughts to the first promise, and to teach him that He is the Second Adam, the seed of the woman who should bruise the serpent's head (Gen. iii. 15), who should undo the mischief wrought by the disobedience of the First Adam, and who should renew man's intercourse with angels, which the First Adam by his sin had forfeited.

INTRODUCTORY NOTE TO CHAPTER II.

Temple.—There were three Temples at Jerusalem. The first was built by Solomon, and completed in seven years, (1 Kings vi. 38,) about 1005 B.C. This was burnt by Nebuchadnezzar, 586 B.C. The second Temple was built by Zerubbabel after the return from captivity, 520 B.C., and was completed in eighteen years. The third Temple was built by Herod the Great. This was a rebuilding of the second Temple. He announced his intention to rebuild it 19 B.C., probably when the people were collected at Jerusalem at the Passover. The completion of the sanctuary itself was celebrated with lavish sacrifices and a great feast, 16 B.C. The courts, cloisters, etc., were added afterwards. Herod's Temple was burnt to the ground during the siege of Jerusalem by Titus, 70 A.D. This happened in the very same month, and on the very same day of the month, (15th July,) as Solomon's Temple had been burnt by Nebuchadnezzar.

The arrangements in Solomon's Temple were identical with those of the Tabernacle, but the dimensions were exactly double. The Temple of Zerubbabel was inferior to that of Solomon in its precious metals, carved ornamentation, and textile fabrics; but it was in almost every dimension one third larger than Solomon's. The internal dimensions of Herod's Temple were the same as those of Solomon; but the whole plan was augmented by the surrounding parts being increased. Zerubbabel's Temple was not larger than an average parish church, Solomon's was smaller. The architectural style of Herod's Temple was Corinthian, that of Zerubbabel's Temple was probably Persian, as it resembles the buildings found at Persepolis and Susa, that of Solomon's is unknown.—Williams's *Holy City*; Smith's *Bib. Dict.*

Herod's Temple.—"Herod, as you may still see from the glorious vaults and passages, visible beneath the Aksa, employed on his works the masons of Athens and Antioch. Indeed, it may be said of Herod's temple, as of Herod himself, that in outward face and polish it displayed far less of the Hebrew genius than of the Greek; yet the core of his new edifice kept its original shape; and the Temple of Herod, like the Temple of Solomon, was a marble tent.

"Deep in the heart of the mass of buildings on Moriah, on the highest level of the rock, the Temple proper, the tent of stone, had been raised by priestly hands. As the tread of any secular foot, whether of Jew or Greek, would have profaned the holy place, the

Ionian builders were thrust aside from this inner range; enough for these heathens to labour on the gates, the colonnades and the open courts. This sacred block was parted like the tabernacle into two grand chambers; the adytum, the Holy of Holies, a square room, in shape a cube, being ten yards in length, in breadth, and in height. This Holy of Holies stood to the west. In front of it, parted from it only by a veil or screen, was the naos, the holy place. As in the old tabernacle, the inner chamber was the dwelling of the Most High; a room now bare and empty, since the Ark had been lost in the Babylonish war; yet not to be trodden, not to be seen, except on rarest occasions by mortal man. In the outer chamber, that lying to the east, stood the candlestick bearing seven lamps, perhaps to typify the seven planets; the table of shew-bread with twelve loaves to represent the months; the altar of incense, having thirteen spices burning night and day, to signify that all the produce of the earth belongs to God. These ornaments were of gold. The veil which divided the Holy of Holies from the Holy Place was a curtain of finest work.

"The true front of this edifice, facing towards the sunrise, stood high and square, having in the middle a great porch or opening like a Roman arch, before which hung a second veil; a magnificent curtain of rich Babylonian art, embroidered with blue and flax, scarlet and purple; colours which were meant to be a reflex and image of the world—the scarlet representing fire, the flax earth, the blue sky, the purple sea. No figures, no sculptures, as in Persian and Egyptian temples, adorned the front. Golden vines and clusters of grapes, the typical plant and fruit of Israel, ran along the wall, and the greater and lesser lights of heaven were wrought into the texture of the veil. The whole façade was covered with plates of gold, which, when the sun shone upon them in the early day, sent back his rays with added glory, so great that gazers standing on Olivet had to shade their eyes when turning towards the Temple mount.

"Twelve steps led down from this platform of the Temple proper, to a second level, occupied by the Court of the Priests. There stood the great bronze laver, the altar of burnt offerings built of unhewn stones, and a number of marble benches on which were laid the flesh of victims waiting to be burnt. Three flights of stairs led down from this court to a third level, occupied by the Court of the Israelites, sometimes called the Sanctuary. Here stood the chief edifices connected with the Temple; houses of priests, offices, guard-room, with the Lishcathha-Gazith, hall of the Sanhedrin. In this Court of the Israelites, facing the porch of the Holy Place, rose a magnificent gate of Corinthian brass, said to have been brought from Alexandria by Nicanor, and sometimes called by his name. It was of Greek design, and some persons believe it to have been that Beautiful Gate by which the lame man sat begging alms when Peter and John went up to pray. Other gates were of wood, but covered with either gold or silver gilding.

"A third flight of stairs, fourteen in number, dropped to an outer court, that of the cloisters, commonly called the Gentile Court, because, not being a part of the Temple, it was open to men of all nations, and had become a kind of sacred exchange and market-place. Here the brokers had their hhanoth, shops or stalls, at which the Jew from Galilee or Perea exchanged his drachm and statu for the sacred shekel; the dove-seller kept his cotes for the accommodation of persons too poor to sacrifice a kid or lamb; and the huckster who sold sheep and oxen for burnt offerings had his pens.

"An open market, lying close to the Altars, was a convenience to the stranger and to the priest; for as no money could be offered in the Temple except sacred shekels, and as no dove or lamb could be slain unless it were of a certain age and breed, many a man might have left Jerusalem without offering his gift, had he not been able, through this arrangement of the dealers, to buy sacred coins and acceptable sacrifices near the Temple gate.

"On this Court of the Gentiles, this market frequented by Greeks and Egyptians, Herod had exhausted the riches of his taste. The Holy of Holies had been left to the priests, who completed their task in about eighteen months; but the surrounding courts had occupied Herod himself for more than eight years; and the porticos, colonnades, and stairs, with many of the halls, offices, and gates, had been left unfinished at his death. At first his son, afterwards the priests, carried on his ambitious work, not to enhance God's glory, but to foster human pride. Cloisters ran round the wall on the inner side, sustained on rows of columns exquisitely wrought, the capitals being ornamented with the acanthus and water-leaf, as in the famous Tower of the Winds. West, north, and east these columns were in three rows; on the south they were in four. The floor made a shaded walk, like the Colonnade in Venice, and the roof an open walk, like the Gallery of Genoa. The pavement was inlaid with marbles of many colours. Leading into this court from the city and the country were many noble gates; one of those on the eastern side, facing the Mount of Olives, was called Solomon's Porch, and a second, near by it, was called the Beautiful Gate.

"When the whole group of buildings,—Temple, courts, halls, cloisters, terraces, and walls,—were seen from a little distance,—say, from the shoulder of Olivet, where the road winds round from Bethany, —they had the appearance of a rough and sparkling pyramid, the base being the line of foundation-wall, the apex being the golden front of the Holy Place."—Dixon's *Holy Land*, vol. ii. p. 43.

"All traces of the Temple have long since disappeared; not one stone has been left upon another, and its exact position has for years been one of the most fiercely contested points in Jerusalem topography."—*Recovery of Jerusalem*, p. 8.

"On one point all are agreed, that the magnificent triple cloister, the Stoa Basilica, built by Herod, stood on the top of the southern wall, and the appearance of this when perfect must have been grander than anything we know of elsewhere. It is almost impossible to realize the effect which would be produced by a building longer and higher than York Cathedral, standing on a solid mass of masonry almost equal in height to the tallest of our church spires; and to this we must add the dazzling whiteness of stone fresh from the mason's hands."—*Recovery of Jerusalem*, p. 9.

CHAPTER II.

1 *Christ turneth water into wine;* 12 *Departeth into Capernaum, and to Jerusalem;* 14 *Where he purgeth the Temple of buyers and sellers;* 19 *He foretelleth His Death and Resurrection;* 23 *Many believed because of His miracles, but He would not trust Himself with them.*

CANA of Galilee, the village where our Saviour turned the water into wine, and where he afterwards healed the nobleman's son, (John iv. 46,) was the home of Nathanael. (John xxi. 2.) There is some doubt as to the true site of the ancient Cana. But the truth of the Gospel narrative is not in any way affected by our uncertainty as to the site of Cana.

1 And the third day there was a marriage in Cana[1] of Galilee: and the Mother of Jesus was there :[2]

---

[1] Cana. "About two miles further, (that is, five miles from Sepporeh,) is Kepher Kenna, where, the Latins say, our Saviour wrought His first miracle of turning water into wine at the marriage of Cana. On the south side of the village is a fountain, out of which, they say, the water was taken that was turned into wine. .... It is certain this situation, so near Nazareth, makes it very probable that it was the place where this miracle was wrought; but the Greeks have a tradition that it was at Cana, on the west side of the plain of Zabulon, about three or four miles north-west of Sepporeh; and it is very extraordinary they should allow that the water was carried from this fountain, which is at the distance of four or five miles from it. Whichever was the place, it seemed to be a matter unsettled about the beginning of the last century, when a writer on the Holy Land (Quaresimus) endeavoured to fix it here, as the most probable place; though Adrichomius seems to give such a description of it from several authors, as would incline to think that it was the other Kana."— Pocock's *Travels*, ii. 66.

Dixon (*Holy Land*, i. 332) discusses the claims of these two places to be the Cana of Scripture at great length, and gives it in favour of Kefr Kenna. Robinson is in favour of Khurbet Kânâ, or Kânâ el Jêlil, as he calls it. (*Bib Researches*, iii. 205.)

"Cana rises at a gentle elevation, facing the south-west. We stopped at a fountain of excellent water, flowing beneath the village through delicious groves of figs and pomegranates, the source, doubtless, of the very water that was made wine."— Lord Lindsay's *Letters on Holy Land*, ii. 84.

[2] And the Mother of Jesus was there. —" Now Mary had very near kindred in this town of Cana, namely, Mary the wife of Alphæus, or Cleopas, and all that family by that relation. For—1. Mary the wife of Cleopas is called her sister (John xix. 25), and that same Mary is called the mother of James and Joses (Matt. xxvii. 56), which were undoubtedly the sons of Alphæus (Mark iii. 18); so that Alphæus and Cleopas were but one and the same name, and Mary his wife was very near allied to the Virgin Mary. 2, Alphæus and his family lived in Cana, as may be collected by this, that one of his sons, namely, Simon, is called a Canaanite to distinguish him from Simon Peter. (Mark iii. 18, and vi. 3.) And he is called a Canaanite, as meaning and importing that he was a man of Cana.

"That this marriage therefore was in

2 (And both Jesus was called), and His disciples, to the marriage.

(Alf. And Jesus also was bidden.)

The Evangelist does not say that the mother of Jesus was invited, but that she was there; that Jesus was invited, and that the invitation was extended to His disciples. All this goes to make it probable that this was the marriage of some intimate friend or relative of the family. Not a word is said about Joseph, the husband of Mary, whether he were at the marriage or not. The last occasion on which he was mentioned, was eighteen years before this, when Jesus was twelve years old. (Luke ii. 41.) Hence it is concluded, with some degree of probability, that Joseph was not living when Jesus began His public Ministry.

The disciples who were invited along with Jesus to the marriage were not His Apostles. Jesus did not choose His Apostles until after John Baptist was cast into prison; (Matt. iv. 12;) and the events related in this chapter took place before that event. (John iii. 24.) The disciples were probably the five mentioned at the end of the last chapter: viz., Andrew and his companion, whose name is not given, but supposed to be the Evangelist St. John; Simon Peter, Philip, and Nathanael. Another ground for thinking that St. John was present at this miracle, is the circumstantiality with which he relates it. It has been observed that he gives to this miracle a minuteness of detail which he only gives to the actions at which he himself was present. His not naming himself is in keeping with his usual custom.

The third day. The events of the last few days St. John records with a chronological exactness that is remarkable. The third day may mean from the event last mentioned, from the conversation which Jesus had held with Nathanael, and His departure into Galilee. This would leave one clear day between His departure into Galilee and the marriage in Cana. Some have thought that the third day is dated from the testimony of John the Baptist. John stood, and two of his disciples, and he testified of Jesus, and they followed Him. And the day following Jesus would go into Galilee, and meeteth with Philip and Nathanael, and the third day there was a marriage. If the latter be the meaning intended, St. John would teach us that Jesus began to work His miracles and to exercise His Ministry publicly on the fourth day after His return from the Temptation.

Alphœus's house may be supposed upon this: That—1. Mary and Jesus their near kindred are invited, and all Jesus' disciples for His sake. 2. That Mary the mother of Jesus is so careful about the wine, lest the feast should be spoiled, and the bridegroom and his family should be disgraced by it. And 3, In that the Evangelist presently after the story of this feast, speaketh of brethren of Jesus, that is, His kinsmen, that went with Him to Capernaum (ver. 12), whereas He had no kinsmen in His company before this feast at all. Now these kinsmen or brethren were James and Judas, and Simon, and Joses (Mark vi. 3)."—Lightfoot, i. 541.

3 [(And when they wanted wine), the Mother of Jesus said unto Him, They have no wine.]

[S.* And they had no wine, because the wine of the marriage was finished. Then said the Mother of Jesus unto Him, There is no wine.]
(Alf. And when wine failed.)

4 [Jesus saith] unto her, Woman, what have I to do with thee? Mine hour is not yet come.

[V. A. And Jesus saith.]

The meaning of our Saviour's reply to His Mother is one of the most difficult passages in the Gospels, as is shown by the number of interpretations that have been given of it in ancient as well as in modern times. The importance of a right view of this subject is a sufficient justification for an explanation of almost any length. But far be it from the presumption of any man to say that our Saviour's words mean this or that and nothing else. The words must certainly be understood in a sense that is consistent with the context, and with what is related of the Virgin Mary, and of our Lord's treatment of her, in other places of the Gospels. The general conclusions here arrived at are:

1. Christ's words do not imply a rebuke to His Mother.
2. They are an explanation of the principle on which He would act throughout His Ministry: viz., that no love of kindred, that no considerations of human relationship would influence Him in His conduct, except on one single occasion, and that had not yet arrived.

1. Our Saviour's own words to His Mother do not necessarily imply a rebuke to her. Conduct in her such as to require a rebuke from her Son would be inconsistent with all her former life. Unless impelled by the unmistakeable sense of the words, why should we select a meaning to this passage which attributes to the Blessed Virgin a weakness which hitherto she had never shown, and which is inconsistent with every action which is recorded of her? At no time, either before this or after it, does she show any love of personal influence, any desire to gain applause among her friends, by her power over her Son, or by her connection with Him in any way. This might be very naturally the conduct of an ordinary woman. But the Blessed Virgin was not an ordinary woman. Human as she was, she had always acted on higher motives than the generality of mankind. In the trial under which Zacharias failed, in the belief of God's promise contrary to the general course of nature, she was triumphant. Zacharias did not believe the word of the angel that a child should be born to him, because he was an old man and his wife well stricken in years. But the Blessed Virgin did not disbelieve the angel's word, that she should conceive in her womb and bring forth a son, because

she was unmarried. Her exclamation was: "Behold the handmaid of the Lord: be it unto me according to thy word." This had been the principle of her life ever since. The angel said unto her: "Hail, thou that art highly favoured, (or full of grace), the Lord is with thee: blessed art thou among women." (28.) Is it reasonable to suppose that she of whom this was said would act on the usual low motives that influence others?

We have the testimony of the angel that up to the time of the Annunciation she had acted on the very highest of motives. Are we then to conclude that her thirty years' intercourse with God—intercourse such as no other being was ever favoured with, are we to conclude that this had no influence with her, or rather that it had a degenerating influence, that it gave her a lower tone of action than before? Was she less holy, more selfish, and more unworthy than before? It would be impossible to conceive this; it would contradict all our experience.

Nor was the Blessed Virgin an uninterested spectator of the mighty events that were taking place around her. We know that she had watched with eager eyes every development of the great Mystery, her miraculous Conception of Jesus, His Birth, His Life. She had kept all these things, and pondered them in her heart (ii. 19). She was probably aware of His Baptism by John, of the visible descent of the Holy Spirit upon Him, it may be, too, of His Temptation, and of the witness of the Baptist.

What had she now said to Him to require a rebuke? His loving subjection to her for thirty years did not embolden her to bid Him, or even to intercede with Him, in behalf of her friends. She simply states their need, and leaves the consideration of it to Himself. Her only words are, "They have no wine." Are these such words as to require a rebuke from our Lord to His Mother, and that Mother, such as the Blessed Virgin was, before all the assembled company, and to be handed down for all ages as a memorial against her?

The term "woman," in our translation, imparts a degree of harshness to the sentence, which it does not possess in the original. Unless our Lord had called her, Mother, no other word in the Greek language would have been so tender or so delicate as the term, which we have translated "woman."

2. Our Saviour's answer to His Mother, is an explanation of the principle, on which He would act throughout His whole public Ministry, which He was then just commencing. No love of kindred, no considerations of mere human relationship would influence Him, except on one single occasion, and that time had not yet come. His miracles must be performed for the glory of God, and the salvation of man, irrespective of all family ties. The public statement of this principle of action was neccessary at the beginning of His Ministry, and an opportunity offers itself in the house of an intimate friend or relation before the working of His very first miracle.

The common opinion, and one very consonant with the usual practice among men, no doubt would be that His power to work miracles might be fairly exercised for the special benefit of His friends and relations. Something of the kind seems to have been the feeling of the woman, who exclaimed, "Blessed is the womb that bare Thee, and the paps which Thou hast sucked." (Luke xi. 27.) A similar feeling He corrected, when those around said unto Him, "Behold Thy Mother and Thy brethren stand without, desiring to speak with Thee." (Matt. xii. 47.)

The Mother of Jesus saith unto Him, "They have no wine." Through the length of the feast, or the number of guests, or, more probably, through the poverty of the bridal party, the wine had failed. He, who was her Son, and their friend or relation, could supply their want. Such might be the current of her thoughts, and our Saviour answers those thoughts. Jesus saith unto her, Woman, what have I to do with thee? or, what is there in common to thee and Me? He inherited from His Mother His Human nature, but that could not perform miracles. His power as God could alone work miracles, and that could not be exerted for the assistance of those who were relations, merely because they were connected by the ties of family or blood. An hour would come when He would fully recognize in His Mother the strong claims of human relationship, the claims which she had upon Him for assistance and support as His Mother. That hour would not be until He was hanging on the Cross, then He would as a Son provide a home for His Mother in the house of His beloved disciple, St. John the Evangelist. (John xix. 26.)

His Mother sees from His answer to her that He will supply the want of wine, though His reason for so doing will not be the one which she had supposed—His relationship to the bridal party, but for the manifestation of His glory, and that His disciples might believe on Him. In this persuasion

5 His mother said unto the servants, Whatsoever He saith unto you, do it.¹

6 (And) there were [set] there six waterpots of stone, after the manner of the purifying of the Jews, (containing) two or three firkins apiece.

[S. Omits, set.]
(Alf. Now—holding.)

7 [Jesus] saith unto them, Fill the waterpots with water. And they filled them up to the brim.

[S. And Jesus.]

---

¹ See note on Chap. xvii. 18.

8 And He said unto them, Draw out now, and bear unto (the governor) of the feast. And they bare it.

(Alf. The ruler.)

The *servants* were required to fill the waterpots, that they might be evidence that no fraud or deception was practised—they were to fill *waterpots*, of which there could be no suspicion—they were to fill them with *water, and up to the brim*, that there might be no possibility of fraud by pouring into them any liquid or drug, so as to impart the taste and colour of wine.

At a very moderate calculation these six stone jars or waterpots would contain 110 gallons, and at the lowest calculation they would hold sixty gallons, a greater quantity of wine than would be consumed at this feast. (Smith's *Bib. Dict.*)

9 When the ruler of the feast (had tasted the water that was made wine), and knew not whence it was : (but the servants (which drew) the water knew :) the governor of the feast (called) the bridegroom.

(Alf. Tasted the water now become wine—which had drawn—calleth).

10 And saith [unto him], Every man (at the beginning doth set forth good wine) : and when men (have well drunk), [then] that which is worse ; [but] thou hast kept the good wine until now.

[S. Omits, unto him : S. V. omit, then : S. but].
(Alf. Setteth on the good wine first—are drunken—omits, but).

The office of ruler of the feast was to regulate all the matters of the feast, and to decide any question of order and precedence that might arise. Whether he was one of the guests, who might be chosen on each occasion to fill this post, or whether he was there for that express purpose, his office was evidently one of considerable consequence. His opinion on all matters would be held decisive, and for several reasons. Besides being invested with authority, his anxiety to preserve order and decorum would restrain him from anything like indulgence himself. Thus the keenness of his own taste would not be blunted. His knowledge as to the quality of wine, as we may fairly suppose, would from his experience be beyond question. But how little did this ruler of the feast know of the depth of meaning which his words contained. When he called the bridegroom, and saith unto him, "Every man at the beginning doth set forth good wine ; and when men have well drunk, then that, which is worse ; but thou hast kept the good wine until now." The real Bridegroom, who was also at this feast, the Bridegroom of the Church, had indeed kept the good wine until now.

The Law was given by Moses, but grace and truth came by Jesus Christ (i. 17). These words are a summary of the difference between the Old and the New Covenant. This difference may also be expressed, and was probably meant to be expressed, in another way. The water, which Jesus at this marriage-feast converts into wine, is as the blessings of the Law; the wine, the good wine, as the richer blessings of the Gospel. In this light the miracle wrought at the very beginning of His ministry is prophetic of the blessings which He should confer on mankind. This miracle not only manifested forth His power as God, and strengthened the feeble faith of his disciples in Him; it was also the key-note of the merciful dispensation which He was then inaugurating. Looking upon this action of our Saviour in its lowest view, not as prophetic, but in its social aspect, the first public display of His Divine power would for ever be associated in the minds of men with the joys of the bridegroom, the festivities of wedded love, and the sanctities of home.

11 This beginning (of miracles) did Jesus in Cana of Galilee, and (manifested forth His glory): and His disciples believed on Him.

(Alf. Of His miracles—manifested His glory.)

About the character of the act which He had just performed there could be no mistake. The witnesses were too many and too independent of each other. Every person at the marriage could bear testimony as to the qualities of the wine which He had made. Thus by suspending the ordinary course of nature, or by acting above and beyond it for a time, Jesus proved that His power was not restrained within the same limits as that of a mere man, and therefore that He was more than a mere man. By this means He prepared the way for His future teaching, that He was sent by the Father, that He was One with the Father, and equal to the Father.[1]

Thus by His presence and first miracle that He wrought, Jesus adorned and beautified the holy estate of matrimony. He teaches that

---

[1] Test of a Miracle—This miracle, as well as all the other miracles that were wrought by Jesus, will amply satisfy every condition required in any fair and exhaustive definition of a miracle, as for instance in the following, which is one of the most recent:

"By a miracle I understand, speaking generally, not the mere use of the common natural powers, accumulated or enlarged, but an operation involving what, I suppose, would be called medically an organic departure from her customary laws: an operation too, which must absolutely be performed upon man himself or some other object, after some manner, which shall be appreciable in its results by his faculties, and calculated to satisfy them, when in their greatest vigilance, that it is a real experience and not a mere delusion of the senses."—Gladstone's *Studies on Homer*, ii. p. 361.

E

in the exercise of His Divine power He could be influenced by no motives of personal intimacy or human relationship; He manifests his power as God; He lays the foundation of faith in Him in the hearts of His disciples, or confirms what already existed in a feeble, wavering condition, and He sets forth, as it were in figure, the rich blessings of the Gospel.

12 After this He went down to [Capernaum], He and His Mother, and His brethren, [and His disciples] : [and they continued] there not many days.[1]

[S. V. Capharnaum : S. omits, and His disciples: A. and He continued].
(Alf. And there they continued.)

Capernaum was a city to the N.E. of Cana, situated in "the land of Gennesaret," which was a rich, busy plain on the west shore of the Sea of Galilee, and which at that time was one of the most prosperous and crowded districts in the whole of Palestine. Being on the shore, Capernaum was lower than Nazareth and Cana of Galilee, from which the road to it was one of descent. Capernaum was better fitted than Nazareth to be the centre from which a knowledge of His teaching and miracles could be disseminated. Nazareth was an obscure village, where He Himself was despised for the supposed lowliness of His Birth and connections.

This appears not to be the journey to Capernaum mentioned in St. Matt. iv. 13, because that was after John Baptist had been cast into prison. This would seem to be before. (John iii. 24; iv. 1).

His Mother, and His brethren, and His disciples are still with Him. Our Lord's *brethren* are mentioned nine times in the Gospel and once in the Acts of the Apostles. Two explanations of this expression are given. 1. The traditional interpretation which dates from Tapias the scholar of St. John, and which has received the sanction of almost all the commentators of antiquity. In a very remarkable fragment, which has come down to our time, Tapias enumerates the various Maries that are mentioned in the Gospels, and he says that our Lord's brethren were His cousins, the children of the Mary who

---

[1] "Capernaum is compounded of two words, Cephar and Naum. Now that Cephar signifieth a village, it is undoubted, for the word occurreth several times in that sense in the Old Testament, (1 Sam. vi. 18; 1 Chron. xxvii. 25; Nehemiah vi. 2, &c.) But whether the latter word Naum were written םיענ or םוחנ is some doubtfulness. The Hebrew map of Canaan writes it םוחנ, the Town of Nahum, or the Town of Consolation, which name suited very well with it, now when Christ had His habitation in it, but it is commonly supposed that it was called םיענ, or the Town of Beauty, because of the pleasant situation of it on the banks of Gennesaret, and because of the beauty of the buildings of the town itself."—Lightfoot, i. 539.

was the wife of Cleopas or Alphæus, and sister to the Blessed Virgin. This would be in strict accordance with the common Jewish custom, which was to call all relatives by the name of brethren. Thus, Abraham was uncle to Lot, and yet he says they were brethren. (Gen. xiii. 8). Laban was uncle to Jacob, and yet he calls him his brother. (Gen. xxix. 15.)

2. The other opinion is that His brethren were the real brothers and sisters of our Lord in the common acceptation of the word. This is quite a modern interpretation, and is chiefly held by a few to whom novelty is a recommendation, rather than otherwise, especially if it gives scope for the nice adjustment of intellectual probabilities. Even if the probabilities were equal, which is by no means the case, an instinctive reverence would incline us to adopt the former interpretation, and rather to shrink from the latter.

13 (And the Jews' Passover) was at hand, and Jesus went up to Jerusalem.[1]

(Alf. And the Passover of the Jews.)

St. John expressly indicates three Passovers by name; the one here, another chap. vi. 4, and the last chap. xviii. 39. He also mentions a Feast of the Jews (v. 1), which most commentators, ancient and modern, agree in explaining of the Feast of the Passover. He thus speaks of four Passovers during our Saviour's ministry, while the other three Evangelists mention only one Passover, namely, that at which Jesus was crucified. But there is no contradiction between St. John and the other three Evangelists as to the number of the Passovers. For none of those three ever utter a single word that in any way implies that the Passover, of which they speak, is the only one that occurred during Christ's Ministry.

The reason that leads the three first Evangelists to allude to one Passover only, while St. John speaks of three at least, was probably this, St. Matthew, St. Mark, and St. Luke, confine themselves almost exclusively to the history of Christ's sayings and doings in Galilee, they never relate any of His works in Judæa, until He went up to Jerusalem the last time for His Crucifixion, while St. John chiefly records his ministry in Judæa, and principally in Jerusalem. To take St. Matthew as a representative of the other three; from chapter iv. to xix. is taken up entirely with our Saviour's work in Galilee. In chap. xix. he sets out on His journey to Jerusalem for the Crucifixion, and from xxi. to the end is contained the history of the last week of His Ministry. Thus only one visit to Jerusalem is here recorded. But it is very different in St. John's Gospel. His special object

---

[1] See Introductory note to chap. viii.

evidently was to record that portion of Our Saviour's work, which he performed in Judæa and Jerusalem, and exceptionally only that in Galilee.

Thus though the Evangelists have given different results, they have been actuated by the same principle, namely to note the time of the Passover when it is in some way connected with the events which they are describing. For instance, it would have been impossible to give anything like a full account of the Crucifixion without recording that it occurred during the celebration of the Passover, and therefore all the four Evangelists refer to this Passover. But it was easy enough to record the Sermon on the Mount, the parable of the sower, or the labourers in the vineyard, etc., without alluding to the Passover, because these were in no way connected with it. They were not delivered either in the place where the Passover was kept, or during the time of its celebration. But to describe the purging of the Temple at the first Passover during His ministry, as related by St. John without giving any intimation that it occurred immediately before the Passover would have been to miss some of the principal points in the action. For it was probably in consequence of the approaching Passover that the market was held in the Temple Court at all. For this market existed chiefly for the convenience of the strangers who flocked to Jerusalem during the celebration of the three great feasts. It was the Passover that collected the immense concourse of people, who by His miracles and His teaching were induced to believe in His supernatural power. It was the nearness of the Passover that would give to the minds of the people a particular significance to His purifying of the Temple. They had assembled a few days before the Passover in order to purify themselves for the worthy celebration of it, and Jesus shows them that God would have his Temple purified as well as the worshippers.

Four Passovers would comprise three years of His Ministry. The time between His Baptism, and this His first Passover is said to be a few months, probably six. St. John enables us to see how part of this time was spent. Forty days were spent in the Fast before the Tempter came to Him. How long the threefold Temptation occupied, we are not informed, nor how long He abode in the wilderness after the Temptation was ended, and when the angels ministered unto Him, or before He returned to John the Baptist. Three days we have account of Him at the Jordan, and going into Galilee (John i. 29, 35, 43), and the next day after that He is at Cana at the Marriage Feast. This was probably the fourth day from His first appearing after He had left the wilderness, and the third since He entertained John's two disciples. We have thus a clear account of six weeks, or thereabouts, of the time which He spent between His Baptism and His first Passover. The rest was probably spent in going about Galilee and preaching the Gospel.

At the time St. John wrote his Gospel, he was living among the Gentile Christians of Asia Minor, and he therefore explains that the

Passover, to be present at which our Saviour now goes up to Jerusalem, was a Jewish feast. His cleansing of the Temple at the commencement of His Ministry had only a temporary effect. When His presence was withdrawn we see the Jews returned to their usual profanation, and He repeats His work in the early part of the last week of His Ministry. (Matt. xxi. 12.)

Our word "temple," is the translation of two Greek words, (1) ἱερόν, which means the whole consecrated precinct, including the outer or unroofed court; (2) ναός, the portion appropriated as the abode of God's Presence. In the following paragraph both these words are used; the first when our Lord drives out the buyers and sellers, etc., from the Temple, and the second, where he says, "destroy this Temple, and I will raise it up in three days."

Every Israelite was bound, within the seven days that the Feast of the Passover lasted, to these two things—1. To appear before the Lord in the Court, and that with a sacrifice. 2. To solemn joy and mirth, and that also with sacrifices. The former was called by the Jews appearance; the latter Chagigah, the festival. God commanded His people thus: "Thou shalt sacrifice the Passover unto the Lord Thy God of the flock and the herd." (Deut. xvi. 2). The Paschal lambs would be taken from the flock, and the after sacrifices the Chagigah from the flock and the herd, or from the herd only. The Targum of Jonathan says: "Ye shall kill the Passover before the Lord your God, between the eves, and your sheep and oxen on the morrow, in that very day, in joy of the feast." (Lightfoot ii. 357.) It was to sell to the people the Paschal lambs, and the sheep and oxen for the Chagigah sacrifices, that the market was held in the Temple Court, either by the priests or by their connivance and authority.

As the Passover was instituted before the establishment of the priesthood, and the services of the Tabernacle, many things were omitted in the first Passover, which were afterwards observed in the later Passovers. The Egyptian Passover was necessarily more simple and less ceremonial than the perpetual Passover. Several injunctions are given in Exodus, which evidently were not intended for the first Passover, and custom introduced other usages, that were not commanded, but which were not inconsistent with the original institution. As instances of this may be mentioned the practice of drinking four cups of wine at the Paschal Supper, which was common in even the poorest households, and of singing the Hallel, or service of praise, consisting of the series of psalms from cxiii. to cxviii. The Passover bullocks offered as the Chagigah were not offered in the Egyptian Passover, though they are plainly alluded to afterwards, Deut. xvi. 2; 2 Chron. xxxv. 7, 8, 9, and are constantly mentioned by the Jewish writers on the Passover.

14 (And found) in the temple (ἐν τῷ ἱερῷ) [those that

sold oxen, and sheep,] and doves, and the changers of money sitting.

[S. That sold sheep and oxen.]
(Alf. And He found.)

15 [And when He had made a scourge of small cords, He drove them] all out of the temple, (and the sheep, and the oxen) : and poured out the changers' money, and overthrew the tables.

[S. He made a scourge of small cords and drove them.]
(Alf. Both the sheep and the oxen—their tables.)

16 (And said unto them that sold doves), Take these things hence : make not My Father's house an house of merchandise.

[A. And make not.]
(Alf. And to them that sold the doves, He said.)

17 [And] His disciples remembered that (it was written, The zeal of Thine house hath eaten Me up).

[S. V. Omit, And. S. V. A. Of Thine house eateth Me up.]
(Alf. It is written, My zeal for Thine house shall eat Me up.)

The market here mentioned was held in the Temple or in the outer Court, and, as mentioned above, was for the sale of such animals as were required for the sacrifices of the Temple. The money-changers were there to facilitate the purchase of these animals as well as the payment of the Temple-rate, the half-shekel, which each man from twenty years old was to pay as an offering to the Lord. (Exod. xxx. 13.) No defence is set up for this traffic on the ground that it had a kind of quasi-religious character about it, as being chiefly in the hands of the priests, or that the animals were required for God's service, and the payment for the maintenance of the Temple and its worship, for incense-wood, shewbread, etc., or that the sale was not exactly in the Temple, but in the outer Court. The house of God was for prayer, and not for trade, and the unhallowed selfish thoughts, which are too apt to mingle themselves with trade.

It is probable that the practice of holding their market in the Temple Court was introduced after their return from the Captivity, as none of the prophets allude to it. This time Jesus accuses them of sacrilege only; the next time, when he expels them from the Temple He accuses them of extortion and injustice : He says they had made His Father's house a den of thieves.) Matt. xxi. 12.)

Some of the ancients were accustomed to look upon our Lord's expulsion of the buyers and sellers, etc., from the Temple as one of His greatest miracles. One man, outwardly like themselves, backed by no earthly authority, ejects from the Temple a multitude, whose gains and whose character He attacks. The awe inspired by His deed, and by the manner of the doer of it, renders them powerless to resist.

A strict translation of the Greek would rather imply that it was the sheep and the oxen which He drove out with a scourge of small cords: "And when He had made a scourge of small cords, He drove all out of the Temple, both the sheep and the oxen." (πάντας ἐξέβαλεν ἐκ τοῦ ἱεροῦ, τά τε πρόβατα καὶ τοὺς βόας.) The holy indignation of His manner, and the power of His words, as well as the consciousness of their own guilt would probably be sufficient to expel the men.

Enraged at their expulsion from the Temple, at the interruption to their traffic, and at the charge of sacrilege, which Jesus brings against them, the Jews in turn accuse Him of acting without authority. They knew that He had received no countenance from the chief priests, and they require of Him a sign to prove that He was commissioned by God to act as He did.

As a proof of His divine power, of His commission from God and Oneness with God, He appeals to His future Resurrection. He does this in language which they misunderstand. This is one of the many instances where in His conversation with the Jews, our Saviour uses words in one sense, which they understand in quite a different sense, but which He does not explain to them. The reason doubtless is, that they are not in a frame of mind to receive such explanation. Either their faith or their knowledge is too imperfect.

18 (Then answered the Jews) and said unto Him, What sign shewest Thou unto us, seeing that Thou doest these things?

(Alf. The Jews therefore answered.)

19 Jesus answered and said unto them, Destroy this Temple,[1] (τὸν ναὸν τοῦτον) and in three days I will raise it up.[2]

---

[1] Destroy this Temple (λύσατε τὸν ναὸν τοῦτον).—"Even recent expositors erroneously take Imperative in John ii. 19; xx. 22, for a Future, supporting their views by a reference to the Hebrew of such passages as Gen. xx. 7; xlv. 18. Inasmuch as every command relates to a future time, the Future tense as a general expression of futurity, may be used for the Imperative; but the special form of the Imperative cannot, vice versâ, be employed for the more general Future. Such a disregard of logical principles would involve speech in inextricable confusion."—Winer's *Grammar of New Testament*, p. 328.

[2] In three days (ἐν τρισὶν ἡμέραις) "does not signify that three whole days are to be spent on something, but that something is to take place *within* that space of time, and, by consequence, before its expiration."—Winer's *Grammar of New Testament*, p. 404.

20 Then said the Jews, Forty and six years was this temple in building, and wilt Thou (rear it up) in three days?

(Alf. Raise it.)

21 But He spake [of the Temple of His Body.]

[S. Of the temple of the Body.]

22 When therefore He was risen from the dead, His disciples remembered that He had said this [unto them]: and they believed the Scripture, and the word which Jesus (had said).

[S. V. A. Omit, unto them.]
(Alf. Omits, unto them—had spoken.)

The Jewish historian, Josephus, confirms the statement of the Jews as to the length of time it had taken to build and to beautify the Temple, which was then standing, and as it then was. Josephus was with the Roman army when, about forty years after this, they besieged and took Jerusalem, and destroyed the Temple.

Roughly speaking there had been three temples. The first was built by Solomon, and was completed in seven years. (1 Kings vi. 37.) This was plundered and burnt by the Chaldæans under Nebuchadnezzar, when he carried the two tribes captive to Babylon, B.C. 584. (2 Kings xxv. 13-15; 2 Chron. xxxvi. 17-20.) The second temple was built by Zerubbabel after their return from the seventy years' captivity at Babylon. (Ezra iii. 12.) This second temple, which was greatly inferior to the first temple in glory and splendour, Herod the Great, about sixteen years before the Birth of Christ, began to rebuild. He did this in order to conciliate the people, and to reconcile them to his usurped rule over them, and his successors had continued to add to it, and adorn and beautify it up to the present time. In this way it could be said that the building of the present Temple had been extended over forty-six years.

Our Lord's words, "Destroy this Temple, and in three days I will raise it up" were prophetic. They had much the same force as if He had said, "You will destroy this Temple, and in three days I will raise it up again." When they quote these words against Him before the Council, they incorrectly represent Him as saying that He would destroy the temple, not that they would. (Mark xiv. 58.) He spake of the Temple of His Body, where dwelt all the fulness of the Godhead. They thought that He spake of the Temple, where God occasionally, but specially, manifested His Presence, which was but a type of His Body. Neither the Jews nor His disciples understood His words at the time. The Jews probably never understood them. After His Resurrection, His disciples called these words to mind, and recognised the fulfilment of them.

23 Now when He was in Jerusalem[1] at the Passover, (on the feast day), many believed in His name (when they saw the miracles) which He did.[2]

(Alf. At the feast—beholding His miracles.)

What was the nature of the miracles which Jesus wrought at the Passover, beyond the cleansing of the Temple, we are not informed. As afterwards they were probably healing the sick and casting out devils. Two instances of the effects which they produced on the mind are mentioned. They convinced Nicodemus that Jesus must be a teacher come from God, and they attracted the favourable attention of the Galilæans (John iv. 45) who were present at this Passover, and bespoke their good will towards Him. It was now four hundred years since the Jews had had among them a prophet who had wrought miracles. Since the day that Daniel closed the mouth of the lions, we have no instance recorded of the working of miracles by any prophet or public teacher, until Jesus turned the water into wine at the marriage in Cana of Galilee.

24 (But Jesus did not commit) Himself unto them, because he knew all men.

(Alf. Yet Jesus did not trust.)

---

[1] City of Jerusalem.—" From year to year as the Holy Family came up from Nazareth to Zion for the feasts of their faith, they would find the great city changing in aspect and in character; becoming less and less Jewish, and more and more Greek: the plain house of stone giving way to the marble front, the portico, the colonnade, and the paved court. All through those years of the Lord's youth, the Temple was in progress; for the princes of Herod's line were all artists and builders, and it was the pride of Archelaus to carry on the structures which his father had commenced."— Dixon's *Holy Land*, i. 232.

[2] The feast-day.—" This feast-day at the Passover, may best be conceived to be the first day of the festival week, or the day after the Passover was eaten; for on that day was the appearance of the people in the Court of the Temple, as the Law appointed, that thrice every year they should appear before the Lord. For 'that appearing mentioned in the Law (saith Rambam) was that every one appear in the Court on the first holy day of the festival, and bring an offering.'—In Haggai, per. i. On that day therefore, the concourse of the people being the greatest, it is most proper to suppose that Christ began to show Himself in His miraculous power, as He had done a day or two before in His prophetic zeal, in driving the market out of the Temple."—Lightfoot, i. 564.

25 (And needed not that any) should testify of man: (for He knew) what was in man.

(Alf. (And because He needed not that any one—for of Himself He knew.)

His knowledge of what was in man, induced Him at the beginning of His Ministry, when His work was still to do, to withhold Himself from the people. But the same knowledge led Him in the fulness of time, when His work was done, to trust Himself to them.

INTRODUCTORY NOTE TO CHAPTER III.

Jordan.—" The absurdity of the etymology of Jordan from Jor and Dan, the supposed names of two sources, is obvious; for the name Jordan is merely the Greek form ($Ιορδάνης$) for the Hebrew יַרְדֵּן Jarden, the Descender, which has no relation to the name Dan. Further, the name Jordan was applied to the river from the earliest times; and we have it constantly in the Scriptures in the time of Abraham, at least five centuries before the name was given to the city at its source. Yet this etymology goes back at least to the time of Jerome. (Comm. in Matt. xvi. 13.) "Jordanes oritur ad radices Libani; et habet duos fontes, unum nomine Jor, et alterum Dan; qui simul mixti Jordanis nomen efficiunt," etc.—Robinson's later *Bib. Res.*, p. 412.

"From the Hasbeya source to the Dead Sea, the direct distance is about 120 miles. I estimate the addition to be made for winding of the channel from the source to the end of the Sea of Galilee as twenty per cent., and for the rest as a hundred per cent. (judging from Warren's outline of that part).

"This would make the water in the first part to be 60 miles long; and in the second part 140 miles, or in all 200 miles of channel, from the source to the Dead Sea.

"The Hasbeya source is 1700 feet above the Mediterranean, and the Dead Sea is 1300 feet below the Mediterranean, so that the total fall of Jordan is 3000 feet, which would be 15 feet per mile of its channel, or 25 feet per mile of its direct distance.

"The surface of the Lake of Tiberias is 653 feet below the ordinary sea-level (its greatest depth is 165 feet).

"From Kerah, at its southern end, the river descends about 650 feet into the Dead Sea. As a general outline, then, it may be said that the Jordan runs 20 miles, falling 1400 feet, into a basin (Lake Hooleh) 12 miles long; then runs 10 miles, falling 700 feet, into another basin (Sea of Galilee) 14 miles long; then runs 65 miles, falling 700 feet, into a basin (Dead Sea) 50 miles long and 1800 feet deep. Here the waters of Jordan being fresh, and therefore lighter than the highly saturated salt water of the Dead Sea, the river stream most probably disperses over the upper surface only, and so, being evaporated before they mingle much with the brine that lies heavy and deep below, they are wafted by the south wind in clouds once more to Hermon, and condensed into snow-flakes, with water from the Abana and Pharpar, also borne up to Hermon, they trickle down again to run along old Jordan's bed, their endless round."—MacGregor's *Jordan*, p. 317.

"During the whole course of the Jordan from source to end there does not seem to be one notable cascade or regular 'fall.'"—p. 309.

"The Jordan seems never to have been navigable for traffic. If any boat went down the lower part before Molyneux (1847), or the upper part before the Rob Roy (1868), it must have been for exploration."

Newbold says (As. Soc. I., vol. xvi. 23), "that we hear no mention of boats or bridges in the different passages of the Israelites." "Ferryboats, however, seem to have been established very early: we hear of one for Jordan in 2 Sam. xix. 18."—MacGregor's *Jordan*, p. 416.

"The Jordan flows through a rent or fissure in the plain some twenty or thirty feet below the level of the broad ancient river-bed; so that the fringe of reeds or canes, which makes the bank bright and cool, is invisible a few yards off."—Dixon's *Holy Land*, i. p. 295.

"Nine hours after leaving Jerusalem, we reached the banks of the river, concealed till you are close upon it by dense thickets of trees, reeds, and bushes, the pride of Jordan, growing luxuriantly to the very edge of the water."—Lord Lindsay's *Letters on Holy Land*, ii. p. 64.

"I found when I came to the river-side, that the track re-appeared upon the opposite bank, plainly showing that the stream had been fordable at this place. Now, however, in consequence of the late rains, the river was quite impracticable for baggage horses. A body of waters, about equal to the Thames at Eton, but confined to a narrow channel, poured down in a current so swift and heavy, that the idea of passing with laden baggage horses was utterly abandoned."—*Eothen*, p. 140.

"We had skirted the band of foliage from the shore of the Lake, delighting in the varied tints of orange, red, and greens of every hue, against the background of dark-blue mountains behind it: now descending into the depth of the ghôr, or deep valley which the rushing Jordan has worn for itself, we entered into the charming shade of the tall fine trees—poplars, willows, tamarisks, planes, terebinths—and a thick jungle of agnus castus and everlastings, both in blossom, the fine tall canes waving their beautiful flowery heads and flaunting leaves in the breeze—'the reeds shaken by the wind.' These reeds are the Arundo donax, the 'Pride of Jordan,' on which the young lions lay when they mourned—because the floods came and hid the reeds, and they were chased away. Zech. xi. 3.

"The plain of the Jordan—now called El Ghôr—would appear to have been always the most important plain in Israel, as its name in Scripture is Ha-arabah (Joshua xviii. 18), the plain *par excellence ;* and the river is the only really large one in the land of Canaan: its three sources we had seen already—that at Hasbeiya—that at Tell el Khady—and that at Banias; but the ancient inhabitants reckoned only the last as its veritable source: the Hebrew name is Yarden, the descender; and the old Arabic writers preserved this in the word 'Ordoun for the upper part of the stream—below the Lake of Galilee it is called Scheriat-el-Kebeer, the great watering-place. The valley is inclosed between ridges, rising with steep precipitous sides, between 1000 and 2000 feet; the eastern side is the loftiest; the breadth of the valley here is about nine or ten miles; but it becomes very much narrower farther north. The river is itself sunk below the level of the valley between *two* sets of banks; those confining the water are low; the upper ones are much higher, and at a considerable distance from the stream: the continuous rush of its volume of water has worn this track for itself: lower down, all along the Jericho plain, there are *three* sets of terrace banks; the middle one is covered with shrubs, canes, and low herbs. The average breadth of the river is about 150 feet.

"Its valley, from being so much depressed below the level of the Mediterranean, is of an intensely hot climate—'a gigantic furnace,' as Van de Weld calls it, in the vivid account he gives of his own sufferings there: he was in the Ghôr in the month of May, when, of course, the inevitable scirocco was constantly upon them, and he says that 'the heat was considerably worse to bear than anything he had ever felt even in South Africa.'"—Beaufort's *Travels in Syria,* ii. p. 136.

"We were particularly struck with the appearance of the Jordan valley, over which far and wide was spread a bright green carpet of turf, a sight we had not seen before in Palestine."—*Recovery of Jerusalem,* p. 374.

CHAPTER III.

1 Christ teacheth Nicodemus the necessity of regeneration; 14 Of faith in His Death; 16 The great love of God towards the world; 18 Condemnation for unbelief; 23 The baptism, witness, and doctrine of John concerning Christ.

THE following conversation between Jesus and Nicodemus was held at Jerusalem, whither He, and the five disciples before mentioned, had gone up for the Passover. His driving out the buyers and sellers, etc., from the Temple, and purging it of all sacrilegious traffic, as well as the other miracles which he had wrought, had begun to draw upon Him the attention of the more earnest among those who were present at this Passover. The reappearing of a Teacher among them who could work miracles, after the cessation of this power for four hundred years, would necessarily excite the greatest interest amongst all classes at Jerusalem.

Among those who had been forcibly struck by the miracles which Jesus wrought was Nicodemus. The Evangelist mentions two points which make the conversion of Nicodemus to the teaching of Jesus the more remarkable—his religious belief and his worldly position. He was a Pharisee, one of the sect which was the bitterest persecutor of Jesus all through His Ministry, and the effect of whose principles was so radically opposed to the humility which He inculcated. He was also a ruler of the Jews, a member of the Sanhedrin, the great Council of the Jewish nation. By principle he was most opposed to the teaching of Jesus, and by his position he had the power to oppose its progress. The conversion of such a man proved at once the power of the Gospel and the sincerity of the man.

1 (There was) a man of the Pharisees, named Nicodemus, a ruler of the Jews.[1]

(Alf. But there was.)

---

[1] " Nicodemus undoubtedly was a spectator and witness of the miracles which Jesus had done at the Passover; and so the Syrian translator seemeth to conclude, when he rendereth the beginning of this chapter thus : ' Now there was one of the Pharisees named Nicodemus there;' and so his own words seem to argue, as spoken not upon hearsay, but upon ocular witness, ' We know that Thou art a Teacher come from God, for none can do such miracles,' &c. He having seen those wondrous workings by day came to Jesus that night, as may in most probability be conjectured and the word νυκτὸς very properly rendered in such a definite and determinate construction."—Lightfoot, i. 562.

2 The same [came to Jesus] by night, and said unto Him, Rabbi, we know that Thou art a teacher come from God: [for no man] can do these miracles that Thou doest, except God be with him.

[S. V. A. Came to Him; S. and no man.]
(Alf. Came to Him.)

It was no great proof of cowardice in Nicodemus to come to Jesus by night. Had he not possessed great sincerity of character, he was just in that position of life, that would have deterred him from coming at all. He was a "master of Israel, a "ruler of the Jews," one who was accustomed to sit in the Council of the nation. On the other hand Jesus was reputed, and as far as Nicodemus would know, correctly reputed, to be the son of a poor carpenter in an ignoble village in the despised districts of Gallilee, and His disciples five poor illiterate fishermen from the same district. To attach himself to such a company as this required in Nicodemus an unusual share of honesty and moral courage. Nothing but a very strong conviction of the truth of what Jesus had said, coupled with an eager desire to learn more about it, could have influenced a man in his rank of life to come even by night to Jesus. Night, too, was probably the only time during which he could gain a private interview with Jesus. If he came, as some have thought, the very next night after he had seen the miracles and heard the doctrine, it would be a proof of his eagerness and earnestness as well as of his courage. This was looked upon as a proof of his sincerity rather than of his fear. In the two other places where Nicodemus is mentioned it is added, as if to his credit, that it was he who came to Jesus by night. (John vii. 50; xix. 39.)

It is uncertain whether Nicodemus meant to imply by the phrase "we know," etc., that the Sanhedrin as a body was convinced of this, or whether he referred to himself personally, using, as is common in many languages, the first person plural for the first person singular, or whether he meant that it was commonly known and acknowledged, as being a matter which was put beyond all question by the miracles which He had wrought.

As far as we can learn from the narrative, the five disciples mentioned in the first chapter were still with Jesus, and it may be that St. John was himself present at the interview between Jesus and Nicodemus. Though this is not stated, there is nothing improbable in the supposition.

3 Jesus answered and said unto him, Verily, verily, I

say unto thee, except a man be born (again), he cannot see the Kingdom of God.¹

[S. Omits, and said unto him.]
(Margin, from above.)
(Alf. Anew.)

---

¹ "Verily, verily, Greek, Amen, amen. Consider these two particulars concerning it: 1. What our Saviour doth properly intend and mean by Amen, when He useth it so oft. And, 2. Why John the Evangelist doth constantly use it doubled, when the other three never use it so at all.

"1. As to the first, it is to be observed that the word Amen is an Hebrew word, and is very commonly used in the Old Testament: but this withall is to be observed, that it is never used in the Old Testament but by way of wishing or appreciation (the 16th verse of Isaiah lxv. only excepted). As when it cometh single, as Deut. xxvii., twelve times over, where the LXX. render it γένοιτο, be it done; 1 Kings i. 36, where the LXX. have it γένοιτο ὄντως, so be it; Nehem. v. 13, Jer. xxviii. 6, Psal. cvi. 48. Or when it cometh double, Numb. v. 22, Psal. xli. 13, and lxxii. 19, and lxxxix. 52, which the LXX. express γένοιτο, γένοιτο, be it done, be it done, or so be it, so be it. In all these places it is used by way of prayer or imprecation, according as the subject matter was to which it was applied, as David Kimchi expresseth it. It is spoken, saith he, either by way of prayer, or by way of undertaking, as that they take upon them a curse if they transgress.

"But in these utterances of our Saviour the sense of it is altered from precatory to assertory, or from the way of wishing, to the way of affirming: for what one Evangelist expresseth, Amen I say unto you, this poor widow, &c., Mark xii. 43; another uttereth Ἀληθῶς λέγω, of a truth I say unto you, Luke xxi. 2; Matthew saith, Amen I say unto you, That some that stand here, &c., which Luke giveth λέγω ἀγηθῶς, of a truth I say unto you (ix. 27). So Ἀμὴν in Matt. xxiii. 36 is rendered ναί, truly, Luke xi. 51. For indeed the word Amen doth properly betoken and signify truth, as is apparent by the construction of that verse forementioned, Isaiah lxv. 16. He who blesseth himself in the earth, shall bless himself in the God of truth; and he that sweareth in the earth, shall swear by the God of truth, as not only our English, but also R. Sol, and David Kimchi, do well render it: and the gloss of Kimchi upon the place is worth the citing. He saith in the earth, because in all the world there shall be one truth, and that shall be the truth of the God of truth. "Now Christ is called Amen, Rev. iii. 14, as being not only the faithful and true witness, but even He, in whom all the promises of God are yea and Amen, 2 Cor. i. 20, and even truth itself.

"Therefore when He cometh to publish the Gospel, which is that one truth that should be in all the world, He speaketh of His own, and useth a different style from the Prophets (which used to authorize their truths with, Thus saith the Lord), and speaketh αὐτοπίστως, upon His own authority as the God of truth. Amen, I say unto you. In this word therefore is included two things, namely, the truth spoken, and the truth speaking it; and the expression doth not only import the certainty of the things delivered, but also recalleth to consider that He that delivers it is Amen the God of truth, and truth itself. And this consideration will help to give a resolution to the second scruple that was proposed, and that is, why John alone doth use the word doubled, and none other of the Evangelists.

"I am but little satisfied with that gloss given by some upon this matter, namely, that John doth constantly double this word, because the matters spoken by him are of a more celestial and sublime strain, than the matters spoken by the other Evangelists, and therefore the greater attention is challenged to them by this gemination: for neither can I see, nor dare I think of any such superiority and inferiority in the writings of the Evangelists.

"Nor do I suppose that Christ used this gemination Himself (for it is very strange that in those speeches that this Evangelist mentioneth He should do so, in the speeches that the others mention He should not do so, when it may be sometimes it was the very same speech); but I conceive that the Evangelist hath doubled the word, that he might express the double sense which the single word in

To see the Kingdom of God is to enter into it, as is plain from verse 5, or to partake of it; as to see corruption, Psalm xvi. 10; to see death, Luke ii. 26, John viii. 51; to see evil, Psalm xc. 15; to see sorrow, Revelations xviii. 7; to see good, Ecclesiastes vi. 6, etc., is to be in these states, or to partake of them. In verse 36, to see life is to have life.

4 Nicodemus saith unto Him, How can a man be born when he is old? can he enter the second time into his mother's womb, and be born?[1]

St. John always doubles the Amen, even when the other Evangelists give it singly. He does not contradict their statement, but he gives the same in a fuller form. Brevity, so far as was consistent with truth, may have been their motive. But writing last of all the Evangelists, and with the special object of recording the sayings and conversations of Jesus at length, he gives if not the very words and in the very way in which He used them, yet in the way which conveys His meaning more fully and unreservedly to the people. He also relates conversations which the others had omitted, or he relates at length what they had recorded in a condensed form.

The word ἄνωθεν translated again, may mean either from above, from heaven, or over again, afresh. From verse 4 it would seem that Nicodemus understood it in the sense of over again.

Every man is born once, of his parents, which is his natural birth, according to the usual course of nature. By this birth he becomes a

---

our Saviour's mouth, and in the other Evangelists includeth. And so he addeth nothing to what Christ spake, but explaineth His speech to the utmost extent. He saith in the other Evangelists Amen singly, but He meaneth thus doubly, This is truth, and I am truth that speak it. Now John, that he might clear this double meaning, doth double the word, Amen, Amen, the one whereof doth refer to the thing that is spoken, and the other to the person that speaketh it.

"But the question proposed is not yet resolved, why John should do thus, rather than any of the other: but the same answer that resolveth why John should relate so many things that none of the other three do ever mention, will resolve this: namely, that it was God's will and disposal, that there should be four that should write the Gospel, and that some writing one thing, and some another, some after one manner, some another, the Story should be divinely made up to its full perfection. Now John wrote last, and he had warrant, and opportunity to relate what the others had omitted. And as for the particular in hand, he saw that the other had only produced this word single, as Christ indeed had continually uttered it, and that they had some of them expounded it in a place or two Ἀληθῶς and Ναί, to show that it was to be taken in these speeches in a meaning different from that precatory strain in which it was constantly used in the Old Testament, but yet that there was something more included in the word, and therefore he is warranted by the Holy Ghost to explain it to the full in two words, Amen, Amen. And thus the counsels of the Lord of old, uttered and revealed by the Prophets, do in the preaching of the Gospel by our Saviour prove Truth, truth. Isaiah xxv. 1."—Lightfoot, i. 535.

[1] Being old.—"So is the Greek verbatim (γέρων ὤν). The Syrian hath kept close to the sense given, 'Can an old man be born?'"—Lightfoot, i. 562.

descendant of Adam, and inherits all the weakness to resist temptation which belonged to Adam after he had yielded to the temptation of the serpent and had disobeyed the command of God. By his natural birth every man is born a child of wrath. (Eph. ii. 3.) By his natural birth every man is born in the power of darkness. (Col. i. 13.) But the Baptist came preaching that another kingdom was about to be established, the kingdom of heaven, or the kingdom of God; and he persuaded men to prepare to enter into this kingdom of heaven. In the next few verses Jesus explains to Nicodemus how to gain admittance into the kingdom of heaven. It must be by birth, but not the birth which he had already passed through. Every man in order to see or to enter the kingdom of heaven must be born afresh, over again, or from above.

In answer to Nicodemus, whose thoughts run entirely on his natural birth, and who asks how it was possible for this to be repeated, how a man after he has grown old, which may have been Nicodemus's own case, can be born again, our Lord explains that this birth is altogether different in character from his first or natural birth.

5 Jesus answered, Verily, verily, I say unto thee, Except a man be born (of water and of the Spirit,) he cannot enter into the kingdom of God.[1]

[S. He cannot see the kingdom of heaven.]
(Alf. Of water and the Spirit.)

---

[1] **Except a man be born of water, &c.**—" The question in hand betwixt our Saviour and Nicodemus, was about his entrance and introduction into the Kingdom of God, or his coming under the days and benefit of Messiah's appearing, which he was sensible was now come.

"And therefore Calvin mistakes and mis-states the question in this place, which made him so resolutely to refuse the general exposition of water for Baptism. 'I can by no means be swayed to think that Christ speaketh of Baptism here, for that would have been unreasonable.' And why unreasonable? Why, he gives this reason, 'Because Christ was exhorting to newness of life.' But that is not the prime and proper question or theme in hand. The matter in hand was about Nicodemus' translation into the days of the Messias (of which the nation had so high thoughts), that is, as he thought, into a changed state of happiness, and, as it was indeed, into a changed principling and profession, to come under new grounds of religion, and under a new manner of profession different from what he was under before. Our Saviour tells him, he must not think to slip into the participation of this Kingdom without any more ado than this, 'Now the days of the Messias are come, I shall have my share of the happiness of them, and they will even drop into my mouth;' but he must be newly moulded, out of his reliance upon his birth prerogative, out of his legal righteousness, out of his carnal performances and ceremonious services, and by a new birth, as it were, must be introduced into this new world and condition. Now, even those that deny that Baptism is spoken of here, yet cannot deny that Baptism was the way which Christ had appointed for introduction into this new profession; and if the introduction thereunto was the question that was in agitation, as indeed it was, they can as little deny that Baptism is meant and spoken of here."—Lightfoot, i. 527.

6 That which (is born) of the flesh is flesh; and that which (is born) of the Spirit is spirit.

(Alf. Hath been born—hath been born.)

Those only can be citizens of the kingdom of heaven who have a spiritual nature. But birth by the union of flesh and blood cannot impart a spiritual nature. Flesh and blood can only impart a carnal nature. Birth through the operation of the Holy Spirit can alone give a spiritual nature. Because it is the law of all creation that like begets like, that the producer infuses his own nature, as far as is possible, into that which is produced.

Jesus warns Nicodemus that he is not to disbelieve in the existence of the birth by the operation of the Holy Spirit because he cannot see it. There are many things that are not subject to the bodily senses which still have a real existence, and which we judge of rather from their effects. What do we know of the wind for instance, or what do we know of the soul? We know them only from certain properties, from certain effects or results. We know nothing of their origin, of their nature, of their final destination, still we believe in their existence; so is every one that is born of the Spirit. The senses are not cognisant of the fact, still we are to believe it. He asserts (1) That the truth and reality of the New birth is as distinctly perceived by the fruits and consequences of it, as the wind is by its sound; (2) That the Spirit accomplishes this work by an agency as free and unlimited as is the wind, which cannot be restrained or confined in its course; (3) That this work is as inscrutable, and as much beyond the power of human reason to fathom, as it is to discover where the course of the wind begins or where it ends.

Not only does Jesus teach Nicodemus this as a doctrine necessary to be understood, but He enforces it almost as a positive command: "Ye must be born again." (δεῖ ὑμᾶς γεννηθῆναι ἄνωθεν.)

7 Marvel not that I said unto thee, Ye must be born (again).

(Margin, from above.)
(Alf. Anew.)

8 The wind bloweth where (it listeth), and thou hearest the sound thereof, but canst not tell whence it cometh, and whither it goeth: so is every one that (is born) of the Spirit.

[A. Or whither it goeth; S. That is born of the water and of the Spirit.]
(Alf. It will—but knowest not—hath been born.)

When Nicodemus still professes his inability to comprehend this, Jesus reminds him that his office as a master or teacher of Israel should lead him to investigate this question, at least so far as to satisfy himself of the truth of it. This was really no new doctrine. The prophets had long before foretold that the heart of man should be changed, and that by the outward washing of the body, and the unseen operation of the Holy Spirit accompanying it. Ezekiel, (xxxvi. 25,) for instance, had said: " Then will I sprinkle clean water upon you, and ye shall be clean; from all your filthiness, and from all your idols, will I cleanse you. A new heart also will I give you, and a new spirit will I put within you; and I will take away the stony heart out of your flesh, and I will give you a heart of flesh. And I will put My Spirit within you, and cause you to walk in My statutes, and ye shall keep My judgments and do them."

The ceremonial washings of the body under the Mosaic Law, with which Nicodemus would be perfectly familiar, did not affect the heart at all. They were never used for that purpose. Those washings were outward in their application and outward in their effects. The Holy Spirit did not operate through them to cleanse the heart. But the Baptism of Jesus in the river Jordan had inaugurated a new era, a new dispensation. By His Own Baptism, and by the visible descent of the Holy Spirit upon Him, He had for ever sanctified the element of water for this purpose. He had given a pledge that the Holy Spirit should for ever accompany the Baptism which He should institute.

9 Nicodemus answered and said unto Him, How can these things be ?

10 Jesus answered and said unto him, Art thou (a master) of Israel, (and knowest not) these things ?[1]

(Alf. The teacher—and understandest not.)

---

[1] **The Teacher of Israel.**) ὁ διδάσκαλος τοῦ Ἰσραηλ.)—Nicodemus is regarded as the teacher of Israel, κατ' 'ἐξοχήν, he in whom all erudition was concentred, so that the contrast καὶ ταῦτα οὐ γινώσκεις may be more fully indicated.—Winer's *Grammar of New Testament*, p. 127.

"Campbell observes that the Article here is remarkable, and that it is omitted in no MS. It must therefore be concluded to have a sense which is indispensable to the passage; and Campbell is certainly right, when he contends that it ought to be expressed in Translations. It is, indeed, the more remarkable, that we should find the Article in all the MSS.

" To determine the precise meaning of the appellation is a task which, I believe, no Commentator pretends to have accomplished. We know that Nicodemus was a person of high consideration, and a member of the Sanhedrin; and some suppose him, and not without reason, to have been the same Nicodemus who is frequently mentioned in the *Talmud;* in which case he was not in wealth and consequence, inferior to any Jew of that time. Still it will be asked, why did our Saviour say to Nicodemus, ' Art thou the Teacher of Israel ?' I have only conjecture to offer; but even this may be tolerated, where nothing certain is known, and when even conjecture has scarcely been attempted. It has been observed, that the Jews gave their Doctors high and sounding titles; in the same manner, probably, as among the Schoolmen in the Middle Ages, one was called the *Angelic* Doctor, another the *Admirable*, and a

11 Verily, verily, I say unto thee, We speak (that we do know), and testify (that we have seen): and ye receive not (our witness).¹

(Alf. That which we know—that which we have seen—our testimony.)

12 If I have told you earthly things, and ye believe not, how shall ye believe (if I tell you of heavenly things)?

(Alf. If I tell you heavenly things.)

13 And (no man hath ascended up to heaven), but He that came down from heaven, even the Son of Man which is in heaven.

[S.V. Omit, which is in heaven.]
(Alf. No one hath ascended into heaven.)

Jesus calls upon Nicodemus to believe the truth of what He had said, not on the ground that he understood it, but on His evidence, on the ground that He, who could not possibly be mistaken, declared it was so.

The subject is one of difficulty to the mere intellect. If Nicodemus could scarcely comprehend His teaching on the birth by the Spirit, when it is explained in terms derived from the natural birth, when it is compared with what takes place in the regular course of nature, and when its operations are illustrated by similar operations in the works of nature such as the wind, how could he possibly understand it, if all these helps and illustrations were withdrawn, and it were presented to him in its full naked aspect. Or, if Nicodemus could not comprehend the doctrine of birth by Baptism, how could he possibly understand other and higher mysteries, such for instance as relate to the Godhead.

In the concluding part of His conversation on the New birth, our Saviour leads Nicodemus on to a more correct knowledge respecting

---

third the *Irrefragable*. Might not, then, Nicodemus have been styled by his followers, ὁ διδάσκαλος τοῦ Ἰσραήλ? On this supposition, nothing is more probable than that our Saviour should have taken occasion to reprove the folly of those who had conferred the appellation, and the vanity of him who had accepted it; and no occasion could have been more opportune than the present, when Nicodemus betrayed his ignorance on a very important subject........ The reproof is more severe in the present form of expression, since it seems to signify not only that the followers of Nicodemus distinguished him by this appellation, but also that he thought himself not altogether unworthy of it."—Middleton on the *Greek Article*, p. 242.

¹ Witness.—"How many readers have read in the English the third chapter of St. John, and missed the remarkable connection between our Lord's words at verse 11, and the Baptist's taking up these words at verse 32; and this because μαρτυρία is translated 'witness,' on the former occasion, and 'testimony' on the latter."— Archbishop Trench on *Authorized Version*, p. 57.

Himself. Nicodemus had addressed Him as a "teacher come from God," and He here instructs him that He is not merely a teacher come from God, He is God Himself, God who fills heaven and earth.

The expression "ascended up to heaven" is used with reference to man, and to his limited intelligence. To God who fills all things such an expression could not be applied in the same sense in which it is applied to man. Man, who lives on earth, can only know what is done in heaven, either by ascending to heaven himself, or by trusting the testimony of one who has already been there. Jesus as God had no need to ascend up into heaven in order to learn the things of heaven. By His nature as God He was already in heaven: He knew what was done in heaven, He knew with a knowledge that mere man can never possess.

The connection of our Saviour's argument is something of this kind. Even earthly things, comparatively speaking, such as the New birth, you could not discover by reason, you can only understand it when revealed to you, and only then by the most familiar explanation; what will you do then in the case of higher mysteries than this, in the case of what may be called heavenly things? You must believe them on the testimony of some one who knows. "I am the only one who can know. For no man has ascended into heaven. I as God fill heaven as well as earth, I therefore know all things, even the things of heaven. Nevertheless you receive not My testimony, you believe not My teaching.

In disbelieving the testimony of Jesus they rejected their own salvation. For the Son of Man, He who was both God and Man, was the great object of all saving faith. Nay, more, the great object of their faith was not simply the Son of Man, but the Son of Man exalted, or crucified. Men must look to the crucified God Incarnate for help, just as the Israelites looked to the brazen serpent. The children of Israel, who had been bitten by the fiery serpents, when they looked upon the brazen serpent, which Moses at God's command had set up, were miraculously healed. (Numb. xxi.) The brazen serpent set upon a pole was a type of the Son of Man, the God Incarnate exalted upon the Cross. The Israelite with his body poisoned by the bite of the fiery serpent, but healed by his looking upon the brazen serpent, was a type of the Christian with his soul poisoned by the bite of the Old Serpent, but healed by his faith in the crucified God.

14 And as Moses lifted up the serpent in the wilderness, even so must the Son of Man be lifted up.

15 That whosoever believeth in Him (should not perish but have eternal life).

[A. On Him; S.V. should have eternal life (omit, not perish but.)]
(Alf. May not perish—but may have eternal life.)

In referring to the account of the brazen serpent in the Pentateuch, does not Jesus Christ give His sanction to the substantial accuracy of the history of the Israelites as received in His time? He gives His testimony not only to the general accuracy of the history of the Israelites, but also to its prophetic character. He accuses them by their traditions of falsifying the meaning, the spirit of their Scriptures, but He never accuses them of altering the Scriptures themselves.

Nicodemus is not represented as asking any further questions during the rest of the interview, but Jesus continues to explain to him the nature of His doctrine. He anticipates any objections that might be made against His being God on the ground of His Crucifixion. So far from that being a proof that He was not God, it was the very proof that He was God. It is the proof of God's love for the world, and of such love as only God can show. Lost in sin as the world was, God sent not His Son to condemn, to punish it, but to save and restore it. Such love as this was the work of God only.

16 For God so loved the world, that He gave [His only begotten Son], that whosoever believeth in Him (should not perish, but have) everlasting life.

[S.V. The only begotten Son.]
(Alf. Might not perish, but might have.)

17 For God sent not [His Son] into the world (to condemn) the world; but that the world through Him might be saved.

[S.V. The Son.]
(Alf. That He might judge.)

He goes on to show Nicodemus that the cause of men's condemnation is their unbelief in the Incarnation. Men refuse to believe that He, Jesus the Son of Mary, was God. This is the cause of their condemnation.

18 He that believeth (on Him is not condemned): [but] he that believeth not (is condemned) already, because he hath not believed in the name of the only begotten Son of God.

[S.V. Omit, but.)
(Alf. In him cometh not into judgment—hath been judged.)

The cause of man's condemnation is his unbelief in the Incarnation. But what is the cause of his want of belief in the Incarnation? Was it the greatness of the Mystery? Was it the difficulty in comprehending or in believing it? Our Saviour says that the cause of their unbelief was their indulgence in sin, their love of sin. Their heart was hardened against proof by indulgence in sin, their eyes were closed against the light by indulgence in sin. The same miracles that had arrested the attention of Nicodemus, and had led him to conclude that Jesus was a teacher come from God, and that no man could do the miracles which He did unless God were with Him, had no influence on the Pharisees, as a body. But the difference was in the state of their heart, of their life, and not in the quality of the proof that was offered to them.

19 And this is (the condemnation, that Light) is come into the world, and men loved (darkness rather than Light), because their (deeds) were evil.

Alf. The judgement—that the Light—the darkness rather than the Light—works.)

20 For every one that doeth evil hateth the light (neither cometh) to the light (lest his deeds should be reproved.[1])

(Margin discovered).
(Alf. And cometh not, lest his works should be detected.)

21 But he that doeth (truth) cometh to the light, that (his deeds) may be made manifest, that they are wrought (of God).

(Alf. The truth—his works—in God.

The effect which this conversation had upon Nicodemus we see in his subsequent conduct. Soon after this we find him defending Jesus against the chief priests and Pharisees, and demanding that he should not be condemned until he had been heard (vii. 50). Later still, he is associated with Joseph of Arimathæa in the holy office of embalming, anointing, and burying the Body of Jesus (xix. 39).

---

[1] That doeth evil. (ὁ φαῦλα πράσσων.) "As there is an opposition here, of *light* and *darkness*; that is, of the truth and error, of a true doctrine and false; so is there an opposition of *doing evil* and *doing the truth*, and the one may be the better understood of the other. Φαῦλα πράσσειν, which is the phrase used here, and ἁμαρτίαν ποιεῖν, which phrase is used by this same Evangelist, (1 John iii. 8,) do not nakedly signify to sin, for the Saints of God do sin, (James iii. 2; 1 Kings viii. 46,) and cannot do otherwise ; Rom. vii. 15, etc. ;) and yet John saith, that whosoever is born of God, (ἁμαρτίαν οὐ ποιεῖ, 1 John iii. 9;) but these phrases, to *do evil*, and *commit sin*, do signify a setting of a man's self to do evil: *dare operam peccato*, as Beza translates it. So, on the contrary, *to do truth* is *dare operam veritati*, as he also renders it here, when a man's bent and desire is to do uprightly ; when gracious desires of doing truth and uprightness lie in the bottom, though the scum of many failings swim aloft in heart, when to will is present, as Rom. vii. 18, and when the mind is to serve the law of God, as Rom. vii. 25. Whosoever is so composed declineth not the light, but delighteth to come to it, and to the touchstone of the truth, that his works may be made manifest."—Lightfoot, i. 580.

After His conversation with Nicodemus, Jesus retired from Jerusalem, the chief city of Judæa, and went with His disciples into the country of Judæa.

22 After these things came Jesus and His disciples into the land of Judæa; and there He tarried with them, and baptized.

In chap. iv. it is said that Jesus made and baptized more disciples than John, though Jesus Himself baptized not, but His disciples. We can scarcely conclude from these two passages taken together that Jesus never baptized at all, but that He did not baptize many or generally. The opinion of the ancient commentators was that Jesus baptized His disciples, or some of them, and they the rest. No disciples have been mentioned by name as yet, except the five in chap. i. He did not appoint His Apostles until after John the Baptist's death.

John did not delegate his baptism to his disciples. He administered it himself only. Jesus administered His Baptism by His disciples. He worked in them and through them. There is no reason to suppose that the Baptism, which Jesus now administered through His disciples, differed in character from that which He administered by His disciples after His Ascension, or that this did not now convey the New birth—the blessings of the Holy Spirit. He had just been instructing Nicodemus in the necessity of the birth by water and the Spirit in order to enter the Kingdom of Heaven.

The Holy Spirit was not given visibly and in its fulness until after His Ascension. But even before His Death He forgave the sins of the paralytic. (Matt. ix. 2.) He forgave the sins of Mary Magdalene, and filled her with the grace of love. (Luke vii. 36-50.) What He could grant by a word He could bestow through the Sacrament, and we have not sufficient reason to conclude that He would withhold His promised blessing, even for a time, even until after His Ascension. If the Sacrament of the Eucharist, which Jesus instituted before His Death, was perfect, may we not safely conclude that the Sacrament of Baptism was equally perfect, even before the visible and full outpouring of the Holy Spirit?

23 (And) John also was baptizing in Œnon near to Salim, because there was much water there: and they came and were baptized.[1]

(Alf. But.)

---

[1] Salim and Œnon.—" One of our main objects in visiting the Ghôr, (a broad valley or plain, described by Josephus as extending from the lake of Tiberias to the Dead Sea,) was to make search after the Ænon and Salim mentioned in connection with John the Baptist. I regret to have to say that our search was fruitless.
" We

Several of the ancient commentators say that Œnon, near Salim, was on the west of Jordan, about eight miles south of Scythopolis. In modern times there is a great diversity of opinion as to the exact site of this place, or in other words, it is one of the places not yet identified. As Œnon indicates the presence of copious springs, it need not necessarily be on the Jordan. In fact, the statement that there was much water there almost implies that it was not on the Jordan.

24 For John was not yet cast into prison.

All the Evangelists refer to the imprisonment of the Baptist, but St. John is the only one who relates any of the works which Jesus wrought before John was cast into prison. He alone records the miracle of the water turned into wine at the marriage in Cana of Galilee, of His driving out the buyers and sellers from the Temple at the beginning of His Ministry, and His conversation with Nicodemus.

John Baptist was not yet cast into prison, but his ministry was fast drawing to a close. The time during which it lasted was in all probability somewhere about twenty months, that is supposing his imprisonment began a little before Jesus departed into Galilee, mentioned in the next chapter. Jesus began His public Ministry when He was thirty years of age, or when He was entering on His thirtieth year, which was the age at which the Levites entered on their term of service. (Numb. iv. 3). The Baptist would doubtless also conform to the same ecclesiastical rule, and having been born six months before Jesus, he would accordingly

---

" We learn from the Scriptural narrative, that John the Baptist was ' baptizing in Œnon near to Salim, because there was much water (many waters) there.' Salim, therefore, was the more important town: and Œnon, apparently, a place of fountains near by.

" According to Jerome, both Œnon and Salim were situated in this part of the Ghôr, eight Roman miles south from Scythopolis. They were probably at a considerable distance from the Jordan; otherwise the Evangelist would hardly have mentioned the abundance of water. In another passage, Jerome regards this Salim as the residence of Melchisedek, and affirms, that in his day the palace of Melchisedek was still shown, which by the magnitude of its ruins attested the ancient magnificence of the work.

" It was natural to infer that, of such extensive ruins, some traces might yet remain. Our inquiries were constant and persevering, but we could obtain no trace of corresponding names or ruins....

" It may further be remarked, that, so far as the language of Scripture is concerned, the place near which John was baptizing may just as well have been the Salim over against Nâbulus."—Robinson's *Later Researches*, p. 333.

" The village of Salim (near Nâbulus) is directly north of Beik Fûrik, on a low hill on the north side of the plain. It was said to have two sources of living water, one in a cavern, and the other a running fountain called ' Aim Kebir.' (p. 298.)

" Nâbulus (the ancient Sychar) is furnished with water in singular abundance in comparison with the rest of Palestine. On the west is the large fountain of Defneh, running off east and turning a mill. On the west are the similar fountains by which we are encamped. In the higher part of the city itself are two large fountains, and another in the ravine above, on the side of Mount Gerezim. The water of these three flows off west, partly along the streets of the city, and partly IN a canal, from which gardens are irrigated, and several mills supplied."—Robinson's *Later Biblical Researches in Palestine*, p. 299.

begin his ministry six months before Him. Shortly after this, in the very next chapter (iv. 35), it is said that it wanted four months to harvest, that would be four months to Passover. If we reckon the time between the Baptism of Jesus and His first Passover as six months, which is most probable, this would give fourteen months since Jesus began His Ministry, and six months added to that would extend the ministry of John Baptist to about twenty months.

Three places are mentioned in which John exercised his ministry. (1) All the country about Jordan. (Luke iii. 3.) (2) Bethabara, or Bethany, beyond Jordan. (John i. 28.) (3) Œnon, near to Salim. (John iii. 23.) The first was on the west, or the Judæa side of Jordan, the second on the east side of Jordan, and the third somewhere on the Judæa side of Jordan. What time he spent in each of these it is scarcely possible to determine with any degree of accuracy. When John baptized Jesus he was on the Judæa side of Jordan, where he had probably been baptizing six months, that is from the commencement of his ministry. When Jesus returned from the Temptation, about six weeks later, He found John at Bethabara, or Bethany, to which place He may have removed soon after the Baptism of Jesus. The rest of his ministry was probably divided between Bethabara and Œnon.

25 Then arose a question (between some of John's disciples [and the Jews]) about purifying.

[S.² V. A. and a Jew.]

(Alf. On the part of John's disciples with a Jew.)

26 And they came unto John, and said unto him, Rabbi, He that was with thee beyond Jordan, to whom (thou barest witness), Behold the same baptiseth, and all men come to him.

(Alf. Thou hast borne witness.)

According to the Vatican and Alexandrine MS. and the Sinaitic too, by a later reading, this question about purifying arose between John's disciples and one Jew. The precise form, which the dispute took, is not expressed, but enough is given to lead us to conclude that it had reference to the comparative merits of the two baptisms, or their relation to each other. The Jew might be disposed to underrate the baptism of John, because it did not cleanse or sanctify those who came to it. The disciples of John would naturally consider themselves interested in his honour and reputation. They knew that he was the first of the two to baptize, that he had baptized great multitudes, and amongst them Jesus Himself. Others might speak of the many miracles that Jesus had wrought, and remind them that John Baptist had wrought no miracle, and that even John in his testimony had preferred Jesus to himself.

27 John answered, and said, A man can (receive) nothing, except it (be given him) from heaven.
(Margin, take unto himself.)
(Alf. Have been given him.)

28 Ye yourselves bear [me] witness that I said, I am not the Christ, but that I am sent before Him.
[S. Omits, me.]

29 He that hath the Bride is the Bridegroom: but the friend of the Bridegroom which standeth and heareth Him (rejoiceth greatly) because of the Bridegroom's voice: this my joy therefore is fulfilled.[1]
(Alf. Rejoiceth with joy.)

30 He must increase, but I must decrease.

In order to check the feeling of jealousy which his disciples were beginning to entertain towards Jesus, and to reconcile them to a still further increase of His fame among men, and to a further decrease of his own, John gives several overwhelming reasons. He is the Christ, while John is but the forerunner; He is the Bridegroom, while John's highest glory is to be the friend of the Bridegroom. He is above all, from Heaven, while John is from the earth. He is the Son of God.

John had already borne witness to Jesus as He who should baptize with the Holy Ghost and with fire; as the Lamb of God which taketh

---

[1] The friend of the Bridegroom.— "No simile could have been more beautiful and true. In the drama of Syrian love and marriage, the friend of the bridegroom plays a conspicuous part, doing kindly, unselfish service; yet earning no other reward than that of feeling how much he has added to the happiness of a man whom he loves. Sometimes this friend of the bridegroom has to select the bride. At all times he has to take the oaths of espousal, and to present the mohar, the bridal gift.

"For the virgin's year, separating the act of betrothal from that of the bringing home, he is the only messenger between youth and maid. With many a laugh and jest, with many a sign and token, he has to pass from the unknown husband to the unknown wife; watching over their common rights, and feeding with his praises their mutual love; for during that virgin's year the husband, though he may possess much of a husband's power, and may even put his wife to death for wrongs against his bed, is never allowed to see her face. His married joy and sorrow come to him only through his chosen friend. Until the day of bringing home, when the veil of the bride is to be lifted up, and with a cry of rapture the husband is allowed to gaze into her eyes and kiss her on the mouth, the function of the bridegroom's friend knows no pause. Then the bridegroom's heart is glad, and the friend rejoices when he hears the bridegroom's voice."—Dixon's *Holy Land*, vol. ii. p. 69.

away the sin of the world, and he now bears witness to Him as the Bridegroom, He, who by His Incarnation had betrothed to Himself the Church, the Body of faithful men, as His Bride. Like a true friend of the Bridegroom, John had prepared and made ready for the marriage. He had shared in His joy at hearing His voice.

So far was he from feeling any jealousy because men began to leave his baptism and come to Jesus, it was the very thing that had been wanting to fill up his joy. The commencement of his joy was when God revealed to him the coming of His Son, it was increased when he beheld and baptized Him, it was now completed, fulfilled, when all men began to leave him and come to Christ.

31 He that cometh from above is above all: he that is of the earth (is earthly), and speaketh of the earth: He that cometh from heaven is above all.

[S. But he that is on the earth.]
(Alf. Is of the earth.)

32 [And what He hath seen and heard, that he testifieth:] and no man receiveth His testimony.

[S. He that cometh from heaven, testifieth what (S.* whom) He hath seen and heard.]
(Alf. Omits, And—and His testimony no man receiveth.)

33 He that hath received His testimony (hath set to his seal[1] that) God is true.[2]

(Alf. Hath set his seal that.)

---

[1] Seal.—The supposed necessity of a seal to attest the signature, is shewn in the following. " At Jezreel, the Chief desired Captain Wilson to make a report to the governor at Jenin, and our dragoman was accordingly directed to write a letter in Arabic, and submit it for signature. . . . . This was duly signed by Captain Wilson; and as the Chief insisted on a seal being appended to the signature, an old monogram was cut off a sheet of note paper and affixed to the letter. This was supposed to prove the genuineness of the document, as a man's seal cannot be forged."—*Recovery of Jerusalem*, p. 460.

[2] That God is true.—" In the Latin, 'verax' and 'verus' would severally represent ἀληθής and ἀληθινός, and in the main reproduce the distinctions existing between them; indeed, the Vulgate does commonly by their aid indicate whether of the two words stands in the original; but the English language, since it has lost, or nearly lost 'very' (vrai) as an adjective, retaining it no otherwise than as an adverb, has only the one word 'true' by which to render them both; so that the difference between the two disappears in our Version; and this of necessity, and by no fault of our translators—unless, indeed, we account it a mistake on their parts that they did not recover 'very,' which was Wiclif's common translation of verus (thus John xv. 1, 'I am the verri wine,') and which to recover would not have been very difficult in their time, would be scarcely difficult in ours. It would have been worth while to make the attempt; for the difference, which we thus efface, is a most real one. What exactly the nature of it is, a single example will at once make evident. God is Θεὸς ἀληθής, and He is Θεὸς ἀληθινός; but very different attributes and prerogatives

34 *For He, whom God (hath sent), speaketh the words of God: [for God giveth not] [the Spirit] (by measure unto Him).*

[S. V. For He giveth not: V.* Omits, the Spirit.]
(Alf. Sent—by measure.)

35 *The Father loveth the Son, and hath given all things into His hand.*

The Baptist uses the same argument to convince his disciples of the truth of what Jesus taught, as Jesus had Himself used to Nicodemus (v. 13). The knowledge of heavenly things can only be gained from one who had been in heaven. No mere man had ever been in heaven. Jesus by His very nature as God, has been and is in heaven. He is the only one who is able to reveal the things of heaven.

And yet no man, very few comparatively, receive His testimony. But whoever receives the words of the Son as true, declares that the Father is also true. For the Father and the Son are one. He that hath receiveth His testimony, hath set his seal that God is true. By this act of believing in the Son, he, so far as in him lies, affirms and declares that the Father is true, as strongly and as solemnly as if he signed and sealed this with his own proper signet.

---

are ascribed to Him by the one epithet, and by the other. God is ἀληθής (John iii. 33; Rom. iii. 4—'verax') inasmuch as He cannot lie, as He is ἀψευδής (Tit. i. 2) the truth-speaking, and the truth-loving God. But He is ἀληθινός (1 Thess. i. 9; John xvii. 3; Isa. lxv. 16—'verus') *very* God, as distinguished from idols and all other false gods, the dreams of the diseased fancy of man, having no substantial existence in the actual world of realities. "It will be seen that it does not of necessity follow, that whatever may be contrasted with the ἀληθινός, must thereby be concluded to have no substantial existence, to be altogether false and fraudulent. Inferior and subordinate realisations, partial and imperfect anticipations of the truth, may be set over against the truth in its highest form, in its ripest and completest development; and then to this last alone the title ἀληθινός will be vouchsafed. . . . . We should frequently miss the exact force of the word, we should, indeed, find ourselves entangled in many and serious embarrassments, if we understood ἀληθινός necessarily as the *true* opposed to the *false*. Rather it is very often the substantial as opposed to the shadowy and outlinear. Thus Heb. viii. 2, mention is made of the σκηνή ἀληθινή, into which our great High Priest entered—which, of course, does not imply that the tabernacle in the wilderness was not also most truly pitched at God's bidding, and according to the pattern which he had shown (Exod. xxv.); but only that it and all things in it, were weak earthly copies of things which had a most real and glorious existence in heaven (ἀντίτυπα τῶν ἀληθινῶν); the passing of the Jewish High Priest into the Holy of Holies, with all else pertaining to the worldly sanctuary, being but the σκιὰ τῶν μελλόντων ἀγαθῶν, while the σῶμα, the filling up of these outlines, was of and by Christ. (Col. ii. 17.) This F. Spanheim (Dub. Evang., 106) has well put: ἀλήθεια in Scriptura Sacra interdum sumitur ethice, et opponitur falsitati et mendacio; interdum mystice, et opponitur typis et umbris, ut ἐικῶν illis respondens, quæ veritas alio modo etiam σῶμα vocatur a Spiritu S. opposita τῇ σκιᾷ."—Archbishop Trench on *Synonyms of New Testament*, p. 25.

John does not declare in direct terms that the Father and the Son are one; but the collective force of the various arguments which he uses in the last six verses of the chapter amounts to this. The time had not come for him to teach this truth in the naked form, in which Jesus afterwards taught it to His disciples.

In the last argument which the Baptist used to allay the jealousy of his disciples, and to induce them to believe in Jesus as the Son of God, is that through Him alone could they obtain everlasting life.

36. He that believeth (on) the Son hath (everlasting life): [and] he that believeth not the Son shall not see life: but the wrath of God abideth on him.[1]

[S. Omits, and.]
(Alf. In—eternal life.)

He speaks of everlasting life as present as well as future. He that believeth on the Son, hath everlasting life: and he that believeth not the Son, shall not see life. This may be explained in two ways. 1. It may be that the life to which he refers, and which he calls everlasting life, does not begin in the present, but in the future state; but that the right to this everlasting life is gained in the present world. Any one, therefore, who has gained in this world a right to everlasting life in the future world, may be now said to have everlasting life, inasmuch as he has the right and title to it. He who believes on the Son, by which belief his claim to everlasting life is established, may be said now to have everlasting life. 2. But far more probably the everlasting life to which he refers begins in this world, and is continued and matured in the world to come. Everlasting life is the same life as our Saviour had explained, in His conversation with Nicodemus. It is the life which a man receives by his birth, of water and the Spirit, and without which he cannot be a citizen of the kingdom of heaven. "Except a man be born again, he cannot see the kingdom of God." Everlasting life is the life to which the Evangelist has already referred, when he said: "But as many as received Him, to them gave He power to become the sons of God, even to them that believe on His Name; which were born, not of blood, nor of the will of the flesh, nor of the will of man, but of God." (Chap. i. 12, 13.)

Thus the chapter begins and ends with the same subject, life. In the beginning of it, Jesus teaches Nicodemus that life, by the birth of

---

[1] Hath everlasting life.—"The thought would be weakened, if ἔχει were taken for ἕξει. The notion which John attached to ζωή admits, and almost requires, the Present. The expression, ἔχειν ζωὴν αἰώνιον might, accordingly, be appropriately applied to one who is not as yet in the enjoyment of eternal life, but who, in the certain hope of attaining it, is already as it were in *possession* of it. In what immediately follows, the Apostle very accurately distinguishes the Future from the Present."—Winer's *Grammar of New Testament*, p. 281.

water and the Spirit, is necessary for the new kingdom, the kingdom of God. In the concluding part of the chapter, the Baptist teaches his disciples that the same life, but which he calls everlasting life, can only be obtained by believing in Jesus as the Son of God. A mere change of opinions, a mere intellectual process, was not the condition required for the kingdom of heaven; it must be a change of being, a new life, a new relation to God, which, imparted at the birth by water and the Spirit, would continue through all eternity.

INTRODUCTORY NOTE TO CHAPTER IV.

Jacob's Well.—" The undoubted scene of our Lord's conversation with the Samaritan woman."—Robinson's *Later Researches*, p. 132.

" At the edge of the plain of Mukna (Moreh) a mile and a half east of the town, is Jacob's well, on the piece of ground he purchased from the Shechemites. Not far from the well is the site of Joseph's Tomb. The identity of the well has never been disputed. Christians, Jews, Moslems, and Samaritans all acknowledge it, and the existence of a well in a place where water-springs are abundant, is sufficiently remarkable to give this well a peculiar history.

" Some men were set to work to clear out the mouth of the well, which was being rapidly covered up. A chamber had been excavated to the depth of ten feet, and in the floor of the chamber was the mouth of the well, like the mouth of a bottle, and just wide enough to admit a man's body. We lowered a candle down the well and found the air perfectly good, and after the usual amount of noise and talking among the workmen and idlers, I, Lieutenant S. Anderson, R.E., was lashed with a good rope round the waist, and a loop for my feet, and lowered through the mouth of the well by some trusty Arabs, directed by my friend Mr. Falcher, the Protestant missionary. The sensation was novel and disagreeable. The numerous knots in the rope continued to tighten and to creak, and after having passed through the narrow mouth I found myself suspended in a cylindrical chamber, in shape and proportion not unlike that of the barrel of a gun. The twisting of the rope caused me to revolve as I was being lowered, which produced giddiness, and there was the additional unpleasantness of vibrating from side to side, and touching the sides of the well. I suddenly heard the people from the top shouting to tell me that I had reached the bottom, so when I began to move I found myself lying on my back at the bottom of the well : looking up at the mouth the opening seemed like a star. It was fortunate that I had been securely lashed to the rope, as I had fainted during the operation of lowering. The well is seventy-five feet deep, seven feet six inches diameter, and is lined throughout with rough masonry, as it is dug in alluvial soil. The bottom of the well was perfectly dry at this time of the year (the month of May), and covered with loose stones. There was a little pitcher lying at the bottom unbroken, and this was an evidence of there being water in the well at some seasons, as the pitcher would have been broken had it fallen upon the stones. It is probable that the well was very much deeeper in ancient times, for in ten years it had decreased ten feet in depth. Every one visiting the well throws stones down for the satisfaction of hearing them strike the bottom, and in this way, as well as from the débris of the ruined church built over the well during the fourth century, it has become filled up to probably more than a half of its original depth. . . . .

" The gardens in the Vale of Shechem were looking very beautiful at this time (May 1st). The fig-trees, the latest of all, were in full leaf, and the people commenced to reap in the plain on this day."— *Recovery of Jerusalem*, p. 467.

"Maundrell, March 24th, 1697, found fifteen feet of water in the well. In April, 1839, my friend, the Rev. S. Calhoun, found water in the well ten or twelve feet deep."—Robinson's *Biblical Researches*, iii. 109.

" A very obvious question presented itself to us upon the spot, viz., How can it be supposed that the woman should have come from the city, now half an hour distant, with her water-pot, to draw water from Jacob's well, when there are so many fountains just around the city, and she must also have passed directly by a large one at mid-distance ? But, in the first place, the ancient city, probably in part, lay nearer to this well than the modern one : and then, too, it is not said that the woman came thither *from* the city at all. She may have dwelt, or have been labouring, near the well ; and have gone into the city only to make her wonderful report respecting the strange prophet. Or, even granting that her home was in the city, there would be nothing improbable and unusual in the supposition, that the inhabitants may have set a peculiar value on the water of this ancient well of Jacob, and have occasionally put themselves to the trouble of going thither to draw. That it was not the ordinary public well of the city, is probable from the circumstance that there was here no public accommodation for drawing water." —Robinson's *Biblical Researches*, iii. 111.

No mention is made of any mechanical contrivance, by which the woman drew the water, and yet considering the great depth of the well there must have been some. She could not raise it with her pitcher. Modern travellers in Palestine have noticed several ways of raising water from the deep wells.

" We came to a well at the foot of a hill, on which there is a village called Perè : the oxen raise the water by a bucket and rope, without a wheel, and so by driving them from the well the bucket is drawn up." —Pocock's *Travels*, ii. 61.

" At the foot of the hill is what the monks call the well of Zabulon: the water is drawn by boys in leathern buckets, and carried in jars up the hill on women's heads."—*Idem*, ii. 62.

"At Ajfûr (between Jerusalem and Gaza) there was an ancient well in the valley, exhibiting quite a pastoral scene of patriarchal days. Many cattle, flocks of sheep, and kids, and also camels, were all waiting around the well : while men and women were busily employed in drawing water for them. These people at once offered, and drew water for us and our thirsty animals, without the expectation of reward. The well was square and narrow; by measuring the rope we found the depth to be sixty feet. A platform of very large stones was built up around it, and there were many drinking troughs. On the platform was fixed a small reel for the rope, which a man seated on a level with the axis wound up, by pulling the upper part of the reel towards him with his hands, while he at the same time pushed the lower part from him with the feet."—Robinson's *Biblical Researches*, ii. 351.

"Here (Sumneil, between Jerusalem and Gaza) is a large public well at the foot of the hillock; it measured 110 feet deep to the surface of the water, and eleven feet in diameter: the walls being circular and composed of hewn stones of good masonry; women were drawing water from the well by a rope passing over a pulley, which they hauled up by running off with it a great distance into the field, in the manner of sailors."—*Idem*, ii. 368.

The Samaritans.—After the Assyrian conquest of Israel, and the removal of its people into captivity, colonies from the East were placed in their deserted cities. The country having been desolated by war, wild beasts multiplied, and became the terror and scourge of the new inhabitants. The barren heights of Hermon and Lebanon, and the deserted jungles of the Jordan valley, are to this day infested with bears, panthers, wolves, and jackals. The strangers attributed the calamity to the anger of the *local deity*, of whose peculiar mode of worship they were ignorant. They therefore petitioned for Jewish priests to instruct them in religious rites; and after they had heard their teachings, "they feared the Lord, and served their own gods." (2 Kings xvii. 24-41.) Such was the origin of the Samaritans. Strangers by blood, they were merely instructed in some of the leading points of the Jewish religion by one or more Jewish priests: and still retained the gods of their own nations. In after times the Jews refused to acknowledge them in any way, and would not permit them to assist in building the second temple, though their refusal cost them many trials. (Ezra iv.)

Being cast off by the Jews, the Samaritans resolved to erect a temple of their own on Gerizim. The immediate occasion appears to have been the circumstances related by Nehemiah, that a son of Joiada, the high-priest, had become son-in-law to Sanballat, and had on this account been expelled from Jerusalem. (Neh. xiii. 28.) The date of the temple may thus be fixed at about B.C. 420. Shechem now became the metropolis of the Samaritans as a sect, and an asylum for all apostate and lax Jews. (Joseph. *Antiq.* xi. 8-6.) These things tended to foster enmity between the two nations, which resulted in the total destruction of the Temple of Gerizim by the Jews, under John Hyrcanus. The very name Samaritan became a by-word and a reproach among the Jews, just as the name Yehûdy, "Jew," is among modern Syrians; and some even supposed that the Jews nicknamed the city of Shechem Sychar, "Falsehood," to mark their opinion of the pretended origin of its inhabitants. In our Saviour's time the Samaritans retained their worship on Gerizim, though the temple was in ruins; and they had some vague expectations of a Messiah. During the reign of Vespasian Shechem was rebuilt, and renamed Neapolis, "New City," an appellation which has run into the Arabic Nabulus— one of the very few instances in which the Greek has supplanted the Semitic name.

The ancient Samaritans and modern Druses appear to have had very much in common both in character and origin. The ancient Samaritan was part heathen, part Jew; and the modern Druse of Mount Lebanon is part heathen, part Christian; and some have thought that the modern Druses derive their origin from the very same tribes as the ancient Samaritans. "After the second captivity of Israel, Esarhaddon re-peopled the wasted strongholds of Samaria with the tribes whose names are given with so much particularity in Scripture, (2 Kings xvii. 24; and Ezra iv. 9,) races of fierce habit and degraded faith, whose heathen practices, engrafted on the corrupt Judaism which lingered amongst the earlier Samaritans, brought down on the new colonies the especial Nemesis of God. Of these fierce tribes there were some who, Cuthites in name, were of the family of the Royal Scythians, or Gordyans, from the Gordiæan mountains, whom in subsequent times the Greeks knew by the name of Carduchi, (Xen. *Anab.*,) and with whom we are familiar as Koords. Some of these were settled in the Lebanon, and from them it has been said that the Druses spring, and draw the tenets of an ancient but unholy worship."—Lord Carnarvon's *Druses of the Lebanon*, p. 42.

Pococke mentions another account of the origin of the Druses. He says: "If any account can be given of the original of the Druses, it is that they are the remains of the Christian armies in the holy war; and they themselves now say that they are descended from the English."—*Travels*, ii. 94.

"If of old the Jews had no dealings with the Samaritans, the latter, the Samaritans of Nàbulus, at the present day reciprocate the feeling: and neither eat nor drink, nor marry, nor associate with the Jews; but only trade with them."—Robinson's *Biblical Researches*, iii. 107.

"There are not now two hundred Samaritans, all told, in the world. They themselves mention one hundred and fifty as the correct census. They are a strange people, clinging to their law and to the sepulchres of their fathers with invincible tenacity."—Thomson's *Land and the Book*, p. 477.

CHAPTER IV.

1 *Christ talketh with a woman of Samaria, and revealeth Himself unto her ;* 27 *His disciples marvel ;* 31 *He declareth to them His zeal to God's glory ;* 39 *Many Samaritans believe on Him ;* 43 *He departeth into Galilee, and healeth the Ruler's son that lay sick at Capernaum.*

JESUS had already paid one visit to Galilee since the commencement of His Ministry, and had then wrought the miracle which this Evangelist describes in the second chapter. He now undertakes a second journey thither. This is most probably the visit of which St. Matthew (iv. 12) and St. Mark (i. 14) both speak. But as neither of these Evangelists relate any of the acts of Jesus between His Temptation and John's imprisonment, they naturally record this His visit into Galilee immediately after their mention of the Baptist's imprisonment.

The reason which St. John assigns for this journey into Galilee, is that the Pharisees or Sanhedrin at Jerusalem were beginning to grow jealous of His increasing influence with the people. The crowds that daily flocked to the baptism of John, had in their opinion become too great either for the public safety, or for the continuance of their power in the nation, and the influence of Jesus was becoming greater even than that of John. Jesus therefore retires for a time into a more remote district. The fulness of time was not yet come for Him to yield Himself up to their malice. By removing into Galilee He would be almost beyond the influence and machinations of the Sanhedrin, and though He would still be within the jurisdiction of Herod, the more distant He was from the place of his abode, the less likely He was to attract Herod's attention, and to cause him in any way to interfere and attempt to put a stop to His Ministry.

1 [When therefore the Lord knew] (how the Pharisees) had heard that Jesus made and baptized more disciples than John.

[S. When therefore Jesus knew.]
(Alf. That the Pharisees.)

2 (Though) Jesus Himself baptized not, but His disciples.

(Alf. Howbeit.)

3 He left Judæa, and departed [again] into Galilee.[1]
[A. V.* Omits, again.]

4 (And) He must needs go through Samaria.
(Alf. Now.)

The expression, "He must needs go through Samaria," has doubtless reference partly to the situation of the countries here mentioned, Samaria lying between Judæa and Galilee. Jesus is now in Judæa, and to reach Galilee he must needs pass through Samaria. Josephus incidentally mentions that it was usual for the Galilæans to travel by the way of Samaria to Jerusalem, upon the celebration of their festivals. But, like so many other expressions, it may have a latent reference to His gracious designs of mercy to this Samaritan woman, or Samaria in general. When he afterwards sent the Twelve Apostles, he said unto them: "Go not into the way of the Gentiles, and into any city of the Samaritans enter ye not." (Matt. x. 5.) He seems to recognise the alien descent of the Samaritans, and to treat them on the footing of Gentiles. He does not forbid his Apostles to pass through Samaria, but not to go of set purpose to preach the Gospel to them. The reason, too, is given. The Gospel must first be preached to the "lost sheep of the house of Israel;" and their prejudice against it must not be excited by preaching to the Gentiles and the Samaritans: their time was not yet come.

5 (Then cometh He) to a city of Samaria, (which is) called Sychar, near to the parcel of ground that Jacob gave to his son Joseph.[2]
(Alf. He cometh therefore—omits, which is.)

---

[1] "From Jerusalem to Nazareth, by way of the hill towns of Shiloh, Sychar, Nain, and Endor, the distance, as a bird would fly, is about sixty-four miles, being nearly the same as that from Oxford to London. By the camel paths, and there are no other, it is eighty miles. A good rider, having little baggage and less curiosity, may get over the ground in two long days; to do so, however, he must make up his mind to spend twelve hours each day in the saddle, on stony hill-sides, with very little water, and still less shade, under the blazing light of a Syrian sun. An easy journey, with time to rest and read, to see the wells, ruins, and cities on the route, may be made in four days; though better still in five.

"The Lord and His disciples went through the land on foot; resting by the wells, under the shade of fig-trees, in the caves of rocks.

"The first part of this journey, a ride of thirty-six miles from the Damascus gate, to be done in about twelve hours, brings you to one of the most lovely and attractive spots in Palestine: the site of Joseph's tomb and Jacob's well, where Jesus, resting from his long walk, begged the woman of Samaria to give him drink."
—Dixon's Holy Land, ii. 72.

"It was the custom of the Galilæans, as they went to Jerusalem to the Festivals, to go through the country of the Samaritans.—Josephus Antiq. xx. vi. 1. "And he that would go soonest thither must go that way, and it is three days' journey that way from Galilee to Jerusalem," in vita sua.

[2] Sychar.—" It is read in some copies and by some expositors, with y in the first syllable, as in the text of Chrysostom, Montanus, the Arabic, the Italian of Brucioli, Chemnitius, Grotius, &c., and by some with i, Sichar, as the Vulgar Latin,

Sychar, or Shechem, must have been a very sacred spot to the Jews as well as to the Samaritans: and Jacob's acknowledged connection with it is, as it were, one of the links that bind the Old and New Testament together. In the book of Joshua, (chapter xxiv. 32,) it is said that this parcel of ground became the inheritance of the children of Joseph, and that Joseph's bones were buried here. St. Stephen implies that others also of the patriarchs or their families were buried here. (Acts vii. 15.)

6 Now Jacob's well was there. Jesus, therefore, being wearied with His journey (sat thus on the well):[1] (And) it was about the sixth hour.

(Alf. Was sitting thus by the well—omits, and.)

Beza, Deodates Italian, the Spanish, French, Dutch, and some Greek copies which these followed. Be it read whether way it is with Sychar or Sichar (as such changes are not strange) the place and city apparently was the same with Sichem, so famous in the Old Testament. And that appeareth plain by this, that it is said, there was the portion of land which Jacob gave to his son Joseph, which plainly was Sichem. (Gen. xxxiii. 18, 19; and xlviii. 22.)—Lightfoot, i. 593.
This name is only found in St. John iv. 5, but it is universally considered to be the same as Sichem or Shechem, which is frequently mentioned in the Old Testament history. Dr. Robinson (*Bib. Res.* iii. 118) says, "In consequence of the hatred of the Jews, and in allusion to the idolatry of the Samaritans, the town Sichem probably received among the Jewish common people the by-name of Sychar, which we find in the Gospel of St. John; while Stephen, in addressing the more courtly Sanhedrin, employs the ancient name. (Acts vii. 16.) Sychar might be derived from a Hebrew root, meaning either falsehood or drunkard."
Josephus describes Shechem as between Mount Gerizim and Mount Ebal. The present Nâbulus is a corruption of Neapolis; and Neapolis succeeded the more ancient Shechem. The city received its new name from Vespasian. The situation of the town is one of surpassing beauty. It lies in a sheltered valley, protected by Gerizim on the south and Ebal on the north. The feet of these mountains, where they rise from the town, are not more than 500 yards apart. The bottom of the valley is about 1800 feet above the level of the sea, and the top of Gerizim 800 feet higher still. The site of the present city, which is believed to have been also that of the Hebrew city, occurs exactly on the water-summit; and streams issuing from the numerous springs there, flow down the opposite slopes of the valley, spreading verdure and fertility in every direction. Travellers vie with each other in the language which they employ to describe the scene that bursts here so suddenly upon them on arriving in spring or early summer at this paradise of the Holy Land.
"Here," says Dr. Robinson (iii. 96) "a scene of luxuriant and almost unparalleled verdure burst upon our view. The whole valley was filled with gardens of vegetables, and orchards of all kinds of fruit, watered by several fountains, which burst forth in various parts, and flow westward in refreshing streams. It came upon us suddenly like a scene of fairy enchantment. We saw nothing to compare with it in all Palestine. Here, beneath the shade of an immense mulberry-tree, by the side of a purling rill, we pitched our tent for the remainder of the day and night . . . . We rose early, awakened by the songs of nightingales and other birds, of which the gardens around us were full."

[1] Sat thus (ἐκαθέζατο οὕτως), "that is, in a weary posture, or after the manner as tired men used to sit down. De Dieu taketh it only for an elegancy in the Greek which might well be omitted; and accordingly the Syriac hath omitted it and not owned it at all. But see it emphatical in other places also: 1 Sam. ix. 13; 1 Kings ii. 7; Acts vii. 8."—Lightfoot, i. 593.

What a mysterious dispensation, that He, who made the body, should feel the hunger and thirst and fatigue incident to the body, that He, who made the sun, should feel exhaustion from its heat; that He, who made all things, should depend for sustenance, and for the support of His life, on the benevolent feelings of his own creatures. Holy women, it is said, ministered to Him of their substance, and He had a common purse with the Twelve Apostles.

The hour may be mentioned either as a reason for His weariness —the sixth hour being the time when the sun was hottest and most exhausting—or as accounting for the presence of the woman, the sixth being the usual hour for drawing water. If St. John calculates time in the same way as the other three Evangelists, *i.e.*, beginning from sunrise, about six o'clock in the morning, the sixth hour would be twelve o'clock at noon. But if, as some think, St. John uses a different mode of reckoning, beginning, like ourselves, at mid-day, the sixth hour would be six o'clock in the evening. This woman appears to be alone. If the evening was the usual time for drawing water, she would scarcely have been quite alone, as the women in Eastern countries generally go in company, in troops, to draw water.

7 There cometh [a woman] of Samaria to draw water: Jesus saith unto her, Give Me to drink.

[S. A certain woman.]

8 For His disciples were gone away into the city to buy (meat.)

(Alf. Food.)

That His disciples should have gone into the village of Sychar, apparently at some distance to buy food: that Jesus should find this Samaritan woman alone, when he could remonstrate with her on the wickedness of her life, nothing of this happened by mere accident. It was part of the same act of mercy, it was all foreseen and ordained. From His dress and dialect, she would easily recognise Him to be a Jew; and she knew the feud that had existed between the Jews and Samaritans for hundreds of years.

" ὅυτως has been considered redundant. But that adverb is thus frequently employed after a participle to imply a repetition of the participial notion: *tired with the journey, sat down thus* (sicut erat, in consequence of being thus fatigued)."—Winer's *Grammar of New Testament*, 640.

On the well (ἐπὶ τῇ πηγῇ).—"It should be rather, *by* the well—in its immediate neighbourhood. On two other occasions, namely, Mark xiii. 29, John v. 2, our translators have rightly gone back from the more vigorous rendering of ἐπὶ, with a dative, to which they have here adhered. Yet it ought to be said that Winer (*Grammar of New Testament*) is on the side of our version as it stands."—Archbishop Trench on *Authorised Version*, 90.

ἐπὶ τῇ πηγῇ "on the well (the margin of the well), the structure round it, was higher than the mouth of the well itself."—Winer's *Grammar of New Testament*, 410.

COMMENTARY ON ST. JOHN'S GOSPEL. 89

9 Then saith the woman of Samaria unto Him, How is it that Thou, being a Jew, askest drink of me, which am a woman of Samaria? for the Jews have no dealings with the Samaritans.[1]

[S. The woman of Samaria saith unto Him: S. omits, for the Jews have no dealings with the Samaritans.]

(Alf. The Samaritan woman therefore—which am a Samaritan woman—for Jews have no dealings with Samaritans.)

The latter clause of this verse is probably the explanation of the Evangelist, and not the words of the Samaritan woman.

10 Jesus answered and said unto her, If thou knewest the gift of God, and who it is that saith to thee, Give Me to drink: thou wouldest have asked of Him, and He would have given thee living water.

In these words Jesus endeavours to excite her desire to learn two things—the gift of God, and the real character of Him who was speaking with her. The gift of God was, by name, "living water," but in reality the Holy Spirit. He was in outward appearance a mere man, a Jew, as she had called Him, but in reality He was God.

The quality of water differs so much, according to the condition in which it exists, that there may be said to be two very different kinds: 1. Water without motion, stagnant, collected in artificial cisterns; 2. Living water, perpetually flowing from a natural spring. Jesus asks of the Samaritan woman water from the well, water more nearly resembling that collected in artificial cisterns; and says, that if she had

---

[1] For the Jews have no dealings with the Samaritans (οὐ γὰρ συγχρῶνται Ἰουδαῖοι Σαμαρείταις).—I. "That translation which the French and English follow, seems to stretch the sense of the word beyond what it will well bear. For granting the Samaritans were mere heathens, yet did not this forbid the Jews having any kind of dealings with them, for they did not refuse merchandising with any of the Gentile nations whatever. . . .

"II. That version, *non utuntur Judæi Samaritis*, as Beza: or *non contuntur*, as the Vulgar, hardly reacheth the sense of the word, or fully comes up to the truth of the thing."

Lightfoot then goes on to prove by quotations from ancient Jewish writings, that the Jews did not refuse to deal with the Samaritans in the way of trade, but they would not borrow anything of them, or accept anything from them gratis, or allow of any interchange of acts of kindness and courtesy between them, and concludes: "Nor, indeed, can the word συγχρῶνται in this place intend anything else. For whereas it was lawful for the Jews to converse with the Samaritans, buy of them, use their labour, answer to their benedictions 'Amen,' lodge in their towns (Luke ix. 52), I would fain know in what sense, after all this, can it be said, Ἰουδαῖοι οὐ συγχρῶνται Σαμαρείταις, but in this only, that they would not be obliged to them for any kindness."—Lightfoot, ii. 538.

known who He was, she would have asked of Him, and He would have given her, "living water." In using the expression, "living water," Jesus means the water that causes life, the Holy Spirit. He is endeavouring to raise her thoughts from earth, from the water of the body to the water of the soul, the Holy Spirit. The woman misunderstands his use of the words, "living water," and expresses her doubts of His power to do this. He has nothing to draw water with, and he is not greater than Jacob, who gave this well. There is no other water here, as she argues, but that of this well: "and the well is deep, and thou hast nothing to draw with; from whence, then, hast Thou that living water."

11 [The woman saith unto Him], Sir, Thou hast nothing to draw with, and the well is deep: from whence [then] hast Thou that living water?[1]

[S. V. She saith unto Him ; S. omits, then.]

12 Art Thou greater than our father Jacob, which gave us the well, [and drank thereof himself,] (and his children) and his cattle?

[S. He drank also thereof himself.]
(Alf. And his sons.)

She praises the water of this well for its goodness and abundance. What Jacob himself and his children drank of must be good, what his cattle drank of, must be plentiful. Jesus does not reply to her question, Art Thou greater than our father Jacob? but leaves her to conclude that He was greater than Jacob, from the superiority of the water which He would give, over that which Jacob had given. The water which He should give had two properties, which no other water had. He who drank of it should never thirst again; and it should be in him a well of water springing up into everlasting life.

13 Jesus answered and said unto her, (Whosoever) drinketh of this water shall thirst again.

(Alf. Every one that.)

14 But whosoever (drinketh) of the water that I shall give him (shall never thirst): but the water that I shall

---

[1] Thou hast nothing to draw with (ὄυτε ἀντλῆμα ἔχεις) Camerarius out of Plautus latins ἀντλῆμα situlam, Beza out of Austin hauritorium .... It seems they brought their buckets with them to draw with, as well as their vessels to carry water in, unless they made the same vessel serve for both uses, by letting it down to draw with a cord."—Lightfoot, i. 593.

give him (shall be) in [him] (a well) of water springing up into (everlasting life).

[S. Omits, him.]
(Alf. Shall drink—shall not thirst for evermore—shall become—a fountain—eternal life.)

The properties of water which ancient writers have mentioned as symbolising the Holy Spirit, are numberless. Two are very striking, its power to purify, and its power to nourish. No stain can be cleansed without water, neither can any life be supported without water.

But the thoughts of the woman still cling to earth. From His conversation with her thus far, she fails to learn either the character of Him who was speaking, or the nature of the "living water." Of the two qualities which He mentions as belonging to the water which He can give, her desires settle upon that which appears most likely to apply to her own bodily wants. She divests His words of their proper meaning, namely, that he who received the gift of the Holy Spirit, should never require any other kind of spiritual strength in his conflict with Satan and his temptations; and she applies them in her own sense to the body, and to the thirst of the body.

15 The woman saith unto Him, Sir, give me this water, that I thirst not, (neither come hither) to draw.

(Alf. Neither come all the way hither.)

The prophets had spoken of "water" and of "living water" with reference to the soul, and as applying to the gift of the Holy Spirit, in such clear unveiled language, that had the woman been a Jew instead of a Samaritan, she would scarcely have failed to see His application of those terms. But this was the defect of her national creed. The Samaritans did not receive as Holy Scripture the prophets, or any portion of the Old Testament except the books of Moses, at least they did not receive them as of the same authority as the writings of Moses. Besides other passages, Isaiah had said, "With joy shall ye draw water out of the wells of salvation" (Isa. xii. 3); "I will pour water upon him that is thirsty, and floods upon the dry ground: I will pour My Spirit upon thy seed, and My blessing upon thine offspring." (xliv. 3.) "My people have committed two evils: they have forsaken Me the fountain of living waters, and hewed them out cisterns, broken cisterns, that can hold no water." (Jer. ii. 13.) "In that day there shall be a fountain opened to the house of David, and to the inhabitants of Jerusalem for sin and for uncleanness." (Zech. xiii. 1.) "And it shall be in that day, that living waters shall go out from Jerusalem," (xiv. 8).

So far Jesus had not succeeded, so to speak, in raising the thoughts of this Samaritan woman beyond her own daily bodily wants. He has apparently excited in her no interest to learn the nature of the "living water," or the character of Him who talked with her. He therefore touches another chord.

16 [Jesus saith unto her], Go, call thy husband, and come hither.

[V. He saith unto her.]
(Alf. He saith unto her.)

17 [The woman answered and said,] (I have no husband). Jesus said unto her, Thou hast well said, (I have no husband).

[V. Answered and said unto Him. S. omits, and said.]
(Alf. I have not a husband.)

18 For thou hast had five husbands: (and he whom thou now hast) is not thy husband: (in that saidst thou truly).[1]

(Alf. And now he whom thou hast—in this thou hast spoken truth.)

If, in the passage, "he, whom thou now hast, is not thy husband" a stress is to be laid on the word "thy," if after having had five legitimate husbands, the one whom she now had was so far from being *her* husband, that he was the husband of some other woman, the case is worse against her than at first sight appears. But when she honestly confesses that she has no husband, Jesus does not rouse her anger by unsparingly denouncing her sin. He first praises her for the truthfulness of her confession.

She now begins to rise to the knowledge of His character, and it may be with a sincere desire to learn where to pray properly—she proposes to Him as a prophet, the great question of the day, whether the Temple of Jerusalem or on Mount Gerizim, which overhung her own city of Sychar, was the right place for the worship of God.

The Patriarch Jacob had offered sacrifice at Sychar, or Shechem. (Gen. xxxiii. 20.) From Mount Gerizim the six tribes had solemnly pronounced the blessings that should be on those who kept the Ten Commandments. (Deut. xxvii. 12.) At Shechem, Joshua before his death had recounted to the assembled Israelites God's merciful dealings with them. (Josh. xxiv.) A temple, if not then standing, had

---

[1] In that saidst thou truly.—τοῦτο ἀληθὲς εἴρηκας, this hast thou spoken true, hoc verum dixisti. On the other hand, τοῦτο ἀληθῶς εἴρηκας (as Kühnöl maintains) would be ambiguous.—Winer's *Grammar of New Testament*, p. 486.

COMMENTARY ON ST. JOHN'S GOSPEL. 93

formerly stood on Mount Gerizim. All this might seem to convey a kind of right and legality to the worship offered there. But God had chosen one place for His worship, one place only for sacrifices to be offered to Him. He had said, "Take heed to thyself that thou offer not thy burnt offerings in every place that thou seest: But in the place which the Lord shall choose in one of thy tribes, there thou shalt offer thy burnt offerings, and there thou shalt do all that I command thee." (Deut. xii. 13.) This place was Jerusalem. Neither length of time, nor the eminence of the worshippers, could invest any other place with the right, which God had given to Jerusalem alone.

19 The woman saith unto Him, [Sir], I perceive that thou art a prophet.

[S. Omits Sir.]

20 Our fathers worshipped in this mountain: and ye say, that in Jerusalem is the place where men ought to worship.

[S. That it is in Jerusalem where.]

21 Jesus saith unto her, [Woman, believe Me,] ([the hour cometh, when ye shall] neither in this mountain, nor yet at Jerusalem, worship) the Father.

[S.V. Believe Me, woman; A. The hour cometh that ye shall.]
(Alf. An hour cometh when neither in this mountain nor in Jerusalem shall ye worship.)

22 Ye worship (ye know not what: we know what we worship: for salvation is of the Jews.)

(Alf. That which ye know not: we worship that which we know, because salvation cometh of the Jews.)

23 (But the hour cometh), and now is, when the true worshippers shall worship the Father (in spirit and in truth): (for the Father seeketh such to worship Him.)[1]

(Alf. Howbeit an hour cometh—in spirit and truth—for such the Father also seeketh them that worship Him to be.)

---

[1] In spirit and in truth.—Ἐν πνεύματι καὶ ἀληθείᾳ, which qualify προσκυνήσουσιν, must not be resolved and degraded into the adverbs πνευματικῶς καὶ ἀληθῶς. The preposition ἐν there denotes the element in which προσκυνεῖν is exercised.—Winer's *Grammar of New Testament*, p. 444.

24 God is a Spirit: and they that worship [Him] must worship [Him] in spirit and in truth.

[S. Omits Him; S. In the spirit of truth.]
(Alf. Must worship in spirit and truth.)

In his answer, Jesus first declares that the worship at present offered to God, whether at Jerusalem or on Mount Gerizim, should shortly, very shortly, be abolished. He then settles the question in dispute between the Jews and the Samaritans, and gives it in favour of the Jews. The Samaritans worship they know not what. The object of their worship, as well as the manner of their worship was wrong. Along with the God of Israel they worship false gods, the knowledge of which their fathers had brought with them from Babylon and its neighbourhood. The Jews know what they worship: for salvation is of the Jews. This was the case both as regards the old dispensation and the new. The will of God respecting Himself, and the way in which He would be worshipped, was in ancient times revealed to the Jews, and so far as it became known to the Gentiles, this knowledge was disseminated from the Jews. In the new dispensation, Jesus, the author of salvation, was born of the Jews, and from them He became a Light to lighten the Gentiles.

But true as is the worship which the Jews offer when compared with that of the Samaritans, it is not to continue, nay, it is already superseded. God has chosen another mode of being worshipped, free from the defects of both these. With the true God the Samaritans worship false Gods. Their worship is not true. The Jews worship the true God, but their worship is not spiritual. It consists chiefly in the sacrifice of animals, in rites which begin and end with the body, and it is limited to one place, the Temple at Jerusalem. But all these are only shadows, types of the worship which Christ should establish. God's worship should be the worship of the heart, by acts of devotion, faith, hope, repentance. These, wherever offered, and by whomsoever offered, should be accepted by God in the place of the victims which had hitherto been offered to Him rightly at Jerusalem, but ignorantly, superstitiously, and unlawfully at Gerizim.

In His Sermon on the Mount which our Saviour delivers only a short time after this, He shows that the righteousness, the practical life of the Christian, must exceed that of the Jew, and in His conversation with this woman He shows that the worship of a Christian must differ from that of a Jew in two great particulars.. It must be the worship of the soul, not the worship offered by the body merely, and it must not be confined to any one locality. He also gives the reason of this: "God is a Spirit: and they that worship Him must worship Him in spirit and in truth."

25 The woman saith unto Him, I know that Messias

cometh, which is called Christ: (when He is come,) [He will tell us] all things.

[S. He telleth us.]
(Alf. When He shall come.)

26 Jesus saith unto her, I that speak unto Thee am He.

The woman only expresses the general expectation, which existed at this time that the coming of the Messiah was at hand. Even if the Samaritans did not receive the prophets and would therefore be ignorant of Daniel's prophecy of the Messiah, the learned among them would be acquainted with the prophecy of Jacob, (Gen. xlix. 10,) and the rest would know it from common rumour.

27 And upon this came His disciples, and marvelled (that He talked with the woman) : (yet no [man said]), What seekest Thou ? or, Why talkest Thou with her.[1]

[S. Said unto Him.]
(Alf. That He was talking with a woman—yet no one said.)

---

[1] With the Woman (μετὰ γυναικὸς). So also Dr. John Lightfoot (17 cent.) translates this passage. His opinion is that though the article is not expressed in the Greek, it is to be understood in the sense. He supposes that the surprise of the disciples was raised, not so much because Jesus was talking with a *woman*, but with a *Samaritan*. This had already been a cause of wonder to herself (ver. 9). He quotes a passage from Maimonides to show that the Jews were allowed to buy meat of, and to sell meat to, those with whom they were not allowed to enter into familiar conversation. "For they might not use any commerce, nor any converse with a person excommunicate (as the Samaritans were to the Jews), but only so much as for the providing of meat."— Maim. in Talmud, torah, per. 7.—Lightfoot, i. 594.

The following is Bp. Middleton's note on this, " Campbell lays some stress on the absence of the article, and thinks the meaning is, with any woman at all. From the absence of the article nothing can be inferred, because of the preposition. On the whole I am inclined to believe that the surprise felt by the Apostles was rather at our Saviour's conversing with this particular woman, than with any woman indiscriminately . . . . . The business of fetching water belonged exclusively to females; and wells had, from that cause, become places of resort for the loose and licentious of both sexes. It is possible, therefore, that the surprise of the disciples might be excited, more especially by our Saviour's conversing with this particular woman, whom He had found in such a place ; and her appearance, probably, bespoke somewhat of her real character, as exhibited in the sequel of the story." —On the *Greek Article*, p. 243.

Alford translates this, with *a* woman, and Dr. J. B. Lightfoot remarks on it: " The English version, ' They marvelled that He talked with *the* woman,' implies that the disciples know her shameful history—a highly improbable supposition, since she is obviously a stranger whose character our Lord reads through His divine intuition alone : whereas the true rendering, ' He talked with *a* woman,' which indeed alone explains the emphatic position of γυναικός, points to their surprise that He should break through the conventional restraints imposed by rabbinical authority, and be seen talking to one of the other sex in public. A rabbinical precept was, Let no one talk with a woman in the street, no not with his own wife."—*Revision of English New Testament*, p. 115.

Between these different translations and different explanations the reader must choose. But the passage can scarcely be cited as a clear instance of careless, or

The surprise of the disciples may have been caused either because He was holding a conversation with a woman, a stranger and in a lonely place, which they looked upon as a breach of Jewish propriety; or, because He was holding a conversation with this particular woman, on the ground, either that she was a Samaritan, or that from certain indications, which the disciples easily recognised, she was a woman of infamous character; but whatever was the source of their surprise, reverence for Jesus prevented them from giving expression to it.

28 The woman then left her waterpot, and (went her way) into the city, and saith to the men,

(Alf. Went away.)

29 Come, see a man, which told me all things that ever I did : is not this the Christ ?[1]

(Alf. Is this the Christ?)

30 [Then] they went out of the city, (and came unto Him.)

(V. A. Omits, Then.]
(Alf. Omits, Then—and were coming to Him.)

She concluded that He was a prophet because He had revealed to her the secrets of her own life, and she believes He is the Messiah on His own word. In the fulness of her faith and zeal she leaves her waterpot, she forgets the errand on which she had been so intent, she neglects the water, with which her mind had been so full that she had no thoughts for the "living water," and hurries into the city to announce to others her good news. Her question, Is not this? or, Is

---

even, of faulty rendering on the part of our Translators, supported as they are by such authorities as Dr. John Lightfoot and Bishop Middleton.

[1] "Is not this the Christ? (μήτι οὗτος ἐστιν ὁ χριστός;) Correcting all our previous translations, our Translators rendered the words, μήτι οὗτός ἐστιν ὁ υἱὸς Δαβίδ (Matt. xii. 23) with perfect accuracy: 'Is this the son of David?' fully understanding that, according to the different idioms of the Greek and English, the negative particle of the original was not to re-appear in the English."—Acts vii. 42 : John viii. 22. I am unable to say when the reading, which appears in all our modern Bibles, 'Is *not* this the Son of David?' first crept in: it is already in Hammond, 1659; but it is little creditable to those who should have kept their text inviolate, that they have not exercised a stricter vigilance over it. It is curious that having escaped error here, our translators should yet have fallen into it in the exactly similar phrase at John iv. 29, μήτι οὗτός ἐστιν ὁ χριστός; where they do render. ' Is *not* this the Christ?' but should have rendered, 'Is this the Christ?' The Samaritan woman in her joy, as speaking of a thing too good to be true, which she will suggest, but dare not absolutely affirm, asks of her fellow-countrymen, 'Is this the Christ? Can this be He whom we have looked for so long? expecting in reply not a negative, but an affirmative answer.'"—Archbishop Trench on *Authorised Version*, p. 101.

this the Christ, as it has been translated, does not imply any hesitancy, or halting in her own belief, but rather a desire that they should draw their own conclusion.

31 In the meanwhile His disciples prayed Him, saying, (Master), eat.

(Alf. Rabbi.)

32 But He said unto them, I have meat to eat that ye know not of.

33 [Therefore] [said the disciples one to another], Hath any man brought Him ought to eat ?[1]

[S. The disciples say one to another (omit Therefore.)]

34 Jesus saith unto them, My meat is (to do the will) of Him that sent Me, and (to finish) His work.

(Alf. That I should do the will—and should finish.)

Our Saviour is gradually unfolding the object of His Own Mission, as well as that of His disciples, in their degree, and he incites them by various considerations zealously to fulfil it. As He had just done in His conversation with the Samaritan woman, so He now acts with His disciples, He kindles their curiosity and interest by using words, that are in common use, in a higher sense. Words that are generally confined to the body and its wants, He applies to the soul. His hunger, His longing for the conversion of the Samaritans was so intense that the hunger of His body was nothing to it. According to your usual mode of reckoning, He says, there are yet four months unto the harvest; but I can point out to you a harvest now ready, fields already ripe for the harvest : a harvest, too, in which those who gather it in shall receive as their wages not an earthly recompense but life eternal.

The fields "white already to harvest" were the city of Sychar and the other cities of Samaria, the firstfruits of which was the body of men who were returning with the Samaritan woman to hear Jesus for themselves. The harvest was their conversion to the faith in Jesus as the Messiah, the Son of God. The reapers were Jesus Himself and His disciples, who by their teaching were bringing to perfection

---

[1] Hath any man, &c.—Mη (μήτι) is used when a negative answer is presumed or expected. Some, however, think that μή sometimes anticipates an affirmative answer in the New Testament. But the speaker, in such case, always leans to a negative answer, and would not be surprised if he received one: John iv. 33. Has any one brought Him anything to eat? (I do not think so; especially as we are here in the country of the Samaritans.—Winer's *Grammar of New Testament*, p. 534.

the first principles of reverence towards God, which Moses and others had sown in their hearts.

35 (Say ye not), There are yet four months, and then cometh harvest? (Behold) I say unto you, Lift up your eyes, (and look on) the fields: for [they are white already to harvest].

[S. V. A. For they are white to harvest. Already (A. adds also) he that reapeth.]
(Alf. Say not ye—lo—and behold—that they are white to harvest already.)

36 And he that reapeth receiveth wages, and gathereth fruit unto life eternal: (that [both] he that soweth and he that reapeth) may rejoice together.

[V. Omits, both.]
(Alf. Omits, And—that both the sower and the reaper.)

37 And herein is that saying true, One soweth, and another reapeth.[1]

(Alf. For herein is [fulfilled] that true saying, One is the sower and another the reaper.)

38 I sent you to reap that whereon (ye bestowed) no labour: (other men laboured), and ye are entered into their labours.

(Alf. Ye have bestowed—others have laboured.)

Of the words "Say ye not there are yet four months and then cometh harvest," other interpretations have been offered; but there is no sufficient reason to reject the literal meaning. If the literal sense be correct, it will fix the date of this conversation.

Lightfoot (ii. 544) explains the words of verse 35 as pregnant with meaning. He quotes several ancient Jewish writers to show that the time for sowing wheat and spelt was during the months Tisri and Marheshvan, or from the middle of September to the middle of November, and that the time for sowing the barley was in the months Shebat and Adar, from January to March, or seventy days before the Passover. The conclusion which he draws from this is that, though

---

[1] That true saying ($\dot{o}$ $\dot{a}\lambda\eta\theta\iota\nu\dot{o}s$).—"A few MSS. are without the article; but as Matthäi well observes, "*et abesse et adesse potest.*" If we render, "in this instance the saying is true," the article must be omitted: but if, "in this is exemplified the true saying," the article is absolutely necessary, as in St. John i. 9; vi. 32; xv. 1. . . . The great majority of MSS. ought, I think, to prevail; they are at least as fifty to one."—Middleton on the *Greek Article*, p. 244.

Jesus says there are yet four months to the harvest, the seed for that harvest was only partially sown, the barley, the hope of the harvest to come, was not yet committed to the ground. The knowledge of this fact helps to throw additional light on our Saviour's words. Directing their attention to the multitudes of Samaritans whom He saw coming towards them, He said, " Lift up your eyes, and look on the fields: for they are white already to harvest." Behold what a harvest of souls are here, where there has been but scanty seed sown. Compared with the Jews, only little seed had been sown among the Samaritans, either in the time of the prophets, or during the Ministry of Jesus Himself. The last eight months He had spent in Judæa and Jerusalem, and this is His first visit to Samaria, and see how ready they are to receive His word and to believe in Him as the Christ.

The harvest of the Jews began at the Passover. On the second day of the Passover the Law enjoined them to bring a sheaf of the firstfruits of their harvest, and wave it before the Lord, and from that day they counted seven weeks to Pentecost. (Levit. xxiii. 10-15.) The Passover was the fourteenth day of the first month—Nisan (the end of March and the beginning of April). Four months before the Passover would be about the end of our November.

39 And many of the Samaritans of that city believed [on Him] for the saying of the woman, which testified, He told me all that [ever] I did.

[S. Omits, on Him; S. V. Omit, ever.]
(Alf. In Him.)

40 (So when the Samaritans were come) unto Him, they besought Him (that He would tarry) with them: and He (abode) there two days.

[V. Were come together unto Him: S. And He abode with them two days.]
(Alf. When therefore the Samaritans came—to tarry—tarried.)

41 And many more believed because of (His Own word).

(Alf. His word.)

42 And said unto the woman, (Now we believe, not because [of thy saying]) [for we have heard (Him ourselves)], and know that this is indeed [the Christ] the Saviour of the world.

[S. Of thy testimony; S. We have heard Him ourselves; S. V. Omit, the Christ.]
(Alf. No longer do we believe because of thy story—for ourselves—omits, the Christ.)

The honesty and sincerity of the Samaritans contrast well with the hardness and unbelief of the Jews. After converse with Him for two days only the Samaritans believe that Jesus is the Saviour of the world. After three years' preaching, after the performance of so many and of such mighty miracles, the Jews as a body refuse to believe in Him. Belief and unbelief in Jesus as God depended not so much on the proofs that were offered, as on the heart and on the previous life of those to whom the proofs were exhibited.

It may be that Jesus remained only two days with the Samaritans out of consideration for the Jews, to avoid the reproach which they would be sure to fix upon Him for it, and the conclusion they would draw, that He could not be the Christ, because Christ was promised not to the Samaritans but to the Jews.

43 Now after (two days) He departed thence, and went into Galilee.

[S. V. He departed thence into Galilee.]
(Alf. The two days—He departed thence into Galilee.)

44 For Jesus Himself testified that a prophet hath no honour in his own country.

45 (Then when He was come) into Galilee, the Galilæans received Him, having seen all the things that He did at Jerusalem at the feast : for they also went unto the feast.

(Alf. When therefore He came.)

Usually Nazareth, His own country, would be included under the term Galilee, but here His own country is used in contradistinction to Galilee. Jesus went not to Nazareth, because He knew that a prophet had no honour in his own country, but He went into Galilee, that is, into the other parts of Galilee.

Continuing his journey from Judæa into Galilee (iv. 3), which had been interrupted by His conversation with the Samaritan woman, our Saviour goes to Cana in Galilee, leaving or passing by Nazareth, (Matt. iv. 13,) because a prophet had no honour in his own country. Nazareth had been His residence, His country from childhood up to manhood, and the inhabitants despised Him, being, as they thought, the son of a carpenter. He probably goes to Cana to confirm by His presence the faith in Him which His former miracle had created.

46 (So Jesus came again into) Cana of Galilee, where

He made the water wine. And there was a certain nobleman, whose son was sick at Capernaum.[1]

[S. So they came again ; V. So He came again ; S.* Where they made.]
(Margin, Courtier, or ruler.)
(Alf. So He came again unto.)

47 [When he heard that Jesus was come out of Judæa into Galilee, he went unto Him], and besought [Him] (that He would come down), and heal his son : for he was at the point of death.

46-47 [S. Now there was a certain nobleman, whose son was sick at Capharnaum (Capharnaum, also V.); he hearing that Jesus was come out of Judæa into Galilee, went therefore unto Him ; S. V. Omit, Him.]
(Alf. The same when he heard, etc.,—to come down.)

48 Then said Jesus unto him, Except ye see signs and wonders, ye will not believe.[2]

(Alf. Ye will never believe.)

---

[1] A certain nobleman (ἦν τις βασιλικὸς) —" It is hard in the variety of constructions that are given of the Greek word βασιλικὸς, to tell what this man was that was so titled. The vulgar Latin and Erasmus render it *regulus*, a little king; the Syriac, one of the king's servants ; which the Arabic followed in sense, though not in words. The Italian hath it *signore*, a great man, or of high degree : Nonnus, βασιλήιος ἀνὴρ, a man of the king's, which is the very epithet that is used by the Arabic, and several other expositions of it are given."—Lightfoot, i. 605.

[2] Signs and Wonders.—" These words (τέρας, σημεῖον, δύναμις, ἔνδοξον, παράδοξον, θαυμάσιον) have this in common, that they are all used to characterise the supernatural works wrought by Christ in the days of His flesh : thus σημεῖον, John ii. 11; Acts ii. 19 ; τέρας, Acts ii. 22 ; John iv. 48 ; δύναμις, Mark vi. 2; Acts ii. 22; ἔνδοξον, Luke xiii. 17: παράδοξον, Luke v. 26: θαυμάσιον, Mark xxi. 15 : while the first three, which are far the most usual, are in like manner employed of the same supernatural works wrought in the power of Christ by His Apostles (2 Cor. xii. 12). They will be found, on examination, not so much to represent different kinds of miracles, as miracles contemplated under different aspects and from different points of view.

"Τέρας and σημεῖον are often linked together in the New Testament (John iv. 48 ; Acts ii. 22; iv. 30 ; 2 Cor. xii. 12), and times out of number in the Septuagint. "The same miracle is upon one side a τέρας, on another a σημεῖον, and the words must often refer, not to different classes of miracles, but to different qualities in the same miracles ; in the words of Lampe (Com. in John, vol. i. p. 513), 'Eadem enim miracula dici possunt *signa*, quatenus aliquid seu occultum seu futurum docent: et *prodigia* (τέρατα) quatenus aliquod extraordinarium, quod stuporem excitat, sistunt. Hinc sequitur signorum notionem latius patere, quam prodigiorum, omnia prodigia sunt *signa*, quia in illum usum a Deo dispensata, ut arcanum indicent. Sed omnia signa non sunt prodigia, quia ad signandum res celestes aliquando etiam res communes adbibentur." . . . . . Origen long ago called attention to the fact that the name τέρατα is never in the New Testament applied to these works of wonder, except in association with some other name. They are often called σημεῖα, often δυνάμεις, often τέρατα καὶ σημεῖα, more than once τέρατα, σημεῖα, καὶ δυναμεῖς, but never τέρατα alone. The observation was well worth making ; for the fact which we are thus bidden to note is indeed eminently characteristic of the miracles of the New Testament,

49 The nobleman saith unto Him, (Sir), come down ere my child die.

[A. Ere my son die.]
(Alf. Lord.)

50 Jesus saith unto him, Go thy way: thy son liveth. [And] the man believed [the word (that Jesus had spoken) unto him, and he went his way.]

[S. V. Omit, And; S. The word of Jesus and went his way.]
(Alf. Omits, And—that Jesus spake.)

51 (And) as he was now going down, [his servants met him, and told him, saying, (Thy son) liveth.]

[S. The servants met him and told that his son liveth; V. Omits, and told him; V. A. That his son liveth.)
(Alf. But—and brought tidings—Thy child.)

52 (Then enquired he of them [the hour when]) he began to amend. (And) they said unto him, Yesterday (at) the seventh hour the fever left him.

[V. The very hour wherein.]
(Alf. He inquired therefore of them the hour in which—So—in.)

53 (So the father knew) that it was (at the same hour) in the which [Jesus said unto him], Thy son liveth: and himself believed, and his whole house.

[S. He said unto him.]
(Alf. The father knew therefore—in that hour.)

---

namely, that a title, by which more than any other these might seem to hold on to the prodigies and portents of the heathen world, and to have something akin to them, should thus never be permitted to appear, except in company of some other, necessarily suggesting higher thoughts about them.

"But the miracles are also σημεῖα . . . . Among all the names which the miracles bear, their ethical end and purpose comes out in σημεῖον with the most distinctness, as in τέρας with the least. It is resolved and declared in the very word that the prime object and end of the miracle is to lead us to something out of and beyond itself: that, so to speak, it is a kind of finger-post of God, pointing for us to this; valuable not so much for what it is, as for what it indicates of the grace and power of the doer, or of the connection with a higher world in which He stands. (Mark xvi. 20; Acts xiv. 3; Heb. ii. 4; Exod. vii. 9, 10; 1 Kings xiii. 3.). . . . . It is to be regretted that σημεῖον is not always rendered sign in our version; that in the Gospel of St. John, where it is of very frequent recurrence, 'sign,' too often gives place to the vaguer 'miracle:' and sometimes not without serious loss; thus see, iii. 2; vii. 31: x. 41; and above all, vi. 26."—Archbishop Trench on *Synonyms of New Testament*, p. 324.

This ruler (βασιλικός), according to the use of the word by Josephus, was probably one of Herod's officers. It is not stated whether he was a Jew or a Gentile. The weakness of his faith and our Saviour's words to him, "Except ye see signs and wonders, ye will not believe," rather favour the opinion that he was a Jew. The Gentiles were far more open to conviction that Jesus was the Christ than the Jews were. The Samaritans had lately given a very striking example of this. The Jews above all others required "signs and wonders," i.e., the exercise of superhuman power, either in accordance with the working of nature, such as suddenly to heal the sick, or in opposition to it, such as to raise the dead.

In this case Jesus had two cures to work, the cure of the father's unbelief, and the cure of his son's fever. The father had perhaps heard of the miracle which a few months before Jesus had performed at Cana, how he had turned the water into wine; or he was one of the Galilæans who had seen all the things that He did at Jerusalem at the feast; or he may have only heard of these, and his faith was less perfect than if he had seen them. Anyhow, he could only connect His power with His presence, and urges Jesus to come down to Capernaum, a distance of twenty-five miles, ere his child died. But on his importunity, Jesus by a word heals both the father and the son : the father of his unbelief, and the son of his fever. By the question which he puts to his servants "when he began to amend," it would seem that even then the father did not expect a sudden but a gradual recovery. On hearing the account of his servants as to the hour when the fever left his son, the father believes still more in Jesus. He believes not only that He has power to heal the sick, but also that He is the Christ.

The fever left the child at the seventh hour. Reckoning from sunrise the seventh hour would be one o'clock at noon, or from midday, it would be seven o'clock in the evening. The latter would readily explain the expression of the servants, "Yesterday, at the seventh hour." Travelling all night, they would meet the father on the morning of the following day. Against this we must set the improbability there is that St. John would put into the mouth of these servants, Galilæans, or living in Galilee, a manner of reckoning time which was never used in any part of Palestine.

This healing of the nobleman's son must not be confounded with the healing of the centurion's son, which St. Matthew (viii. 5) and St. Luke (vii. 1) record. They are different cases. In the case of the Centurion's son, Jesus had entered into Capernaum, but here the nobleman comes to Jesus, who was still at Cana. In the former Jesus expressed great willingness to go to the house, but the centurion deemed it unnecessary, and himself unworthy of His presence, and that His word was sufficient; but the nobleman entreats Jesus to go down ere his child die. In the former case "palsy" is mentioned as the malady, in the latter "fever." In the centurion's case the sick might be, and most probably was, his servant (παις) ; in the nobleman's case it was his son (υἱός). The difference between them will be more striking when seen in juxtaposition.

St. Matthew viii.	St. John iv.
5 And when Jesus was entered into Capernaum. There came unto Him a centurion (ἑκατόνταρχος) beseeching Him. 6 And saying, Lord my servant (ὁ παῖς μου) lieth at home, sick of the palsy (παραλυτικὸς) grievously tormented.	
7 And Jesus saith unto him, I will come and heal him. 8 The centurion (ἑκα τόν ταρχος) answered and said, Lord, I am not worthy that Thou shouldest come under my roof, but speak the word only, and my servant (ὁ παῖς μου) shall be healed. 9 For I am a man under authority, having soldiers under me: and I say to this man, Go, and he goeth, and to another, Come and he cometh, and to my servant, Do this, and he doeth it.	46 And there was a certain nobleman (τις βασιλικὸς) whose son (ὁ υἱὸς) was sick at Capernaum. 47 When he heard that Jesus was come out of Judæa into Galilee, he sent unto Him and besought Him that He would come down and heal his son (αὐτοῦ τὸν υἱὸν) for he was at the point of death.
10 When Jesus heard it, He marvelled, and said to them that followed, Verily I say unto you, I have not found so great faith, no, not in Israel. 11 And I say unto you, That many shall come from the east and west, and shall sit down with Abraham, and Isaac and Jacob, in the Kingdom of Heaven, 12 But the children of the kingdom, shall be cast out into outer darkness: there shall be weeping and gnashing of teeth.	48 Then said Jesus unto him, Except ye see signs and wonders, ye will not believe. 49 The nobleman (ὁ βασιλικὸς) saith unto Him, Sir, come down ere my child (τὸ παιδίον μου) die.
13 And Jesus said unto the centurion, (τῷ ἑκατοντάρχῳ), Go thy way ; and as thou hast believed, so be it done unto thee. And his servant (ὁ παῖς αὐτοῦ) was healed in the selfsame hour).	50 Jesus saith unto him, Go thy way : thy son (ὁ υἱὸς σου) liveth: And the man believed the word that Jesus had spoken unto him, and he went his way. 51 And as he was now going down his servants met him, and told him, saying thy son (ὁ παῖς σου) liveth. 52 Then enquired he of them the hour when he began to amend. And they said unto him, yesterday at the seventh hour the fever (ὁ πυρετὸς) left him. 53. So the father knew that it was at the same hour, in the which Jesus said unto him, Thy son (ὁ υἱὸς σου) liveth : and himself believed, and his whole house.

Both the centurion and the nobleman lived at Capernaum. The miraculous cure of the nobleman's son by a word from Jesus, who was dwelling at Cana, twenty-five miles off, would be known to every one in Capernaum. This may have produced the vigorous faith in the centurion, which drew forth the praise of Jesus Himself, when a short time after this he said, " Speak the word only and Thy servant shall be healed."

54 (This is again the second miracle that Jesus did), when he was come out of Judæa into Galilee.

(Alf. This again, a second miracle did Jesus.)

The Authorised English Version has imparted a degree of obscurity to this verse which does not belong to the Greek. The simple translation is, " This again, a second miracle, did Jesus, when He was come out of Judæa into Galilee." On His first visit to Cana in Galilee, after He had left Judæa, He made the water wine, now on His second visit direct from Judæa He heals the nobleman's son.

INTRODUCTORY NOTE TO CHAPTER V.

The Water Supply, or system by which Jerusalem was furnished with a constant supply of water was one of the most wonderful things in that wonderful city. The following extracts will tend to throw some light upon it :—

" The cisterns, in what is now called the Sanctuary, appear to have been connected by a system of channels cut out of the rock; so that when one was full the surplus water ran into the next, and so on until the final overflow was carried off by a channel into the Kedron. One of the cisterns, that known as the Great Sea, would contain two million gallons; and the total number of gallons which could be stored probably exceeded ten millions."—*Recovery of Jerusalem*, p. 17.

" The ancient supply of water appears to have been obtained from springs, wells, the collection of rain in pools and cisterns, and water brought from a distance by aqueducts. The extensive remains of cisterns, pools, and aqueducts show that little dependence was placed on any natural springs existing in or near the city; and, indeed, from the formation of the ground it is doubtful whether any existed besides the Fountain of the Virgin in the Kedron Valley. There may have been a source in the Tyropæon Valley, but it could only have been a small and not very lasting one."—*Idem*, p. 19.

" Water was brought into the city by two aqueducts, the 'low level' and the 'high level;' but the course of the former can alone be traced within the walls of the city."—*Idem*, p. 23.

" In this investigation the interesting question of the supposed spring inside the walls of Jerusalem and under the Temple Courts has been for the first time followed to the bottom, and the result appears to be that while there is no actual spring within the walls, the whole mount is so honeycombed with cisterns as to give ample materials for the conjecture of Tacitus and for the imagery of Scripture."—*Recovery of Jerusalem* (Introduction), xvii.

Pool of Bethesda.—" Immediately to the east of the hill is a small valley, which falls into the Kedron about 100 yards south of St. Stephen's Gate. On its left bank stands the Church of St. Anne, and in its bed has been formed the traditional Pool of Bethesda, called in the most ancient MSS. of the New Testament Bethzatha*, a name not unlike that of the fourth hill—Bezatha."— p. 11.

---

* Not quite correct (S. Bethzatha, V. Bethsaida).

"The Pool of Bethesda was made across the valley, and not in the direction of its length."—*Recovery of Jerusalem*, p 12.

"Pool of Bethesda (Birket Israel) lies in the valley which runs past St. Anne's Church; but the drainage of this is not sufficient to supply such a large tank, and it must have been fed from some other source. Though partly filled with rubbish, it still has a depth of forty feet; it is out of repair, and does not now hold water."—p. 22.

Siloam.—"The two pools of Siloam are at the bottom of the Tyropæon Valley, and were probably made for the irrigation of the gardens below. They derive their supply partly from the surface drainage, and partly from the Fountain of the Virgin, the water of which is brought to them by a subterranean channel."—p. 22.

"The present supply of water is almost entirely dependent on the collection of the winter rainfall, which is much less than has generally been supposed, as by a strange mistake the rain-gauge was formerly read four times higher than it should have been. According to Dr. Chaplin's observations the average rainfall during the years 1860-64 was 19·86 inches, the maximum being 22·975 inches, and minimum 15·0 inches."—p. 25.

II.

THE ACTS OF JESUS IN JUDÆA.—SECOND PASSOVER. (V. 1.)

CHAPTER V.

1 *Jesus on the Sabbath day cureth him that was diseased eight-and-thirty years;* 10 *The Jews therefore cavil, and persecute Him for it;* 17 *He answereth for Himself, and reproveth them, showing by the testimony of His Father,* 32 *of John,* 36 *of His works,* 39 *and of the Scriptures, who He is.*

1 After this there [was a feast] of the Jews : and Jesus went up to Jerusalem.

[S. Was the feast.]
[Alf. After these things.]

FROM the earliest times a difference of opinion has existed with respect to the nature of this feast. Some have supposed that the Passover, and others that the Feast of Pentecost is meant. The following considerations are offered in favour of this feast being the Passover.

The Passover was held to be the greatest of all the Jewish feasts, so much greater than the others that it was considered *the* feast of the Jews, so much so that it is generally admitted that if the article were prefixed to ἑορτή, scarcely a doubt could remain that the Passover was here meant. Though the article is not found in all the MSS., and is wanting in some of those of the greatest authority, it is found in the Sinaitic Manuscript, which, as Prof. Tischendorf thinks, is the most ancient and the most important of all, and which is certainly one of very great antiquity and of very great authority. On this and other grounds the article before ἑορτή has been admitted by Prof. Tischendorf into the text.—*Greek Testament*, last edition.

In the last chapter Jesus said there were yet four months to the harvest, or to the Passover. The Passover would be the next great feast that occurred after this. If, therefore, this be not the Passover, but the Feast of Pentecost, as Chrysostom, Cyril, and others have thought, it implies that a Passover has been celebrated fifty days before this feast, and which St. John has omitted to record. But St. John has mentioned by name the first, the third, and the fourth Passover during our Saviour's Ministry, is it not therefore probable that he would mention the second? But if this be the Feast of Pentecost and not the Passover, it still proves there were four Passovers during His Ministry. For the mention of the Feast of Pentecost as much implies that a Passover had taken place fifty days before, as if that were expressly stated. No feast was kept during the four months immediately preceding the Passover, except the Feast of Dedication. But the Jews were not commanded to assemble at Jerusalem to keep this feast, nor was it celebrated at Jerusalem with very much greater solemnity than it was in any other place. Another consideration that goes to show that this feast was the Passover is this: St. Mark (ii. 13, &c.), and St. Luke (v. 27 and vi. 1, &c.,) place the rebuking of the disciples for plucking the ears of corn on the Sabbath day as the next event after the call of Levi. But St. Luke fixes the day on which the plucking of the ears of corn took place, and calls it by a name which implies that a Passover had occurred just before it. It happened ἐν σαββάτῳ δευτεροπρώτῳ, or on the first Sabbath after the second day in the Passover week.[1] On this second day they offered their first fruits sheaf (Levit. xxiii. 11), and from this second day they counted their weeks and Sabbaths until Pentecost. Until the offering of the first sheaf had sanctified the corn it was not lawful either to put in the sickle, or to pluck the ears of corn to eat. On this ground harmonists are generally agreed in placing the feast here mentioned by St. John between the call of Levi and the rebuke of the disciples by the Pharisees for plucking the ears of corn on the Sabbath day.

In St. John's narrative there is an interval of about four months between this chapter and the last. But the other Evangelists enable us to fill in this interval with a fair account of the works which our Saviour wrought during that time. After Jesus had said there were

---

[1] The first Second-day Sabbath (Σαββατον δευτεροπρωτον). " The law enjoined that the next morrow after the eating of the Passover should be kept holy like a Sabbath (Exod. xii. 16), and accordingly it is called a Sabbath. (Levit. xxiii. 7, 11.) And there the Law also enjoins that the next day after that Sabbatical day they shall offer the sheaf of first-fruits to the Lord, and from that day they should count seven Sabbaths to Pentecost, which was their solemn festival and thanksgiving for that holy harvest, viz., barley-harvest, which they had then inned. (Levit. xxiii. 15, 16, 17.) That day, therefore, that they offered their first barley sheaf, and from which they were to count the seven Sabbaths or weeks forward, being the second in the Passover week, the Sabbaths that followed did carry a memorial of that day in their name till the seven were run out; as the first was called Σαββατον δευτεροπρωτον, the first second-day Sabbath; the next Σαββατον δευτεροδευτερον, the second second-day Sabbath; the next Σαββατον δευτεροτριτον, the third second-day Sabbath; and so the rest of all the seven through. Now let it be observed (1) That no corn—no, not ears of corn—might be eaten till the first-fruits sheaf was offered and waved before the Lord (Levit. xxiii. 14); (2) That it was waved the second day of the Passover week; (3) That this was the first Sabbath after that second day, when the disciples pluckt the ears of corn, and it will plainly evince that we must look for a Passover before this story, and so it will show the warranty and justness of taking in the fifth of John next before it."—Lightfoot, i. 222.

four months to the harvest or Passover, He tarried two days in Sychar, then He goes into Galilee, avoiding His own city Nazareth (John iv. 43). After some delay in Galilee teaching in their synagogues, (Luke iv. 14, &c.), He goes to Nazareth. The inhabitants of Nazareth having endeavoured to take His life He went to Capernaum, called four disciples, cast out a devil, healed Peter's mother-in-law and others that were diseased, goes and preaches in the synagogues of Galilee (Mark i. 23-39), cleanses and heals a leper in one of those cities (Luke v. 12), returns to Capernaum and recovers a man sick of the palsy, and calls Levi from the receipt of custom (Mark ii.). Such are some of the works which Jesus wrought between His healing of the nobleman's son and the Feast of the Passover, for which He now goes up to Jerusalem.

2 Now there is (at Jerusalem, by the sheep market) a pool, which is called in the Hebrew tongue Bethesda, having five porches.[1]

[By (S.ᵃ A., in) the sheep market a pool: S. A sheep pool: S. Bethzatha: V. Bethsaida.]
(Margin, gate.)
(Alf. In Jerusalem by the sheep gate.)

The word "gate" completes the meaning better than the word

---

[1] **Now there is at Jerusalem** (ἔστι δὲ ἐν τοῖς Ἱεροσολύμοις). "No expositor of any judgment would admit the possibility that ἐστὶ could be put for ἦν. On the other hand, the use of the Present does not necessarily prove that the locality is still as described by the latter."—Winer's *Grammar of New Testament*, 283.

Gates of Jerusalem. "The modern city is entirely surrounded by a massive well-built wall, provided with numerous flanking towers, and is protected on the north by a ditch partly cut in the rock. There are five gates now open, and five closed. Of the former the Jaffa Gate is on the west, the Damascus Gate on the north, St. Stephen's on the east, and the Zion and Dung Gates on the south. Of the latter the Bab er-Zahire is on the north, the Golden Gate on the east, and the Single, Double, and Triple Gates on the south."—*Recovery of Jerusalem*, p. 7.

In the Hebrew tongue (ἑβραϊστί). "They mean the Chaldee language, which, from their return out of Babylon, had been their mother tongue; and they call it the language of those beyond Euphrates (although used also in common with the Syrian on this side Euphrates), that with respect to the Jews they might distinguish it from the ancient holy tongue as not being the tongue they used before they went into captivity, but that which they brought along with them beyond Euphrates."—Lightfoot, ii. 545.

"Bethesda is conceived by some to be derived or compounded of two words which signify *the place of effusion*, a falling in of waters, either, say some, because the rain water falling off the houses gathered here; or as others, because the waters used in the Temple fell through an underground channel hither; or as yet some others, because water ran out of another pool into this; nay yet some further have dreamed of the blood of the sacrifices running in hither. But certainly (to omit to examine these opinions) the title of *the place of effusion* is a note but little distinctive of a peculiar pool (and it is apparent enough that the Evangelist would put a distinction upon this pool here), since it may be given to any pool near Jerusalem, or near any city whatsoever. The Syriac, therefore, hath more pertinently and properly expressed it as signifying the *place of mercy* or compassion, in regard of the virtue that it had of healing those that were diseased."—Lightfoot, i. 661.

COMMENTARY ON ST. JOHN'S GOSPEL. 111

"market," for the sheep-gate was a well-known gate in Jerusalem. Nehemiah relates that, on their return from captivity, the high priest rose up with his brethren the priests, and they builded the sheep-gate; they sanctified it and set up the doors of it. (Neh. iii. 1.) Through this gate the sheep required for the daily service of the Temple would be brought into Jerusalem from the neighbouring country.

Some have supposed that the Pool of Bethesda was used for washing the animals preparatory to their being offered in sacrifice. Lightfoot, whose opinion can seldom be safely despised on subjects connected with the Jews or the Temple worship, is strongly opposed to this, on the ground (ii. 545) (1) That the practice of washing the animals prior to their being sacrificed is nowhere alluded to in Holy Scripture; and (2) That he has searched the traditional writings in order to discover such a custom, and cannot find a trace of it. It is true that the entrails were washed after the animal was slain, but for this purpose a room was set apart in the Temple itself called the washing-room. In his opinion the original purpose of this pool with its five porticoes or cloister-ways covered above and open on one side was for the washing of men and not of animals, of men who were unclean either from some legal or traditionary defilement. Each class of the unclean might have its own separate portico according to the nature of the defilement, and through which they entered the water. The cases of purification on account of uncleanness either legal or traditional were so numerous that if all the pools in Jerusalem had been used for this purpose, they would scarcely have been more than sufficient. The Syriac interpreter renders this passage, *There was at Jerusalem a certain place of baptistery.* By this he may have intended the washing of unclean persons and not of animals. This pool was probably of considerable size. In some of the old translations (see Fulke's *New Testament*) it is called "a pond."

The Evangelist mentions only three kinds of diseased people who came to this pool to be healed, probably as specimens of the rest: these being among the diseases that were the most difficult to cure, and which most impeded their descent into the pool.

3 In these lay (a great multitude of impotent folk), of blind, halt, withered, waiting for the moving of the water.[1]

[S. V. Omit, great: S. V. A.* Omit, waiting for the moving of the water.]
(Alf. A multitude of the sick—omits, waiting for, &c.)

4 For an angel[2] went down at a certain season into the

---

[1] Withered (ξηρῶν). "Sinew-shrunk, as in 1 Kings xiii. 4; Matt. xii. 10."— Lightfoot i. 661.
[2] For an angel, &c. "Tertullian clearly recognises these verses ('Piscinam Bethsaidam angelus interveniens commonebat,' de Bapt. 5), as do Cyril, Chrysostom, Ambrose (twice), Theophy-

112   COMMENTARY ON ST. JOHN'S GOSPEL.

pool, and troubled the water: whosoever then first after the troubling of the water stepped in was made whole of whatsoever disease he had.

[S. V. Omit, this verse: A. An angel of the Lord washed at a certain season.]
(Alf. Omits, this verse.)

The Sinaitic, Vatican, and Alexandrine MSS. omit the last clause of the third verse, and the whole of the fourth. Some have therefore concluded that these words were added by a later hand, and by way of explanation. But the passage must have been in the text in very early times. For Tertullian (A.D. 160-245) quotes the passage, probably a hundred years before any one of these three manuscripts was written, and his copy of St. John certainly contained the words in dispute. (*De Baptismo*, 5: i. 1205, Migne.)

5 (And a certain man was there, which had an infirmity thirty and eight years.)

[S. And there was a certain man which had.]
(Alf. And there was a certain man there, which had been thirty and eight years in his infirmity.)

6 When Jesus saw him (lie), and knew that he had been [now] a long time in that case, He saith unto him, (Wilt thou) be made whole?[1]

[S. Omits, now.]
(Alf. Lying—Desirest thou to.)

7 (The impotent man) [answered Him], Sir, I have no man, when the water is troubled, to put me into the pool; but while I am coming another (steppeth) down before me.

[A. Saith unto Him.]
(Alf. The sick man—goeth.)

---

lact, and Euthymius. No other ecclesiastical writers allude to the narrative, unique and perplexing as it is.—Scrivener's *Introd. to Criticism of New Testament*, p. 438.

"It may be reasonably thought that a portion of these various readings, and those among the most considerable, had their origin in a cause which must have operated at least as much in ancient as in modern times, the changes gradually introduced after publication by the authors themselves into the various copies yet within their reach. Such revised copies would circulate independently of those issued previously, and now beyond the writer's control; and, thus becoming the parents of a new family of copies, would originate and keep up diversities from the first edition, without any fault on the part of transcribers."—*Idem*, p. 16.

[1] Wilt thou be made whole? " There is sometimes an ellipsis of even a sentence. In John v. 6, 7, the answer ἄνθρωπον οὐκ ἔχω, ἵνα βάλῃ με, &c., does not seem to correspond directly to the question, θέλεις ὑγιὴς γενέσθαι; so that a simple *yes, certainly*, may be supplied. But the sick man did not stop at this simple affirmation, but immediately proceeded to state the obstacle which had hitherto prevented the fulfilment of his wish."—Winer's *Grammar of New Testament*, 621.

8 Jesus saith unto him, [Rise, take up] thy bed and walk.

[A. Rise and take up.]

9 [And immediately] the man was made [whole, and took up] his bed and walked; (and on the same day was the sabbath.[1])

[S. Omits, And immediately : S. Whole, and rose and took up.]
(Alf. Now on that day was the sabbath.)

Knowing, either by His own power, or by the information of the bystanders, or from the man himself, that he had been now a long time in that case, Jesus saith unto him, Wilt thou be made whole? He does this to raise in him a longing for help, and an expectation of this help from Jesus Himself. It would seem that an expectation of help from Jesus was a necessary condition in all the cases in which He exercised His divine power to heal.

It does not appear whether the angel was ever visible to the spectators, or whether his presence was only indicated by the moving of the water. But they all knew that the healing of the water was superhuman, and was not by any virtue inherent in the water itself. To heal the impotent man close to the pool, yet without any application of the water of the pool, would naturally suggest to a reflecting mind the similarity which there was in the power of Him who healed by His word, and the power of Him who healed through the water. He, who could heal the impotent man, who had been in this state for thirty and eight years, whether through the water or by His word, must be more than man. He must be God. Thus not merely by the miracle, but also by the locality in which the miracle is wrought, does Jesus lead both the man who had been healed, and those who had witnessed his healing, to draw some such conclusion as this for themselves.

On other occasions, when He had wrought a miracle our Saviour adds some circumstance, either to show them the perfection of His work, or in some way to call their special attention to it. When He had multiplied the bread so as to feed 5000 men with five barley loaves and two fishes, He orders the fragments to be gathered up. (Matt. xiv. 20.) When He cleansed the leper He sent him to show himself to the priest. (Matt. viii. 4.) When He had raised Jairus's daughter from death He commanded that something should be given her to eat. (Mark v. 43.) When He had turned the water into wine He bade them bear it unto the governor of the feast. (John ii. 8.)

---

[1] Thy bed (τὸν κράββατόν σου). The bed, according to the custom of the country, would be a thick mat, rug, or quilt, as in the following:—" Beds were spread for us in our upper room, consisting of thick quilts underneath, and another quilt of silk in which to wrap ourselves."
—Robinson's *Biblical Researches*, iii. 33.

I

To the impotent man, whom He had now healed, He said, "Rise, take up thy bed and walk."

We have reason to believe that in ordering the man to take up his bed and walk Jesus had another object in view besides proving the completeness of the cure, and therefore that He must be God. He did this to bring before the Jews His claim to be God in another form.

10 The Jews therefore said unto him that was cured, It is the sabbath day: [it is not lawful] for thee (to carry thy bed.)[1]

[S. V. A. And it is not lawful.]
(Alf. To take up thy bed.)

11 [He answered] them, He that made me whole, the same [said unto me, Take up thy bed and walk.]

[S. V. A. But he answered: S. Told me to take up the bed and walk.]

The reasoning of the man who was cured was unanswerable. He who made me whole was the man who commanded me to take up my bed and walk. He who could make me whole could not command me to do what was not lawful, or wrong.

12 ([Then] asked they him, What man is that) which [said unto thee (Take up thy bed and walk.])

[S. V. Omit, Then: Told thee to take up and walk.]
(Alf. They asked him, who is the man—Take up and walk.)

13 And he that was healed wist not who it was: for Jesus had (conveyed Himself away), a multitude [being in that place.][2]

[S. Being present.]
(Margin, from the multitude that was.)
(Alf. Escaped his notice—being in the place.)

---

[1] The Sabbath.—"It was only in the synagogue and the Temple, chiefly in the Temple, that the Jewish rule could be set at nought. A law which put an end to gifts and sacrifices in the Temple would not have suited the chief priests and high priests, and these smiling Sadducees taught the old sacerdotal rule that there was no sabbath in holy things. A cripple could not carry his rug a mile, a hungry man could not pluck a grain of wheat; but the Temple fires might be lit, the shew-bread might be baked, the altars might be trimmed and guarded, the shekels might be paid in to the receivers, the doves and heifers might be slain, and the victims might be burnt with fuel. In the Temple courts the seventh day was the busiest of all the week, for, on the Sabbath every Jew who made an offering to God was expected to present two shekels instead of one shekel, two doves instead of one dove, and two rams instead of one ram."—Dixon's *Holy Land*, ii. 117.

[2] Had conveyed Himself away, ἐξένευσεν. This word by some expositors

There is nothing unreasonable in the man's ignorance of Jesus, even so far as not to know His name. For only about eighteen months had elapsed since Jesus had been baptized by John, soon after which He had commenced His Ministry, and only once before during that time had He been in Jerusalem. Great as His fame in Jerusalem might be from His driving out the buyers and sellers from the Temple, it might not be such as to reach the ears of a poor destitute cripple lying in one of the porches near the pool of Bethesda. This was in all probability the first time that he had ever seen Jesus, and that but for a moment or two, for He had at once conveyed Himself away. He had done this to avoid the inconvenient praise and admiration of the impartial multitude, and the malice of the unjust among them, and to leave the man's own testimony more free and less open to suspicion than it would have been by His presence.

14 Afterward Jesus [findeth him in the Temple, and said unto him,] Behold thou art made whole : sin no more, (lest a worse thing come unto thee).

[S. Findeth him that had been healed in the Temple, and saith.]
(Alf. Lest some worse thing befall thee.)

The gratitude of the man who had been healed was shown by his going to the Temple. As soon as he had carried away his bed he returns to the Temple, no doubt to give thanks to God for his cure. Jesus had healed his body by the pool of Bethesda, and thus had given him a proof that He was God, and in the Temple he reveals to him secrets known only to himself, and thus gives him another proof of His divine power. He calls to his recollection his sin, a sin which had been committed before Jesus was born of the Blessed Virgin. He shows him the heinous nature of his sin in the sight of God, who had punished it with thirty-eight years of suffering, and warns him that a repetition of his sin would be followed by a greater punishment.

God's judgments are sent upon men in this world partly to try their patience and faith in God, as in the case of Job, and partly to check their further career and to punish their sin, as in the case of this man. Apparently his chastisement had been good for him. Everything here related of him is in his favour. He shows a right feeling by his strong belief in the goodness of Him who had so unexpectedly and so miraculously restored him to the use of his limbs. Failing to find Him who had wrought the cure, he returns thanks to God in as public a manner as was possible by going to the Temple.

is made of a questionable derivation, whether from ξενευω or from ἐκνεύω. The latter is the more undoubted, both as better suiting with the sense of the place, and having also its parallel in the Old Testament, as 2 Kings xxiii. 16. And as

Josiah turned himself he saw the graves, &c. The Septuagint have it καὶ ἐξένευσεν Ἰωσίας καὶ ἴδε, &c. So Jesus, when He had done this cure upon the man, turned Himself away and was gone."—Lightfoot, i. 662.

When he found his benefactor, in the fulness of his heart he departed and told the Jews that it was Jesus which had made him whole. He did this doubtless in the overflowing of his gratitude, and that the Jews also might believe in Him. Fear lest his punishment should return, or lest a worse thing should come to him, would prevent him from informing the Jews, except from the very best of motives. He would be quite aware that Jesus, who could reveal his secret deeds, which had happened thirty-eight years before, could read his heart at the present time.

15 [The man] [departed (and told the Jews)] that it was Jesus (which had made) him whole.[1]

[A. And the man: S. Departed, and said unto the Jews.]
(Alf. And brought the Jews word—which made.)

16 (And therefore did the Jews persecute Jesus) [and sought to slay him], (because He had done) these things on the sabbath day.[2]

[S. V. Omit, And sought to slay Him.]
(Alf. And for this cause the Jews persecuted Jesus—omits, and sought, &c.—because He did.)

The reason which the Jews alleged for their persecution of Jesus was because He had broken the Sabbath; but the real secret reason was not their zeal for the observance of God's ordinance, but their personal envy and hatred. His teaching laid bare their sins and hypocrisies too unsparingly to escape their bitterest persecution.

By commanding the man to take up his bed and walk on the Sabbath Day He had broken the sabbath, the rest enjoined to be observed on the Sabbath. He justifies the deed, not by saying it was

---

[1] "The Jews (οἱ Ἰουδαῖοι), that is the Sanhedrin or the Rulers, for so it is very common with the Evangelists, especially with this, to mean by that expression, as i. 19. The Jews sent priests and Levites from Jerusalem: vii. 1. The Jews sought to kill Him: ix. 22. The Jews had agreed to put out of the synagogue, &c., xviii. 12. The officers of the Jews took Jesus: verse 14. Now, Caiaphas was he that gave counsel to the Jews, &c. So that Christ is here convented before the Sanhedrin, although the Evangelist hath not expressed so much *totidem verbis*, and is put to answer for His life about the violation of the Sabbath, which they laid to His charge, upon what He had done and commanded to the man that He had recovered."—Lightfoot, i. 662.

[2] **Because He had done** (ὅτι ταῦτα ἐποίει). "It is admitted by all that an aorist, under certain conditions, may have the sense of a past behind another past; nor, according to some, can this force be altogether denied to the imperfect; but a pluperfect force is given in our version to these terms where certainly no sort of necessity requires it. Thus for the words 'because *He had done* these things on the Sabbath' (John v. 16) read, because *He did* (ἐποίει) these things on the Sabbath. And, again, in the same chapter read, 'For Jesus *conveyed Himself away*' (ἐξένευσεν); that is, so soon as this discussion between the Jews and the healed man arose, not, '*had conveyed Himself away*' previously, as our version would imply."—Archbishop Trench on *Authorised Version*, p. 98.

done in the service of humanity, in the cause of suffering human nature, or that it was such an act as was not forbidden by the law; but He justifies His deed by saying that God had always ever since the Creation worked on the Sabbath, and that He therefore worked on the Sabbath because God was His Father.

17 [But Jesus answered] them, My Father worketh (hitherto), and I work.

[S. V. But He answered.]
(Alf. Even until now.)

God had commanded the Sabbath or seventh day to be observed as a day of rest because He had finished the works of creation on that day. He had ceased to create new kinds of life besides those which had been already enumerated. But God did not cease to work at the end of the sixth day. He worked on the seventh day by preserving and upholding the works which He had already made. He has continued the same preserving care over His works every Sabbath Day since hitherto. By restoring the impotent man to the perfect use of his limbs on the Sabbath Day Jesus had only exercised the same power which God who was His Father exercised every Sabbath.

18 [Therefore] the Jews sought the more to kill him, because He not only (had broken) the sabbath, (but said also that God was His Father), making Himself equal with God.

[S. Omits, Therefore.]
(Alf. For this cause therefore—broke—but also called God His Own Father.)

Jesus calls God His Own ($\iota\delta\iota o\nu$) Father. The Jews interpreted this not in the lower subordinate sense, in which the expression is sometimes used, and in which it may be used by mere men, who call God their Father. They understand it in the highest sense, and in understanding it in the highest sense they did not mistake His meaning. They saw Jesus in appearance a mere man like themselves, they believed that he was born in Nazareth of Galilee, and that He was the son of a carpenter, and they heard Him say that God was His Own, His natural ($\iota\delta\iota o\nu$) Father, and that He was equal with God; that He, a mere man in appearance, was equal with God the Creator of heaven and earth.

So far from correcting the sense which the Jews had given to His words, Jesus in the following verse confirms it and asserts His claim to be equal with God in language different from that which He had used before, but not less strong, and which He ushers in with the words "Verily, verily."

19 [(Then answered Jesus) and said unto them, Verily, verily, I say] unto you, The Son can do nothing of Himself, (but what) He seeth the Father (do); for what things soever He doeth, these also doeth the Son (likewise).

[S. Then Jesus said unto them, Verily, I say.]
(Alf. Jesus answered therefore—save what—doing—in like manner.)

The Son can do nothing of Himself, nothing without the Father, not from deficiency of power, but from their inseparability of nature. The Father and the Son are One; they cannot therefore do different or separate things. Whatever things the Father doeth, the same things, not similar things, the Son also doeth in like manner (ὁμοίως) with a similar power and a similar will. The acts of the Son are not an imitation of the Father, but a co-operation, a participation with the Father, as being One with the Father.

In this conversation with the Jews Jesus uses the language that men would use to express the closest possible union between a father and a son.

The word to "see," as well as the kindred word to "show," has a special meaning in Holy Scripture. They mean to participate or to share in the nature of another by sight, and to communicate a participation in the nature of another by sight. This is evidently the meaning, at least in a certain degree, in another passage of St. John, "We shall be like Him, for we shall see Him as He is." (1 John, iii. 2.) In St. Matthew too the word to "see" is used in this sense. "Blessed are the pure in heart, for they shall see God." (Matt. v. 8.)

Thus to "see" and to "show" are used here to indicate the most intimate union and relation possible between God the Father and God the Son. To express the participation of the Son in the Father's work the Son is said to "see" the Father; to express the participation of the Son in the Father's power and will, the Father is said to "show" the Son.

20 For the Father loveth the Son, and sheweth Him all things that Himself doeth: (and He will shew Him greater works than these), that ye may marvel.

[Alf. And greater works than these will He show Him.)

I am Man as well as God, nevertheless I and the Father are One. The healing of the impotent man on the Sabbath Day is My work, and it is the work of My Father, for We are One. But the Father will show Me greater works than these, the Father will work through Me, the Son, God and Man, greater works than healing the sick. He will through Me, God Incarnate, raise the dead, and judge the quick and the dead: and the effect of this upon you hardened Jews will be not that ye will believe, but that ye will marvel.

The first of these greater works, which the Father will show the Son, is the resurrection of the dead, and the second the judgment of the quick and dead. The Father will not raise some to life and the Son raise others, for there is a unity of will between the Father and the Son. When God the Father raises from the dead and quickens, the Son, God Incarnate, shares in that quickening. The Father in Person will judge no man, but he will judge through the Son. God the Son, the Son of Man alone will be visible as the Judge, on the great Day of Judgment, and he will then receive equal honour with God the Father. Even now those who honour not the Son, lowly as He may appear, in so doing detract from the honour due to God the Creator and Preserver of all things, and whose special claim to our honour is that He hath sent His Son.

21 (For as) the Father raiseth up the dead, and quickeneth them: even so the Son quickeneth whom He will.

(Alf. For like as.)

22 (For the Father judgeth no man), but hath committed (all judgment) unto the Son.[1]

(Alf. For neither doth the Father judge any one—judgment altogether.)

23 (That all men should honour) the Son, even as they honour the Father. He that honoureth not the Son honoureth not the Father (which hath sent him.)

(Alf. That all may honour—which sent Him.)

Jesus calls the attention of the Jews to the importance of what He is about to utter, by the repetition of that forcible exclamation, Amen, Amen.

24 Verily, verily I say unto you, He that heareth My word, (and believeth on Him) that sent Me, (hath everlasting life, and shall not come into condemnation: but is passed from death unto life.)[2]

(Alf. And believeth Him—hath eternal life and cometh not into judgment, but hath passed out of death into life.)

---

[1] Hath committed all judgment unto the Son (τὴν κρίσιν πᾶσαν δέδωκε τῷ υἱῷ). "πᾶσαν is quite appropriately placed immediately before δέδωκε, as it belongs to it. He gave it to Him not in part, but all."—Winer's *Grammar of New Testament*, 570.

[2] He that heareth My word, &c. (ὁ τόν λόγον μου ἀκύων). The continuous action of faith is very strikingly shown in

Life and death are words that are constantly used by the sacred writers, and especially by St. John, without any reference to the separation of the soul from the body. They rather refer to the union between the soul and God, which is the fruit of the Incarnation, and which can only be obtained by a belief in the Incarnation. The Evangelist had already said (i. 4) that in Jesus was life and the life was the light of men, and that, as many as received Him, to them gave He power to become the sons of God, even to them that believe on His name—which were born not of blood, nor of the will of the flesh, nor of the will of man, but of God. (i. 12, 13.) He who believes, with, of course, all the obedience which a sincere belief implies, in God the Father and in His Son, whom He hath sent, has passed out of the state of death, out of the condition, in which the soul is dead through sin and unbelief into the life of grace, which will gradually be matured into the life of glory hereafter.

25 Verily, verily, I say unto you, (The hour is coming), [and now is], when the dead shall hear the voice of the Son of God; [and they that hear shall live.]

[S.* Omits, And now is: S.* and when they hear, they shall live.]
(Alf. An hour cometh.)

It may be that Jesus is still speaking of the resurrection of the soul from death; and the construction of the whole sentence rather favours that view. Others think that He is passing on from the resurrection of the soul to the resurrection of the body, not at first to the general resurrection of the body preceding the Day of Judgment, but to that exercise of His power to raise the dead during His Ministry, shown in the case of Jairus's daughter, the widow's son, and Lazarus, indicated here by the expression, "The hour cometh and now is."

26 (For as) the Father hath Life in Himself: (so hath He given to the Son) to have Life in Himself.

(Alf. For like as—even so gave He to the Son also.)

---

the fifth chapter of St. John, where our Saviour in the original Greek almost invariably uses the present active participle when speaking of the relations between Himself and the believer. It is not as in our Version, "He that believeth in Me;" "He that eateth My Flesh and drinketh My Blood;" "He that cometh unto Me;" but he *believing* in Me, *eating* My Flesh and *drinking* My Blood, *coming* unto Me; all indicating that the specific act is continuous, not performed once and then over for ever, but always going on. Believing in Christ, coming to Him, eating His Flesh and drinking His Blood, is no mere transient act, but a habit. Faith is an active, continuous habit of the soul: it is the constant expression of life, and life is eternal.—Macmillan on the *True Vine*, p. 256.

27 (And hath given Him) authority to execute judgment [also] because He is the Son of Man.[1]

[S. A. Omit, also.]
(Alf. And gave Him—omits, also.)

Jesus Christ will raise the dead because He is God and One with the Father, who is the source of life, but He will judge the world not because He is God, but because He is Man. The Head of man will judge man, He who came to save man will also be the Judge of man.

From what He had already said about the resurrection, where some should rise and others not, "when the dead shall hear the voice of the Son of God; and they that hear shall live," from this Jesus passes on to a subject of still greater wonder, to the great Day of Resurrection, where all would rise, both those that had done good and those that had done evil, and He introduces His statement with the words, "Marvel not."

28 Marvel not at this; (for the hour is coming) in the which all that are in the graves shall hear His voice.

(Alf. For an hour cometh.)

29 And shall come forth: they that have done good, unto the resurrection of life: and they that have done evil, unto the resurrection of (damnation.)[2]

(Alf. Judgment.)

---

[1] Because He is the Son of Man.— "Some divide this seven and twentieth verse, and join the latter part of it 'because He is the Son of Man' to the verse following, and read it in this sense and juncture, because He is the Son of Man. Marvel not at this—that is, marvel not at this that I speak, although ye see Me to be a Man, &c. And thûs readeth the Syriac and Chrysostom, and some that follow him. . . . . . As for the pointing that we follow, joining the clause, because He is the Son of Man, to the words preceding and not to those that follow, it is plainly cleared and asserted by the very sense and construction of the place itself. And withal it hath this consent and concurrence of antiquity in the words of Beza, "ut plane appareat Latinam Ecclesiam semper ita legisse. Consentiunt veteres omnes Græci codices quos videmus. Cyrillus quoque non aliter distinguit.' To which I may add the Arabic pointeth as we do."—Lightfoot, i. 663.

[2] Unto the resurrection of life.—" The genitive may be called the whence-case. Its import is that of issuing out of, or proceeding from. The genitive, especially in the writings of John and Paul, denotes internal relations still more remote, as John v. 29, ἀνάστασις ζωῆς, κρίσεως, resurrection to life, resurrection to condemnation."—Winer's *Grammar of New Testament*, 201.

Evil.—" That which is morally evil may be contemplated on two sides and from two points of view; either on the side of its positive malignity, its will and power to work mischief, or else on that of its negative worthlessness, and so to speak its good-for-nothingness. Πονηρός contemplates evil from the former point of view, and φαῦλος from the latter.
. . . . . There are words in most languages, and φαῦλος is one of them, which contemplate evil under the aspect of its good-for-nothingness, the impossibility of any true gain ever coming forth from it.

122 COMMENTARY ON ST. JOHN'S GOSPEL.

Before, when speaking of a resurrection, but not the general resurrection at the Last Day, He says, "The hour is coming and now is;" here, when speaking of the general resurrection, which was future, He says, "The hour is coming," and omits the words, "and now is." In many places of Holy Scripture where the general resurrection of the body is mentioned the good only are expressly named as rising. In Dan. xii. 2, it is directly asserted that the bodies of the unjust as well as of the just shall rise again. This passage of St. John and Acts xxiv. 15 are the only places in the New Testament where the resurrection of the unjust is expressly declared. In many passages it is implied with more or less of fulness.

30 I can of Mine Own self do nothing: as I hear, I judge: [and] My judgment is just: because I seek not Mine Own will but the will [of the Father which hath sent me.][1]

(S. V. A. Omit, the Father.)
[S.* Omits, and: S. V. A. Of Him that hath sent Me.]
(Alf. Of Him that sent Me.)

Jesus had before reasoned that His work of healing the impotent man on the Sabbath Day must be right, because God, who was His

---

Thus 'nequam' (in strictness opposite to frugi) and 'nequitia' in Latin, 'vaurien' in French, 'naughty' and 'naughtiness' in English, taugenichts, 'schlecht,' schlechligkeit in German. This notion of worthlessness is the central notion of φαῦλος, (by some identfied with 'faul,' foul) which in Greek runs successively through the following meanings: light, unstable, blown about by every wind, small, slight, mediocre, of no account, worthless, bad; but still bad predominantly in the sense of worthless.

"Φαῦλος, as used in the New Testament, has reached this latest stage of its meaning; and τὰ φαῦλα πράξαντες, are set over against τὰ ἀγαθὰ ποιήσαντες and condemned as such to the 'resurrection of damnation' (John v. 29)."—Archbishop Trench on *Synonyms of the New Testament*, p. 302.

[1] As I hear I Judge, &c.—"Our Saviour seemeth in these words to allude to two customs and traditions of the Jews, and to plead with them from their own principles.

"(1) The Talmudic tract Sanhedrin, speaking concerning men's inquiring of the judicatories in matters of difficulty, hath this tradition: 'They ask first of the Sanhedrin in their own city. If they had heard it they resolve them. If not they go to a Sanhedrin near their city. If they had heard it they resolve them. If not they go to that in the gate of the Mountain of the House. If they had heard it they resolve them, &c. (Terek 11), where by the words, 'If they had heard,' they mean if the Sanhedrin had heard by tradition what was to be the determination of such a matter, they judge accordingly; but if they had not heard then the last recourse was to the great Sanhedrin of seventy-one, which was the very treasury of traditions. Christ being come now before the Sanhedrin, seemeth here to speak to them according to their own rule, as you judge according as you hear and receive by tradition, so I judge as I hear, &c.

"(2) Ramham, in his tract about Messengers and Partners, and the Talmudists occasionally in the treatises about contracts, espousals, &c., concludes this for a maxim, that a messenger doeth that upon which he is sent, all his acts are good in law, &c. Upon this very ground Christ's arguing here is clear and frequent, and cometh home to their own position. My judging is just, because I being sent of the Father do not Mine own will, but I do the errand that He sent Me upon, and do His will."—Lightfoot, i. 680.

own Father had, ever since the Creation, continued to work on the Sabbath Day. He now teaches the Jews that His judgment, at the Day of Judgment, as well as at all other times, must be right, because He will only judge as he hears of the Father. I can of Mine Ownself do nothing; as I hear, I judge. This is so not from any inability, not from any deficiency of power, but from their inseparability of nature. They are One, God the Father and Jesus His Son, God Incarnate, are One. They cannot, therefore, give differing or opposite judgments.

Man's knowledge of the unity between the Persons in the Godhead can only be apprehended partially, according to their finite capacity to receive it, and the limited power of language to convey it. Man's senses are the limits of his knowledge. It is, therefore, by words derived from the senses that Jesus chiefly imparts to the Jews a knowledge of the unity between the Persons in the Godhead in the only way in which they could comprehend it. In every variety of phrase, in this very conversation with the Jews, Jesus has expressed His equality, his Oneness with the Father. For instance, the Son can do nothing of Himself, but only what he seeth the Father do. Whatever things the Father doeth, the same and in the same manner the Son also doeth. (v. 19.) The Father loveth the Son, and showeth Him all things that Himself doeth. (20.) As the Father raiseth up the dead and quickeneth them, even so the Son quickeneth whom he will. (21.) The Father judgeth no man, but hath committed all judgment unto the Son. (22.) That all men should honour the Son, even as they honour the Father. He that honoureth not the Son honoureth not the Father which hath sent Him. As the Father hath Life in Himself: so hath He given to the Son to have Life in Himself. (26.) I can of Mine Ownself do nothing : as I hear, I judge : I seek not Mine Own will, but the will of Him which hath sent Me. (30.)

Jesus anticipates the objection, which he knew the Jews would make to all that he had just said. He knew that they would urge that His own witness of Himself was not true, not legal, not admissible in evidence. He therefore turns from His own witness and adduces three kinds of evidence, which, even in their eyes, ought to be above all suspicion. God the Father had borne witness to Him when, at His Baptism, a voice came from heaven saying, "This is my beloved Son, in whom I am well pleased. (Matt. iii. 17.) John the Baptist had borne witness to Him when he cried, "Behold the Lamb of God, which taketh away the sin of the world." (John i. 29.) Surely the Baptist was a man whom they could believe. Such had been their admiration for his holiness and zeal in the service of God, that they themselves had sent to inquire of him if he were not the Christ. They had been willing for a season to rejoice in his light, to boast themselves in the holiness of his life and in the purity of his teaching, they were willing to believe that he was the Christ, but when he reproved their sins and bore witness that Jesus of Nazareth, the carpenter's son as they thought, was the Christ, and that he himself was only sent to bear witness of Him, and was unworthy to stoop down and unloose the latchet of His shoe; then they despised him. Jesus did not require the witness of John. The works that He was daily working in the midst of them were sufficient of themselves to prove that He was God. He produced the evidence of John because they looked upon him as a holy man and worthy of all credence. To remove every possible ground of prejudice against Him, and in order that they may believe in Him and be saved, He recalls to their recollection the testimony that John had given that he was the Christ. John bore witness unto the truth, but if John's witness could be suspected of undue favour towards Him the miracles that He wrought among men could not. They must prove that the Father hath sent Him.

31 If I bear witness (of Myself), My witness is not true.
(Alf. Concerning Myself.)

32 (There is another) that beareth witness of Me: [and I know] that the witness which He witnesseth of Me is true.
[S. And ye know.]
(Alf. It is another.)

33 (Ye sent) unto John, and (he bare) witness unto the truth.
(Alf. Ye have sent—hath borne.)

34 (But I receive not testimony from man): but these things I say, that (ye might) be saved.
(Alf. Yet the witness, which I receive, is not from man:—ye may.)

35 (He was a burning and a shining light): [and] ye were willing (for a season to rejoice) in His light.[1]
[S. Omits, and.]
(Alf. He was the lamp that burneth and shineth—to rejoice for a while.)

---

[1] He was a burning and a shining light.—"More passages than one would gain in perspicuity by a re-arrangement of the words rendered 'light,' 'lamp,' &c., and mainly through the clear distinction between φῶς and λύχνος, which would then be apparent. One of these is John v. 35. 'He was a burning and a shining light.' So our translation; but in the original, ἐκεῖνος ἦν ὁ λύχνος ὁ καιόμενος καὶ φαίνων: or, as the Vulgate has it, ille erat lucerna ardens et lucens, not obliterating, as we have done, the whole antithesis between Christ, the φῶς ἀληθινόν (John, i. 8), φῶς ἐκ φωτός, that Eternal Light, which, as it was never kindled, so should never be quenched, and the Baptist, a *lamp* kindled by the hands of Another, in whose brightness men might for a season rejoice, and which was then extinguished again."—Archbishop Trench on *Synonyms of New Testament*, p. 162.

"Thus rendered the expression ap-

36 (But I have greater witness than that of John) : for the works which the Father (hath given) Me to finish (the same works that I do) bear witness of Me, that the Father hath sent Me.

(Alf. But the testimony, which I have, is greater than John :—gave—the very works that I am doing.)

Jesus appeals to the miracles which He wrought as proving that He was the Messiah, the Son of God. Apart from the witness of the Baptist, and even above this, the miracles which He was working among them were of such a nature as to convince any but the most hardened and unfair that He was God. They were wrought with the purpose of proving this, and they proclaimed, as plainly as a voice from heaven, that He was God. He wrought the very same miracles which the prophet foretold that God, who should come amongst them, would work. Isaiah had said, "Behold, your God will come with vengeance, even God with a recompense; He will come and save you. Then the eyes of the blind shall be opened, and the ears of the deaf shall be unstopped. Then shall the lame man leap as an hart, and the tongue of the dumb sing," &c. (Is. xxxv. 4, 6.) Some of the prophets, or holy men of old, occasionally wrought miracles, but none ever wrought such miracles as Jesus, or so many in number. When the prophets wrought miracles they never professed to do so in their own name, or by their own power. The miracles which the prophets wrought were their credentials to man that they were God's servants. But the miracles which Jesus wrought were always in His own name and by His own power, and were appealed to by Him as proving that He was God, One with the Father and equal to the Father. Some of His miracles had a peculiar relation to Himself, as for instance, His Birth of the Blessed Virgin, the foretelling His Death and Passion, His Resurrection and Ascension, the Descent of the Holy Spirit upon

---

pears as intended simply to glorify John. But this is not the sense which the context requires, and it is only attained by a flagrant disregard of the article. Commentators have correctly pointed out that John is here called ὁ λύχνος, the lamp; he was not τὸ φῶς, the Light : for Christ Himself, and Christ only, is the Light (i. 9, iii. 19, ix. 5, &c.). Thus the rendering of ὁ λύχνος is vitally wrong, as probably few would deny. But it has not been perceived how much the contrast between the Baptist and the Saviour is strengthened by a proper appreciation of the remaining words ὁ καιόμενος καὶ φαίνων. The word κάιειν is to burn, to kindle, to set alight, as in St. Matt. v. 15, οὐδὲ κάιουσιν λύχνον, 'Neither do men light a candle ;' so, too, Luke xii. 35, δι λύχνοι καιόμενοι, Rev. iv. 5, viii. 10. Thus it implies that the light is not inherent, but borrowed; and the force of the expression will be, 'He is the lamp that is lighted, and (then) shineth.' Christ Himself is the centre and source of light; the Baptist has no light of his own, but draws all his illumination from this greater One. He is only as the light of a candle, for whose rays, indeed, men are grateful, but which is pale, flickering, transitory, compared with the glories of the Eternal flame from which itself is kindled."—Dr. J. B. Lightfoot on *Revision of New Testament* (1871), p. 117.

His Disciples, &c. We might have supposed that if this or that individual miracle had failed to convince them that Jesus was God, the ever-existing, ever-active power in Him to work miracles would have had its due effect on them. But the fault was in the heart, not in the reason.

37 [And the Father Himself, which hath sent Me], hath borne witness of Me. Ye have neither heard His voice at any time (nor seen) His shape.

[S.V. And the Father, He which hath sent Me.]
(Alf. And the Father, which sent Me, Himself hath—nor have seen.)

38 And ye have not His word abiding in you: for whom (He hath sent) Him ye believe not.
(Alf. He sent.)

39 Search the Scriptures: (for in them ye think) ye have eternal life: and they are they which testify of Me.[1]
(Alf. Because ye think that in them.)

---

[1] **Search the Scriptures.**—(ἐρευνᾶτε τὰς γραφὰς). " I rather construe it in the Indicative sense, ye search the Scriptures, upon these reasons. 1. Because of what is said in the verse itself, ye think ye have eternal life in them; in which words our Saviour intendeth not so much to show what they might have in the Scriptures, for then it had been proper to have said, In them ye have eternal life, as He meaneth to touch upon the erroneous conceit of the Jews, who thought they obtained eternal life by the study of the law *ex opere operato*. 2. Because of the context in the verse following, which lieth fairer in this sense, Ye study the Scriptures scrutinously, and they are they that testify of Me, and yet ye will not come unto Me—than taken thus: Search ye the Scriptures, for they testify of Me, and ye will not come to Me."—Lightfoot, i. 664.

" Besides, consider—1. That Christ is speaking to the doctors of the Sanhedrin, the most acute, diligent, and curious searchers of the Scripture of all the nation. Men that made that their glory and employment; and howsoever it was their arrogancy that they thought their skill in Scripture more than indeed it was, yet was their diligence and scrutinousness in it real and constant even to admiration. It was exceedingly in fashion among the nation to be great Scripture men, but especially the great masters of the Sanhedrin were reputed as the very *foundations of the law and pillars of instruction*, as Maimony styles them in the treatise *Mamrim*, cap. i. And therefore it cannot be proper to think that Christ in this clause sets them to the study of the Scripture, upon which they spent all their wits and time already, as confessing their studiousness, yet showeth them how unprofitably they did it and to little purpose.

" 2. They did exceeding copiously and accurately observe and take up the prophecies in Scripture that were of the Messias, and though they missed in expounding some particulars concerning Him, yet did they well enough know that the Scriptures did testify of Him abundantly.

" 3. The word that is used, ἐρευνᾶτε, which betokeneth a narrow search, seemeth to be intended purposely to answer the word דרש, which they themselves attribute to themselves in their unfolding of the Scriptures," &c., &c.—Lightfoot, i. 684.

40 (And ye will not come) to Me, that ye (might have) life.

(Alf. And yet ye are not willing to come—may have.)

The difficulty of connecting the train of thought in this passage is shown by the number of interpretations that have been given to it. In the following an attempt has been made to keep as close to the text as possible:—Jesus enumerates the various sources of belief in Him, the different kinds of testimony there were that He was God. First, there was the witness of John the Baptist, and, greater than that, there was the evidence of His own miracles, and there was also the witness of the Father. All these had so far failed to produce in the Jews a belief in Jesus as the Son of God. They would not come to Him, that they might have life. But there was one source of belief in Him still left. If they would be saved, if they would inherit eternal life, He bids them search the Scriptures, the writings of the Old Testament. In the Scriptures they think they have eternal life, but they do not suppose, as they will find on a close investigation, that eternal life consists in believing in Jesus as the Son of God. They must not expect any communication from the Father except through the Son. Such had never been the case. No man had at any time heard His voice or seen His shape. In bidding them search the Scriptures in order to obtain eternal life our Saviour again bears witness to the general accuracy of the Scriptures as received by the Jews in His time.

The object of Jesus was not to gain honour from man, but this was the great object of the Jews, and it was this that kept them from believing in Him. This same want of love towards God, this same longing for the applause of men, which had influenced them to reject Jesus, though He had come in His Father's name to perform His Father's will and to fulfil the promises made unto them by His Father, would induce them to receive another, though he should come in his own name, led on by his own ambition, and to gain his own ends, and not the glory of God.

41 I receive not (honour) [from men.]

[A. From man.]
(Alf. Glory.)

42 But I know you, that ye have not the love of God in you.

43 I am come in My Father's name, and ye receive Me not: if another shall come in his own name, him ye will receive.

44 How can ye believe, which receive (honour) one of another, and seek not (the honour that cometh from God only ?)

[V. That cometh from the only (omits, God.)]
(Alf. Glory—the glory which is from the only God ?)

The Fathers looked upon this passage as a prophetic intimation that in punishment for their rejection of Jesus as a deceiver the Jews should be seduced by the arch-deceiver, the Antichrist (2 Thess. ii. 8), and by many who should precede him and partake of his spirit. Commentators mention 60 as the number of antichrists who have already appeared.

45 Do not think that I will accuse you to the Father: [there is one that accuseth you,] even Moses, in whom (ye trust.)

[V. There is one that accuseth you to the Father.]
(Alf. Ye hope.)

46 For had ye believed Moses, (ye would have believed) Me : for he wrote of Me.

(Alf. Ye would believe—)

47 But if ye believe not his writings, [how shall ye believe My words ?]

[V. How believe ye My words?]

At the Day of Judgment the condemnation of the Jews for refusing to believe in Jesus as the Christ will not be because they disbelieved His own teaching, but because they disbelieved the teaching of Moses, in whom they professed to trust. They looked upon Jesus as a deceiver, and, therefore, it was not to be expected that they would believe His words, but they regarded Moses as a true prophet, as one to whom God had spoken (ix. 29), and yet they did not believe his teaching respecting Jesus, and this would be the ground of their condemnation.

INTRODUCTORY NOTE TO CHAPTER VI.

The Lake.—" This lake or sea has had four names, Chinnereth, Gennesareth, Galilee, Tiberias.

" The lake is called Chinneroth in the Old Testament, either from Chinnereth, one of the fenced cities, or from the district, or perhaps from the oval harp-like form of its basin. Now that the real shape of the lake can be seen in our map, the word ' oval ' does not apply, but the form is more than ever seen to be harp-like. De Saulcy says that in Joshuà xi. 2, the Hebrew text has ' south of Chinnereth,' and the Chaldaic text has ' south of Gennesar.' It was called Gennesa·reth from a town or district on the shore. When the lake is called by St. John (vi. 1), ' The Sea of Galilee, which is the Sea of Tiberias ' (the Sea of Galilee, of Tiberias), it may be to distinguish this lake from that other sea of Galilee, Lake Hooleh. The earlier Evangelists call it Lake of Gennesareth, for Tiberias was then a new and unimportant town, but St. John, who wrote later, calls the lake by the name of the town which had by that time become important."—(MacGregor, 322).

" The Sea of Galilee itself is a great hollow, and at the bottom it is about 800 feet depressed into the crust of the earth. The surface of the water is so low that if St. Paul's Cathedral were set upon the shore, and the lofty spire of Salisbury on the top of that, the summit of this pile would still be lower than the Mediterranean Sea."—(MacGregor, 405).

" From north to south the lake is twelve and a-half miles long. Across the widest part from Magdala is six and three-quarter miles. Soundings show its depth to be less than 200 feet in any part.

" The length of the lake given by Josephus is 140 stadia, or sixteen miles, which is much too large, unless he means the distance by land, which would then be nearly correct. He gives the breadth as forty stadia, or about four miles and a-half, which, again, is much too small, unless he reckons it from opposite Tiberias, where it is only about four miles and three-quarters.

" Abulfeda gives the length as twelve miles, and the breadth six (Buckingham, 345). All modern travellers, except Robinson, have erred in their estimates, and usually make them too large, but Buck-

K

ingham gives eight miles long and six miles broad, and says the plain above is ten miles square."—MacGregor, 412.

"The Sea of Galilee has a beauty of its own which would always make it remarkable. The hills, except at Khan Minyeh, where there is a small city, are recessed from the shore of the lake, or rise gradually from it; they are of no great elevation, and their outline, especially on the eastern side, is not broken by any prominent peak; but everywhere from the southern end the snow-capped peak of Hermon is visible, standing out so sharp and clear in the bright sky that it appears almost within reach, and towards the north, the western ridge is cut through by a wild gorge, 'the Valley of Doves,' over which rise the twin peaks or horns of Hattin. The shore-line, for the most part regular, is broken on the north into a series of little bays of exquisite beauty; nowhere more beautiful than at Gennesareth, where the beaches, pearly white with myriads of minute shells, are on one side washed by the limpid waters of the lake, and on the other shut in by a fringe of oleanders, rich in May with their blossoms red and bright.

"The surrounding hills are of a uniform brown colour, and would be monotonous, if it were not for the ever-changing lights and the brilliant tints at sunrise and sunset. It is, however, under the pale light of a full moon that the lake is seen to the greatest advantage, for there is then a softness in the outlines, a calm on the water in which the stars are so brightly mirrored, and a perfect quiet in all around, which harmonise well with the feelings that cannot fail to arise on its shores. It is perhaps difficult to realize that the borders of this lake, now so silent and desolate, were once enlivened by the busy hum of towns and villages: and that on its waters hostile navies contended for supremacy. But there is one feature which must strike every visitor: and that is the harmony of the Gospel narrative with the places which it describes; giving us, as M. Renan happily expresses it, 'un cinquième évangile lacéré, mais lisible encore.'

"The lake is pear-shaped, the broad end being towards the north; the greatest width is six and three-quarter miles, from Mejdel, 'Magdala,' to Khersa, 'Gergesa,' about one-third of the way down, and the extreme length is twelve and a quarter miles. The Jordan enters at the north, a swift muddy stream, colouring the lake a good mile from its mouth, and passes out pure and bright at the south. On the north-western shore of the lake is a plain, two and a-half miles long and one mile broad, called by the Bedawin El Ghuweir, but better known by its familiar Bible name of Gennesareth; and on the north-east, near Jordan's mouth, is a swampy plain, El Batihah, now much frequented by wild boars, formerly the scene of a skirmish between the Jews and Romans, in which Josephus met with an accident that necessitated his removal to Capernaum. On the west there is a recess in the hills, containing the town of Tiberias; and on the east, at the mouth of Wadys Semakh and Fik, are small tracts of level ground. On the south the fine open valley of the Jordan stretches

away towards the Dead Sea, and is covered in the neighbourhood of the lake with luxuriant grass. The water of the lake is bright, clear, and sweet to the taste, except in the neighbourhood of the salt springs, and where it is defiled by the drainage of Tiberias. Its level, which varies considerably at different times of the year, is between 600 and 700 feet below that of the Mediterranean—a peculiarity to which the district owes its genial winter climate. In summer the heat is great, but never excessive, as there is usually a morning and evening breeze. Sudden storms, such as those mentioned in the New Testament, are by no means uncommon. : . . . .
" There does not appear to be anything volcanic in the origin of the lake, which is simply part of the great Jordan depression. The hills on either side are limestone, capped in places with basalt, which has three distinct sources ; one at Kurn Hattin, or in its neighbourhood ; another near Khan Jubb Yusuf, north of the lake, and a third in the Jaulan district. Earthquakes are frequent, and sometimes extremely violent ; as, for examples, that of 1837, which laid Tiberias in ruins, and caused the death of 700 persons ; and the scarcely less terrible one which occurred in 1759. There are in the basin of the lake a number of warm springs, which are said to have increased both in volume and temperature after the earthquake of 1837."—*Recovery of Jerusalem*, p. 337.

Storm on the Lake.—" Sudden storms, such as those mentioned in the New Testament, are by no means uncommon ; and I had a good opportunity of watching one of them from the ruins of Gamala on the eastern hills. The morning was delightful : a gentle easterly breeze, and not a cloud in the sky to give warning of what was coming. Suddenly, about midday, there was a sound of distant thunder, and a small cloud, ' no bigger than a man's hand,' was seen rising over the heights of Lubieh to the west. In a few moments the cloud appeared to spread, and heavy black masses came rolling down the hills towards the lake, completely obscuring Tabor and Hattin. At this moment the breeze died away, there were a few minutes of perfect calm, during which the sun shone out with intense power, and the surface of the lake was smooth and even as a mirror : Tiberias, Mejdel, and other buildings stood out in sharp relief from the gloom behind ; but they were soon lost sight of as the thunder gust swept past them, and rapidly advancing across the lake lifted the placid waters into a bright sheet of foam; in another moment it reached the ruins, driving myself and companion to take refuge in a cistern, where for nearly an hour, we were confined, listening to the rattling peals of thunder and torrents of rain. The effect of half the lake in perfect rest, whilst the other half was in wild confusion, was extremely grand : it would have fared badly with any light craft caught in mid-lake by the storm ; and we could not help thinking of that memorable occasion on which the storm is so graphically described as ' coming down' upon the lake."—*Recovery of Jerusalem*, p. 340.

"I have seen it lashed into fury for thirty consecutive hours by a tempest that would have wrecked a hundred fleets such as that of Josephus, had they been exposed to its violence."—Thomson's *Land and the Book*, p. 392.

On the taking of Tarichœa by Titus, Trajan, Vespasian, and Agrippa, being also present, a sharp fight took place with the Jews on the plain outside (*Jewish Wars*, iii. 10, 1-6), and a day or two afterwards there was a sea-fight near the same place. Josephus says that 6500 men were killed in the two engagements, the lake was coloured with blood for some distance round, and the air tainted with the number of bodies on the shore. This was probably the last great display of ships upon this lake.

"Nowadays one single Armstrong gun at Gamala would command the whole Sea of Tiberias."—MacGregor, p. 353.

" The following shows the state of the navy of this sea in various years, according to travellers' statements :—

"In A.D. 1738, Pococke found one boat on the lake of Gennesareth. In A.D. 1806, Seetzen saw one boat, but it was useless; 1812, Burckhardt, the only boat had fallen to pieces in 1811; 1817, Richardson, two boats; 1818, Irby and Mangles, ' no boat whatever :' 1822, Berggren, no boat; 1822, Buckingham, ' not a boat nor a raft, large nor small ;' 1829, Prokesch, no boat ; 1834, 1835, Smith, one boat ; 1838, Robinson, one boat; 1852, Vandevelde, one; 1856, Newbold, one; 1857, Thomson, no boat, once only in his other visits he saw a sail ; 1869, MacGregor, six boats besides the Rob Roy."—MacGregor, 357.

III.

HIS WORKS IN GALILEE AND JUDÆA, INCLUDING CHAPTERS VI., VII., VIII., IX., X., XI., ABOUT THE THIRD PASSOVER (vi. 4) BEFORE AND AFTER.

CHAPTER VI.

1 *Christ feedeth five thousand men with five loaves and two fishes;* 15 *Thereupon the people would have made him king;* 16 *But withdrawing Himself, He walked on the sea to his disciples;* 26 *Reproveth the people flocking after Him, and all the fleshly hearers of His Word;* 32 *Declareth Himself to be the Bread of Life to believers;* 66 *Many disciples depart from Him;* 68 *Peter confesseth Him;* 70 *Judas is a devil.*

IN the first verse of this chapter the Evangelist represents Jesus as going over the sea of Galilee (πέραν τῆς θαλάσσης.) But this does not necessarily mean crossing over from one side of the Jordan to the other. Most probably he here uses the word over the sea (πέραν τῆς θαλάσσης) in the sense in which Josephus used it with reference to this very lake, namely, of going by sea from one place to another on the same side of the lake. Thus it is said that the people followed Him on foot from one city to another while He went by sea, which they could do much more easily, if He crossed over from one city to another on the same side of the lake, than if he crossed over from the west side to the east, or from the east to the west.

1 After these things Jesus went over the sea of Galilee, which is the sea of Tiberias.[1]

2 And a great multitude followed Him, because [they

---

[1] The Sea of Galilee, &c. (ἡ θάλασσα τῆς Γαλιλαίας τῆς Τιβεριάδος.) "The sea of Galilee, of Tiberias. That sea only once again occurs under that name in John xxi. i. Probably for the sake of foreign readers, John annexed the more definite to the more general designation. Beza *in loc.* takes a different view. Kühnöl's conjecture, that the word Τιβεριάδος is a gloss, is rash. The explanation proposed by Paulus—*near Tiberias*—if not at variance with classic Greek, is at least opposed to the diction of the New Testament, which, in such circumstances, prefers to the combination by cases alone, more explicit phraseology by the use of prepositions, Τιβεριάδος cannot depend on the ἀπὸ in ἀπῆλθεν."—Winer's *Grammar of the New Testament*, 205.

saw His miracles] which he did on them that were (diseased.)

[S. V. A. They saw the miracles.]
(Alf. They beheld the miracles—sick.)

3 And Jesus [went up into] (a mountain) and [there] He sat with His disciples.

[S. Went into: S.* Omits, There.]
(Alf. The Mountain.)

4 And the Passover, (a feast) of the Jews, was nigh.
(Alf. The feast.)

After these things, but not immediately after, for nearly a whole year elapsed between the events recorded in chap. v. and those in chap. vi. The healing of the impotent man on the Sabbath Day, and our Lord's defence of it to the Jews, took place at the beginning of the second year of His Ministry (v. 1); and the feeding of the 5000 about the end of the same year. (vi. 4.) St. John omits almost all the transactions of the second year. During the second year Jesus chooses His Twelve Apostles, He delivers his Sermon on the Mount, and He sends the Twelve to preach the Gospel. St. John records none of these, and probably for the reason that they had been fully related by the other Evangelists. He refers to other miracles that were wrought on them that were diseased (vi. 2), and selects this though it is related by the other three Evangelists quite as fully as by himself. The reason, doubtless, is that the feeding the 5000 with five barley loaves and two fishes gave occasion to Jesus for His discourse on the Bread which gives life to the soul here and life to the soul and body hereafter for ever, which discourse none of the other Evangelists had recorded.

It has been observed that in the following miracle, as related by each of the four Evangelists, there are several slight verbal differences which are not easy to reconcile, but that on every point of importance all the four historians are entirely and absolutely agreed.

5 (When Jesus then lifted up his eyes, and saw) a great company (come) unto Him, he saith unto Philip, Whence (shall we buy) bread, that these may eat?

(Alf. Jesus then lifting up His eyes, and seeing that—cometh—are we to buy.)

6 ([And] this He said to prove him): [for] He Himself knew what He (would do.)

[S. For—but.]
(Alf. But this He said proving him—was about to do.)

7 [Philip answered] Him, two hundred pennyworth of bread is not sufficient [for them], that every one [of them] may take a little.¹

[S. Then Philip answereth: S. Omits, for them: S. V. A. Omit, of them.]

8 One of His disciples, Andrew, Simon Peter's brother, saith unto Him,

9 There is a lad here, which hath five barley loaves and (two small fishes): but what are they among so many?
(Alf. Two fishes.)

Jesus receives the multitudes and heals their sick, and when evening draws on His disciples urge Him to send them away, that they may go and buy themselves food. He bids the disciples supply them with food, and appeals personally to Philip, with the question, Whence shall we buy bread, that these may eat? This He said to prove him, for He Himself knew what He would do. It may be that He thus called Philip's special attention to the miracle as proving that He was God, because Philip had before called Him the son of Joseph (i. 45), or because Philip had been one of those most urgent for Him to send the multitudes away, or because this happened in the desert near Bethsaida, Philip's own city, or because he was of a frank, open disposition, and would, therefore, give a ready answer, or for some other reason which we cannot understand.

---

¹ **Two Hundred Pennyworth.**—" The denarius, a silver piece of the value originally of ten and afterwards of sixteen asses, is always in the English authorised Version rendered a *penny*. Its absolute value, as so much weight in metal, is as nearly as possible the same as the French franc. Its relative value, as a purchasing power, in an age and country where provisions were much cheaper, was considerably more. Now, it so happens that in almost every case where the word denarion occurs in the New Testament, it is connected with the idea of a *liberal* or *large* amount; and yet in these passages the English rendering names a sum which is absurdly small. Thus the Good Samaritan, whose generosity is intended to appear throughout, on leaving takes out ' two pence' and gives them to the innkeeper to supply the further wants of the wounded man. Thus again, the owner of the vineyard, whose liberality is contrasted with the niggardly envious spirit, the evil eye of others, gives, as a day's wages, a penny to each man. It is unnecessary to ask what impression the mention of this sum will leave on the minds of an uneducated peasant, or shopkeeper of the present day. Even at the time when our version was made, and when wages were lower, it must have seemed wholly inadequate. The inadequacy again appears, though not so prominently, in the two hundred pence, the sum named as insufficient to supply the bread to the five thousand.

" The rendering a penny was probably handed down in this familiar parable (the vineyard) from the time when this sum would be no inadequate remuneration for a day's labour; but long before the Versions of the Reformed Church were made, this had ceased to be the case. Even in Henry VIII.'s reign, a labourer earned from sixpence to eightpence a-day (Froude, i. p. 29, sq.): though after the Restoration the rate of wages does not seem to have advanced much upon this amount (*see* Macaulay, i. p. 413)."—Dr. J. B. Lightfoot on the *Revision of the New Testament*, 166.

The mention of purchasing two hundred pennyworth of bread suggests the probability that these five barley loaves and two fishes were purchased, and that the "lad here" did not belong to the Apostles or to their party.

10 [And] Jesus said, Make the men sit down. Now there was much grass in the place. So the men sat down, in number [about five thousand.[1]]

[S. Omits, And: S.* About three thousand.]
(Alf. Omits, And.)

11 [And Jesus] took the loaves : [and when He had given thanks, He distributed to the disciples, and the disciples to them that were set down] (and likewise) of the fishes as much as they would.

[V. A. Therefore Jesus : S. And gave thanks and gave to them that were set down: V.A. Omit, to the disciples, and the disciples.]

(Alf. Jesus therefore—omits, to the disciples, and the disciples—and in like manner.)

Nothing that is related in the account of this miracle is too trifling or too minute in its nature to be observed. Much is recorded, not only for its historical value because it really took place, but because it forms a prophetic precedent, so to speak.

Before the five loaves and the two fishes were distributed they were brought to Jesus, and, looking up to heaven, He returned thanks to the Father, He blessed them and brake them. Then, in all probability, it was that He imparted to them the power to multiply, not a physical power, not according to the ordinary working of nature, but a miraculous, superhuman power. He who, at the Creation, could give to the seed when placed in the ground the power to multiply itself, could by blessing the bread and distributing it with His own hands impart to it the power to multiply at His will. He distributes the bread thus miraculously multiplied to the multitude through the hands of His Twelve Apostles, who had been called in the interval between the healing of the impotent man, the last event recorded by St. John, and this miracle of feeding the 5000 with five barley loaves and two fishes.

Jesus prayed or gave thanks to the Father before performing this miracle. He did this, not because He had not power of Himself to work the miracle, as is clear from one single reflection. He did not pray or give thanks before all His miracles, but only before some of them.

---

[1] In number about 5000.—" Sitting in 50 ranks, of 100 each rank, the men would exactly number 5000. Baskets were carried by the Jews when travelling in the Passover time, for their food and other things, lest they should be defiled."
—MacGregor's *Jordan*, 376.

He sometimes prayed before He performed some of those which, humanly speaking, were less difficult, and He did not pray before those which to us appear more difficult. For instance, when He forgave the sins of the man sick of the palsy, when He gave away Paradise to the thief on the Cross, when He raised the widow's son, when He calmed the raging of the sea, when He revealed the secret thoughts of men's hearts, when He cured the eyes of the blind, He used no prayer to His Father before performing any of these works. But all these were miracles which none could work but God or one sent by God. The reason why Jesus prayed to His Father before performing His miracles, as He sometimes did, was that it was done for our sakes, to teach us that He was One with the Father, that He was sent by the Father, and was working the works of the Father.

By being seated in companies by hundreds and by fifties (Mark vi. 40), the number of the multitude could be more easily ascertained, order would be preserved among them, and the wants of each would thus be better supplied.

12 (When) they were filled, (He said) unto His disciples, Gather up the fragments (that remain), that nothing be lost.

(Alf. Now when—He saith—that remain over.)

13 (Therefore) they gathered them together, and filled twelve baskets (with the fragments) of the five barley loaves, (which remained over and above) unto them that had eaten.

(Alf. So—with fragments—which remained over.)

14 Then those men, when they had seen [the miracle that Jesus did], said, This is of a truth (that prophet that should come) into the world.

[S. The miracle that He did: V. The miracles which He did.]
(Alf. The men therefore, seeing the miracle that He did—the prophet that is to come.)

The twelve baskets are first mentioned when the fragments are gathered up, but it is probable that Jesus brake the five loaves and two fishes into the baskets, and in breaking multiplied them and gave the baskets to the Twelve Apostles, one to each, to distribute the bread among the people. The bread would be first distributed from the twelve baskets, and after the 5000 had eaten, the fragments would be gathered into the same twelve baskets, and thus the miraculous nature of the action would be made to appear more striking.

The multitudes were honest in their conclusion that He who could perform such a miracle must be the Messiah, the Prophet, but their conception of the Messiah was of too gross and earthly a nature. They saw that He could multiply the bread at His will, and they wished to have for their King one who could thus supply the daily wants of their body. They had probably no care for the Messiah, except as one who had unlimited power to relieve their hunger.

15 (When Jesus therefore perceived that) they would come and take Him by force, (to) make Him a king, (He departed) again into (a mountain) Himself alone.

[S. And take Him by force and appoint Him king, He fleeth again]
(Alf. Jesus therefore knowing that—that they might—withdrew—the mountain.)

16 (And) when even was come, His disciples went down into the sea.

(Alf. But.)

17 And entered into a ship [(and went) over the sea] toward [Capernaum.] [And it was now dark, and Jesus was not come to them.][1]

[S. And come over the sea: S. V. Capharnaum: S. And the darkness overtook them, and Jesus was not yet come to them.]
(Alf. And were going—and darkness had now come on, and Jesus was not yet come to them.)

18 (And the sea arose by reason of a great wind that blew).

(Alf. And the sea was rising, for a strong wind was blowing.)

19 (So when) they had rowed about five-and-twenty or thirty furlongs (they see) Jesus walking on the sea, and drawing nigh unto the ship; and they were afraid.

(Alf. When then—they behold.)

20 [But] He saith unto them, It is I: be not afraid.
[S. And.]

21 [Then they willingly received·Him] into the ship:

---

[1] It was now dark (σκοτία ἤδη ἐγεγόνει).—" An οὔπω with ἤδη preceding, would, to say the least, be unnecessary. It was already dark, and Jesus had not come."—Winer's *Grammar of the New Testament*, 618.

and immediately the ship was at the land [whither they went.]

[S. Then they came to receive Him: S. Whither it went.]
(Alf. They were willing, therefore, to receive Him.)

22 [The day following, [when] the people which stood on the other side of the sea saw that there was none other boat (there save that) one whereinto His disciples were entered), and that Jesus went not (with) His disciples into (the boat), but that His disciples (were gone) away alone.]

[S. The day following the people which stood on the other side of the sea saw that there was none other boat there, save that whereinto the disciples of Jesus were entered, and that Jesus went not with them into the boat, but His disciples alone: V. Omits, when—V. A. Save one (omit, whereinto, &c.)]
(Alf. Omits, When the multitude—save one—together with—the ship—went).

23 (Howbeit there came other boats) from Tiberias nigh unto the place where they (did eat) bread, (after that) the Lord had given thanks.)

[S. When, therefore, the boats came from Tiberias, which was nigh unto where they did also eat bread, after that the Lord had given thanks, and when they saw that —they took shipping and came to Capharnaum. V. Omits, Howbeit.]
(Alf. Yet other boats came—ate—when.)

24 When (the people) therefore saw that Jesus was not there, neither His disciples, (they [also] took shipping) and came [to Capernaum], seeking for Jesus.

[V. S. Omit, Also: V. To Capharnaum.]
(Alf. The multitude—they themselves entered into the boats.)

25 And when they had found Him on the other side of the sea, they said unto Him, Rabbi, when camest Thou hither?

THE SCENE OF THE FEEDING OF THE 5000, AND THE MIRACLE ON THE LAKE.

The following is a synopsis of the passages which enable us to fix the localities with respect to the feeding of the 5000, and the miracle on the Lake :—

St. Matthew xiv.	St. Mark vi.	St. Luke ix.	St. John vi.
13 He departed thence by ship into a desert place apart.	32 They departed into a desert place by ship privately.	10 And He took them and went aside privately into a desert place [belonging to the city called Bethsaida.] [S². V. Privately into the city called Bethsaida: S.* omits, belonging to a city called Bethsaida.]	1 After these things Jesus went over (πέραν) the sea of Galilee, which is the sea of Tiberias.
15 This is a desert place.	35 This is a desert place.	12 For we are here in a desert place.	
22 [And straightway Jesus constrained His disciples to get into a ship] and to go before Him unto the other side. (εἰς τὸ πέραν). [S. And He constrained the disciples. V. And straightway He constrained His disciples: S. into the ship.]	45 And straightway He constrained His disciples to get [into the ship] and to go to the other side before (εἰς τὸ πέραν) (unto) Bethsaida. [S. Into a ship.] (Margin, over against.)		
34 And when they were gone over (καὶ διαπεράσαντες) they came into the land of Gennesaret. [S.V. They came to land unto Gennesaret.]	53 And when they had passed over (καὶ διαπεράσαντες) they came into the land of Gennesaret, and drew to the shore.		22 The day following, when the people which stood on the other side of the sea (πέραν τῆς θαλάσσης) saw that there was none other boat there, save that one whereinto His disciples were entered, and that Jesus went not with His disciples into the boat, but that His disciples were gone away alone.
			[S. The day following, the people which stood on the other side of the sea, saw that there was none other boat there, save that whereinto the disciples of Jesus were entered, and that Jesus went not with them into the boat, but His disciples alone ; A. omits, when ; V. A. save one (omit, whereunto, &c.) and that]
			23 (Howbeit there came other boats from Tiberias, nigh unto the place where they did eat bread, after that the Lord had given thanks):
			24 When the people, therefore, saw that Jesus was not there, neither His disciples, they also took shipping and came to Capernaum, seeking for Jesus.
			[S. When therefore the boats came from Tiberias, which was nigh unto where they did also eat bread, after that the Lord had given thanks, and when they saw that—they took shipping and came to Capharnaum. 23. V. omits Howbeit ; 24. V. A. omit, also ; V. to Capharnaum.
			25 And when they had found Him on the other side of the sea (πέραν τῆς θαλάσσης) they said unto Him, Rabbi, when camest Thou hither?

From an inspection of this synopsis it will appear that the Greek Text, of which the English Version is a translation, makes St. Luke say that the scene of the feeding of the 5000 was in a desert place near the city called Bethsaida. The Alexandrian MS. confirms this. The Vatican says that they entered into the city called Bethsaida, omitting "the desert place," and the Sinaitic has the same, but by a later hand; in fact, an addition to the original text.

The Greek Text of the English Version says that other boats came from Tiberias nigh unto the place where they did eat bread, after that the Lord had given thanks. If there could be any doubt as to the exact meaning of these words, whether they meant that boats came from Tiberias to some place near the scene of the feeding of the 5000, or that the boats came from Tiberias, which was near the scene of the miracle, this doubt is removed by the Sinaitic MS., which expressly says that the boats came from Tiberias, which was nigh unto the place where they did eat bread.

The inference, which naturally follows from this, is that the place in which Jesus fed the 5000 lay somewhere between Tiberias and Bethsaida, and probably nearer Bethsaida than Tiberias.

Jesus sent away the disciples while He Himself dismissed the people. We gather from St. John that the disciples set sail from Tiberias, and from St. Mark (vi. 45) that their destination was Bethsaida or the neighbourhood of it. Their purpose apparently was not to go to a distant place, but to hover about near the coast until Jesus had dismissed the multitude. For if the Bethsaida, for which, according to St. Mark, they set out, were a different place from the Bethsaida near which, according to St. Luke, lay the desert place in which Jesus fed the 5000, we might reasonably expect that some intimation of this would have been given in some way or other. A storm came on, and the disciples were driven out of their course and beyond their destination. After taking up Jesus they finally land at Capernaum.

The explanation of this passage, which was anciently received, is that Bethsaida lay on the west shore of the lake, and the desert place between Bethsaida and Tiberias. With this agree the old local traditions of the country as is testified by the early travellers, Arculf, Sœwulf, and others.

Arculf, the French Bishop, who travelled in the Holy Land a little before A.D. 700, says:—

"He further saw, on this side of the sea of Galilee, to the north of the city of Tiberias, the place where our Lord blessed the loaves and fishes, a grassy and level plain, which has never been ploughed since that event, and shows no traces of buildings, except a few columns round the fountain, where, as they say, those persons drank after they had eaten their fill."

"Those who wish to go from Jerusalem to Capernaum, take the direct way by Tiberias, and from thence along the sea of Gennesareth, to the place where the loaves were blessed, from which Capernaum is at no great distance."—*Early Travels in Palestine*, Bohn's ed., p. 8.

Sœwulf, an Anglo-Saxon pilgrim who travelled in the Holy Land about A.D. 1102, says : " The sea of Galilee is about six miles from Mount Tabor to the east and north-east, and is about ten miles long by five in breadth. The city of Tiberias stands on the sea-shore on one side, and on the other side are Corozaim and Bethsaida, the city of Andrew and Peter. About four miles to the north-east of the city of Tiberias is the castle of Gennesareth, where the Lord appeared to the disciples when fishing, as we learn from the Gospel. About two miles to the east of Gennesareth is the mount on which our Lord Jesus fed 5000 men with five loaves and two fishes. This mount is called by the inhabitants our Lord's Table ; and at its foot stands a very beautiful church of St. Peter, but deserted."—*Early Travels in Palestine*, p. 46.

Pococke, who travelled in the East about the middle of the eighteenth century, says :—" Twelve miles north-east from Nazareth we came to the Mount of Beatitudes, where our Saviour delivered His remarkable sermon. It is about ten miles north of Mount Tabor. From the plain to the south it appears like a long low hill, with a mount at the east and west end, from which it seems to have the name of Kern-el-Hutin (the horns of Hutin), the village of Hutin being under it. At the first sight the whole hill appears to be rocky and uneven, but the eastern mount is a level surface, covered with fine herbage ; and here, they say, it was that those blessings proceeded out of the mouth of the Redeemer of mankind. The mount is ninety paces long, and sixty wide. About the middle of this eastern mount are the foundations of a small church twenty-two feet square, on a ground a little elevated, which probably is the place where they supposed our Saviour was when He spoke to His disciples. To the west of it there is a cistern underground, which might serve for the use of those who had the care of the church. About two miles to the east, near the brow of high ground which runs to the sea of Tiberias, there are several large black stones ; two of these stand together, and are larger than the rest ; and it is said Christ blessed the loaves on them when He fed the 5000, whom He made to sit down on the grass."—Pococke's *Travels*, ii., p. 67.

Again, he says :—"On the north side of the hill, over the plain of Gennesareth, there is a fortress cut into the perpendicular rock a considerable height, with a great number of apartments, the ascent to which is very steep ; it is said by some to be the work, or at least the improvement, of Feckerdine. The reason of my mentioning this pass so particularly is because south of it is the plain of Hutin, and about two miles west of the sea of Tiberias are the ruins of a town or large village which is now called Baitsida, and must have been the ancient Bethsaida of Galilee so often mentioned in the Gospel. I cannot find that this has been yet thoroughly settled by any authors ; and the writers on ancient geography finding that there was a Bethsaida east of the sea of Tiberias or of Jordan, in Gaulonitis, have very much doubted whether there was another to the west of that sea, and consequently have concluded that our Saviour spoke of that on the east; but, as the town in the east had its name changed to Julias by Philip the Tetrarch, before our Saviour frequented those parts, it may easily be concluded that the eastern place was never intended, but always this town, which is in Galilee; and, though it be two miles distant from the sea or lake, yet it may be said, without any impropriety, to be by the sea of Tiberias."—Pococke's *Travels*, ii. 68.

The following statement made by a very recent traveller, though inaccurate as to the time when the tradition first arose, is valuable as a modern testimony to the suitability of Kurn Hattin for the Mount of Beatitudes:—"The tradition which makes Kurn Hattin the Mount of Beatitudes is of Latin origin, and not older than the twelfth or thirteenth century; but the place is so well adapted for the delivery of a discourse to a large multitude that in this case we may well believe it was correctly chosen by those who first selected it."—*Recovery of Jerusalem*, p. 357.

From the earliest times down to the Reformation it was universally believed that the site of the feeding of the 5000 was on the west side of the lake of Gennesareth, somewhere between Bethsaida and Tiberias. In the sixteenth century Adricomius, a native of Holland, published his work on the *Geography of the Holy Land*. This writer missing the meaning of the word (πέραν) across, concluded that as Capernaum was on the west side of the lake, the Bethsaida mentioned in this chapter must be somewhere on the east side, and suggested that Julias, which had formerly been called Bethsaida, must be the site of this miracle. In the seventeenth century Cornelius à Lapide published his invaluable *Commentary on Holy Scripture*, in which he pointed out the error into which Adricomius had fallen with respect to the site of Bethsaida. Early in the eighteenth century (1714) Reland, also a native of Holland, published his work on the *Geography of the Holy Land*, and repeats the mistake already made by Adricomius. Such were the insufficient grounds on which a tradition of fifteen centuries was put aside, and a new interpretation set up in its place. Strange to say almost all modern English commentators have eagerly accepted this new opinion as to the site or sites of Bethsaida—Bishop Wordsworth, Dean Alford, Dean Stanley, Dr. Robinson the American traveller, Smith's *Biblical Dictionary*, and the *Handbook on Palestine*, a work of considerable research, have all adopted the explanation that besides a Bethsaida on the west side of the lake, there was another on the north-east, where the miracle of feeding the 5000 was wrought. The writer of the article "Bethsaida" in *Smith's Dictionary* evidently looks upon the suggestion of two Bethsaidas as a discovery that has disposed of all the difficulties in the case.

During the last few years a slight reaction has arisen against the explanation of this passage by means of two Bethsaidas (Thomson's *The Land and the Book*, p. 373). The latest writer on this subject (*Recovery of Jerusalem*, p. 380) is inclined to place the scene of this miracle on the west side of the lake, very much in the spot which tradition has handed down, partly from the character of the country which he has inspected, and of which he appears a very competent judge, and partly because he thinks it need not be near Bethsaida at all. He adopts this opinion because the Sinaitic MS., (p.m.) does not mention Bethsaida in St. Luke ix. 10. But a reading which is found in our own text, and which receives the support which this does from the Vatican and Alexandrian MSS., cannot be rejected, on the ground that it is supported only by a later reading in the Sinaitic MS.

The following considerations are offered in support of the old tradition that the Bethsaida here mentioned was on the west side of the lake, and that the scene of this miracle lay somewhere between Bethsaida and Tiberias.

Of the four Evangelists two, St. Matthew (xiv. 15) and St. Mark (vi. 35), state that Jesus fed the 5000 men with five barley loaves and two fishes in a "desert place" (τόπος ἔρημος). St. Luke (ix. 10) says it was in "a desert place belonging to the city called Bethsaida," and St. John (vi. 23) that it was near Tiberias.

In English the expressions "in a desert place" (ἐν τόπῳ ἐρημῷ), and "in the desert" (ἐν τῇ ἐρήμῳ), have a very different meaning, and a similar difference exists in the Greek. Jesus fed the 5000 "in a desert place," their fathers did eat manna "in the desert" (John vi. 31), or in the wilderness. Any waste or unoccupied land free from habitations around a city or village would be a desert place (τόπος ἔρημος). In such a place it was, not far from Bethsaida, that this miracle was wrought, and not "in the desert."

All that is known of Bethsaida or Julias in the north-east of the lake is told by Josephus, who says Philip (the Tetrarch), for his part beautified and enlarged Paneas at the head of the river Jordan, and gave it the name of Cæsarea; and so for the village of Bethsaida upon the bank of the lake of Gennesareth, he built it up to the bulk and appearance of a magnificent city, rich and populous, and gave it the name of Julias, out of respect to Julia, the daughter of Cæsar. (*Antiq.* xviii. 2, 1.) Again he says, "Philip the Tetrarch built a city at Paneas, which he called Cæsarea. It was erected at the very head of the river Jordan. And he raised another also in Gaulonitis, which he called Julias. Tiberias in Galilee was built by Herod, and so was also Julias in Peræa."—*Jewish Wars*, ii. 9, 1 (L'Estrange's Translation).

At the time of this miracle Julias would be at the height of its glory, for Philip died there A.D. 34, that is about two years after this, and was buried there with great pomp and expense in a monument which he had prepared for himself. (*Antiq.* xviii. 4, 6.) Is it, therefore, credible that, if by Bethsaida St. Luke had meant this place, he would have given it the name by which it had once been called when a mere village, and not the name which it then had, and when it was a magnificent city rich and populous?

The name of Paneas was also changed by this very Philip the Tetrarch into Cæsarea, and where it is mentioned in the New Testament it is called Cæsarea (Matt. xvi. 13; Mark viii. 27), and never Paneas. Neither would it be strictly true that this place was "called Bethsaida," either at the time of the miracle or at the time when St. Luke wrote his Gospel. It was then called Julias, not Bethsaida.

The word Bethsaida occurs only in one place besides in St. Luke, and that is in the very next chapter (x. 13), where a woe is denounced against it, in company with Chorazin and Capernaum. But it will scarcely be questioned that the cities here meant are all cities of Galilee, and on the west shore of the lake. Nor is it at all probable that St. Luke would use the word Bethsaida in two consecutive chapters, meaning by that name two very different places, one a village and the other a magnificent city rich and populous, one on the west shore of the lake of Tiberias, and the other on the north-east, and give no intimation of this. If there were two cities called Bethsaida, and if our Saviour wrought part of His miracles in one of these places, and part in the other, which did He mean when He said, "Woe unto thee, Bethsaida?" (Luke x. 13.)

There is no difficulty in the expressions used by the Evangelists, and translated "the other side" (Matt. xiv. 22), "gone over" (34), "other side" (Mark vi. 45), "passed over" (53), "over the sea" (John vi. 17), and "the other side of the sea" (25). All these expressions are translations of one and the same Greek word πέραν and its compounds. But its meaning is amply satisfied by over the sea to some other part, and not necessarily from one cardinal point of the compass to another. Πέραν would mean to the opposite side from whatever point and in whatever direction the start was made. If they set sail from the west coast πέραν and διαπεράσαντες would not of necessity mean that they sailed due east to the opposite shore, but that they crossed over by sea to some other part, it may be on the same side of the lake. This use of the word is strikingly exemplified by Josephus, and quoted by Macgregor. He says: " The words εἰς τὸ πέραν translated to the other side, need not, perhaps, mean to the opposite side of the lake, east or west of the Jordan. Josephus, departing from Tiberias, says he 'sailed over to Tarichæa' διεπεραιώθεν (*Life*, sec. lix.), while 'Tiberias and Tarichæa were on the same western side of Jordan, and without any deeply indented bay between them." (MacGregor's *Jordan*, p. 376.) This is the more valuable, as being the opinion of a sailor, and of one who had examined the coast.

Not wishing to import into this examination any extraneous difficulty by identifying Capernaum or Bethsaida with the modern Tell

L

Hum, Khan Minyeh, or any other site, the following rough sketch has been taken from Smith's *Biblical Dictionary*, which no doubt is approximately correct. There it will be seen that the distance from Tiberias to Capernaum is greater than the distance from Bethsaida or Julias in the north-east to Capernaum. The expression across or over the sea (πέραν) would therefore be more applicable to the former voyage than to the latter.

St. Mark says (vi. 45) that their destination was at first Bethsaida. If they were going from the neighbourhood of a Bethsaida in the north-east to a Bethsaida in the west, would not this have been so unusual as to require from the Evangelist some explanation, some distinction between the two places? The fair conclusion from all this is that the old local tradition is in this case tolerably correct, and this places the scene of the miracle of the feeding of the 5000, the place from which the disciples set sail (Tiberias), the place of their destination (Bethsaida), and the place at which they in the end arrived (Capernaum), all on the west shore of the lake.

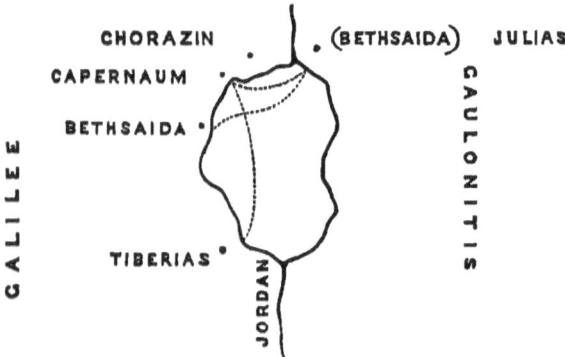

To their question, "When," which also implies the other question, "How," "camest Thou here?" Jesus does not reply. But He shows them that their motive in seeking Him was a wrong one. Their object was not to witness His miracles, and from thence to learn the nature of His office, to conclude from His works that he was the Messiah promised to them of old. They sought Him simply and solely for the bread, to have their hunger supplied without labour, without any regard to the miraculous manner in which it was provided for them. He bids them labour, but not for the meat, which perisheth, but for that meat which endureth unto everlasting life, which He the Son of Man, God Incarnate, could give them, because God the Father had sealed Him.

When conversing with the woman of Samaria Jesus had raised her thoughts from the water of the well to the living water, to life everlasting, so here he leads the Jews on from the food of the body to the food of the soul, from "the meat which perisheth to that meat which endureth unto everlasting life." That He could give the former of these, the food of the body, they were themselves witnesses. He here declares His power, as well as the reason of His power, to give the other. "For him hath God the Father sealed." On Him hath God the Father set the seal of His approval, and hath given Him the Impress of Himself. God the Father sealed the Son of Man, when at His Baptism there came a voice from heaven, saying, "This is My beloved Son, in whom I am well pleased." (Matt. iii. 17.) The Son of Man is elsewhere (Heb. i. 3) called the Brightness of His Father's Glory, and the Express Image of His Person or of His substance. When God the Son took unto Him human nature He gave to it His Impress, the Seal of His Father. When the Word was made Flesh, the human nature received the Seal, the Impress of the Divine.

26 Jesus answered them and said, Verily, verily, I say unto you, ye seek Me, not because ye (saw the miracles), but because ye (did eat) of the loaves, and were filled.

(Alf. Saw miracles—ate.)

27 (Labour not) for the meat which perisheth, [but for (that meat) which] endureth unto (everlasting life), [which the Son of Man shall give unto you]: (for Him hath God the Father sealed.)

[S. But for that which: S. which the Son of Man giveth unto you.]
(Margin. Work not.)
(Alf. Work not—the meat—eternal life—for Him the Father sealed, even God.)

Jesus could give them "the meat which endureth unto everlasting life," because Him had God the Father sealed. But Jesus had said that they must work for it. They therefore ask Him what the works were which they must do in order to obtain this meat. He replies that they must believe on Him, whom God hath sent, *i.e.*, on Himself. Belief or faith is here, as often in Holy Scripture, put for all the active virtues that spring from belief. Belief is the root from which all these grow naturally as its fruit. It is therefore used alone, but includes them all.

28 [Then said they] unto Him, (What shall we do), that we may work the works of God?

[A. They said.]
(Alf. They said therefore—what must we do?)

29 Jesus answered and said unto them, This is the

work of God (that ye believe on Him whom He hath sent.)

(Alf. That ye should believe in Him whom He sent.)

The Jews then reply that, before they can believe in Him they must see some works adequate to produce in them this belief. He had only fed them, 5000 of them, with superhuman food for a single day, and yet on the strength of this He required them to believe that He was God, whereas Moses only required their fathers to believe that he was God's servant, and yet to produce in them this belief he fed them, 600,000 of them, continually for forty years with manna.

So gross and carnal are the Jews that they cling to the miracle of multiplying the bread, and overlook all the other miracles which Jesus had wrought among them; how He had healed the sick, cast out devils, opened the eyes of the blind, none of which Moses had done. Jesus wrought His miracles with the express purpose of proving to them that He was God: Moses wrought his miracles to prove that he was God's servant. On the strength of the miracles which he performed their fathers had believed Moses that he was, what he professed to be, God's servant. But they had not believed Jesus that He was, what He claimed to be, God, in consequence of His miracles.

30 They said therefore unto Him, (What sign shewest Thou [then]) that we may see, and believe Thee? What dost Thou work?

[S. Omits, Then.]
(Alf. What doest Thou then as a Sign?)

31 Our fathers (did eat manna in the desert): as it is written, He gave them bread from heaven to eat.[1]

(Alf. Ate the manna in the wilderness.)

In answer to this Jesus shows that He was greater than Moses, and that the bread, which He gave, was greater than that which Moses gave.

32 (Then said Jesus) unto them, Verily, verily, I say unto you, Moses gave you not (that bread) from heaven; but My Father giveth you the true bread from heaven.

(Alf. Jesus therefore said—the bread.)

---

[1] See note on John iii. 33.

33 For the bread of God (is He which) cometh down from heaven, and giveth life unto the world.

(Alf. Is that which.)

In these words He contrasts the manna, with the "true bread," and points out several important distinctions between them. The manna was given by Moses, who was a mere man; the "true bread" was given by God the Father. The manna was given to their fathers only, to the Israelites in the desert, but the true bread is given by God the Father to the world. The manna did not really come from heaven, but only apparently so. It was formed in the air at God's command, like the frost, or snow, or hail, and it is only called the bread of heaven as a type or figure of the true bread of heaven, but the true bread of heaven, the Word, came down from the bosom of the Father. The manna nourishes the body only, and that only for a time: the true bread nourishes both soul and body, and that for ever.

The dulness of these Jews in apprehending our Saviour's meaning of the words, "true bread from heaven," is not unlike that of the Samaritan woman with respect to His use of the expression, "living water." After all the explanation which He had given her of the "living water," her thoughts had never risen above the water of the well, and she exclaims, Sir, give me this water that I thirst not, neither come hither to draw. (iv. 4.) In like manner, the highest aim of these Jews was to obtain the food of the body, and without the necessary labour.

34 (Then said they) unto Him, Lord, evermore give us this bread.

(Alf. They said therefore.)

Though Jesus had identified Himself with the meat which endureth unto everlasting life, or with the "true bread from heaven," yet up to this point He had spoken of Himself in the third person, now He begins to use the first person and speak of Himself in such a manner that they can scarcely mistake His meaning, at least so far as that He Himself is "the true bread from heaven."

35 [And Jesus] said unto them, I am the Bread of Life: he that cometh to me (shall never) hunger; and he that believeth (on Me shall never thirst.)

[V. Omits, And: S. Then Jesus.]
(Alf. Omits, And—shall not—in Me shall never thirst.)

In the expression, "the bread of life," there is probably some allusion to the "tree of life." (Gen. ii. 9.) If our first parents had eaten of the tree of life it would have prolonged their life, even though their life was one of misery. "The bread of life" imparts immortality not to the body only, but to the soul also, and Jesus is the bread of life. Those who believe in Him, those who come to Him, shall never lack strength in their contest with Satan. They shall never hunger nor thirst any more. They shall never faint for want of supernatural grace.

36 But I said unto you (That ye also have seen [Me]), and believe not.

[S. A. Omit, Me.]
(Alf. That ye have even seen Me.)

Either He had said these very words at some other time, and St. John has not recorded them, or they were the substance of what He had said above.

37 (All that) the Father giveth Me shall come unto Me : and him that cometh to Me, I will in no wise cast out.

(Alf. All which.)

38 [(For I came) down from heaven, not to do] Mine own will, but the will of Him that sent Me.

[S. For I came not down from heaven to do.]
(Alf. For I am come.)

39 [And this is the Father's will, (which hath] sent) Me, that of all which He hath given Me I should lose nothing, but should (raise it up again at the last day.)

[S. V. A. And this is the will of Him which hath.]
(Alf. That sent—raise it up at the last day.)

40 (And this is the will of Him that sent Me, that every one which seeth the Son, and believeth on Him, may have everlasting life : and I will) raise him up at the last day.

[S. V. A. For this is: S. V. The will of My Father that.]
(Alf. For this is the will of My Father, that every one which looketh on the Son, and believeth in Him, should have eternal life : and that I should.)

They had seen Jesus, they had seen, too, the miracles which He wrought before them, they had heard the testimony of John the Baptist, and yet, as a nation, the Jews did not believe in Him. Some of them would believe, and those He would not reject. To believe in

Him was the gift of the Father, and was the reward of His Passion. The prophet had long before said, "He shall see of the travail of His Soul, and shall be satisfied." (Isa. liii. 11.) Eternal life, the life of grace in the soul here, to be matured into the life of glory hereafter for ever, is given to those who believe on Jesus the Son of God, who is the bread of life. He would not cast out those who came to Him, because the Father had given them to Him as the reward of His Passion, and because He came down from heaven, *i.e.*, because He was made Flesh, in order to do the will of His Father. So far from permitting them to perish, He would raise them up at the last day. Their coming to Him, their belief in Him, and union with Him, would be the very cause of their resurrection.

41 (The Jews then) murmured at Him, because He said, I am the Bread which came down from heaven.

(Alf. The Jews therefore.)

42 And they said, Is not this Jesus, the Son of Joseph, [whose Father and mother we know]? [(how is it then that He saith,] I came) down from heaven?

[S.* Whose father also we know: V. How now saith He?]
(Alf. How then doth He say, I am come.)

43 [Jesus therefore answered and said] unto them, Murmur not among yourselves.

[V. Omits, Therefore: S. Answered them and said.]
(Alf. Omits, Therefore.)

44 No man can come to Me, [except the Father which] hath sent Me draw him: and I will raise him up at the last day.[1]

[A. Except he which.]

45 It is written in the prophets, And they shall be all taught of God. Every man [therefore] that (hath heard, [and hath learned of the Father]), cometh unto Me.[2]

[S. V. Omit, Therefore: A. And hath learned the truth of the Father.]
(Alf. Heareth from the Father, and learneth.)

See note on xii. 32.
 Taught of God (διδακτοι του θεου.)—
"That is, taught by God, as in St. Matt.

xxv. 34, οἱ εὐλογημένοι τοῦ πατρὸς, means blessed by the Father."—Winer's *Grammar of the New Testament*, 202.

46 Not that any man hath seen the Father, [save He which is (of God), He hath seen the Father.]

[S. Save He, which is of the Father, He hath seen God.]
(Alf. From God.)

Jesus bids the Jews not to murmur at what He had just said to them. The fault, the cause of their murmuring, lay not in His words, for they were true, but in the state of their own hearts, in their own want of divine light. Their belief, or their want of belief, in Him depended on the previous preparation of their heart. Those who had previously listened to the teaching of the Father would believe in Him. Those who had hitherto faithfully and conscientiously obeyed the laws of God the Father would be led on to believe in His future revelation of His Son.

The conditions under which God effectually draws some men to believe in Him and others not are beyond man's knowledge. Practically all men are free to choose and free to refuse Him. As a rule, we see that men are drawn from one degree of perfection to another. This is strikingly seen with respect to the Incarnation. All those whom God chose as His instruments to bring about the Incarnation, or to whom it should be first revealed, were already eminent for their devout lives under another and less perfect dispensation. This is expressly stated in the case of the Blessed Virgin Mary (Luke i. 28); Joseph (Matt. i. 19); Zacharias and Elizabeth (Luke i. 6); Simeon (Luke ii. 25); and Anna (v. 37).

Thus, according to the rules which had been already observed and displayed in God's providence those in that very crowd of Jews who were diligently striving to do the will of the Father as declared under the Mosaic dispensation would be convinced by the works which Jesus wrought, that He was the Christ. Conviction so as to produce belief in Jesus was not the effect of miracles unless acting on a teachable, obedient, devout spirit. No amount of miracles would succeed in persuading those whom the Father had not already drawn. But the reward of those who were drawn by the Father to believe in Him would be unlimited, it would be resurrection to eternal life.

47 Verily, verily, I say unto you, He that believeth (on Me) hath (everlasting life.)

[S. V. Omit, On Me.]
(Alf. In Me—eternal life.)

48 I am (that bread) of life.
(Alf. The bread.)

49 Your fathers (did eat manna in the wilderness, and are dead.)
(Alf. Ate the manna in the wilderness, and died.)

50 This is the bread, which cometh down from heaven, that a man may eat thereof, and not die.

51 I am the living bread, which came down from heaven: if any man [eat of this bread,] he shall live for ever: ([and] [the Bread that I will give is My Flesh), [which I will give] for the life of the world.]

[S. Eat of My bread: S. Omits, and: S. The bread that I will give for the life of the world, is My Flesh: V. Omits, which I will give.]
(Alf. Yea, and the Bread that I will give is My Flesh.)

52 The Jews therefore (strove among themselves), saying, [How can This Man] give us His Flesh to eat?
[S. How therefore can This Man.]
(Alf. Contended among themselves.)

If we review the last twenty-five verses we shall find that the chief subject of them, and that which connects them all, like a vein running from one end to the other, is that Jesus is the author of life, of life to the soul here, and of life to the soul and body hereafter. Every variety of expression is used to convey this knowledge to them. He is the meat which endureth unto everlasting life. He is the true bread from heaven. He is the bread of life. He is the living bread which came down from heaven.

The Jews said that Jesus was a mere man, the son of Joseph, and that His father and mother were living among them. Jesus Himself claimed to be God, as well as man, and therefore the author of life to man. If they wished to partake in eternal life they must believe that He was God, One with the Father, and equal to the Father. In order to partake of life they must believe in Him, they must believe that He, Jesus, whom they supposed to be the son of Joseph, was God, and therefore the source of life, and able to impart life to them. This was the first step in order to obtain life eternal; the next was to eat His Flesh and drink His Blood.

The first objection of the Jews was that He could not be the author of life, because He was only a man like themselves and descended from men like themselves. Their second objection was that no man could give them his flesh to eat.

In answer to the objection of the Jews, " How can this Man give us His Flesh to eat?" Jesus, in the next six verses, declares that this is possible, and, more than that, it is absolutely necessary. He does not explain to the Jews how they can eat His Flesh and drink His Blood, but He repeats, in almost every possible form, that in order to obtain life in the soul here, and life in the soul and body hereafter, they must believe that He, Jesus the Son of Mary, was God, and they must eat His Flesh and drink His Blood.

53 (Then Jesus said) unto them, Verily, verily, I say unto you, Except ye eat the Flesh of the Son of Man, and drink His Blood, ye have [no life] in you.

[S. Not everlasting life.]
(Alf. Jesus therefore said.)

54 (Whoso) eateth My Flesh, and drinketh My Blood, hath eternal life: and I will raise him up at the last day.[1]

(Alf. He that.)

55 For My Flesh [is meat indeed,] and My Blood [is drink indeed.]

[V. Is true meat: V. Is true drink.]

56 He that eateth My Flesh, and drinketh My Blood, dwelleth in Me, and I in Him.

57 As the living Father (hath sent) Me, and I live (by the Father): (so) he that eateth Me, (even he) shall live (by Me.)

(Alf. Sent—by reason of the Father—even so—he also—by reason of Me.)

58 This is (That Bread) which came down from heaven: [not as your fathers did eat manna, and are

---

[1] **Whoso eateth My Flesh** (ὁ τρώγων μου τὴν σάρκα).—" It is very interesting to notice that our Saviour, in the sixth chapter of St. John's Gospel, uses two Greek synonyms φάγω and τρώγω, to express the act of eating as applied to Himself. When speaking of Himself as the True Bread, the archetype of the manna in the wilderness, He invariably employs, φάγω, which is a general term, meaning to eat any kind of substance, and in any way. But when speaking of His own Flesh, He suddenly uses the word τρώγω, which is a specific term, and means to chew food like a ruminating animal, to eat vegetable substances alone. It is one of those delicate refinements of the Greek text which we lose in our English Version, and which seems to have been intended by Him who is the Word, to connect more closely His Flesh and Blood with the manna and the bread. He limits the general term, applied to animal and vegetable food indiscriminately, to the manna and the bread. He enlarges the specific term applied exclusively to vegetable food, so as to embrace His Flesh and Blood. His Flesh is Bread, and Bread is His Flesh. The broken Bread of the Supper is His broken Body; and we are to eat of It in both the senses signified by φάγω and τρώγω."—Macmillan on the *True Vine*, p. 69.

dead] : he that (eateth of This Bread) shall live for ever.

[S. The bread which cometh down from heaven is not: S. V. Not as the fathers did eat, and are dead.]
(Alf. The Bread—not as the fathers ate and died—eateth This Bread.)

59 These things said He in the synagogue, as He taught in Capernaum.[1]

[S. V. In Capharnaum.]

---

[1] "Capernaum was a busy bright little town; a station on the great road: a garrison for Roman troops: a port for collecting dues by land and lake: a place of tanners, dyers, soap-boilers: a market for oilmen, shepherds, cheesemongers and fruit grocers: a halting ground for the buyers and sellers of every kind, the cornchandlers, the fishermen, the woolstaplers, the vinters and the gardeners. Being the first town on the lake of Tiberias, as you ride in from Damascus, as Arona is the first town on Lago Maggiore as you come from Turin, it was the port at which any one coming that way would embark for cities lying south and east on the shore. Standing on a hill of limestone, rough and rich with the flow of the basaltic rocks from higher volcanic hills; having the rich plain and cool lake of Gennesareth at its feet, with the palm, the orange, and the pomegranate blooming everywhere about, Capernaum became, like Como or Palanza nearer home, a retreat for the rich as well as a field of labour for the poor. Most of the Jewish inhabitants, netmakers, fishermen, farmers, were believers in a physical Messiah: followers of Herod, of Judas, of Simon, of John: Jews of an earnest and yet of a most worldly type. The strangers who dwelt among those Jews, like every one trained in the Hellenic schools, were liberal and tolerant in affairs of faith. Had not the Roman governor built a synagogue for the Jews at his own expense?

"Capernaum, properly spelt Caphar na Hum, was one of the towns most favoured by the Lord. It was the first place to which He came after His Baptism by John. There He dwelt for a little while with His early disciples, Peter and Andrew, James and John. Here lived the good nobleman whose son He cured. There too He healed the demoniac in the synagogue; relieved the mother-in-law of Peter, healed the man sick of the palsy, and restored the withered hand. There He made whole the centurion's servant, and raised the daughter of Jairus from the dead. From the blue waters of the lake, He obtained the tribute money: and on its slimy shores, among the brambles and vines, He spoke the parables of the Tares, of the Sower, of the Treasure, of the Merchant, of the Net. In the White Synagogue, built by the Roman soldier, He pronounced His discourses on Faith, on Fasting, on Humility of Spirit, on Brotherly Love. Near to Capernaum He fed the five thousand, walked on the sea, and preached His Sermon on the Mount. He loved the busy, basaltic town, and after His expulsion from Nazareth, He made it the scene of His ministry. In the words of St. Matthew, a native of the place, it became His own city. Where then was this favoured spot?

"Strange to say, the great Churches of East and West, while bent on fixing the sites of events in the sacred story . . . . . . kept no clear record of the scene of so many miracles and sermons as Capernaum."—Dixon's *Holy Land*, ii. 160.

"As regards Capernaum, what may be called the intrinsic arguments in favour of Tell Hum had been often urged; and in recent /years the recognition of the remains of a Jewish Synagogue in the great ruin on that spot, gave much additional interest to the question. But what is new and, it seems to me, almost decisive, is the identification of the fountain at Tabigah with the fountain of Capernaum, by the discovery that the tract round the rock of Khan Minyeh is an aqueduct carrying the waters of the fountain into the plain of Gennesareth. This at once elevates the claim of Tell Hum to be the ancient Capernaum to the very highest rank."—*Recovery of Jerusalem*, xix.

In order to obtain eternal life they must believe that Jesus was God, and they must eat His Flesh and drink His Blood. As He had introduced and enforced the first of these with the solemn declaration, Verily, verily, so also He does the second. As He had used a variety of expressions in order to convey the knowledge of the first requisite for life, so He does also in the case of the second.

In these verses Jesus once more reiterates the absolute necessity of eating His Flesh and drinking His Blood in order to obtain eternal life, and to be raised up at the last day. He shows that the effects of His Flesh and His Blood will not be physical, not according to the usual working of nature, but spiritual and supernatural. In the case of common eating whatever is eaten is assimilated to the body of the person who eats. He who eats the Flesh of Jesus and drinks His Blood is united to Jesus, to the God Man personally, to the Second Person in the Godhead. But He declares that His Flesh is really Flesh, and that His Blood is really Blood, not figuratively so only. The union produced by eating the Flesh of Jesus and drinking His Blood is a real, actual union, though supernatural, and not a union through the affections only. He likens the union between Himself and those who eat His Flesh and drink His Blood to the union between the Father and Himself.

The Jews go away with the impression that He meant them to eat His Flesh and drink His Blood in the usual acceptation of the words. He does not explain to them that this was not the case. Either the time for this was not yet come, or the Jews were not in a state of mind to receive further explanation. Jesus does not give this explanation until when in the Eucharist He offers His Body or His Flesh and His Blood for the Life of the world. Then He shows His Apostles how they were to eat His Flesh and drink His Blood, not only then but to the end of the world, and not only they but all faithful earnest believers in Him, as the God Incarnate, the Word made Flesh.

He did not give them His Body to eat and His Blood to drink until He had offered Them in the Eucharist for the life of the world. The Body which He then gave them to eat, and the Blood which He then gave them to drink, were not different from His Body and from His Blood, which He would give to all time, not different from the Flesh and the Blood which He had just told the Jews they must eat and drink in order to obtain eternal life. His miracle of multiplying the bread just before this discourse had prepared us for this. No limits can be put to His power. The only question for us to consider is, What did He mean?

Jesus delivered this discourse not to His disciples or to the Twelve Apostles, but to the Jews in the most public place in Capernaum, in the synagogue. The synagogue-days were the second and fifth day of the week. (Lightfoot, i. 235.)

COMMENTARY ON ST. JOHN'S GOSPEL.   157

60 Many therefore of His disciples, when they (had heard) this, said, (This is an hard saying): who can hear it?
(Alf. Heard—This saying is hard.)

61 [(When Jesus knew) in Himself] that His disciples (murmured at it), [He said] unto them, Doth this offend you?
[S. Jesus therefore knew in Himself—and He said.]
(Alf. But Jesus knowing—were murmuring at this.)

62 (What, [and] if ye shall see the Son of Man ascend up) where He was before?
[S. Omits, And.]
(Alf. What then if ye should behold the Son of Man ascending up.)

63 It is the Spirit (that quickeneth): the flesh profiteth nothing: the words that (I speak) unto you, (they are Spirit and they are Life.)
[S. They are Spirit and Life.]
(Alf. That giveth life—have spoken—are spirit and are life.)

64 But there are some of you that believe not. [For Jesus knew] from the beginning who they were [that believed not, and (who should) betray him.]
[S. For the Saviour knew: S. That believed, and who it was which should betray Him.]
(Alf. Who it was that should.)

65 And He said, (Therefore said I) unto you, that no man can come unto Me, except it (were given) [unto him of My Father.]
[S. Omits, Unto him: S. V. Of the Father.]
(Alf. For this cause have I said—be given.)

The Jews, as we have already seen, murmured and called in question His power to give life, and especially through the eating of His Flesh and the drinking of His Blood. The latter they called a hard saying. But though Jesus knew that they murmured at what He had just said He did not soften down His statement, He meets it with one equally hard, and said unto them, "Doth this offend you? What and if ye shall see the Son of Man ascend up where He was before?" He calls to their recollection what He had before taught them, that He was God and came down from heaven, and that He should ascend up where He was before.

Jesus does not say, "My Flesh profiteth nothing," but "the flesh," mere flesh, mere human nature profiteth nothing, that is, has no power to give life. But His was not mere flesh, mere human nature, He was the Word made Flesh. The Divine Nature communicated life-giving power to the Human Nature which He took of the Blessed Virgin, and He communicates life to men through their eating His Flesh and drinking His Blood.

In all the instances where He teaches that life in the soul here and life in the soul and body hereafter is the fruit of eating the Flesh and drinking the Blood of the Son of Man, He, of course, implies a corresponding belief that He is God and a frame of mind in keeping with such a belief.

Jesus shows them that the cause of their unbelief was not because His saying was hard, but because their hearts were hard. They had not been taught of God, they had not been drawn to Him by the desire to learn how to serve God. He knew from their first coming to Him which of them would continue to believe in Him.

By the saying which they called hard Jesus was not breaking the bruised reed, nor quenching the smoking flax. This was a test to sever the earnest and sincere among them from the selfish and indifferent, those who followed Him merely for the sake of the bread, which they saw He could provide, from those who really believed that He was God.

66 [(From that time) many of His disciples] went back, and walked no more with Him.

[S. From that *time* therefore many of the disciples.]
(Alf. Upon this.)

67 (Then said) Jesus unto the twelve, (Will ye also go away?)

(Alf. Therefore said—do ye also wish to go away?)

68 [Then] Simon Peter answered Him, Lord, to whom shall we go? Thou hast the words of eternal life.

[S. V. Omit, Then.]
(Alf. Omits, Then.)

69 And we (believe and are sure [that Thou art that Christ, the Son of the living God.)]

[S. V. That Thou art the Holy One of God.]
(Alf. Have believed and know that Thou art the Holy One of God.)

From that time, and in consequence of that hard saying, that they must eat His Flesh and drink His Blood in order to have life in them, many of His disciples went back. But neither Judas nor the rest of the Twelve went away. Judging from the difference in their characters, and from their subsequent conduct, we may safely conclude that they remained with Jesus from very different motives. Judas, we know, was a thief and had the bag. That would be sufficient to retain him. The reason why the others did not go away is contained in their own answer—Peter, either as entitled by his age or as influenced by the strength and sincerity of his zeal, speaks in the name of the rest. Some one they must follow. None but He had the words of eternal life. Peter only repeats with slight variation our Saviour's Own words, "The words that I have spoken unto you are spirit and are life." (63.) Though they might not fully understand His words, they had unbounded confidence in Him. From the testimony of John Baptist, from His Own miracles, from the holiness of His life and teaching, they believed and were sure that He was the Holy One of God. This Peter says, not as a single individual, not as his own belief only, but in the name of the Twelve Apostles and as their belief, " Thou hast the words of eternal life. And we believe and are sure that Thou art the Christ, the Son of the Living God. This, Peter says, is the belief of them all. But Jesus tells him that he is mistaken, for though He had chosen twelve as Apostles, one of them was a devil.

70 [Jesus answered them, (Have not I chosen) you twelve, and one of you is a devil ?]

[S. Jesus answered and said unto them: S. And among you is a devil.]
(Alf. Did I not choose.)

71 He spake ([of Judas Iscariot the son of Simon]: for he it was that should betray Him), being one of the twelve.

[S. Of Judas the son of Simon, who was of Cariotus: S. That should also betray Him.]
(Alf. Of Judas the son of Simon Iscariot: for it was he that was about to betray Him.)

It is the Evangelist who adds that Judas Iscariot was meant by the expression "Have not I chosen you twelve, and one of you is a devil?" Jesus does not mention His name. He does not discover him to the rest of the Apostles, but He says sufficient to convince Judas himself that his real character was known to Him, and sufficient to put the other Apostles on their guard against trusting too much to their own strength and to the sincerity of their own belief. Jesus calls him " a devil," probably to imply that he was His Adversary, a thief and a liar like the devil, and, in short, a mere instrument of the devil.

The way in which the name of Judas the traitor is associated (71) with this discourse of Jesus, almost seems to imply that his hardness of heart, which eventually led him to betray, to deliver up the Son of God, took its rise, or at least, assumed its more positive form after he had heard it, that this discourse which might have been the means of imparting to him life eternal, became the occasion of increasing his hardness of heart.

What is the exact meaning of Iscariotes is not known. Many conjectures have been made, such as ish Kerioth (אִישׁ קְרִיוֹת), a native of Kerioth in Judah. (Josh. xv. 25.) Similar compounds can be produced, as for instance, Isbosheth, Ishtob. Nothing seems to be known for certain about Judas before his call to be an Apostle. Lightfoot (ii. 176) suggests three explanations. If the title Iscariotes were given to Judas while he was alive, he thinks it may have been derived from the word אסקירטא (Iskortja), which means a leathern apron, and upon such aprons purses were usually sewn. Thus Judas with the leathern apron would mean much the same as Judas "who had the bag;" or, the leathern apron might indicate his trade, that of a tanner: Judas, called the son of Simon the tanner; and in the Acts ix. 43 we read of a Simon who was a tanner. If the title were given him upon his death he would suggest that אסכרא (Iscara), which means strangling, was the root from which the term Iscariot was derived. In this sense Judas Iscariot would imply Judas who died by strangling.

INTRODUCTORY NOTE TO CHAPTER VII.

THE JEWS' FEAST OF TABERNACLES.

The following calendar from the beginning of the month Tisri to the Feast of Tabernacles is taken from Lightfoot, ii. 554, who substantiates almost all the statements by references to ancient Jewish writers.

I. The first day of the month Tisri, was the beginning of the year, for stating the years, the intermissions of the seventh year, and the Jubilees. Upon this day was the blowing of Trumpets, Levit. xxiii. 24, and persons were sent out to give notice of the beginning of the year. On this day began the year of the world 3960, in the middle of which year Christ was crucified.

II. The second day, observed also as holy by the Jews that were in Babylon, that they might be sure not to miss the beginning of the year.

III. A Fast for the murder of Gedaliah: for so they expound those words, Zech. viii. 19. The fast of the seventh month.

IV. This day was the High-Priest in the apartment called προεδρον or παρεδρον, to which he then betook himself from his own house; that he might inure himself by exercise to the rights of the day of atonement approaching, and be ready and fitted for the service of that day.

V. All those seven days, after he betook himself from his own house to this
VI. chamber until the day of atonement, he sprinkles the blood of the daily
VII. sacrifice, offers the incense, snuffs the lamps, and brings the head and legs
VIII. of the sacrifice to the altar, that he may be the more handy in his office upon the expiation day.

IX. Whereas for the whole seven days they permitted him to eat according to his usual custom, the evening of this day approaching, they diet him more sparingly, lest a full stomach should occasion sleep. They spend the whole night waking.

X. The day of Expiation. The solemn Fast. On this day began the year of Jubilee when it came about, Levit. xxv. 9. And indeed this year, which is now under our consideration, was the twenty-eighth Jubilee, reckoning from the seventh year of Joshua, wherein the land was subdued and rested from war, Josh. xi. 23.

XI. The multitude now gather together toward the Feast of Tabernacles, that they
XII. might purify themselves before the Feast, and prepare necessaries for it, viz.,
XIII. little tents, citrons, bundles of palms, willows, &c. But if any were defiled by the touch of a dead body, such were obliged to betake themselves to Jerusalem before the Feast of Expiation, that they might undergo seven days' purification before the Feast of Tabernacles.

XIV. They were generally cut or trimmed on the Vespers of the Feast for the honour of it.

XV. The first day of the Feast of Tabernacles. A feast day. Thirteen young bullocks offered, &c., Numb. xxix. 13. The preparation of the Chagiga. They lodge that night in Jerusalem.

XVI. The second day of the feast. Twelve young bullocks offered. The appearance of all the males in the Court.

XVII. The third day. Eleven young bullocks.
XVIII. The fourth day. Ten.
XIX. The fifth day. Nine.
XX. The sixth day. Eight.
XXI. The seventh day. Seven.
XXII. The eighth day. One young bullock offered.

Upon all these days there was a pouring out of water upon the altar with wine (a thing not used at any other time); and for the sake of that, great joy and singing and dancing; such as was not all the year besides.

At the close of the first day of the Feast they went down into the Court of the Women, and there prepared a great stage, that is, benches on which the women stood above and the men below. Golden candlesticks were then fixed to the walls, over these were golden cups, to which were four ladders set, by which four of the younger priests went up, having bottles in their hands that contained 120 lags, which they emptied into every cup. Of the rags of the garments and girdles of the priests they made wicks to light those lamps; and there was not a street throughout all Jerusalem that did not shine with light.

The religious and devout danced before them, having lighted torches in their hands, and sang songs and doxologies. The Levites, with harps and psalteries, cymbals and other instruments of music without number, stood upon those fifteen steps by which they went down from the Court of Israel to the Court of the Women, according to the fifteen Psalms of degrees, and sung. Two priests also stood in the upper gate, which goes down from the Court of Israel to the Court of the Women, with the trumpets in their hands. When the cock crew, or the president gave his signal, the trumpets sounded; when they came to the tenth step they sounded again: when they came to the Court they sounded; when they came to the pavement they sounded, and so went on sounding the trumpets till they came to the east-gate of the Court; when they came thither they turned their faces from the east to the west, and said, "Our fathers in this place turning their backs upon the Temple, and their faces toward the east, worshipped the sun, but we turn our faces to God."

CHAPTER VII.

1 *Jesus reproveth the ambition and boldness of His kinsmen;* 10 *Goeth up from Galilee to the Feast of Tabernacles;* 14 *Teacheth in the Temple;* 40 *Divers opinions of Him among the people;* 45 *The Pharisees are angry that their officers took Him not, and chide with Nicodemus for taking His part.*

After His miracle of feeding the 5000, of walking on the sea of Galilee, and His discourse with the Jews on the Bread of life, there occurs in St. John's narrative an interval of six months. Those events took place about the time of the Passover (vi. 4), and the Passover was observed in the month Nisan from 14th to 21st, or from April 16th to 23rd. The acts related in the following chapter took place about the Feast of Tabernacles, which was observed from 15th of the month Tisri, or from October 7th, and for eight following days.

After this Feast of Tabernacles Jesus continued His Ministry on earth for six months longer. Thus all His sayings and doings which St. John from this time records, took place in the last six months before His Crucifixion. St. John omits all His acts during the first half of His last year, that is, from April to October. He does not mention that, during the first six months of the year, Jesus had defended His disciples against the complaint of the Pharisees, because they eat with unwashen hands; that He had cast out a devil from the daughter of a woman of Canaan; that He had fed 4000 men besides women and children with seven loaves and a few little fishes; that He had questioned His disciples as to what men thought of Him, with St. Peter's answer. He relates nothing of all this, nor of His Transfiguration on the Mount, nor of His healing the lunatic child, nor of His paying the tribute money, nor of His reproving His Apostles, who disputed which of them should be the greatest. St. John omits all these, and most probably for the reason that they had been fully recorded by the other Evangelists.

1 (After) these things Jesus walked in Galilee: for He would not walk (in Jewry), because the Jews sought to kill Him.

(Alf. And after—in Judæa.)

2 Now the Jews' feast of tabernacles was at hand.

3 His brethren therefore said unto Him, Depart hence, and go into Judæa, that Thy disciples also (may see the works that Thou doest.)

(Alf. May behold Thy works which Thou doest.)

4 (For there is no man that doeth anything in secret, and he himself seeketh) to be known openly. (If Thou do) these things (shew Thyself) to the world.[1]

(Alf. For no man doeth any thing in secret, and seeketh himself—if Thou doest—manifest Thyself.)

5 (For neither did His brethren) believe in Him.

(Alf. For even His brethren did not.)

It would seem that Jesus had not, according to His usual custom, and as the law of Moses enjoined, gone up to Jerusalem either at the last Passover or at the Feast of Tabernacles, and probably for the reason here alleged, that He would not walk in Jewry, because the Jews sought to kill Him. It was not that He feared death, but because the time for His Death was not yet come.

No argument has been advanced in modern times sufficient either to prove that our Saviour's "brethren" were the sons of the Blessed Virgin, or to disprove the old opinion that they were her relations, probably her nephews, and sons of her sister, the wife of Cleophas. This being the case, it is surely in harmony with God's works, if we select that meaning, which attributes the least of human passion and the utmost of self-restraint to the persons, who were the most nearly interested as instruments in bringing about the Incarnation. Thus no violence is done to the reason, and scope is given for the exercise of a healthy feeling of devotion.

In the eyes of His brethren Galilee was no field for Jesus in which to manifest Himself. They did not believe in Him. But it was not that they did not believe that He had the power to work miracles. When they considered His works only, they might be inclined to believe in His claims to be God, but when they beheld His poverty, the lowliness of His condition, which was only equal to their own, they could not believe that He was God, the Creator of all things. Jerusalem was the place in which His pretensions could be proved or disproved, and no time could be better than one of the great annual

---

[1] *For there is no man, &c.*—"Sometimes a clause or simple sentence is grammatically resolved into two, which are connected by καί. Thus in οὐδείς ἐν κρυπτῷ τι ποιεῖ καὶ ζητεῖ αὐτὸς ἐν παρρησίᾳ εἶναι, the two unconnected acts are freely combined in parallelism (nobody does both at the same time), as if John had written οὐδείς—ποιεῖ ζητῶν αὐτός, &c."—Winer's *Grammar of New Testament*, 652.

feasts, when multitudes would be gathered from all parts. Though they did not believe that He was God, they could not deny the truth of His miracles, and they might feel a secret satisfaction in their connection with Him, and a mixture of hope and belief that they would gain by the publicity of His works.

6 ([Then] Jesus said) unto them, My time [is not yet come]: but your time is alway ready.

[S. Omits, Then: S. Is not come.]
(Alf. Jesus therefore saith.)

7 The world cannot hate you: but Me it hateth, because I testify [of it], that the works thereof are evil.

[S. Omits, of it.]

8 Go ye up unto (this feast): [I go not up yet unto this feast]: (for) My time is not yet full come.[1]

[V. Unto the feast. S. I go not up unto this feast.]
(Alf. The feast—because.)

9 (When) [He had said these words unto them, He abode] still in Galilee.

[S. Said these words, He Himself abode.]
(Alf. And when—He remained.)

The time for Jesus to go up to Jerusalem was not come. It was usual for the people to assemble at Jerusalem a few days before the feast. But by delaying His journey a few days until the multitude had assembled, and by entering Jerusalem privately, unattended by the usual crowd of honest admirers, He would avoid the hatred of the Scribes and chief priests. By His constant exposure of their worldliness He had already incurred their bitterest hatred, and if no caution were used in administering fresh fuel to their hatred, they would anticipate the time appointed by the Father, and would put Him to Death before the salvation of man was perfected. His brethren had incurred no such hatred by their conduct, and there was therefore no risk in their going up to Jerusalem any time. Their time was alway ready.

It is not improbable that our Saviour's very words to His brethren were, as the Sinaitic MS. expresses it, "I go not up," but meaning, "not yet." The expression "not yet" might have given an oppor-

---

[1] I go not up yet (εγω ουπω, &c.) "Ουπω is a correction. If we read ουκ, we cannot remove an ethical difficulty, by introducing a literary one in its place."— Winer's *Grammar of New Testament*, 619.

tunity to His brethren to propose to wait for Him, until He did go up. The sense of the passage is, however, the same, whether the precise words were "not," or "not yet," (ὄυ, or ὄυπω.)

10 But when His brethren (were gone up, then went He also up unto the feast, not openly, but [as it were] in secret.)

[S. Omits, as it were.]

(Alf. Were gone up unto the feast, then went He also up, not openly, but as in secret.)

Jesus was now in Galilee, and it is not stated by what route He went up to Jerusalem, whether He kept on the west side of the Jordan and passed through Samaria, which was the more usual route; or whether He crossed to the east side, going through Peræa, the region on the farther side of the Jordan, and then recrossed the river not far from Jericho. The latter would be the more private.

11 (Then the Jews) sought Him at the feast, and said, Where is He?

(Alf. The Jews therefore.)

12 And there was much murmuring among (the people) concerning Him: for some said, He is a good man: others said, Nay: but He deceiveth (the people.)

(Alf. The multitudes—the multitude.)

13 Howbeit no man spake openly of Him for fear of the Jews.

On the first days of the feast they sought Jesus without success. By the very form of their question they expressed their scorn for Him, saying literally, Where is that? deceiver or impostor being, as their manner indicated, the word naturally required to complete the sense.

Here, as elsewhere, the people and the Jews are represented as taking opposite sides. The former implied the common people, the multitude, men who had witnessed His miracles, and who spake of Him as their conviction led them. The latter term referred to the rulers of the people, the chief priests, the scribes, and pharisees. When speaking of the enemies of Jesus St. John seldom distinguishes them by the name of chief priests, scribes, and pharisees, but seems to prefer to call them by the general expression "the Jews." Those among the multitude who thought Jesus a good man did not dare to speak openly of Him for fear of the Jews. Those who thought Him a deceiver were under no such fear; they spake openly enough.

14 (Now about the midst) of the feast Jesus went up into the temple, and taught.

(Alf. But when it was now the midst.)

These words do not necessarily imply that Jesus was absent from Jerusalem at the commencement of the feast, but that He did not appear in the Temple until the middle of the feast. We ought not rashly to conclude that He neglected anything that was appointed in the Law.

Either Jesus left Galilee after the departure of His brethren, and arrived at Jerusalem in the middle of the feast, and went to the Temple the same day, or He left Galilee so as to reach Jerusalem for the beginning of the feast, but did not go up to the Temple until the middle of it. The Feast of Tabernacles was not celebrated in the Temple, but in booths erected in the city of Jerusalem, or in the suburbs, and it lasted eight days. It was the custom, at the beginning of the feast, for each man to construct a booth and to dwell in it, during the time of the feast. Either Jesus may have done this for Himself, or He may have dwelt in the booth of some friend or disciple.

We have here in Jesus an example of prudence in avoiding danger and also of courage in meeting it. During the first half of the feast He shrinks from irritating the enraged Jews, during the last half He teaches boldly in the Temple.

He teaches with such power that He turns their hatred into wonder. Knowing, as many of them must have done, His bringing up, and that He had passed His days in the workshop of Joseph the carpenter, and not in the acquisition of knowledge, they naturally ask, How knoweth this Man letters, having never learned? This should have led on the scribes and chief priests to conclude that He must be supernaturally taught by God; that His teaching, which could not be the fruit of human learning, must be the display of divine knowledge.

15 [And the Jews] marvelled, saying, How knoweth this man letters, having never learned?[1]

[S. V. Therefore the Jews.]
(Margin, learning.)
(Alf. The Jews therefore.)

16 Jesus answered them, and said, (My doctrine) is not Mine, but His that sent Me.

[S. V. Therefore Jesus.]
(Alf. Jesus therefore—My teaching.)

---

[1] Having never learned (μὴ μεμαθηκώς). "Since He has not yet learned; since we know Him to be such a one as has never learned."—Winer's *Grammar of New Testament*, 505.

The doctrines which Jesus taught were not invented by Him, nor acquired by His labour and study, but they were the promptings of the Divine nature which He shared with the Father, and in which He was One with the Father, the Father who sent Him.

He gives them two tests by which they might prove whether the doctrines which He then taught them were the inventions of a mere man, which they supposed Him to be, or were the dictates of the Godhead. What He then taught them is in harmony with that which God the Father had formerly taught them under the law of Moses; those who formerly did God the Father's will, who were the most devout worshippers of God the Father under the law of Moses, are the very men who now most eagerly accept His doctrines. This is the first test.

It was not their understanding that was in fault, but their will, their heart. The reason why they did not believe in Him was not the hardness of His sayings or the strangeness of His doctrines, but because of their perverted will. Their understanding could easily have been convinced; but it was not so easy to persuade the heart. If any man did God the Father's will he would know whether the doctrines which Jesus taught, were invented by Himself or were commanded by God the Father. The disposition most favourable to belief in Jesus and the reception of His doctrines was a devout performance of God the Father's will under the former dispensation.

The next test is, that by the doctrines which He taught them, He was not seeking His Own glory, but the glory of Him who sent Him, the glory of God the Father.

17 If any man (will do) His will, he shall know (of the doctrine) whether it (be) of God, or whether I speak (of Myself.)

(Alf. Be willing to do—concerning the teaching—is—from Myself.)

18 He that speaketh (of Himself) seeketh his own glory: [but] He that seeketh His glory that sent Him, the same is true, and no unrighteousness is in Him.

[S. And.]
(Alf. From himself.)

Jesus then objects to them, that though they made a great boast of Moses and of the law of Moses, yet none of them kept the law. For if they kept the law of Moses they would not go about to kill Him, for the law forbade murder. The people, evidently ignorant of the design of their rulers, reply that they had no such intention, and that He, in saying so, spake like one possessed with a devil. For a devil only could have instigated Him to impute to them anything so false.

19 Did not Moses give you the law, and yet none of you keepeth the law? (Why go ye about) to kill Me?[1]

(Alf. Why seek ye?)

20 (The people) answered [and said,] Thou hast a devil: (who goeth about) to kill Thee?

[S. V. Omit, and said.]
(Alf. The multitude—who seeketh.)

Jesus replies that He had done one work, He had healed a man on the Sabbath Day, and that their surprise and indignation at such a breach of the Sabbath had led them on to seek His life. In order to lessen their indignation, He goes on to draw an argument in defence of His healing the man on the Sabbath from their own practice with regard to circumcision.

21 Jesus answered and said unto them, (I have done) one work, and ye all marvel.

(Alf. I did.)

22 (Moses [therefore] gave unto you circumcision): (not because it is of Moses, [but of the fathers];) and ye on the sabbath day circumcise a man.

[S. Omits, therefore: S. But because it is of the fathers.]
(Alf. For this cause hath Moses given you circumcision—not that it is of Moses.)

23 If a man on the sabbath day receive circumcision, (that the law of Moses (should not) be broken): are ye angry at Me, because (I have made a man every whit whole) on the sabbath day?

(Margin, without breaking the law.)
(Alf. May not—I made a man whole every whit.)

24 Judge not (according to the appearance), but judge righteous judgment.

(Alf. According to appearance.)

---

[1] Why go ye about to kill Me? (τί με ζητεῖτε ἀποκτεῖναι;) "In such passages as, John vii. 19, 20 'Why go ye about to kill Me?' 'Who goeth about to kill Thee?' Acts xxi. 31, 'As they went about to kill Him,' it can hardly occur to the English reader that nothing more is meant than 'seek to kill,' as the same phrase ζητεῖν ἀποκτεῖναι is translated elsewhere, and even in the very context of the first passage (John vii. 25). In Acts, xxiv. 5, 6, again the misunderstanding is rendered almost inevitable by the context, 'A mover of sedition among all the Jews throughout the world . . . . who also hath gone about to profane the Temple:' where the expression represents another verb similar to ζητεῖν in meaning, τὸ ἱερὸν ἐπείρασεν βαβηλῶσαι."—Dr. J. B. Lightfoot on *Revision of New Testament*, 178.

A child born on the Sabbath Day must, according to the command given unto the fathers, be circumcised on the eighth day after its birth, that is, on the following Sabbath. But if this is done the command which was given to Moses to do no work on the Sabbath Day is broken. It is in this case impossible to observe both these commands, one must give way to the other. If the observance of the law of the Sabbath has to give way to the observance of the law with respect to circumcision, surely the observance of the law with respect to the Sabbath should also give way to the observance of God's universal law of charity to the afflicted. If they on the Sabbath Day were allowed to perform an operation which required some labour and preparation, and which inflicted pain and suffering, surely He could be allowed to make a man every whit whole on the Sabbath Day, especially when that required no servile work, but was performed by His word only.

He concludes His argument by bidding them form their judgment of any work according to the goodness of it, and not according to the condition in life of the man who performs it.

25 Then said some of them of Jerusalem, Is not this He, whom they seek to kill.

26 But, lo, He speaketh boldly, and they say nothing unto Him. [Do the rulers know indeed that this is the very Christ?]

[S. Do the chief priests know ; S. V. is the Christ (omit, very.)]
(Alf. Have the rulers come to know indeed that This Man is the Christ?)

27 Howbeit we know This Man, whence He is: [but] when (Christ) cometh, no man knoweth whence He is.

[S. Omits, but.]
(Alf. The Christ.)

As being the chief city in Judæa, and as being the place in which God had chosen to place His name, and to have the Temple erected for His worship, Jesus frequently taught in Jerusalem and wrought many of His mighty works in its streets. Thus many of its inhabitants were convinced by what they heard and saw that He was the Christ, who dared not openly confess their belief in Him for fear of the rulers. Nicodemus was an instance of this in the higher ranks of society.

One great stumbling-block to many of the Jews, and which prevented their believing in Him was His supposed Birth in Galilee. This was the case with some of these inhabitants of Jerusalem. They seem to have held, what was a very common opinion among the unlearned, that when the Messiah should appear it would be in Bethlehem, that He would appear to them a full grown man, but as to the time of His birth, or who were His parents, none would know. The Jews in general thought the Messiah would be an extraordinary prophet raised up by God, but they had no expectation that He would be God Himself. Certain passages in the Scriptures which related to the divine nature of the Christ, but which they had understood of His human nature, had probably given rise to this misapprehension. Such, for instance, were Isaiah's words, "Who shall declare his generation?" (liii. 8); and Micah's words, "Whose goings forth have been of old, from everlasting." (v. 2.) The Jews in general thought that the Messiah would be a great prophet, an extraordinary deliverer raised up by God, but they had no expectation that He would be God Himself.

Because they knew, or thought they knew, whence Jesus was, that is, who His parents were, these inhabitants of Jerusalem concluded that He could not be the Christ whose parents would be unknown. In the most public place in Jerusalem, in the Temple, and with a loudness of voice to be heard by all who were present, Jesus exposes the fallacy of this argument.

28 Then cried Jesus [in the temple as He taught, saying], Ye both know Me, and ye know whence I am: and I am not come of Myself, but He that sent Me is true, whom ye know not.

(Alf. Teaching in the temple, and saying.)

29 But I know Him: (for) [I am from Him], and He (hath sent) Me.

[S. I am with Him.]
(Alf. Omits, But—because—sent.)

They said they knew Jesus, whence He was, that is, who His parents were. Even supposing they were correct as to the place of His Birth and the name of His parents, which they were not, they were having regard only to His human nature, and quite overlooked, or were ignorant of, His Divine nature. He was both God and Man. He was from the Father, One with the Father, and He was sent into the world, He was born of the Blessed Virgin Mary.

The miracles which induced the straightforward, honest multitude to conclude that Jesus must be the Christ had no such influence on the Pharisees and the chief priests. The people reason thus: It was not foretold that the Christ would perform more miracles than these which Jesus does; therefore Jesus must be the Christ. For instance, Isaiah prophesied that when the Christ should come, "Then the eyes of the blind shall be opened, and the ears of the deaf shall be unstopped. Then shall the lame man leap as an hart, and the tongue of the dumb sing: for in the wilderness shall waters break out, and streams in the desert." (xxxv. 5.) But all these miracles has Jesus wrought. He must therefore be the Christ here foretold. But the Pharisees and chief priests send officers to take Jesus, and probably on the plea of creating disturbances among the people. But they were powerless against Him until the hour appointed for His Death should have fully come.

30 (Then they sought) to take Him : (but) no man laid (hands) on him, because His hour was not yet come.

(Alf. Therefore sought they—and yet—his hand.)

31 (And many of the people) believed on Him, and said, When (Christ cometh), will He do more miracles[1] than these which This Man hath done ?[2]

[S. Than those which This Man doeth.]
(Alf. But many of the multitude—the Christ shall come.)

32 [The Pharisees] (heard that the people murmured such things) concerning Him : (and the Pharisees and the chief priests) sent officers to take Him.[3]

[S. Now the Pharisees.]
(Alf. Heard the multitude murmuring these things—and the chief priests and the Pharisees.)

Then in the hearing of the officers who were sent to apprehend Him, Jesus declares that at present they had no power to take Him, that He should remain with them a little longer, and that when His Death should come, it would not be against His will, but by a voluntary surrender of Himself He should "go" to the Father.

---

[1] See note to iv. 48.
[2] "**Will He do more miracles,** &c., (μὴ πλείονα σημεῖα ποιήσει:) μη (μητι) is used, when a negative answer is presumed or expected, 'Will He do more miracles than these ?' (that is not conceivable)."— Winer's *Grammar of New Testament,* 533.
[3] "**Officers.**—Ὑπηρέτης is a word drawn originally from military matters ; he is the rower (from ἐρέσσω, remigo) as distinguished from the soldier on board a war-galley ; then the performer of any strong and hard labour ; then the subordinate official that waits to accomplish the commands of his superior, as the orderly that attends a commander in war. (Xenophon, Cyr, vi. 2, 13.) In this sense, as a · minister to perform certain defined functions for Paul and Barnabas, Mark was their ὑπηρέτης (Acts xiii. 5: and in this official sense of lictor, apparitor, and the like, we find the word constantly, indeed prominently, used in the New Testament (Matt. v. 25 ; Luke iv. 20 ; John vii. 32 : xviii. 18 ; Acts v. 22). The mention of both δοῦλοι and ὑπηρέται together (John xviii. 18) would be alone sufficient to indicate that a difference is there observed between them ; and from this difference it would follow that he who struck the Lord on the face (John xviii. 22) could not be, as some have supposed, the same whose ear the Lord had but just healed (Luke xxii. 51), seeing that this last was a δοῦλος, that profane and petulant striker a ὑπηρέτης of the High Priest." —Archbishop Trench on *Synonyms of New Testament,* p. 32.

33 (Then said Jesus) [unto them], Yet a little while am I with you, (and then I go) unto Him that sent Me.

[S. V. Omit, unto them.]
(Alf. Jesus said therefore,—and I go.)

34 Ye shall seek Me and shall not find Me; and where I am (thither ye cannot come).
(Alf. Ye cannot come.)

Many interpretations have been given of these words, none of which seems entirely satisfactory. It may be that the stress is to be laid on the latter part of them, on the words "Ye shall not find Me." Jesus may have meant no more than that, if they should seek Him, they would not find Him, because He should no longer be with them in bodily presence, at least in the sense in which He had been present with them hitherto.

35 (Then said the Jews) [among themselves], Whither (will He go), that we shall not find Him?[1] Will He go unto the dispersed among (the Gentiles, and teach the Gentiles?)[2]

[S. Omits, Among themselves.]
(Alf. The Jews therefore said—will this Man go—the Greeks and teach the Greeks.)

---

[1] **We shall not find Him** (ποῦ οὗτος μέλλει πορεύεσθαι (λέγων), ὅτι ἡμεῖς οὐχ εὑρήσομεν αὐτόν.) The future indicative is quite according to rule; whether will He go, that (according to His statement, verse 34) we shall not find Him? In οὐχ εὑρήσομεν, the words uttered by Him (verse 34) are repeated in Tense and mood of the direct discourse.—Winer's *Grammar of New Testament*, 315.
We find in the New Testament several regularly framed verbal forms, which are rejected as unclassical by ancient grammarians, on the ground that they do not occur in Greek authors, or only in the later. Among such forms are classed a number of Futures Active, for which standard writers use Future Middle; instance, Future 'ῥεύσω, John vii. 38, for 'ῥεύσομαι.—*Idem*, p. 94 and 101.

[2] **The dispersed among the Gentiles** (ἡ διασπορὰ τῶν Ἑλλήνων). "The dispersion (the dispersed) among the Greeks."

"I confess Ἕλληνες in the Apostles' writings does very frequently denote the Gentiles; but here I would take Ἑλλήνων in its proper signification for the Greeks. It is doubtful indeed whether the διασπορὰ Ἑλλήνων ought to be understood the dispersed Greeks, or the Jews dispersed among the Greeks. There was no nation under heaven so dispersed and diffused throughout the world as these, both Greeks and Jews, were.

"Into what countries the Jews were scattered, the writings both sacred and profane do frequently instance. So that if the words are to be taken strictly of the Greeks, they bear this sense with them, Is He going here and there, amongst the Greeks, so widely and remotely dispersed in the world?

"If of the Jews (which is most generally accounted by expositors) then I would suppose the διασπορὰ Ἑλλήνων set in distinction to the διασπορὰ Βαβυλωνίων καὶ Περσῶν. That distinction between the Hebrews and the Hellenists explains the thing. The Jews of the first dispersion, viz., into Babylon, Assyria, and the countries adjacent, are called Hebrews,

36 (What manner of saying is this) that He said, Ye shall seek Me and shall not find Me; and where I am (thither ye cannot come.)

(Alf. What is this saying—Ye cannot come.)

The Jews did not understand the expression used by Jesus, "Him that sent Me," as referring to God the Father; and they ask among themselves whether Jesus will go and teach the Jews, who were scattered over the various countries belonging to the Gentiles. The Jews of Jerusalem seemed to have held their brethren who were dispersed among other nations, cheap, as being neither so highly favoured as themselves with respect to the privilege of worshipping in the Temple, and in the land of the patriarchs, and as liable to be infected with the heretical customs or opinions of the different countries in which they dwelt.

These words do not imply that the truth, that the doctrines of Jesus, should be preached to the Gentiles, was beginning to dawn on them.

The Feast of Tabernacles lasted eight days, and the last was the principal day of the feast. God had thus commanded Moses, "Seven days ye shall offer an offering made by fire unto the Lord; on the eighth day shall be a holy convocation unto you: and ye shall offer an offering made by fire unto the Lord: it is a solemn assembly; and ye shall do no servile work therein." (Levit. xxiii. 36.) On the last day of the feast, prior to the departure of the people to their respective homes in the different parts of Palestine, and elsewhere, Jesus makes one more appeal to them.

It has been generally held that in the following verses an allusion is made to the practice of carrying a pitcher of water in triumphant procession from the pool of Siloam to the Temple, accompanied with

---

because they used the Hebrew, or Trans-Euphratensian language. How they came to be dispersed into those countries we all know well enough, viz., that they were led away captive by the Babylonians and Persians. But those that were scattered amongst the Greeks used the Greek tongue, and were Hellenists. It is not easy to tell upon what account, or by what accident they came to be dispersed amongst the Greeks or other nations about. Those that lived in Palestine, they were Hebrews indeed as to their language, but they were not of the διασπορά, the dispersion, either to one place or another, because they dwelt in their own proper country. The Babylonish dispersion was esteemed by the Jews the more noble, the more famous, and the more holy of any other. The land of Babylon is in the same degree of purity with the land of Israel. (Rabbi Solom in Gittin, fol. 26, 1.) The Jewish offspring in Babylon is more valuable than that among the Greeks, even purer than that in Judæa itself. (Kidduth, fol. 69, 2.) Whence for a Palestine-Jew to go to the Babylonish dispersion was to go to a people and country equal, if not superior, to their own. But to go to the dispersion among the Greeks, was to go into unclean regions, where the very dust of the land defiled them: it was to go into an inferior race of Jews stained in their blood; it was to go into nations most heathenised."
—Lightfoot, ii. 558.

the blowing of trumpets and the singing of the Psalms of Hallel. (Ps. cxiii.-cxviii.) This ceremony was observed on the first seven days of feast, not on the eighth; but it was so prominent a feature in the feast that a reference to it would be sure to arrest the attention of the Jews at any time, and especially the very day after it had been observed for seven days.

37 (In the last day, that great day) of the feast, Jesus stood and cried, saying, If any man thirst [let him come unto Me and drink].[1]

[S. Let him come and drink.]
(Alf. Now in the last day, the great day.)

38 He that believeth (on Me), as the Scripture (hath said,) out of his belly shall flow rivers of living water.[2]

(Alf. In Me—saith.)

---

[1] In the last day, that great day of the feast.—"The Evangelist speaks according to a received opinion of that people; for from divine institution it does not appear that the last day of the feast had any greater mark set upon it than the first; nay, it might seem of lower consideration than all the rest. For on the first day were offered thirteen young bullocks upon the altar; on the second, twelve; and so fewer and fewer, till on the seventh day it came to seven, and on this eighth and last day of the feast there was but one only; as also for the whole seven days there were offered each day fourteen lambs, but on this eighth day seven only. (Numb. xxix.) So that if the number of the sacrifices add anything to the dignity of the day, this last day will seem the most inconsiderable, and not the μεγάλη, the great day of the feast. But what the Jews' opinion was about the matter, and this day, we may learn from themselves."

Lightfoot then quotes from several ancient Jewish authorities to show that they believed that the seventy bullocks, which were offered during the seven days of this feast, were offered in behalf of the nations of the world, and that the single bullock, which was offered on the eighth day, was offered for the Jewish nation, and concludes:

"Hence, therefore, this last day of the feast grew into such esteem in that nation above the other days: because on the other seven days they thought supplications and sacrifices were offered, not so much for themselves as for the nations of the world; but the solemnities of the eighth day were wholly on their own behalves. And hence the determination and finishing of the feast when the seven days were over, and the beginning, as it were, of a new one on the eighth day. For

"They did not reckon the eighth day as included within the feast, but a festival day separately and by itself.

"On this day they did not use their booths, nor their branches of palms, nor their pome-citrons; but they had their offering of water upon this day as well as the rest."—Lightfoot, ii. 559.

[2] Out of his belly shall flow rivers of living water.—"To this offering of water perhaps our Saviour's words may have some respect, for it was only at this feast it was used, and none other.

"They filled a golden phial containing three lags, out of Siloam, when they came to the water-gate [a gate of the Temple so called, as some would have it, because that water which was fetcht from Siloam was brought through it] they sounded their trumpets and sung. Then a priest went up by the ascent of the altar, and turning to the left, there were two silver vessels. . . . one with water, the other with wine; he poured some of the water into the wine, and some of the wine into the water, and so performed the service (Succah).

"Whosoever hath not seen the rejoic-

176 COMMENTARY ON ST. JOHN'S GOSPEL.

39 But this spake He of the Spirit, which they that believe (on Him) (should receive): for the [Holy Ghost was not yet given]: (because that) Jesus was not yet glorified.¹

[S. Omits, Holy. V. was not yet given.]
(Alf. In Him—were about to receive: for the Holy Spirit was not yet:—because.)

If any man has an insatiable longing for the salvation of his soul, a longing only to be described by the intense desire which a man has to supply the thirst of the body, let him go unto Jesus and drink, let him believe in Him and learn His doctrine, and he shall receive the life, the spirit which He has to impart.

No single place in Scripture can be pointed out in which are found the very words which Jesus here says the Scripture saith. There are many passages which contain a portion of these words, but none so

ing that was upon the drawing of this water, hath never seen any rejoicing at all."—(Succah, fol. 51, i.)
"I. They bring for it the authority of the Prophet Isaiah, xii. 3. Therefore with joy shall ye draw water out of the wells of salvation.
"This rejoicing they called the rejoicing of the Law, or for the Law: for by waters they often understand the Law, as Isaiah lv. 1, and several other places, and from thence the rejoicing for these waters.
"II. But they add, moreover, that this drawing and offering of water, signifies the pouring out of the Holy Spirit.
"Drawing of water, therefore, took its rise from the words of Isaiah, they rejoiced over the waters as a symbol and figure of the Law, and they lookt for the Holy Ghost upon this joy of theirs.
"And now let us reflect upon this passage of our Saviour, 'Whosoever believeth in Me, out of his belly shall flow rivers of living water.' They agree with what He had said before to the Samaritan woman, chap. iv. 14, and both expressions upon the occasion of drawing of water.
"I. Our Saviour calls them to a belief in Him from their own boast and glorying in the Law; and therefore I rather think those words καθὼς εἶπεν ἡ γραφὴ, as the Scripture hath said, should relate to the foregoing clause, whosoever believeth in Me, as the Scripture hath spoken about believing in Isaiah xxviii. 16; Habak. ii. 4; Amos v. 6.
"II. Let those words then of our Saviour's be set in opposition to this rite and usage in the Feast of Tabernacles, of which we

have been speaking. 'Have you such wonderful rejoicing at drawing a little water from Siloam? He that believes in Me, whole rivers of living waters shall flow out of his own belly.' Do you think that the waters mentioned in the prophets do signify the Law? They do indeed denote the Holy Spirit which the Messiah will dispense to those that believe in Him: and do you expect the Holy Spirit from the Law, and from your rejoicing in the Law? 'The Holy Spirit is of faith, and not of the Law.'" (Gal. iii. 2.)—Lightfoot, ii. 560.

¹ "For the Holy Ghost was not yet given (οὔπω γὰρ ἦν πνεῦμα Ἅγιον). In our English version διδόμενον is properly expressed, though not found in the original. And with this should be compared Acts xix. 2, which exactly answers to it in the Greek, though it is strangely translated in our Version, 'We have not so much as heard whether there be any Holy Ghost.' Ἀλλ' οὐδὲ εἰ πνεῦμα ἅγιον ἐστιν, ἠκούσα μεν."
—I.S. note to Bishop Middleton on Greek Article, 250.

"Proclivi Scriptioni præstat ardua: the more difficult the reading the more likely it is to be genuine. It would seem more probable that the copyist tried to explain an obscure passage, or to relieve a hard construction, than to make that perplexed which before was easy: thus in John vii. 39, Lachmann's addition of δεδομένον to οὔπω γὰρ ἦν πνεῦμα ἅγιον is very improbable, though countenanced by the Vatican MS., and of course by the versions."— Scrivener's Introduction to Criticism of New Testament, p. 372.

distinctly as to be identified as the passage to which He refers. It has therefore been supposed that Jesus did not refer to any particular words of Scripture, but to the sense. As His reference is a general one to "Scripture," and not any particular book of prophet, it will bear this meaning without the least straining of His words. The sense of our Saviour's words is contained in many passages. The following among many others bear some resemblance to His words: "When the poor and needy seek water, and there is none, and their tongue faileth for thirst, I the Lord will hear them, I the God of Israel will not forsake them. I will open rivers in high places, and fountains in the midst of the valleys; I will make the wilderness a pool of water, and the dry land springs of water." (Isa. xli. 17, 18.) "For I will pour water upon him that is thirsty, and floods upon the dry ground; I will pour out My spirit upon thy seed, and My blessing upon thine offspring." (xliv. 3.) " Ho, every one that thirsteth, come ye to the waters, and he that hath no money; come, ye, buy and eat ; yea, come, buy wine and milk without money and without price." (lv. 1.) " Then will I sprinkle clean water upon you, and ye shall be clean; from all your filthiness and from all your idols will I cleanse you. A new heart also will I give you, and a new spirit will I put within you; and I will take away the stony heart out of your flesh, and I will give you an heart of flesh. And I will put My spirit within you, and cause you to walk in My statutes, and ye shall keep My judgments and do them." (Ezek. xxxvi. 25-27.) " A fountain of gardens, a well of living waters, and streams from Lebanon." (Cant. iv. 15.)

The words of this verse have a far greater depth of meaning than at first meets the eye. Jesus is Himself the source, the spring, the fountain of the living water. The heart is to the soul, to the inner man, what the belly is to the body. From the heart of him that believeth in Jesus shall flow no scanty trickling drops, nor even a stream, but streams of living water, abundance and diversities of the gifts of the Spirit. (1 Cor. xii. 4.) The true believer in Jesus will be actuated by the influences of the Holy Spirit through his union with Jesus, the author, the source, and fount of life. His life will be a continual exhibition, a daily bringing forth of the fruits of Christian charity. But there must be the same longing, eager desire to gain this living water, these gifts of the Spirit, as there is to obtain water to allay the parching thirst of the body.

The Evangelist states a fact, and adds the reason for it. The Holy Ghost was not yet given—that is, was not given visibly and in the fulness in which it would be on the day of Pentecost, because Jesus was not yet glorified. The faithful under the old dispensation were partakers of the gifts of the Holy Spirit, but not in the same degree as they were who lived after Christ's Ascension into heaven. The outpouring of the Holy Spirit was thus made the reward of His Passion, the fruit of the travail of His soul. (Isa. liii. 11, 12.) "When He ascended up on high He led captivity captive, and gave gifts unto men." (Ephes. iv. 8.) By the outpouring of the Spirit on the day of Pentecost, when devout Jews from every nation under heaven were assembled at Jerusalem, the knowledge of the great mysteries of the Incarnation was dispersed throughout the world. The disciples of Jesus might not be in a state of mind before His ascension to receive such "gifts." Their views were too low and carnal, and they clung too much to His visible presence among them. But His crucifixion, His resurrection, His instruction during the forty days, and His ascension into heaven had prepared their hearts for the reception of the Holy Spirit in its fulness.

40 (Many of the people) therefore, when they heard [this saying,] said, Of a truth This is the Prophet.[1]

[S. Some of the people. S. These His sayings. V. These sayings.]
(Alf. Some of the multitude.)

41 Others said, This is the Christ. [But some said], Shall Christ come out of Galilee?[2]

[S. Others said.]

42 Hath not the Scripture said, That (Christ) cometh of the seed of David, (and out of the town of Bethlehem, where David was?)

(Alf. The Christ—and from Bethlehem, the town where David was.)

43 So there was a division among (the people) because of Him.

(Alf. The multitude.)

44 And some of them (would have taken Him): (but no man laid hands) on Him.

[S. Some of them said they should take Him.]
(Alf. Were minded to take Him—nevertheless no man laid his hands.)

---

[1] This is the Prophet (οὗτός ἐστιν ἀληθῶς ὁ προφήτης). "Connected with the title of the Messiah is that of the prophet, who occupied a large space in the Messianic horizon of the Jews—the prophet whom Moses had foretold, conceived by some to be the Messiah Himself, by others an attendant in his train. In one passage only (John vii. 40) is ὁ προφήτης so used, rightly given in our Version. In the rest (John i. 21, 25; vi. 14) its force is weakened by the exaggerated rendering *that* prophet."—Dr. J. B. Lightfoot on *Revision of New Testament*, 102.

[2] Shall Christ come out of Galilee? (μὴ γὰρ ἐκ τῆς Γαλιλαίας ὁ χριστὸς ἔρχεται).—"The essentially inferential force of γάρ (ἄρα) is in many passages perceptible: Do you then think that the Messiah is to come out of Galilee? You surely do not; num igitur putatis, Messian, &c. The peculiar force of such questions with γάρ consists in their being prompted by the very words of the other party, or by the circumstances; a right being thus conferred to demand an answer."—Winer's *Grammar of New Testament*, 467.

Jesus had wrought the very same works, and all the works, which the Prophets had foretold that the Christ when He came should work. He had opened the eyes of the blind, and the ears of the deaf. He had made the lame man to leap as a hart, and the tongue of the dumb to sing. (Isa. xxxv. 5.) The one and only point which appeared to oppose His claim to be Christ was that, as they thought, He was born in Galilee, and the Prophet Micah had declared that the Christ should be born in Bethlehem. (Micah v. 2.) Instead of examining into this apparent contradiction, and learning from Jesus Himself, they rest in ignorance of the real state of the case, and continued their opposition, the people actuated by indifference and their rulers by malice.

It was among the people that a division in favour of Jesus was made. Some accused Him as a deceiver, and others took up His defence. There was no division among the rulers. As a body they remained opposed to Him from first to last.

The officers, who were sent by the Pharisees to take Jesus, had probably been observing Him for some time, either watching for a convenient opportunity to seize Him, or because their intention to do so had been gradually weakened as they listened to His instruction. They are mentioned as sent to take Him (verse 32).

45 (Then came the officers) to the chief priests and Pharisees; [and they said] unto them, Why have ye not brought Him?[1]

[S. And they say.]
(Alf. The officers therefore came.)

46 [The officers] answered, [Never man spake like this Man.]

[S. But the officers: S. Never man spake thus as this Man speaketh: V. Never man spake thus.]

47 [Then answered them the Pharisees], Are ye also deceived?

[S. The Pharisees answered them.]

48 Have any of the rulers or of the Pharisees believed on Him?

[S. Doth any of the rulers or of the Pharisees believe on Him?]
(Alf. Hath any of the rulers believed in Him, or of the Pharisees?)

---

[1] They said unto them (εἶπον αὐτοῖς ἐκεῖνοι). "Ἐκεῖνοι relates to the members of the Sanhedrin (ἀρχιερεῖς καὶ Φαρισαῖοι), regarded, through the collective force of the Article, as *one* college. In such a combination, οὗτος refers to the more remote subject, and ἐκεῖνος to the nearest." Winer's *Grammar of New Testament*, 170.

49 But (this people) who knoweth not the law are cursed.[1]

(Alf. The multitude.)

Though the reason which these officers give is itself a confutation of their employers, that is, of those who sent them, they boldly state that the reason why they had not brought Jesus was, their admiration for Him. A conviction may also have been lurking in their minds that they had not the power to apprehend Him, that they were withheld from this by some invisible restraint stronger than the mere force of His gracious words.

Those who did not know the law believe in Him who gave the law, and those whose office it was to teach the law, did not believe in Him. When the Pharisees see that they have not convinced the officers either by any reason which their reply may contain, or by the contemptuous tone of it, they attempt to frighten them by quoting the curses of the law against those who continue not in its precepts. This, like many garbled quotations, misrepresents the sense. The words of Moses are, " Cursed be he that confirmeth not all the words of this law to do them " (Deut. xxvii. 26) ; or, " Cursed is every one that continueth not in all things which are written in the Book of the Law to do them." (Gal. iii. 10.) But the Pharisees imply that those who forsake the law of Moses in order to believe in Jesus are cursed.

50 [Nicodemus saith unto them, (he that came to (Jesus) by night), being one of them.]

[S. But Nicodemus said unto them, being one of them.]
(Margin. Him.)
(Alf. He that came to Him before.)

51 (Doth our law judge any man [before it hear him, and know] what he doeth ?)[2]

[S. Before it hear and know.]
(Alf. Doth our law judge a man, except it first hear from him, and learn what he doeth ?)

---

[1] This people who knoweth not the Law (ὁ ὄχλος οὗτος, ὁ μὴ γινώσκων τὸν νόμον). μὴ γινώσκων conveys a censure, ὁν γινώσκων would be a simple predicate: unacquainted with the Law."—Winer's *Grammar of New Testament*, 508.

[2] Before it hear him. (ἐὰν μὴ ἀκούσῃ), where ὁ νόμος personified as a judge, is to be repeated.—Winer's *Grammar of New Testament*, 545.

Nicodemus saith unto them, &c.— "The turn which Nicodemus gave to the debate appears to have been this: the Pharisees had made a [charge, but they had offered no evidence in support of it. Could the court proceed without proof? To arrest a man was to accuse him ; and what evidence of crime were the Sanhedrin in a position to lay before a Roman judge?

" Until evidence were laid before it, the Council could take no further steps ; and Jesus went on preaching and teaching ; vexing the Pharisaic mind by openly sitting down to meat with sinners, and by doing good deeds on the Sabbath. He taught His followers a new prayer, in

52 They answered and said unto him, Art Thou also of Galilee? Search (and look): for out of Galilee ariseth no prophet.[1]

(Alf. And see.)

These words appear to contain an unusual depth of scorn and contempt, and probably mean, Art thou of those Galilæans who believe in this Galilæan?

---

which they were to ask forgiveness of God only so far as they forgave their fellowmen. He stood on the Temple Court and told the people a story of a Good Samaritan. A *good* Samaritan! on the Sabbath next after that scene in which Nicodemus saved him from arrest by the Sanhedrin, He exasperated His accusers by curing the blind man."—Dixon's *Holy Land*, ii. 227.

[1] **Search and look** (ἐρεύνησον καὶ ἴδε). —" When two Imperatives are connected by καί, sometimes the first contains the condition (supposition) under which the action indicated by the second will take place, or the second expresses an inevitable result. The expression ἐρεύνησον καὶ ἴδε is more forcible than if it had been καὶ ὄψει. The result of the search is so certain, that the exhortation to search is felt as equivalent to an invitation to look at, behold, what is asserted."—Winer's *Grammar of New Testament*, 327.

" Galilæans.'—There never has been a time in which this beautiful province (Galilee) was not peopled by a mixture of races from the East and the West.

" At the time when our Lord was a child in Nazareth, one of its midland towns— lying on the slope of a hill about four miles from the capital, Sepphoris—Galilee was inhabited by a population of Greeks, Jews, Egyptians, Cypriotes, Italians, Arabs: men speaking separate idioms, following hostile fashions, and kneeling to rival gods.

" Thus the people of Galilee had become a mixed though not a blended community. Most of the reapers and sowers of grain were of Syrian stock: of the Canaanite rather than of the Arab branch. The vine-dressers and husbandmen were mostly Jews; but Jews who were considered by the men of Judah as provincials. Many of the artizans, most of the traders dwelling in towns, were descended from those princes of Tyre and Sidon, who had been driven by Alexander and Pompey from the sea. Other artizans and traders had come in the ranks of foreign armies from Antioch, Alexandria, and Rome. In cities which lay along the coast, like Ptolemais and Tyre, and in strong inland forts like Sepphoris and Gadara, lived the more supple and artistic Greeks, the workers in gold and marble, the rhetoricians and painters, the orators, dancers, amatory poets, the professors of every art, and as the Jews considered them, the propagators of every vice. From Italy, from Gaul and Spain, a more robust, and perhaps a more licentious rabble had been poured over the country to eat it up; legionaries, lawyers, gladiators, courtezans, charioteers, procurators and police. But the most picturesque figure in this picturesque group has still to be named. Through the midst of these peasants of the soil, these Jews of the hamlet, these Greek and Egyptian strangers of the city, roved the wild and pastoral tribes, the untamed children of Ishmael and Esau, men who still dwelt under their black tents, driving their flocks and herds from valley to valley, coming with the verdure, going with the dearth, and owning no allegiance to either Cæsar or to his tributary kings.

" The only tongue that could pretend to be a common vehicle for all these families was that of Greece. Every man of a higher grade than a hewer of wood and a drawer of water, every man who had to move about the province, who had to deal with the stranger, to appeal in a law court, to consult a physician, to discharge any public function, in fact, the merchant, citizen, priest, and courtier, was compelled to practise Greek. It was the only medium of the court, the college, and the camp. In the time when our Lord was a child at Nazareth, this noble language had that predominance in Galilee which English has acquired in Calcutta, French in Algiers, and Turkish in Stamboul."—Dixon's *Holy Land*, i. 187-195.

Nicodemus does not announce himself a believer in Jesus; but he lays down a general principle sanctioned by the law of Moses, and by the law of nature. His cautious answer may have been dictated by a constitutional timidity, or by a hope that if the Pharisees would only have the fairness to examine the doctrine and the claims of Jesus before they condemned Him they would not wish to condemn Him; that, like the officers who were sent to apprehend Him, they too would be filled with admiration for Him.

But the Pharisees, who are blinded by envy and spite, see not the want of truth, or the falsehood as well as the irrelevancy of their answer to Nicodemus. Many prophets had come out of Galilee. But if not, that was no reason why prophets should not still arise in Galilee. Deborah the Prophetess was from the country of Galilee. She dwelt between Ramah and Bethel in Mount Ephraim. (Judges iv.) Anna the Prophetess was from Galilee, of the tribe of Asher. (Luke ii. 36.) The prophet Jonah was of Gathhepher, a town of Lower Galilee in Zebulun. (2 Kings xiv. 25.) There is also a general consent among commentators that the Prophecies of Hoshea were delivered in the kingdom of Israel. It was also anciently believed that Hosea belonged to the tribe of Issachar, which would be included in the more modern district of Galilee. Nahum was born in Elkosh, a small village in Galilee; hence he was called Nahum the Elkoshite. (i. 1.) The Prophet Elijah the Tishbite was born, according to some, at Thisbe in the tribe of Naphtali, in Galilee; according to others in Gilead, on the east side of the Jordan. Elisha was born at Abel-Meholah, in the northern part of the valley of the Jordan. Though neither of these were strictly in the district called Galilee, they were neither of them in the country of Judæa, or in the kingdom of Judah, but both in the kingdom of Israel.

Nicodemus simply asks that they should hear Him before they condemn Him. The answer of the Pharisees shows that they had already condemned Him, and unheard. It was impossible, they said, that He could be the Christ, because the Christ should come from Bethlehem, in Judah, and Jesus was born in Galilee.

53 [And every man went unto his own house.]
[S. V. Omit, this verse.]

INTRODUCTORY NOTE TO CHAPTER VIII.

The Temple consisted of two parts, the first of which was called the Holy Place. In this were placed the golden altar of incense (Exod. xxx. 1-10), the seven-branched golden candlestick (Exod. xxv. 31-39), and the table of shittim wood overlaid with gold, on which the shew-bread was placed. Into this the priests alone entered and performed their priestly offices. Here every morning and evening they burnt incense to God upon the altar of incense. Their office was also to see that the seven lamps of the candlestick of pure gold were continually burning before the Lord. Every Sabbath Day they had to remove the twelve loaves of the shew-bread from off the table of shew-bread, and replace them with twelve new loaves.

The inner portion of the Temple was called the Holy of Holies. Into this the high priest alone entered, and that only once a year, on the day of atonement. Here was placed the Ark of the Covenant, an oblong chest of wood covered with gold, two golden figures of cherubims; the lid of the ark of pure gold, or "the mercy-seat," the two tables of stone, the Book of the Law, a pot of manna, and Aaron's rod that budded. (Heb. ix. 2-4.)

But Jesus, who was of the tribe of Judah, and not of the tribe of Levi, would enter into neither of these, neither the Holy Place nor the Holy of Holies. In addition to this there were courts around the Temple open to the air. The innermost of these was the Court of the Priests. Here they performed all public services of religion, and offered sacrifices on the altar of burnt offerings. The court adjoining to this was called the Court of the People. In this the people prayed and beheld the sacrifices that were offered by the priests. Here it was that Jesus so often taught the people. Around this Court were porches or corridors, cloisters or arcades, covered above, under which they could retire when the weather did not permit them to walk in the open air. Here Jesus was walking when the Jews came round about Him, not in the Temple proper, nor in the Court of the Temple, but in the porch, the covered portion that went round the Court.

"We have in our Version only the one word 'Temple,' with which we render both ἱερόν and ναός; nor is it very easy to see in what manner we could have indicated the distinction between them, which is yet a very real one, and one the marking of which would often add much to the clearness and precision of the sacred narrative. Ἱερόν (=templum) is the whole compass of the sacred inclosure, the τέμενος, including the outer courts, the porches, porticoes, and other buildings subordinated to the Temple itself. But ναός (=ædes), from ναίω, habito, as the proper *habitation* of God (Acts vii. 48; xvii. 24; 1 Cor. vi. 19): the οἶκος τοῦ θεοῦ (Matt. xii. 4; cf. Exod. xxiii. 19) is the Temple itself, that by especial right so called, being the heart and centre of the whole; the Holy, and the Holy of Holies, called often ἁγίασμα. (1 Macc. i. 37; iii. 45.) This distinction, one that existed and was acknowledged in profane Greek, and with reference to heathen temples, quite as much as in sacred Greek, and with relation to the Temple of the true God (see Herodotus i. 181-3; Thucydides v. 18; Acts xix. 24-27) is, I believe, always assumed in all passages relating to the Temple at Jerusalem, alike by Josephus, by Philo, by the Septuagint translators, and in the New Testament. . . . .

"The distinction may be brought to bear with advantage on several passages in the New Testament. When Zacharias entered into 'the *Temple* of the Lord' to burn incense, the people who waited his return, and who are described as standing 'without' (Luke i. 10) were in one sense in the Temple too—that is, in the ἱερόν, while he alone entered into the ναός, the 'Temple' in its more limited and auguster sense. We read continually of Christ teaching 'in the Temple' (Matt. xxvi. 55; Luke xxi. 37; John viii. 20), and perhaps are at a loss to understand how this could have been so, or how long conversations could there have been maintained, without interrupting the service of God. But this is ever the ἱερόν, the porches and porticoes of which were eminently adapted to such purposes, as they were intended for them. Into the ναός the Lord never entered during His earthly course; nor, indeed, being made under the law, could He do so, that being reserved for the priests alone. It need hardly be said that the money-changers, the buyers and sellers, with the sheep and oxen, whom the Lord drives out, He repels from the ἱερόν, and not from the ναός. Irreverent as was their intrusion, they yet had not dared to establish themselves in the Temple properly so called. (Matt. xxi. 12; John ii. 14.) On the other hand, when we read of another Zacharias slain 'between the Temple and the altar' (Matt. xxiii. 35) we have only to remember that 'Temple' is ναός here, at once to get rid of a difficulty, which may perhaps have presented itself to many—this, namely, Was not the altar *in* the Temple? How, then, could any locality be described as *between* these two? In the ἱερόν, doubtless was the brazen altar to which allusion is here made, but not in the ναός, '*in the court* of the House of the Lord (cf. Josephus *Antiq.* viii. 4, 1), where the sacred historian (2 Chron. xxiv. 21) lays the scene of this murder, but not in the House of the Lord, or ναός itself. Again, how vividly does it set forth to us the despair and defiance of Judas, that he presses even into the ναός itself (Matt. xxvii. 5), into the 'adytum' which was set apart for the priests alone, and there casts down before them the accursed price of blood. Those expositors who affirm that here ναός stands for ἱερόν should adduce some other passage in which the one is put for the other."—Archbishop Trench on *Synonyms of New Testament*, p. 10.

(186)

CHAPTER VIII.

1 *Christ delivereth the woman taken in adultery;* 12 *He preacheth Himself the Light of the world, and justifieth His doctrine;* 33 *Answereth the Jews that boasted of Abraham;* 59 *And conveyeth Himself from their cruelty.*

ON the last day of the Feast of Tabernacles Jesus had been teaching the people in the Temple. At the end of the last chapter it is said, "And every man went unto his own house," and in the beginning of this it is said, "Jesus went unto the Mount of Olives." The probability is that, from fear of the Pharisees, none of the Jews dared to invite Him to their house, and that He retired to the Mount of Olives, where, as on other occasions, He spent the night in prayer. Bethany, where Lazarus and his sisters Mary and Martha dwelt, was "at the Mount of Olives" (Mark xi. 1), and unless they supplied Him with food, or unless His disciples had procured it in the city, He would be fasting.

The first eleven verses of this chapter are omitted in the Sinaitic and Vatican MSS. They were also omitted in the copies of St. John which St. Cyril and St. Chrysostom and other Greek commentators read. They are contained in the Vulgate, which received the sanction of the Council of Trent.

The omission of the whole paragraph respecting the woman taken in adultery in early copies of St. John's Gospel is not a discovery of modern scholars. It was known, and discussed, and accounted for, in very early times. St. Augustine thinks it was omitted from some of the Greek and Latin copies of St. John, lest our Saviour's meaning should be perverted, and it should be thought that He dealt leniently with adultery as being a human frailty. (Aug. de Conjug. Adult., i. 10; vi. 458, Migne.)

1 Jesus went unto the Mount of Olives.[1]

[S. V. Omit all these verses (1-11)].

---

[1] " **Pericope Adulteræ.**—On no other grounds than those just intimated (see note to i. 43) can this celebrated and important paragraph, the pericope adulterœ as it is called, be regarded as a portion of St. John's Gospel. It is absent from too many excellent copies not to have been wanting in some of the very earliest: while the arguments in its favour, internal even more than external, are so powerful, that we can scarcely be brought to think it an unauthorised appendage to the writings of one who in another of his inspired books deprecated so solemnly the adding to or taking away from the blessed testimony he was commissioned to bear. (Apoc. xxii. 18, 19.) If chap. xx. 30, 31 show signs of having

COMMENTARY ON ST. JOHN'S GOSPEL. 187

2 And early in the morning He came again into the Temple, and all the people came unto Him; and He sat down and taught them.

3 And the Scribes and Pharisees brought unto Him a woman taken in adultery; and when they had set her in the midst,

4 They say unto Him, Master, this woman was taken in adultery, in the very act.

5 Now, Moses, in the law commanded us that such should be stoned, but, what sayest Thou?[1]

6 This they said, tempting Him, that they might have

---

been the original end of this Gospel, and ch. xxi. be a later supplement by the Apostle's own hand, which I think with Dean Alford is evidently the case, why should not St. John have inserted in this second edition both the amplification in chap. v. 4, and this most edifying and eminently Christian narrative? The appended chapter (xxi.) would thus be added at once to all copies of the Gospels then in circulation, though a portion of them might well overlook the minuter change in chap. v. 4; or from obvious though mistaken motives, might hesitate to receive for general use or public reading the history of the woman taken in adultery."—Scrivener's *Introd. to Criticism of New Testament*, p. 439.

"The passages (in the English Authorised Version) which touch Christian sentiment or history or morals, and which are affected by textual differences, though less rare than the former (instances in which doctrine is directly or indirectly involved) are still very few. Of these the pericope of the woman taken in adultery holds the first place in importance. In this case a deference to the most ancient authorities, as well as a consideration of internal evidence, might seem to involve immediate loss. The best solution would probably be to place the passage in brackets, for the purpose of showing, not indeed that it contains an untrue narrative (for, whencesoever it comes, it seems to bear on its face the highest credentials of authentic history), but that evidence external and internal is against its being regarded as an integral portion of the original Gospel of St. John. The close

of St. Mark's Gospel should possibly be treated in the same way. If I might venture a conjecture, I should say that both the one and the other were due to that knot of early disciples who gathered about St. John in Asia Minor, and must have preserved more than one true tradition of the Lord's life and of the earliest days of the Church, of which some at least had themselves been eye-witnesses."
—Dr. J. B. Lightfoot on *Revision of New Testament*, p. 27.

"I am convinced that the first occasion of the omission of these memorable verses was the lectionary practice of the primitive Church, which, on Whitsunday, read from St. John vii. 37 to viii. 12, *leaving out the twelve verses* in question. Those verses, from the nature of their contents (as Augustine declares) easily came to be viewed with dislike or suspicion. The passage, however, is as old as the second century, for it is found in certain copies of the old Latin. Moreover, Jerome deliberately gave it a place in the Vulgate."
—Burgon on *The Last Verses of St. Mark's Gospel*, p. 219.

[1] *That such should be stoned.*—"The censuring and judging of this woman belonged to a judicial bench at the least of twenty-three judges, and it would have carried a fair accusation against Him had He gone about to judge in such a matter. The woman was espoused and not yet married, as see Deut. xxii. 24, for their judicials punished him that lay with an espoused maid with stoning (Sanhedr. per 7. Nalac. 4), but him that lay with a married wife with strangling (Ibid. per ii. Nalac 1.)"—Lightfoot, 1. 244.

to accuse Him. But Jesus stooped down, and with His finger wrote on the ground, as though He heard them not.
7 So when they continued asking Him, He lifted up Himself, and said unto them, He that is without sin among you, let him first cast a stone at her.¹
8 And again He stooped down and wrote on the ground.²

---

¹ Let him first cast a stone at her (πρῶτος τὸν λίθον ἐπ' αὐτῇ βαλέτω.)—"I regard it as a circumstance rather in favour of the authenticity of these verses that λίθον has the Article prefixed. The allusion is to the particular manner of stoning, which required that one of the witnesses (for two at the least were necessary, see Deut. xvii. 6) should throw the stone, which was to serve as a signal to the bystanders to complete the punishment. There is, therefore, strict propriety in calling this stone τὸν λίθον, in order to distinguish it from other stones. But would an interpolater have been thus exact in his phraseology? or would he have adverted to this apparently trifling circumstance? Probably he would not, especially since the expression of βάλλειν τὸν λίθον is not elsewhere found in the New Testament."—Bp. Middleton on *The Greek Article*, 251.

² But Jesus stooped down, &c.—The following, though long, is a good explanation of the several actions of our Saviour in this matter:—"I. The matter in hand was judging a woman taken in adultery, and therefore our Saviour in this matter applies Himself conformably to the rule made and provided for the trial of an adulteress by the bitter water.—(Num. v.)

"II. Among the Jews this obtained; in the trial of a wife suspected. If any man shall unlawfully lie with another woman the bitter water shall not try his wife. . . . For it is said, if the husband be guiltless from iniquity, then shall the woman bear her iniquity."—Maimon. in *Sotah*, c. 2.

"When the woman hath drunk the bitter water, if she be guilty, her looks turn pale, her eyes swell, &c. . . . same hour that she dies the adulterer also, upon whose account she drank the water, dies too, wherever he is. But this is done only upon condition that the husband has been guiltless himself. For if he have lien with any unlawfully himself then this matter will not try his wife."—*Ibid*, c. 3.

"You may see by these passages how directly our Saviour levels at the equity of this sentence, willing to bring these accusers of the woman to a just trial first. You may imagine you hear Him thus speaking to them, 'Ye have brought this adulterous woman to be adjudged by Me, I will therefore govern Myself according to the rule of trying such by the bitter waters: You say, and you believe according to the common opinion of your nation, that the woman upon whom a jealousy is brought, though she be indeed guilty, yet if the husband that accuseth her be faulty that way himself she cannot be affected by those waters, nor contract any hurt or danger by them. If the divine judgment proceeded in that method, so will I at this time. Are you that accuse this woman wholly guiltless in the like kind of sin? Whosoever is so, let him cast the first stone, &c. But if you yourselves stand chargeable with the same crimes, then your own applauded tradition, the common opinion of your nation, the procedure of divine judgment in the trial of such, may determine in this case, and acquit Me from all blame if I condemn not this woman when her accusers themselves are to be condemned.'

"III. It was the office of the priest when he tried a suspected wife to stoop down and gather the dust off the floor of the sanctuary, which when he had infused into the water, he was to give the woman to drink: he was to write also in a book the curses or adjurations that were to be pronounced upon her. (Numb. v. 17, 23.) In like manner our Saviour stoops down, and making the floor itself His book, He writes something in the dust, doubtless against these accusers, whom He was resolved to try, in analogy to those curses

9 And they which heard it, being convicted by their own conscience, went out one by one, beginning at the eldest, even unto the last. And Jesus was left alone, and the woman standing in the midst.
10 When Jesus had lifted up Himself, and saw none but the woman, He said unto her, Woman, where are those thine accusers? hath no man condemned thee?
11 She said, No man, Lord. And Jesus said unto her, (Neither do I condemn thee: go, and sin no more.)

(Alf. Neither do I condemn thee: go, henceforth sin no more.)

The Scribes and Pharisees intend to found an accusation against Jesus, however He may decide the case. If He should acquit the woman, they would charge Him with giving sentence contrary to the law of Moses. If He should command her to be stoned, they would accuse Him to the people as a severe, merciless interpreter of the law, and as acting contrary to that spirit of mercy and forgiveness, which He had so often inculcated on them. But they were rather expecting from His accustomed gentleness that He would acquit the woman.

Jesus made no claim to be a judge at all, especially of crimes, of breaches of the law, civil or ceremonial, of the sins which one man commits against another. He came to be the Physician, the Saviour of the world. He who was the judge of the secret thoughts of the heart knew the difference which existed between the Scribes and Pharisees and the woman whom they accused. The chief difference between them was, that the one was detected and the other not. They had committed sins similar, or as great, or greater, but they were known only to God; her sin was known to man likewise.

Different conjectures have been made as to the words which He wrote on the ground, which, of course, can be nothing beyond conjecture. The purport of it doubtless was, to lead the Scribes on to

---

and adjurations written in a book by the priest against the woman that was to be tried.

"IV. The priest, after he had writ these curses in a book, blots them out with the bitter water. (Numb. v. 23.) For the matter transacted was doubtful. *They do not make the suspected wife drink, unless in a doubtful case.*" (*Bemidhar Rabba*, fol. 233, 2.)

"The question is, whether the woman was guilty or not. If guilty, behold the curses writ against her, if not guilty, then behold they are blotted out. But Christ was assured that those whom He was trying were not innocent, so he does not write and blot out, but writes and writes again.

"V. He imitates the gesture of the priest, if it be true what the Jews report concerning it, and it is not unlikely, viz., that he first pronounced the curses, then made the woman drink, and after she had drunk pronounced the same curses again. So Christ, first He stoops down and writes, then makes them, as it were, drink, in that searching reflection of His, Whosoever of you is without sin, and then stoops down again, and writes upon the earth." —Lightfoot, ii. 568.

discover for themselves their own misdeeds. They press Him to give a definite answer to their question, and they feel more sure, from His hesitation and delay, that He is in a strait, and that they shall catch Him.

He appeals to them as men, whose conscience, if they would listen to it, would bear witness that they had committed sins as great as this woman, and thus He would urge them to pass the same judgment on her which they pass on themselves.

In bidding the man who was without sin among them to cast the first stone at this adulteress, or, rather, as our Saviour's words mean, who was without this particular sin of adultery, He did not strike at the root of all civil judicature. Judges must pass sentence on the guilty, whether they are conscious that they themselves have been guilty of the same crimes or not. But these men were probably not the authorised judges, or if they were, they were judging the case in an informal way. They profess to accuse this woman, out of the abundance of their zeal for God's laws. But the words of Him, who will one day be the righteous judge of all mankind, teach them that if they are so anxious to eradicate all sin against God, they must begin with themselves.

Jesus again stoops down, in order to give the Scribes and Pharisees an opportunity to depart without any interruption. Conscious that they had committed sin as great, nay, even the very same sin as the woman, whom they, in their pretended zeal for God, had denounced, they go out one by one, the older first, probably as burdened with a greater load of sin. Silently but effectually conscience, quickened by the divine power of Jesus, works its work in them. They might even have some fear that He who, as they saw, could read the thoughts of their hearts, could also lay their secret sins open to the public gaze. With shame and confusion they one by one draw off and retire, and thus confess their guilt before the whole crowd. This transaction is little less than a miracle.

Jesus was left alone, and the woman standing in the midst. Jesus was left alone with His disciples and the multitude, and the woman standing in the midst of them. The term alone would seem to exclude only the Scribes and Pharisees who had brought the woman to Jesus.

He, the only one who was without sin, does not condemn her. He came to seek and to save, and not to condemn. We know not what signs of repentance He, the Judge of the secrets of men's hearts, could see in her. He bids her "Go, and sin no more." By these words He probably means the same as when He utters the fuller and more usual formula, "Go in peace." Thus, as God He forgives her sins, and points out to her the life which she must henceforth lead. He did not absolve her from the legal punishment of her sin; neither did He condemn her. He left that to the Scribes and Pharisees. But He absolved her from guilt in the eyes of God.

It may be that the expression, "Then spake Jesus again," implies some connection with His dismissal of the woman taken in adultery, and that it may connect them somewhat in this way : " Do not wonder that I have delivered this woman from the darkness of sin, in which she was living, for I am the Light of the World; I am God." Others, and perhaps more correctly, connect these words with the second verse. Early in the morning Jesus had gone again into the Temple, and all the people came unto Him; and He sat down and taught them. The Scribes and Pharisees interrupt His instruction by bringing to Him the woman taken in adultery. After the Scribes and Pharisees had gone out of themselves, and Jesus had dismissed the woman, He turns again to the people and resumes His teaching, which they had broken off.

12 (Then spake Jesus) again unto them, saying, I am the Light of the world: he that followeth Me (shall not walk in darkness), [but shall have] the light of life.[1]

[S. But he hath.]
(Alf. Jesus therefore spake—shall in nowise walk in the darkness.)

It was early morning (v. 2) when Jesus spake these words, and this may have suggested to Him the form in which to throw the instruction which He now gives to the people. He may have drawn His subject from the rising of the sun, that most glorious of all the works of creation. From the sun in creation to Himself, the Light of the world, the transition was natural and striking. Or it may be, as some think, that when He said, " I am the Light of the world," He alluded to one of the well-known ceremonies in the Feast of Tabernacles, which had just been concluded. In the evening of the seven days of the feast both men and women assembled in the Court of the Women, expressly to hold a rejoicing for the drawing of the water of Siloam. At the same time there was set up in the Court two lofty stands, each supporting four great lamps. These were lighted on each night of the festival, and the light of these illuminated the whole of Jerusalem. Many think that Jesus took occasion from this to speak of Himself as the Light of the World.

Jesus was the Word made Flesh, God born into the world to lighten the Gentiles and to be the glory of His people Israel. (Luke ii. 32.) The Prophets had all a limited sphere, their business was to instruct God's ancient people, either in the kingdom of Judah or Israel. The Christ came to be the Saviour, not of any particular nation, but of the world. In using this term, " the world,"

---

[1] **I am the Light of the world.—** " Has with great probability been referred to the lighting up the colossal candlestick in the Feast of Tabernacles: the more remarkable in the profound darkness which, then as now, reigned through the night of an Oriental town."—Stanley's *Sinai and Palestine*, 428.

Jesus had doubtless a reference to the reception of the Gospel by the Gentiles.

He who followeth Jesus shall not walk in darkness. As the Lord went before His people Israel by night in a pillar of fire to give them light (Exod. xiii. 21), so Jesus offers Himself as a Light and a Guide to all who will follow Him. Those who believe in Him shall not lead a life of sin and of blind speculation about the present and the future; they shall lead a life of holiness, of active goodness here, and of rest in the revelation which He has made of the life everlasting hereafter. Nay, this life everlasting shall begin here, for the life of glory will not be a new life, but a continuation, a development, and a more perfect condition of the present life. Through union with Jesus, the life-giving Light, we receive light, and we receive it here; but it will be expanded and perfected into a more glorious state at the resurrection.

The Pharisees object to Him, Jesus, that He bears witness of Himself, and that therefore His witness is not "true," in the sense of not trustworthy, not admissible in evidence. These are probably not the same individuals, who only a short time before had left the Temple convicted by their own conscience and by His appeal to it. There might be other Pharisees in the crowd, equally anxious to show their opposition to Him at any fitting opportunity.

13 The Pharisees therefore said unto Him, (Thou bearest record of Thyself: Thy record) is not true.

(Alf. Thou art bearing witness concerning Thyself: Thy witness)

14 [Jesus answered and said unto them] (though I bear record of Myself, yet My record is true: for) I know whence I came, and whither I go: [but] ye (cannot tell) [whence I come, (and) whither] I go.

[S. Jesus said unto them: S. omits, but: V. whence I come or whither]
(Alf. Though I bear witness concerning Myself, My witness is true: because—know not—or)

Jesus replies that His testimony is true, true in itself, and admissible in evidence. He is the Light of the world, and a light does not require any one to bear witness of its presence. As a light bears testimony to itself by its own brightness, so does the Light of the world by His own works.

But still He says that His own testimony is confirmed by that of the Father. "I know whence I came and whither I go," Who sent Me and on what mission, and My work on earth being finished I shall return to the Father that sent Me. Jesus was God of God, very God of very God. Such is the union between the Father and the Son, that He does not leave the Father in coming to us, and He did not desert us in returning to the Father. Jesus does not say, in a direct naked form, that He is God, or the Son of God, probably not to raise the angry opposition of the Jews to anything further which He had to say. He clothes His meaning in such words, that it is only gradually unfolded to them, and in proportion to their docility and anxiety to hear the truth. Their power to understand His meaning depends very much on their readiness to receive it, that is, on the state of their own hearts. It is the same sun, which shines on the face, of the man who has eyes to see, and of the man who is blind, but very different is the effect which it has on them. So too the effect, which the instruction and the works of Jesus, the Light of the world, have on His hearers, depends on their power to receive it. He reminds them how radically wrong their judgment concerning Him is. They judge Him after the flesh, that is, after the senses of the flesh. They see Him in appearance a man, they hear the rumour that He is the son of Joseph the carpenter, and they consider not how His teaching and His miracles prove Him to be more than a man, nay how they substantiate His claim to be God, the express object for which He wrought them.

15 Ye judge after the flesh : I judge no man.[1]

16 (And yet if I judge,) My judgment is true: (for) I am not alone, [but I and the Father that sent Me.]

[S. But I and He who sent Me.]
(Alf. Yea and if I should judge—because.)

17 (It is also written) in your law, that the testimony of two men is true.

(Alf. Moreover it is written).

18 (I am one that bear witness of Myself,) and the Father that sent Me beareth witness of Me.

(Alf. I am He that beareth witness concerning Myself.)

19 (Then said they) unto Him, Where is Thy Father ? [Jesus answered,] (Ye neither know Me nor) My Father :

---

[1] Ye judge after the flesh I judge no man (ὑμεῖς κατὰ τὴν σάρκα κρίνετε, ἐγὼ οὐ κρίνω οὐδένα.)—" The second clause is completed by οὐδένα, and nothing whatever requires to be supplied: Ye judge according to the flesh, but I judge no one," (not merely no one according to the flesh, but no one in any manner whatever.) The supplying of κατὰ τὴν σάρκα, from the foregoing clause, could only be justified by incongruity in the sense without such addition. With Olshausen and Lücke, I am unable to perceive that the words in the text are not entirely sufficient."— Winer's *Grammar of New Testament*, 606.

if ye had known Me, (ye should have known) [My Father also.]

[S. Jesus answered and said: S. The Father also.]
(Alf. They said therefore—Ye know neither Me, nor—ye would know.)

At verse 18 the question of testimony, its legality or admissibility in evidence, is raised, and it is not concluded until verse 19. When then Jesus says, "I judge no man," it is not easy to see the connection of His words with the context, if we interpret them in the sense of passing sentence. To give testimony, and to weigh the value of testimony, which is the office of the judge, are kindred actions. It has therefore been thought that by these words He meant to imply that in no man's case did He decide on the testimony offered, nor did He himself offer testimony, but that, if He did offer testimony, it would be admissible in proof, because it would be confirmed by the Father.

The law said, "one witness shall not rise up against a man for any iniquity, or for any sin, in any sin that he sinneth: at the mouth of two witnesses, or at the mouth of three witnesses, shall the matter be established." (Deut. xix. 15.) Thus according to the law the testimony of two men is sufficient for proof. In the case of Jesus there is the testimony of two, who are not men, but who are infinitely more than men, who are God. There is the testimony of God the Father, and the testimony of God the Son, both bearing witness, that Jesus the son of Mary is the Christ, the Word made Flesh. Christ was one Person, but in him were two natures, the Godhead and Manhood. Christ as He is God, bears witness of Himself as He is Man.

The Pharisees ask Jesus where His Father is? not in sincerity and with a desire to learn, but to lead Him on to commit Himself—that they may have, as they think, grounds to accuse Him of blasphemy. He does not answer, as they hoped, so as to give them occasion to take hold of His words. But He replies that they know neither Him nor His Father. They did not know Him, because they believed Him to be a mere man, while He was God. They did not know His Father, because they believed Joseph to be His father, but Joseph was not even the father of His Human nature. They did not know God, who was His Father, otherwise they would serve Him.

20 These words [(spake Jesus)] in the treasury, [(as He taught) in the temple]: and no man laid hands on Him: (for) His hour was not yet come.

[S. V. Spake He in the: S. omits, as He taught in the temple.]
(Alf. Spake He—as He was teaching—because.)

The treasury was the place, in which was kept the chest which contained the offerings of the people for the payment of the sacrifices, for the repair of the fabric, and the relief of the poor. This was the most public part of the Temple. (2 Kings xii. 9; 2 Chron. xxiv. 8.) In these words it is intimated that the Jews had every opportunity of taking Jesus, for He did not teach in secret, but in the most public part of the most public place in Jerusalem, in the treasury of the Temple. The reason why they did not lay hands on Him is also given. They were supernaturally withheld by an invisible influence on them, because the time appointed for His Death was not yet come.

21 [(Then said Jesus again) unto them,] (I go My way), and ye shall seek Me, and shall die in your (sins): whither I go, ye cannot come.

[S. Then said He unto them.]
(Alf. Therefore said He again—I go away—sin.)

22 (Then said the Jews,) Will He kill Himself? Because He saith, Whither I go, ye cannot come.
(Alf. The Jews therefore said.)

The particle "then" or "therefore" (in v. 21) may be merely the introductory word to a new portion of His teaching; or it may be meant to join this on to the preceding, and to indicate that this was said at the same time and place as the last: or it may connect this with the last sentence, "No man laid hands on Him, because His hour was not yet come." Jesus saw that the Pharisees were burning with a desire to take Him, but were withheld by a secret power, therefore He said unto them, "I go my way," &c.

He had already said the same words to the officers, who were sent by the Pharisees to take Him (vii. 33); and He now repeats them to the Pharisees themselves. He uses the expression "I go My way," because His Death will be voluntary, and a continued proceeding. He will not remain in a state of Death, but through Death He will go to the Father. They will die in a condition of sin, in consequence of their unbelief in Jesus, the only One who could have delivered them from this. He will go to a state of eternal happiness, they to one of eternal punishment. The Pharisees cannot go to the former, because they have not now the will or the affections for such a state.

When Jesus had said these same words, "Ye shall not find Me," to the officers who were sent by the Pharisees to take Him, they said, "Whither will He go that we shall not find Him? will He go unto the dispersed among the Gentiles, and teach the Gentiles? But the Pharisees are so blinded by anger and hatred, and are so intent on His Death, that in their eyes the only alternative to their not finding Him and killing Him is His killing Himself." They do not see that death, whether brought on by them or by Himself, cannot be the place He meant, because they will also die. He is referring to their place or condition after death: He in heaven with the Father, they in hell with the devil.

23 And He said unto them, Ye are from beneath: I am from above: ye are of this world: I am not of this world.

[S. He said therefore.]

24 I said [therefore] unto you, that ye shall die in your sins: for [if ye believe not that] I am He, ye shall die in your sins.

[S. Omits, therefore: S. If ye believe Me not that.]

He states the reason why they cannot go to the place where He is. He says their origin is different and their nature is different, and their final abode will be different. They are from beneath, of this world. The origin of the Pharisees is earthly, and their nature is gross and earthly, and they shall return to a place suitable for such earthly natures. He is from above, from the Father, and will return thither. Not only is their origin earthly, but their natures, their tastes and habits and aims are earthly, bounded by the enjoyments and pleasures of the body, and of the present world. None but He could deliver them from their sins and sinful nature; but, if they refuse to believe in Him, they will die in their sins.

25 [Then said they] unto Him, Who art thou? [And Jesus saith unto them], (Even the same that I said unto you from the beginning.)[1]

[S. They said: S. Then Jesus said unto them.]
(Alf. Therefore said they—in very deed that same which I also speak unto you.)

26 I have many things to say and judge of you: [(but) He that sent Me] is true: (and I speak to the world those things which I have [heard of Him.])

[S. But the Father that sent Me: S. Heard with Him.]
(Alf. Howbeit—and the things which I heard from Him, these speak I unto the world.)

---

[1] That I said unto you from the beginning (τὴν ἀρχὴν ὅ, τι καὶ λαλῶ ὑμῖν.) "Τὴν ἀρχὴν throughout, altogether, which in all probability is to be understood in John viii. 25 (see Lücke's careful examination of the passage): altogether what I say unto you (I am entirely what in My discourses I profess to be.) The context furnishes no ground whatever for preferring the interrogative to the positive form of expression."—Winer's *Grammar of New Testament*, 485.

27 They understood not that He (spake) to them [of the Father.]

[S. Of the Father God.]
(Alf. Was speaking.)

The difficulty of the 25th and 26th verses is confessed by all who have attempted to explain and to connect them. Each commentator sees them in a different light.

Jesus had just said to the Jews that they should die in their sins, because they did not believe in Him. They then ask Him who He is, and He replies to this effect: "I am He who, from the beginning of the Creation, spake unto you as the Word, and Who now speak unto you the Word made flesh. He then goes on to say that He had many things to say and to judge against them, but not now, for this is not the time for judgment. Now He will speak only what will confute their unbelief in Him, viz., that the Father who sent Him is true, and the things which He speaks to them are true, because He hears them of the Father.

Jesus did not say that God is His Father in direct terms. He rather suggests it to their thoughts to dwell upon and become familiar with. Had they clearly understood that this was His meaning some of them would have believed it, but probably the greater part not. Those who did believe it would have shrunk from taking any part in His Crucifixion. Those who did not believe it would have been for putting Him to death as a blasphemer immediately. The economy by which men's Redemption was to be accomplished by the Death of the God Incarnate would have been interfered with. Those who were drawn by the Father came to believe that Jesus was God gradually, and probably not fully until after His Death.

28 [Then said Jesus unto them], When ye have lifted up the Son of Man, then shall ye know that I am He, and that I do nothing of Myself: ([but as My Father] hath taught Me,) [I speak these things.]

[S. Then said Jesus again: V. Omits, Unto them: S. As the Father: S. So I speak.]
(Alf. Jesus therefore said—but according as the Father taught Me.)

29 And He that sent Me is with Me: the Father[1] hath

---

[1] The Father hath not left Me alone.—"In no part of the New Testament does the Aorist express what *is wont to be done*. Οὐκ ἀφῆκέ με μόνον ὁ πατηρ, the Father left Me not alone (on the earth), that is, He granted Me, after having sent Me (πέμψας), also (hitherto) His unceasing aid."—Winer's *Grammar of New Testament*, 293.

not left Me alone: (for) I do always those things that (please) Him.

[S. And He that sent Me hath not left Me alone: He is with Me, for I do.]
(Alf. Because—are pleasing to.)

He speaks of His Crucifixion as an exaltation. He was lifted up upon the Cross, and He was lifted up so as to become an object of worship to all generations. His Crucifixion was intended by the Jews as an act of dishonour and ignominy. He was by it exalted above all things. He foretells that their unbelief would be overcome by His Crucifixion, His Death and Resurrection, by His patience, love and zeal for their salvation, by His miracles, and wondrous works. The centurion was but one out of many who were struck with awe and with the belief that this was the Son of God. He asserts that after His Crucifixion they would believe that He had taught with the authority of the Father, and was One with the Father, that the Father who had sent Him into the world had been with Him and had worked with Him all through His sojourn among men.

30 As He spake these words, many believed (on Him.)
(Alf. In Him.)

31 (Then said Jesus) to those Jews which (believed on Him), If ye continue in My word, [(then) are ye My disciples indeed.]

[S. Ye are disciples indeed.]
(Alf. Jesus therefore said—had believed Him—omits, then.)

32 And ye shall know the truth, and the truth shall make you free.

The many who believed in Him would doubtless be from the simple, honest, unbiassed multitude, and but few from the Pharisees, whose pride and strong prejudices kept them, as a body, aloof from Jesus. These had probably given some outward expression of their belief in Him which is not mentioned; either by words, or by ranging themselves along with His other disciples. If they continue in their belief in Him and in His teaching, which they had embraced, they should be His disciples in more than name, and they should receive the reward of His disciples. They should know the truth not by mere hearing, but they should realize it by the knowledge of actual experience. For this belief in Him and the doctrine which He taught them should deliver them from the yoke and servitude of sin. Belief in Him will lead them on to repent and forsake their sins, and to lead a life of love to Him. Wilful indulgence in sin cannot exist in the heart along with hatred of sin and love to God.

33 They answered Him, We be Abraham's seed, and (were never) in bondage to any man: how sayest Thou, Ye shall be made free?

(Alf. Have never been.)

The Jews who make this answer are either not the same who had believed in Him, or they are some who believed but whose faith in Him was still very imperfect. What they say might be strictly true of the Jews of our Saviour's own time, but the statement is almost too general to be meant to be confined to them. The probability is that, in their eagerness to vindicate themselves from the reflection which, as they imagine, Jesus had cast on them, they have overstepped the bounds of historical accuracy. But Jesus, who had a very different meaning, in His answer takes no notice of what they had said.

34 Jesus answered them, Verily, verily, I say unto you, (Whosoever) committeth sin is the (servant) of sin.

(Alf. Every one that—bondman.)

35 (And the servant) abideth not in the house for ever: [but the Son abideth ever].

[S. Omits, but the Son abideth ever.]
(Alf. Now the bondman—the Son abideth for ever.)

36 (If the Son therefore) shall make you free, ye shall be free indeed.

(Alf. If then the Son.)

Though Jesus speaks in general terms here, and in the third person, His words have evidently a personal application to the men before Him. They were living in the daily practice, in the habitual commission, of sin, they were therefore the bondmen of sin. He personifies sin and represents it as a master, to give a more lively idea of the hard tyranny of sin, and to represent more forcibly that the devil is the tempter, the person who seduces men to sin, and leads them captive and punishes them for their compliance.

The boast of these Jews was that they were the seed of Abraham. The events of Abraham's own household give an apt illustration of their relation, and of their position with respect to Abraham. He had two kinds of seed, the son of the bondwoman and the son of the free. Ishmael, the son of the bondwoman, was cast out, while Isaac, the son of the free, remained in his father's house and inherited his goods. They, though the seed of Abraham, if they continued the bondmen of sin, would be cast out from God's kingdom. The only condition, on which they could remain in His house, was to receive freedom from sin, by belief in Jesus the Son of God, whom Isaac prefigured.

37 I know that ye are Abraham's seed : (but) ye seek to kill Me, because My Word (hath no place in you).
(Alf. Nevertheless—gaineth no ground in you).

38 I speak that which I have seen [with My Father] : (and ye) do that [which ye have seen (with) your father.¹]
[V. With the Father: S. Which ye have seen from your father: V. Which ye have heard from your father.]
(Alf. And ye likewise—from.)

39 They answered and said unto Him, Abraham is our father. [Jesus saith unto them], If ye were Abraham's children ye would do the works of Abraham.
[S. Jesus answered them.]

40 But now ye seek to kill Me, a Man that hath (told you) the truth, which (I have heard of God) : this did not Abraham.²
(Alf. Spoken unto you—I heard from God.)

In this conversation with the Jews Jesus makes a distinction between Abraham's seed (σπέρμα) and Abraham's children (τέκνα). He admits that they were Abraham's seed, that is descended from Abraham according to the flesh ; but by their actions they were so degenerated from Abraham that they could not be called his children. If they were Abraham's children they would do the works of Abraham. But Abraham always sought to save life and not to kill ; but they sought to kill Him, a Man who taught them the truth, which God only could teach them. The reason of this degeneracy was because His Word, His teaching had no influence with them.

41 Ye do the (deeds) of your father. [Then said they to Him,] (We be not) born of fornication : we have one Father, even God.
[S. V. They said to Him.]
(Alf. Works—we were not.)

---

¹ And ye do that which ye have seen with your father (καὶ ὑμεῖς οὖν ὃ ἑωράκατε παρὰ τῷ πατρὶ ὑμῶν, ποιεῖτε.)—" The οὖν is far from being a mere expletive. It strikingly contrasts the character of Jesus with that of the Jews (*you also, therefore*), representing both as respectively springing, as it were, from one and the same principle—conformity to paternal direction and example."—Winer's *Grammar of New Testament*, 476.

² The truth which I have heard of God (τὴν ἀλήθειαν, ἣν ἤκουσα παρὰ τοῦ θεοῦ.)—" Of verbs of *perception* ἀκούω is construed with the Genitive (to hear *from*, *out of* one.) Here ἀκούω is construed with the accusative, because the object is the whole connection, and the hearing meant is intellectual ; while in the previous case the object is simply certain sounds or words received by the ear." — Winer's *Grammar of New Testament*, 213.

The conduct of the Jews to Jesus was of a piece with the rest of their actions. They were not by that acting out of character. It was all through in keeping with the other works of him who was their father, the prompter and author of all their thoughts and works. As Jesus spake and taught what He had heard of His Father so they did what they heard from their father. When the Jews perceive that He is not speaking so much of natural descent from Abraham, but of spiritual likeness by imitation of faith and life, they reply that they are not born of fornication, but have one Father, even God. Fornication was the word by which the prophets stigmatised idolatry, the forsaking the One true God for the worship of idols. The Jews reply that they are not the descendants of idolators, such as the Gentiles, or such as the Samaritans were, but they worship the One true God, and so did their fathers. Abraham was called from the midst of the heathen to worship the true God, and they are his children, and continue to worship the same God as he.

42 Jesus said unto them, If God were your Father, ye would love Me: for I proceeded forth, and (came) from God: (neither came I) of Myself, but He sent Me.

(Alf. Am come—for neither am I come.)

They say that God is their Father, and Jesus brings this to the test. If God were their Father they would love Him, for He is God in the most perfect sense of the word, by Eternal Generation from the Father, and by mission from the Father to take upon Him the nature of man. The expression, " I proceeded forth from and am come from God," is remarkably full and unusual, and its meaning would scarcely be satisfied by being confined to the Incarnation.

He complains that they cannot understand His speech, His meaning, the drift of His words, not from any natural impossibility, but because of the hardness, the aversion of their own hearts.

43 Why do ye not understand My speech ? (even because) ye cannot hear My word.[1]

(Alf. Because.)

---

[1] **Speech, Word.**—" Λαλιά and λόγος are here set in a certain antithesis to one another, and in the seizing of the point of this must lie the right understanding of the verse. What the Lord intended by varying λαλιά und λόγος has been very differently understood. Some, as Augustine, though commenting on the passage, have omitted to notice the variation. Others, like Olshausen, have noticed, only to deny that it had any significance. Others again, admitting the significance, have failed to draw it rightly out. It is clear that as the inability to understand His 'speech' (λαλιά) is traced up as a consequence to a refusing to hear His word (λόγος); this last as the root and ground of the mischief, must be the deeper and anterior thing. To hear His word can be nothing else than to give

44 Ye are of your father the devil, and the lusts of your father (ye will do). He was a murderer from the beginning, (and abode not) in the truth, because there is no truth in him. When he speaketh a lie, he speaketh of his own : (for) he is a liar, and the father (of it).[1]

(Alf. Ye love to do—and standeth not—because—thereof.)

Words could scarcely express more distinctly the personality of the devil—viz., that man does not sin—because the properties of certain things accidentally fall in with his passions, or with the constitution of his nature, but because a being of power and intelligence infinitely superior to his is ever plotting his ruin, always on the alert to originate and suggest some action, or some course of action, to withdraw him from the allegiance which he owes to his Creator.

The devil is their father, and they are his children, not by natural descent, but by imitation, because they love to do his lusts. Jesus alludes to two points in particular, in which they loved to do the lusts of their father—viz., murder and lies. He does this because they were at that very time devising the means how to accomplish His Death, and because they said that He was a false prophet, a deceiver, and had a devil.

The devil was a murderer from the beginning, even from the beginning of the Creation. It was he who brought about the fall of Adam and Eve, and through them the death of the whole human race. When one man rises against his fellow man, as Cain against Abel, and commits murder, the devil is the author, the suggestor of the murder ; and man is merely his instrument in executing it, the doer of his lusts.

The devil, too, is the author of all that is false. Truth may be considered in several aspects as regards the heart, the mouth, and also

---

room to His truth in the heart. They who will not do this must fail to understand His speech, the outward form and utterance which His word assumes. They that are of God hear God's words, His ῥήματα as elsewhere (John iii. 34; viii. 47), His λαλιά, as here it is called, which they that are not of God do not and cannot hear."—Archbp. Trench on *The Synonyms of New Testament*, 275.

[1] The lusts of your father ye will do (τὰς ἐπιθυμίας τοῦ πατρὸς ὑμῶν θέλετε ποιεῖν.)—" The lusts of your father you will (are resolved and inclined to) do (carry into effect, either in general (your hearts impel you to follow the will of Satan), or because ye go about to kill Me." (Verse 40.)—Winer's *Grammar of New Testament*, 489.

For he is a liar and the father of it (ψεύστης ἐστὶ καὶ ὁ πατὴρ αὐτοῦ.)—"'Αυτός sometimes refers to an abstract deduced from a preceding concrete, or vice versâ. (ψεύστης ἐστὶ καὶ ὁ πατὴρ αὐτοῦ.) (ψεύδους) see Lücke *in loc*. The other explanation, *Father of the liar*, appears neither grammatically simpler nor substantially preferable. *Father of falsehood* is a notion more appropriate to John, who had a predilection for abstract terms."—Winer's *Grammar of New Testament*, 158.

Bishop Middleton (on *Greek Article*) disagrees with this interpretation, but is unable, with the present reading, to suggest any other that is entirely satisfactory. See his very interesting note, p. 251.

with respect to action. The devil abode not in the truth, he abode not in the true and right course, in the lawful position in which God had created him, when through pride he rebelled against Him. He abode not in the obedience, in the allegiance which he owed to God, he was created an angel of light, and through his own deed he became darkness. The devil abode not in the truth, when through lies and misrepresentations he deceived Eve, and succeeded in bringing death upon mankind.

When men speak a lie they are not the author of it—the devil is the author, the inventor of it. They are themselves the victims of "the liar," and are merely his instruments in uttering it. The devil was the author of the first lie, of the whole system or art of lying, and also of every individual lie.

45 (And because I tell you) the truth, ye believe Me not.

(Alf. But because I speak.)

46 Which of you (convinceth) Me of sin? [And] (if I say the truth,) why do ye not believe Me?

[S. V. Omit, And.]
(Alf. Convicteth—If I speak truth.)

47 He that is of God heareth (God's words): (Ye therefore) hear them not, because ye are not of God.

(Alf. The words of God—for this cause ye.)

They loved to do the lusts of the devil because he was their father. They would not believe Jesus, though He spake the truth, because God was not their Father. He challenges them to convict Him of sin in His life, or of falsehood in His teaching, and presses on them the conclusion that the sinlessness of His life and truth of His teaching would have ensured the reception of His words, if they had been, as they professed, of God. Unable to answer this unanswerable argument, the Jews replied that He was a Samaritan, and had a devil.

48 [Then answered the Jews], and said unto Him, Say we not well that Thou art a Samaritan, and hast a devil?

[S. V. The Jews answered.]
(Alf. The Jews answered.)

It is nowhere recorded that the Jews were in the habit of calling Jesus a Samaritan, and yet these words would seem to imply as much. The religion of the Samaritans was a corruption of the Jewish, a mixture of Jewish worship with the worship of false gods, the knowledge of which they had brought with them from Assyria. A Samaritan, therefore, was with the Jews a term of reproach for one who was half a Jew and half an idolater, an idolatrous schismatic. By this term they might mean that Jesus kept the law of Moses in part, but mixed up with it much that was new and false.

The characteristic of devils is to arrogate to themselves the honour and glory that belong only to God. The Jews in saying that Jesus had a devil charged Him with taking to Himself, who was a mere man, the honour which belonged to God alone. To this which is the most serious part of their charge, He replies, but makes no reference to the first part—viz., that of being a Samaritan.

49 [Jesus answered], I have not a devil: but I honour My Father, and ye do dishonour Me.

[S. Jesus answered and said.]

50 (And) I seek not Mine Own glory: (but there is) One that seeketh and judgeth.

(Alf. But—there is.)

51 Verily, verily, I say unto you, If a man keep My (saying), he shall never see death.

(Alf. Word.)

He denies in express words that He has a devil, or the qualities of a devil. For a devil seeks his own glory, but He seeks the glory of His Father. Jesus honours the Father, but the Jews, in dishonouring Him dishonour the Father. Jesus seeks not His Own glory, but God the Father is seeking His glory, and is even now judging between Him and the Jews. The term judging here has no reference to the Last Judgment. In the Last Judgment it is expressly said that the Son of Man shall be the Judge. It rather refers to the daily visitations and judgments by which God chastises His disobedient people. Here, too, in all probability Jesus alludes to the sufferings which the Jews are on the very point of enduring at the hands of the Romans, for their rejection and crucifixion of Him.

In spite of the malignity and the venom of their reproach that He had a devil, Jesus still continues to press on them the offer of eternal life. With the strongest form of asseveration amounting, as some think, almost to an oath, He declares that if they will keep His saying they shall never die. He does not refer to the death of the body, for that is not really death, any more than the life of the body is really life. If they will keep His word, He will impart to them life, the life of grace in the soul, and they shall never fall into such sin as will quench the life of the soul, which shall be purified and strengthened until it ripens into the life of glory everlasting hereafter.

52 [Then said the Jews] unto Him, Now we know that Thou hast a devil. Abraham (is dead), and the prophets, and Thou sayest, If a man keep My (saying,) [he shall never (taste of death.)]

[S.V. The Jews said: V. He shall never see death.]
(Alf. Died—word—taste death.)

53 Art Thou greater than our Father Abraham, which (is dead)? and the prophets (are dead): whom makest Thou Thyself?

(Alf. Died.)

After all His instruction the Jews as yet could only grasp the idea of one kind of life, and of one kind of death, viz.: that of the body. They declare that His offer to keep them from tasting death is only another confirmation of their conviction, that He had a devil. Nothing in their opinion could account for such language, as He used, except the supposition that He was possessed with a devil. Not only was He a mere man making Himself greater than Abraham, and greater than the prophets, but even greater than God himself. Abraham kept God's word, and so did the prophets, and yet they all died. God's word conferred on them no such immunity from death, as Jesus here declares that the observance of His word will do. They are at a loss to conceive to whom He likens himself.

The mistake of the Jews, which runs through all this, is in thinking of Abraham and the prophets as dead, and in confining death to the body. Even their bodies, which were dead, Jesus could raise up again at the last day. The souls of the righteous could never die, could never taste death, could never experience eternal separation from God.

54 Jesus answered, If I (honour) Myself, My (honour) is nothing: It is My father that (honoureth) Me: [of Whom ye say, (that He is your God).]

[A. Of Whom ye say, He is our God.]
(Alf. Glorify—glory—glorifieth—He is our God.)

55 (Yet) ye have not known Him: but I know Him: and if I should say, I know Him not, I shall be a liar like unto you; but I know Him and keep His (saying).

(Alf. And—word.)

If the honour or glory, which is given to Jesus, were given to Him by Himself, it would be of no value. But it is given to Him by the

Father, whom the Jews claim as their God. Though they say the Father is their God, they do not know Him. They do not show that they have any knowledge of Him, either by sincerely worshipping Him, and by living according to His commands, nor do they show that they know anything of His nature, otherwise they would have understood that Jesus the Messiah was the Son of God. They do not know that in the Godhead there are Three Persons, though but One God. The Jews proved themselves to be liars by saying that they knew God, when they worshipped Him not. Jesus is not like them, He knows Him and therefore He fulfils all His word.

The Jews despised Jesus, but Abraham, whose children they boasted they were, did not; He looked forward with delight to Him as his Saviour. The boast and glory of the Jews was in Abraham, but Abraham's glory was in Jesus.

56 Your father Abraham rejoiced to see My day: and He saw it and was glad.

57 (Then said the Jews) unto Him, Thou art not yet fifty years old, [and hast Thou seen Abraham]?

[B. And hath Abraham seen Thee?]
(Alf. The Jews therefore said.)

In their use of the term fifty years the Jews had probably some reference to the time at which the Levites began to be superannuated with respect to the service of the Temple. Their time of service lasted from thirty to fifty years. (Numb. iv. 3.) And the Jews had an opinion, that whoever died before fifty or at least fifty-two, died untimely, and as it were by cutting off. Thus their words imply: Thou art not yet come to the common years of superannuation, and dost Thou talk of having seen Abraham?

58 Jesus said unto them, Verily, verily, I say unto you, Before Abraham (was) I am.[1]

(Alf. Was made.)

---

[1] Before Abraham was, I am (πρὶν Ἀβραὰμ γενέσθαι, ἐγὼ εἰμί).—"It is important to mark the distinction between εἶναι and γενέσθαι, where our translators have not observed it. Thus our English rendering of John viii. 58, 'Before Abraham was, I am,' loses half the force of the original, πρὶν Ἀβραὰμ γενέσθαι, ἐγὼ εἰμί, 'Before Abraham was born, I am.' The *becoming* only can rightly be predicated of the patriarch, the *being* is reserved for the Eternal Son alone. Similar in kind, though less in degree, is the loss in the rendering of Luke vi. 36 γίνεσθε οἰκτίρμονες καθὼς [καὶ] ὁ πατὴρ ὑμῶν οἰκτίρμων ἐστίν. Be ye merciful, as your Father also *is* merciful. Here also the original expresses the distinction between the imperfect effort and the eternal attribute."—Dr. J. B. Lightfoot on *Revision of New Testament*, 75.

"Sometimes a Past Tense is included in the Present, when, for instance, a verb expresses a state which commenced at an earlier period, but still continues—a state in its whole duration as John viii. 58,

The day which Jesus here calls "My day" and which Abraham rejoiced to see, which he saw and was glad, was the day of Christ's appearance in the Flesh, the day of His Birth and life among men, the Incarnation, when the Word was made Flesh and dwelt among us. Abraham is here but the representative of the righteous. He saw it with a faith, which realized it as though present. He saw it as revealed to Him by God, at different times, and in divers manners, as for instance in the ram caught in a thicket by his horns, and which he was to offer up for a burnt-offering in the stead of his son. (Gen. xxii. 13).

He may have seen it too in another sense. The good tidings which caused so much joy to the angels, and to the shepherds, and to the saints on the earth, to Zacharias and Elizabeth, to Simeon and Anna and others, may not have been confined to them; these good tidings may have been conveyed to the righteous, who were already removed from the earth, and who were awaiting the fulness of time for their redemption.

Jesus here appropriates to Himself the form "I Am," by which God the Father had of old described Himself (Exod. iii. 14): the Eternal, without change, without beginning or ending. In this sense the Jews understood Him and took up stones to stone Him as speaking blasphemy.

59 Then took they up stones to cast at Him: [but] Jesus hid himself and went out of the temple, [going through the midst of them, and so passed by.]¹

[V. Omits, but : S. V. omits going through the midst of them, and so passed by.]
(Alf. Omits, going through the midst of them, and so passed by.)

The Jews had a tradition that the murder of Zacharias in the Temple by their fathers had (Lightfoot ii. 237) entailed upon the nation a fearful punishment. Yet so exasperated are they with Jesus that undeterred by this story which was commonly believed among them they attempt His life in the Court of the Temple, taking up the stones, which in all probability lay there for the completion or the repair of some portion of the building.

He hid Himself, probably not by secreting Himself in any part of the building, but by rendering Himself invisible to them, and thus went out of the Temple. The words going through the midst of them are not found in the Sinaitic and Vatican MSS. but they may contain a very good explanation of the way in which He hid Himself.

πρὶν Ἀβραὰμ γενέσθαι ἐγὼ εἰμί.—Winer's *Grammar of New Testament*, 283.
¹ Going through the midst of them, &c.—"The Vatican and Sinaitic MSS. and Codex Bezæ are alone among MSS. in omitting the clause διελθὼν διὰ μέσου αὐτῶν· καὶ παρῆγεν οὕτως. The omission is to be accounted for by the fact that just then the Church lesson for Tuesday in the fifth week after Easter came to an end."—Burgon on *The Last Verses of St. Mark*, 222.

INTRODUCTORY NOTE TO CHAPTER IX.

Jewish Parties.—" When John began to preach, the Jews proper—excluding Samaritans and Galilæans—were divided into the three great bodies of the Sadducees, Pharisees, and Essenes. Most of the Sadducees were men of birth and rank: princes of the royal house, sons of high priests, heads of great houses, and their kin. Annas was a Sadducee. As a rule all the old families, and most of the rich families, belonged to this aristocratic school. . . . . These Sadducees—in other words the party of nobles, the friends of Annas—supported Pilate, and lent no countenance to the policy of revolt.

" The Pharisees, the second party in point of age, the first in strength of numbers, were a body of men professing to be set apart, selected from the mass. A Pharisee was one of the saints, one of those for whom the earth was made, a special object of Almighty care. These Separatists believed that it was only for a time, and only for their good that God was ruling them by a Roman sword. A little while and they would chase these legions into the sea. The Lord had promised them this deliverance from of old, written it down in their sacred books. They were always quoting this great charter, always expecting a Deliverer to arrive.

" In the sense which the Separatists put on the word patriot, they were patriots in the first degree, men to whom the Roman yoke was odious, and liberty sweeter than love and life.

" The Essenes, youngest and meekest of the three great parties, were a protest of nature against the easy unbelief of certain priests and princes of the Church. They ran into a wild extreme of faith. But, like the Sadducees, they took no part in street politics, dreamt of no Messiah, and strongly opposed the theory of revolt.

" Herod the Great had given his favour to these harmless breeders of bees and birds, and Menachem, one of their chiefs, had exercised a merciful influence in the tyrant's court."—Dixon's *Holy Land*, i. 268-280.

The Sanhedrin.—" When Jesus began to speak more openly of being sent down from heaven to save the world from death, the Temple Courts in which He prayed and taught were filled with tumultuous crowds; men who had come from all parts of Jewry to keep the feast, and were eager to see whether this Jesus of Nazareth was the Christ whom they had sought. Some believed in His words: still more believed in His acts; for in His last few weeks on earth His miracles increased in number and in power.

"The two great parties which divided Jewry treated these tumults in a different way.

"If the Sadducees gave them any thought it was only in so far as they disturbed the public peace. Having much to risk, and nothing to gain by change, the aristocratic party were anxious to keep things safe, so as to prevent any action on the side of Rome. Avoiding the mistake of Gratus Pilate left the priests alone, so that Annas remained sagan, and his son-in-law high priest; and Annas being content, his partisans were calm. Having no expectation of a Messiah's kingdom, the rich and ancient families of Judæa preferred a government of priests and nobles, supported by Roman legions, to the license of a new Judas of Gamala, and the exactions of a new Simon the Slave. They cared nothing for the delusions of a mob; but in the cause of order even these unbelieving Sadducees might act.

"The Pharisees took other ground. As a body they might have changed their demeanour towards Jesus even now, had He consented to declare Himself a prince of their royal house, an upholder of the Separatist policy, an admirer of the Oral Law, a restorer of their independent rule; in one word, a king of the Jews. But Jesus urged on them more than ever the necessity of adopting a new law, a new commandment, a new form of prayer, a new religious life. He profaned their Sabbath, He abolished their ceremonies, He decried their righteousness. When they found that He would make no terms with them they went up to the Temple and laid a charge against Him before the Sanhedrin of preaching false doctrine and leading the people astray.

"This Sanhedrin, the Great Council of Jewry, met at Lishcath ha-Gazith (Paved-hall), the largest of many cells, or chambers, built on the Temple hill, and used as offices for the guard and watch; just as the domed houses under the high terraces of the rock are still used by the dervishes who watch and guard the holy Mosque. The Lishcath ha-Gazith seems to have stood on the great wall, part of it being in the Israelites' Court, part in the Gentile Court, so as to admit of the entrance of Jew and Greek; probably on the western side, facing towards Zion, near the most public entrance into the Temple Courts.

"The great council before whom the Pharisees laid this charge of false teaching against Jesus, consisted of seventy, seventy-one, perhaps seventy-two members, chosen by vote from among the wise, aged, and wealthy Jews, not of Jerusalem only, but of every city in which they dwelt, even from Egypt, Babylon, and Greece. Until the times of Herod the Great, the powers of this body had been royal, and more than royal. . . . .

"But the Sanhedrin's strength had been reduced, first by Herod

P

the Great, afterwards by the Roman governors of Judæa. Herod, on capturing Jerusalem, had seized the whole body of the Sanhedrin, thrown them into prison, and, with two illustrious exceptions, put them all to death. Around Hillel and Shammai, the men whom Herod had spared, a new council had been formed; but the prestige of the Sanhedrin could never be restored. Pilate abridged their rights, taking from them more particularly the faculties of life and death; yet, even after they had lost the right to torture prisoners and stone offenders, they still exercised a vast authority in Jerusalem, and in every other Jewish city.

"Pilate himself could not dispute their jurisdiction over Jews, in whatever land they dwelt, as to all that concerned their faith, ritual, and education. They had a right to fix all festivals, to judge all doctrines, to expel all sinners from the Church, to regulate colleges and schools, to punish offenders against the law so long as, in the exercise of their rights, they refrained from encroaching on the civil power. . . . . They could still condemn a man to death; though they could only proceed to execution after their sentence had been confirmed by a Roman judge."—Dixon's *Holy Land*, ii. 220.

CHAPTER IX.

1 *The man that was born blind restored to sight;* 8 *He is brought to the Pharisees;* 13 *They are offended at it, and excommunicate him;* 35 *But he is received of Jesus, and confesseth Him;* 39 *Who they are whom Christ enlighteneth.*

The healing of this blind man took place, as we know, on the Sabbath Day (v. 14); and there is a probability, though not a certainty, that it was the same day as that on which Jesus had held His conversation with the Scribes and Pharisees, as recorded in the last chapter, and only a short time after He had escaped from the infuriated Jews in the Temple. The opening words of this chapter are looked upon as lending support to this view.

1 (And as Jesus passed by) He saw a man which was blind from his birth.

(Alf. And as He was passing by.)

The fact that he was blind from his birth is mentioned to indicate that his blindness was not of a passing, temporary nature, but one of long standing and incurable.

2 And His disciples asked Him, saying, (Master, who did sin), this man or his parents, that (he was) born blind?[1]

(Alf. Rabbi, who sinned—should be.)

---

[1] Who did sin, this man or his parents?—" It was a received doctrine in the Jewish schools that children, according to some wickedness of their parents, were born lame, or crooked, or maimed, or defective in some of their parts, &c., by which they kept parents in awe lest they should grow remiss and negligent in the performance of some rites which had respect to their being clean, such as washings and purifyings.

" It appears that the ancient opinion of the Jews was that the infant from its first quickening had some stain of sin upon it. . . . Nay, they went a little further, not only that the infant might have some stain of sin in the womb, but that it might in some measure actually sin, and do that which might render it criminal. To which purpose this passage of the disciples seems to have some relation, Did this man sin that he was born blind? that is, did he, when his mother carried him in her womb, do any foul or enormous thing that might deserve this severe stroke upon him that he should bring this blindness with him into the world."—Lightfoot, ii. 568.

" This is to be explained by the Jewish theory of causes with which, in its national exaggeration, the disciples were fully imbued. Heavy, mysterious bodily afflic-

This question seems to proceed from a belief that all affliction in this world is the punishment of sin. This was the position which Job's friends vainly endeavoured to maintain against him. Many explanations have been given of the train of thought which led the disciples to put their question to Jesus in this particular form. But none seems entirely satisfactory. It is not easy to understand in what way they thought this man, who had been blind from his birth, could have brought on his blindness by sin. The suggestion has been made that the disciples used the words of their question in a general way, without intending any very accurate or close application of them to the circumstances of the case, as for instance, Did this man, or since it is out of the question that he could have sinned himself, so as to bring on his present blindness, was it from his parents' sin? But after all explanation there still remains a degree of uncertainty as to the exact meaning of the disciples' question.

3 Jesus answered, Neither (hath this man sinned) nor his parents; but that the works of God should be made manifest in him.

(Alf. Did this man sin.)

4 [I must work] the works of Him [that sent Me] while it is day: the night cometh, when no man can work.

[S. V. We must work: S. That sent us.]

5 (As long as) I am in the world, I am the Light of the world.

(Alf. When.)

By "the day" Jesus means His continuance among men, and by "the night" His departure from them. Day and night are well expressed by the shining and the withdrawal, the departure, of the Light of the world. He must work the works which the Father hath sent Him to work for the salvation of man, while He is present with them on earth, and before His departure from them. This He says as a preparation for the miracle, which He is just about to perform on the blind man.

The property of light is to shine and to enlighten. Jesus, the Light of the world, proceeds to open the eyes of the body as well as the eyes of the soul of this man, who was born blind, born without light either of the body or of the soul.

---

tions must be punishments which God has annexed to sin. Who by sins has provoked divine justice so as to cause this person's having been born blind? The necessary, though not intentional consequence of ἁμαρτάνειν is meant." See Lücke in loc.—Winer's Grammar of New Testament, p. 480.

6 When He had thus spoken He spat on the ground, and made clay of the spittle, [and He anointed the eyes of the blind man with the clay,¹]

[S. And He anointed his eyes with His clay: V. And He put His clay upon his eyes: A. With His clay.]
(Margin, Spread the clay upon the eyes.)
(Alf. And spread the clay upon his eyes.)

Two views, very different and almost opposite, have been taken in ancient and modern times with respect to the object, which Jesus had in spreading the clay upon the eyes of the blind man.

Besides calling the attention of the bystanders to the similarity of His works with those of the Creator, who had at first formed man from the dust or clay of the earth, and thus leading them to see the union which there was between God the Father and Jesus, who claimed to be His Son: besides all this, the ancients thought that Jesus had a still further object in anointing his eyes with clay, and that He meant to show them that the cure which He then wrought was not brought about in a natural way, but by means that were altogether supernatural. For they would themselves see that the natural effect of the clay was to cause blindness and not to give sight. They thought that He also made clay of His spittle to show them that illumination and salvation was the special property, the natural effect, so to speak, of His Humanity.

An opinion, which has found some favour in modern times, is that Jesus anointed the eyes of the blind man with clay as an accommodation to the prejudices or opinions of the people, and perhaps even with the view of increasing the belief of the blind man in His power to cure him. It is maintained that there was, at this very time, a widely spread belief that clay spread over the eyes was in some cases a cure

---

¹ He spat on the ground, &c.—" It was prohibited amongst them to besmear the eyes with spittle upon the Sabbath Day upon any medicinal account, although it was esteemed so very wholesome for them."
Both these statements Lightfoot proves by quotations from Jewish writers.
" So that in this action of our Saviour's we may observe:—1. That He does not heal this sick man with a word as He did the others, but chooseth to do a thing, which was against their canonical observation of the Sabbath, designing thereby to make a trial of the man, whether he was so superstitious that he would not admit such things to be done upon him on the Sabbath Day. He made an experiment not much unlike this upon the man at Bethesda.
" 2. While He mingles spittle with dust, and of that makes a clay to anoint the eyes of the blind man, He thereby avoids the suspicion of using any kind of charm, and gives rather a demonstration of His own divine power when He heals by a method contrary to nature. For clay laid upon the eyes, we might believe, should rather put out the eyes of one that sees than restore sight to one that had been blind. Yea, and further, He gave demonstration of the divine authority He Himself had over the Sabbath, when He heals upon that day by the use of means which had been peculiarly prohibited to be used in it."—Lightfoot, ii. 570.

for blindness, and that the spittle of any person who was fasting was commonly looked upon as efficacious in some cases of disease of the eye, or even of blindness. The authorities that are quoted are sufficient to prove that these opinions were at this time, or rather a little later, common among the Romans, and they may even have been known to these Jews. But when the Pharisees tried to disprove the truth or reality of the miracle, they never allude to the possibility of the cure having been wrought by the use of mere human means. Their silence as to the possibility of the clay and the spittle having healed the man's blindness by their natural properties was doubtless not caused by any want of will to pervert them for their own objects. They institute a rigid examination into the case, and all their ingenuity is used to prove that the man had never been blind. When that fails they silence him; but they never give the slightest hint that either clay or spittle had ever before had any healing power. The reason of their silence is plain enough, because they had never heard of such an opinion.

Jesus, having anointed the eyes of the blind man with clay, sends him to the Pool of Siloam, probably that the multitude may see him as he goes, and with the clay on his eyes, that thus they may more distinctly perceive both the blindness and the inadequacy of the means which had been used to effect a cure.

7 And said unto him, [Go, wash in the Pool of Siloam] (which is by interpretation, Sent). He went his way therefore, and washed, and came seeing.[1]

[A. Go to the Pool of Siloam, and wash.]
(Alf. Which is interpreted, Sent.)

---

[1] **Which is by interpretation sent** (ὁ ἑρμηνεύεται ἀπεσταλμένος.) — "The spring of Siloam discharged itself by a double stream into a twofold pool. (2 Kings xviii. 17; Isaiah vii. 3; Nehem. iii. 15.) The *upper* pool, which was called שִׁילוֹחַ the pool of Siloah; and the *lower*, which was called שֶׁלַח the pool of Shelah. Now, the former plainly and properly signifies ἀπεσταλμένος, but not so the latter. Probably the Evangelist added this parenthesis on purpose to distinguish which of the pools the blind man was sent to wash in, viz., not in the pool Shelah, which signifies κῳδίων fleeces, but in the pool of Shelohh, which signifies ἀπεσταλμένος, sent."—Lightfoot, ii. 571.

"There are two pools of Siloam, a small one, into which the waters from the Virgin Fount fall after issuing from the tunnel; the other a larger pool, now nearly filled up. This latter I suppose to have been the pool dug by Hezekiah, and to be that going under the name of Siloam in Josephus (Wars, v. 10, 4), and the King's pool in Nehemiah (ii. 14.)"—*Recovery of Jerusalem*, p. 238.

"Passing under the rocky face of Ophel, we came to the Pool of Siloam. We were surprised to find it so entire, exactly resembling the common prints of it. It is in the form of a parallelogram, and the walls all round are of hewn stones. The steps that lead down into it, at the eastern end, are no doubt the same which have been there for ages. The water covered the bottom to the depth of one or two feet. At the western end, climbing a little way into a cave hewn out of a rock, we descended a few steps into the place from which the water flows into the pool. It is connected by a long subterranean passage, running quite through the neck to the Fountain of the Virgin, or more

The Sinaitic and Vatican MSS. connect the Pool of Siloam with the verb "wash," and not with "Go." This is rendered by the Authorised Version, as well as by Alford's Revision, "Go, and wash in the Pool of Siloam." The Alexandrine MS. reads "Go to the Pool of Siloam and wash."

Jesus was the Sent. He had so often repeated to the Jews the phrase that He was sent that it could scarcely fail to attract their attention. Siloam also means Sent. What the Pool of Siloam was to this blind man—viz., the source and fount of light—Jesus was to the world. He may have sent this blind man to wash in the Pool of Siloam, and to receive sight through the instrumentality of its waters, to remind them that He Himself was the Shiloh, "the Messiah," "the Sent" by the Father. That Jesus had in His mind some typical reference when He sent the blind man to the Pool of Siloam is rendered almost certain by the interpretation of its name being given by the Evangelist. The Evangelist did not give any interpretation of the term Bethesda, which was also a Hebrew word, and probably for the reason that no typical allusion was intended in the latter name.

It had been already foretold that the Messiah or Shiloh, or the Sent, as the Jews understood it, would open the eyes of the blind. (Isa. xxix. 18; xxxv. 5.) He, who declared Himself again and again to be the Sent, had just opened the eyes of a man born blind through the instrumentality of the waters of a pool called Sent. Yet all this awakened in the mind of the Jews no insight into the real character of Jesus.

8 The neighbours therefore, and they which before had seen him that he was [blind] said, Is not this he that (sat and begged?)

[S. V. A. Beggar.]
(Alf. A beggar—sitteth and beggeth.)

The Sinaitic, Vatican, and Alexandrine MSS. all read, and they which before had seen him that he was a beggar. It has been well remarked that the question of identity would be much more likely to

---

properly the Fountain of Siloam, the entrance to which is a considerable way farther up the Valley of Jehoshaphat. Through this passage the water flows softly from the fountain till it finds its way into the pool, not as generally represented in pictures by pouring over the mouth of the cave, but secretly from beneath. Wild flowers, and among other plants the caper-tree, grow luxuriantly around its border."—*Mission to the Jews from Scotland*, p. 154.

"Go wash in the pool (ὕπαγε νίψαι εἰς τὴν κολυμβήθραν.)—εἰς τὴν κολυμβήθραν is, in regard to the sense, to be connected with ὕπαγε. Comp. verse ii: Go into the pool and wash thyself in it. (Comp. Luke xxi. 37.) See Lücke. Though νίπτεσθαι εἰς ὕδωρ is as proper an expression as in aquam macerare, so Jer. xli. 7, ἔσφαξεν αὐτοὺς εἰς τὸ φρέαρ, he slew (and cast) them into the pit. Comp. 1 Macc. vii. 19.—Winer's *Grammar of New Testament*, 484.

turn on whether he was really the person who had sat and begged. That proved—the whole city would remember—that it was a blind beggar who used to sit there.

The greatness of the miracle, and the alteration of the face from that of a blind man to that of one, who sees for the first time in his life, of one delighted and amazed by the first sight of creation, must have been immense, enough surely to cause them to doubt, whether he were the same man or not.

9 Some said, This is he : [others said, He is like him] : (but he said) I am he.

[S. V. Others said, No, but he is like him.]
(Alf. Others said, Nay, but he is like him—he said.)

10 Therefore said they unto him, [How] were thine eyes opened ?

[S. How, therefore.]

11 He answered [and said], A man that is called Jesus made clay, and anointed mine eyes, and said unto me, [Go to the pool of Siloam], and wash : [and I went] and washed, (and I received sight.)

[S. V. Omit, And said : S. V. Go to Siloam : S. V. I went therefore.]
(Alf. Omits, And said—Go to Siloam—I went therefore—and received sight.)

12 [Then said they] unto him, (Where is He? He said,) I know not.

[S. V. And they said : A. They said.]
(Alf. They said—Where is the Man ? He saith.)

The man himself does not in any way attribute his recovery to the natural effect of the water of Siloam. He speaks of it merely as the instrument in the hand of Jesus for his recovery. He does not yet know that Jesus is God, he knows that his name is Jesus, either by common rumour, or by the report of the bystanders. He could not see Him before the miracle, and after it Jesus had withdrawn Himself.

13 (They brought) to the Pharisees him that aforetime was blind.

(Alf. They bring.)

14 (And it was the sabbath day when) Jesus made the clay, and opened his eyes.

(Alf. Now it was the Sabbath, on the day when.)

15 (Then) again the Pharisees also asked him how he (had received) his sight. [He said unto them], He put clay upon mine eyes, and I washed, and do see.

[A. He said also unto them.]
(Alf. Therefore—received.)

16 Therefore said some of the Pharisees, This man is not (of God), because he keepeth not the sabbath day. [Others] said, How can a Man that is a sinner do such miracles? And there was a division among them.

[S. V. But others.]
(Alf. From God.)

17 [They say unto the blind man again], What sayest thou of Him, that He hath opened thine eyes? He said, He is a prophet.

[S. V. A. They say therefore: S. Unto the formerly blind man.]
(Alf. They say therefore.)

The neighbours of the blind man are the unwitting instruments of furthering the designs of God. It was probably from no feeling of kindliness, but rather of hostility towards Jesus, or from fear of the Pharisees, that they bring him to the Pharisees to be examined by them. But this was the very way to render this miracle the best attested and the most widely known of all His works.

These Pharisees seem invested with legal authority, and were probably a court of the Sanhedrin. They are divided in opinion respecting the matter. The one, and probably the smaller party, and which might include in it Nicodemus, Joseph the Arimathæan, and Gamaliel, Pharisees, who sat in the Sanhedrin, and who on other occasions counselled fairness and moderation, this party wished to form their conclusion solely on the evidence of the case itself. The animus of the other party is shown by the prominence which they give to the fact that the cure was wrought on the Sabbath Day. They wish to prejudge the miracle solely on this ground, without any reference to its own merits. This pretended miracle could not be real, or true, because it was wrought in violation of God's command to keep the Sabbath Day holy. This is their sole argument. Being unable to agree, they appeal to the man's own opinion of Jesus. He, grateful and sincere, and uninfluenced by any inferior motives, frankly and openly declares that Jesus is a prophet—that is, one commissioned by God to fulfil His work. They then turn to examine the evidence for the fact, or rather to see what flaw they can find in the evidence, for that is plainly their object.

18 (But the Jews) did not believe concerning him, that he had been blind, and received his sight, until they called the parents of him that had received his sight.

(Alf. The Jews, therefore.)

19 And they asked them [saying], Is this your son, who ye say was born blind? how then doth he now see?

[S. Omits, Saying.]

20 [His parents] answered them, and said, We know that this is our son, and that he was born blind.

[S. V. His parents, therefore: A. But his parents.]
(Alf. His parents answered and said.)

21 But by what means he now seeth, we know not: or who (hath opened) his eyes, we know not: [he is of age; ask him]: he (shall) speak for himself.

[V. Ask him, he is of age: S. Omits, Ask him.]
(Alf. Opened—ask him: he is of age—will.)

22 These words (spake) his parents, because they feared the Jews: for the Jews had agreed already, that if any man (did confess that He was Christ) he should be put out of the synagogue.[1]

(Alf. Said—should acknowledge Him as Christ.)

---

[1] He should be put out of the synagogue (ἀποσυνάγωγος γένηται)—" So chap. xvi. ii. ἀποσυναγώγους ποιήσουσιν ὑμᾶς, granting that this is spoken of as excommunication, the question may be whether it is to be understood of the ordinary excommunication, that is, from this or that synagogue, or the extraordinary, that is, a cutting off from the whole congregation of Israel.

"Whosoever is excommunicated by the President of the Sanhedrin is cut off from the whole congregation of Israel: and if so then much more so, if it be by the vote of the whole Sanhedrin. And it seems by that speech ἐξέβαλον αὐτὸν ἔξω, they cast out (verse 34) that word ἔξω (out) was added for such a signification."—Lightfoot, ii. 572.

Christ.—To us Christ has become a proper name, and as such rejects the definite article. But in the Gospel narratives, if we except the headings or prefaces and the after-comments of the Evangelists themselves (e.g. Matt. i. 1; Mark i. 1; John i. 17), no instance of this usage can be found. In the body of the narratives we read only of ὁ Χριστὸς the Christ, the Messiah, whom the Jews had long expected, and who might or might not be identified with the person "Jesus," according to the spiritual discernment of the individual. Χριστὸς is nowhere connected with Ἰησοῦς in the Gospels with the exception of John i. 8, where it occurs in a prophetic declaration of our Lord, ἵνα, γινώσκωσιν, τὸν μόνον ἀληθινὸν Θεὸν καὶ ὃν ἀπέστειλας Ἰησοῦν Χριστόν: nor is it used without the definite article in more than four passages, Mark ix. 41, ἐν ὀνόματι ὅτι Χριστοῦ ἐστέ; Luke ii. 11, σωτηρ ὅς ἐστιν, Χριστὸς κύριος; xxiii. 2, λέγοντα ἑαυτὸν Χριστὸν; John ix. 22, αὐτὸν ὁμολογήσῃ Χριστόν, where the very exception strengthens the rule. The turning point is the Resurrection: then,

COMMENTARY ON ST. JOHN'S GOSPEL.   219

23 (Therefore) said his parents, He is of age: [ask him].
[A. And ask him.]
(Alf. For this cause.)

There was no denying that the man then saw. Their object, therefore, was to prove that he had never been blind. His parents, cautious and afraid of the Pharisees, undertake to answer only what was perfectly known to them, not what they had learnt, from the report either of their son or of others. Thus their evidence, though unsatisfactory to the Pharisees, becomes a more valuable testimony in favour of the miracle.

24 (Then again called they) the man that (was) blind, and said unto him, (Give God the praise): we know that This Man is a sinner.
(Alf. So they called the second time—had been—Give glory to God.)

25 [He answered and said], Whether He (be) a sinner or no, I know not: [one thing] I know, (that, whereas I was blind, now I see.)[1]
[S. V. A. Omit, And said: S. But one thing.]
(Alf. He therefore answered—is—that I, a blind man, now see.)

26 [Then said they to him again], What did He to thee? How opened He thine eyes?
[V. Therefore they said to him: S. They said to him.]
(Alf. They said therefore.)

---

and not till then we hear of Jesus Christ from the lips of contemporary speakers (Acts ii. 38; iii. 6), and from that time forward Christ begins to be used as a proper name with or without the article. This fact points to a rule which should be strictly observed in translation. In the Gospel narratives ὁ Χριστὸς should always be rendered *the* Christ, and never Christ simply. In some places our translators have observed this (e. g. Matt. xxvi. 63; Mark. viii. 29), and occasionally they have even overdone the translation, rendering ὁ Χριστὸς by *that* Christ, John i. 25; vi. 69, or *the very* Christ, John vii. 26, but elsewhere under exactly the same conditions the article is omitted, e. g. Matt. xvi. 16; xxiv. 5; Luke xxiii. 35, 39, &c."—Dr. J. B. Lightfoot on *Revision of New Testament*, p. 100.

Bishop Middleton in an interesting note (*Greek Article*, p. 193) reviews this subject and gives the arguments for and against, and arrives at a different conclusion from the above. He says, "On the whole it can hardly be doubted that the word Χριστὸς, even during our Saviour's lifetime, had become a Proper Name, though its appellative use was very much the more frequent."

[1] "Whereas I was blind, now I see (τυφλὸς ὢν ἄρτι βλέπω). ὢν joined to a Preterite, or an adverb of time, not unfrequently is the Participle Imperfect. But τυφλὸς ὢν ἄρτι βλέπω is, perhaps, being blind (from my infancy). Very probably, it is only inasmuch as ἄρτι refers to the past that ὢν can be rendered, whereas I was blind."—Winer's *Grammar of New Testament*, 358.

27 He answered them, I have told you already, and ye did not hear: wherefore would ye hear it again? Will ye also (be) His disciples?

(Alf. Would ye also become.)

By the expression, "Give God the praise," the translators of the Authorised Version have missed the sense of the words. The meaning is not, Give God the praise of this miracle, as their rendering necessitates. They are all the time attempting to disprove the truth of the miracle. The correct translation is that adopted by Alford, "Give glory to God;" and these words are a common form of charging any one to speak the truth, amounting almost to an adjuration. Thus, Joshua said to Achan, "My son, Give, I pray thee, glory to the Lord God of Israel, and make confession unto Him; and tell me now what thou hast done: hide it not from me." (Josh. vii. 19.) The Pharisees conjure this man, by an appeal to God, to confess to them the truth of his blindness and its cure, which they imply he is not doing. Under the pretext of religion they wish to force him to unsay what he had already said. But he refuses to argue with them on subtleties which are beyond him, and which do not concern him. One thing he realizes without any possibility of mistake, and on that he is willing to give evidence, on the difference of his present condition from his former. He was born blind; he now sees. As to how that was brought about he sees no good use that will be served in repeating it. Such is his gratitude to Jesus that it only knows one limit—viz., that they and all should become His disciples, whatever he may mean by that term.

28 [Then they reviled him,] and said, Thou art His disciple: but we are (Moses' disciples.)

[A. Omits, Then: S. V. And they reviled him.]
(Alf. Disciples of Moses.)

29 We know that God (spake) unto Moses: as for this (fellow) we know not from whence He is.

(Alf. Hath spoken—Man.)

30 The man answered and said unto them, Why herein is a marvellous thing, that ye know not from whence He is, and yet He (hath opened) mine eyes.[1]

(Alf. Opened.)

---

[1] Why herein is a marvellous thing (ἐν γὰρ τούτῳ θαυμαστόν ἐστι).—"In a cultivated prose style γὰρ (for) is the causal particle most usually employed. Agreeably to its origin (contracted from γε and ἄρα, it commonly expresses a corroboration or admission (γε) of what precedes (ἄρα). Sane igitur, certe igitur, sane pro rebus comparatis. In ἐν γὰρ τούτῳ θαυμαστόν ἐστιν, the reply specially refers

31 [Now] we know that God heareth not sinners: but if any man be a worshipper of God, and (doeth) His will, him He heareth.[1]

[S. V. Omits, Now.]
(Alf. Omits, Now—do.)

32 Since the world began (was it not heard) that any man opened the eyes of (one that was born blind.)

(Alf. It was never heard—a man born blind.)

33 If This Man were not (of God) He could do nothing.[2]

(Alf. From God.)

In reply to the assertion of the Pharisees that they know not whence Jesus is, that is, whether He has been sent by God, or by the devil, the beggar expresses his utter astonishment that, after Jesus has opened the eyes of one born blind, they who were skilled in the Law and who were the authorised interpreters of it should be at a loss to determine whence He is and by whom He has been sent. He then proceeds to prove to them that God must have sent Him.

34 They answered and said unto him, Thou wast (altogether born) in sins, and dost thou teach us? And they (cast him out.)

(Margin. Excommunicated him.)
(Alf. Wholly born.)

Jesus Himself said that He was sent by God, and God, as the beggar argues, was not accustomed to allow miracles to be wrought for the confirmation of lies and hypocrisy. From the very beginning of

---

to the statement of the Pharisees in verse 29 (ἄρα), and then subjoins an assertion (γε): sane quidem mirum est; in this at least it is assuredly wonderful."—Winer's *Grammar of New Testament*, 467.

[1] And doeth His will (καὶ τὸ θέλημα αὐτοῦ ποιῇ.)—"As in other passages in the Authorised Version we have a Subjunctive instead of an Indicative, an actual fact dealt with as though it were only a possible subjunctive conception, so here we have just the converse, an Indicative instead of a Subjunctive. It is true that in modern English the Subjunctive is so rapidly disappearing, that 'If any man doeth His will' might very well pass. Still it was an error when our Translators wrote; and there is, at any rate, an incongruity in allowing the Indicative '*doeth*' in the second clause of the sentence to follow the subjunctive '*be*' in the first, both equally depending upon 'if': one would gladly therefore see a return to 'do His will,' which stood in Tyndale's Version."—Archbishop Trench on *Authorised Version*, p: 29.

[2] If this man were not of God he could do nothing (εἰ μὴ ἦν οὗτος παρὰ θεοῦ, οὐκ ἠδύνατο ποιεῖν οὐδέν). "In the consequent clause ἄν joined with the Imperfect may sometimes be omitted, as when there is Imperfect in the condition and Imperfect in the conclusion, as in John ix. 33, 'were He not from God, He could do nothing.'"—Winer's *Grammar of New Testament*, 321.

the world it had never been heard that any man, however great, had ever opened the eyes of one born blind. Moses and the prophets wrought many miracles, but it was the special prerogative of Jesus to open the eyes of the blind. Jesus therefore was greater than Moses. The Pharisees prefer to be the disciples of Moses, he prefers to be the disciple of Jesus. For unless He were from God He could do nothing, He could have no power whatever to open the eyes of the blind. That is a supernatural work and could only be wrought by express permission from God.

Unable to answer his reasoning, the Pharisees accuse him of presumption in attempting to teach them. He was altogether born in sin, as his very blindness showed, and he had learnt nothing but sin ever since his birth, for him to think of teaching them! In their headlong haste the Pharisees do not see that their two charges against this man cannot be both true, the one that he had never been blind at all, but was an impostor, the other that his very blindness even from his birth was a proof of his sinfulness. They cast him out from the house or building in which they were then assembled, and they cast him out of the society of the synagogue.

The very means, which the Pharisees have adopted all through this transaction to disprove the truth of the miracle, bring the truth and perfection of it more plainly to the light and proclaim to all future ages that the evidence for it was such as could not be overthrown. Here is the case of a man born blind miraculously cured by Jesus, who works this miracle as a proof of His claim to be God. The witnesses respecting it are various, and they are influenced rather by the fear of the Pharisees and the consequences of their testimony. They are cautious in their evidence and show no officious readiness to testify beyond what they actually knew as eye-witnesses. The Pharisees have them all before them and sift their evidence to detect any possible inaccuracy in it. The neighbours who had known the beggar before testify as to his identity, and to that only, that this is the man who had been accustomed to sit there and beg. The parents of the man in question give evidence, but they scrupulously confine themselves to the knowledge of two facts: he is their son, and he was born blind. The man himself gives evidence as to the Person who had healed him, and as to the means, the instruments, which He had used for that purpose. It was the Man called Jesus who had put clay upon his eyes and bid him go wash in the Pool of Siloam, and he went and came seeing. He says nothing as to the way in which He had made the clay, because he had not seen it, and knew it only by report. They themselves are witnesses that the man can now see. To all this strictly legal evidence, and accumulated as it is, the Pharisees are unable to offer a single objection. Their only answer is, that it was the Sabbath Day on which Jesus had made clay to put upon his eyes, and that this amounted to a profanation of the day which God had commanded to be kept holy. It was therefore impossible, they said, that God could have permitted a miracle to be wrought by a man who had thus profaned the Sabbath.

35 [Jesus] heard that they had cast him out: (and when he had found him, He said) [unto him], Dost thou believe [(on) the Son of God?]

[S. And Jesus : S. V. Omit, unto him : S V. On the Son of Man.]
(Alf. And He found him and said—in.)

36 [He answered and said] [(Who) is he, Lord,] that I (might believe on Him?)[1]

[V. Omits, Answered and said: A. Omits, and said: S. Lord, and who is He: V. And who is He, Lord.]
(Alf. And who—may believe in Him.)

37 [And] Jesus said unto him, Thou hast both seen Him, (and it is He that talketh with thee.)

[S. V. Omit, And.]
(Alf. Omits, And—and He that talketh with thee is He.)

38 And he said, (Lord, I believe, And he worshipped Him.)

[S.* Omits this verse.]
(Alf. I believe Lord, and worshipped Him.)

When Jesus knew that the Pharisees had cast out the beggar, He sought for Him. He had already, when He gave him the bodily blessing of sight, imparted to him some seeds of divine grace. These he had used aright. They had brought forth in him abundant fruit. As yet no man had ever defended Jesus and confessed himself His disciple more openly and in the face of greater danger than this beggar. Jesus now seeks him out to impart to him some greater blessing. He had opened his eyes solely on his obedience to His command to Go and wash in the Pool of Siloam. On his cure the beggar had at once come to the conclusion that Jesus must be a prophet, a prophet even greater than Moses. But he did not yet know that He was the Son of God. Nay, so far was he from having the slightest suspicion of this, that when Jesus found him and put to him the question, "Dost thou believe on the Son of God?" he replied, "Who is he, Lord, that I may believe on Him?" When informed that Jesus, who stood before him, and whom, in consequence of his former blindness, he had then seen for the first time, but to whom he owed the gift of sight, that He was the Son of God, he falls down and worships Him.

---

[1] " Who is He, Lord, that I might believe in Him (καὶ τίς ἐστι, κύριε, ἵνα πιστεύσω εἰς αὐτόν; Sc. I wish to know, in order that, &c. Comp. i. 22."—Winer's *Grammar of New Testament*, p. 642.

It may be that Jesus turned immediately to the people, or it may have been after a lapse of some little time when recurring to the healing of the blind beggar. The first appears the most probable.

39 [And Jesus said,] For judgment (I am come) into this world, that they which see not (might) see: and that they which see (might be made) blind.

[S.* Omits, And Jesus said.]
(Alf. Came I—may—may become.)

40 [And] some of the Pharisees which were with him [heard (these words) and said] unto Him, Are we blind also?

[S. V. Omit, And: S. Heard it, and said.]
(Alf. And those of the Pharisees—these things—Are we also blind.)

41 Jesus said unto them, If ye were blind, ye should have no sin: but now ye say, We see: [therefore] your sin remaineth.

[S. V. Omit, Therefore.]
(Alf. Ye would not have sin—omits, therefore.)

For judgment Jesus came into the world. The Incarnation was a trial of men's character, such as had never been before. The poor humble souls who, like this beggar, had lived in sin and ignorance from want of better instruction were brought to the knowledge of salvation through Jesus the Incarnate God. The Pharisees, who in the pride of intellect and of superior knowledge despised others, also despised the lowly estate of the Son of God. Their blindness was the effect of their pride followed by its natural punishment in this world, that is, by an increase of blindness. In the world to come it would receive another and a greater punishment. If they were ignorant and blind, but humble, and sensible of their blindness, they would ask from Him a remedy for their blindness, and they would obtain it. If their rejection of Jesus was the result of invincible ignorance, of their unavoidable ignorance of Holy Scripture, their sin would be slight in comparison with what it is. Now through malice and arrogance they persist in their denial of Jesus, they refuse to acknowledge the truth and the power of the miracles which He works to prove that He is sent by God, there remains therefore no remedy for their ignorance and unbelief. The blind man, who does not know that he is blind, will of course refuse the blessing of sight if offered to him. There can be no hope of cure for those who are blind but unconscious of it, whether their blindness be that of the body or that of the soul. So far from seeking for a remedy they do not admit that they require one. Like these Pharisees they indignantly repudiate the slightest imputation of blindness.

INTRODUCTORY NOTE TO CHAPTER X.

Shepherds and Sheep.—"The encampment, as viewed in the grey morning light, was one vast forest of camels, with a dense underwood of sheep and goats. Presently the whole was in motion. The smaller animals assembled in groups, obedient to the call of their masters, and followed them away into the distance. Thus disappeared flock after flock, each knowing and following its own shepherd. Occasionally the masses mingled, and for a few moments united; but this caused no confusion, for 'a stranger will they not follow: they know not the voice of a stranger.'"—Porter's *Five Years in Damascus*, p. 51.

"Often in my wanderings have I sat beside a fountain in the midst of these wild-looking shepherds. I have seen their flocks gathered round them in one dense mass; and I have been astonished and pleased to observe that this mingling creates no confusion. Each shepherd, when he has finished his repast, or when the time of rest is over, rises from his place and walks away, calling his sheep or goats, and immediately his own flock leaves the throng and follows him."—p. 313.

"We were struck here, as elsewhere, with the wondrous facility with which a shepherd managed his flock. His sheep knew his voice, and followed him. We noticed him going before them, and them coming after him in rank and file. On his uttering a peculiar cry they scampered off to the watering-place; and he had only to raise his voice again to recall them to the pastures. The goats were not so obedient, and they were sure to be in the rear. Yet he had command of them also."—Wilson's *Lands of the Bible*, ii. p. 222.

"The East is and has ever been the land of sheep. . . . . Job had 14,000 sheep, and Solomon sacrificed 120,000 at the dedication of the Temple. Nor will these numbers seem incredible when examined and compared with what now exists in this country. Every year sheep are brought down from the north in such multitudes as to confound the imagination. In 1853 the interior route was unsafe, and all had to be passed along the seaboard. During the months of November and December the whole line of coast was covered with them; they came from Northern Syria and from Mesopotamia, and their shepherds, in dress, manners, and language closely resemble those of Abraham and Job, as I believe. . . . . The shepherds 'put a space between drove and drove,' and then lead on softly as Jacob's shepherds did, and for the same reason. If they over-drive them the flock dies; and even with the greatest care many give out, and, to prevent their dying by the wayside, are slaughtered and sold to the poor, or are eaten by the shepherds themselves. The flocks are also constantly thinning off as they go south by selling on all occasions, and thus the whole country is supplied. How vast must be the numbers when they first set out from the distant deserts of the Euphrates!"—*The Land and the Book*, p. 331.

CHAPTER X.

1 *Christ is the Door, and the Good Shepherd;* 19 *Divers opinions of Him;* 24 *He proveth by His works that He is Christ the Son of God;* 39 *Escapeth the Jews;* 40 *And went again beyond Jordan, where many believed on Him.*

THIS chapter is intimately connected with the one before it. For it was the conduct of the Pharisees in the last chapter which gave rise to our Saviour's teaching in this. After Jesus had opened the eyes of the man born blind, he boldly defended Him as one sent by God and professed himself to be one of His disciples. The Pharisees, unable either to answer his arguments or to resist the force of his testimony in favour of Jesus, expelled him from the society of the synagogue. They did not expel him from being a member of their own, or of any other sect within the Church, but they excommunicated him so far as they were able, and cut him off from being any longer a member of the Church of God at all. To cast out the man because he believed in Jesus was as much as to say that neither was Jesus a member of their communion, that so far was Jesus from being the Messiah, that He was not even a member of the Jewish Church.

On this Jesus directs His public teaching so as to explain the nature of communion with God through His Church on earth. He delivers two parables, or rather two allegories. In the first of these he shows that He, Jesus, is the door of the sheepfold, that is, of God's Church on earth, and that all who enter the fold either as shepherds or as sheep must enter through Him, by faith in Him. In the second He shows that He is the Good Shepherd, and that the pastors and rulers of the Church are good in proportion as they resemble Him. These two parables, explained as they are by Himself, must have proved to the people most clearly and in a manner which they could scarcely mistake, who Jesus was and what was the character of His adversaries the Scribes and Pharisees.

Though these two parables, or allegories, are intended to teach a distinct lesson, they are partly mixed up together in their structure. The parable of the Door is contained in the first ten verses of the chapter, and that of the Good Shepherd in the eight following.

1 Verily, verily, I say unto you, he that entereth not

(by) the door into the sheepfold, but climbeth up some other way, the same is a thief and a robber.[1]

(Alf. Through.)

2 But he that entereth in (by) the door (is the shepherd of the sheep.)[2]

(Alf. Through—is shepherd of the sheep.)

3 To him the porter openeth : and the sheep hear his voice: and he calleth his own sheep by name, and leadeth them out.

4 (And when he putteth forth [his own sheep]) he goeth before them, and the sheep follow him : (for) they know his voice.[3]

[S. His own (omits, sheep): V. All his own (omits, sheep.)]
(Alf. Omits, And—when he had put forth all his own—because.)

5 (And) a stranger (will they not) follow, but will flee from him : (for) they know not the voice of strangers.

(Alf. But—they will not—because.)

6 This parable spake Jesus unto them: [but] they understood not what things they were which He spake unto them.

[S. And.]

7 (Then) said Jesus [unto them again], Verily, verily, I say unto you, I am the door of the sheep.

[S. Omits, Unto them again.]
(Alf. Therefore.)

---

[1] See note on xviii. 40.
[2] **Sheep-fold.**—" It now began to rain (on the Lebanon), and at 8.15 we stopped for an hour at a Merâh or goat house. We had seen several of those along the road. They consisted of a large yard, enclosed by a wall of stone like a house, eight or ten feet high: a portion being covered with a rude flat roof. In the present instance the single doorway was so low that our horses could not enter. We therefore took refuge under the high northern wall.—Robinson's *Later Researches*, p. 39.

[3] **They know his voice.**—" A traveller once asserted to a Syrian shepherd, that the sheep know the *dress* of their master, not his *voice*. The shepherd, on the other hand, asserted it was the *voice* they knew. To settle the point, he and the traveller changed dresses, and went among the sheep. The traveller in the shepherd's dress, called on the sheep, and tried to lead them : but 'they knew not his voice,' and never moved. On the other hand they ran at once to the call of their owner, though thus disguised."— *Mission to the Jews from Scotland*, p. 174.

8 All that ever came [before me] are thieves and robbers: but the sheep did not hear them.

[S. Omits, before Me.]

9 I am the door: (by) Me if any man enter in, he shall be saved, and shall go in and out, and (find) pasture.

(Alf. Through—shall find.)

10 The thief cometh not, but for to steal and to kill, and to destroy: (I am come that ye) [might have life], and (that ye might have it more abundantly.)

[S. Might have everlasting life.]
(Alf. I came that they—that they might have it abundantly.)

The pith of the allegory lies in the meaning of the following terms, the fold, the door, the porter, the sheep, and the shepherd. Not only do these words contain the substance of this allegory, but they contain the substance of His whole teaching. If we understand these terms aright, we shall comprehend the main drift of the Gospel, the great object of the Incarnation.

It is seldom possible in a parable to make the two things that are compared correspond accurately in every point. Probably all that is required or intended is a general resemblance, strong in the particular, for which the comparison was instituted.

The Sheepfold is the Church of God. Formerly this was co-extensive with the nation of the Jews, and almost limited to it. After the Incarnation the door was opened, and the Gospel preached throughout the world, so that men from every nation under heaven could enter the fold. It was from the synagogue, the local representative of this fold, that the Pharisees cast out the man who was born blind. The sheepfold, the Church, is to the world at large what the Ark was to Noah and his family in the Deluge, the one place of refuge and salvation provided by God from the destruction hanging over the world through sin.

The Door of the fold is Jesus Himself. This is the principal point in the parable. The Pharisees had cast out the man born blind because he believed in Jesus, and by this parable He teaches them that He is the door of the fold, that the only way in which they can enter the fold of God is through Him, through faith in Him, as the Messiah, the Son of God. There is but one door, through which both shepherds and sheep must enter the fold, and Jesus is that door. When speaking of the shepherds (verses 2, 7, and 8), He says He is the door through which they must enter, and that those who do not enter through Him are thieves and robbers, whose object is not the good of the sheep, but to gratify their own love of gain, or their own malice, "to steal, and to kill, and to destroy." When speaking of the sheep (v. 9), He says that He is the door through which all who desire to be saved must enter. The abundance of grace and of spiritual nourishment provided for those who are in the fold, as well as their security from evil and from fear of evil through Satan and his agents, is beautifully expressed in the words, "shall go in and out and find pasture."

Jesus the Shepherd may be said to enter through the door, that is, through Himself, because He enters the fold by His own authority. Other shepherds enter it by the authority which He gives them.

The prophets and other holy men of old were shepherds over God's sheep, before the coming of Christ in the Flesh, but they too entered the fold through Him, the door. They came in His name and by His authority. They are not those who climb up some other way. Nor is it very easy to see exactly who are meant by these words. For we have no accurate account of falseteachers who came before Jesus, and who assumed to themselves either the title of Messiah, or who laid claim to His power, and whose object was their own personal gain, or to kill and destroy the sheep. It has been thought that Jesus has reference here to the devil, of whom He had spoken in the last chapter as a murderer from the beginning.

In one respect the character of the door into the sheepfold in Palestine is singularly calculated to represent the lowly estate of the Son of Man. As a rule they are made remarkably low. Thus they are fitting emblems of Him who was God, and who yet became Man. Thus too they should remind His followers, the shepherds of the Church, of the lesson which they have to learn of Him, to be meek and lowly in heart.

The Porter is the Holy Spirit. He openeth when by His influence He draws men into the Church of God, or when He reveals to them the meaning of Holy Scripture. Faith to believe in Jesus, as the Son of God, the Saviour of the world, is especially the gift of the Holy Spirit.

If the expression the porter openeth is to be applied to Jesus, who is the Shepherd, the Good Shepherd, it must be in a sense different from that in which it is understood of others. It may be that He opened to Jesus, when at His Baptism He descended upon Him, and bore witness that He was the Son of God, and thus openly and before men gave Him a commission to be the Head over the Church, the Good Shepherd of the fold. It may also refer to the public sanction which all through His Ministry the Holy Spirit gave to Jesus by working cures and miracles and casting out devils at His will and command.

The Sheep are all the disciples of Jesus, all who have ever been in covenant with Him, all who are in the Church. The division into sheep and goats is not made until the Day of Judgment. All in the fold are treated as sheep, they are tended with the same care of the Shepherd, and they feed on the same pasture. Some have thought that by the sheep here is meant only the true sheep, only those who shall be acknowledged as such at the Day of Judgment. Others think, and it would seem with greater probability, that all who enter the sheepfold are meant. For Jesus is setting forth his relation to the whole fold, to the Church militant on earth, He is the door through which they must all enter.

The Shepherd is Jesus Himself. He is the Chief Shepherd, others are subordinate to Him. In this parable Jesus lays down several marks or notes of a true Shepherd. He enters through the door. To him the porter openeth. The sheep hear and know his voice. He calls his own sheep by name and leadeth them out. He goeth before them, and the sheep follow him.

The habits of the shepherds in Palestine, and their almost affectionate attention to their flocks, are well suited to represent the tender care and concern which the shepherd of souls should feel in the welfare of his flock. The shepherd of the country goes before his sheep, and they follow him. So the Christian shepherd should lead his sheep on by his example. He should be first in danger, first in all Christian graces, and first in all holy and devout ways. His is not the stinted service of the hireling who feels no personal interest in their well-being, but the love of one who regards them as his own, of one who loves them.

In the last verse of the parable Jesus compares the object of those, whom He had before described as thieves and robbers, with His object. They came to steal, and to kill, and to destroy. He came, He the Word was made Flesh, in order that they might enter the fold, and become His sheep, and that they might have life, and that they might have it abundantly. The great object of the Incarnation was that His brethren in the flesh might be delivered from the bondage of Satan, and might receive grace to enable them to walk in His steps, and afterwards to ascend with Him in glory everlasting.

From the parable of the door into the sheepfold Jesus passes on to that of the Good Shepherd.

11 I am the Good Shepherd: the Good Shepherd (giveth) His life for the sheep.

(Alf. Layeth down.)

12 [But] he that is an hireling, and not the shepherd, whose own the sheep are not (seeth) the wolf coming, and leaveth the sheep, and fleeth : and the wolf (catcheth) them, and scattereth [the sheep.]

[V. Omits, But: S. V. Omit, the sheep.]
(Alf. Beholdeth—teareth.)

13 [(The hireling fleeth)], because he is an hireling, and careth not for the sheep.

[S. V. A.* Omit, the hireling fleeth.]
(Alf. Omits, the hireling fleeth.)

14 I am the Good Shepherd, and (know My sheep), [and am known of Mine.]

[S. V. And Mine know Me.]
(Alf. I know Mine own.)

15 (As) the Father knoweth Me, (even so know I) the Father: and I lay down My life for the sheep.

(Alf. Even as—and I know.)

16 And other sheep I have, which are not of this fold: them also I must bring, and they shall hear My voice: (and there shall be one fold and one shepherd.)[1]

(Alf. And they shall become one flock, one shepherd.)

17 (Therefore) doth My Father love Me, because I lay down My life, that I (might) take it again.

(Alf. For this cause—may.)

18 [(No man) taketh it] from Me, but I lay it down of Myself. I have power to lay it down, and I have power to take it again. This commandment (have I received of My Father.)[2]

[S. V. No man hath taken it.]
(Alf. None—received I from my Father.)

---

[1] This fold—One fold. (τῆς αὐλῆς ταύτης—μία ποίμνη)—" Something of precision and beauty is lost at John x. 16, by rendering αὐλὴ and ποίμνη both by fold. 'And other sheep I have, which are not of this fold, (αὐλῆς) : these also I must bring, and they shall hear My voice: and there shall be one fold (ποίμνη) and one shepherd.' It is remarkable that in the Vulgate there is the same obliteration of the distinction between the two words, ovile standing for both. Substitute 'flock' for 'fold' on the second occasion of its recurring (this was Tyndale's rendering, which we should not have forsaken), and it will be at once felt how much the verse will gain. The Jew and the Gentile are the two 'folds' which Christ, the Good Shepherd, will gather into a single 'flock.'"—Archbishop Trench on *Authorised Version*, p. 69.

"Much attention has been directed by recent writers to the synonyms of the New Testament. They have pointed out what is lost to the English reader by such confusions as those of αὐλὴ *fold* and ποίμνη *flock* in John x. 16, where in our Version the same word stands for both, though the point of our Lord's teaching depends mainly on the distinction between the many folds and the one flock."—Dr. J. B. Lightfoot on *Revision of New Testament*, p. 71.

[2] This Commandment have I received of My Father. (ταύτην τὴν ἐντολὴν ἔλαβον παρὰ τοῦ πατρός μου.) "After

In the former parable Jesus lays down the qualities or characteristics of a good shepherd, and in this He claims them for Himself. He declares Himself the Good Shepherd. He knows His sheep individually, their excellencies and their deficiencies, He knows the requirements of each, and He alone is able to supply them.

Whether the wolf come to scatter the sheep by disseminating heresy, or immorality, or by any other device of Satan, the hireling, whose eye is fixed solely on the rewards of the office, and who has but slight regard for the interests of the sheep, is unable to offer any resistance. He shrinks from the attack, and the reason which is given for this is, that he is only an hireling and not the owner of the sheep, and consequently that their welfare is not the chief thing which he has at heart. The hireling's object is the greatest reward with the least labour.

In the Authorised Version, verse 15 has not been happily rendered. It should not stand as an independent sentence. It is intimately connected with verse 14, and should not be separated from it. Verse 15 continues the comparison, and indicates the strength and origin of His love for the sheep. It may be paraphrased somewhat in this way, As the Father knows and loves Me as His Own Son, and I know and love Him as My Father, so in like manner I know and love My sheep, and they know and love Me. The standard of love is the love between the Father and the Son. This too is the cause, as well as the measure, of the love between the Son and the sheep. The nearer the human love approaches the divine the more pure and perfect it is. The origin and the measure of His love for the sheep is the love between Himself and the Father, and the proof of His love for the sheep is that He lays down His life for them.

The expression, "I lay down My life" would almost of itself imply that the act was voluntary and only for a time. But this is not left to rest on the probable meaning of a single word. It is stated in distinct formal propositions as clearly as language can express it. The act of laying down His life was so far from being a sign of compulsion, or of inferiority to the Father, that it was the mark of union and love between Them. The way of Humility, His Passion, His Death on the Cross, was the way to bring Honour and Glory and Exaltation to the Godhead.

Jesus here foretells His Death and Resurrection, and He is at some pains to make them comprehend that His Death was voluntary, that He had the power but not the will to avoid it. In His instruction to the Jews He shows that His Death was by His Own will, and

---

verbs of receiving, borrowing, &c. ἀπὸ has merely the general meaning of *whence*. In the expression λαμβάνειν παρά τινος the τις denotes the person actually delivering or tendering: in λαμβάνειν ἀπὸ τινος, it de- notes merely the proprietor. Christ says with strict precision ταύτην τὴν ἐντολὴν ἔλαβον παρὰ τοῦ πατρός μου."—Winer's *Grammar of New Testament*, p. 388.

all through His Passion He gave proofs of this. He, who, by His secret power, could cause the band of soldiers and officers who were sent to take Him to go backward and fall to the ground (xviii. 6); He, who, by His touch could heal the ear of Malchus (xviii. 10); He, who, after such hours of exhaustion as human nature had never before experienced, had strength at the last moment before His Death to cry with a loud voice, "Father, into Thy hands I commend My Spirit" (Luke xxiii. 46); He who could do this showed that He had power successfully to resist Death.

In this parable too we get a glimpse of the nature of the Hypostatic Union. Through His Manhood, through His nature as Man, He laid down His life. Through His power as God He took it again and rose again from the dead. But to lay down His life was not the result of His Own single, individual will only, so to speak, it was the joint act of Himself and the Father. His Own will is expressed by laying down His life, and His Father's will is expressed by giving the command, and by loving Him because He laid down His life.

But Jesus has other sheep beside those of the Jewish nation, for whom He lays down His life. He here intimates that after His Death and Resurrection He would send His Apostles and disciples to preach to the Gentiles and to gather sheep from among them, sheep who would hear His voice. The Jews though His sheep, as a nation, refused to hear His voice. Through the preaching of the Gospel the Gentiles would be converted to Him and would obey His commands. The fold should no longer be confined to the seed of Abraham after the flesh, but it should be enlarged so as to contain all who walked in the steps of Abraham's faith. They should become one flock under Him, the One Shepherd, and in one fold, the Church. Though dispersed among different nations and over different quarters of the world, the Church forms but one fold, and but one flock, of which Jesus Christ is the One Shepherd.

19 There was a division [therefore] again among the Jews (for) these sayings.

[S. V. Omit, Therefore.]
(Alf. Because.)

20 [(And) many] of them said, He hath a devil, and is mad: why hear ye Him?

[S. V. Therefore many.]
(Alf. For.)

21 [Others] said, These are not the words of Him that hath a devil. Can a devil open the eyes of the blind?

[S. But others.]

The answer of those who defend Jesus plainly connects these two parables with the miraculous healing of the man born blind. That event is still so fresh that they appeal to it as a refutation of the possibility of His being possessed with a devil. "Can a devil open the eyes of the blind?"

It is the custom of devils to arrogate to themselves the power and the honour due to God only. The Jews therefore say that Jesus is possessed with a devil, because He said that God was His Father, and that He was the Son of God. They accused Him of being mad, or raving like a madman, because He said that He lay down His life and that of His Own accord. The first of these appeared contrary to fact, for He was then alive; and the second contrary to the nature of things, because no man willingly laid down his own life. To these accusations Jesus makes no reply. He leaves His defence to those who believe in Him.

22 [(And) it was] at Jerusalem the feast of the dedication, [and] it was winter.[1]

[V. It was then: S. V. Omit, and.]
(Alf. Now it was the feast of the dedication at Jerusalem. It was winter.)

The Feast of the Dedication was the anniversary feast of some former dedication of the Temple, and what that was is fixed by the time of the year in which it was held. There are descriptions of two dedications in Canonical Scripture and one in Apocryphal. There is a very full relation of the dedication of the first Temple, of that built by Solomon (1 Kings viii.), which seems to have been a model for subsequent dedications. This took place in the month Ethanim (v. 2) that is part of September and October. Zerubbabel's temple was finished after their return from Babylon in the month Adar, that is part of February and March (Ezra vi. 15). The account of the dedication which Ezra gives, implies that it was held immediately after (v. 16). In this temple Antiochus Epiphanes king of Syria set up an idol altar and otherwise polluted it with every mark of profanation B.C. 167. After it had remained

---

[1] The Feast of the Dedication.—"The Rabbins have a tradition: From the five and twentieth day of the month Chisleu there are eight days of the Encenia or Feast of Dedication, in which time it is not lawful either to weep or fast. For when the Greeks entered into the Temple they defiled all the oil that was there. But when the kingdom of the Asmoneans had conquered them, they sought and could not find but one single vial of oil, that had been laid up under the seal of the chief Priest. Nor was there enough in it but to light for one day. There was a great miracle: for they lighted up the lamps from that oil for eight days together: so that the year after, they instituted the space of eight days for the solemnizing that Feast. (Schabb, fol. 21, 2).

"The Feast was instituted in commemoration of their Temple and religion being restored to them: the continuance of the Feast for eight days was instituted in commemoration of that miracle; both by the direction of the Scribes, when there was not so much as one prophet throughout the whole land.

"The Passover, Pentecost, and Feast of Tabernacles might not be celebrated in any place but Jerusalem, but the Encenia were kept everywhere throughout the whole land."—Lightfoot, ii, 577.

deserted for three whole years, Judas Maccabæus re-dedicated the Temple and replaced the holy vessels, &c. They celebrated the feast for eight days, and ordained that the days of the dedication of the altar should be kept in their season from year to year by the space of eight days, from the five and twentieth day of the month Casleu, with mirth and gladness. (1 Maccabees iv. 59.) The month Casleu or Chisleu, was made up of parts of November and December. It was the anniversary of this dedication that is here referred to in verse 22.

23 (And Jesus walked) in the temple in Solomon's porch.[1]

(Alf. And Jesus was walking.)

24 Then came the Jews round about Him, and said unto Him, (How long dost Thou make us to doubt)? If Thou (be) the Christ, tell us plainly.

(Alf. How long dost Thou hold our mind in suspense?—art.)

The interval between the Feast of Tabernacles and the Feast of Dedication was about two months. For the former was celebrated at the end of September and the latter early in December. Thus all that is recorded by St. John between chapter vii. 2, and chapter x. 22. must have taken place within these two months. The time which intervened between this Feast of Dedication and the Passover, at which He was crucified, was about three months. All therefore, that St. John relates from this time to the end of his Gospel, happened in the last three months of our Saviour's life on earth.

The Evangelist adds that it was winter, either to indicate the approach of the Passover, at which He would have to suffer, which was in the spring, or, which is far more probable, to account for His walking not in the Court of the Temple which was in the open air, but in the porch or arcade or colonnade which ran along the side of the Court and which was roofed above as a protection from the weather.

The Jews were not sincere in saying, "How long dost Thou make make us to doubt? If Thou be the Christ, tell us plainly." Their object was not to certify themselves of the truth, but to entrap Jesus and to cause Him to commit Himself, and to say something on which they could found a charge against Him, either of blasphemy against God, or of treason against the regal power.

In reply to their words Jesus says, That He has already declared

---

[1] Solomon's Porch.—" Along the eastern side of the Temple Court extended Solomon's Porch, where Jesus was wont to walk (John x. 23), and where the multitude crowded round Peter and John after they had cured the lame man. (Acts iii. 2.) This porch, or *stoa*, consisted of a double range of cloisters, between three rows of columns. It was of great height, and its commanding position on the eastern brow of Moriah, over the deep valley of the Kidron, made it look still more so. There were also ranges of cloisters along the other two sides, but Josephus does not speak specially of them."—*Handbook of Palestine*, p. 119.

who He is, and more than that, He has confirmed His declaration by such works as no mere man could work: that the Father has testified in His behalf, by allowing Him to use supernatural power in confirmation of the truth of what He had said. Since they had believed neither His words nor His works, no further declaration would have any weight with them. He then goes on to assign the reason of their unbelief. He had already done this before in words very similar to those which He now uses. This was not the want of plainness or distinctness in His language, it was not the want of proof of His divine power, but the want of will in themselves to become His disciples. Their own schemes of ambition and worldly policy would not allow them to believe that the son of a carpenter could possibly be the Messiah, whatever might be the arguments by which He proved His Oneness with the Father, or whatever might be the works by which He showed that He was sent by Him.

25 Jesus answered [them], I told you, and ye (believed) not: the works that I do in my Father's name, (they bear witness) of Me.

[S. Omits, them.]
(Alf. Believe—these bear witness.)

26 (But) ye believe not, (because) ye are not of My sheep, [as I said unto you.]

[S. V. Omit, as I said unto you.]
(Alf. Nevertheless—for.)

27 My sheep hear My voice, and I know them, and they follow Me.

28 And I give unto them eternal life: and they shall never perish, (neither shall any man pluck them) out of My hand.

(Alf. And none shall tear them.)

29 [My Father], (which gave them Me) is greater than all: and (no man) is able (to pluck them) out of [My Father's hand.]¹

[S. The Father: S. V. the Father's hand.]
(Alf. Which hath given them to Me—none—to tear them.)

---

¹ **My Father—My Father's hand.**— "In these and similar places (xix. 13; xxi. 1), while the phraseology is exceedingly simple, the variations which the text exhibits, are so exceedingly numerous, that when it is discovered that a *Church Lesson begins in those places*, we may be sure that we have been put in

30 I and (My Father) are One. (ἐγώ καὶ ὁ πατὴρ ἕν ἐσμεν.)
(Alf. The Father.)

He invites them to become His disciples, and promises them eternal life, the life of grace here, and the life of glory hereafter. He shows them that if they become His disciples, human and weak as He may appear, no one will be able to draw them from under His protection against their own consent. If they become His disciples and still perish, it will not be because He cannot deliver them, but because they remove themselves from under His hand. No one could take them from God the Father, because He is above all. In like manner no one could take them from Jesus, because He and the Father are One. Two Persons, they are one substance; the plural verb (ἐσμεν) expressing the plurality of Persons, and the neuter singular adjective (ἕν) the unity of substance. Because they are One in essence, in Godhead, therefore they were One in will and in power.

This passage thus understood was used by the early Church to refute some of the heresies of that day. Arguments were drawn from the use of the plural verb "we are" (ἐσμεν) to disprove the doctrine of Sabellius and his followers, who in the third century denied that there was a plurality of Persons in the Godhead. From the use of the neuter singular adjective one (ἕν), arguments were also drawn to refute the opinions of Arius and his followers, who in the fourth century denied that the Father and the Son were of one essence or substance. Hence arose the use of the word Homoousion, Consubstantial, to guard the true faith of the Church, and to denote that the Father and the Son were of the same, not of a like, or different, essence or substance.

That this was the sense, in which the Jews understood these words, there can be no question. They took up stones to stone Him, because that He, being a Man, made Himself God. His words would have been blasphemy, had they not been true.

31 ([Then] the Jews) took up stones again to stone Him.
[S.V. Omit, Then.]
(Alf. The Jews therefore.)

---

possession of the name of the disturbing force."—Burgon on *The last twelve verses of St. Mark*, p. 223.
"At times the repetition of a noun (instead of a pronoun) is employed to denote an emphatic antithesis. .... Accordingly, it will be perceived that the repetition of the noun in the following passage is not without special import ὁ πατὴρ μου, ὃς δέδωκέ μοι, μείζων πάντων ἐστί καὶ οὐδεὶς δύναται ἁρπάζειν ἐκ τῆς χειρὸς τοῦ πατρός μου."—Winer's *Grammar of New Testament*, p. 157.

32 Jesus answered them, Many good works have I shewed you [from My Father]: for which of (those works) do ye stone Me?¹

[S. V. From the Father.]
(Alf. The Father—these works.)

33 The Jews answered Him, [saying], For a good work we stone Thee not: but for blasphemy: [and] because that Thou being a man, makest Thyself God.

[S. V. A. Omit, saying—S. omits, and]

The Jews had themselves requested Him to tell them, without any reservation, or indistinctness of language, whether He were the Christ, intimating that if He were they would worship Him as such. Now when He declares that He is God in language which they cannot misunderstand, they take up stones to stone Him, giving as their reason, that He, being a Man, made Himself God. In the very act of hurling the stones at Him they are withheld by some secret power, and Jesus, in order as it would seem, to bring out more strongly than ever His equality and Oneness with the Father, puts a question to them. He had used words, which, as the Jews well saw, could have but one meaning, to make Himself equal with God. When they take up stones to stone Him, He asks them, For which of the many good works it was that they did this? Was it for raising the dead, or healing the sick, or opening the eyes of the blind? They reply it was not for any of His works, but for His words, for the blasphemy of His words, because that He, being a Man, made Himself God.

Jesus acknowledges that they had understood His words aright. But He does not withdraw them, He does not retract in the least. He does not soften down His meaning but repeats and enforces it in a different form. He shows them that the word God is used in Scripture in two senses; (1) In a lower sense it is applied to those who have a power delegated to them by God: and (2) in the highest sense it is the name of the Creator of all things. In the first sense they were gods, they were judges and rulers set over the people by God. In the second sense He was God; He it was who gave them their power and authority.

34 Jesus answered them, Is it not written [in your law], I said, ye are gods?

[S. In the law.]

---

¹ For which of those works do ye stone Me? (διὰ ποῖον αὐτῶν ἔργον λιθάζετέ με.) "Sometimes the Present is employed to denote what is just about to take place—what one is intending to effect, and what he has already made the necessary preparations to do, as in John x. 32. διὰ ποῖον αὐτῶν ἔργον λιθάζετέ με; "they had already taken up stones.") Winer's *Grammar of New Testament*, p. 280.

35 If He called them gods, unto whom the word of God came, and the Scripture cannot be (broken);
(Alf. Made void.)

36 Say ye of Him, whom the Father (hath sanctified and sent) into the world, Thou blasphemest: because I said, I am the Son of God?
(Alf. Sanctified and sent.)

They were called gods by the Psalmist (Ps. lxxxii. 6-8) and He was God, but the difference between them was this, they were called gods because the word of God came to them, and gave them a certain authority: He was God, because the Father sanctified Him, and sent Him into the world, that is, because the fulness of the Godhead dwelt in Him bodily. They knew from the testimony of John the Baptist, that the Holy Spirit had descended upon Him, and that a voice from the Father had set His seal upon Him, had given His highest sanction to Him, and declared that Jesus was His Beloved Son, in whom He was well pleased. There was, as His words imply, the same difference between Himself and them, mere man though he seemed, as the Psalmist had made between the Most High and those, who were His children, between those who should die like men, and the God that judgeth the earth.

Jesus then appeals to His words as proving His unity with the Father. If they will not believe His teaching, that He is One with the Father, that the Father is in Him, and He in the Father, He calls on them to examine the character of His works. His works are such as no mere man could perform. They must either admit, that He wrought them by His power as God, or they must admit, that the Father permitted Him to exert supernatural power in confirmation of a claim, which is not true, nay of a claim, which they themselves say is blasphemy, the highest blasphemy, if it be not true. Reduced to this extremity their exasperation knows no bounds, and they attempt again to take Him, but He escapes out of their hands, probably by giving them another proof of His Almighty power as God, by rendering Himself invisible to them.

37 If I do not the works of My Father, believe Me not.[1]
38 (But if I do) though ye believe not Me, believe the

---

[1] If I do not the works of My Father, (εἰ οὐ ποιῶ τὰ ἔργα τοῦ πατρός μου, &c.). "If I neglect My Father's works (and thus withheld from you the proofs of My divine mission, &c.). In the New Testament generally 'if not' is expressed more frequently by εἰ οὐ than by εἰ μή, which latter form most commonly signifies 'except."—Winer's *Grammar of New Testament*, p. 499.

works [that ye may know, and (believe)], that the Father is in Me, [and I in Him.]

[V. That ye may know and understand :—S. V. And I in the Father.]
(Alf. But if I do them—understand—and I in the Father.)

39 Therefore they sought [again] to take Him: (but He escaped) out of their hand.

[S. Omits, again.]
(Alf. And He passed.)

40 [And went away again] beyond (Jordan)[1] [into the place] where John at first baptized: (and He abode there.)[2]

[S. Omits, into the place: A. He went away therefore again.]
(Alf. The Jordan—and there He tarried.)

41 And many (resorted) unto Him, and said, (John did)

---

[1] And went away again beyond Jordan.—" To go down this road, (leading from Jerusalem towards the Jordan) as Jesus went down, on foot and with a company of men, made a journey of two days. A mile below Bethany, in a wild glen, they came upon a little spring of pure water, then called En-Shemesh, and now known to travellers and pilgrims as the Apostles' Fountain. Beneath that spring on the hill-side and Jericho in the great plain, there was only one spot in which a man could find shade and drink: the half-way house, the khan at which caravans rested and travellers slept for the night.

" In going to and fro, between Galilee and Judæa, Jesus must have often lodged in the arches of this khan. The wild glen, the desert country dividing two rich cities, offered every temptation to daring thieves, and nothing was more usual than for the people lodging at this inn for the night to see unhappy men, who had been robbed, disabled, and left in the sun to die. Such a sight must have suggested the parable of the Good Samaritan, spoken in the Temple Court: for the Lord's habit was to illustrate moral truths by circumstances which were as familiar to His hearers as light and air.

" Early on the second day of His journey, Jesus would reach the City of Palms, and crossing the Ford into Perea, would find Himself in the dominions of Antipas Herod, comparatively free and safe."—Dixon's *Holy Land*, ii. 227.

[1] And there He abode.—" In its lower course, the sacred stream divided the Roman province of Judæa from the semi-independent province of Perea, as in its upper course it parted Galilee from Trachonitis. The eastern bank lying in another country to the western, a man living near the Ford had the privilege of being able to select his own time for accepting any process of arrest: unless, indeed, Herod, who was still conducting operations on the desert frontier against Aretas, should think proper to give him up to Pilate: an event unlikely to occur, even if Pilate could be persuaded to ask it, since it was well known in Jewry that the procurator was on very bad terms with the prince. Pilate had been the cause of a great crime, which Antipas considered, and justly considered, an infringement of his sovereign rights. This offence is known in history as the Massacre of the Galilæans.

" Under the safeguard of these suspicions and animosities between the two rulers, Jesus could remain near the Ford : preaching to the crowds who followed Him from Jericho and the hamlets of Perea: and waiting for the time of the great Feast, when He proposed to go up with the Galilæan caravan to Jerusalem and accept His appointed crown of thorns.' —Dixon's *Holy Land*, ii. 232.

no miracle: but all things (that) John spake of this Man were true.

(Alf. Came—John indeed did—whatsoever.)

42 And many believed (on Him) there.

(Alf. In Him.)

Jesus withdrew to Bethabara or Bethany beyond Jordan where John had baptized Him. He went there probably to recall to the minds of those who accompanied Him the testimony which John had at His Baptism borne to Him, as well as the testimony of the Father. They seem to have held the memory of John in great reverence, and to have treasured up his sayings. They reason like men who were open to conviction, anxious only to learn the truth. John, as they say, did no miracles, and yet we believed his words. Jesus has wrought many miracles, and in confirmation of the truth of what He says, why then should we not believe Him? Besides, whatever John said respecting Jesus, so far as we are able to judge, was true; He is, as John said He would be, greater than John in His miracles, in the gracious words that fall from His lips, and in the sanctity of His life; we see that John's words are true so far, why should we not believe that they are true in all that he said respecting Him: why should we not believe that Jesus is, as John said, the Messiah, the Lamb of God that taketh away the sin of the world? This honesty of heart prepared the way for their reception of the truth, and many believed on Jesus. Here Jesus remained till within a short time of the Passover, at which He should suffer, when He returned again to Jerusalem.

INTRODUCTORY NOTE TO CHAPTER XI.

Bethany.—" Sixty generations of men have come and gone since that day, yet Bethany (Beth-anyah, House of the Poor) is still the abode of poverty, a heap of stone sheds, mixed with some ruins, and peopled by a rabble of Arab peasants too lazy to work, too abject to thieve. Only two miles from Jerusalem, only one mile from Galilæans' Hill, it is yet out of the world: standing on a ledge of bare rock, looking down into the Cedron Gorge, across to the opposite ridge of Abu Dis, then into the intricate maze of limestone hills which go dropping from shelf to shelf into the plain of the Dead Sea. A track from Jerusalem to Jericho winds through it, over slippery sheets of stone, on which horse and camel find it difficult to keep their feet. A carob here, and a fig tree there, make the absence of verdure more keenly felt.

" The situation of Bethany, if lonely and exposed, is also commanding and picturesque. At the head of two wadies, covering the chief tracks through the wilderness, it is a needful outpost for Jerusalem, and must have been used as a watch-tower from the earliest times. Some old foundations of Jewish style and bevel would seem to show that Bethany was one of those places on the desert edge in which the Kings of Judah built watch-towers to protect the walls. Around this tower poor people would creep and huddle, throwing up their booths and houses beneath its walls, and nothing is more likely in Palestine than that such a village should be called by the name of Bethany (Beth-anyah) House of the Poor."—Dixon's *Holy Land*, ii. p. 205.

On the derivation of the word Bethany, see a learned dissertation by Mr. Deutsch in Dixon's *Holy Land*, ii. p. 214.

CHAPTER XI.

1 *Christ raiseth Lazarus, four days buried;* 45 *Many Jews believe;* 47 *The high priests and Pharisees gather a council against Jesus;* 49 *Caiaphas prophesieth;* 54 *Jesus hid Himself;* 55 *At the Passover they inquire after Him, and lay wait for Him.*

THE Evangelist St. John here omits many of the sayings of Jesus, and at once passes on from the events of December to those of March, that is, from His discourse at the Feast of Dedication and His retirement to Bethany beyond Jordan to the raising of Lazarus from the dead only a few days before His Crucifixion.

1 Now a certain man was sick, named Lazarus, (of Bethany, the town) of Mary and [her sister] Martha.
[A. His sister.]
(Alf. There was a certain man sick—from Bethany, of the town.)

2 It was that Mary which anointed the Lord with ointment, and wiped His feet with her hair, whose brother Lazarus was sick.[1]

---

[1] It was that Mary which anointed the Lord, &c., (ἦν δὲ Μαρία ἡ ἀλείψασα)— "The Participle Aorist is never employed instead of the Participle Future; certainly not in John xi. 2, where the Evangelist alludes to an event long past, which he narrates for the first time in chap. xii."
—Winer's *Grammar of New Testament*, p. 359.
The following contains the reasons that may be urged against referring this to the anointing mentioned in the next chapter.
"The words of xi. 2, 'It was that Mary which anointed the Lord with ointment, and wiped His feet with her hair,' are most generally construed as pointing to that story in the next chapter, xii. 3. 'Then took Mary a pound of ointment of spikenard very costly, and anointed the feet of Jesus, and wiped His feet with her hair,' which seemeth very improper and unconsonant upon these reasons.
"1. To what purpose should John use such an anticipation? It was neither

material to the story that he was entering on chap. xi, to tell that Mary anointed Christ's feet a good while after He had raised her brother: nor was it any other than needless to bring in the mention of it here, since he was to give the full story of it in the next chapter.
"2. The word ἀλείψασα is of such a tense as doth properly denote an action past, and so is to be rendered, if it be rendered in its full propriety, 'It was Mary which had anointed.'
"3. Whereas no reason can be given why John should anticipate it here, if he meant it of an anointing that was yet to come, a plain and satisfactory reason may be given, why he speaks of it here, as referring to an anointing past, namely because he would show what acquaintance and interest Mary had with Christ, which did embolden her to send to Him about her sick brother, for she had washed and anointed His feet heretofore. The words of John therefore point to an action past, and indeed they point at that story of the

3 (Therefore his sisters) sent unto Him, saying, Lord, behold, he whom Thou lovest is sick.

(Alf. His sisters therefore.)

This is not the beggar Lazarus, whom Jesus described as sitting at the gate of the rich man. This Lazarus, from the entertainment which he gave to Jesus and from the number of guests that were invited, seems to have lived in circumstances of comfort and plenty. He is generally considered to have been a man of rank as well as of wealth. The number of Jews who came to console the sisters on the death of their brother, the tomb of Lazarus himself, and the costly ointment, all go to prove that the family was wealthy.

Whether there were two anointings of Jesus or three, and whether these were by different persons or by the same, has been a fruitful source of discussion from the earliest times, from the second century to the present. It has been occasionally held, though by very few, that there were three anointings: but the generality of commentators, and certainly those of most weight, have maintained that there were only two, the first recorded by St. Luke (vii. 37) in the Pharisee's house, but where is not named; the second in Bethany, recorded by St. Matthew (xxvi. 6); by St. Mark (xiv. 3); and by St. John (xii. 3).

Another question is whether these two anointings of Jesus were by different women or by one and the same. The second anointing, that at Bethany, is expressly stated to be by Mary the sister of Lazarus. The other anointing is said to have been by "a woman in the city, which was a sinner." What was the city or who was the woman is not mentioned. A few verses after St. Luke relates that Jesus was accompanied by the Twelve and by certain women who ministered to Him of their substance, and whom He had healed of evil spirits and infirmities, and among them He names Mary, called Magdalene, out of whom went seven devils. Hence it has been concluded that it was Mary Magdalene that anointed Jesus here. From the heading which the translators of the Authorised Version prefixed to chapter vii., it is evident that this was their opinion. But it is nowhere expressly stated that it was Mary Magdalene. Supposing this to be correct, there still remains another question, Was Mary Magdalene the same person as Mary of Bethany, the sister of Lazarus? Among the Fathers, names of very high authority can be quoted as holding this opinion. The Church of Rome has founded her office for Mary

---

woman-sinner washing the feet of Christ with tears and anointing them with ointment, and wiping them with her hair. (Luke vii.) It is true indeed that John who useth these words that we are upon, had not spoken of any such anointing before, hereunto to refer you in his own Gospel, but the passage was so well and renownedly known and recorded by Luke before, that he relateth to it as to a thing of most famous notice and memorial."— Lightfoot, i. 249.

Magdalene on this supposition. It may be said that writers in the Western Church, as a rule, held that Mary Magdalene and Mary of Bethany were the same, while writers in the Eastern Church thought they were different persons. Of late years the opinion that they were not the same seems to have gained ground, but no new arguments for it have been adduced.

Jesus had lately been living at Bethabara, or Bethany, on the east side of Jordan, but the Bethany, where Lazarus dwelt, was on the west side, about two miles from Jerusalem, at the Mount of Olives. (Mark xi. 1.)

To explain the connection of Jesus with the family of Lazarus, and the interest which He naturally took in its welfare, the Evangelist adds, " It was that Mary which anointed the Lord with ointment and wiped His feet with her hair, whose brother Lazarus was sick." Does this anointing refer to the one before the sickness of Lazarus, or to the one after it? There is nothing in the form of the expression itself to decide this. It may refer to an event which had already taken place, or it may by anticipation be intended by the Evangelist to refer to the anointing, which he himself relates in the next chapter. If it refer to a former anointing, then Mary, the sister of Lazarus, and Mary Magdalene may have been one and the same.

The sisters do not ask Jesus to come and heal their brother. But their message seems almost to imply a prayer. They state that their brother is sick, and remind Jesus of His love for him.

4 (When Jesus heard that), He said, This sickness is not unto death, but for the glory of God, that the Son of God (might) be glorified thereby.

(Alf. But when Jesus heard it—may.)

In language which they could not understand at the time, but which, when afterwards understood, would serve as a further confirmation of their faith, Jesus intimates to his disciples, and probably also to the messenger that was sent to Him, that the sickness of Lazarus will not end in his final removal from the scene of trial, but only for a time. He will be restored to it, and in a way that will increase the honour and glory of God among men. For, beholding his miraculous restoration to life by Jesus, they will be compelled to believe that He is the Messiah, the Son of God.

This was one way in which the sickness of Lazarus would be for the glory of God. It is also probable that in using this expression Jesus had reference to His Own Death. He knew that the raising of Lazarus would be the occasion of His Own Crucifixion. When He opened the eyes of the man born blind the fury of the Scribes and Pharisees was wellnigh without bounds. The raising of Lazarus from the dead would add fuel to their malice. They would spare no pains to accomplish His Death.

5 Now Jesus loved Martha, and her sister, and Lazarus.

No reason is given why Jesus loved Martha and her sister and Lazarus. Doubtless it was from what He knew of them. His love was not from the instinctive feeling which a man has to his fellow creatures. It was from His admiration of their lives, of their deeds, and from His knowledge of their hearts. With the exception of the Evangelist St. John, it is said of only one other, besides this family at Bethany that Jesus "loved" them, and that other was the young man who had great possessions. (Mark x. 21.) Hence it has been suggested (Smith's *Bible Dictionary*, *Article Lazarus*), perhaps on too slender grounds, that Lazarus might be this young man. Their age might not be unlike, both young men, their social position would seem to correspond, and they both possessed virtues in an uncommon degree so as to draw forth the love of Jesus.

The sickness of Lazarus would not appear to have been of a lingering nature, but sudden and rapid, as if from one of the fevers of the country, which terminate fatally in a day or two, and sometimes even in the course of a few hours. Hence his death, on the very day on which the messenger is despatched to Jesus, is no indication of remissness on the part of his sisters, but of the rapid progress of his sickness after his first attack.

In remaining where He was two days after He received the news of Lazarus's sickness, Jesus was consulting for their good, that they might have stronger grounds for believing that He was God. In all probability Lazarus was dead before the messenger from his sisters arrived. For when Jesus came to Bethany he found that he had lain in the grave four days already. According to the custom of the country he would be buried either on the day of his death or certainly on the following day. Two days Jesus had delayed, one day was taken up with the journey of the messenger, and one whole day or part of another with the journey of Himself and disciples on foot. In allowing Lazarus to be buried, and his body to become decomposed, it would scarcely be possible for the Jews to deny the reality of the miracle. They could not allege that the vital powers had been, as it were, suspended for a time by sickness, and then restored by the force of nature. The Jews had endeavoured to evade His miracle of opening the eyes of the man born blind by declaring that he had never been blind. Here there would be no possibility of escape. Having been buried four days they must acknowledge that Lazarus had been dead, seeing him alive, they would be compelled to admit that he had been raised from the dead by superhuman power.

6 (When He had heard, therefore) that he was sick, He abode two days still in the same place where He was.

(Alf. When, therefore, He heard—at that time He continued two days.)

7 Then (after that saith He) [to his disciples], Let us go into Judæa [again].

[A. To His disciples: S. Omits, Again.]
(Alf. After this He saith.)

8 (His disciples) say unto Him, (Master, the Jews of late sought to stone Thee): and goest Thou thither again?

(Alf. The disciples—Rabbi, the Jews were but now seeking to stone Thee.)

9 Jesus answered, Are there not twelve hours in the day? If any man walk in the day, he stumbleth not, because he seeth the light of this world.

10 But if a man walk in the night he stumbleth: because (there is no light in him).

(Alf. The light is not in him.)

It is not usual for Jesus to announce beforehand to His disciples the place to which He is next going, or the route which He will take. On this occasion He does so, because the last time they were in Jerusalem the Jews had attempted to stone Him. By way of calming their fear, before going into Judæa, He declares to them His intention to do so. They remind Him of the treatment which He had received when last there, and so vivid is their recollection of it that though it is now two months since, they speak of it as "of late," or "but now." He replies that as the time for man's work and man's rest, the hours of the day and the night, are arranged by God, so the life of Him who is the Light of the world, the time for Him to accomplish the salvation of man is fixed by God, and cannot be shortened or altered by the fickle will of man. Neither have His disciples anything to fear for themselves in accompanying Him into Judæa. So long as He remains with them they need have no fear of persecution. The time will come when the Jews will persecute them, but that will be in the night, when He, the Light of the world, shall have been removed from them. Jesus is the Light. Whoever walks without this Light illuminating his soul by His Holy Spirit, and does not direct his life by His example, he will wander from the path of duty, and will stumble and fall into sin and error.

11 These things said He; and (after that) He saith unto

them, Our friend Lazarus (sleepeth) : but I go, that I may awake him out of sleep.¹

(Alf. After this—is fallen asleep.)

12 [Then said His disciples], Lord, if (he sleep), he (shall do well).

[S. V. Then said the disciples unto Him : A. Then said they unto Him.]
(Alf. He is fallen asleep—will recover.)

13 Howbeit Jesus spake of [his death] : but they thought that He (had spoken of taking) of rest in sleep.

[S. Of death.]
(Alf. Was speaking of the taking.)

14 (Then said Jesus) unto them plainly, Lazarus is dead.²

(Alf. Then said Jesus therefore.)

15 And I am glad for your sakes that I was not there,

---

¹ These things said He, and after that said unto them (ταῦτα εἶπεν, καὶ μετὰ τοῦτο λέγει αὐτοῖς) neither ταῦτα εἶπεν, nor μετὰ τοῦτο is redundant. The latter expression indicates a pause.—Winer's *Grammar of New Testament*, p. 630.

² Then said Jesus therefore (τότε οὖν εἶπεν)—Dr. J. B. Lightfoot points out several inadvertencies where the same word is twice rendered in the English Version, or where conversely the same English word is made to do duty for two Greek words. Of the latter, examples occur in John xi. 14. " *Then* (τότε οὖν) said Jesus unto them plainly," where " then " stands for two words—" then " local and " then " argumentative ; or Rom. vi. 21, " What fruit had ye *then* (τίνα οὖν καρπὸν εἴχετε τότε) in those things whereof ye are now ashamed?" where exactly the same error is committed. Of the converse error— the double rendering of the same word— we have an instance in James v. 16, πολὺ ἰσχύει δέησις δικαίου ἐνεργουμένη, " The effectual fervent prayer of a righteous man availeth much," where the word effectual is worse than superfluous. This last rendering I am disposed to ascribe to carelessness in correcting the copy for the press. The word would be written down on the copy of the Bishops' Bible, which the revisers used, either as a tentative correction or an accidental gloss; and, not having been erased before the copy was sent to the press, would appear in the text. In the Bishops' Bible, which the translators had before them, the passage runs, " The fervent prayer of a righteous man availeth much."—*Revision of New Testament*, p. 182.

Fountain of the Apostles.—We were momentarily in expectation of reaching San Saba, when coming to a fountain (welcome object !) I recognised it as the one we had passed the day before, within an hour of leaving Bethany—the ' Fountain of the Apostles,' it is called—and doubtless they often quenched their thirst at it; and He too, who became man, and hungered and thirsted for our sake! Why might it not have been there, resting before the ascent to Bethany, that ' Jesus said unto them plainly, Lazarus is dead ! '—*Lord Lindsay's Letters in Holy Land*, ii. 67.

to the intent ye may believe: nevertheless let us go unto him.[1]

16 (Then said Thomas, which is called Didymus), unto his fellow disciples, Let us also go, that we may die with Him.

(Alf. Thomas therefore, which is called Didymus, said.)

Jesus is now in Bethabara, or Bethany, on the east side of Jordan, a day's journey from Bethany near Jerusalem, where Lazarus had lived with his sisters. As a preparation for the exertion of his superhuman power in raising Lazarus from the dead, He shows His disciples that, though absent from Lazarus, He knew in what condition he was. The messenger had stated that he was sick; Jesus says that he is asleep; he is dead. To them he was dead, to Him he was asleep, because He could and would shortly raise him to life again. None of His disciples seem to have understood the expression, "he sleepeth;" not even the three, who had already heard Him use it in a similar case once before. (Matt. ix. 24.) But neither the words, nor the miracle that had then followed, suggested to their minds His meaning on the present occasion.

The feeling to which Jesus gives utterance, is not sorrow for the death of His friend Lazarus, but joy that He was not present. He was glad for their sakes, as well as for the sake of others. The restoration of Lazarus to life would strengthen their faith in Him as God, and it would induce many of the Jews to believe in Him. Had He been present Lazarus might not have died; had He been present sooner, his body would not have become so decomposed; his resurrection to life would not have appeared a miracle so decisive or so striking in the eyes of men.

Generally it is Peter who is most forward in zeal and devotion to his Master; here it is Thomas, which name is the Hebrew for Didymus, which is the Greek for Twin-born. Some suppose that he was born in some place that was inhabited by Jews and Greeks promiscuously, and that the Jews called him by his Hebrew name, and the Greeks by his Greek name. His devotion to Jesus is such that he proposes to his fellow disciples to accompany Him into Judæa again, and if He be put to death they, like true and faithful disciples, should

---

[1] To the intent ye may believe (καὶ χαίρω δι᾿ ὑμᾶς, ἵνα πιστεύσητε). "*Ἵνα πιστεύσητε is added to δι᾿ ὑμᾶς by way of illustration: I rejoice on your account (that I was not there), that ye may believe, *i.e.*, now ye cannot but believe."—Winer's *Grammar of New Testament*, p. 480.

COMMENTARY ON ST. JOHN'S GOSPEL.   251

die with Him. It is not weariness of life, or indifference to death, that Thomas wishes to express, but devotion to his Master. He does not say, Let us also go that we may die with Lazarus, but, Let us also go that we may die with Jesus.

17 (Then when) Jesus [came], He found that He had lain in the grave four days already.

[A. Came to Bethany.]
(Alf. When therefore.)

18 Now Bethany was nigh unto Jerusalem, about fifteen furlongs off:¹

19 And many of the Jews (came) to Martha and Mary, to comfort them concerning their brother.

(Alf. Had come.)

20 Then Martha, (as soon as) she heard that Jesus was coming, went (and met Him): but Mary (sat still) in the house.

(Alf. When—to meet Him—was sitting.)

The nearness of Bethany to Jerusalem is mentioned to account for the number of Jews who came to console the sisters on their loss, induced by the ties either of kindred or of friendship.

Martha, probably as the elder sister, or at least as the active practical manager of the house, who is busied with the affairs of every-day life, receives the first intimation of the approach of Jesus, and goes to meet him. Mary remains at home, wrapt in silent meditation and sorrow, and, in all probability, still ignorant that Jesus is at hand.

---

¹ **Bethany was nigh unto Jerusalem, about fifteen furlongs off** (ἦν ἡ Βηθανία ἐγγὺς τῶν Ἱεροσολύμων ὡς ἀπὸ σταδίων δεκαπέντε, and John xii. 1, six days before the Passover (πρὸ ἓξ ἡμερῶν τοῦ πάσχα). "These expressions, it has been thought should regularly run thus: ὡς σταδίους δεκ. ἀπὸ Ἱερος, and ἐξ ἡμέραις πρὸ τοῦ πάσχα. It would appear, however, that in *local* specifications, Greek phraseology was regulated by a different point of view, ἀπὸ σταδίων δεκ. (properly situated at a distance of fifteen furlongs, as in Latin, Liv. xxiv. 46. "Fabius cum a quingentis fere passibus castra posuisset." If it were necessary to specify the speaker's point of view, it would be expressed in the Genitive. The same applies to *temporal* specifications. As it is usual to say πρὸ ἓξ ἡμερῶν, the form of expression was retained when it was necessary to indicate the point of time from which the period in question was counted, as πρὸ ἓξ ἡμερῶν τοῦ πάσχα. However the matter may be considered, the fact is, that both these forms of expression (the *temporal* and the *local*) were of frequent occurrence in later Greek.—Winer's *Grammar of New Testament*, p. 579.

21 (Then said Martha) unto Jesus, Lord, if Thou hadst been here, my brother had not died.

(Alf. Martha then said.)

22 [(But I know that even now)] whatsoever Thou shalt ask of God, God will give it Thee.[1]

[S. V. Even now I know that.]
(Alf. And even now I know that.)

Martha's first words to Jesus express her belief in His power and in His love toward her brother—that is, her belief in His power as a mighty prophet, but not in His power as God. Of that she seems as yet scarcely to have entertained a thought. She is also ignorant that His object in coming is to raise her brother from the dead. She very naturally concludes that it is to comfort her sister and herself in their distress. Considering the miracles which Jesus had wrought, and the love which He had shown for Lazarus, the sisters may have indulged a kind of undefined hope that God, at His intercession, would restore their brother to life. Martha does not seem to believe that Jesus, by His Own power as God, could raise up her brother, but that God, at His intercession might. This was the lesson, which she had now to be taught. To lead her into a right state of mind, and to prepare her for a fuller and more correct belief in Him, for a belief in Him, not as a mighty prophet, but as God.

23 Jesus saith unto her, Thy brother shall rise again.

24 Martha saith unto Him, I know that he shall rise again in the resurrection at the Last Day.

The doctrine of the Resurrection is evidently not new to Martha. It may be that Jesus, in His conversations with the family at Bethany, had instructed them in it; or it may have been the common belief of the Jews at that time, or at least of a portion or school among them. Perhaps both these suppositions are true. It is plain that, in the time of the Maccabees about B.C. 160, a belief in the Resurrection was widely spread among the Jews (2 Maccab. xii. 43, &c.), and a few years after the Crucifixion the Pharisees are mentioned as prominently holding this belief. (Acts xxiii. 8.)

From the general Resurrection at the Last Day Jesus leads the thoughts of Martha on to a special and immediate Resurrection, and from a belief in Himself as a prophet to a belief in Him as God.

---

[1] See note on John xvi. 23.

Martha had said, Even now I know, that whatsoever Thou shalt ask of God, God will give it Thee. He teaches her that He Himself is God, that it is He who raises up the dead, and who gives life to the living, that through Him the dead shall rise, and through Him the living live.

Before Jesus exercised His power as God He seems always to have required either from those for whose benefit it is exerted, or from the friends who make the request, a belief in His power as God, in His ability to work the cure which they ask. Probably it was in cases, where the patient was from physical causes unable himself to entertain any belief, that Jesus required from his friends this belief in His power. Before He healed the lunatic child He required the father to believe in His power as God. He intimates, too, that the exercise of His divine power in healing his son would be in proportion to the father's belief in it. (Mark ix. 23.) He healed the man sick of the palsy when He saw the great faith of those who brought him. (Mark ii. 5.) Lazarus is dead, and Martha makes her request that, by His intercession with God, her brother may be restored to life again. Jesus explains to her that before He can restore her brother to life she must believe that He can do this by His power as God, not by His prayer to God.

25 [Jesus said] unto her, I am the Resurrection and the Life : he that believeth in Me, (though he were dead), yet shall he live :

[S. But Jesus said.]
(Alf. Though he die.)

26 (And whosoever liveth and believeth in Me shall never die). Believest Thou this ?

(Alf. And every one that liveth and believeth in Me shall not die for evermore.)

Jesus is the Resurrection and the Life. He alone can raise the dead, and He alone can give life to the living. His words imply that if Martha can believe this, her brother shall rise again, even before the last day. Jesus is the life of the soul, as well as the life of the body ; and when speaking of life He in general means the life of the soul. But the subject to which He now more immediately refers is the resurrection of Lazarus from the grave. He therefore uses the word life, partly but not entirely with respect to the body. Lazarus, who is dead, shall be raised from bodily death through the belief of his sister. Those who are still living, and who believe in Jesus, shall never die. Their bodies shall rest in the grave for a time, and then shall rise again. Their souls shall be quickened by His grace here, and shall dwell with Him hereafter in glory. Jesus is the source of life, both to the soul and to the body; but those who would partake of this life must believe in Him as such.

27 She saith unto Him, Yea, Lord : (I believe) that Thou art the Christ, the Son of God, (which should come) into the world.

(Alf. I have believed—which is to come.)

This confession of Martha has been variously interpreted. Some have supposed that by His words, "I am the Resurrection and the Life," &c., Jesus had opened her eyes as to His real character, and that she now for the first time saw clearly that Jesus, the Son of Mary, and her brother's friend, was in the highest sense the Son of God, the source of life to the dead and to the living. Others again have held that Martha may have used these words without entering much into their meaning.

28 And when she had so said, she went her way, and called Mary her sister secretly, saying, The Master (is come, and calleth for thee).

(Alf. Is here, and calleth thee.)

29 [As soon as] she heard that, she arose quickly, and came (unto Him).

[S. V. And as soon as.]
(Alf. When she heard that—to Him.)

30 Now Jesus was not yet come into the town, [(but was in that place)] where Martha met Him.

[S. V. But was still in that place.]
(Alf. But was still in the place.)

31 The Jews then which were with her in the house, (and comforted her), when they saw Mary, that she rose up hastily and went out, followed her, [saying, She goeth] unto the grave to weep there.

[S. V. Thinking, she goeth.]
(Alf. And were comforting her—thinking that she was going.)

The Evangelist does not relate that Jesus asked for Mary, but leaves this to be inferred from Martha's message to her sister. She delivers her message secretly to avoid the tumult which she feared might take place if the Jews knew that Jesus was there. Thinking that Mary was going to the grave to weep the Jews accompany her, for such was the custom of the country, and thus they became eyewitnesses of the raising of Lazarus from the grave. Jesus had probably remained at the entrance to the town, because the grave of Lazarus would be outside.

32 (Then when Mary was come) where Jesus was, and saw Him, she fell down at His feet, saying unto Him, Lord, if Thou hadst been here my brother had not died.

(Alf. Mary therefore when she came.)

Both the sisters greet Jesus with the same words, though Mary stops short, prevented perhaps by the excess of her grief, and does not say all that her sister had said. But the abundance of her sorrow does not prevent the expression of her reverence for Him. Both declare that the death of their brother would not have taken place had He been present; meaning either that His love for their brother would have saved him from death, or that no such profanation as death could possibly take place in His presence. Mary does not go on to express in words, as Martha had done, either her conviction or her hope that God would, at His intercession, raise up her brother from the grave. Whatever the heart may have felt the lips refused to utter it.

33 (When Jesus therefore saw) her weeping, and the Jews also weeping which came with her, (He groaned in the spirit), and was troubled,

(Margin, He troubled Himself.)
(Alf. Jesus therefore, when He saw—was greatly moved in His spirit.)

Few single words in St. John's Gospel present greater difficulties than the verb which is here translated, "He groaned," ($\dot{\epsilon}\nu\epsilon\beta\rho\iota\mu\eta\sigma\alpha\tau o$.) Perhaps the simplest way to ascertain its meaning is to examine the sense in which it is used in other places where it occurs. The same verb is used three times in the New Testament, but never in the Septuagint. According to St. Matthew (ix. 30) and St. Mark (i. 43) it is the word which Jesus used after He had opened the eyes of the blind and had cleansed the leper, when he "straitly charged them ($\dot{\epsilon}\nu\epsilon\beta\rho\iota\mu\eta\sigma\alpha\tau o$ $\alpha\dot{v}\tau o\hat{\iota}\varsigma$) that no man should know it." Again the same word is used by the Jews (Mark xiv. 5) when "they murmured against Mary ($\dot{\epsilon}\nu\epsilon\beta\rho\iota\mu\hat{\omega}\nu\tau o$ $\alpha\dot{v}\tau\hat{\eta}$) for the pretended waste of the ointment which she had poured upon the head of Jesus. Somewhat of the nature of rebuke enters into all these meanings.

As applied to Jesus here and in connection with the expression, He troubled Himself, it may be that He groaned to give an outward indication of the conflict which was going on internally in His spirit. The same kind of struggle may have been going on as afterwards took place more sharply in the Agony in the Garden. The cause assigned for His groaning was the death of Lazarus, and the sorrow of his sisters and their friends. In other words, it was sin and the sorrow which He saw around Him, and which sin had caused. The two feelings which seemed to animate Him especially at this time were sympathy and indignation; sympathy with the bereaved sisters, and indignation at sin and the author of sin, who had caused their distress. It is probable that Jesus groaned, not to repress His indignation but to give expression to it. Indignation with Him was not an involuntary overpowering, irregular rising of the anger, as it is in mere man. In Jesus indignation was the holy feeling of anger in all its original purity. The object of His indignation was Satan and sin, and men only so far as they were the willing instruments of Satan. When Jesus saw the havoc of sin, the distress which sin had caused to these sisters, and their sorrow was but a specimen of the sorrow which filled the world, He groaned in the spirit and troubled Himself.

34 And said, Where have ye laid Him? (They said) unto Him, Lord, come and see.

(Alf. They say.)

35 [Jesus] wept.

[S. And Jesus.]

Except in special instances, and then only with the object of convincing the people of His power as God, Jesus does not exercise either His divine power or His divine knowledge in the transactions of daily life, but confines Himself to that which He could do and could know as Man. He therefore asks, "Where have ye laid him?" By this question he arouses their attention, perhaps too He might raise in them the expectation of some miraculous work.

The Man of Sorrows sheds His tears at the sorrows of His friends, and weeps with them. The misery of sin, and especially of the sin of unbelief, of which He saw the Jews would soon give an almost incredible proof, may have been one cause of His tears. Lazarus had been now four days in the grave, to restore him to life again was beyond the power of mortal man. But Jesus foresaw that if He should raise Lazarus from the dead, the Jews would be so far from confessing, that He had done this by His power as God, that they would seek to kill both Himself, because He had made this claim, and Lazarus, because His living presence among them was a proof of the truth of His claim. This might be one reason why Jesus wept. The sorrow of the sisters He could heal, by raising their brother from the dead;

for the unbelief of the Jews, according to the economy of salvation, He had no cure to offer.

Jesus is but three times recorded to have wept, once here at the death of Lazarus; again, when He wept over the rebellious city Jerusalem (Luke xix. 41); and again when His Own sufferings were the cause (Heb. v. 7.)

36 (Then said the Jews), Behold how He loved him!

(Alf. The Jews therefore said.)

37 (And) some of them said, Could not (this man), which opened the eyes of (the blind) (have caused that even this man) should not have died ?

(Alf. But—this person—the blind man—have caused also that this man.)

Only three months before this Jesus had opened the eyes of a man born blind. Through the examination of that miracle by the Pharisees the public attention had been drawn to it in an extraordinary degree. It had become known throughout all Judæa. When then the Jews saw Jesus standing over the grave of Lazarus and weeping for his death, they were at a loss to understand why the Man, who plainly had the power, had not given a proof of His love for Lazarus by preserving him from death. They were ignorant that the object of Jesus was to do more than prevent Lazarus from dying, that it was to raise him to life again after he had been dead and buried four days. His power they had witnessed. Of His affection for Lazarus they could not entertain a doubt. They beheld how He groaned and troubled Himself when He saw Mary weeping and the Jews weeping with her. On His way to the grave they had seen how He wept. When he arrived at the grave they were again witnesses of His trouble.

38 Jesus therefore again (groaning in Himself) cometh to the grave. (It was) a cave, and a stone (lay upon it.)[1]

(Alf. Greatly moved within Himself—now it was—lay against it.)

---

[1] Tombs.—The following are some of the different forms of tombs existing in Palestine.

"The numerous sepulchral chambers around Jerusalem are all excavated horizontally in the natural or artificial face of the rock . . . . The entrance is always at the side, and never from above."—Robinson's *Later Researches*, p. 181.

"There are in Syria and Egypt numbers of these tombs, which the Arabs erect to the memory of any man who they think has led a holy life. Their tombs are generally placed in some conspicuous spot, frequently on the top of a mount. The sepulchre consists of a small apartment with a cupola over it, white-washed externally."—*Irby* and *Mangles*, p. 57.

"Three miles from Mount Tabor there are many sepulchres cut in the rock; some of them are like stone coffins above ground, others are cut into the rock, like graves, some of them having stone covers over them."—Pocock's *Travels*, ii. 65.

Tombs in Palestine are of two kinds, either dug down in the ground like modern graves, to which our Saviour compares the Scribes and Pharisees, "for ye are as graves which appear not, and the men, that walk over them, are not aware of them" (Luke xi. 44); or they are hewn in the rock or mound, and are entered at the side like a room. These are often natural caves excavated and enlarged at the will of the owner. Along the side of this hollow cave or room niches are excavated from time to time, as they are required, and in them the dead are deposited. The word ($\epsilon\pi i$) rendered by our translators "upon" might have been translated quite as correctly "against." Its meaning here must depend on the nature of the tomb, whether it was dug in the ground or excavated at the side of a rock. The latter is the traditional opinion, and the word cave ($\sigma\pi\dot{\eta}\lambda a\iota o\nu$) rather points to this kind of tomb.

Jesus orders the stone to be removed. Thus they would have sensible proofs of the decomposition of the body of Lazarus, proofs both by the sight and the smell. Against this Martha gently remonstrates. Either she shrunk from the thought of Jesus seeing her brother in the condition in which he would now be, or she doubted whether it was possible for even Him to restore to life again one who had been dead four days. Our Lord's answer to her would rather imply the latter, it rather indicates some want of belief in Martha. She had said, "Even now I know that whatsoever Thou shalt ask of God, God will give unto Thee," but when the trial came her faith wavered, and she failed to see a ray of hope in His command to remove the stone.

39 Jesus (said), Take ye away the stone. Martha, the sister of him that was dead, saith unto him, Lord, by this time he stinketh : (for he hath been dead four days).

(Alf. Saith—for he hath been four days).

40 Jesus saith unto her, Said I not unto thee, (that, if thou wouldest believe, thou shouldest see) the glory of God?

(Alf. If thou believe, thou shalt see.)

"Instead of the acres of inscriptions which cover the tombs of Egypt, not a single letter has been found in any ancient sepulchre of Palestine."—Stanley's *Sinai and Palestine*, p. 149.

"Every hill and valley round the Holy City is thickly studded with these memorials of man's mortality. The summits of Zion and Bezetha: the slopes of Olivet and Moriah, the rocky plateau on the N.W. and the deep valleys of Hinnom and Jehoshaphat, are all cemeteries. The tombs of Jerusalem are far more numerous than her houses. Many of them are evidently very ancient, and a few are interesting from their historic and sacred associations."—*Handbook to Palestine*, p. 137.

It is nowhere recorded that Jesus had said these identical words to Martha. The substance of them He had said, perhaps more than once. To her messenger He had said, "This sickness is not unto death, but for the glory of God, that the Son of God may be glorified thereby." (v. 4.) To herself He had said, "Thy brother shall rise again" (v. 23); and again, "I am the Resurrection and the Life: He that believeth in Me, though he were dead, yet shall he live. And whosoever liveth and believeth in Me shall never die. Believest thou this?" (v. 25.)

He promises Martha that, if she will believe, He will work a work, which will convince the people that its author must be God, and as such they will honour Him and worship Him. That work is the miraculous restoration of Lazarus to life. One condition, which Jesus requires for this is, that Martha should believe that He is able to do it.

41 (Then) they took away [the stone (from the place where the dead was laid)]. And Jesus (lifted up His eyes), and said, Father, I thank Thee that Thou (hast heard Me).

[A. The stone where he was: S. V. Omit from the place where the dead was laid].
(Alf. So—omits, from the place where the dead was laid—lifted His eyes upward—heardest Me.)

42 (And) I knew that Thou hearest Me always: but (because of the people which stand by) I said it, that they may believe that Thou hast sent Me.

(Alf. Yet—for the sake of the multitude which stand around.)

Such is the nature of the Hypostatic Union, that the Father always hears the prayers of His Son. Jesus has not to plead to bend the will of a dissentient Father. For there is a unity of will between Him and the Father. He gives thanks and offers prayers to the Father for the sake of the people, who stand around Him, to prove to them, that He is one with the Father and is sent by the Father. In the presence of the Jews Jesus prays to God, the Father of heaven, that, as a proof of their union, Lazarus, who had been dead four days may rise from the grave. Jesus does not pray for power to perform the miracle, but as a proof to the people of the unity of will and power, which there is between the Father and Himself. For their sakes too it is that He declares, that He is heard, and that the miracle will take place, and in confirmation of His words.

43 And when He (thus had spoken, He cried) with a loud voice, Lazarus, come forth.

(Alf. Had thus spoken, He cried out.)

44 (And he that was dead) came forth, bound hand and foot with grave clothes: and his face was bound about with a napkin, Jesus saith unto them, Loose him and let him go.[1]

(Alf. And the dead man).

Jesus calls with a loud voice, as a sign of His authority over the dead; perhaps also to indicate, that the separation of the soul and body of Lazarus had already taken place, and that the soul was not in the grave with the body but in some more distant abode. Jesus

---

[1] *Manner of Burial.*—"On the following morning (Oct. 26th) very early, I looked from the window, and saw a bier close to the door of a neighbouring house. It was a painted wooden stand, about seven feet by two, raised slightly on four legs, with a low gallery round it, formed of uprights far apart, and two cross bars. Two strong poles projected at each end from the corners. Above it a canopy was raised, made of freshly-gathered elastic palm branches. They were bent like half hoops, and then interlaced and secured lengthways, with straight fronds. I sketched it, and presently I saw the dead body of a man, handsomely dressed, brought out and placed upon it. His face was covered with a shawl. Four men lifted the bier from the ground, and resting the poles on their shoulders, bore it to the mosque. After a little while, it was carried slowly along, passing the Consulate on its way to the Moslem burial-ground, preceded by about forty men solemnly silent, and followed by at least fifty women and children, shrieking wildly, singing and screaming.

"Between the palm-fronds I could plainly see the figure of the dead man, the head was foremost.... He had died just before midnight, after a few hours' illness.—Rogers' *Domestic Life in Palestine*, p. 144.

The Raising of Lazarus from the Grave.—" Why do the three earlier Evangelists not even mention this most stupendous of Christ's miracles? The following answer has been suggested. They wrote in the lifetime of Martha, Mary, and Lazarus. Well might one about whom there hung the mystery of having passed through death desire privacy. Nay, his own personal safety required it: for we read that the Sanhedrin sought his life, because that by reason of him many of the Jews went away and believed on Jesus! "Not, therefore, till that generation had passed away was the miracle published. The last of the Apostles, writing sixty years or more after the event, far away at Ephesus, records with all the vividness of an eye-witness what had sunk deep into the memory of all the Twelve. So, too, and doubtless for like reason, he alone of the Evangelists publishes the name of him who came to Jesus by night, and brought spices to His tomb."—Canon Norris's *Key to the Four Gospels*, p. 62.

"The argument from the silence of the Synoptists, which is much insisted upon by some critics who have not formed for themselves a clear and accurate conception of what the Synoptic Gospels are, really counts for but little . . . .'.

" The significance of their silence, too, has been exaggerated by looking at it in the light of modern ideas. To us the raising of the dead stands apart from other miracles, is a class by itself as peculiarly unexampled and incredible. But that it was not so regarded at the time when the Gospel was written appears from this very narrative, where the Jews are made to ask whether He who opened the eyes of the blind could not have prevented the death of Lazarus altogether. So, in the Synoptists, the answer that Jesus gives to the disciples of John groups together every class of miracle, the raising of the dead amongst them, without distinction. Similar narratives in the Synoptists, in the Acts, and in the Old Testament, are given without any special relief or emphasis. And if the fourth Evangelist himself does lay more stress upon them, this belongs rather to his own peculiar conceptions than to the circle of popularly current ideas."—Sanday's *Historical Character of the Fourth Gospel*, p. 185.

addresses Lazarus by name and as if living, because the result of His command is the re-union of his soul and body, as will also take place in the resurrection at the last day. (1 Thess. iv. 16).

Jesus had before bid the Jews remove the stone, and by that means, to become more than mere eye-witnesses of the condition in which the body of Lazarus then was. Now He commands them to loose him, and let him go. By making the Jews themselves assist in the circumstantial details, they became, as it were, co-operators with Him in the performance of the miracle. They were thus more able to bear witness to the truth of the miracle, and were more interested in doing so, than if they had been mere spectators of it.

It is not improbable that his legs were tied together, and his hands bound to his side, to keep them in a straight position, and his face covered with a napkin, to prevent the distortion of his features from being seen as he was carried to the tomb.

45 [Then many] of the Jews which (came) to Mary, (and had seen) [the things which Jesus did,] believed (on Him).

[S. And many—V. A. What He had done.]
Alf. Many therefore—had come—and beheld—in Him).

46 But some of them (went their ways) to the Pharisees, and told them what things Jesus had done.

(Alf. Went away.)

From the way in which these two sets of Jews are contrasted, it is plain that the latter went to the Pharisees with no friendly intention towards Jesus. Their object is not to persuade them of the truth of the miracle, or to mollify their hatred towards Jesus, but to assist them in getting up some accusation against Him.

47 (Then) gathered the chief priests and the Pharisees[1]

---

[1] Then gathered the chief priests and the Pharisees a Council.—" The high priests, hitherto so calm, appear to have grown uneasy about the public peace. A meeting of the Sanhedrin being called to consider these reports, Caiaphas went over from his palace on Zion to the Lishcath ha-Gazith to preside. As official high priest he had a right to the chief seat; but in what he laid before the elders, he must be taken as speaking, not only for himself, but for Annas, for the Sadducees, and for all those politicians who leaned on Rome. Details are not given, but his line of argument is suggested by St. John. People were expecting a Messiah, one who could command the secrets of nature, who could free them from the stranger's yoke, and a man who was reported to have raised the dead to life, would be sure to draw away the multitude, to excite disturbance, and bring on their city and nation the wrath of Rome. Caiaphas said nothing about false teaching, for what could a philosophic Sadducee care whether a mob of dyers and porters believed in a resurrection, in rewards and punishments or not? Caiaphas had faith

a council, and said, (What do we?¹ for) this man doeth many miracles.

(Alf. Therefore—What are we doing, seeing that.)

48 If we let Him thus alone, [all men will believe (on) Him]: and the Romans will come and take away both our place and nation.²

[S. All men believe on Him].
(Alf. In Him).

So blinded are these Jews by hatred, that they do not see that their machinations can have no power against Him, who can open the eyes of the blind, and raise the dead. They are unable to question the reality of His last miracle, the raising of Lazarus from the dead, nay they admit that Jesus has wrought many miracles. They foresee that all the people will believe in Him. They reason that the people will wish to make Him their king, and that the Romans will use this as a plea to take away their political status, their place among nations, and to reduce their country into greater subjection than it is even now. All this they propose to avert by a course of the most flagrant injustice and iniquity. They have evidently no belief in the principle, that righteousness exalteth a nation.

49 (And one) of them, named Caiaphas, (being the high priest that same year), said unto them, Ye know nothing at all,

(Alf. And a certain one—being high priest that year.)

in the power of Cæsar, and a riot in Jerusalem meant to him a visit from Pilate, an addition to the garrison, perhaps a change of high priest. He hinted that though they had lost much by tumults, they might lose yet more. Was it not better that one man should die, than that a whole people should be swept away.

"Then the Sanhedrin agreed to consider Jesus a dangerous man, a disturber of the public peace. Orders to arrest Him were given, and every one who knew of His coming and going was warned to send news of it to Caiaphas.

"To avoid this proclamation until His time should come, Jesus left Bethany and the living witness of His power, going first to Ephraim, a place on the edge of the wilderness of Judæa, eight or nine miles from Jerusalem on the north, near Salem and those springs at which He had parted from John the Baptist, making thence a secret and obscure journey, through a part of Samaria, perhaps of Galilee, passing thence to the lower Jordan and the ford from which He had first set out."—Dixon's *Holy Land*, ii. 237.

¹ What do we? (τί ποιοῦμεν:) "The Indicative Present sometimes occurs also in indirect questions, when, in Latin, the Conjunctive would be used, as John xi. 47, τί ποιοῦμεν; quid faciamus? what can we do? what is to be done? The Indicative, however, here strictly denotes that something must undoubtedly be done. The question τί ποιῶμεν invites deliberation (comp. Acts iv. 16). On the contrary, τί ποιοῦμεν implies that something is to be done, and inquires what that is.— Winer's *Grammar of New Testament*, p. 299.

² The Romans shall come, &c. "ἐλεύσονται οἱ 'Ρωμαῖοι refers to the approach of the Roman armies."—Winer's *Grammar of New Testament*, p. 630.

50 (Nor consider) that it is expedient [for us], that one should die for the people, and that the whole nation perish not.

[S. Omits, for us—V. For you.]
(Alf. Nor do ye consider.)

51 (And this) he spake not of himself: but being high priest that year, he prophesied that Jesus. (should die for that nation).

(Alf. Now this—was about to die for the nation.)

52 And not for (that nation) only, but that also He should gather in one the children of God that (were scattered) abroad.

(Alf. The nation—are scattered.)

The priesthood was hereditary in the family of Aaron, and the firstborn of the oldest branch of it, if he had no legal blemish, was always the high priest. After their return from the Captivity this rule was frequently violated. Of late years the Roman governors had deposed one high priest and had substituted another in his place, very much according to their own pleasure without any regard to the Law of Moses. It was never limited to one year or to two, but by the caprice of the governors some had been allowed to continue high priests for a few months only, others for many years. But there is no reason to suppose that the Evangelist here refers to this malpractice. His words simply mean that Caiaphas was high-priest during that year, that year when events of such mighty importance were taking place. Caiaphas or Joseph Caiaphas had been appointed high-priest by the Procurator Valerius Gratus, and he continued high-priest for eleven years, during the whole procuratorship of Pontius Pilate.

Caiaphas did not understand the words which he uttered. It is plain from the Evangelist's explanation that Caiaphas by these words meant one thing, and that the Holy Spirit intended quite another. Caiaphas meant that it was better that one man should die than that many should die, that it was better that Jesus should die than that He should be the occasion of involving the whole nation in ruin. But the words, which the Holy Spirit put into his mouth as high-priest, apparently mean that it is expedient that Jesus should die for the whole nation, that is, in behalf of the whole nation, instead of, as a sacrifice or propitiation for the whole nation.

Caiaphas gave his advice as a piece of state policy with a reckless indifference as to the innocence of Jesus, or the truth of His claims to be God. These he seems never to have considered. The political status must be preserved. The claims of no one individual, of whatever nature they might be, could be allowed to interfere with that. Such was his mode of reasoning. The consequence of it was not the preservation of its political status, not the prosperity of Judæa as a nation, but its utter ruin and desolation.

We have the authority of St. John that though Caiaphas himself did not attribute any such sense to his words, that the meaning conveyed in them by the Holy Spirit was that Jesus should die for the salvation of the Jewish nation, and not of the Jewish nation only, but of all nations, that by His Death He should gather together in one Church all His children, out of every nation under heaven.

53 (Then from that day) forth they took counsel together (for to put) Him to death.

(Alf. Therefore from that day—to put.)

54 Jesus therefore walked no more openly among the Jews; but (went thence unto a country near to the wilderness, into a city) called Ephraim, and there (continued) [with His disciples].[1]

[S. V. With the disciples.]
(Alf. Departed thence into the country near the wilderness, to a city—tarried.)

Several times during His Ministry the people, mistaking what He had said for blasphemy against God, and incited by their rulers, had taken up stones to stone Him. Now it is a deliberative assembly, the great Council of the Jewish nation, led on by Caiaphas the High Priest, which resolves to kill Him, and which decides upon this course of action after mature deliberation. Jesus as God knows this their decree, and as Man He takes the same precaution against it which other men would have done. He retires from Jerusalem to Ephraim, a city which is about five miles to the north-east of Bethel, and about twenty miles from Jerusalem, and not very far from the brook Cherith, near the

---

[1] Ephraim.—" Further still is the dark conical hill of Tayibeh, with its village perched aloft, like those of the Apennines, the probable representative of Ophrah of Benjamin (Josh. xviii. 23 ; 1 Sam. xiii. 17): in later times ' the city called Ephraim,' near to the wilderness, to which our Lord retired, after the raising of Lazarus."—Stanley's *Sinai and Palestine*, p. 214.

"This ancient site appears to correspond with the position of Ophrah, a city of Benjamin, to which one band of the Philistine spoilers went from Michmash. It stood, according to Jerome, five miles east from Bethel, which accords exactly with this place. It is also highly probable that the city Ephraim, which Abijah, king of Judah, took from Jeroboam (2 Chron. xiii. 19) was the same as Ophrah) —the names are radically identical. With this too we may identify the city Ephraim of the New Testament, which was 'near to the wilderness,' and to which our Lord withdrew with His disciples after the raising of Lazarus. Josephus mentions Ephraim as one of the towns taken by Vespasian."—*Handbook to Palestine*, p. 209.

Jordan, where about 900 years before the prophet Elijah had hid himself from the anger of Ahab and his wife Jezebel. Here Jesus retires with His disciples, probably to prepare Himself by prayer and meditation for the great struggle with the powers of darkness, which He is just about to commence.

55 (And the Jews' Passover was nigh at hand) : and many (went out of the country up to Jerusalem) before the Passover, to purify themselves.

(Alf. Now the Passover of the Jews was nigh—went up out of the country to Jerusalem.)

56 (Then sought they) for Jesus, (and spake) among themselves, as they stood in the temple, What think ye, that He will not come to the feast?

(Alf. So they sought—and said.)

57 Now [both] the chief priests and the Pharisees [had given (a commandment)] that, if any man knew where (He were), he should shew it, that they might take Him.

[S. V. A. Omit, Both : S. V. Had given commandments.]
(Alf. Commandment—He was.)

The Passover was near at hand, the Passover at which Jesus was to offer up Himself as the Lamb that taketh away the sin of the world. The people were already flocking from the country into Jerusalem. It was the custom to repair to Jerusalem some days before the commencement of the Feast, in order that those who laboured under any legal uncleanness might purify themselves by the requisite sacrifices and prayers, and might thus be duly prepared to keep the Passover. The rulers and Pharisees had already become impatient of delay, and were beginning eagerly to ask each other, whether He would come to the Feast.

(266)

INTRODUCTORY NOTE TO CHAPTER XII.

Gathering for the Feast.—"Coming into Bethany, the nearest point of the great road to Galilæans' Hill, the caravan broke up; the company dispersed to the south and north, some seeking for houses in which they could lodge, others fixing on the ground where they meant to encamp. Those marched round Olivet to the south, following the great road, crossing the Cedron by a bridge, and entering the Holy City by the Sheep Gate, near Antonia; these mounted by the short path to the top of Olivet, glancing at the flowers and herbage, and plucking twigs and branches as they climbed. Some families, having brought their tents with them from Galilee, could at once proceed to stake the ground; but the multitude were content with the booths called Succoth, built in the same rude style as those in which their father Israel dwelt.

"Four stakes being cut and driven in the soil, long reeds were drawn, one by one, round and through them. These reeds, being in turn crossed and closed with leaves, made a small green bower, open on one side only, yielding the women a rude sort of privacy, and covering the young ones with a frail defence from both noontide heat and midnight dew. The people had much to do, and very little time in which it could be done. At sundown, when the shofa sounded, Sabbath would begin; then every hand must cease its labour, even though the tent were unpitched, the booth unbuilt, the children exposed, the skies darkening into storm. Consequently the poles must be cut, the leaves and branches gathered, the tents fixed, the water fetched from the wells, the bread baked, the cattle penned, the beds unpacked and spread, the supper of herbs and olives cooked before the shofa sounded from the Temple wall. But every one helped. While the men drove stakes into the ground and propped them with stones, the women wove them together with twigs and leaves, the girls ran off to the springs for water, the lads put up the camels and led out the sheep to graze. In two or three hours a new city had sprung up on the Galilæans' Hill—a city of booths and tents—more noisy, perhaps more populous, than even the turbulent city within the walls.

"This Galilæans' Hill made only one field in a great landscape of booths and tents. All Jewry had sent up her children to the feast, and each province arrayed its members on a particular site. The men of Sharon swarmed over Mount Gideon, the men of Hebron occupied the Plain of Rephaim. From Pilate's roof on Mount Zion the lines and groups of this vast encampment could be followed by an observer's eye down the valley of Gihon, peeping from among the fruit-trees about Siloam, dotting the long plain of Rephaim, trespassing even on the Mount of Offence, and darkening the grand masses of hill from Olivet towards Mizpeh. All Jewry appeared to be encamped about the Temple Mount.

" From sundown all was quiet on the hill-sides and on the valley, only the priests and doctors, the Temple guards, the money-changers, the pigeon-dealers, the bakers of shew-bread, the altar-servants being astir and at their work. There was no Sabbath in sacred things. But everywhere, save in the Temple Courts, traffic was stayed, movement arrested, life itself all but extinct."—Dixon's *Holy Land*, ii. p. 244.

Lazarus.—" These cowering Arabs still call Bethany El Azariyeh, from the name of Lazarus, said in their country traditions to have been the village sheikh. From what is told by St. John it may be inferred that Lazarus was rich, well known, and of good repute—to wit, from his dwelling in a large house, from his habit of receiving guests, from the costly unguents used by his sister, from his owning a rock-hewn sepulchre, from the concourse of Jews who came over to mourn for him when he died. He may have been all that these Arabs say—the sheikh of a poor village of lepers and paupers—in which case the excavated chamber now shown may have been his tomb."—Dixon's *Holy Land*, ii. p. 206.

(268)

IV.

HIS PASSION IN JERUSALEM DURING THE WEEK OF THE FOURTH PASSOVER. HIS RESURRECTION, &C., INCLUDING CHAPTERS XII.—XXI.

CHAPTER XII.

1 *Jesus excuseth Mary anointing His feet;* 9 *The people flock to see Lazarus;* 10 *The high priests consult to kill Him;* 12 *Christ rideth into Jerusalem;* 20 *Greeks desire to see Jesus;* 23 *He foretelleth His Death;* 37 *The Jews are generally blinded;* 42 *Yet many chief rulers believe but do not confess Him;* 44 *Therefore Jesus calleth earnestly for confession of faith.*

THE following Calendar of the Passover-week is taken from Lightfoot (ii. 586) :—

THE DAY OF THE MONTH:	WEEK.	THE EVANGELISTS' ACCOUNT.
Nisan IX.	The Sabbath.	VI Days before the Passover, Jesus sups with Lazarus at the going out of the Sabbath, when according to the custom of that country their suppers were more liberal.
X.	Sunday.	V Days before the Passover, Jesus goes to Jerusalem on an ass, and in the evening returns to Bethany (Mark xi. 11). On this day the lamb was taken, and kept till the Passover (Exod. xii.), on which day this Lamb of God presented Himself, who was the Antitype of that rite.
XI.	Monday.	IV Days before the Passover, He goes to Jerusalem again : curseth the unfruitful fig-tree (Matt. xxi. 18 ; Mark xi. 12); in the evening He returns again to Bethany (Mark xi. 19).
XII.	Tuesday.	III Days before the Passover, He goes again to Jerusalem: His disciples observe how the fig-tree was withered (Mark xi. 20). In the evening going back to Bethany, and sitting on the Mount of Olives, He foretelleth the destruction of the Temple and city (Matt. xxiv.), and discourses those things which are contained in Matt. xxv.
XIII.	Wednesday.	This day He passeth away in Bethany. At the coming in of this night, the whole nation apply themselves to put away all leaven.
XIV.	Thursday.	He sends two of His disciples to get ready the Passover. He Himself enters Jerusalem in the afternoon. In the evening eats the Passover, institutes the Eucharist: is taken, and almost all the night had before the Courts of Judicature.
XV.	Friday.	Afternoon, He is crucified.
XVI.	Saturday.	He keeps the Sabbath in the grave.
XVII.	The Lord's Day.	He riseth again.

In the last two verses of the preceding chapter we are told how the chief priests and the Pharisees were eagerly watching for the arrival of Jesus at Jerusalem, and how they had given commandment, that if any man knew where He was, he should show it, that they might take Him. In the first verse of this chapter it is related how six days before the Passover Jesus came not to Jerusalem, but to Bethany. The distance between Bethany and Ephraim, the place last named as the abode of Jesus, would be much the same as between Jerusalem and Ephraim, that is, about twenty miles.

1 (Then Jesus) six days before the Passover came to Bethany, where Lazarus was [which had been dead, whom He raised] from the dead.[1]

[S. V. Omit, which had been dead: S. V. A. whom Jesus raised.]
(Alf. Jesus then—whom Jesus raised.)

The Passover was on the fourteenth day of the month Nisan, which this year happened on a Thursday. Six days, or the sixth day before the Passover, would be the Jewish Sabbath, which lasted from sunset on Friday to the same hour on Saturday. This supper, therefore would be on the evening of Saturday, the day on which the Sabbath ended. Lightfoot (ii. 586) says on the authority of Maimonides, that the Jews were accustomed to have a more liberal supper than usual in the evening of the day on which the Sabbath ended. We are not told whether Jesus had come direct from Ephraim, or how much of the journey he had travelled on the day on which He came to Bethany, or at what part of the day He arrived there.

The expression, " where Lazarus was," does not preclude the possibility of his having accompanied Jesus with His other disciples to Ephraim. This conjecture receives some countenance from the mention incidentally made in the 9th verse, that much people of the Jews came to Bethany that they might see Lazarus, whom Jesus had raised from the dead, as if they had not been able to satisfy their curiosity in the interval since his resurrection, on account of his absence from Bethany.

At Bethany they made Him a supper. The Evangelist does not say who made Him a supper. It was probably the sisters and Lazarus who did this, as they are the only persons here mentioned by name. St. Matthew (xxvi. 6) and St. Mark (xiv. 3), both relate that He was received on this occasion in the house of Simon the leper. St.

---

[1] Where Lazarus was, which had been dead (ὅπου ἦν Λάζαρος ὁ τεθνηκώς)—
" Markland rightly censures the Latin Versions for rendering, ubi Lazarus fuit mortuus, and thus overlooking the Article.

The sense, as he observes, is, 'where Lazarus was, he who had been dead.' His objection does not, and is not, meant to apply to the English Version."—Bishop Middleton on *Greek Article*, p. 257.

John relates that Martha and Mary and Lazarus are present. Martha serves, Lazarus is one of the guests, and Mary, who is evidently no stranger in the house, anoints the feet of Jesus with the precious ointment. The probability is, that Simon the leper was a near relative of Lazarus and his sisters. Some have supposed that he was their father, and that he is called the leper because he was once a leper, and had been miraculously cleansed by Jesus. If he were a leper and still living, he would not be able to entertain guests, but would be cut off from all social intercourse with his friends.

2 (There they made Him a supper): and Martha served: but Lazarus was one of them that sat at the table with Him.

(Alf. So they made Him a supper there.)

3 Then took Mary a pound of ointment (of spikenard)[1], very costly, and anointed the feet of Jesus, and wiped his feet with her hair; and the house was filled with the odour of the ointment.[2]

(Alf. Of pure spikenard.)

As a guest at the table Lazarus would prove the reality of his resurrection, and would amply dispose of any rumours to the effect that

---

[1] Spikenard.—Dr. Johnson in his Dictionary gives the following account of spikenard:—"A plant, and the oil or balsam produced from the plant. "There are three sorts of spikenard. 1. The Indian spikenard is most famous. It is a congeries of fibrous substances adhering to the upper part of the root, of an agreeable aromatic and bitterish taste. It grows plentifully in Java. It has been known to the medical writers of all ages. 2. Celtic spikenard is an oblong root, of an irregular figure, a fragrant and aromatic but not very pleasant smell. It had its name from Celtic Gaul, and is still found in great abundance on the Alpine and Pyrenean mountains. 3. Mountain spikenard is a moderately large oblong root of a plant of the valerian kind, its smell and qualities resembling those of the Celtic spikenard" (ed. 1765).

"Alexander now led his army into the Gedrosian desert. The march, at the outset, did not threaten that accumulation of suffering and calamity by which it was subsequently attended. It lay through a part of the province where the heat of the climate favoured the growth of aromatic plants. The myrrh-bearing shrub grew there in profusion, and the herb which produces nard was equally abundant. The latter, trodden under foot by the Grecian host, sent forth into the air 'a stream of rich distilled perfume,' which delighted the sense. Following the army for commercial purposes were some Phœnician merchants who loaded their cattle with a rich burden of nard and myrrh, which, however, they did not long retain."
—Milford's *History of Greece*, chap. lix. vol. viii. p. 177.

[2] With the odour of the ointment (ἐκ τῆς ὀσμῆς τοῦ μύρου)—"We must not regard ἐκ τῆς ὀσμῆς as merely equivalent to a Genitive, but as denoting especially that *whence* the filling of the house was come: it was filled with (from) the odour of the ointment (with fragrance)."—Winer's *Grammar of New Testament*, p. 214.

Jesus had only raised a spectre from the grave, and not the veritable body of Lazarus himself.

The literal translation is ointment of nard pistic (νάρδου πιστικῆς) very costly. Nothing whatever is known respecting the meaning of the word "pistic." Five or six different meanings have been assigned to it, but all founded on conjecture.[1] Some have supposed that it referred to the place from which the nard was obtained, others to the nature or quality of the nard itself. In this uncertainty as to its real meaning, Bishop Taylor, in his Life of Christ (sect. 15) prefers to leave tho word untranslated thus, "Ointment of Nard Pistick."

St. John says that it was Mary who anointed Jesus on this occasion. St. Matthew (xxvi. 7), and St. Mark (xiv. 3) merely say it was a woman. St. John wrote His Gospel last and at a time when all cause for silence as to her name may have disappeared. St. John says that she anointed the feet of Jesus. St. Matthew and St. Mark say that she poured the ointment on His head, and St. Mark adds that she brake the box and poured it on His head. The probability is that she brake the box and poured the ointment on His head, and then with the remainder anointed His feet, or the reverse. The wiping His feet with her hair is supposed by many to have preceded the anointing of them. There is nothing in the language of the narrative itself which is inconsistent with this view. She would wipe them to remove the dust which the open sandal would have allowed to gather round them on His journey, and thus to prepare them for the ointment which was too costly to be wiped off His feet by her hair. Besides Mary's object was to anoint the feet of Jesus, not her own hair. Jesus would reach Bethany perhaps wearied with the heat of the sun, and the toil of His journey. Mary would deem no office unbecoming her that would prove her love to Him who had shown them, in a manner which they could most thoroughly appreciate, that He was indeed the Resurrection and the Life. Instead of ministering to personal vanity and to sin, her hair would receive honour in being employed to wipe off the dust from the wearied feet of the Son of God.

4 ([Then saith] one of His disciples, Judas Iscariot, [Simon's son], which should betray him),

[S. V. But saith: S. V. Omit, Simon's son.]

(Alf. Then saith Judas Iscariot, Simon's son, one of His disciples, which was about to betray Him.)

5 Why was not this ointment sold for three hundred pence, and given to the poor?[2]

---

[1] See Cornelius à Lapide. See also Winer's *Grammar of New Testament*, p. 110.

[2] Three hundred pence.—" Judas, son of Simon, the last and lowest of the Twelve, was a Jew of Judæa, not of Galilee; a man close and secret, fond of money and of power, inclined to Essenic views and habits, a narrow bigot in heart

6 This he said, not (that) he cared for the poor: but because he was a thief, ([and had the bag, and bare what] was put therein).[1]

[S. V. And having the bag bare what.]
(Alf. Because—and kept the bag, and took away what was put therein.)

St. John said it was Judas who murmured. The other Evangelists do not mention Judas by name. St. Matthew (xxvi. 8) says, "When His disciples saw it, they had indignation, saying, to what purpose is this waste?" St. Mark (xiv. 4) says, "There were some that had indignation in themselves." The explanation probably is that it was Judas who began the murmuring, who first gave utterance to this feeling of dissatisfaction, and who, by representing it as a waste, and a waste of what might have been so useful to the poor, induced the others to join in his indignation. From what we elsewhere know of the other disciples, their indignation would be sincere and honest, though misplaced, that of Judas would be only a cloak to hide his disappointment at missing so much from his grasp.

St. Matthew (xxvi. 9) says the ointment might have been sold "for much;" St. John "for three hundred pence;" and St. Mark (xiv. 5) "for more than three hundred pence." This is another of those apparent discrepancies between the Evangelists, but where there is in reality no contradiction.

---

and brain. His office among the brethren was not to teach and preach, but to carry the bag, to pay the bills for food and lodging, to dispense alms to the needy. The fund was perhaps getting low in his purse, for they had been living much in the desert, making many quick journeys from place to place, followed by swarms of the poor and ailing, whom they were often obliged to feed. That box of unguent would have sold for three hundred denarii, a large addition to his chest. A denarius was a silver coin, the size and value of a Tuscan lira, eight pence of our English money. It was a labourer's wages, and something above a soldier's pay. Three hundred denarii made ten pounds, a very large sum in the miser's eyes."—Dixon's *Holy Land*, vol. ii. 249.

See note on St. John vi. 7.

[1] And bare what was put therein (καὶ τὰ βαλλόμενα ἐβάσταζεν)—"I cannot but think that it was St. John's intention to say not merely that Judas 'bare,' but that he 'bore away,' purloined or pilfered what was put into the common purse. It has the appearance of a tautology to say that He 'had the bag and *bare* what was put therein,' unless indeed the latter words are introduced to explain the op-portunity which he enjoyed of playing the thief, hardly, as it appears to me, a sufficient explanation. On the other hand the use of βαστάζειν, not in the sense of portare, but of auferre, is frequent: it is so used by Josephus, Antiq. xiv. 7, 1, and in the New Testament, John xx. 15; and such, I am persuaded, is the use of it here. We note that already in Augustine's time the question had arisen which was the right way to deal with the words: for, commenting on the 'portabat' which he found in his italic, as it has kept its place in the Vulgate, he asks, 'Portabat an exportabat? Sed ministerio portabat, furto exportabat.' Here he might seem to leave his own view of the passage undecided: not so however at Epist. 108, 3. 'Ipsi (Apostoli) de illo scripserunt quod fur erat, et omnia quæ mittebantur de dominicis localis auferebat.' After all is said, there will probably always remain upholders of one translation and upholders of the other, yet, to my mind, the probabilities are much in favour of that version which I observe that the Five clergymen have also adopted."—Archbishop Trench on *Authorised Version*, p. 104.

Why Jesus should have allowed Judas to carry the bag, when He knew that he could not resist the temptation to which it exposed him, is one of those mysteries which we shall only be able to answer when we understand why God allows any man to be exposed to temptation, which He knows he will not be able to resist. It may be that Judas was first selected for this purpose, because he showed an aptitude for making such arrangements as were required for supplying the daily wants of the disciples, and for relieving the poor, and that the opportunity—the possession of the bag—had developed in him the hitherto latent feeling of avarice. His sin consisted in appropriating to his own individual use some of the money, which was given to him for the general good of Jesus and the disciples and the poor. That Judas was not an unblushing peculator, that he did not practise his thefts openly, but with the utmost secrecy, and with every outward appearance of upright dealing, is plain from the fact that the disciples do not seem to have suspected his motives on this occasion. They join with Judas in representing, that the value of the ointment might have been better spent in distributing to the poor, because they had not the slightest suspicion of his honesty.

The fearful lesson, which the conduct of Judas teaches us, is the intimate relation which, in the nature of things, exists between appropriating to oneself the goods given to us in charge for Christ and His poor, and the betrayal of Christ Himself, between avarice and treason to Christ. The latter of these is the necessary consequence of the former, not the accidental but the moral consequence, not in Judas only, but in every man. Betrayal of Christ, in some form or other, follows the love of money as regularly and as certainly as night follows day.

7 Then said Jesus, [(Let her alone: against the day of My burying hath she kept this)].[1]

[S. V. Let her alone, that she may keep this against the day of My burying.]
(Alf. Let her alone, that she may keep it against the day of My burying.)

8 For the poor (always ye have with you): but Me ye have not always.

(Alf. Ye have always with you.)

Of the three Evangelists who record this murmuring against Mary, St. Mark gives our Saviour's answer the most fully, and St. John the

---

[1] Against the day of my burying hath she kept this (εἰς τὴν ἡμέραν τοῦ ἐνταφιασμοῦ τετήρηκεν αὐτό). "Here τετήρηκεν is to be regarded as strictly a Perfect (she has kept it, and has thus used it now), as Jesus meant figuratively that this anointing was part of the preparation for His interment."—Winer's *Grammar of New Testament*, p. 289.

least so. But they all agree in giving the substance of it, the prophetic signification of the act. Mary was led by the Holy Spirit thus to anoint His Body. This anointing is preparatory to His Burial, which would shortly take place. She had done "what she could." (Mark xiv. 8.) She had beforehand done what she could not do then; she had paid the reverential honour due to His Body, and which she would wish to pay at His Burial, but which the peculiar circumstances attending His Death would not permit her then to offer to Him.

He says that the wants of the poor have to be relieved, and will have to be relieved for all time to come; but that can form no plea for not paying honour, even costly honour, to His Body. So far from rebuking Mary as wasting the ointment, He says that she had "wrought a good work" on Him, and promises that wherever this Gospel shall be preached in the whole world there shall also this, that she hath done, be told for a memorial of her. He extols the reverential devotion of Mary, He rebukes the ill-judged censure of Judas and the rest; but He neither divulges the dishonest acts in which Judas is secretly indulging, nor reproaches him with his avarice and hypocrisy.

			St. Luke vii.
			36 And He went into the Pharisee's house, and sat down to meat.
			37 And behold a woman in the city, which was a sinner, when she knew that Jesus sat at meat in the Pharisee's house, brought an alabaster box of ointment,
			38 And stood at His feet behind Him weeping, and began to wash His feet with tears, and did wipe them with the hairs of her head, and kissed His feet, and anointed them with the ointment.
St. Matthew xxvi.	St. Mark xiv.		St. John xii.
			1 Then Jesus six days before the Passover came to Bethany, where Lazarus was which had been dead, whom He raised from the dead.
6 Now when Jesus was in Bethany, in the house of Simon the leper,	3 And being in Bethany, in the house of Simon the leper, as He sat at meat,		2 There they made Him a supper: and Martha served: but Lazarus was one of them that sat at the table with Him.
7 there came unto Him a woman having an alabaster box of very precious ointment,	there came a woman having an alabaster box of ointment of spikenard very precious:		3 Then took Mary a pound of ointment of spikenard, very costly,

St. Matthew xxvi.	St. Mark xiv.	St. John xii.
and poured it on His head, as He sat at meat.	and she brake the box, and poured it on His head.	and anointed the feet of Jesus, and wiped His feet with her hair: and the house was filled with the odour of the ointment.
8 But when His disciples saw it they had indignation saying to what purpose is this waste?	4 And there were some that had indignation within themselves, and said, Why was this waste of the ointment made?	4 Then saith one of his disciples, Judas Iscariot, Simon's son, which should betray Him.
9 For this ointment might have been sold for much, and given to the poor.	5 For it might have been sold for more than three hundred pence, and have been given to the poor. And they murmured against her.	5 Why was not this ointment sold for three hundred pence, and given to the poor?
		6 This he said, not that he cared for the poor: but because he was a thief, and had the bag, and bare what was put therein.
10 When Jesus understood it, He said unto them, Why trouble ye the woman? for she hath wrought a good work upon Me.	6 And Jesus said, Let her alone: Why trouble ye her? she hath wrought a good work on Me.	7 Then said Jesus Let her alone: against the day of My burying hath she kept this;
11 For ye have the poor always with you: but Me ye have not always.	7 For ye have the poor with you always, and whensoever ye will ye may do them good: but Me ye have not always.	8 For the poor always ye have with you: but Me ye have not always.
12 For in that she hath poured this ointment on My Body, She did it for My burial.	8 She hath done what she could: she is come aforehand to anoint My Body to the burying.	
13 Verily I say unto you, wheresoever this gospel shall be preached in the whole world, there shall also this, that this woman hath done, be told for a memorial of her.	9. Verily I say unto you, wheresoever this gospel shall be preached throughout the whole world, this also, that she hath done shall be spoken of for a memorial of her.	

9 Much people of the Jews therefore knew that He was there : and they came not (for Jesus' sake only), but that they might see Lazarus also, [whom He had raised] from the dead.

[A. Whom Jesus had raised.]
(Alf. On account of Jesus only.)

10 But the chief priests (consulted) that they might put Lazarus also to death.

(Alf. Took counsel.)

11 Because that by reason of him many of the Jews (went away, and believed on Jesus).

(Alf. Were going away, and believing in Jesus.)

The rulers of the Jews do not themselves believe that Jesus is God, but they believe that He has raised Lazarus from the dead, and they see that in consequence of this others are beginning to believe that He is God. At the same time such is their infatuation, that they take counsel to put to death both Jesus and Lazarus. They seek to put Jesus to death because He claims to be God: they would put Lazarus to death because he was a living witness of the truth of His claim, an undeniable proof of His power as God.

12 On the next day much people (that) were come to the feast, (when they heard) that Jesus was coming (to) Jerusalem.

(Alf. Which—having heard—into).

13 Took branches of (palm trees),[1] and went forth to meet Him, [and cried, Hosanna: (Blessed is the King of Israel that cometh in the name of the Lord.)][2]

[S. A. And cried saying: S. V. Blessed is He who cometh in the name of the Lord, and the King of Israel].

(Alf. The palm trees—Blessed is He that cometh in the name of the Lord, the King of Israel.)

---

[1] Took branches of palm-trees (ἔλαβον τὰ βαΐα τῶν φοινίκων). Dean Alford (Greek Testament) and Dr. J. B. Lightfoot think that the presence of the two Articles here, the branches of the palm-trees, imply that the palm-trees were growing on the spot. "They were the palm-trees with which the Evangelist himself was so familiar, which clothed the eastern slopes of the Mount of Olives."—*Revision of New Testament*, p. 108.

"The Greek word for branches in the Gospel of St. John, xii. 13, 'Took branches of palm-trees and went forth to meet Him'—is not κλῆμα as in chapter xv. 2, &c., but βαΐα, derived from a Coptic root, and applied to the palm-tree exclusively. It does not signify branches properly, for the palm-tree has no branches like the vine, but the huge fibrous leaves which form the crown on the top of the stem."—Macmillan on the *True Vine*, p. 76.

[2] "Hosanna ('save, we pray'), the cry of the multitude as they thronged in our Lord's triumphal procession into Jerusalem (Matt. xxi. 9, 15; Mark xi. 9, 10; John xii. 13). The Psalm from which it was taken, cxviii. was one with which they were familiar from being accustomed to recite the 25th and 26th verses at the Feast of Tabernacles. On that occasion the Hallel, consisting of Psalms cxiii., cxviii. was chanted by one of the priests, and at certain intervals the multitude joined in the responses, waving their branches of willow and palm, and shouting as they waved them Hallelujah, or Hosanna, or, 'O Lord, I beseech Thee, send now prosperity.' (Ps. cxviii. 25.) On each of the seven days during which the feast lasted, the people thronged in the Court of the Temple, and went in procession about the altar, setting their boughs bending towards it, the trumpets sounding as they shouted Hosanna. It was not uncommon for the Jews in later times to employ the observances of this feast, which was pre-eminently a feast of gladness, to express their feelings on other occasions of rejoicing. (1 Macc. xiii. 51; 2 Macc. x. 6, 7.)—Smith's *Dictionary of the Bible*.

The Passover is at hand, and Jesus is preparing to offer up Himself. For He is the One true Paschal Lamb, that can deliver His people from death. All the lambs which had been offered at the Passover since its first institution, did but prefigure Him. A tradition, which can be traced back to the third century (Origen in Matt. xxi. iii. 743, Migne), and which is probably older, describes Bethphage as a village belonging to the priests. Here in all likelihood it was, as being conveniently near Jerusalem, that the lambs were kept, that were required for the sacrifices of the Temple.

The lamb, which the Jews were to kill in the evening of the fourteenth day of the month Nisan, they were ordered to select and take up from the rest of the flock, on the tenth day of the month. (Exod xii. 3). On this tenth day of the month the Passover lambs, one for each household, would be taken from Bethphage to Jerusalem, to be kept there ready to be slain on the evening of the fourteenth. Jesus, who fulfilled in Himself all the conditions required in the lamb, did not overlook even such an apparently trivial circumstance as this. For St. John relates that six days before the Passover Jesus came to Bethany where He was entertained at supper, when Mary anointed His Body preparatory to His Burial, and that on the next day, the tenth day, He is conducted by the people from Bethphage in triumphal procession to Jerusalem.

The multitude took the branches of the palm trees which were growing on the spot, as if to grace the triumphal entry of a conqueror. They know not what the triumph is over, which they are thus helping to celebrate,—but Jesus knows. He knew that in a few days, and by the hands of these very men, He would triumph over death and Satan.

The other three Evangelists record at length, how Jesus sent two of His disciples to procure an ass, on which He might ride into Jerusalem. St. John briefly relates that He obtained an ass, on which to ride, and omits both the command to His disciples, and the circumstances attending it. The site of Bethphage is not known. But we know that the distance between Jerusalem and Bethany is fifteen furlongs, about two miles, and that Bethphage lay somewhere between them. In no other journey which Jesus made, do we read that He rode. We know that He walked from Judæa to Galilee, a distance of sixty miles at least, and that He was wearied (iv. 6) with His journey. The only time we read that Jesus rode was on this occasion, and that the short distance between Bethphage and Jerusalem, perhaps a mile. For this purpose He had expressly sent two disciples to procure the ass. Evidently there was some significance in this act of riding. He had some object in it besides bodily convenience, such as to fulfil the prophecy of Zechariah, " Rejoice greatly, O daughter of Zion : shout O daughter of Jerusalem : behold thy King cometh unto thee : He is just and having salvation : lowly and riding upon an ass, and a colt the foal of an ass." (ix. 9).

The people hear that Jesus, who had raised Lazarus from the grave, is on His way to Jerusalem. Some of the people had been present when He called Lazarus out of the grave, and others had heard their testimony, and they meet Him, and conduct Him into the city as becometh a conqueror. They attend Him with all the ceremonies and indications of rejoicing, which they are accustomed to use on the Feast of Tabernacles. They were led to this conduct by their feelings of delight and gratitude to Jesus as the benefactor of mankind, and in acting thus they were unconsciously fulfilling the prophecies, which God had given them a thousand years before. But these prophecies neither the people nor His disciples either recollected or understood at the time. Afterward when the Holy Spirit had opened their understanding, the disciples recollected the prophecies, and understood their application and fulfilment in these events, in what they had done to Jesus on this occasion.

14 (And) Jesus, (when He found) a young ass, sat thereon: as it is written,

(Alf. But—having found.)

15 Fear not, daughter of Sion: behold, [thy King cometh], sitting on an ass's colt.

[A. The King cometh.]

16 These things understood not His disciples at the first: but when Jesus was glorified, then remembered they that these things were written of Him, and that they had done these things unto Him.

17 (The people) therefore that was with Him when He called Lazarus out of (his grave), and raised him from the dead, (bare record).

(Alf. The multitude—the grave—bare witness.)

18 [For this cause (the people] also met Him), for that they had heard that He had done this miracle.

[S. For this cause much people.]
(Alf. The multitude also went to meet Him.)

St. Matthew xxi.	St. Mark xi.	St. Luke xix.	St. John xii.
7 and brought the ass and the colt, and put on them their clothes,	7 And they brought the colt to Jesus, and cast their garments on him:	35 And they brought him to Jesus: and they cast their garments upon the colt,	
and they set Him thereon.	and He sat upon him.	and they set Jesus thereon.	14 And Jesus, when He had found a young ass, sat thereon:
			15 As it is written, Fear not, daughter of Sion: behold thy king cometh, sitting on an ass's colt.
			16 These things understood not His disciples at the first: but when Jesus was glorified, then remembered they that these things were written of Him, and that they had done these things unto Him.
8 And a very great multitude spread their garments in the way: others cut down branches from the trees, and strawed them in the way.	8 And many spread their garments in the way: and others cut down branches off the trees, and strawed them in the way.	36 And as He went they spread their clothes in the way.	
		37 And when He was come nigh, even now at the descent of the mount of Olives, the whole multitude of the disciples began to rejoice and praise God with a loud voice for all the mighty works that they had seen: saying, Blessed be the King that cometh in the name of the Lord: Peace in heaven, and glory in the highest.	17 The people therefore that was with Him when He called Lazarus out of his grave, and raised him from the dead, bare record.
			18 For this cause the people also met Him, for that they had heard that He had done this miracle.

All the four Evangelists relate that the people went to meet Jesus on His way to Jerusalem, and that they acted thus towards Him, but St. John alone gives the reason for their conduct, viz., that they knew that He had called Lazarus out of the grave, and raised him from the dead.

19 The Pharisees therefore said among themselves,

Perceive ye (how) ye prevail nothing? behold the world (is gone) after Him.

(Alf. That—is gone away.)

The Pharisees are conscious that their opposition to Jesus does not prevent the people from believing in Him, and that the number of those who believe in Him is increasing daily, that in their own expressive language the world is gone away after Him. But this does not seem to have suggested to them the question, whether the world might not be right and themselves in the wrong. They go on hardening themselves in their unbelief.

At the very time that these Pharisees, with the High Priest at their head, are taking counsel to kill Jesus, certain devout Gentiles are seeking an interview with Him. With this object they come to Philip. Why they should select Philip is not mentioned. Whether he was known to them, or whether they were induced to address themselves to him from the benignity of his countenance, or from some other reason, is quite uncertain. Before Philip mentions their desire to Jesus he consults with Andrew. Jesus had chosen Andrew as his disciple first of all, and that circumstance may have given him some degree of weight or authority with the other disciples.

20 (And) there were certain Greeks among (them) that came up to worship at the feast:

(Alf. Now—those.)

21 The same came therefore to Philip, which was (of) Bethsaida of Galilee, and (desired) him, saying, Sir, we would see Jesus.

(Alf. From—prayed.)

22 Philip cometh and telleth Andrew: [and again (Andrew and Philip tell Jesus.)]

[V. A. Omit, And again : S. V. A. Andrew and Philip come and tell Jesus.]
(Alf. Andrew and Philip come and tell Jesus.)

The reason why the disciples hesitate to convey the request of these Greeks to Jesus is, because when sending them to preach the Gospel He had said to them, " Go not into the way of the Gentiles." (Matt. x 5.)

In His answer to them Jesus implies that this command, which He had given them in the beginning of His ministry, was meant to be only for a time, and that the time had now come for it to cease. These Gentiles had come to Him, prompted by a desire to reverence and to worship Him, and their worship must not be rejected. Nay, more, the hour is at hand when He will be worshipped alike by Jew and Gentile, when by His Death He will draw all men unto Him. He is glorified when He is worshipped among men. His worship will be widely increased only after and through His Death. The hour of His Death, which is at hand, will also be the hour of His Glorification.

23 (And) Jesus [answered] them, saying, The hour is come, that the Son of Man should be glorified.[1]

[S. V. Answereth.]
(Alf. But.)

He goes on to teach them that men's faith in Him and worship of Him can be secured only by His Death, and that this is according to an established natural law, that it must be so according to the very nature of things.

24 Verily, verily, I say unto you, Except (a corn) of wheat fall into the ground and die, (it abideth alone): but if it die, it bringeth forth much fruit.

(Alf. A grain—it abideth by itself alone.)

The same law which is seen in the works of creation, viz., increase by death, and which holds good in the case of the Son of God Himself, applies also in its degree to His disciples. They, too, shall live by death.

25 He that loveth (his life) [shall lose] it: and he that hateth (his life) in this world shall keep it unto life eternal.

[S. V. Loseth.]
(Alf. His soul or life.)

He who loves his life, who prefers his life to his faith in God, who saves his life by denying God, shall lose his soul and his life eternally. But he who hates his life in this world, who prefers his faith in God to his life, shall keep it unto eternal life, he shall live for ever with God. Also He who loves His soul, who prefers to gratify the carnal desires of his soul, who prefers to follow his own lusts rather than the commands of God, he shall lose his soul in hell. But he who hates

---

[1] The hour is come, that the Son of Man should be glorified (ἐλήλυθεν ἡ ὥρα ἵνα δοξασθῇ ὁ υἱὸς τοῦ ἀνθρώπου). "The time is come in order that, that is, the time appointed. The theory of final causes is implied in the expression, which is peculiar to John. The hour is (by God's decree) come, that I should, &c. comp. xiii. 1; xvi. 2, 32. Inaccurate expositors suppose that in these passages, ἵνα is used for ὅτε or ὅταν."—Winer's Grammar of New Testament, pp. 355 and 481.

his soul, by resisting and by mortifying those desires of it that are contrary to God's commands, he shall keep it, he shall obtain eternal life hereafter.

26 If any man serve Me, let him follow Me: and where I am, there shall also My servant be: [if] any man serve Me, him will (My Father) honour.

[A. And if.]
(Alf. The Father.)

Jesus does not say that if any serve Him He will honour him, but that His Father will honour him. This may be either to indicate the unity of will between Himself and the Father, or because their opinion of Him was as yet so imperfect, that they would value honour from the Father more than honour from Jesus.

Jesus was perfect God and perfect Man, but such was the nature of the Hypostatic Union that it did not deliver Him from suffering, or from the dread of suffering. It is probable that the perfection of His Human Nature increased the intensity both of His suffering and of His dread of it. No man ever exhibited such signs of acute mental suffering as Jesus.

It was not by precept only that He taught His disciples. He showed them an example even by exhibiting the weakness incidental to human nature. They could not retort that it was easy for Him to harangue on the duty of preferring death to sin, because He could not experience what was man's natural love of life, or his dread of death. He has just alluded to His Death, which is so near at hand, when His soul is filled with trouble. The weakness of His Human Nature seeks some refuge, and flies in prayer to the Father to be saved from this hour. Strength is supplied sufficient to support Him in the hour of need, and He prays the Father to perfect His work in Him, that by His Death He may make satisfaction for sin and draw all men unto Him. It may even be that He prays the Father to glorify His Name by giving, at that very moment, some proof by which the Jews and Gentiles, who are gathered round Him, may understand that He, Jesus, the Son of Mary, is sent by Him to redeem mankind and to do His will.

27 Now is My soul troubled: and what shall I say? Father, save Me from this hour: (but) for this cause came I unto this hour.

(Alf. But yet.)

28 Father, [glorify Thy Name]. Then came there a

voice from heaven, (saying), I have both glorified it, and will glorify it again.
[V. Glorify My Name.]
(Alf. Omits, saying.)

29 The (people) [therefore], that stood by, [and heard it], said that it (thundered) : others said, An angel (spake) to Him.
[V. Omits, therefore: S. When they heard it.]
(Alf. Multitude—had thundered—hath spoken.)

30 Jesus answered [and said], This voice came not (because of Me), but for your sakes.
[S. Omits, and said.]
(Alf. For My sake.)

People describe the same things differently, because they look at them from different sides, but it does not always follow that the two descriptions are inconsistent with each other. Probably the two descriptions which the people gave of the voice which came from heaven, and which St. John is careful to record, contain a full and true account of it. The voice was like thunder because of its majesty and awfulness, like no mere earthly voice. It was like the voice of an angel because, besides being grand and awful and unearthly, it was articulate and distinct, not a rumbling, continuous sound. It has generally been held that this voice was the voice of an angel representing God the Father, who, in answer to the prayer of Jesus to glorify His name, replied that He had both glorified it and would glorify it again. He had glorified it at His Baptism and at the Transfiguration by the voice from heaven, which said, "This is My beloved Son, in whom I am well pleased, hear ye Him." (Matt. iii. 17; xvii. 5.) He had glorified it by all the miracles and wonderful works which Jesus had wrought, and by which God the Father gave testimony to the truth of His words. He would glorify it again at His Death, and after His Death, when, by His Resurrection and Ascension and the Descent of the Holy Spirit, all nations should believe in Him and should worship Him as God.

The voice came not for the sake of Jesus, to give Him strength and support to fulfil His mission, but for the sake of the people, to convince those who disbelieved in Him that He was the Son of God, and to confirm those who believed in Him but whose faith was weak and wavering.

31 Now is the judgment of this world: now shall the prince of this world be cast out.

Jesus here declares that the deliverance of the world from the power and tyranny of the devil is at hand, so near, that He says, "Now is." His Passion, which is to begin within three days, shall be the judgment, the deliverance, the salvation of the world. In these words He refers to the world as in two different conditions, as the oppressed captive, and as the willing slave. By His Death Satan's power over men shall be broken. He, as represented by sin and darkness and idolatry, shall be cast out. His worship, or the worship of idols, shall be replaced by the worship of Jesus, the Son of Man. In the great conflict with Satan He will bruise his head, He will diminish the power which hitherto he has had over both the bodies and the souls of men.

The presence of the Gentiles, who desired to see Him, may have prompted these words. When He looked around He saw the Gentile world entirely given up to idolatry and to the power of Satan. A few there were who, by contact with the Jews, gained a knowledge of the true God, and desired to worship Him. His heart yearned over them, and He seemed to long for the time of His Death to be hastened that the Gospel might be preached among all nations.

32 And I, if I be lifted up from the earth, will draw [all men] unto (Me.)[1]

[S. All things.]
(Alf. Myself.)

[1] **To drag, draw** (σύρειν, ἑλκύειν)— "These words σύρω and ἑλκύω differ, and with differences not theologically unimportant. We best represent their differences in English, when we render σύρειν, to drag, ἑλκύειν, to draw. In σύρειν, as in our drag, there lies *always* the notion of force, as when Plutarch (De Lib. Ed. 8) speaks of the headlong course of a river, πάντα σύρων καὶ πάντα παραφέρων; and it will follow, that where persons, and not merely things, are in question, σύρειν will involve the notion of violence (Acts viii. 3; xiv. 19; xvii. 6). But in ἑλκύειν this notion of force or violence does not of necessity lie. It may be there (Acts xvi. 19; xxi. 30; Jam. ii. 6) but not of necessity, any more than in our 'draw,' which we use of a mental and moral attraction, or in the Latin 'traho' ('trahit sua quemque voluptas.')

"Only by keeping in mind the difference which thus exists between ἑλκύειν and σύρειν, can we vindicate from erroneous interpretation two doctrinally important passages in the Gospel of St. John. The first is xii. 32. 'I, if I be lifted up from the earth, *will draw* all men [πάντας

ἑλκύσω] unto Me.' But how does a crucified, and thus an exalted, Saviour draw all men unto Him? Not by force, for the will is incapable of force, but by the divine attraction of His love. Again (vi. 44) 'No man can come to Me, except the Father which hath sent Me *draw* him :' (ἑλκύσῃ αὐτόν). Now as many as feel bound to deny any gratia irresistibilis, which turns man into a mere machine, and by which, willing or unwilling, he is dragged to God, must at once allow, must indeed assert, that this ἑλκύσῃ can mean no more than the potent allurements, the allective force of love, the attracting of men by the Father to the Son ; compare Jer. xxxi. 3: ' With loving kindness *have I drawn thee* (εἵλκυσά σε), and Cant. i. 3, 4. Did we find σύρειν on either of these occasions (not that I can conceive this possible), the assertors of a 'gratia irresistibilis,' might then urge the declarations of our Lord as leaving no room for any other meaning but theirs; but not as they now stand.

In agreement with all this, in ἑλκύειν is predominantly the sense of a drawing to a certain point, in σύρειν merely of

33 This He said, signifying (what death He should die.)

(Alf. By what manner of death He was about to die.)

St. John explains that this had reference to the manner of His Death. By His Death on the Cross He would withdraw men from the power of the devil to Himself. Jesus is represented as fighting with Satan and spoiling His goods, as carrying off from Satan those souls which He had before taken captive.

Some have thought that the expression "lifted up" had some reference to the advantage which one raised higher than another has over him in conflict, that the Crucifixion would give Jesus the same advantage in His conflict with Satan, that fighting on higher ground does to an ordinary antagonist.

Jesus lifted up on the Cross as the one Mediator reconciled heaven and earth, Jews and Gentiles, God and man. Christ crucified is the ransom, the example, the object of love for all. Hitherto men had been drawn to believe in Jesus by God the Father; henceforth He draws men to Himself. Christ crucified is to be the object of faith to all nations.

The Jews at once understood our Saviour's meaning of being "lifted up," and from that they raised an objection against His being the Messiah. From certain passages of the Old Testament, which they call the Law, they had erroneously concluded that the Messiah would remain with His people on earth for ever.

34 [The people] answered Him, We have heard out of the Law that (Christ) abideth for ever: and how sayest Thou, The Son of Man must be lifted up? who is this Son of Man?

[S. V. Therefore the people.]
(Alf. The multitude therefore—the Christ.)

The passages to which they allude were probably such as the following, but which refer to the continuance of Christ's Kingdom rather than to the continuance of His presence with them on earth.

dragging after one: Thus Lucian (De Merc. Cond. 3), likening a man to a fish already hooked and dragged through the water, describes him as συρόμενον καὶ πρὸς ἀνάγκην ἀγόμενον. Not seldom there will lie in σύρειν the notion of this dragging being on the ground, inasmuch as that will trail upon the ground (cf. σύρμα σύρδην; and Isa. iii. 16) which is forcibly dragged along with no will of its own: as for example, a dead body (Philo. In Flac. 21). We may compare John xxi. 6, 11, with ver. 8 of the same chapter, in proof of what has just been asserted. At ver. 6 and 11 ἑλκύειν is used: for there a drawing of the net to a certain point is intended: by the disciples to themselves in the ship, by Peter to himself upon the shore. But at ver. 8, ἑλκύειν gives place to σύρειν for nothing is there intended, but the dragging of the net, which had been fastened to the ship, after it through the water. Our Version has maintained the distinction; so too the German of De Wette by aid of Ziehen (=ἑλκύειν) and nachschleppen (=σύρειν): but neither the Vulgate, nor Beza, both employing 'traho' throughout." — Archbishop Trench on Synonyms of New Testament, p. 69.

The prophet Micah had said (v. 2) "But thou, Bethlehem Ephratah, though thou be little among the thousands of Judah, yet out of thee shall He come forth unto Me that is to be ruler in Israel: whose goings forth have been from of old, from everlasting." The Psalmist had said (cx. 4.), "The Lord hath sworn, and will not repent, Thou art a Priest for ever after the order of Melchizedek;" again, "His seed also will I make to endure for ever, and His throne as the days of heaven." (Ps. lxxxix. 29.) "His seed shall endure for ever, and His throne as the sun before Me." (ver. 36.) But these and many similar passages refer rather to the permanence of Christ's Kingdom than to His continuance with them in bodily presence for ever. They overlook the passages, and many such there are, which foretell the Messiah's Death. Isaiah (liii.); the Psalmist (xxii. 12, &c.); Daniel (ix 26); and Jeremiah (xi. 19), all expressly teach of the Death of the Christ.

To their argument that, if the Son of Man must be lifted up, He cannot be the Messiah, Jesus does not give a direct reply. It may be that He saw they were not in a state of mind either to understand or to profit by such explanation.

35 (Then Jesus) said unto them, Yet a little while is the Light [with you]. Walk while ye have the Light, (lest darkness come upon you) : (for) he that walketh in darkness knoweth not whither he goeth.

[B. V. Among you.]
(Alf. Jesus therefore—that darkness overtake you not—and.)

36 While ye have (Light), believe in the Light, that ye (may be the children of Light). These things spake Jesus (and departed), and did hide Himself from them.

(Alf. The Light—may become sons of Light—and He departed.)

The Jews could not understand how Christ could die and still remain with His people for ever. Jesus does not explain this to them. But He speaks of Himself, as He had often done before, as the Light of the World. He says that He will remain with them only for a short time longer, a few days ; and He bids them in the meantime believe in Him. Thus they will become sons of Him who is the Light of the World, and shall receive illumination so as to understand this and other like difficulties.

Having said this Jesus removed Himself from them, probably because He judged, from the spirit in which they received His words, that they would otherwise have taken Him and put Him to death before the time and in a manner different from that which the salvation of mankind required. He withdrew, as we have reason to believe, to the Mount of Olives, where He passed the night, or to Bethany.

COMMENTARY ON ST. JOHN'S GOSPEL. 287

37 But though He had done so many miracles before them, yet they believed not (on) Him.

(Alf. In.)

38 That the saying of (Esaias) the prophet might be fulfilled, which he spake, Lord, who hath believed our report? and to whom (is the arm of the Lord revealed)?

(Alf. Isaiah—hath the arm of the Lord been revealed?)

39 (Therefore) they could not believe (because that Esaias) said again,

(Alf. For this cause—for that Isaiah.)

40 He hath blinded their eyes and hardened their heart: that they should not see with their eyes, (nor) understand with their heart, and be converted, and I should heal them.

(Alf. And.)

41 These things said (Esaias), [when he saw] His glory (and spake) of Him.

[S. V. A. Because he saw.]
(Alf. Isaiah—and he spake.)

Miracles do not necessarily carry conviction along with them. Unless the heart is in a previous state of preparation to receive conviction, no matter what is the number of the miracles, or what is the force of them, they would fail to convince the people. The preparation required for further conviction is the conscientious performance of their duty to God, so far as they have been taught it.

The unbelief of the people was not the effect of Isaiah's prophecy; but Isaiah's words, inspired by God, accurately foretold what turned out to be the true state of the case. In one sense their unbelief, the blinding of their eyes, and the hardening of their hearts, was produced by God. It is the effect which God attached to sin as its punishment. The more sin they committed, the greater would be their inclination to disbelieve the proofs which Jesus gave, that He was the Son of God, the more their eyes would be blinded, and the more their hearts would be hardened, and this as the natural effect which God had attached to sin.

These words Isaiah spake in the person of Jesus Himself. He is there foretelling the very small number of the Jews that would believe in His Gospel as preached by Himself and His Apostles, and to express this in the strongest possible form He says, Who, what single man, hath believed our word, our preaching? To whom, to what single individual hath the arm of the Lord been revealed? By the arm of the Lord He may mean either Himself the Word made Flesh, of the same substance with the Father, and by whom the Father made all things; or He may mean the power of God, which displayed itself in the miracles and in the wonderful works which He wrought. He here laments, and foretells while He laments, the very small number, in comparison, of those who would recognise the power of the Godhead in His actions and in His daily life.

The glory which Isaiah saw was a glorious appearance, which was made to him, as far as could be shown to man, to represent the Holy Trinity. (Isa. vi. 1.) St. John here testifies that the glory of Jesus, a glorious representation of Jesus, as One of the Three Persons in the Holy Trinity, was here shown to Isaiah.

42 Nevertheless (among the chief rulers also) many believed on Him: but because of the Pharisees (they did not confess Him), (lest they should) be put out of the synagogue:

(Alf. Even of the rulers—they confessed it not—that they might not.)

43 For they loved (the praise of men more than the praise of God).

(Alf. The glory that is of men more than the glory that is of God.)

Two among the rulers, who believed in Jesus, but who did not confess Him because of the Pharisees, are mentioned by name, Nicodemus and Joseph of Arimathæa. Afterwards they came boldly forward and professed themselves His disciples. Probably even now the love of the praise of men was less strong in them than in others.

When Jesus saw that some believed on Him who did not confess their belief in Him for fear of the Pharisees, He endeavours to strengthen their wavering faith, and to draw from them a confession of it. He uses a loudness of voice not usual with Him, partly, perhaps, to arrest their attention, and to set them an example of boldness, partly, too, because the time pressed, only a few days remaining before His Crucifixion. Some think that He uttered these words before He withdrew from them as related in verse 36, and that they are the continuation of what He then said, and are only separated from them by the explanation of the Evangelist. Others again think, that Jesus spake these words on some other occasion. There is nothing in the language itself to decide which opinion is the more correct.

44 (Jesus) cried and said, He that believeth (on) Me, believeth not on Me, but (on) Him that sent Me.
(Alf. But Jesus—in.)

45 And He that (seeth) Me (seeth) Him that sent Me.
(Alf. Beholdeth.)

This is true only because God the Father and Jesus His Son are One in nature or substance, majesty and power, two Persons in the same Godhead.

We make a distinction between believing a person and believing in a person. We believe a person when we believe his words, his statement. We believe in a person when we make him the object of our faith. We believe the Evangelists, that they relate what is true; we believe in Jesus; we believe that He is God, One with the Father, and equal to the Father.

46 I am come a Light into the world, [that whosoever believeth] (on) Me (should not abide in darkness).
[V. That he who believeth.]
(Alf. In—may not remain in the darkness.)

The Light of the World is the peculiar description of the Word made Flesh, who is Light of Light, Very God of Very God. Jesus is to the soul what the sun is to the body. The sun is the source of all light and heat, of all life and growth to the body. So Jesus, the Incarnate God, is the source of light and life in the soul, of the life of grace here, and of the life of glory hereafter. Take away the sun from the world and all natural life would die, and chaotic darkness would once more return. Take away Jesus as the life and hope of the soul, and the soul becomes dead in sin, without God and without hope in the world.

47 And if (any man) hear My words [and believe not], I judge him not: for I came not (to judge) the world, but (to save) the world.
[S. V. A. And keep them not.]
(Alf. A man—and keep them not—that I might judge—that I might save.)

48 He that rejecteth Me, and receiveth not My words, hath one that judgeth him: the word that I (have spoken), the same shall judge him in the last day.
(Alf. Spake.)

He teaches them that this life is the time of mercy, and that the
U

last day will be the time of judgment. At that day Jesus will be the Judge ; but it will not be He who will condemn them, it will not be His arbitrary sentence that will condemn them, but their own present unbelief. The words which He now speaks to them will rise up and condemn them. He personifies, as it were, the words, and speaks of them as a living person, who will bring an accusation against them, and will thus be the cause of their condemnation.

In the next verse He goes on to give the reason why these words will have the power to condemn them, because they are the Father's words. Though they might not believe that He, the Son of Mary, was God, yet the words that He had spoken to them were from the Father, and proved to be from the Father by the miracles which He wrought among them. The cause of their condemnation in the last day would therefore be, that they had rejected the words of the Father in whom they professed to believe.

It may be that under the terms "should say" and "should speak" He intends to include all His teaching, whether contained in His more formal instruction, or in His familiar addresses to them, that all His words, whether in public or in private, were from the Father, or in agreement, in unity with the will of the Father.

49 (For I have not spoken) of Myself: but the Father which sent Me, He gave Me (a commandment), what I should say, and what I should speak.

(Alf. Because I spake not—commandment.)

50 And I know that His commandment is (life everlasting) : whatsoever I speak therefore, even as the Father (said) unto Me, so I speak.

(Alf. Eternal life—hath said.)

Thus it is, that our Saviour concludes His public teaching on this day. It was Palm Sunday, the day on which He had entered Jerusalem in triumph, and as if to fix them in their memory for ever, He concludes with these memorable words, "I know that His commandment is life everlasting," &c. His last appeal to them is to invite them to keep God's commandment by the hope of eternal life. This was the only way in which they could obtain eternal life. He does not state what the punishment for neglecting His commandment would be. He leaves them to draw that inference for themselves, and says, "I know that His commandment is life everlasting."

INTRODUCTORY NOTE TO CHAPTER XIII.

"**Passover Cake** is made of the finest wheaten flour and water, rolled into a very thin paste, and quickly baked. Many Jews go out in the previous year to watch the growth of the corn until it is reaped and threshed, and stored away in a clean place; it is ground with much care, as, if water should fall on it, fermentation might ensue, and it would then be unclean. . . . . . Very often a patch of corn is sown separately for the Passover bread, and is then carefully watched. The ovens in which to bake it are hired by the Synagogue authorities some days before, and are thoroughly cleaned out, plastered within anew, and large flag-stones laid down, on which to bake the bread; these are afterwards taken up again, and locked up in some place belonging to the Synagogue till the next year."—Beaufort's *Travels* ii. 266.

It would be Passover bread like this, that Jesus would use in the institution of the Eucharist.

"All these minute observances made the Passover bread very expensive, and difficult for the poor to obtain for a whole week's sustenance; the Synagogue gives away a rottl to each person, and the richer Jews also give it away to their poorer brethren, but, at the best, they are always very poor and starving after Passover, having spent every piastre they can beg or borrow to observe the feast with due honour."—*Idem*, ii. 267.

"The Jews were celebrating their Passover: and our friends had received a present of some of their unleavened bread. It was spread out into very thin sheets, almost like paper, very white, and also very delicate and palateable."—Robinson's *Biblical Researches*, i. 329.

Eastern Customs at Meals.—"Before eating, each one of us had water poured on our hands over the marble basin : for the Christian Arabs, as well as the Moslems, 'and all the Jews, except they wash their hands, eat not.' This is particularly necessary, considering they do not use knives and forks: but each one 'dips his hand into the dish' with his neighbour."—Rogers's *Domestic Life in Palestine*, p. 183.

"Supper was announced, and we were conducted to another room. Water was poured over our hands as we entered, then we, seven in number, sat on the matted floor, round a circular tray, raised about six inches from the ground, and literally crowded with food. A very long narrow towel was placed in front of the guests, and reached all round, resting on our knees, and its fringed ends met and crossed where I was invited to take my seat. There were six round dishes of heaped-up rice, boiled in butter: six dishes of boiled wheat, mixed with minced meat and spices: a few plates of fowls and lamb, and bowls of lebbany, or sour cream, and a good supply of sweet cream, cheese, olives, and salad. A cake of bread was before each person. Directly Salikh Agha was seated, he began eating silently, and (as it seemed to me) voraciously, quite in Bedouin style, making pellets of the hot rice or wheat in the palm of his hand, and with a skilful jerk tossing them into his mouth. He divided the fowls with his fingers, and did me the honour to pass the most delicate morsels to me. At this rate the contents of the dishes soon disappeared, for all the gentlemen followed the example of Salikh Agha, and as, one by one, they were satisfied, they rose and washed their hands."—*Idem*, p. 179.

"The meal generally consists of camels', goats', or sheep's milk, boiled wheat and milk, lentil soup, or melted butter, and bread to dip into it: as soon as the meal is ready, the landlord pours out water for all his guests in turn, who, therewith wash the right hand. The ablution finished, every one commences: the host retires, not eating with his guests, but welcoming them with frequent exclamations of conta, conta, (eat it all, eat it all). The repast ended, the attentive master again brings the water for washing the hands, and then eats of what remains."—Irby & Mangles, p. 85.

"The staple of the Arabs' food, however, is leban and bread. The milk was usually presented in a wooden bowl, and the liquid butter in an earthenware dish. The party being seated round, dipped their bread in, endeavouring to make it imbibe as much as possible. The Arabs were very expert at this, pinching the thin cake in such a form as to make a sort of spoon of it. This mode of eating is alluded to in Scripture."—*Idem*, p. 149.

CHAPTER XIII.

1 *Jesus washeth the disciples' feet; exhorteth them to humility and charity;* 18 *He foretelleth and discovereth to John by a token, that Judas should betray Him;* 31 *Commandeth them to love one another;* 36 *And forewarneth Peter of his denial.*

AT the first institution of the Passover God commanded the children of Israel thus, "Ye shall keep it (the lamb) up until the fourteenth day of the same month; and the whole assembly of the congregation of Israel shall kill it in the evening." (Exod. xii. 6.) And again : "In the first month, on the fourteenth day of the month at even, ye shall eat unleavened bread until the one-and-twentieth day of the month at even." (ver. 18.) The Passover Feast was the first meal of unleavened bread.

St. Matthew (xxvi. 17-29), St. Mark (xiv. 12-25), and St. Luke (xxii. 7-39), who give substantially the same account, relate that on the first day of unleavened bread Jesus sent two of His disciples to prepare the Passover; that in the evening, when the hour was come, He sat down with the twelve in the upper room, and eat the Passover with them, that He then instituted the Holy Eucharist, and foretold His betrayal by Judas. St. John, in this chapter, relates that, "Before the Feast of the Passover," ($\pi\rho o$ $\delta\epsilon$ $\tau\hat{\eta}s$ $\dot{\epsilon}o\rho\tau\hat{\eta}s$ $\tau o\hat{v}$ $\pi a\sigma\chi a$), &c., supper being ended, Jesus washed the feet of His disciples, and foretold His betrayal by Judas, &c. St. John says nothing about the institution of the Eucharist. Does St. John here mean the same supper as the other three Evangelists, and which, according to their account, took place in the evening of the first day of unleavened bread? St. John's use of the words, "Now before the Feast of the Passover," has given a difficulty to this question which it would not otherwise have possessed.

At least three different answers have been given to this question. Some think that St. John is not giving an account of what took place at the Feast of the Passover on the first day of unleavened bread, but at a supper one or more days before the Passover Feast. Others think that St. John is referring to the same supper as the other Evangelists, and that this was the Passover Feast, and that Jesus kept it on the thirteenth day of the month Nisan instead of the fourteenth, that He eat the Passover with His disciples on the thirteenth, when He offered up Himself a sacrifice for the whole world, and that on the fourteenth He completed this sacrifice of Himself on the Cross.

The opinion most generally received is that St. John is here describing the Paschal Supper which Jesus kept with the Twelve on the evening of the fourteenth Nisan, that He omits many particulars which the other Evangelists record, and relates some which they omit. There is no difficulty in reconciling the accounts of the other three Evangelists together. The difficulty consists in making St. John's account of this supper fairly and without any straining fit in with what the other three Evangelists have related respecting the Passover Supper.

As no new considerations can be adduced in addition to those which have been brought forward again and again, it is not here proposed to repeat these arguments, but to accept the supposition that St. John is in this chapter describing what took place at the Passover Supper, and which the other three Evangelists expressly say was in the evening of the first day of unleavened bread.

By way of reconciling St. John's account with the other Evangelists a suggestion has been made, which is here repeated, and which can be accepted or not, according to the force it may seem to contain. It has been proposed to limit the application of the words 'Now before the Feast of the Passover' to the first verse, and not to understand it as applying to the time when this supper took place.

1 Now before the Feast of the Passover, (when Jesus knew) that His hour was come that He should depart out of this world unto the Father, having loved His own which were in the world, He loved them unto the end.

(Alf. Jesus knowing, &c.—loved them.)

2 [And supper being ended], the devil having now put [into the heart of Judas Iscariot, Simon's son, to betray Him].[1]

[S. V. And during supper: S. V. Into His heart that Judas Iscariot, Simon's son, should betray him.]
(Alf. And when supper was begun.)

3 [Jesus] knowing that the Father had given all things into His hands, and that (He was come) from God, and (went) to God.[2]

[S. V. Omit, Jesus.]
(Alf. Omits, Jesus—He came forth—was going.)

---

[1] The devil having now put into the heart (τοῦ διαβόλου βεβληκότος εἰς τὴν καρδίαν). The received reading, or that adopted by Lachmann and Tischendorf, may be followed. At all events, βάλλειν has an active (not a middle) signification."—Winer's *Grammar of New Testament*, p. 267.
[2] See note on i. 29.

4 He riseth from (supper), and (laid) aside His garments: and took a towel, and girded Himself.

(Alf. The supper—layeth.)

5 After that He poureth water into (a bason), and began to wash the disciples' feet, and to wipe them with the towel wherewith He was girded.[1]

(Alf. The bason.)

The meaning of the word "Passover" is passing over, and it has reference to two events, the angel of death passing over the houses of the children of Israel (Exod. xii.), and the children of Israel themselves passing out of Egypt over the Red Sea. (Deut. xvi. 1.) To the meaning of the word Passover Jesus has evidently an allusion when He says that the time is at hand when He should ($\mu\epsilon\tau\alpha\beta\hat{\eta}$) depart, pass out of this world, when by His death on the Cross He should pass out of this world unto the Father.

The Passover Lamb was a type of Himself. The death, from which it delivered the people, was a type of the death from which He by His Death would deliver His Own, those who believed on Him. Having loved them up to this time before His Death He gives them proofs of the continuance of His love. These proofs were washing the feet of His twelve disciples, and the institution of the Eucharist. The latter of these St. John does not relate.

St. John alone relates that Jesus washed the feet of His twelve disciples, which He does with great circumstantiality, noting all the minute details incident to such an event. But before He proceeds to this, He mentions two facts—(1) That the devil had already put it into the heart of Judas to betray Him; (2) That Jesus knew that the Father had given all things into His hand, and that He came forth from God, and was going to God. The object of the Evangelist evidently is to enhance the love and the humility of Jesus. He who was God, into whose hands the Father had given all things, who came from God and was going to God, He washes the feet of His twelve disciples. He does this though He knows that one of them had already agreed with the chief priests to deliver Him up, and was even then watching for an opportunity.

In Eastern countries, where the open sandal is worn, it is common

---

[1] Began to wash the Disciples' feet ($\mathring{\eta}\rho\xi\alpha\tau o \nu\acute{\iota}\pi\tau\epsilon\iota\nu \tau o\grave{\upsilon}s \pi\acute{o}\delta\alpha s$).—"$\mathring{\eta}\rho\xi\alpha\tau o$ is not redundant, but indicates the commencement of an action, the completion of which is recorded in verse 12."—Winer's *Grammar of New Testament*, p. 636.

Eἰs τὸν νιπτῆρα.—"The Article seems to indicate, that only one basin or ewer was used on this occasion."—Bishop Middleton on *Greek Article*, p. 257.

to wash the feet after a journey, and before reclining to a meal, and to wash the hands after a meal. To wash the feet during a meal was not in accordance with the custom of the country. Jesus does it here as a symbolic act; He washes the feet, but the meaning, the lesson, which He would thereby convey, related entirely to the soul and its affections —viz., to the love which they should mutually bear to each other, and to the purity of life with which they should walk.

It is not stated in what part of the supper the washing of the disciples' feet took place. The rendering of the English Authorised Version, "Supper being ended," (δείπνου γενομένου; Sinaitic, γεινομένου, Vatican, γινομένου) is unfortunate. It was during the supper, or when the supper was begun, that Jesus washed the feet of the Twelve. Both Jesus Himself, as well as His disciples, sat down to the table again (v. 12 and 28), and afterwards when He dipped the sop He gave it to Judas Iscariot (v. 26). If, as many think, the washing of the feet took place between the Paschal Supper and the institution of the Eucharist, what a significance it gives to the preparation, to the purity required before partaking of His Body and His Blood.

The probability is that the feeling expressed by Peter in the following verses was felt by all the disciples with the exception, of course, of Judas, and that they would have given expression to it, if Jesus had begun with them instead of with Peter. An opinion which has found favour with many, and which has much about it to recommend it, is that Jesus first of all washed the feet of Judas, in order that, by showing him the first and greatest attention, He might soften the hardness of his heart, and lead him to repent of his treachery in time, and that Judas allowed this without remonstrance; that Jesus then came to Peter who expressed the feeling which all the rest shared with him; that they as well as Peter felt too much reverence for Jesus to allow Him to perform for them an office so menial.

6 (Then cometh He) to Simon Peter: [and Peter saith unto Him, Lord,] dost Thou wash my feet?[1]

[S. V. And; V. Omits, he saith unto Him: S. Omits, Lord.]
(Alf. He cometh, therefore.)

7 Jesus answered and said unto him, What I do thou knowest not now: but thou shalt (know hereafter).
(Alf. Understand, afterwards.)

8 Peter saith unto Him, (Thou shalt never wash my

---

[1] Lord, dost Thou wash my feet? (κύριε, σύ μοῦ νίπτεις τοὺς πόδας). "Sometimes the Present is employed to denote what is just about to take place, what one is intending to effect, and what he has already made the necessary preparations to do. Here He had already prepared to wash them."—Winer's *Grammar of New Testament*, p. 281.

feet). Jesus answered him, If I wash thee not, thou hast no part with Me.

(Alf. Never shalt Thou wash my feet.)

9 [Simon Peter] saith unto Him, [Lord,] not my feet only, but also my hands and my head.

[V. Peter Simon: S. Omits, Lord.]

10 Jesus saith unto him, (He that is washed (ὁ λελουμένος) [needeth not) save to wash his feet (τοὺς πόδας νίψασθαι), but] is clean every whit (καθαρὸς ὅλος) : and ye are clean, (but) not all.[1]

[S. Needeth not to wash, but.]
(Alf. He that hath been bathed hath no need—yet.)

---

[1] He that is washed needeth not save to wash his feet (ὁ λελουμένος οὐ χρείαν ἔχει ἢ τοὺς πόδας νίψασθαι). "There is a certain poverty in English, which has but the one word, 'to wash,' with which to render these three Greek words πλύνω, νίπτω, λούω, seeing that the three have each a propriety of its own—and one which the inspired writers always observe. Thus πλύνειν is always to wash inanimate things, as distinguished from living objects, or persons, oftenest garments; sometimes nets, Luke v. 2. Νίπτειν and λούειν, on the other hand, express the washing of living persons; although with this difference, that νίπτειν and νίψασθαι almost always express the washing of a part of the body,—the hands (Mark vii. 3 : Exod. xxx. 19), the feet (John xiii. 5); the face (Matt. vi. 17); the eyes (John ix. 7); while λούειν, which is not so much 'to wash,' as 'to bathe,' and λούσθαι, to bathe oneself, imply always not the washing of a part of the body, but of the whole (thus λελουμένοι τὸ σῶμα, Heb. x. 22; Acts ix. 37 ; 2 Peter ii. 22; Rev. i. 5). This limitation of νίπτειν to persons as contradistinguished from things, is always observed in the New Testament.

"The passage where it is most important to mark the distinction between νίπτειν, to wash a part, and λούειν or λούσθαι, to wash the whole, of the body, and where certainly our English Version loses something in clearness, from the absence of words which should note the changes of the original, is John xiii. 10. 'He that is washed (ὁ λελουμένος) needeth not save to wash (νίψασθαι) his feet, but is clean.every whit.' The foot-washing was a symbolic act. St. Peter had not perceived this at the first, and not perceiving it, had exclaimed, 'Thou shalt never wash my feet.' But so soon as ever the true meaning of what his Lord was doing flashed upon him, he who had before refused to suffer his Lord to wash even his feet, now prayed to be washed altogether. 'Lord, not my feet only, but also my hands and my head.' Christ replies, that it needed not this: Peter had been already made partaker of the great washing, of that forgiveness which reached to the whole man: he was λελουμένος, and this great absolving act does not need to be repeated, as, indeed, it was not capable of repetition. 'Now ye are clean through the word which I have spoken unto you.' (John xv. 3.) But while it was thus with him in respect of the all-inclusive forgiveness, he did need at the same time to wash his feet (νίψασθαι τοὺς πόδας) evermore to cleanse himself, which could only be through suffering his Lord to cleanse him from the defilement which even he, a justified, and in part also, a sanctified man, should gather as he moved through a sinful world. One might also suppose, as it has been suggested, that there was allusion here to the Levitical ordinance, according to which Aaron and his sons, in the priesthood, were to be washed once for all from head to foot at their consecration to their office (Exod. xxvii. 4 ; xl. 12): but were to wash their hands and their feet in the brazen laver, as often as they afterwards

11 For He knew (who should betray Him): (therefore) said He, Ye are not all clean.

(Alf. Him that was betraying Him—for this cause.)

From the language which Jesus uses to Peter, it is plain that this act of washing contained in it at least two distinct meanings, one which refers to the body, and another which has reference to the soul, and to the economy of grace, which He was then instituting for the salvation of man. He says that Peter did not then know what He was doing to him, but that he should understand it afterwards. After He had washed their feet Jesus Himself explains what He had done to them, as far as relates to the body. He says that He meant it as an example to them of love and humility, that as He their Lord and Master had done to them, so should they do to each other.

After this act of love and condescension, which Jesus showed to them, and especially which He showed to Judas—for He knew that at this very time he was meditating how most conveniently to betray Him—after this act of love and humility, no circumstances in which the disciples could ever be placed, would relieve them from the obligation of showing love to each other, and of humbling themselves in the service of others. In no circumstances could they ever experience treachery and ingratitude equal to that of Judas, and never could they show love equal to that of Jesus.

Jesus Himself explains to them what the washing of their feet meant as far as regards the body, that it was an example to them in showing love and humility. What it meant as it related to the soul and to the economy of grace He did not explain, and Peter probably did not understand it until after the Descent of the Holy Spirit. That he did then understand it, we can have no question. Even now he had a dim perception that unless Jesus washed his feet he should forfeit some privilege of fellowship with Him. What that fellowship was he did not then understand, but lest he should in any way diminish or lose it he withdrew the opposition which had arisen only from love and reverence for Him.

---

ministered before the Lord. (Exod. xxx. 19, 21; xl. 31.) Yet this would commend itself more, if we did not find *hands and feet* in the same category there, while here they are not merely disjoined, but set over against one another. (John xiii. 9, 10.) Of this, however, I cannot doubt, that the whole mystery of our justification, which is, once for all, reaching to every need, embracing our whole being, and of our sanctification, which must daily go forward, is wrapped up in the antithesis between the two words. This Augustine has expressed clearly and well

(in John xiii. 10)."—Archbishop Trench on *Synonyms of New Testament*, p. 156.
The bath.'—The writers, after describing a Turkish bath in Alexandria, say, "We were then conducted back to the room where we had undressed.... The custom of passing from the bath to the dressing-room, during which the feet might easily be soiled, reminded us of the true rendering of the precious words of our Lord: 'He that hath been in the bath needeth not, save to wash his feet, but is clean every whit.'"—*Scottish Mission of Enquiry to the Jews*, 1839.

Two acts are here narrated as referring to the body, but which have a meaning beyond the body, and both of them as necessary and preparatory in order to have a part in Jesus. (1) The washing in the bath by which a man becomes clean every whit; (2) the washing of his feet.

(1) What is the meaning which the Church has in all ages put upon these words? Her interpretation must have weight with every man interested in the subject, either as indicating the teaching handed down from the Apostles, who, as we cannot doubt, were taught it by the Holy Spirit, or as indicating the inspiration of the Church by the Holy Spirit and her preservation in the faith which Jesus promised when He said, Lo, I am with you alway even unto the end of the world.

He that hath been washed in the bath is clean every whit. What bath? History shows that neither the Church at large, nor any body of men in the Church, has ever held that there was any bath but the bath of Baptism, in which, by washing a man's body under certain conditions, his soul was cleansed from sin every whit. Divisions have not seldom arisen in the Church as to the conditions, on which they should be washed in this bath, but none as to the efficacy of the bath of Baptism itself. The words of the Nicene Creed have expressed the belief of the Church from the earliest times and in all countries. "I acknowledge one Baptism for the remission of sins."

Our Saviour's words to Peter, "He that is washed needeth not save to wash his feet, but is clean every whit," express the same teaching which He had already given to Nicodemus, "Except a man be born of water and of the Spirit, he cannot enter into the kingdom of God." (John iii. 5.) Out of the numberless passages in Holy Scripture which contain the same doctrine, the following are selected as expressed by the same Greek verb or by its corresponding substantive.

"And such were some of you: (but ye are washed), but ye are sanctified, but ye are justified in the name of the Lord Jesus, and by the Spirit of our God."—1 Cor. vi. 11.

(Alf. But ye washed them off (ἀπελούσασθε.)

"Let us draw near with a true heart in full assurance of faith, having our hearts sprinkled from an evil conscience, and our bodies washed (λελουμένοι τὸ σῶμα) with pure water."—Heb. x 22.

"Not by works (of righteousness which we have done), but according to His mercy He saved us, (by the washing of regeneration) and renewing of the Holy Ghost."—Titus iii. 5.

(Alf. Wrought in righteousness which we did—through the font (δια τοῦ λουτροῦ) of regeneration.)

St. Paul, speaking of the Church says:

"That He might sanctify and cleanse it with the washing of water by the word."—Ephes. v. 26.

(Alf. That He might sanctify her, cleansing her by the laver (τῷ λουτρῷ) of the water in the word.)

(2) Jesus does not explain to them the meaning of His act of washing their feet, as far as it referred to the soul. He says that by this act of washing their feet He had cleansed them, but not all of them. When they were washed in the bath of Baptism they had all been cleansed every whit, and when He now washes their feet, outwardly as regards the body they were all equally cleansed, but inwardly in the soul one of them was not cleansed, for he was meditating the betrayal of his Lord.

By the feet have generally been understood the affections, the passions which influence men to go hither and thither, on this course of action' and on that. These, though cleansed in Baptism, like feet washed in the bath, coming into contact with earth and earthly things, require washing again before they can have part with Jesus. Different methods have been prescribed in different parts of the Church, but each and all with the same object of cleansing the affections stained by sin. Fasting and prayer, repentance in its manifold forms, confession sometimes to God alone, and sometimes to His ministers, are the principal means which have been prescribed for washing the feet, for cleansing the affections before partaking of Jesus. In the bath of Baptism a man is washed clean every whit. All disqualification of nature, all sins actually committed, are there washed away. This can take place only once in the lifetime of each person. But his feet, his affections, must be washed repeatedly, the sins daily committed through weakness of nature, through surprise, and from other causes, must be acknowledged and repented of before God, as an act necessary and preparatory in order to have a part with Jesus.

St. John does not relate, as the other Evangelists do, that during this Supper Jesus "Took bread, blessed It, and brake It, and gave It to the disciples, and said, Take, eat: This is My Body. And He took the cup and gave thanks, and gave It to them, saying, Drink ye all of it: For This is My Blood of the New Testament, which is shed for many for the remission of sins." (St. Matt. xxvi. 26, 28.) There is every reason to believe that Jesus referred to the act of eating His Body and drinking His Blood when He spoke of their having a part with Him. This was their last night together. No other act is recorded as taking place. Washing their feet could not be necessary in order that they might have mental sympathy with Him. This they had already, and this Peter had already expressed when from love he had hesitated to allow Him to wash his feet. It was doubtless to this mystery of cleansing their affections, by washing their feet in order that they might communicate in His Body and Blood, to which Jesus refers when He says, "What I do thou knowest not know, but thou shalt understand afterwards," and "If I wash thee not, thou hast no part with Me."

12 So after He had washed their feet, [and had taken

His garments, and (was set) down again], He said unto them, Know ye what I have done (unto) you?
[S. A. He took His garments and sat down again. He said.]
(Alf. Had sat—to.)

13 Ye call Me Master and Lord: and ye say well: for so I am.¹

14 If I then, your Lord and Master, have washed your feet: ye also ought to wash one another's feet.

15 For I (have given) you an example, that (ye) should do (as I have done) to you.
(Alf. Gave—ye also—according as I did.)

16 Verily, verily, I say unto you, (The servant is not) greater than his lord: neither he that is sent greater than He that sent Him.
(Alf. There is no servant—nor apostle.)

As ever Jesus teaches His disciples as much by His example as by His words. He knew their proneness to dispute which of them should be the greatest, and how soon a strife would again arise among them on this very subject (Luke xxii. 24), and He here gives them an example which, if followed, would for ever cut off all feeling of this kind.

17 If ye know these things, (happy) are ye if ye do them.
(Alf. Blessed.)

18 I speak not of you all: [I know] whom I (have chosen): but that the Scripture may be fulfilled, He that eateth bread with Me (hath lifted) up his heel against Me.²
[S. A. For I know.]
(Alf. Chose—lifted.)

---

1 Ye call Me Master and Lord (ὑμεῖς φωνεῖτε με, ὁ διδάσκαλος, καὶ ὁ κύριος). "The editions of Erasmus, Colin, and Bogard omit the latter Article. No MS., however, warrants the omission. Though both titles are meant to be applied to our Saviour, yet they are not spoken of as being applied at the same time, but distinctly and independently, as if our Saviour had said, one of you calls Me ὁ διδάσκαλος, another ὁ κύριος."—Bishop Middleton on Greek Article, p. 257.

² But that the Scripture may be fulfilled (ἀλλ ἵνα ἡ γραφὴ πληρωθῇ). "I speak not of you all, I know those whom I have chosen, but (I have made this choice) that... might be fulfilled," etc.—Winer's Grammar of New Testament, p. 333.

One of them never could be happy or blessed, for he never would do these things, and of him He spake not. He had not chosen Judas as one of the Twelve in ignorance of his character, or of the way in which he would yield to the temptations of Satan, and betray Him. He had elected Judas among the Twelve, bad as he was, in order to make use of him and to fulfil the Scripture and to accomplish His Passion, and by that the salvation of mankind.

The words which Jesus here quotes from Psalm xli. 9 is evidently not intended as a quotation from the Septuagint, for it differs from it in several words. Both this and the Septuagint may be regarded as exact translations from the Hebrew, and differ from each just as much and no more than we might naturally expect in the case of any two accurate and independent translations. Here, as in other places, Jesus applies the words of the Old Testament to Himself; and without any explanation, as if that were the principal and natural meaning of these passages. In quoting the Scriptures of the Old Testament, and making no exception at least to their general accuracy, we may fairly conclude that He bears a positive testimony to it.

19 (Now) I tell you before it (come), that, when it is come to pass, ye may believe that I am He.

(Alf. From this time—come to pass.)

His choice of Judas to be one of the Twelve was not the effect of human frailty, of ignorance. He had not been deceived in Him. It was a proof of Divine foreknowledge, for he had chosen him for this very purpose, because He knew that he would become a traitor and deliver Him up to the chief priests. His Passion, too, which He now foretold and which was close at hand, ought not to be to them a cause of distrust and disbelief in Him, as if it had come upon Him unawares and as if He was unable to avert it. His Passion should rather be a cause of greater belief in Him as having been foretold by Him, and as having been foretold for this very purpose to increase their belief in Him.

20 Verily, verily, I say unto you, He that receiveth whomsoever I send receiveth Me: and he that receiveth Me receiveth Him that sent Me.

The meaning of these words in themselves is plain enough, but it is not easy to see their connection with what Jesus had said before, or what is His intention in giving utterance to them just at this particular time. Some have thought that He uttered them to comfort and encourage His Apostles under the persecutions which they should meet with in preaching the Gospel. Others that He has reference to the enormity of the sin of Judas in being faithless in such a trust as that with which he was charged. Others, that as Jesus had before commanded the Apostles to wash the feet and to show acts of love and condescension to His faithful ones, so He now commands the faithful to receive His Apostles with the utmost honour and reverence, as sent by the Father. Others again have thought that by these words He further enforces on the Apostles the duty of receiving and caring for all who came in His name.

St. John in his narrative of the Last Supper omits to record the institution of the Eucharist. The question therefore naturally arises, where in his account should the institution of the Eucharist come in? The difficulty of answering this question is increased by the fact that St. Matthew and St. Mark relate His disclosure of the treachery of Judas before they relate His institution of the Eucharist, while St. Luke does not relate his disclosure of the traitor until after the Eucharist. It seems impossible to reconcile these different accounts unless in some such manner as that proposed by St. Augustine,[1] that is, to suppose that Jesus spake to His disciples of His betrayal by Judas, more than once during this evening. Though this is not actually stated, it would not be unnatural to suppose that Jesus might mention this more than once, considering the agitation and the sorrow which it caused Him, nor would it be inconsistent with the narrative itself. None of the Evangelists but St. John relate the actual giving of the sop to Judas, so that it would not strain the narrative to suppose that St. Matthew and St. Mark record the words, which Jesus used about the traitor before the institution of the Eucharist, and St. Luke and St. John those which He used after. There seems to be no other way of reconciling the account, unless we suppose that the Evangelists record the events of the evening but without regard to the exact order in which they occurred, that St. Luke has related the disclosure of the treachery of Judas after he relates the institution of the Eucharist, though it occurred before, or that St. Matthew and St. Mark anticipate the order and relate the disclosure of the treachery of Judas before the institution of the Eucharist, though it really took place after, or, that each of the Evangelists relates in one account the words which Jesus spake at twice, part before the institution of the Eucharist and part after.

On the supposition either that Jesus spake to His Disciples of His betrayal by Judas more than once during the evening, both before and after the institution of the Eucharist, or that St. Matthew and St. Mark record His words respecting Judas before they relate the institution of the Eucharist, though part of them at least were spoken after; on either of these suppositions the account of the institution of the Eucharist would naturally come into St. John's Gospel somewhere

---

[1] (De consensu Evangelistarum iii. 1: vol. iii. part i. 1158, Migne.)

about the 20th verse of this chapter, probably between the 20th and 21st verses, or, as some think, after the 22nd verse.[1]

The following might be the order of events during the evening. The Paschal supper being concluded, and their ordinary supper having begun, Jesus rose from the table and washed the feet of his disciples. Having sat down again, He spake the words which John has related from 12th to 20th verses. Then being troubled in spirit He spake of His betrayal. Jesus then institutes the Eucharist and commands them to offer it as His Memorial. After this He again speaks of His betrayal as related by St. Luke and St. John. Peter beckons to John to ask Him, who it was, and Jesus replied, He it is, to whom I shall give a sop, when I have dipped it. And when He had dipped the sop He gave it to Judas Iscariot: and after the sop Satan entered into him. Judas having received the sop immediately went out, and Jesus then delivered the discourse which St. John records.

21 When Jesus had thus said, He was troubled (in spirit), and testified and said, Verily, verily, I say unto you, that one of you shall betray Me.

(Alf. In His spirit.)

22 [Then] the disciples looked one on another, (doubting) of whom He spake.

[V. Omits, Then.]
(Alf. Omits, Then—being in doubt.)

23 [Now] there was (leaning on) Jesus' bosom one of His disciples, whom Jesus loved.

[V. Omits, Now.]
(Alf. Omits, Now—reclining at meat in.)

24 Simon Peter therefore (beckoned) to him, [that he should ask who it should be of whom He spake.]

[V. And saith unto him, Say who it is of whom He speaketh: He spake.]
[S. And saith unto him, Say who it is of whom He speaketh.]
(Alf. Maketh a sign—Tell us who it is of whom He speaketh.)

The custom of the country was to recline at meals two or three on one couch. Nearness to Jesus their Lord and Master was the

---

[1] **The institution of the Eucharist.—** "There is no reason whatever to suppose, with some critics, that the foot washing is intended to take the place of the institution of the Eucharist. The random guesses that have been made to account for the omission of the latter, are sufficient to refute the theories of which they form a part. The simple explanation is, that the subject was too familiar to need repetition."—Sanday's *Historical Character of the Fourth Gospel*, p. 217.

post of honour. This was not allotted to Philip or to Andrew, who were the disciples first called; but to John the disciple whom Jesus loved. The reason is not assigned, why He loved him: it is generally believed to have been on account of his youthful, gentle, loving character. A proof of his modesty is given in the very way in which he relates this, omitting any mention of his own name.

Besides reclining the nearest to Jesus at supper, St. John in his Gospel enters the most fully into the great Mystery of the Incarnation. He brings before us more fully than the other Evangelists Jesus the Son of Mary as the Resurrection and the Life. Though it is not anywhere said, that the nature of St. John's Gospel was influenced by the innocence, meekness, and gentleness of his youth, and by his close communion with Jesus in his life, it would not be very unnatural to suppose that this was the case.

As on other occasions, so here too, the zeal of St. Peter makes him one of the most prominent among the Twelve. It was probably not mere curiosity on his part that prompted this inquiry, but a desire to counteract the treachery. His zeal in the garden afterwards led him to offer resistance to the apprehension of Jesus by the soldiers.

25 ([He then lying]) on Jesus' breast saith unto Him, Lord, who is it?[1]

[S. He therefore lying.]
[V. He lying thus.]
(Alf. He then leaning back thus.)

26 ([Jesus answered]), He it is, (to whom I shall [give a sop]), when I have dipped it. And when he had dipped the sop, [He gave it] to Judas Iscariot, the son of Simon.

(V. Jesus therefore answereth,—All MSS. give the sop : V. He taketh and giveth it.]
[S. Jesus answereth and saith.]
[Alf. Jesus therefore answereth—for whom I shall dip the sop, and give it to him —He taketh it and giveth it.)

---

[1] He then lying on Jesus' breast (ἐπιπεσὼν δὲ ἐκεῖνος ἐπὶ τὸ στῆθος τοῦ Ἰησοῦ).—"The English Version makes no distinction between the reclining position of the beloved disciple throughout the meal, described by ἀνακείμενος, and the sudden change of posture at this moment introduced by ἀναπεσών. This distinction is further enforced in the original by a change in both the prepositions and the nouns, from ἐν to ἐπί, and from κόλπος to στῆθος. St. John was reclining on the bosom of his Master, and he suddenly threw back his head upon His breast to ask a question. Again, in a later passage, a refer-ence occurs—not to the reclining position, but to the sudden movement—in xxi. 20, ὃς καὶ ἀνέπεσεν ἐν τῷ δείπνῳ ἐπὶ τὸ στῆθος αὐτοῦ καὶ εἶπεν, where likewise it is mis-understood by our translators, 'which also *leaned on* His breast and said.' This is among the most striking of those vivid descriptive traits which distinguish the narrative of the fourth Gospel generally, and which are especially remarkable in these last scenes of Jesus' life, where the beloved disciple was himself an eye-witness and an actor."—Dr. J. B. Lightfoot on *Revision of New Testament*, p. 72.

On the sign made to him by St. Peter, St. John withdraws himself a little from Jesus towards Peter to hear what he had to say. Peter seems to have concluded that John as the beloved disciple would know who the traitor was. St. John who was reclining on Jesus' bosom (ἐν τῷ κόλπῳ) now moved nearer to Him and leaned back on His breast (ἐπὶ τὸ στῆθος) and asked the question secretly. The answer which Jesus made to St. John was apparently not intended for the ear of the rest, and did not reach them. The words "to whom I shall give a sop," &c. were not spoken aloud, but privately to John, who then probably communicated them to Peter.

In common with the rest of the Twelve, Judas was present at the Paschal Supper, at the washing of the feet, and at the institution of the Eucharist. But he alone received the sop, which would not be part of the bread which Jesus had blessed, but a portion of the unleavened bread which remained on the table.

Bread taken from the table and given to another has been, in all ages and among all nations, a sign of peace and friendship between them. Thus by this sop Jesus might not only point out to John who the traitor was, but also under what guise he would act the traitor, under the form of love and friendship. The giving of the sop too might be one more act on the part of Jesus, to inform Judas that his intended treachery was known, and to recall to his recollection the words of the Psalmist, "Yea, Mine own familiar friend, in whom I trusted, which did eat of My bread, hath lifted up his heel against Me," and thus if possible to deter him from his purpose.

27 And after the sop (Satan) entered into him. (Then said Jesus) unto him, (That) thou doest, do quickly.[1]

(Alf. Then Satan—Jesus therefore saith—What.)

28 [Now] no man at the table knew for what intent He (spake this unto him.)

[V. Omits, Now.]
(Alf. Spake unto him.)

29 For (some of them) thought, because Judas (had) the bag, that Jesus (had said) unto him, Buy (those things) that we have need of against the feast: or that he should give something to the poor.

(Alf. Some—kept—said—the things.)

---

[1] That thou doest, do quickly (ὃ ποιεῖς ποίησον τάχιον). "More quickly than you seem disposed to do, hasten the execution.

The Imperative must not be taken as simply permissive."—Winer's *Grammar of New Testament*, p. 327.

30 He then having received the sop went immediately out: [and it was night.]

(A. And it was night, when he went out, Jesus said, Now, &c.)

It was before stated (Ver. 2) that Satan had put it into the heart of Judas to betray Jesus, now it is said that after the sop Satan entered into him. Satan took possession of him, and hurried him on to complete his work. There was no connection between Satan and the sop. This was not the medium of Satan's entering into Judas, but merely the occasion of his doing so. The sop was to St. John the sign who should betray Jesus, but to Judas it was a mark of honour, of good will and love. Kindly as this was meant towards Judas, his evil conscience no doubt looked upon it, only as a sign intended to discover him to the rest, and conscious of his treacherous designs towards Jesus, he becomes desperate in his resolve to execute his dreadful purpose. Even if the giving of the sop to Judas was in any way a sign to the others that Judas was the traitor, still it did not lead either them or St. John, who at least knew the sign, to understand the meaning of the words, which Jesus spake to him. Though they might conclude that he it was who should betray Jesus, they did not imagine it would be that very night, that very hour. They supposed that these words had reference to some of the business which Judas usually transacted for the company. No doubt it was then as it is now. The poor are unable to make the necessary provision for the Passover week without assistance. The disciples probably remembered that Jesus had been accustomed on such occasions, to give something to the poor out of their common fund. They little thought that by these words Jesus, though He was not persuading, was permitting and foretelling His Own betrayal to Death. Nay so eager is Jesus for the salvation of man, that he is represented as reproving the tardiness of Judas.

The Evangelist is careful to record the time. "It was night." As soon as his new master takes possession of him, he gives him no rest, but forces him to go at once on his horrible undertaking. Night is the most fitting hour, in which to accomplish such a work as Judas purposes, most expressive too of the nature of his work, and of the state of his soul. "It was night."

31 Therefore, when he was gone out, Jesus (said), Now is the Son of Man glorified, and God is glorified in Him.[1]

(Alf. Saith.)

---

[1] Now is the Son of Man glorified (νῦν ἐδοξάσθη ὁ υἱὸς τοῦ ἀνθρώπου). "It is only in appearance that the Aorist is used for the Future. Jesus says, 'Now is the Son of Man glorified,' the traitor Judas having gone away, and, as it were, completed his treason,"—Winer's Grammar of New Testament, p. 292.

32 If God be glorified in Him [God shall also glorify Him in Himself], and shall straightway glorify Him.

[S. V. And God shall glorify Him in Himself (Omit, If God be glorified in Him.)]

As soon as Judas had gone out Jesus said, "Now is the Son of Man glorified, and God is glorified in Him," intimating that the process of glorification was already begun, that Judas had gone out to betray Him to Death, and that His Death would be not for the ignominy but for the highest glorification of the Son of Man. By His Death He would be proved to be not only Man, and the Son of Man, but God, and the Son of God.

That the Godhead tabernacled in the body, that in Jesus there dwelt all the fulness of the Godhead bodily, would be shown by the darkening of the sun, by the quaking of the earth, by the rending of the rocks, and the opening of the graves, and by the resurrection of the saints who slept. All these things would prove clearly that it was not Man only who suffered, and gave up His Life on the Cross, but God.

Some think that a distinction is intended to be made between the glorifying in the 31st verse, and that in the 32nd. The first is spoken of as already begun and nearly completed, and refers to the glorifying of God by Jesus on earth, in His course of obedience as the Son of Man, and which was completed by His Death. The second is spoken of as future, and is thought to refer to the manifestation of Jesus to be the Son of God with power, by His Resurrection and Ascension to the Father, to sit at the right hand of God.

The expression "God shall also glorify Him in Himself" applies to God the Father, and expresses the glory which the Word had with the Father before His condescension to be born of a virgin, and which after His Resurrection and Ascension He would again receive as the "Word made Flesh." With His Human Body Jesus would ascend to the Father and share with Him the glory which He had before the Incarnation. These words are explained by those which Jesus used a little later, "And now, O Father, glorify Thou Me with thine Own Self, with the glory which I had with Thee before the world was." (xvii. 5.)

33 Little children, yet a little while I am with you. Ye shall seek Me: and as I said unto the Jews, Whither I go, ye cannot come: so now I say to you.

34 A new commandment I give unto you, That ye love one another: [(as I have loved you), that ye also love] one another.

[S. As I have loved you, love ye also.]
(Alf. Even as I loved you.)

35 (By this shall all men know) that ye are My disciples, if ye have love one to another.

(Alf. Herein shall all men perceive.)

Using the expression which a mother would use to her new-born offspring, "Little children" (τεκνία) Jesus may intend to express the tenderness of His affection for His disciples, as well as the weakness of their condition, of their faith in Him. In a few short hours He would leave them. For in that time Judas would have betrayed Him to the chief priests.

His departure was nothing new. He had already announced it to the Jews. To them He had said, "Whither I go, ye cannot come," because they should die in their sins. (viii. 21.) The disciples cannot go, because they have a work to do, a commandment to fulfil, and to exhibit the fulfilment of it to the world. He had inaugurated a new Dispensation, and love to each other was to be the distinguishing mark of this Dispensation. He had united them in One, in Himself the Head. They had just partaken of His Body and of His Blood, the Sacrament of the New Covenant, and they must show forth the fruits of this, by keeping the commandment of the New Covenant. They were no longer individuals, so to speak; they were members of One Body, and they must henceforth show the love and the sympathy which members of the same Body have for each other.

36 Simon Peter (said) unto Him, Lord, whither goest Thou? Jesus answered [him], Whither I go, thou canst not follow Me now: but thou shalt follow Me afterwards.

[V. Omits, Him: S. V. A. But thou shalt follow afterwards.]
(Alf. Saith.)

37 Peter saith unto Him [Lord], why cannot I follow Thee now? I will lay down my life (for Thy sake).

[S. Omits, Lord.]
(Alf. Saith—for Thee.)

38 [Jesus answered him,] Wilt thou lay down thy life (for My sake)? Verily, verily I say unto thee, The cock shall not crow, till thou hast denied Me thrice.

[S. V. A. Jesus answereth.]
(Alf. For Me.)

St. Peter's question was dictated not by mere curiosity to know whither Jesus is going, but by an earnest feeling of devotion to Him.

But he could not follow Him now, either because he had not the strength of resolution so to do, or because there was work on earth for him to accomplish first. When the Holy Spirit should have been given, he should acquire the strength to labour in his Master's cause, and then to follow Him in the mode of His Death by a similar death on the Cross. When Peter, with more zeal than knowledge, persists, Jesus, in order to prove to him his own weakness without the help of the Holy Spirit, foretells and permits his fall.

INTRODUCTORY NOTE TO CHAPTER XIV.

The Advocate.—After showing from the derivation of the word that Advocate and not "Comforter" is the proper rendering of the term παράκλητος, Dr. J. B. Lightfoot goes on to say :—"If Advocate is the only sense which παράκλητος can properly bear, it is also (as I cannot but think) the sense which the context suggests whenever the word is used in the Gospel. In other words, the idea of pleading, arguing, convincing, instructing, correcting, is prominent in every instance. Thus in xiv. 16, &c., the Paraclete is described as the Spirit of *truth* whose reasonings fall dead on the ear of the world, and are vocal only to the faithful (ὅ ὁ κόσμος οὐ δύναται λαβεῖν . . . ὑμεῖς γινώσκετε αὐτό.) In xiv. 26, again, the function of the Paraclete is described in similar language. He shall *teach* you all things and *remind* you of all things. In xv. 26, He is once more designated the Spirit of Truth, and here the office assigned to Him is to *bear witness* of Christ. And lastly, in xvi. 7, &c., the idea of the *pleader* appears still more definitely in the context, for it is there declared that He shall convince or convict (ἐλέγξει) the world of sin and of righteousness and of judgment. And generally it may be said that the Holy Spirit, the Paraclete, is represented in these passages as the Advocate, the Counsel, who suggests the true reasonings to our minds and true courses of action for our lives, who convicts our adversary the World of wrong and pleads our cause before God our Father. In short, the conception (though somewhat more comprehensive) is substantially the same as in St. Paul's language when describing the function of the Holy Ghost : 'The Spirit itself beareth witness with our spirit that we are children of God.' 'The Spirit helpeth our infirmities : for we know not what we should pray for as we ought, but the Spirit itself maketh intercession for us with groanings which cannot be uttered.' (Rom. viii. 16, 26.)

"Thus whether we regard the origin of the word, or whether we consider the requirements of the context, it would seem that 'Comforter' should give way to 'Advocate,' as the interpretation of παράκλητος. The word 'Comforter' does indeed express a true office of the Holy Spirit, as our most heartfelt experiences will tell us. Nor has the rendering, though inadequate, been without its use in fixing this fact in our minds : but the function of the Paraclete, as our Advocate, is even more important, because wider and deeper than this.

Nor will the idea of a 'Comforter' be lost to us by the change, for the English *Te Deum* will still remain to recall this office of the Paraclete to our remembrance, while the restoration of the correct rendering in the passages of St. John's Gospel will be in itself an unmixed gain. Moreover (and this is no unimportant fact) the language of the Gospel will thus be linked in the English Version, as it is in the original, with the language of the Epistle. (1 John ii. 1.) In this there will be a twofold advantage. We shall see fresh force in the words thus rendered. He will give you *another* ' Advocate : ' when we remember that our Lord is styled by St. John our 'Advocate:' the advocacy of Christ illustrating and being illustrated by the Advocacy of the Spirit. At the same time we shall bring out another of the coincidences tending to establish an identity of authorship in the Gospel and Epistle, and thus to make valid for the former all the evidences external and internal which may be adduced to prove the genuineness of the latter."
—Dr. J. B. Lightfoot on *Revision of New Testament*, p. 53.

CHAPTER XIV.

1 *Christ comforteth His disciples with the hope of heaven;* 6 *Professeth Himself the Way, the Truth, and the Life, and One with the Father;* 13 *Assureth their prayers in His Name to be effectual;* 15 *Requesteth love and obedience;* 16 *Promiseth the Holy Ghost the Comforter;* 27 *And leaveth His peace with them.*

This their last Passover had been overclouded with sorrow, it had ended in sadness. They are still in the Upper Room. But how different are their feelings now from what they were a few hours ago, when they first entered that Room to keep the Feast in memory of their deliverance from the angel of death, and from the bondage of Egypt. They had eaten the usual Passover. Jesus had shown them an unwonted mark of His love. He had washed the feet of His Twelve Disciples. He had instituted a New Memorial of Himself, and had bound them to Himself and to each other under stronger ties of love than ever before. But with all this He had mingled His instruction with words that filled their hearts with sadness. He had spoken of His immediate departure from them, and that by the treachery of one of their own number, of the denial of Peter, and of the desertion of the rest. (Matt. xxvi. 31.) Judas had already left them, and sadness had filled the hearts of the rest.

To leave them would be to crush all the hopes they had ever built upon Him. The more firmly they believed that Jesus was the Messiah, the more disappointment His departure would cause them. For the Apostles, like the rest of the Jewish nation, had indulged in the expectation that the Messiah would restore the temporal kingdom to Israel (Acts i. 6), that He would rescue them from the yoke of the Gentiles (Luke xxiv. 21), and would invest His followers with the ensigns of kingly pomp, triumph, and splendour. Hitherto they had seen nothing but poverty, contempt, reproach, and persecution as the rewards of their attachment to Him: should He leave them, all their hopes of improvement and of earthly grandeur would be destroyed for ever. No wonder their heart was troubled. To comfort them in this their trouble and disappointment Jesus said unto them,

1 Let not your heart be troubled: (ye believe in God), believe also in Me.

(Alf. Believe in God.)

2 In My Father's house are many mansions : if it were not so, I would have told you. ([I go to prepare]) a place for you.

[S. V. A. For I go to prepare.]
(Alf. For I go to prepare.)

3 [And if I go and prepare] a place for you, I will come again, and (receive) you unto Myself: that where I am, there ye may be also.¹

[A. And if I go, I will prepare.]
(Alf. Will receive.)

4 [(And whither I go ye know, and the way ye know.)]

[S. V. And whither I go, ye know the way.]
(Alf. And whither I go ye know the way.)

The remedy for their trouble was not only to believe that there was One True God, who directed and superintended all the affairs of men, but also that He, Jesus, their Lord and Master was that One God.

He had already promised Peter that he should follow Him after a time. He now extends the promise to the rest. But first He must depart from them, and prepare a place for them. They could not ascend into heaven before He, by His Ascension, had prepared the way. As yet no man had ever ascended into heaven. Until He, the Head of the Church, in His glorified Human Body, had ascended into heaven, none of His members could ascend thither. To show how great is the Mystery of the Human Body ascending into heaven at all, the Psalmist represents the angels as expressing the utmost surprise, admiration, and exultation at the Ascension of Jesus, the God-Man in His risen Body.

(1st Choir.) Lift up your heads, O ye gates, and be ye lift up, ye everlasting doors, and the King of Glory shall come in.
(2nd Choir.) Who is the King of Glory?
(1st Choir.) It is the Lord strong and mighty, even the Lord mighty in battle. Lift up your heads, O ye gates, and be ye lift up, ye everlasting doors, and the King of Glory shall come in.

---

¹ And if I go, I will come again and receive you, etc. (ἐὰν πορευθῶ πάλιν ἔρχομαι καὶ παραλήψομαι). " The Present tense is used only in appearance for the Future, when, exactly as in Latin, German, English, etc., an action still future is mentioned as already present, either because it is unalterably determined, or is about to take place by some unchanging arrangement."—Winer's *Grammar of New Testament*, p. 280.

(2nd Choir.) Who is the King of Glory ?
(1st Choir.) Even the Lord of Hosts, He is the King of Glory.
(Psalm xxiv. 7-10.)

But before He ascended in His glorified Body into heaven, Jesus had to show Himself the Lord strong and mighty, even the Lord mighty in battle, He had through Death to destroy Him that had the power of death, that is, the devil. (Heb. ii. 14.)

Not only had Jesus to prepare a place for them by His Own Ascension into heaven, He had also to prepare them for the place, by sending down the Holy Spirit to sanctify them, and to fit them to dwell with Him. If they remembered what He had said unto them they would understand this, they would know whither He was going, and also the way. They would know that through His Death on the Cross He would return to the Father, and they would know the way by which they were to follow Him.

5 Thomas saith unto Him, Lord, we know not whither Thou goest: [and how (can) we know the way ?]
[V. Omits and: V. How know we the way ?]
(Alf. Do.)

6 Jesus saith unto him, I am the way, (the Truth), and the Life: no man cometh unto the Father but (by) Me.[1]
(Alf. And the Truth—through.)

7 [If ye had known [Me,], ye (should have) known] My Father also : [and] from henceforth ye know Him, and have seen Him.[2]
[A. Omits, Me: S. If ye have known Me, ye shall know: V. Omits, and.]
(Alf. Would have.)

---

[1] The way.—" It is true of Christianity, as it is true of no other religious system, that the religion is identified with, is absorbed in, the Person of its founder. The Gospel is Christ, and Christ only. This fact finds expression in many ways: but more especially in the application of the same language to the one and to the other. In most cases, this identity of terms is equally apparent in the English and the Greek. But in one instance, it is obliterated by a mistranslation of the definite article. Our Lord in St. John's Gospel, in answer to the disciple's question, ' How can we know the way ?', answers, 'I am the way.' Corresponding to this, we ought to find that in no less than four places in the Acts of the Apostles the Gospel is called ' the way' absolutely : ix. 2, ' If he found any that were of the way, (ἐάν τινας εὕρῃ τῆς ὁδοῦ ὄντας) : xix. 9. ' Divers believed not, but spake evil of the way :' xix. 23. ' There arose no small stir about the way :' xxiv. 22. ' Having more perfect knowledge of the way :' but in all these passages, the fact disappears in the English Version, which varies the rendering between ' this way' and ' that way,' but never once translates τὴν ὁδόν the way."—Dr. J. B. Lightfoot on Revision of New Testament, p. 104.

[2] From henceforth ye know Him,

To the objection made by Thomas, that they did not know whither or to whom He was going, and therefore how could they know the way by which to follow Him, Jesus replies that He is going to the Father, and that the way by which they are to follow is by belief in Him. For He is the way, the Truth and the Life, and no man can come to the Father except through Him.

Jesus by His Passion opens the way to heaven for man. By His doctrine He delivers His followers from the darkness and errors in which others wander. By His Holy Spirit He sanctifies their lives and leads them to prepare for the life to come. By His own perfect Life He has given them an example, He has first trod the way, and they are to follow in His steps.

But not only is Jesus the way to the Father, but He is also One with the Father, One with the Father not in a secondary sense, but in the very highest and most perfect sense. This was a subject which as yet the disciples did not comprehend. Though Jesus had been "so long time," three years, with them, they had not from their intercourse with Him gathered a sufficiently correct and full idea of the relation between Him and the Father.

8 Philip saith unto Him, Lord, shew us the Father, and it sufficeth us.

From the miracles which Jesus had wrought they could not doubt that He was, as He said, the Son of God. Still there was about Him somewhat, that contradicted their expectations of what God would be. He was subject to the same human weakness as themselves; He was almost as much in the power of His enemies, so far as they could see, as themselves. Hence arose at times their fears, their misgivings. If once they could only see the Father, they would be satisfied, their fears would all be removed.

They formed their opinion of the union between God the Father and Jesus His Son, from what they saw existed on earth between a father and his son. They have a common nature alike in both, they possess equal or similar power, they occupy a similar station or rank in the world, have individual wills and individual characteristics. But in no sense can they be called one. If the relation between God the Father, and God the Son, were such as exists between a father and his son on earth, they would be two independent Gods, two, it might be, equal, but two independent Gods. In the following verses Jesus shows that such is not the relation between Himself and the Father.

---

etc. (καὶ ἀπ' ἄρτι γινώσκετε αὐτὸν καὶ ἑωράκατε αὐτόν), must be rendered from this time, ye know Him, and ye have seen Him, not with Kühnöl: cum mox accura- tius cognoscetis et quasi oculis videbitis. —Winer's *Grammar of New Testament*, p. 289.

9 Jesus saith unto him, Have I been so long time with you, and yet (hast thou not known) Me, Philip? He that hath seen Me hath seen the Father: [and] how sayest thou then, Shew us the Father?

[S. V. Omit, and.]
(Alf. Dost thou not know.)

10 Believest thou not that I am in the Father, and the Father in Me? The words that I speak unto you I speak not of Myself: [but the Father that dwelleth in Me, He doeth the works.]

[V. But the Father dwelling in Me, doeth His works.]
[S. But the Father in Me, doeth His works.]
(Alf. Doeth His works.)

11 Believe Me that I am in the Father, [and the Father in Me]: or else believe Me for the very works' sake.[1]

[A. Omits, and the Father in Me: S. Or else believe the very works.]

> The union between Jesus and the Father is such that,
> He, who hath known Jesus, hath known the Father,
> He, who hath seen Jesus, hath seen the Father.
> Jesus is in the Father, and the Father in Jesus.
> The words, which Jesus speaks, He speaks from the Father.
> The works, which Jesus does, the Father doeth.

No language could express Oneness, equality, between the Father and Jesus His Son, more strongly than this. Such union as this is inconceivably beyond the relation, that exists between an earthly father and his son, and could never be gathered from it. Nothing but express revelation from God could communicate this knowledge. To put these expressions into other language is to say, that God the Father and Jesus His Son are One in essence or divine nature, but distinct in Person, One God, and Two Persons.

If they will not believe His words that the Father is in Him, He appeals to His works as proving it. If it is not sufficient to gain their credence, that He says the Father is in Him, He appeals to them to believe it, because they see the Father working in Him. They cannot see with their bodily eyes the soul, but still they believe that the soul

---

[1] That I am in the Father, and the Father in Me (ὅτι ἐγὼ ἐν τῷ πατρὶ καὶ ὁ πατὴρ ἐν ἐμοί). Two different forms of the verb substantive are suppressed in this same compound sentence. In general, in the simple diction of the New Testament, it is easy to perceive from the connection what words are to be supplied."—Winer's *Grammar of New Testament*, p. 608.

exists in the body, because they can see its works. They see the body performing operations, which it could not do of itself, unless the soul were in it. In like manner they see Jesus performing miracles, working supernatural works, which He could not do if He were a mere Man, which He could not do unless the Father were working with Him and in Him.

12 Verily, verily, I say unto you, He that believeth (on) Me, the works that I do, shall he do also: and greater works than these shall he do: because I go ([unto My Father.])
[S. V. A. Unto the Father.]
(Alf. in—unto the Father.)

13 And whatsoever ye shall ask in My name, that will I do, that the Father may be glorified in the Son.

14 If ye shall ask anything in My name, [I will do it.]
[V. A. That will I do.]

Another proof that the Father is in Jesus, and works in Him, is that he who holds this belief has also, by this very faith, power to work similar or even greater miracles than He Himself did while on earth.

Some have thought that in the expression, "greater things than these shall he do," He had reference to the conversion of the Gentile world by His Apostles. By His Own Personal preaching and miracles Jesus converted only a small number, a few hundreds at most. His Apostles converted a great part of the world as then known. The conversion of the world was the effect of His Resurrection and of the descent of the Holy Spirit. But this did not take place until Jesus had ascended to the Father. This, too, is the reason assigned why they should work greater things than He had done, because He should go to the Father. Having gained the victory, having triumphed over sin and death and hell, He ascends to the Father and sends down the Holy Spirit, to enlighten and sanctify and strengthen the Apostles, so as to convert the world.

Though he should not be present with them in the same sense as formerly, still He promised to grant, whatever they asked in His name consistently with the glory of the Father, and this promise is repeated in two consecutive verses.

15 If ye love [Me], [keep] My commandments.
[S. Omits, Me: V. Ye shall keep.]

16 And I will pray the Father, and He shall give

you another Comforter, ([that He may abide]) with you for ever :[1]

[S. V. That He may be.]
(Alf. That He may be.)

17 Even the Spirit of truth : whom the world cannot receive, because it (seeth) Him not, neither knoweth Him : [but] ye know Him : for He dwelleth with you, ([and shall be in you.])

[S. V. Omit, but: V. And is in you.]
(Alf. Beholdeth—and is in you.)

He asks for a proof of their love, which would be shown by keeping His commandments, and on this He promises to send another Advocate or Comforter, to supply His place after His departure from them, which would be after His Ascension, and this promise He fulfilled at the Day of Pentecost. To keep in their minds His Oneness with the Father, He expresses His promise to send the Comforter with the form of a prayer to the Father to send Him.

The word translated Comforter is literally a Paraclete or Advocate. The disciples are in trouble at the thought that Jesus is going to leave them, and at the loss which they shall experience thereby,—a loss, which, as they think, cannot possibly be made up to them. What they therefore require is, one who shall supply the place of Jesus to them : one who can be their Advocate, the defender of them and their cause against their adversaries ; who can intercede with the Father for them, and can be their leader and adviser in all the attacks of their enemies on earth.

1. He will be with the Apostles and those, whom they represent, the Church, for ever.
2. He is the Spirit of Truth. He will lead them into all the truth and fulness of the Gospel, and will preserve them from the errors of Satan.
3. The world, or the men whose minds are set upon this present world without regard to the future, cannot receive Him. Their thoughts and desires are taken up with the things that concern the body only, and care not for the salvation of the soul, which is the object of the Paraclete.
4. The Apostles, the Church, know Him, because He dwelleth with them, and in them. He is not an object for their senses, but for their faith. They cannot feel His presence by the senses of the body, but still they recognise His holy influence over them.

---

[1] See note on John xvi. 23.

18 I will not leave you (comfortless): I will come to you.

(Margin, Orphans.)
(Alf. Orphans.)

19 Yet a little while, and the world (seeth) Me no more: but ye (see) Me: because I live, ye shall live also.

(Alf. Beholdeth—behold.)

At the beginning of this discourse to them, He called them little children (τέκνια) now He says that He will not make them " orphans " (ὀρφανούς) by His departure. He will come to them again. This promise He fulfilled on the Day of Resurrection, when He appeared to them in His glorified Body, and on the Day of Pentecost, when He sent down the Holy Spirit upon them.

He then speaks of His Resurrection and of the effects of His Resurrection. Of the immediate future He uses the present. Of His own Resurrection He speaks as present, and of theirs, which will not be until the Day of Judgment, and which will be the effect of His Resurrection, as future. In a little time—in the space of a few hours —the world should see Him no more though they should see Him. When risen from the dead, He should not appear to all the people, but unto witnesses chosen before of God. (Acts x. 41.)

After His Resurrection, when they had been enlightened by the descent of the Holy Spirit, they should understand doctrines which now it was difficult for them to comprehend, and which, though He had explained to them more than once, they could not fully understand and receive now.

20 (At) that day ye shall know that I am in My Father, and ye in Me, and I in you.

(Alf. In.)

These three propositions are not to be understood in the same way, but each according to its own relation. Jesus is not in the Father in the same sense as He is in His disciples, and as they are in Him. Jesus is in the Father as being of the same essence, of the same divine nature, One with the Father and equal to the Father. He is in His disciples because He, through the Holy Spirit, dwelt in them. They are in Him because they were engrafted into Him the God Man. As an illustration it has been said, that Jesus is in the Father as a ray is in the Sun, of the same nature. They are in Jesus as branches grafted into the Vine. He is in them as the Vine is in the branches, supplying life and sustenance to them.

But the effect of Christ's resurrection should not be confined to the Apostles. It should be extended to all who loved Him, whether living at the time of His resurrection or afterwards.

COMMENTARY ON ST. JOHN'S GOSPEL. 321

21 He that hath My commandments, and keepeth them, he it is that loveth Me: and he that loveth Me, shall be loved (of) My Father, and I will love him, and will manifest Myself to him.

(Alf. By.)

The proof of their love to Jesus is to keep His commandments. The effect of their love is that God will love them and will manifest Himself unto them.

22 Judas saith unto Him, not Iscariot, [Lord, how is it] that Thou wilt manifest Thyself unto us, and not unto the world?[1]

[S. Lord, and how is it.]

To the inquiry of Judas why Jesus would manifest Himself unto them and not unto the world, He, in effect, replies that the manifestation of Himself after His resurrection, will be made to them only and to a few other witnesses chosen before of God (Acts x. 41), but that He will manifest Himself in another way to all who love Him and keep His words.

23 Jesus answered and said unto him, If a man love Me, he will keep My (words): and My Father will love him, and We will come unto him, and make Our abode with him.

(Alf. Word.)

God is everywhere, and fills all things, and therefore when He is said to abide in one place and to remove to another, such expressions are used with reference to our limited capacities. Jesus uses these terms here to indicate the various operations of the Holy Spirit on

---

[1] Jude, or Judas, Lebbæus, and Thaddeus (Luke vi. 16 'Ἰούδαν 'Ἰακώβου Authorised Version, "Judas the brother of James") one of the Twelve Apostles. "The name Judas only, without any distinguishing mark, occurs in the lists given by St. Luke vi. 16; Acts i. 13; and in John xiv. 22 (where we find 'Judas not Iscariot' among the Apostles), but the Apostle has been generally identified with Lebbæus, whose surname was Thaddeus (Matt. x. 3; Mark iii. 18). Much difference of opinion has existed from the earliest times as to the right interpretation of the words 'Ἰούδας 'Ἰακώβου. The generally received opinion is, that the Authorised Version is right in translating 'Judas the brother of James.' But we prefer to follow nearly all the most eminent critical authorities, and render the words 'Judas the son of James.' The name of Jude only occurs once in the Gospel narrative (John xiv. 22). Nothing is certainly known of the later history of the Apostle. Tradition connects him with the foundation of the Church at Edessa.—Smith's *Biblical Dictionary*.

men's minds. God comes to a man when He imparts His grace and influences His heart, and the more love He shows by keeping His commandments the longer He abides with him, the more grace He imparts to Him.

As love is shown by keeping God's commandments, so not to keep them is a proof of the want of love.

24 He that loveth Me not keepeth not (My sayings): and the word which ye hear is not Mine, but the Father's which sent Me.

(Alf. My words.)

To keep prominently before their minds His Oneness with the Father He says that the word which they hear Him speak is not His, but His Father's, who sent Him.

25 These things have I spoken unto you (being yet present with you).

(Alf. While yet abiding with you.)

26 But the Comforter (which is the Holy Ghost), whom the Father will send in My name, He shall teach you all things, and (bring all things to your remembrance, whatsoever I have said) unto you.

(Alf. Even the Holy Spirit—bring to your remembrance all things which I spake.)

Many things Jesus had said unto them, which they could not then understand, either on account of their own incapacity or on account of the deep nature of the things themselves, and there were many things which He had not said unto them for the same reasons. All these, as well as all the other Mysteries of the Incarnation, the Holy Spirit would enable them to comprehend. He would instruct them in all things necessary for the foundation, and for the future growth of the Church.

He says "Whom the Father will send in My name," to indicate the unity between the Three Persons in the Holy Trinity, and the mission of the Holy Spirit from the Father and the Son, and that His coming to them was the fruits of His Passion, and to supply His place to the Church.

27 Peace I leave with you, My peace I give unto you: [not as the world giveth give I unto you]. Let not your heart be troubled, neither let it be afraid.

[S. Not as the world giveth unto you give I unto you.]

The world, men in general, when departing from each other, say, "Peace be unto you." They wish peace in words, but they cannot by that give peace. It is a mere form of speech, expressive of goodwill to each other. Jesus, when now departing from them, gives them His peace, peace in the highest sense, peace with God, and in such a degree that they have no cause for trouble or fear. For a time He will depart from them, but only for a time. At this they ought rather to rejoice because, by His departure, He will fulfil the Mystery of the Incarnation. He will take captivity captive, and will receive for them gifts, the reward of His Passion.

28 Ye have heard how I said unto you, I go away, and come again unto you. If ye loved Me, ye would ([rejoice because I said I go) unto the Father: for My Father] is greater than I.[1]

[S. V. A. Rejoice because I go: V. A. For the Father.]
(Alf. Have rejoiced that I go.)

The latter part of this passage has at times been misunderstood. This has arisen from explaining the relation between God the Father and Jesus His Son, by reference to the relation which exists on earth between a father and his son. But the nature of the union which exists between an earthly father and his son is far too imperfect, ever to be a measure of the union which is between God the Father and God the Son, or even to convey an adequate conception of it. This can only be understood from the consistent interpretation of the language in which this union is revealed. No better summary of this language has ever been made than is contained in the Creed called the Creed of St. Athanasius. "Equal to the Father, as touching His Godhead, and inferior to the Father as touching His Manhood." In this His inferior part, in His Manhood He was now about to ascend to the Father, and to receive the reward of His Passion. At this they ought to rejoice. To rejoice at His exaltation rather than to mourn at His departure was a proof of their love to Him.

29 And now I have told you before it come to pass, that, when it is come to pass, ye (might) believe.
(Alf. May.)

Jesus foretold to His disciples His departure from them, His Death, His Resurrection, and return to them, not that they might condole with Him, or that they might take measures for their own

---

[1] "If ye loved Me, ye would rejoice (εἰ ἠγαπᾶτέ με, ἐχάρητε ἄν) if ye loved Me, ye would have rejoiced: After conditional clauses with εἰ we find ἄν in the apodosis with the Indicative to denote hypothetical reality."—Winer's *Grammar of New Testament*, p. 320.

conduct, but that they might believe in Him more fully, that they might believe that He foreknew all that came upon Him, and that He laid down His Life of His Own will, and for the salvation of man, and that they might believe that He is the Messiah, the Son of God, the Saviour of the world.

30 (Hereafter I will not talk) much with you : for the prince [of this world] cometh, and hath nothing in Me.¹

[S. V. A. Of the world.]
(Alf. I will no more talk—of the world.)

31 But that the world may know that I love the Father : and as the Father gave Me commandment, even so I do. Arise, let us go hence.

"The Prince of the World" comes through his agents, by their voluntarily yielding to his temptations. But Satan will find nothing in Jesus. He will have no right over Him ; he will find no sin in Him, and therefore not the right which sin gives him over other men. Though He die it will be because He lays down His life voluntarily that He may save mankind, and not because He is vanquished by Satan. His Death will be another proof to the world of His love to the Father, of His Oneness with the Father, and of His obedience to His commands.

Jesus was free from sin, and obeyed the commands of the Father, by reason of the Hypostatic Union of the Word with the Flesh. The divine power directed all the passions and affections of the Flesh, so that they were without sin. The weakness incident to the flesh, such as hunger, and thirst, and fatigue He underwent. But the weakness of the flesh, as the effect of man's fall, in the irregularity of passion, all these were rectified and sustained by the union of the Word with the Flesh.

Though Man, He fulfilled all the commands of the Father, and not by constraint. Necessity or constraint are terms which cannot be applied to the Son of God. The beatific Vision, the sight of God which the Saints will enjoy, will assimilate them to Him in their love

---

¹ xiv. 30, 31. "In punctuating these verses, expositors vary between ἐν ἐμοὶ οὐκ ἔχει οὐδέν, ἀλλ' ἵνα—ποιῶ. ἐγείρεσθε, and οὐδέν. ἀλλ ἵνα—ποιῶ, ἐγείρεσθε. In general, such discrepancies of punctuation, occurring in the New Testament, are not to be regarded as of much importance."—Winer's *Grammar of New Testament*, p. 72.

* Arise, let us go hence.—"This discourse is apparently intended to be conceived of as only momentarily broken at verse 31. Our Lord and His disciples arise from the table as if to go. But we see from xviii. 1 ((ἐξῆλθε) that they had not yet left the house, or at least the city. We must, therefore, suppose that the contents of chapters xv. and xvi., with the prayer of chap. xvii. were still spoken in the upper room, though after the first motion for departure."—Sanday's *Historical Character of the Fourth Gospel*, p. 221.

and in all their affections. They will desire but Him. In a similar way we may describe the obedience which Jesus rendered to the commands of the Father, not as the effect of constraint, but of love, and of such love as mere man knows not.

Some have thought that when Jesus said, "Arise, let us go hence," He and the eleven arose from the table, and set out towards Gethsemane, and that on the way thither He uttered these His farewell words to them, from chapters xv. to xviii. Others, and with more probability, think that Jesus and His disciples arose from the table, and that before they left the Upper Room, in which they had spent the evening, He delivered to them the following discourse, His last words to them before His Death.

INTRODUCTORY NOTE TO CHAPTER XV.

Johannean Words.—"The vocabulary of St. John's Gospel is eminently characteristic. It has several peculiar terms—such as the Word, the Light, the Life, the Truth, the World, Glory, Grace,—which, perhaps more than all others, bear upon them the clear stamp of the Divine signet. They are key-words, which open up new realms of thought to us, as suggestive as the streak of dawn along the Eastern hills. Like the jewels in the breast-plate of the Jewish High Priest they glow among the commoner terms with a mystic radiance which dispels the shadows of earth and time, and reveals the unseen and eternal. To these peculiar words may be added the word 'true,' which occurs no less than twenty-two times in the Gospel of St. John, as against five times in all the rest of the New Testament. It illustrates in a remarkable way the meditative simplicity of St. John's writings, in which all the ideas reduce themselves to a few comprehensive terms."—Macmillan on *The True Vine*, p. 19.

CHAPTER XV.

1 *The consolation and mutual love between Christ and His members, under the parable of the vine;* 18 *A comfort in the hatred and persecution of the world;* 26 *The office of the Holy Ghost and of the Apostles.*

THE eleven Apostles were now about to be put to their severest trial. Their faith in Jesus, as well as their love for Him, were both shortly to be brought to the proof. To prepare them for this, He delivers the parable of the Vine and its branches. He shows them the close union between Himself and them, and the bearing which their future conduct would have on this. Their union with Him was the great blessing of their lives, and their future happiness or misery would depend on the way in which they responded to this. The trials, to which they were on the point of being exposed, had not happened to them by chance; they were sent by the Father, and for the very purpose of causing them to bear fruit corresponding with their condition as members of Him, the God Incarnate.

1 I am the True Vine, and My Father is the Husbandman.[1]

Jesus, the Word made Flesh, is the True Vine, God the Father is the Husbandman, and the disciples are the branches. The disciples did not become branches in Him the Vine by their natural birth, or after the usual course of nature. Of no other man, and of no other Person in the Holy Trinity, but of Jesus, could it be said that He was the Vine and they the branches. They became branches in Him by being grafted into Him. This relation was the effect of a mysterious supernatural working. It was not a relation existing merely in the imagination, a mental process only. It was a union more real in the nature of things than that of the branches and the vine. This is the relation by birth, to which the Evangelist had before alluded in these words:—"As many as received Him, to them gave He power to become the sons of God, even to them that believe on His name: which were born, not of blood, nor of the will of the flesh, nor of the will of man, but of God (i. 12).

Many reasons have been given why Jesus selected the vine to illustrate the union between Himself and His disciples. The proba-

---

[1] See note iii. 33.

bility is that He has a reference to the Eucharist, which He had instituted only a short time before, perhaps within the last hour, with the fruit of the vine. (Luke xxii. 18.) He had then instituted and left them a new Memorial of Himself, a new means of renewing their union with Him, as well as their belief in that union. It may be that there is something in the very nature and organism of the vine, that renders it peculiarly suitable to indicate the closeness of His union with His disciples.

Jesus is the True Vine. Compared with Him all the other vines and their branches are but reflections, shadowy imitations. They are called by the same name, because they have somewhat of the same effect on the body as the True Vine has on the soul, to strengthen and to refresh.

The God-Man is the True Vine because He alone can give the Holy Spirit to His branches. He is the True Life, because He alone can enlighten the soul of man. He is the True Light, because He alone can quicken the soul dead in sin. He is the True Bread, because He alone can give His Own Body to nourish the soul.

Beyond the statement that He is the True Vine He says nothing respecting the Vine, but goes on to describe the condition of the branches and the nature of their culture by the Father.

2 Every branch in Me that beareth not fruit He taketh away ; and every branch that beareth fruit (He purgeth it, that it may bring forth) more fruit.[1]

(Alf. He cleanseth, that it may bear.)

Jesus says this primarily with reference to the Apostles, and then to all the faithful. Judas had been chosen as one of the Twelve. He had gone in and out with Jesus for three whole years. He had witnessed His miracles, and had Himself shared in His miraculous powers.

---

[1] Branch.—" These words (κλῆμα, κλάδος) are related to one another by descent from a common stock, derived as they both are from κλάω frango; the *fragile* character of the branch, the ease with which it may be broken off, to be planted or graffed anew, constituting the basis and leading conception in both words. At the same time there is a distinction between them, this namely, that κλῆμα (= palmes) is especially the branch of *the vine* (ἀμπέλου κλῆμα, Plato, Rep. i. 353, *a*) : while κλάδος (= 'ramus') is the branch, not the larger arm, of any tree : and this distinction is always observed in the New Testament, where κλῆμα only occurs in the allegory of the True Vine (John xv. 2, 4, 5, 6 ; of Numb. xii. 24 ; Ps. lxxix. 12 ; Ezek. xvii. 6) : while we have mention of the κλάδοι of the mustard-tree (Matt. xiii. 32), of the fig-tree (Matt. xxiv. 32), of the olive-tree (Rom. xi. 16), and of trees in general (Matt. xxi. 8)."— Archbishop Trench on *Synonyms of New Testament*, p. 174.

" Fruitfulness is the consummation of all that God has done in creation, in human history, and in the work of redemption. All sacraments and ordinances, all providences and dispensations of goodness or of severity, are working together, like the seasons of the year, and the influences of nature in ripening the natural harvest, in promoting the one great end of general and individual fruitfulness."—Macmillan on *The True Vine*, p. 131.

He had even received the last tender mark of His love; Jesus had washed his feet that very night. But with all this Judas did not bear fruit, and the Father had removed him from the company of the Apostles.

The rest of the Apostles had borne some fruit. They had one and all expressed great faith in Jesus, and great love and zeal for Him. But secretly, unknown, perhaps, to themselves, their love for Him was mixed up with a stronger love of life and fear of the Jews. After the most earnest protestations of devotion to Him even to death, in a few hours they would all either deny or desert Him. After the Day of Pentecost we see them delivered from this fear. The Father had purged them that they might bring forth more fruit. He had filled them with the Holy Ghost, and the boldness of Peter and John even excited the attention of the High Priest and his friends. (Acts iv. 13.)

3 (Now ye are clean through the word), which I have spoken unto you.

(Alf. Ye are clean already, by reason of the word.)

The Father has many ways of cleansing His disciples, such as by His word, or by personal affliction in one of its manifold forms. His Apostles, He says, are clean already, by reason of the word which He had spoken unto them, probably alluding to the words which He spake to them at the table after supper. By this word He had freed them from much ignorance and vain confidence. Peter had been taught that he could not follow Him now. Thomas had learnt whither He was going, and the way. Judas (not Iscariot) now knew that he who had seen Jesus had seen the Father. They had all been taught to depend less on His sensible presence with them, and to rely less on the strength of their own resolution in time of temptation. These were some of the human frailties, from which He had cleansed them by His conversation with them this night.

4 Abide in Me, and I in you. (As) the branch cannot bear fruit of itself, except it abide in the vine : no more can ye, except ye abide in Me.

(Alf. Even as.)

5 I am the Vine, ye are the branches: He that abideth in Me, and I in Him, the same (bringeth forth) much fruit: for (without Me) ye can do nothing.[1]

(Alf. Beareth—apart from Me.)

---

[1] Without Me ye can do nothing (χωρὶς ἐμοῦ οὐ δύνασθε ποιεῖν οὐδέν).— "Two or more negations produce one negation, which is the more frequent case, and serve to make the principal negation more distinct and forcible, and

6 If a man abide not in Me, he is cast forth as a branch, and is withered: [and men gather them and cast them] into the fire (and they are burned).[1]

[S. And men gather it, and cast it.]
(Alf. And they burn.)

7 If ye abide in Me, and My words abide in you [ye shall ask] what ye will, and it shall be done unto you.

[V. A. Ask.]
(Alf. Ask whatsoever ye will.)

8 Herein is My Father glorified, that ye bear much fruit: (so shall ye be) My disciples.

(Alf. And become.)

9 As the Father hath loved Me, so have I loved you: (continue ye) in My love.

(Alf. Abide ye.)

10 If ye keep My commandments, ye shall abide in My love: even as I have kept [My Father's commandments], and abide in His love.

[V. The Father's commandments.]

11 These things have I spoken unto you, that My joy [might remain in you], and that your joy (might be) full.

[V. A. Might be in you.]
(Alf. May be in you—may be.)

He exhorts them to abide in Him, and on this He promises to abide in them. He urges them to this by seven kindred reasons or considerations.

---

exhibit the sentence as negative in all its parts, χωρὶς ἐμοῦ οὐ δύνασθε non potestis facere quidquam, that is, nihil potestis facere."—Winer's *Grammar of New Testament*, p. 521.

[1] If a man abide not in Me, he is cast forth, &c.—"It is only in appearance that the Aorist is used for the Future, ἐὰν μή τις μείνῃ ἐν ἐμοί, ἐβλήθη ἔξω ὡς τὸ κλῆμα, in such case, should such a thing happen, *it is cast away*, not, *it will be cast away* (its not abiding has the instan-

taneous consequence; whoever has fallen away from Christ resembles a branch broken off and thrown away). With βληθῆναι the Presents συνάγουσιν, &c. are connected."—Ibid. p. 292.

And men gather them (καὶ συνάγουσιν αὐτά).—"Words referring to something antecedent are used in a loose relation. Here αὐτά refers to the Singular τὸ κλῆμα, which is in opposition to εἴ τις."—Ibid. p. 654.

1. (v. 4) Because without Him they can bear no fruit.
2. (v. 5) If they abide in Him they will bear much fruit.
3 (v. 6) If a man abide not in Him he is cast forth as a branch and is withered.
4 (v. 7) If they abide in Him, whatever they ask of God they shall obtain.
5 (v. 8) Herein is the Father glorified, that they bear much fruit.
6 (v. 9) Because He has loved them, and it is right that they should love Him in return, and continue in His love.
7 (v. 11) That their joy may be full.

The first and second considerations are drawn from their power to bear fruit, the third from their punishment, the fourth from their reward. The fifth consideration refers to the way in which they will be able to magnify the glory of God by their success in converting the heathen to His worship. The sixth shows that, if they abide in Him the Vine the love which will exist between Himself and them will resemble the love which there is between Him and the Father, and that the effect will be similar; that they will keep His commands with an earnestness which will resemble the unity of will between Himself and the Father. The seventh refers to the joy which their perfect union with Him will cause.

As the branches to the vine, they must be united to Him the God-Man sacramentally, by the sacraments of Baptism and of the Eucharist, and also spiritually or mentally—that is by the affections of the soul. Where this is the case they will bear much fruit. Where the former exists without the latter, the branches though in the Vine become unfruitful, withered and dead here, and in the world to come will be cast out and burnt.

12 This is My commandment, That ye love one another (as I have loved) you.
(Alf. As I loved.)

13 Greater love hath no man than this, that a man lay down his life for his friends.

14 [Ye are] My friends, if ye do (whatsoever) I command you.
[S. For ye are.]
(Alf. The things which.)

15 (Henceforth I call you not) servants: (for) the servant knoweth not what his Lord doeth: but I have

called you friends : for all things that I have heard of My Father, I have made known unto you.

(Alf. I call you no longer—because—because I made known unto you all things that I heard from My Father.)

16 Ye (have not chosen) Me, but I (have chosen) you, and (ordained) you, that ye should go and [(bring forth fruit)] and that your fruit should remain : [that] whatsoever (ye shall ask) of the Father in My name [He may give] it you.

[A. Bring forth much fruit: S. Omits, that : S. He shall give.]
(Alf. Did not choose—choose—and bear fruit—ye ask.)

17 These things I command you, that ye love one another.

The distinguishing mark of the New Dispensation was to be the love which they had for each other. Here he calls it, "My commandment," before (xiii. 34) He called it "a new commandment." Their love for each other was to be the characteristic of the brethren. His love to them was to be the standard and model for their love to each other. Those whom He calls "My friends" are not those who love Him, but those whom He loves, and who may not be friends but enemies to Him. Hence there is no opposition between this passage and that (Romans v. 6, &c.), in which St. Paul magnifies the love of Christ because He laid down His Life for His enemies.

He is still specially addressing the Apostles, and He enumerates several proofs of the love, which He had shown to them in particular.

He had called them and treated them as His friends, not as servants but friends. The proof of this was the instruction which He had given them. To show them that it was not mere human knowledge, man's wisdom, the fruit of man's natural faculties, He calls it "all things that I have heard of My Father." This was what He had already communicated to them, so far as they were in a condition to receive it, and He would impart it still more to them after the descent of the Holy Spirit.

They had not chosen Him to be their Master. He had chosen them to be His Apostles. He had appointed them to go and convert the world. Whatever they should ask God in furtherance of the salvation of the world, in the name of the Saviour, He would grant it. This promise relates not to their own personal private interest or convenience, but to the fulfilment of their mission as Apostles, for the bearing of the fruit which may remain.

18 If the world (hate you), ye know that it (hateth Me) before it hated you.

(Alf. Hateth you—hath hated Me.)

19 If ye were of the world, the world would love his own: but because ye are not of the world, but I have chosen you out of the world, therefore the world hateth you.

20 Remember the word that I said unto you, (The servant is not) greater than his lord. If they (have persecuted) Me, they will also persecute you: (if they have kept My saying), they will keep yours also.
(Alf. There is no servant—persecuted—if they kept My Word.)

21 (But) all these things will they do unto you for My name's sake, because they know not Him that sent Me.
(Alf. Howbeit.)

He forewarns the Apostles of the persecutions they would meet with, in their attempt to convert the world. In this, as in all other things, He was their Leader and Example. What had happened to Him, must also happen to them so far as they walked in His steps. The world are the men who are given up to the enjoyment of this world, without regard to the future, whether Jews or Gentiles. The world's hatred was a proof of their righteousness, the world's love a proof of their sin. He reminds them of His former saying to which, at the time of its utterance, He had called their most earnest attention, " Verily, verily, I say unto you, The servant is not greater than his Lord." (xiii. 16.) The servant cannot refuse to do and suffer what his Lord does and suffers. He is the Lord, they are the servants. The persecution and death which He suffers they must not expect to escape. As they have persecuted Him, so they would His Apostles; as they have believed Him, so they would His Apostles. The reason assigned for this is their disbelief in Him as the Messiah, their disbelief in the proofs which He gave, that He was sent by the Father, that He was God.

22 If I had not come and spoken unto them, they had not sin: [but] now they have no (cloke) for their sin.[1]
[S. Omits, But.]
(Margin, Excuse.)
(Alf. They would not have—excuse.)

23 He that hateth Me, hateth My Father also.

---

[1] If I had not come, &c.—" Aorist in the condition, Imperfect in the conclusion—εἰ μὴ ἦλθον . . . ἁμαρτίαν οὐκ εἶχον— if I had not come, they would not have had sin."—Winer's *Grammar of New Testament*, p. 321.

24 If I had not done among them the works which none other man did, (they had not had) sin; but now have they both seen and hated both Me and My Father.

(Alf. They would not have.)

25 But (this cometh to pass) that the word might be fulfilled that is written in their Law, They hated Me without a cause.

(Alf. Note not expressed in the original.)

In these words He makes two distinct propositions. (1) In hating Him, they hated the Father. (2) They were inexcusable in refusing to believe in Him, on the proofs that He gave them. So many and so convincing were the proofs that He gave them of His Mission from the Father that in disbelieving them they were guilty of the sin of hatred and unbelief.

The unbelief of the Jews had a moral origin not an intellectual one. The seat of it was in the heart, not in the head. It was not that they were unable to understand, how Jesus could be the Son of God. They refused even to investigate His claims, to hear His words and examine His works. Before the coming of Jesus they were anxiously looking forward for the Messiah. Jesus wrought the same miracles down to the very letter, which the prophet Isaiah had foretold the Messiah would. (Isa. xxxv. 5, 6.) The reason why they refused to acknowledge Him, and why they hated Him, was that He broke through their traditions, that He set at naught their oral law, that He reproved their vices, their hypocrisies, that He preached to them a new life, and repentance of their past sins, that He laid claim to no earthly kingdom, and declined to deliver them from the yoke of the Romans.

The Psalmist had foreseen and had foretold their hatred of Him, as well as the nature of it, thus : " Let not them that are Mine enemies wrongfully rejoice over Me, neither let them wink with the eye that hate Me without a cause (Ps. xxxv. 19); and " They that hate Me without a cause are more than the hairs of Mine head : they that would destroy Me, being Mine enemies wrongfully are mighty." (Ps. lxix. 4.) Jesus again applies the words of the Old Testament to Himself as the natural object of them. Again, by His silence He bears testimony to the general accuracy of their " Law."

26 [But] when the Comforter is come, whom I will send unto you from the Father, even the spirit of truth, which proceedeth from the Father, He shall (testify) of Me.[1]

[S. Omits, But.]
(Alf. Bear witness.)

---

[1] See note to xiv. 16.

27 And ye also (shall bear witness), because ye have been with Me from the beginning.

(Alf. Are witnesses.)

This is one of the passages from which we gather what we know respecting the nature of the Holy Spirit.
1. He is the Third Person in the Holy Trinity, distinct from both the Father and the Son. He is said to proceed from the Father and to be sent from the Father by the Son. But He who proceeds from another, or is sent by another, is distinct from Him from whom He proceeds, or by whom He is sent.
2. He is God, of the same nature as God the Father, because He proceeds from the Father.
3. He is said to proceed from the Father, and to be sent by the Son.
4. He is said to proceed from the Father, not to be begotten by the Father.

It is impossible to express the deductions, which necessarily follow from this verse, more briefly or more correctly than in the words of the Creed called the Creed of St. Athanasius.

"The Father is God, the Son is God, and the Holy Ghost is God." And again, "The Holy Ghost is of the Father and of the Son: neither made nor created, nor begotten, but proceeding." This is but the legitimate expansion of our Saviour's Own words. This is but another form of expressing the same truths which He here taught.

The Holy Spirit will bear witness that Jesus is the Son of God through the Apostles; inwardly, by enlightening their minds, by enabling them to understand and to receive more fully than before the truths of the Gospel: outwardly, by giving them power to work miracles in proof that Jesus is God. The Holy Spirit will choose the Apostles through whom to bear witness, because they are naturally the most suitable instruments for this purpose. The people will most readily believe them, because they have had the best chance of knowing the truth, they have been the longest with Jesus. In the economy of grace as in the economy of nature everything is ordered and carried out with Divine wisdom, with the utmost perfection, and in all its stages. No want of unity in plan is anywhere perceptible.

INTRODUCTORY NOTE TO CHAPTER XVI.

Synagogue.—"The origin of the Synagogue is of uncertain date. Some think they find traces of it in very early times, but little is known for certain until long after their return from the Captivity. Before a synagogue could be erected there must be not less than ten men of leisure and reputation resident in the place. Synagogues were erected in the highest part of the city, and one of their canons forbade a house to be built higher than the synagogue. According to Jewish writers, in the time of our Saviour the land was full of synagogues. In Jerusalem alone it is said there were 460, or, as others say, 480 synagogues. There were three days of meeting in the week, the second day (Monday), the fifth (Thursday), and the seventh (Sabbath)."—See Lightfoot.

The White Synagogue (Capernaum).—The synagogue, built entirely of white limestone, must once have been a conspicuous object, standing out from the dark basaltic background; it is now nearly level with the surface, and its capitals and columns have been for the most part carried away or turned into lime. The original building is 74 feet 9 inches long by 56 feet 9 inches wide: it is built north and south, and at the southern end has three entrances. In the interior we found many of the pedestals of the columns in their original positions, and several capitals of the Corinthian order buried in the rubbish. There were also blocks of stone which had evidently rested on the columns and had supported wooden rafters. Outside the synagogue proper, but connected with it, we uncovered the remains of a later building, which may be those of the Church which Epiphanius says was built at Capernaum, and was described by Antoninus A.D. 600, as a Basilica inclosing the house of Peter. It may be asked what reason there is for believing the original building to have been a Jewish synagogue, and not a temple or church. Seen alone there might have been some doubt as to its character; but, compared with the number of ruins of the same character which have been lately brought to notice in Galilee, there can be none. Two of these buildings have inscriptions in Hebrew over their main entrances; one in connection with a seven-branched candlestick, the other with figures of the Paschal lamb, and all without exception are constructed after a fixed plan, which is totally different from that of any church, temple, or mosque in Palestine. For a description of the very marked peculiarities, which distinguish the synagogues from other buildings, I would refer the reader to an article on the subject in the Second Quarterly Statement of the Palestine Exploration Fund. If Tell Hum be Capernaum, this is, without doubt, the synagogue built by the Roman centurion (Luke vii. 4, 5), and one of the most sacred places on earth. It was in this building that our Lord gave the well-known discourse in John vi., and it was not without a certain strange feeling that on turning over a large block we found the pot of manna engraved on its face, and remembered the words, 'I am the Bread of Life. Your fathers did eat manna in the wilderness, and are dead.'"—*Recovery of Jerusalem*, p. 344.

CHAPTER XVI.

1 *Christ comforteth His disciples against tribulation by the promise of the Holy Ghost, and by His resurrection and Ascension;* 23 *Assureth their prayers made in His name to be acceptable to His Father;* 33 *Peace in Christ, and in the world affliction.*

1 These things have I spoken unto you, that ye should not be offended.

The things which Jesus had spoken to them last, and which He terms "these things," were the persecutions which they should suffer, and the descent of the Holy Spirit upon them. They were not to be offended and fall away because of the persecutions, and for two reasons, because they had not been taken by surprise, He had forewarned them, and because He had given them the Holy Spirit to support them under all these trials, however severe they might be. And severe they would be. For not only would they put them out of the synagogue, which in itself would be a civil death, a renunciation of all social comfort and distinction, but they would actually put them to bodily death, and in so doing they would think that they were doing God service, that they were offering to God an acceptable sacrifice.

2 [They shall] put you out of the synagogues: yea, (the time cometh), that (whosoever) killeth you will think that he (doeth God service.)[1]

[S. For they may: A. Doeth service to the Lord.]
(Alf. An hour cometh—every man that—offereth a service unto God.)

3 And these things [will they do unto you], because they have not known the Father, nor Me.

[S. They may do unto you: V. A. Omit, unto you.]
(Alf. Omits, unto you.)

The reason which He gives for these persecutions is not of a nature to excuse the persecutors, but rather to increase their condemnation.

---

[1] Put out of the synagogue.—"A heretic cannot be a Jew: cannot live in Jewry. When there is no longer a place for a man in the synagogue, there is no longer a home for him in the city in which that synagogue stands. With that compact and terrible body of men, religion and society are one. An outcast from one is an outlaw from the other."—Dixon's *Holy Land*, ii. 156.

It is their disbelief in Jesus as the Son of God, their refusal, in spite of the proofs offered to them, to believe that Jesus is sent by the Father.

4 (But) these things have I (told you), that [when (the time shall come)], ye may (remember [that I told you of them]). (And these things I said not unto you) at the beginning, because I was with you.

[V. A. When their time shall come: S. That I spake of them.]
(Alf. Nevertheless—spoken unto you—their hour is come—remember them—But these things I told you not.)

Either Jesus had not before spoken of the persecutions which they should suffer at all, or He had not foretold them to the extent, and in the severity, and with the minuteness with which He now speaks of them: or He had then spoken of them when far distant, but now when close at hand, on the very point of taking place. When before foretelling the persecutions which they should suffer, He had not, as now, promised the remedy for them, the Holy Spirit to enable them to bear them.

While He was with them, whatever hatred the Jews might feel, whatever violence they might be guilty of, would be directed against Him and not against His disciples. Now that He was going away, both Jews and Gentiles would persecute them. He therefore forewarns them of this, and promises to strengthen them by the gift of the Holy Spirit, in order that they might not faint under them.

5 But now I go My way to Him that sent Me: and none of you asketh Me, Whither goest Thou?

6 ([But] because I have said) these things unto you, sorrow hath filled your heart.

[A. Omits, But.]
(Alf. Yet because I have spoken.)

Thomas had, it is true, asked Him, "Whither goest Thou?" But beyond that they had manifested little interest in the matter. They had scarcely understood the answer, and had not followed it up with further inquiry, so as to draw out from Him any information as to the advantages which they would derive from His departure. Advantages they certainly were to receive by His leaving them, but this, in consequence of their present sorrow, they could not understand.[1]

7 Nevertheless I tell you the truth: It is expedient for

---

[1] See note on Chap. xiv. 16.

you that I (go away): for if I (go not away,) the Comforter will not come unto you : but if I (depart), I will send Him unto you.

(Alf. Depart—depart not—go.)

To console them in their sorrow, and to convince their judgment in spite of their sorrow, He condescends to use an unusual mode of speaking, and to add, as it were, asseveration to His simple assertion. "I tell you the truth, It is expedient for you that I go away." The disciples were like children who have to be weaned for their good, but against their own will, in order that they may receive food more suited to their age and condition. So long as Jesus remained with them, He would be the object of all persecution, not they. When once He should depart from them a totally new scene of trial would begin. Their condition would appear more desolate, but it would not in reality be so. The Advocate or Comforter, whom He would send to supply His place, though unseen, would be present with them. Their position in the world would be more prominent than before, but the Holy Spirit would enable them to fill it. Their temptations would be increased tenfold, but the Holy Spirit would increase their power to withstand temptation more than tenfold. All this would be the fruit of His Ascension to the Father. They ought therefore rather to rejoice than to sorrow at this new and fuller dispensation.

8 And when He is come, (He will reprove the world) of sin, and of righteousness, and of judgment.[1]

(Margin. He will convince the world.)
(Alf. He will convict the world.)

---

[1] He will reprove the world, &c.—(ἐλέγξει τὸν κόσμον).—"One may rebuke another without bringing the rebuked to a conviction of any fault on his part: and this, either because there was no fault, and the rebuke was therefore unneeded or unjust: or else because, though there was such fault, the rebuke was ineffectual to bring the offender to own it: and in this possibility of ' rebuking' for sin, without ' convincing' of sin, lies the distinction between 'ἐπιτιμᾶν and 'ἐλέγχειν. In ἐπιτιμᾶν lies simply the notion of rebuking ; which word can, therefore, be used of one unjustly checking or blaming another; in this sense Peter 'began to rebuke' Jesus (ἤρξατο 'ἐπιτιμᾶν, Matt. xvi. 22; cf. xix. 13; Luke xviii. 39):—or ineffectually, as without any profit to the person rebuked, who is not thereby brought to see his sin; as when the penitent thief ' rebuked' ('ἐπετίμα) his fellow malefactor (Luke xxiii. 40 ; cf. Mark ix. 25). But ἐλέγχειν is a much more pregnant word : it is so to rebuke another, with such effectual wielding of the victorious arms of the truth, as to bring him, if not to a confession, yet at least to a conviction, of his sin, just as in juristic Greek, 'ἐλέγχειν is not merely to reply to, but to refute, an opponent.

"When we keep this distinction well in mind, what a light does it throw on a multitude of passages in the New Testament, and how much deeper a meaning does it give them. Thus our Lord could demand, 'Which of you *convinceth* ('ἐλέγχει) Me of sin?' (John viii. 46). Many rebuked Him: many laid sin to His charge (Matt. ix. 3 ; John ix. 16), but none brought sin home to His conscience. Other passages also will gain from realizing the

He first states what are the three principal offices of the Holy Spirit with respect to the world, the Jews and Gentiles who refused to believe in Him, and then re-states each particular separately with an explanation of it.

9 Of sin, because they believe not (on) Me.

(Alf. In.)

The Holy Spirit, whom He would send upon them on the day of Pentecost, would convince and convict the unbelieving Jews and Gentiles of the sin which they committed in refusing to believe in Him, after the proofs which He offered them that He was the Son of God, after the many works which He wrought among them of every kind and degree of the miraculous. The Holy Spirit would convince the world of this, partly by the preaching and by the miraculous works of the Apostles, and partly by His secret working on their hearts. In refusing to believe on Jesus as the Son of God they refused to believe on Him, who alone could save them, who alone could be a sacrifice for their sins, who alone could sanctify their hearts, and enable them to live without sin for the time to come.

10 Of righteousness, because I go [to My Father], and ye (see) Me no more.

[S. V. To the Father.]
(Alf. Behold.)

The Holy Spirit will convince and convict the world, that is, the Jews and Gentiles who believe not in Him, of righteousness; by showing that they are not righteous, and that He alone is righteous and the source of righteousness to all others. And this He will prove by going to the Father. He will prove that the Jew, as tested by the law of Moses, is not righteous, and that neither is the Gentile as tried by the law of conscience or the law of nature. He will prove that the words which Jesus spake of Himself as being the Son of God were

---

fulness of the meaning of $\ell\lambda\epsilon\gamma\chi\epsilon\iota\nu$, as John iii. 20; viii. 9; 1 Cor. xiv. 24, 25; but above all, the great passage, John xvi. 8: 'When He (the Comforter) is come, He will *reprove* the world of sin, and of righteousness, and of judgment;' for so we have rendered the words, 'following in our reprove the Latin' ' arguet :' although few, I think, that have in any degree sought to sound the depth of our Lord's words, but will admit that ' convince,' which unfortunately our Translators have relegated to the margin, would have been the preferable rendering, giving a depth and fulness of meaning to this work of the Holy Ghost, which ' reprove' in some part fails to express. ' He who shall come in My room, shall so bring home to the world its own sin,' My perfect ' righteousness,' God's coming ' judgment,' shall so ' convince' it of these, that it shall be obliged itself to acknowledge them ; and in this acknowledgment may find, shall be in the right way to find, its own blessedness and salvation."—Archbishop Trench on *Synonyms of New Testament*, p. 13.

true. He would prove the truth of this by the very fact of His going to the Father, and by sending His Holy Spirit upon men. The Holy Spirit would also prove it to be true, by the miracles He would enable the Apostles to perform in attestation of it.

The world would not see Jesus after His Crucifixion. Neither would the Apostles themselves see Him after His Ascension to the Father.

11 Of judgment, because the prince of this world (is judged.)

(Alf. Hath been judged.)

The Holy Spirit will convince the world, that is, those who refuse to believe that Jesus is God, that they are mistaken in acting thus, and that they have already been judged and condemned for it. When they see Satan their own prince vanquished, cast out of his possessions by the power of the Holy Spirit, when they see the Apostles through the name of Jesus casting out devils, they must be convinced that they are wrong, and that their condemnation is certain, nay that it has already taken place.

12 I have yet many things to say unto you, but ye cannot bear them [now].

[S. Omits, Now.]

St. Luke has recorded (Acts i. 3) what was the general subject of our Saviour's conversation with the Apostles during the forty days between His Resurrection and His Ascension. It was on "the things pertaining to the Kingdom of God." On many of these things they would require further instruction, though they might not be able to bear it before His Resurrection. As yet they had heard little about the Mysteries of the Faith, little about the foundation and the ruling of the Church, which was to be planted in all the world. When the Holy Spirit came He would lead them into all the truth. But He did not lead them into all the truth at once, but gradually as they were able to receive it. They were led into it step by step, at different times, as circumstances arose which required further guidance, further instruction. He did not reveal to them until after the Day of Pentecost, that the Gospel was to be preached to the Gentiles as well as to the Jews (Acts x.), and later still, that the Gentiles need not be circumcised or keep the Law of Moses. (Acts xv.)

13 Howbeit, when He, the Spirit of truth is come, He will guide you into all (truth): for He shall not speak of

Himself: but whatsoever He shall hear, that shall He speak : and He shall (shew you things) to come.[1]

(Alf. The truth—tell you the things.)

To express that God the Son and God the Holy Spirit would not teach things contrary to each other, but that what Jesus had already taught would be confirmed by what the Holy Spirit should teach, and at the same time to express the Oneness of the Holy Spirit with the Father and the Son, He says, "He shall not speak of himself: but whatsoever He shall hear, that shall He speak."

The Holy Spirit would guide them into all the truth, into all the truth that concerned them in their office as Apostles and Teachers, both in what had reference to the future as much as to the past and present. Whatever was required to enable them to fill the office of Apostle, Evangelist, or even Prophet, the Holy Spirit would supply.

14 He shall glorify Me: for He shall receive of Mine, and [shall (shew) it unto you].

[S. And showeth it unto you.]
(Alf. Tell.)

15 All things that the Father hath are Mine: (therefore) [said I that He] [(shall take of Mine, and shall shew)] it unto you.

[S. Said I unto you that He: S. V. That He taketh of Mine and shall show.]
(Alf. For this cause—receiveth of Mine, and shall tell.)

The Holy Spirit shall glorify Jesus by convincing men both outwardly by miracles, and inwardly by working on their hearts, that Jesus was the Son of God the Saviour of the world.

He (the Holy Spirit) shall receive of Mine (the Son's),
All things, that the Father hath, are Mine,
For this cause said I that He (the Holy Spirit) shall take of Mine.

These three verses are of themselves almost sufficient to furnish adequate grounds for every statement contained in the following:

The Catholic Faith is this: That we worship one God in Trinity, and Trinity in Unity.

Neither confounding the Persons: nor dividing the Substance.

---

[1] **All the truth** (πᾶσαν τὴν ἀλήθειαν).— "It is frequently difficult, and even impossible, to ascertain when the Article should be used before abstract nouns, yet there is not the same difficulty when such nouns are preceded by πᾶς. The examples adduced prove that ἀλήθεια, in this place, is not truth universally, but only in reference to the particular subject. 'He shall lead you into all the truth,' as Campbell has translated it, though without any remark."—Bishop Middleton on *Greek Article*, p. 258.

For there is one Person of the Father, another of the Son, and another of the Holy Ghost.
But the Godhead of the Father, of the Son, and of the Holy Ghost is all one: the glory equal, the majesty co-eternal.
Such as the Father is, such is the Son: and such is the Holy Ghost.

16 A little while, and ye [(shall not see Me)]: and again a little while and ye shall see Me, [(because I go to the Father.)]

[S. V. No longer see Me: S. V. Omit, because I go to the Father.]
(Alf. Behold Me no longer—omits, because I go to the Father.)

In these words Jesus foretells His Death and Resurrection. Of His Death, and that as close at hand, He had frequently spoken of late, of His Resurrection but seldom. His Death the disciples were quite prepared to expect. Of His Resurrection in three days they had not the least expectation. The thought of such an event seems never to have occurred to them. A little while, a few hours at most, and He would be seized by the Jews, crucified, dead and buried, and they should not see Him, and again a little while, three days, and He would rise again, and then they should see Him.

But the disciples did not understand His words in this way. He had but just said to them that when the Holy Spirit should come He would convince the world of righteousness, "because I go to My Father, and ye see Me no more. (ver. 10.) They did not understand that what He now said would take place in the interval, before He went to the Father.

Others have explained these words in this way. A little while and ye shall not see Me, because I ascend to the Father: again a little while, that is, after the time of this your mortal life is over, and ye shall see Me, that is, at the Day of Judgment.

17 (Then) said some of His disciples (among themselves), What is this that He saith unto us, A little while, and ye (shall not see Me): and again, a little while, and ye shall see Me: and, Because I go to the Father.

(Alf. Therefore—one to another—behold Me not.)

18 They said therefore, [What is this that He saith, (A little while? We cannot tell] what He saith.)

[S. What is this little while: V. What is this little while that He saith? we cannot tell.]
(Alf. This little while? we know not of what He speaketh.)

Several reasons have been given why the disciples did not understand this. (1) Because the words themselves are expressed with a certain degree of obscurity. (2) The disciples were too much overwhelmed with grief for His departure to see their meaning. (3) They could not understand them from their ignorance that on the third day after His Burial He would rise again.

Perhaps to give them another proof of His power, another reason why they should trust Him, He shows them that He knows the thoughts of their hearts, or the discussions which they had held among themselves.

19 [(Now)] Jesus knew [that they were desirous to ask Him], and said [unto them], Do ye enquire among yourselves (of that I said), a little while, and ye (shall not see Me): and again a little while, and ye shall see Me.

[S. V. Omit, Now: S. That they were going to ask Him: A. Omits, unto them.]
(Alf. Omits, Now—because I said—behold Me not.)

20 Verily, verily, I say unto you, (That) ye shall weep and lament, but the world shall rejoice: [(and)] ye shall be sorrowful, but your sorrow shall be turned into joy.

[S. V. Omit, And.]
(Alf. Omits, That—omits, and.)

A little while, a few hours, and ye shall see me bound, crucified, dead and buried, then ye shall lament with bitter sorrow, but the world the unbelieving Jews, shall exult because they have, as they think, overcome Me: but on the third day I shall rise again, and then your sorrow shall be turned into joy, but their rejoicing shall be turned into vexation and disappointment. Such will be the sense of this passage if we regard ver. 16 as referring to the Death and Resurrection of Jesus, as seems most probable.

But if we regard the " little while " in ver. 16 as meaning the whole of this present life, then we must interpret ver. 20 with reference to the persecution and labour and toil which the Apostles would endure after His Ascension to the Father, and to the joy with which they should be greeted at the Day of Judgment.

21 A woman when she is in travail hath sorrow, because her hour is come; but as soon as she is delivered of the child, she remembereth no more the anguish, (for joy) that a man is born into the world.

(Alf. For her joy.)

22 (And ye now therefore) [have sorrow] : but I will see you again, and your heart shall rejoice, and your joy no man (taketh) from you.

[A. Shall have sorrow.]
(Alf. So ye also now—shall take.)

In the first of these verses Jesus delivers a parable, He institutes a comparison, and in the second He applies it. He compares His Death and Passion to the travail of a woman when her hour is come, and His Resurrection to her joy after the birth. At the time of His Passion His Soul was "exceedingly sorrowful." (Matt. xxvi. 38.) His disciples too shared in some degree in that sorrow. After His Resurrection when He saw of the travail of His soul, He was satisfied. (Isa. liii. 11.)

He likens the sorrows of His Passion to the sorrow of a woman in travail, and the joy of His Resurrection to the joy of a woman at the birth of a child : because by His Death and Resurrection He purchased the life, the resurrection, of both the body and soul of man. The joy of the woman is described as the joy of a woman who has given birth to a man-child, as the greatest joy possible, as joy not diminished by any human drawback.

As the woman in travail had sorrow because her hour was come, so the disciples were in sorrow because the hour of His Passion is come, but as the woman rejoices when the child is born, so after His Resurrection He would see them again and their hearts would rejoice, and this their joy in consequence of His Resurrection should never be removed from them.

23 And in that day ye shall ask Me nothing. Verily, verily, I say unto you, whatsoever ye shall [ask the Father in My name, He will give it you.][1]

[S. V. Ask the Father, He will give it you in My name.]
(Alf. Ask of the Father, He will give it you in My name.)

---

[1] In that day ye shall ask Me nothing —whatsoever ye shall ask the Father, &c. (ἐν ἐκείνῃ τῇ ἡμέρα ἐμὲ οὐκ ἐρωτήσετε οὐδὲν—ὅσα ἂν αἰτήσατε τὸν πατέρα,) &c.— "These words, αἰτέω and ἐρωτάω, are often rendered by our Translators as though they covered one another : nor can we object to their rendering, in numerous instances, αἰτεῖν and ἐρωτᾶν alike by our English 'to ask.' Yet sometimes they have a little marred the perspicuity of the original by not varying *their* word, where that has shown them the way. For example, the obliteration at John xvi. 23, of the distinction between αἰτεῖν and ἐρωτᾶν suggests very often a wrong interpretation of the verse—as though its two clauses were in near connection and direct antithesis—being indeed in none. In our Version we read : " In that day *ye shall* ask Me nothing (ἐμὲ οὐκ ἐρωτήσατε οὐδέν). Verily, verily, I say unto you, Whatsoever ye shall ask (ὅσα ἂν αἰτήσητε) the Father in My name, He will give it you.' Now every one competent to judge is agreed, that ' ye shall ask' of the first half of the verse has nothing to do with 'ye shall ask' of the second ; that in the first Christ

COMMENTARY ON ST. JOHN'S GOSPEL. 347

Jesus knew that they had been greatly perplexed by what He had said to them just before, and had only been prevented by fear from asking Him what He had meant. He here promises that after His Resurrection He by His own instructions and by the descent of the Holy Spirit, would so open their understanding that they would have no need

---

is referring back to the ἤθελον αὐτὸν ἐρωτᾶν of ver. 19: to the questions which the disciples would fain have asked of Him, the perplexities which they would gladly have had resolved by Him, if only they dared to set them before Him. In that day, He would say, in the day of My seeing you again, I will by the Spirit so teach you all things, that ye shall be no longer perplexed, no longer wishing to ask the questions (cf. John xxi. 12) if only you might venture to do so. Thus Lampe well: ' Nova est promissio de plenissima cognitionis luce, quâ convenienta œconomiæ Novi Testamenti collustrandi essent. Nam sicut quæstio supponit inscitiam, ita qui nihil amplius quærit abunde se edoctum existimat, et in doctrinâ plene expositâ ac intellectâ acquiescit.' There is not in this verse a contrast drawn between asking *the Son*, which shall cease, and asking *the Father* which shall begin: but the first half of the verse closes the declaration of one blessing, namely, that hereafter they shall be so taught by the Spirit as to have nothing further *to inquire;* the second half of the verse begins the declaration of a new blessing, that, whatever they shall *seek* from the Father in the Son's name, He will give it to them. Yet who will affirm that this is the impression which the English text conveys to his mind.

"The distinction between the words is this: Αἰτέω, the Latin peto is more submissive and suppliant, indeed the constant word for the seeking of the inferior from the superior (Acts xii. 20): of the beggar from him that should give alms (Acts iii. 2): of the child from the parent (Matt. vii. 9; Luke xi. 11; Lam. iv. 4): of the subject from the ruler (Ezra viii. 22): of man from God (1 Kings iii.11; Matt. vii.7; James i. 5; 1 John iii. 22; cf. Plato Euthyph. 14; εὔχεσθαι (ἐστιν) αἰτεῖν τοὺς Θεούς.) Ἐρωτάω, on the other hand, is the Latin rogo; or, sometimes (as John xvi. 23) interrogo, its only meaning in classical Greek, where it never signifies ' to ask,' but only to 'interrogate' or 'to inquire.' Like rogare, it implies that he who asks, stands on a certain equality with him from whom the boon is asked, as king with

king (Luke xiv. 32), or, if not equality, on such a footing of familiarity as lends authority to the request.

"Thus it is very noteworthy, and witnesses for the singular accuracy in the employment of words, and in the record of that employment, which prevails throughout the New Testament, that our Lord never uses αἰτέω or αἰτεῖσθαι of Himself, in respect of that which He seeks on behalf of His disciples from God: for His is not the *petition* of the creature to the Creator, but the *request* of the Son to the Father. The consciousness of His equal dignity, of His potent and prevailing intercession, speaks out in this, that often as He asks, or declares that He will ask, anything of the Father, it is always ἐρωτῶ, ἐρωτήσω, an asking, that is, as upon equal terms (John xiv. 16; xvi. 26; xvii. 9, 15, 20), never αἰτέω, or αἰτήσω. Martha, on the contrary, plainly reveals her poor unworthy conception of His person, that she recognises in Him no more than a prophet, when she ascribes that αἰτεῖσθαι to Him, which He never ascribes to Himself: ὅσα ἂν αἰτήσῃ τὸν Θεὸν, δώσει σοι ὁ Θεός (John xi. 22); on which verses Bengel observes: ' Jesus de se rogante loquens 'ἐδεήθην dicit (Luke xxii. 32), et 'ἐρωτήσω, at nunquam αἰτοῦμαι. Non Græce locuta est Martha, sed tamen Johannes exprimit improprium ejus sermonem, quem Dominus benigne tulit: nam αἰτεῖσθαι videtur verbum esse minus dignum;' compare his note on 1 John v. 16.

"It will follow that the ἐρωτᾶν, being thus proper for Christ, inasmuch as it has authority in it, is not proper for us; and in no single instance is it used in the New Testament to express the prayer of man to God, of the creature to the Creator. The only passage seeming to contradict this assertion, is 1 John vi. 16. The verse is difficult, but whichever of the various ways of overcoming its difficulty may find favour, it will be found to constitute no true exception to the rule, but perhaps, in the substitution of ἐρωτήσῃ for the αἰτήσει of the earlier clause of the verse, will rather confirm it."—Archbishop Trench on *Synonyms of New Testament*, p. 140.

to ask Him any question, that they should understand whatever it concerned them to know as the Apostles of His Church. The word here rendered in the English Authorised Version ask, in the expressions "ye shall ask (ἐρωτήσατε) Me nothing" and "Whatever ye shall ask (αἰτήσατε) the Father," is in the Greek represented by two different words. The first generally means to ask for information, and the second to ask for a gift or for alms. But some have thought that both words, as here used, imply presenting a petition.

Jesus is henceforth to be the medium of all prayer to the Father: the medium through whom all prayer will be granted. All grace will henceforth be granted through the economy of the Incarnation, so to speak.

24 Hitherto have ye asked nothing in My name: ask, and ye shall receive, that your joy may be full.

Whatever pertains to salvation they can have by asking for it in the name of the Saviour. Hitherto they had asked nothing in the name of the Saviour, they had cared little how to obtain salvation, they had been ignorant that the way to it was through union with Jesus.

St. James says that the reason why men ask and receive not, is because they ask amiss (iv. 3.) either because they do not ask for right things, or because they do not ask for them in a right way. All the promises made in Holy Scripture of hearing and granting prayer are made subject to these conditions, that they ask right things and in the right way: that they ask for things pertaining to salvation and not to bodily comfort or to worldly aggrandisement, and that they ask them in the Saviour's name, with all the degree of faith and repentance and perseverance that this implies. If they asked in this way, they would obtain a fulness of grace, of which, hitherto, they had never thought.

25 These things have I spoken unto you in (proverbs): but (the time cometh), when I shall no more speak unto you in proverbs, but I shall (shew you plainly of the Father.)

(Margin, Parables.)
(Alf. The hour cometh—tell you plainly concerning the Father.)

He had spoken these things unto them in parables—in language so dark and enigmatical, so clothed in figure, that they did not understand His meaning; as for instance when He had spoken to them respecting the "little while" (ver. 16) or of the Holy Spirit, or of His own departure, or of their rejoicing. Now He promises that after the

Resurrection He will so open their hearts to understand the Scriptures, that they shall have no difficulty in understanding whatever He reveals to them.

26 [At that day ye shall ask] in My name : and I say not unto you, that I will pray the Father for you.

[S. At that day ask ye.]

27 For the Father Himself loveth you, because ye have loved Me, and have believed that I came ([out from God].)

[V. From the Father.]
(Alf. Forth from the Father.)

His object in these words apparently is to show them that the Holy Spirit will supply His place to them : that though He Himself will have departed from them, they will not be left without One, who will both pray for them and teach them also how to pray. By His prayer for them to the Father the Holy Spirit will be sent down upon them, and He, when He comes, will teach them how to pray to the Father in the name of Jesus. The Father also will grant all that they pray for, for He loves them, because they have believed that Jesus is His Son.

28 I came forth from the Father, and am come into the world : again I leave the world, and go to the Father.

These words have been thought to intimate to the disciples more than lies on the mere surface, and to teach them that Jesus came forth from the Father by being born in the world of the Virgin Mary, and also more than this, that He came forth from the Father by being the Son of God by Eternal Generation. That He was "God, of the Substance of the Father, begotten before the worlds : and Man, of the Substance of His Mother, born in the world." (Creed of St. Athanasius.)

29 [(His disciples] said [unto Him)] Lo, now speakest Thou plainly, and speakest no (proverb).

[S. The disciples: V. Omits, unto Him.]
(Margin, Parable.)
(Alf. His disciples say unto Him.)

30 Now are we sure that Thou knowest all things, and needest not that any man should ask Thee : by this we believe that Thou camest forth from God.

(Alf. Now know we.)

The disciples did not understand the words which Jesus spake to them (ver. 16), "A little while," &c. They were anxious to ask Him but were withheld by a kind of fear and awe. He, by His Divine power, knew their thoughts and their desire to question Him on this point, and in His reply He reveals to them that He knew the cause of their perplexity. This was to them a further proof that He was the Son of God, a great confirmation of their faith in Him.

But how weak this their faith really is, strong as they themselves think it, Jesus shows them in the following words:

31 Jesus answered them, (Do ye now believe) ?

(Alf. Ye do now believe.)

32 Behold, (the hour) cometh, [yea, is now come], that ye shall be scattered, every man to (his own), and shall leave Me alone : and yet I am not alone, because the Father is with Me.[1]

[S. V. A. Omit, now: S. Yea the hour is come.]
(Margin, His own home.)
(Alf. An hour.)

It was now night, and before the morning should dawn they would all fly and desert Him, whom they profess to believe came forth from God. They would fly, not in a body and with a preconcerted arrangement to assemble together again, but each one for himself, each his own way and to His own place of refuge as fear dictated. But this their desertion of Him was their dishonour not His loss, for Himself He needed not their protection.

33 These things I have spoken unto you, that in Me ye (might have) peace. [In the world ye shall have] tribulation : but be of good cheer : I have overcome the world.

[S. V. A. In the world ye have.]
(Alf. May have peace—in the world ye have.)

By the world here He evidently means Satan, the Prince of the world, and those whom he influences not to believe that Jesus is the Son of God. Through them the Apostles and their followers would have persecution and tribulation of every kind. In Jesus they would have peace. So long as they remained united to Jesus by faith and

---

[1] That ye shall be scattered, every man to his own (ἵνα σκορπισθῆτε ἕκαστος εἰς τὰ ἴδια).—" The verb is not to be directly referred to ἕκαστος, but ἕκαστος is annexed, as explanatory, to the Plural."— —Winer's *Grammar of New Testament*, p. 539.

love, they would have inward peace—peace in the soul—in spite of all bodily persecution and suffering. The world He had already overcome by His holy life and by the exercise of His divine power, and He would still more overcome it by His Death and Resurrection. He overcame the world for them not for Himself, that He might set them an example, and that He might gain for them the power and the grace to overcome it. Thus He would also overcome the world through them. They would be the combatants and He the author of the victory.

INTRODUCTORY NOTE TO CHAPTER XVII.

NATURAL CULTURE IN RELATION TO SUPERNATURAL, WHICH CAN ONLY BE THROUGH THE INCARNATION.—" The tendency of the system (the Olympian religion) was to exalt the human element by proposing a model of beauty, strength, and wisdom, in all their combinations, so elevated, that the effort to attain them required a continual upward strain. It made divinity attainable: and thus it effectually directed the thought and aim of man—

'Along the line of limitless desires.'

" Such a scheme of religion, though failing grossly in the government of the passions, and in upholding the standard of moral duties, tended powerfully to produce a lofty self-respect, and a large, free, and varied conception of humanity. It incorporated itself in schemes of notable discipline for mind and body, indeed, of a lifelong education: and these habits of mind and action had their marked results (to omit many other greatnesses) in a philosophy, literature, and art, which remain to this day unrivalled or unsurpassed.

" The sacred fire, indeed, that was to touch the mind and heart of man from above, was in preparation elsewhere. Within the shelter of the hills that stand about Jerusalem, the great Archetype of the spiritual excellence and purification of man was to be produced and matured. But a body, as it were, was to be made ready for this angelic soul. And as when some splendid edifice is to be reared, its diversified materials are brought from this quarter and from that, according as nature and man favour their production, so did the wisdom of God, with slow but ever sure device, cause to ripen amidst the several races best adapted for the work, the several component parts of the noble fabric of a Christian manhood and a Christian civilisation. ' The kings of Tharsis and of the isles shall give presents: the kings of Arabia and Saba shall bring gifts.' (Ps. lxxii. 10.) Every worker was, with or without his knowledge and his will, to contribute to the work. And among them an appropriate part was thus assigned both to the Greek people, and to what I have termed the Olympian religion."
—Gladstone's *Juventus Mundi*, p. 376.

CHAPTER XVII.

1 Christ prayeth to His Father to glorify Him; 6 To preserve His Apostles; 11 In unity; 17 And truth; 20 To glorify them and all other believers with Him in heaven.

THIS chapter contains the prayer, which Jesus offered to the Father before He left the Upper Room where He and the Twelve had kept the Passover, and where He had washed their feet and had instituted the Eucharist. Judas had left them before He offered this prayer, and had gone to the chief priests to arrange with them the place and manner of His betrayal.

1 These words spake Jesus, and lifted up His eyes to heaven, and said, Father, the hour is come: glorify Thy Son, [that Thy Son also may glorify Thee.]

[S. V. That the Son may glorify Thee: A. Omits, Also.]

In the first five verses (1-5) Jesus prays for Himself, in the next fourteen verses (6-19), He prays for His disciples, and in the remainder of the chapter (20-26), for them and for those who should believe with them.

The Evangelist minutely records both the words and even the attitude, which Jesus uses on this occasion.

Father, the hour is come; glorify Thy Son, that Thy Son also may glorify Thee. Such language as this could not have been used by a mere man, and only by One who was equal to the Father. Jesus prays, because He is inferior to the Father as touching His Manhood; He prays thus, because He is equal to the Father as touching His Godhead.

He prays that at His Death there should be such a manifestation of Him as the Son of God, that men may believe in Him. There was the more need for this, because He was about to die as a malefactor, as a breaker of the law. This would have the effect of eclipsing His spotless life, of creating false impressions of Him in men's minds, and thus of preventing them from believing that He was the Christ the Son of God. He, therefore, thirsting for the salvation of mankind, prays that His name, even at His Death, may be rendered so glorious, that men may believe on Him, and may thus be saved.

His prayer to the Father to glorify His Son was answered in part, when the veil of the Temple was rent in twain from the top to the bottom; and when the earth did quake, and the rocks rent, and when all nature was so convulsed that the Centurion and those who kept the watch with Him cried, "Truly, This was the Son of God." (Matt. xxvii. 51, &c.)

Jesus desired this not for Himself, but that the glory of the Father, that the knowledge of the Father's power and mercy might be diffused among men, and that thus the salvation of many among all nations might be secured.

2 (As Thou hast given Him) power over all flesh (that He should give eternal life to as many as Thou hast given Him).

(Alf. According as Thou, gavest Him—that whatsoever Thou hast given Him, to them He should give eternal life.)

Jesus prays that as the Father had given Him power over all flesh, over all men, so also He would grant Him glory commensurate with His power; that, as His power over men was unlimited, so also His glory, the worship paid to Him as the Son of God, might also be unlimited.

3 And this is (life eternal), (that they might know) Thee the only true God, (and Jesus Christ, whom Thou hast sent).

(Alf. Eternal life—to know—and Him, whom Thou didst send, even Jesus Christ.)

In these words Jesus gives the reason why He prays to the Father to glorify Him. It is because this His glorification consists in the diffusion of the knowledge of God and of Jesus as His Son, and because this is the only way by which men can obtain eternal life. He prays for glorification, in order that men may obtain eternal life by this glorification of the Father and of the Son, by acknowledging that the Father is the true God, and that Jesus is His Son, whom He hath sent to be the redeemer of the world. The only way to eternal life is to believe and to confess that the Father is the true God, and that Jesus is His Son. This belief, and their union with God in consequence of this belief, causes them to have eternal life, the life of grace here, and the life of glory hereafter. The increase and the diffusion of this belief is the glorification of the Father and the Son.

The expression, "the only true God," applied to the Father is not meant to exclude the other Persons in the Holy Trinity, but merely to exclude false gods. This is plain from the whole tenor of the argument.

Our Saviour's words here show, that a belief in the Incarnation is as necessary for eternal life, as a belief in the Father is, or a belief in the Trinity.

" It is necessary to everlasting salvation : that he also believe rightly the Incarnation of our Lord Jesus Christ.

" For the right Faith is that we believe and confess : that our Lord Jesus Christ, the Son of God, is God and Man." (Creed of St. Athanasius.)

He makes no mention of the Holy Spirit here. Of late He had spoken much respecting the Holy Spirit. It may be that now it was necessary to draw their attention exclusively to a belief in Himself as the Son of God. For a belief in the Incarnation is the foundation of all right belief in God, and of all acceptable approach to Him.

The practice of using Christ as a proper name, and joining it with Jesus did not begin until after the Resurrection, by which Jesus was more especially proved to be the Christ. This is the only instance in the Gospels where Jesus is joined to Christ, and that occurs in His last address to His disciples the very night in which He was betrayed, and so but a few hours before His Resurrection.

4 (I have glorified) Thee [on the earth: (I have finished) the work] which Thou (gavest) Me to do.[1]

[S. V. A. On the earth, having finished the work.]
(Alf. I glorified—by finishing—hast given.)

The work for which He was sent was to redeem mankind, and to preach to them the Gospel of Redemption. In the course of a few hours He by His Death and Passion would finish His work of Redemption. The work of preaching He would finish by giving His Apostles a commission to go and teach all nations. He had glorified the Father by offering up Himself the Sacrifice for the sin of the world, and by making Him known to man. For God is glorified when He is preached to men, and when they believe on Him and worship Him.

5 And now, O Father, glorify Thou Me with Thine Ownself, with the glory which I had with Thee before the world was.

In these words Jesus prays, that after His Resurrection He may receive with the Father the same glory, as the Word made Flesh, which He had with Him before as the Word, that He may sit at the Right Hand of the Father in His glorified Human Body with the same undiminished glory, which He had with the Father before He condescended to be born of a Virgin.

---

[1] I have glorified Thee on the Earth, &c. (ἐγώ σε ἐδόξασα ἐπὶ τῆς γῆς, τὸ ἔργον ἐτελείωσα).—" It cannot be distinctly shown from any passages that could be adduced, that the Aorist stands for a Perfect. In this passage the action is viewed as filling only one point of time past, as simply a past event."—Winer's *Grammar of New Testament*, p. 291.

The glory here mentioned has reference to three different manifestations of it. (1) His glory as God, which He had with the Father before the world was. (2) His glory as Man, that His Manhood may ascend to heaven. But His Manhood could not ascend to the Father, unless it were united to the Godhead. This second manifestation, therefore, implies the first. He prays the Father, that the glory which He had as God He may after His Resurrection have, as God and Man. (3) That His glory may be manifested to His Apostles and other followers. This was fulfilled to the Apostles when they beheld Him ascend to Heaven in the presence of angels (Acts i. 9, &c.): when they received from Him the promised gift of the Holy Spirit, with power to work miracles in His name.

Thus the glory which He had as God was made manifest by the Ascension of His Human Body into heaven; and this glory was made manifest to His Apostles and disciples.

In the next fourteen verses Jesus prays for His disciples.

6 I (have manifested) Thy name unto the men, which Thou (gavest) Me out of the world: Thine they were, and Thou (gavest) them Me: and they have kept Thy Word.

(Alf. Manifested—hast given.)

To manifest the name of the Father to the men whom He had given Him out of the world, was the work which the Father had given Jesus to do, and which He says (ver. 4) He had finished. It was not the name of God which Jesus was to manifest. This had been known long before among men. It was the name of the Father, the Father of His Son Jesus Christ which He was to manifest among men, that is, to make known to them the Mystery of the Incarnation.

The disciples of Jesus, the men who had believed in Him, the Father had selected out of the world, and had given them to Him by drawing them to Him and influencing them to believe on Him. Jesus is now about to leave the world, and He prays the Father still to preserve and protect them. The argument, so to speak, by which He enforces His petition, is that before they believed in Him they were the Father's. They had righteously observed the law of Moses, they had walked in all the commandments and ordinances of the Lord blameless, and thus they had been led on to believe in Him as the Messiah the Son of God. They were the Father's in every sense. They had faithfully observed the law of God before the preaching of John the Baptist, and then they had believed in His Son Jesus Christ, and had kept His word.

7 [(Now they have known)] that all things, whatsoever Thou hast given Me, (are of Thee).

[S. Now I have known.]
(Alf. Now they know—are from Thee.)

COMMENTARY ON ST. JOHN'S GOSPEL. 357

8 For I have given unto them the words which Thou gavest (Me): and (they have received) them, and (have known) surely that I came (out from Thee) and (they have believed) that Thou didst send Me.

(Alf. Unto Me—they received—knew—forth from Thee—they believed.)

The plea which Jesus here urges in behalf of His disciples, is that they have believed that He is God Incarnate, that He, the Son of Mary, is the Son of God.

9 (I pray) for them : (I pray not) for the world, but for them which Thou hast given Me : for they are Thine.[1]

(Alf. I am praying—I am not praying.)

10 [(And all Mine) are Thine, and Thine are Mine]: and I am glorified in them.[2]

[S. And thou hast given them to Me.]
(Alf. And all things that are Mine.)

Jesus does not mean that He never prays for "the world," but at this particular time, in this His farewell address, He is praying for His Apostles, and for those who should believe through their preaching. On His Cross He prayed for "the world," for them who believed not in Him, but who crucified Him. Jesus had before said that His disciples were the Father's, now He repeats it, and proves it by saying, All things

---

[1] See note on John xvi. 23.
[2] I am glorified in them (δεδόξασμαι ἐν αὐτοῖς). "Here ἐν αὐτοῖς undoubtedly signifies something more than δι' αὐτῶν. He would have been glorified *through them*, if they had merely carried into effect, objectively, something conducive to the glory of Christ: He would have been glorified *in them*, only in as far as they had, in their own persons, *in themselves*, subjectively contributed to Christ's glory. In the same way, the phrase, living or being *in God*, appears to indicate with greater force and precision, than could be done by διά, one's taking root, as it were, in the strength of God:

When ἐν and διά are joined together in one and the same sentence, διά expresses the external means, while ἐν points to what has been done *in* or *on* somebody, and what, as it were, remains in or on him, Ephes. i. 7. ἐν ᾧ (Χριστῷ) ἔχομεν τὴν ἀπολύτρωσιν διὰ τοῦ αἵματος αὐτοῦ

(iii. 6). Even when things and not persons, are in question, the distinction between 'ἐν (referring to mental states or powers) and διά (of the means) is preserved, as 1 Peter i. 5, τοὺς 'ἐν δυνάμει θεοῦ φρουρουμένους διὰ πίστεως: i. 22, ἡγνικότες ἐν τῇ ὑπακοῇ τῆς ἀληθείας διὰ πνεύματος, and Heb. x. 10. Lastly, passages in which ἐν and διά, in reference to things, and not persons, are interchanged, merely show that both prepositions are there employed to express the same meaning, but with different degrees of precision, or under different aspects, Col. i. 16: 2 Cor. vi. 4, 8: 1 Cor. xiv. 19. Even in Matt. iv. 4, 'ἐν παντὶ ῥήματι, does not appear to be exactly equivalent to ἐπί in ἐπ' ἄρτῳ μόνῳ. The latter (ἐπί) denotes the ground, foundation ; ἐν the spiritual element of life. At all events, it would be incorrect to render ἐν here by *through*."—Winer's *Grammar of New Testament*, p. 407.

that are Mine are Thine, and Thine are Mine. By their belief in Him as the Messiah, by their union with Him as the Head, they glorified Him, and they would glorify Him yet more when they preached His Gospel through the world.

11 (And now I am) no more in the world, (but) [these] are in the world, and I come to Thee. Holy Father, [(keep through Thine Own name those whom Thou hast given Me)], that they may be one, [(as We are.)]

[S. V. They: S. V. A. Keep them through Thine Own name wherein Thou hast given them to Me: V. As we are also.]

(Alf. And I am—and—keep them in Thy name which Thou hast given Me—even as we are.)

The word merciful is more often applied to the Father by those who pray to Him, than the word holy is. Jesus uses the term because He is here asking the Father to keep His disciples holy, separate, uncontaminated by the sins of the world, the unbelievers among whom they will have to dwell after His departure from them.

The principal subject of His prayer is that His disciples may be one as He and the Father are One. He had just united them in One in Himself. By giving them His Own Body and His Own Blood He had made them one in a sense in which they had never been one before. Their oneness before, so far as it existed, was the effect of agreement in intellect, because they held the same opinion. Their oneness now arose from their union with Jesus the God Incarnate. Now they were one because they had been made one bread, one body, for they had all partaken of that one bread. (1 Cor. x. 17.) Amidst the unbelief of those around them, Jesus prays the Father to keep them one, one in heart and will and love, as He and the Father were One in nature, in essence, as we speak.

12 While I was with them [(in the world)], (I kept them [in Thy name: those that Thou gavest Me I have kept)], (and none of them is lost,) but the son of perdition : that the Scripture (might be) fulfilled.

[S. V. Omit, in the world: V. In Thy name, wherein Thou gavest them to Me, and guarded them: S. In Thy name and guarded them.]

(Alf. Omits, in the world—I kept them in Thy name whom Thou hast given Me, and guarded them—and not one of them perished—may be.)

Jesus had kept all those whom the Father had given Him in the true belief, and in the sincere worship of Him as God, except Judas. He, yielding to the temptation of avarice, had betrayed Him to the Jews, as though He were a mere man unable to resist. He is the son of perdition as having brought perdition upon himself by his own deeds, as having incurred the penalty of perdition.

It is plain that, in His prayer to the Father, that His disciples may be kept from the evil of the world, and that they may be one, Jesus does not include Judas. When Judas left the Upper Room he had cut himself off from communion with Jesus and His disciples.

The expression "that the Scripture might be fulfilled" does not imply that there was a necessity, that there was a line of action fixed which led to perdition, and that Judas was not a free agent and had not the power to avoid this. The phrase is used here and elsewhere, to express in the strongest possible form God's foreknowledge of the events here related. St. Peter quotes the prophecies in which the end of Judas was foretold, Let his habitation be desolate, and let no man dwell therein (Ps. lxix. 25): and his bishoprick let another take. (Ps. cix. 8; Acts i. 20.)

13 And now come I to Thee: and these things I speak in the world, that they (might have) My joy fulfilled in themselves.

(Alf. May have.)

Jesus is on the point of returning to the Father through His Death and Resurrection, and He prays this prayer aloud, that His disciples may know that He has prayed thus for them, for their peace and safety in the world, and may rejoice as feeling sure that His prayer will be accomplished in them.

14 I have given them Thy word: and the world (hath hated) them, because they are not of the world, even as I am not of the world.

(Alf. Hated.)

15 I pray not that Thou shouldest take them out of the world, but that Thou shouldest keep them from the evil.

16 They are not of the world, even as I am not of the world.

Jesus uses the expression that His disciples are not of the world twice in these three verses: once as a reason why the world hated them, and again as a reason why the Father should keep them from the evil. His disciples had relinquished the unbelief and the sinful pursuits of those around them, and had given themselves up to the service of Jesus as the Son of God. This He urges as a reason why the Father should keep them from the evil, from sin and its punishment, as well as from him who is the tempter to all sin, the devil.

17 Sanctify them [(through Thy truth)]: Thy word is [truth.]

[S. V. A. Through the truth: V. Thy word is the truth.]
(Alf. In the truth.)

The sanctification of which Jesus here speaks was not an initiative act. He had already said, after He had washed their feet, that, with the exception of Judas, who had now left them, they were clean (xiii. 10), since that they had partaken of His Own Body and Blood, whereby there would be a further sanctification of them body and soul. Here, therefore, He probably refers to the more complete sanctification of them by the descent of the Holy Spirit at the day of Pentecost.

The sanctification of which heathen philosophers treat is obtained by following the dictates of reason, by performing some acts and abstaining from others. But high and noble as this often was, it failed to reach the depraved nature of man, it offered no remedy for a corrupt source of action.

The sanctification aimed at by the law of Moses was partial and prophetic. It removed all disqualification to an acceptable approach to God, but it did not cleanse the heart. It concerned the body rather than the soul, and foreshadowed that sanctification by the Holy Spirit which alone could cleanse the heart.

The sanctification of which Jesus here speaks is a supernatural work. It is derived to His disciples as the fruits of their union with Him, the Word made Flesh, and through the operation of the Holy Spirit the Third Person in the Trinity. This alone is true sanctification.

The revelation which Jesus had delivered them, as distinguished from the false teaching of the heathen, and from the imperfect teaching of the law of Moses, alone taught them the truth. The Incarnation with its consequences, God made Man, and man made God, the Word made Flesh, and man united to Him, was the truth, the full and true teaching of Jesus to His disciples.

18 As Thou (hast sent) Me into the world, even so (have I also sent) them into the world.[1]

(Alf. Didst send—I also sent.)

This is an additional reason why the Father should keep them and sanctify them. As the Father had sent His Son into the world to redeem and to sanctify the world, lost as it was in sin, so the Son

---

[1] Even so have I also sent them. (κἀγὼ ἀπέστειλα αὐτούς). "'Ἀπέστειλα is = I sent them forth (referring to the election of the Apostles)."—Winer's *Grammar of New Testament*, p. 292.

had likewise sent His Apostles into all nations to teach and to sanctify them. The Apostles had need of a sanctification continually renewed for their work, lest in their intercourse with the world they should be infected by its sins, or overcome by its temptations.

19 And for their sakes I sanctify Myself, that they also (might be sanctified through the truth.)

(Margin, Truly sanctified.)
(Alf. May be sanctified in truth.)

In a few hours Jesus would sanctify Himself, He would offer Himself on the Cross the Sacrifice for the whole world. By His Death He would make Himself the Victim, the Oblation, and would thus make atonement for the sins of the world. The effect of this His sanctification on His Apostles would be, that they also in their degree would be sanctified, and would devote themselves and their lives as victims in the service of the world, in preaching to them the truth, the Gospel of Jesus.

Hitherto Jesus has been praying for His disciples, for the Apostles, and those who had been converted by His own teaching. In the rest of the chapter He prays also for those who should be converted by the preaching of His Apostles, that is, for the whole Church, for all in all ages who should believe in Him.

20 (Neither pray I for these alone), but for them also [(which shall believe on Me)] through their word.

[S. V. A. Which believe on Me.]
(Alf. Yet not for these alone do I pray—that believe in Me.)

21 That they all may be one : (as Thou, Father, art in Me, and I in Thee), that they also may be one in Us : that the world may believe that Thou (hast sent) Me.

(Alf. Even as Thou Father in Me, &c.—didst send.)

As before, when Jesus prays for the Church, the substance of His prayer is that they may be one, that His disciples may be one in faith, one in love, as He and the Father are One in nature or essence. Their union with Jesus is the root of their union, of their oneness, with each other. Their love to Jesus is the root of their love to each other. Their oneness with each other is but the natural effect of their union with Jesus. Their love to each other is but the necessary fruit of their love to Jesus. Whatever in them is earthly and selfish is absorbed by their love to Jesus. Like fire, the love of Jesus is the source of life and zeal ; like light, it refreshes and invigorates everything within its reach.

A union through agreement in opinion would not convince the unbeliever in Jesus. It must be a union through love, and the centre of that union and of that love must be Jesus.

22 And the glory which Thou (gavest Me) I have given them: that they may be one, [even as we are one.]
[V. Even as we are one; S. Even as we.]
(Alf. Hast given Me.)

23 I in them, and Thou in Me, that they may be made perfect in one: [and that] the world may know that Thou (hast sent) Me, and (hast loved) them, as Thou (hast loved) Me.
[S. Omits, that: V. Omits, and.]
(Alf. That the world—didst send—lovedst.)

The glory, of which Jesus here speaks, has been explained in two ways. Some have thought that it means the glory of Sonship with the Father. This Jesus as God had naturally, so to speak; as Man by the Hypostatic Union with the Divine nature. This glory He had given to them: "To as many as received Him, to them gave He power to become the sons of God" (i. 12), not by nature but by adoption, not by natural birth, nor of the will of the flesh, nor of the will of man but of God.

Others have explained this glory with reference to the communication of Christ's Divine and Human nature to man in the Eucharist. This is the highest glory that can be conferred on man while on earth. By this mystical union with Him the many members of His Body are united in one. It may be that Jesus here prays that as His disciples, those who believe on Him, have already been united in one by the communication to them of His Divine and Human nature in the Eucharist, this oneness may be ratified and continued and increased by the descent upon them of the Holy Spirit on the day of Pentecost.

Thus they see both the privileges which belong to them here as His disciples, and the reward which awaits them hereafter. The privileges are a share in the glory, a portion of the love, which is shown by the Father to the Son, so far as this can be communicated to man. The reward is, that they may dwell with Him hereafter, and enjoy the beatific Vision, that they may behold His glory with all the transforming effects of that Vision.

24 Father, I will (that they also, whom Thou hast given Me), be with Me where I am: that they may behold My glory, which Thou hast given Me: (for) Thou lovedst Me before the foundation of the world.
(Alf. That what Thou hast given Me, even they—because.)

25 O righteous Father, the world (hath not known Thee) : but I (have known Thee), and these (have known) that Thou (hast sent) Me.

(Alf. Knew Thee not—knew Thee—knew—didst send.)

26 And I (have declared) unto them Thy name, and will (declare it) : that the love [wherewith Thou (hast loved) Me] may be in them, and I in them.

[S. Wherewith Thou hast loved them.]
(Alf. Made known—make it known—lovedst.)

Before (ver. 11) Jesus addressed the Father as Holy Father, here as Righteous Father. Then He had reference to their sanctification by the Holy Spirit : here He refers to the justice which the Father shows in giving them His glory, the beatific Vision, as a reward for believing in Jesus His Son, and for believing in Him in spite of the unbelief of men generally.

During His own Ministry on earth He had made known to them the name of the Father, not merely the knowledge of Him as God, but as God the Father. As they were able to bear it, He had revealed to them the knowledge of the Holy Trinity and of the Incarnation ; and He here promises to do that still more by the Holy Spirit, whom He will send to them on the day of Pentecost. The effect of the mission of the Holy Spirit upon earth will be the continuance of their union with Him, and the increase of their love to Him and to each other.

With these words Jesus closes His prayer for His Church, which He had offered to the Father in the hearing of His eleven Apostles.

In delivering His instructions to His Apostles, and in offering up His prayer to the Father for them, He had occupied a considerable portion of time. But in this He was only acting in accordance with the custom of the Jews at the Passover supper. On that evening it was their custom to draw out their discourse to an unusual length, and to recount one by one some of God's merciful dealings with His people of old.

(364)

INTRODUCTORY NOTE TO CHAPTER XVIII.

GOVERNMENT OF JUDÆA FROM THE DEATH OF HEROD THE GREAT UNTIL THE DESTRUCTION OF JERUSALEM BY TITUS.

[Compiled from Greswell's *Dissertations*, Vol. iv. part ii. p. 735, etc.]

EMPERORS.	TETRARCHS.	HIGH PRIESTS.
B.C.	B.C.	B.C.
31. Augustus.	4. Archelaus.	3. Eleazar, son of Boethus.
		A.D.
	PROCURATORS.	(?) Jesus, son of Sie.
	A.D.	(?) Jozar, son of Boethus.
	7. Coponius.	7. Ananus, son of Seth.
	10. Marcus Ambivius.	22. Ishmael, son of Phabi.
A.D.	13. Annius Rufus.	24. Eleazar, son of Ananus.
14. Tiberius.	15. Valerius Gratus.	25. Simon, son of Camithus.
	26. Pontius Pilatus.	26. Josephus or Caiaphas.
	36. Marcellus.	
37. Caligula.	37. Maryllus.	37. Jonathan, son of Ananus.
		Theophilus, son of Ananus.
		41. Simon Cantheras, son of Boethus.
		42. Matthias, son of Ananus.
		43. Elionæus, son of Cantheras.
	44. Cuspius Fadus.	44. Josephus, son of Cami.
	46. Tiberius Alexander.	46. Ananias, son of Nebedæus.
	48. Ventidius Cumanus.	49. Jonathan, son of Ananus.
54. Nero.	50. Antonius Felix.	56. Ismael, son of Thaboi.
	58. Porcius Festus.	61. Josephus Cabi, son of Simon.
	62. Albinus.	62. Ananus, son of Ananus.
68. Galba.	64. Gessius Florus.	Jesus, son of Damnæus.
69. Otho.	70. M. Antonius Julianus.	63. Jesus, son of Gamaliel.
Vitellius.		65. Matthias, son of Theophilus.
Vespasian	72. Liberius Maximus.	67. Phannias, son of Samuel.

—*Williams's Holy City*, i. 487.

High Priest.—The following passages from Josephus show the capriciousness with which the Roman Governors changed the High Priest and also the time during which Caiaphas retained that office:

"Tiberius Nero, the stepson of Augustus, and the son of Livia his wife, succeeded Augustus, being the third Emperor of the Romans, and sent Valerius Gratus to be Governor of Judæa instead of Annius Rufus. He removed Ananus from the Pontificate, and put Israel, the son of Fabius in his place, who was soon after deposed, and the honour transferred to Eleazar, the son of Ananus, the High Priest. It was taken from him in one year and given to Simon, the son of Camith, who, after another year, was commanded to deliver it up to Joseph, whose surname was Caiaphas. Gratus having been now eleven years in his government, went back to Rome, and Pontius Pilate succeeded him."—*Antiq.* xviii. 4.

"Vitellius (a person of consular dignity and at that time Governor of Syria) upon this sent his friend Marcellus to take charge of the government of Judæa, and ordered Pilate to Rome to answer before Cæsar the accusations that were exhibited against him. He had now been ten years in his government, and upon this order put himself upon a journey to Rome, but Tiberius died before he got thither."—*Idem*, xviii. 5.

"Vitellius took away the High Priesthood from Joseph, called Caiaphas and gave it to Jonathan, the son of the High Priest Ananus, and so went his way back to Antioch."—*Idem*, xviii. 6.

CHAPTER XVIII.

1 Judas betrayeth Jesus; 6 The officers fall to the ground; 10 Peter smiteth off Malchus's ear; 12 Jesus is taken, and led unto Annas and Caiaphas; 15 Peter's denial; 19 Jesus examined by Caiaphas; 28 His arraignment before Pilate; 36 His kingdom; 40 The Jews ask Barabbas to be let loose.

AFTER Jesus had ended His prayer to the Father He and His disciples left the Upper Room and went over the brook Cedron. Probably the strife among his disciples as to which of them should be the greatest (Luke xxii. 24) had occurred before Jesus delivered His address to them. Whether they had sung the hymn before this discourse or after it is uncertain. Some have concluded that St. Matthew (xxvi. 30) meant to imply, that the singing the hymn took place after the discourse of Jesus, and immediately before they left the room. But it would seem to have occurred more naturally after the eating of the Passover. The Hallel, or service of praise sung at the Passover consisted of the series of Psalms from cxiii. to cxviii. The first portion, comprising Psalms cxiii. and cxiv., was sung in the early part of the meal, and the second part after the fourth or last cup of wine. This is supposed to have been the "hymn" sung by Jesus and His disciples, as mentioned by St. Matthew (xxvi. 30) and St. Mark (xiv. 26). St. John omits all mention of "the hymn" probably because he omits all express mention both of the Paschal supper, and of the institution of the Eucharist.

The following may have been the order in which the events of this evening thus far occurred. They eat the Passover, singing the Psalms of Hallel in the proper place. Jesus then having washed the feet of His Twelve Disciples instituted the Eucharist. After that He indicated to St. John, by the giving of a sop to Judas, who should be the traitor. Judas now left the room, and Jesus began His discourse to His Disciples, and last of all He offered his prayer to the Father. This being ended Jesus and His Eleven Disciples leave the Upper Room, and cross over the brook Cedron or Kidron to the Garden of Gethsemane.

1 When Jesus had spoken these words, He went forth with His disciples over the brook Cedron, where was a garden into the which He entered, and His disciples.[1]

---

[1] Over the brook Cedron (πέραν τοῦ χειμάρρου τῶν Κέδρων. S. τοῦ Κέδρου)— "The bed of the Kidron although it lies at the bottom of a deep ravine, which is spoken of as a valley by Josephus, is in Scripture almost uniformly designated not

2 (And) Judas also, which (betrayed Him), knew the place: (for) Jesus ofttimes resorted thither with His disciples.[1]

(Alf, Now—delivered Him up—because.)

3 Judas then, having received (a band) of men and officers from the chief priests [and Pharisees], cometh [thither] with lanterns and torches and weapons.[2]

[S. And from the Pharisees: S. Omits, thither.]
(Alf. The band.)

as the *valley*, but as the *brook*: a distinction of usage which it is important to observe. The Kidron itself is no more than a winter torrent: and such is the strict meaning of the Greek word which is applied to it in the New Testament: (χείμαρρος. John xviii. 1). Even in winter but little water is to be found in it except during the heavy rains, and only at intervals are any traces of a continuous watercourse descernible. The meaning of the name Kidron, denoting *dark* or *blackish* (or, according to Gesenius, *turbid*) is illustrated by a passage in the Book of Job, in which the corresponding Hebrew participle is employed. The Kidron is one of those brooks ' which are *blackish* by reason of the ice, and wherein the snow is hid: what time they wax warm, they vanish; when it is not they are consumed out of their place.' (Job vi. 16, 17.) "— Thrupp's *Ancient Jerusalem*, p. 211.

" Kidron was so called from blackness: the waters being blackened by the mud and dirt that ran into it, it being indeed rather the sink or common sewer of the city than a brook."—Lightfoot, ii. 607.

"An objection has been drawn from the reading τῶν κέδρων, which, as in so many other instances turns out upon examination to be favourable to the view against which it is directed. Arguing from the plural article which has the authority of a majority of MSS., it has been inferred that the Evangelist was ignorant of the true derivation of the name Cedron or Kidron, which does not stand for ' cedars,' but is a Hebrew word meaning 'black' or 'dark.' But the Codex Sinaiticus reads τοῦ κέδρου, and a respectable minority of MSS. read τοῦ κέδρων, which may be restored to the text with little hesitation. If the original reading was τοῦ κέδρων, it is easy to understand how each of the two corruptions came to be substituted for it by copyists knowing only Greek. But on the other hand it is difficult to see how either τοῦ κέδρου could be corrupted into τῶν κέδρων or vice versâ, or how either of them could sink into such a monstrosity to a Greek eye and ear as τοῦ κέδρων. To suppose that this last was a correction on critical grounds would be a mistaken modernism. Even upon the supposition that τοῦ κέδρου or τῶν κέδρων was the right reading, it would still be credible that a person who was thoroughly acquainted with Hebrew might yet be struck by the similarity in form (he might think also in meaning) of the Greek word, and so be led to use it as a translation. I suspect that the history of geographical nomenclature would furnish analogies to such a case.

"It ought however to be noticed that a majority of the best professed critics (Tischendorf, Tregelles, Westcott) retain τῶν κέδρων; and the niceties of text-criticism are such that a positive opinion ought not be expressed except by those who are thoroughly conversant with them. The genuineness of the Gospel, however, is not affected whichever way the decision may go."— Sanday's *Historical Character of the Fourth Gospel*, p. 240.

[1] For Jesus ofttimes resorted thither, &c.—" It is probable that Jesus often resorted to this place, not only because of its retirement, but also because it formed a fit place of meeting when his disciples, dispersed through the city by day, were to join His company in the evening and go with Him over the hill to Bethany. And this seems the real meaning of the original words, πολλάκις συνήχθη ὁ Ἰησοῦς ἐκεῖ μετὰ τῶν μαθητῶν αὐτοῦ. Jesus ofttimes rendezvoused at this spot with His disciples."—*Mission to the Jews from Scotland*, p. 162.

[2] The band (τὴν σπεῖραν).—"This is

Through the same gate and by the same path along which David had passed with his followers, when he fled from his son Absalom (2 Sam. xv. 23) through the very same gate (now St. Stephen's) and along the very same path Jesus leads His Eleven Apostles sad and perplexed. Enough had happened during the evening to fill their hearts with sorrow, and they were in ignorance as to how all this would end.

The brook Kidron or Cedron is the channel of the valley of Jehoshaphet, the deep ravine which lies on the east of Jerusalem between the City and the Mount of Olives. Though the mere bed of a wintry torrent, it is occasionally swept over by a large volume of water. In

---

spoken of definitely, as being the particular cohort which, by order of the Procurator, attended on the Sanhedrin at the great festivals and preserved tranquillity."—Middleton on *Greek Article*, p. 261.

Then Judas having received a band, &c.—" Our English Version gives little idea of the exactness of the description in the verse which follows: Ὁ οὖν Ἰούδας λαβὼν τὴν σπεῖραν καὶ ἐκ τῶν ἀρχιερέων καὶ [ἐκ] τῶν Φαρισαίων ὑπηρέτας ἔρχεται, &c. Σπεῖρα is a Roman cohort, ἡ σπεῖρα that which garrisoned the citadel of Antonia. It is probable that part only was present: but it is called ἡ σπεῖρα from its being under the command of the chief officer, or Chiliarch, of the cohort, who is mentioned in verse 12. The ὑπηρέται are the servants or apparitors of the Sanhedrin. Dr. Scholten raises another objection which only recoils upon his own theory, founded on the introduction of the Roman soldiers. He thinks they were unnecessary and that their presence is improbable. But it is obviously accounted for by the fear of the chief priests that the arrest of Jesus would cause an uproar among the people. At a time when 3,000,000 people were assembled in and round a city which usually held about 50,000, it must have been easy to collect a crowd anywhere; and Josephus testifies to the excitable condition of mind and frequent disturbances and bloodshed among the pilgrims attending the Passover. A little spark might easily set so much inflammable material into a blaze, especially if it arose from the Messianic expectations. Thus we read that 3000 men were slain in a sedition at the time of the Passover on the accession of Archelaus in B.C. 4. A little later there is an outbreak against Sabinus at the Feast of Pentecost, in putting down which Varus crucified 3000 men. Under the oppressions of Pilate the Jews were constantly

upon the verge of insurrection, and the great centres of sedition were the religious feasts. The presence of the Chiliarch and his soldiers was therefore a natural and necessary precaution."—Sanday's *Historical Character of the Fourth Gospel*, p. 241.

With lanterns and torches (μετὰ φανῶν καὶ λαμπάδων.)— " In rendering λύχνος and λαμπάς our Translators have done the best in their power with the words which they had at their disposal. Had they rendered λαμπάς by 'torch' not once only (John xviii. 3) but always, this would have left 'lamp,' now wrongly appropriated by λαμπάς, disengaged. Altogether dismissing 'candle,' they might have rendered λύχνος by 'lamp' wherever it occurs. At present there are so many occasions where 'candle' would manifestly be inappropriate, and where, therefore, they are obliged to fall back on 'light' that the distinction between φῶς and λύχνος nearly, if not quite, disappears in our Version.

" Λύχνος is not a 'candle' (candela from candeo, the *white* wax light, and then any kind of taper), but a hand-lamp fed with oil. Neither is λαμπάς a ' lamp,' but a ' torch,' and this not only in the Attic, but in the later Hellenistic Greek as well, and so, I believe, always in the New Testament. It may be urged that in the parable of the Ten Virgins the λαμπάδες are furnished with oil, and must needs therefore be lamps. But it is not so. Elphinstone (*History of India*, vol. i. p. 333,) shows that in the East the torch as well as the lamp is fed in this manner. These are his words : The true Hindu way of lighting up is by torches held by men, who feed the flame with oil from a sort of bottle (the ἀγγεῖον of Matt. xxv. 4) constructed for the purpose."—Archbishop Trench on *Synonyms of New Testament*, p. 161.

all probability when Jesus and His disciples now went over the Kidron it was dry, for this was the month of April. Across the Kidron and leading up to the Mount of Olives is a garden where Jesus ofttimes resorted with His disciples.

There is no reason to limit the expression "for Jesus ofttimes resorted thither with His disciples," to this His last visit to Jerusalem. Either here in this garden, or in the neighbouring village of Bethany, it is supposed that He spent each night in His several visits to Jerusalem. There is no record that He ever spent a night within the City of Jerusalem itself. During the daytime he taught in the Temple, and in the evening He retired either to Gethsemane or to Bethany. St. John does not record the prayer of Jesus in the Garden of Gethsemane: he says nothing either of His Agony or of the heaviness of the disciples, which the other three Evangelists have so minutely related, but he hastens on at once to the events connected with His apprehension by the soldiers.

The care taken to provide the band with everything, that they might require in their attempt to apprehend Jesus, indicates the determination of the chief priests and Pharisees to make sure of Him. Though it was full moon they had with them various kinds of lights, lanterns, and torches, either for searching under the trees or within the caves with which the neighbourhood abounded, as the occasion might require. They had also weapons, swords and staves (Matt. xxvi. 55), in case His disciples should offer resistance. Probably soldiers and officers were employed who were well acquainted with Jesus, but lest there should be any mistake, and to prevent any possibility of His escape through their ignorance of His Person, as a sign a kiss was to be given Him by Judas. (Matt. xxvi. 48.)

4 [Jesus therefore, knowing] all things (that should come upon Him), went forth, [and said] unto them, Whom seek ye ?

[S. But Jesus knowing: V. And saith.]
(Alf. That were coming upon Him.)

5 They answered Him, Jesus of Nazareth. [Jesus saith unto them, I am He.] (And) Judas also, (which betrayed Him) (stood with them.)

[V. He saith unto them, I am Jesus.]
(Alf. Now—which delivered Him up—was standing with them.)

6 As soon [then] as (He had said) [unto them], I am He, they went backward, and fell to the ground.

[A. Omits, then: S. Omits, unto them.]
(Alf. He said.)

2 B

The Evangelist is careful to point out, that Jesus was not taken by surprise at the arrival of Judas with a band of armed men, and that He voluntarily offered Himself up to them, that, so far from showing the least trace of a desire to avoid them or escape from them, He even thrust Himself, so to speak, on their notice.

Both the kiss of Judas and the declaration of Jesus Himself indicate to them the object of their search, but for a time they lack the power to execute their commission. A blindness or a powerlessness bodily or mental seems to have seized them. All this was doubtless done, to show that Jesus was not a malefactor prevented from escaping, but a Sacrifice who willingly gave Himself up to Death.

It has been thought that Judas, though He came with the band of armed men, did not wish to appear to belong to them—that He advanced a little in front in order to give the kiss to Jesus, but that when he received from Him the rebuke "Judas, betrayest thou the Son of Man with a kiss?" (Luke xxii. 48) that he again withdrew into the midst of the band and remained standing with them.

Whether they went back a little and then fell with their face to the ground, or, as some have thought, went back and fell backwards, the cause was the same, the Divine power of Jesus. Either this supernatural power was exerted over the band through a visible cause, as by some irresistible terror conveyed by His voice or countenance, or by some awe which suddenly and secretly filled their hearts without any visible agency to account for it. Perhaps the very terms of His answer, "I am," carried with them a power which they could not withstand until He expressed His permission for them to take Him.

7 (Then asked He them again), Whom seek ye? And they said, Jesus of Nazareth.

(Alf. He asked them therefore again.)

8 Jesus answered, (I have told you) that I am He; if therefore ye seek Me, let these go their way.

(Alf. I told you.)

9 That the same might be fulfilled, which He spake, Of them which (Thou gavest Me have I lost none.)

(Alf. Thou hast given Me I lost none.)

The words "let these go their way" do not convey a mere request to the soldiers, but the intimation of His Divine will, the accomplishment of His purpose.

With the exception of Judas, He had allowed none of the Twelve to perish, either bodily by the violence of the soldiers, or spiritually by treachery towards Himself. They showed fear and timidity even so far as to deny and desert Him, but this was the effect of surprise or of the weakness of the flesh. None of them but Judas had acted with a settled resolution to betray Him, and that for worldly gain. Their love to Jesus was undoubted, but their belief in Him as God was not perfect as yet, it was not unmixed with some considerable drawback.

10 Then Simon Peter having a sword, drew it, and smote the high priest's servant, and cut off his right ear. The servant's name was Malchus.

11 (Then said Jesus) unto Peter, [Put up thy sword] into the sheath : the cup which My Father hath given Me, shall I not drink it ?[1]

[S. V. A. Put up the sword.]
(Alf. Jesus therefore said.)

Of the four reasons which Jesus gave why Peter should put up the sword and not offer any further resistance to those who came to apprehend Him, St. John mentions only the last.
1. For all they that take the sword shall perish with the sword. (St. Matt. xxvi. 52.) All who shed blood, except by lawful authority, are guilty of death. God had commanded Noah, Whoso sheddeth man's blood, by man shall his blood be shed. (Gen. ix. 6.)
2. That He had no need of such resistance. For had He wished to resist His capture, He could have had twelve legions, an infinite number, of angels to defend Him.
3. That to offer resistance was the way to render void the Scriptures, which had foretold the redemption of mankind through His Death and Passion. " But how then shall the Scriptures be fulfilled, that thus it must be ? "
4. " The cup, which My Father hath given Me, shall I not drink it ? " The cup of suffering, the death which is the lot of all men, He as the Word made Flesh must undergo. The Flesh, the Body, which He had received from His Mother, naturally shrunk from this, but the Godhead willed it.

St. John omits the first three of these reasons and gives only the fourth, which is omitted by the other three Evangelists.

All the four Evangelists relate the cutting off of the ear of the high priest's servant. St. Luke and St. John describe it more exactly than the others, and say it was the right ear. St. John alone says that the servant's name was Malchus, and that it was Peter who drew his sword and cut off his ear. The others merely state in general terms that it was one of them which were with Jesus (St. Matt. xxvi. 51), or " one

---

[1] The cup—shall I not drink it? (τὸ ποτήριον ὃ δέδωκέν μοι ὁ πατήρ, οὐ μὴ πίω αὐτό).—" The pronoun is here used for the sake of emphasis."—Winer's *Grammar of New Testament*, p. 160.

of them that stood by" (St. Mark xiv. 47). At the late period at which St. John wrote his Gospel, probably all the reasons which had formerly existed for withholding the name, either of the servant or of St. Peter were then removed.

When Jesus had asked the band of armed men a second time, "Whom seek ye?" had invited them to take Him and let the disciples go, they appear to have moved towards Him. Then it was that Peter drew his sword and struck a servant of the high priest's and smote off his ear, probably as being one of the most eager to lay hold on Jesus. When He had healed the servant's ear, and had rebuked first His disciples for offering resistance, and then the soldiers and officers for coming out against Him as against a thief, then they lay hands on Him and lead Him away. Comparing the several accounts of the Evangelists together, it is plain that they had not laid hands on Him before, though a strict and literal interpretation of St. Matthew would almost seem to imply that they had. St. John says that when they took Jesus they bound Him, which must have been after He had touched the ear of Malchus. The Evangelist mentions with a wonderful minuteness who took Jesus and bound Him, the band, the captain, and the officers of the Jews. These are they who had been struck to the ground, and they are still filled with awe and fear of His power. Like Isaac, like the lamb for sacrifice, He too must be bound.

St. Matthew xxvi.	St. Mark xiv.	St. Luke xxii.	St. John xviii.
51 And, behold, one of them which were with Jesus, stretched out his hand, and drew his sword, and struck a servant of the high priest's, and smote off his ear.	47 And one of them that stood by drew a sword, and smote a servant of the high priest, and cut off his ear.	50 And one of them smote the servant of the high priest, and cut off his right ear.	10 Then Simon Peter having a sword drew it, and smote the high priest's servant, and cut off his right ear. The servant's name was Malchus.
		51 And Jesus answered and said, Suffer ye thus far. And He touched his ear, and healed him.	
52 Then said Jesus unto him, Put up again thy sword into his place: for all they that take the sword shall perish with the sword.			11 Then said Jesus unto Peter, Put up thy sword into the sheath:
53 Thinkest thou that I cannot now pray to My Father, and He shall presently give Me more than twelve legions of angels?			the cup which My Father hath given Me, shall I not drink it?
54 But how then shall the scriptures be fulfilled, that thus it must be?			

12 (Then the band) and the captain and (officers) of the Jews took Jesus, and bound Him.[1]
(Alf. So the band—the officers.)

13 [And led Him away to Annas first] : for he was father-in-law to Caiaphas, (which was the high priest) that same year.
[S. V. And led Him to Annas first.]
(Alf. Which was high priest.)

14 Now Caiaphas was he which gave counsel to the Jews, that it was expedient that one man should die for the people.

Caiaphas, or Joseph Caiaphas, was high priest during the whole three years of our Saviour's Ministry on earth. He was son-in-law to Annas, who had himself been high priest, and who had acquired a great and unusual influence in affairs at Jerusalem. The influence of Annas was either the result of a sort of recognised official or quasi-official authority, which he possessed as ex-high priest, or as Sagan, that is, deputy: or it was the effect of his personal character, as the head of a very powerful Jewish party, and as the father-in-law to Caiaphas.

Some have supposed that it was with Annas that Judas had negotiated, when he agreed to deliver up Jesus for thirty pieces of silver; and that this was the reason why Jesus was first carried to Annas, in order that Judas, on producing his Prisoner, might receive his thirty pieces.

All commentators are agreed that Jesus was first examined by Annas, and then by Caiaphas: by Caiaphas at first probably alone, or with only a few of the Scribes and Pharisees, and then by Caiaphas at the head of the whole Jewish Council or Sanhedrin, and afterwards by Pilate. The point on which they are not agreed is, whether the examination, which Annas made of Jesus, is recorded by any of the Evangelists, or whether they merely allude to it.

Some think that only one examination of Jesus before "the high-priest" is recorded by the Evangelists, viz.: His examination before Caiaphas, either before Caiaphas alone or with a few of his friends, or before him at the head of the whole Council. Others think that two examinations of Jesus before "the high-priest" are related by the Evangelists; the first before Annas recorded by St. John here, and the second before Caiaphas as recorded by the other three Evangelists.

---

[1] Then the band and ... took Jesus (συνέλαβον τὸν Ἰησοῦν).—" According to the other Evangelists (Matt. xxvi. 50; Mark xiv. 46) the seizing and binding preceded Peter's striking in with his sword. John, however, would seem to imply that Peter used his sword at the moment the soldiers were about to lay hands on Jesus."—Winer's *Grammar of New Testament*, p. 291.

Those who think that only one examination of Jesus before " the high-priest," viz., that in the house of Caiaphas, is related by the Evangelists, have a difficulty in translating and explaining verse 24. They are obliged to have recourse to the explanation that it is out of its place, and ought properly to have come in after verse 18th. But still, though the interpretation which makes all the four Evangelists relate only one examination of Jesus is not without its difficulties, many have thought that it presented fewer than the other. Of the two, this has been perhaps the more generally received.[1]

15 And Simon Peter followed Jesus, and so did (another disciple) : that disciple was known unto the high priest, and went in with Jesus into the palace of the high priest.[2]

(Alf. The other disciple.)

---

[1] **The examination of Jesus.**—Bishop Wordsworth gives several arguments and a list of authorities to prove that all the four Evangelists are describing one and the same examination, that in the house of Caiaphas, at different stages of it.—See Greek Testament.

Dean Alford held that St. John is here describing the examination of Jesus before Annas, while the other three Evangelists are describing his examination before Caiaphas, and he gives a long list of authorities, ancient, and modern chiefly German, to support his opinion. — See Greek Testament, on John xviii. 13.

[2] **And so did the other disciple** (καὶ ὁ ἄλλος μαθητής).—" This phrase obviously implies *the remaining one of the persons* who not only were, in common with many others, disciples of Christ, but between whom some still closer relation might be recognised to exist ; and if it could be shown that Peter and John stood towards each other in any such relation, the term *the other disciple* might not unfitly be used, immediately after the mention of Peter, to designate John: especially, if from any cause whatever John was not to be spoken of by name. Now it does appear that a particular and even exclusive friendship existed between Peter and John: the circumstance has been noticed in that admirable manual of Christian piety, the *Companion for the Fasts and Festivals.* Upon the news of our Saviour's Resurrection, they two hasted together to the sepulchre. It was to Peter that John gave the notice of Christ's appearing at the sea of Tiberias in the habit of a stranger ; and it was for St. John that St. Peter was solicitous what should become of him. (John xxi. 21.) After the Ascension of our Lord, we find them both together going up to the Temple at the hour of prayer, both preaching to the people, and both apprehended and thrown into prison, and the next day brought forth to plead their cause before the Sanhedrin. And both were sent down by the Apostles to Samaria to settle the plantations Philip had made in those parts, where they baffled Simon Magus." (p. 77.) It might have been added that the same two were sent by Christ to prepare the last Passover. (Luke xxii. 8.) " It is moreover to be observed that the same expression of ὁ ἄλλος μαθητής, with some addition indeed, occurs in this Evangelist (xx. 2), where, however, I do not perceive that the addition affects the question: it is repeated also in verses 3, 4, and 8 of the same chapter, in a manner which to the modern reader will appear extraordinary, but which, combined with the circumstances already related, leads me to infer that this phrase, when accompanied with the mention of Peter, was readily, in the earliest period of Christianity, understood to signify John : and it is not impossible that the Evangelist may have employed this expression in order to remind his readers that of the Twelve Apostles two were distinguished from the rest by their chosen friendship and connection. If this be a reasonable solution of the difficulty the Article ought to be expressed in all future Translations: by the omission of it we withhold from the readers' notice a circumstance of considerable interest and beauty."—Bishop Middleton on the *Greek Article*, p. 262.

16 But Peter stood at the door without. Then went out (that other disciple), which was known unto the high priest, and spake unto her that kept the door, and brought in Peter.

(Alf. The other disciple.)

It has been universally agreed that by "the other disciple" St. John meant himself. He may have intended the expression to have some reference to the disciple whom Jesus loved (xiii. 23). Some have supposed that he used this form of speech, as the special friend and constant companion of St. Peter, as though the presence of one almost necessarily implied that of the other too. They certainly were often joined together, either by mutual affection or by accidental circumstances.

When the disciples fled, Peter still followed at a distance, influenced partly by love to his Master and partly by a desire to see the end. As a prominent disciple of Jesus, and as the one who, but a few hours before, had cut off the ear of the high priest's servant, Peter would be well known to the band which had apprehended Jesus. He had therefore reason to fear detection, and to follow at a distance, and to stand at the door without.

It has been supposed that this was the official residence of the high priest, and that both Annas the late high priest, and Caiaphas the present high priest, may have resided here, or at least may have both been present on this occasion. None of the Evangelists call it the palace of Caiaphas or the palace of Annas, but "the high priest's palace." The house was probably quadrangular with an entrance from the street, and a court-yard in the centre, a form of house very common in Eastern countries, and well-suited to keep out the strong rays of the sun.

The difference between the social position of the high priest, and that of St. John or any other of the disciples, must have been very great, and though many conjectures have been formed, no clue has been given to lead us to the right explanation of the way in which "the other disciple" was known unto the high priest.

17 Then saith the damsel that kept the door unto Peter, (Art not thou also) one of this man's disciples? He saith, I am not.

(Alf. Art thou also.)

18 (And the servants and officers stood there, who had made) a fire of coals: (for) it was cold: (and they warmed

themselves) : and Peter [stood with them] and warmed himself.[1]

[S. Also stood there : S. V. And Peter also stood.]
(Alf. Now the servants and the officers were standing there, having made—because —and were warming themselves.)

St. Matthew says that Peter sat with the servants (xxvi. 58), and St. John that he stood with them (xviii. 18). Both doubtless are correct. For neither term excludes the other. During the time Peter was with the servants he most probably both sat and stood. St. John, by his expression that Peter stood with the servants, may not have meant to express any particular posture, but merely to state that he was present with the servants.

It seems not to have been uncommon for women to act as keepers of the doors. Another instance is mentioned in the Acts of the Apostles (xii. 13). From Peter's behaviour here, we may estimate the nature of the change which afterwards took place in his character, we may learn the wonderful effect which the Holy Spirit had on his mind. Here he trembles at the bare hint that he is a disciple of Jesus, though expressed by a woman, and by one who holds one of the lowest offices in the household of the high priest. After the descent of the Holy Spirit, he confesses before Caiaphas himself that he is a disciple of Jesus, and boldly refuses to obey the commands of the whole Sanhedrin.

It was the nature of her office, which was partly to notice who went in, and who went out by the gate, which led her to detect Peter.

---

[1] **Servant.**—" The δοῦλος, opposed to ἐλεύθερος (Rev. xiii. 16; xix. 18) being properly the bond-man, from δέω, ' ligo,' is one in a permanent relation of servitude to another, and that, altogether apart from any ministration to that other at the present moment rendered; but the θεράπων is the performer of present services, without respect to the fact whether as a freeman or slave he renders them, as bound by duty, or impelled by love : and thus, as will naturally follow, there goes constantly with the word the sense of one whose services are tenderer, nobler, freer than those of the δοῦλος . . . .

It will be seen, then, that the author of the Epistle to the Hebrews, calling Moses a θεράπων in the house of God (iii. 5), implies that he occupied a more confidential position, that a freer service, a higher dignity was his, than that merely of a δοῦλος, approaching more closely to that of an διάκονομος in God's house : and, referring to Num. xii. 6-8, we find, confirming this view, that a special dignity is here ascribed to Moses, lifting him above other δοῦλοι of God, cf. Deut. xxiv. 5, where he is οἰκέτης κυρίου given to Moses (Wisd. of Sol. x. 16), but not to any other of the worthies of the old Covenant mentioned in the chapter cf. xviii. 21. It would have been well if in our Version it had been in some way sought to indicate the exceptional and more honourable title here given to him who 'was faithful in all God's house.' The Vulgate has very well rendered θεράπων by 'famulus' (so Cicero, famulae Idaeae matris,) Tyndall and Cranmer by 'minister,' which perhaps is as good a word as in English could have been found."—Archbishop Trench on *Synonyms of New Testament*, p. 29.

For it was cold.—" I was surprised at the severity of the cold in Jerusalem. Twice I saw the city shrouded with snow, but the sun soon melted it away, leaving only white fleecy wreaths on the northern sides of the domes and cupolas."—Rogers' *Domestic Life in Palestine*, p. 384.

Probably she marked his agitated manner, along with other signs which he might give of being a disciple of Jesus. The question arises, Why this maid did not discover "the other disciple," why she did not recognise St. John as one of His disciples? The form of her question to Peter would almost seem to imply that she had already discovered others: "Art not thou also, or Art thou also, one of this man's disciples? (μή καὶ σὺ ἐκ τῶν μαθητῶν εἶ τοῦ ἀνθρώπου τούτου;) though nothing is said on this subject in the Gospels. It was evidently the object of the Evangelists to notice the events connected with the denial of Peter, because it had been foretold by Jesus and was so signally fulfilled, but not to relate every incident connected with the trial.

19 The high priest then asked Jesus of His disciples, and of His doctrine.

20 [Jesus] answered him, (I spake) openly to the world: I ever taught in the synagogue, and in the temple, [whither the Jews always resort]: and in secret (have I said nothing.)

[S. And Jesus: S. V. A. Whither all the Jews resort.]
(Alf. I have spoken—spake I nothing.)

21 Why askest thou Me? ask them (which heard Me), what (I have said unto them): behold, (they know) what I said.

(Alf. Which have heard Me—I spake unto them—these know.)

22 And when He had (thus spoken), one of the officers (which stood by) struck Jesus with the (palm of his hand,) saying, Answerest thou the high priest so?

(Margin, With a rod.)
(Alf. Thus said—who was standing by.)

23 [Jesus answered him], (If I have spoken) evil, bear witness of the evil; but if well, why smitest Thou Me?

[S. But Jesus said unto him.]
(Alf. If I spoke.)

Caiaphas is sitting as President either of the whole Council of Seventy-one, or at least of twenty-three of its members, the number required by their traditionary canons (Lightfoot, ii. 609); and his object in this preparatory examination evidently is to discover something, on which to found a charge before Pilate the Roman Prætor, that Jesus, by His teaching, was a disturber of the public peace; that

He was preparing the people for a revolt against the Roman power, a subject on which the Roman governors were at all times exceedingly sensitive. Their continuance in favour at the Court of the Cæsars, and therefore their continuance in office depended very much on their success in keeping the Jews quiet. The object of Caiaphas, therefore, is to be prepared to substantiate the charge, that Jesus was dangerous to the public welfare. A charge of heresy, false doctrine, or blasphemy, Pilate would not take cognizance of. It must be a charge of causing danger to the State, to the peace of Judæa, and not to the religion of the Jews. We may form some conjecture, as to the unscrupulous way in which Caiaphas would get up a charge of this kind, from the advice which he gave (xi. 49) in a former sitting of this very Council.

For his teaching Jesus refers Caiaphas to the testimony of those who had heard Him teach. He does not send him to His disciples, but to any who had heard him, either in the Temple at Jerusalem, or in the synagogues of the provinces, whether friends or enemies. Surely nothing could be more reasonable or fairer than this proposal. But it is looked upon as disrespectful to constituted authority by men, who are influenced only by a spirit of servile flattery, perhaps, too, by a desire to repair the confession, which the officers who had been sent to apprehend Him had made, that never man spake like this man. (vii. 46.) This zeal in injustice, in order to conciliate the favour of superiors, Jesus promptly rebukes in the most mild and dignified manner. But He corrects the officer for his unjust spirit, not for the blow.

In their relation of this examination of Jesus before the high priest, and of the three denials of Peter, as well as in many other matters, the Evangelists differ considerably; but their accounts are not inconsistent with each other. None of them professes to give the whole that took place. One gives one portion, and each of the others give another. Probably these are independent relations, and they have the appearance of not being written in concert, nor intended to fit in with each other, and thus to make one perfect and exhaustive whole. Doubtless other things occurred which none of them relate. The Evangelists agree so far as to leave on the mind of the impartial reader the conviction, that if we knew the whole 'circumstances of the case their accounts would be in perfect agreement.

24 (Now Annas had sent him) bound, unto Caiaphas, the High Priest, (ἀπέστειλεν οὖν αὐτόν ὁ ʼΑννας δεδεμένον πρὸς Καϊάφαν τὸν ἀρχιερέα.)
(Alf. Annas therefore sent Him.)

In the English Authorised Version this verse has been translated so as to favour the view of those who hold that the examination of Jesus, which St. John is here relating, took place in the house of Caiaphas. A slight violence has been done to the original, in order to give it the appearance of a recapitulation of an event which had happened some time before rather than a narration of what had taken place just at this precise time.

Those who think that the examination which is recorded by St. John, took place in the house of Annas, must also believe that Peter's first denial of Jesus occurred in the court-yard of the palace of Annas. They must also believe that the house of Annas and Caiaphas were in the same range of buildings, and surrounded the same court-yard. As being the official residence of the high priest this might not be at all improbable. There are several things to indicate that all the three denials of Peter occurred in and about the same court-yard—viz., that attached to the palace, where Caiaphas the high priest dwelt.

25 And Simon Peter (stood and warmed himself). (They said therefore unto him), (Art not thou also) one of His disciples ? [He denied it and said], I am not.
[A. He denied it, and saith.]
(Alf. And Simon Peter was standing and warming himself—They said unto him—Art thou also.)

26 One of the servants of the high priest, (being his kinsman) whose ear Peter cut off, saith, Did not I see thee in the garden with Him ?
(Alf. Being a kinsman of him.)

27 (Peter then denied again) : and immediately the cock crew.
(Alf. So Peter denied again.)

St. Matthew says that Peter "sat without in the palace," that is, he was in the court-yard of the palace, which he had entered by the door which the damsel kept, but he was not in the Council chamber where Jesus was being examined. The Council chamber was probably raised a little above the level of the court-yard, as St. Mark says, that Peter was beneath in the palace. This would enable Jesus to see Peter, when He turned and looked upon him after the second crowing of the cock, and by this look recalled him to the recollection of what He had before said unto him, which the first crowing had failed to do.

By his temptation and fall Peter furnished a warning to men in all future ages—(1) Against confidence in their own strength to resist temptation ; (2) Against rashness in putting themselves in the way of temptation, and mixing unnecessarily with the enemies of Jesus ; (3) As one of the future chief pastors of the Church he would learn a lesson from his own fall, to have compassion on those who are overcome by the temptation of Satan. St. John is silent respecting the examination of Jesus before the whole Council and His treatment there as related by St. Matt. (xxvi. 59, &c.), St. Mark (xiv. 55), and St. Luke (xxii. 66).

PETER'S FIRST DENIAL OF CHRIST.

St. Matthew xxvi.	St. Mark xiv.	St. Luke xxii.	St. John xviii.
69 Now Peter sat without in the palace; and a damsel came unto him,	66 And as Peter was beneath in the palace, there cometh one of the maids of the high priest, and when she saw Peter warming himself she looked upon him,	56 But a certain maid beheld him as he sat by the fire, and earnestly looked upon him.	
			17 Then saith the damsel that kept the door unto Peter,
saying, Thou also wast with Jesus of Galilee.	and said, And thou also wast with Jesus of Nazareth,	and said, This man was also with Him.	
			Art not thou also one of this man's disciples?
70 But he denied before them all, saying, I know not what thou sayest.	68 But he denied, saying, I know not neither understand I what thou sayest: and he went out into the porch: and the cock crew.	57 And he denied Him, saying, Woman, I know Him not.	He saith I am not.

SECOND DENIAL.

St. Matthew xxvi.	St Mark xiv.	St. Luke xxii.	St. John xviii.
			18 And the servants and officers stood there, who had made a fire of coals; for it was cold: and they warmed themselves: and Peter stood with them, and warmed himself.
		58 And after a little while	
71 And when he was gone out into the porch,			
			25 And Simon Peter stood and warmed himself.
another maid saw him, and said unto them that were there, This fellow was also with Jesus of Nazareth.	69 And a maid saw him again, and began to say to them that stood by, This is one of them.	another saw him, and said, Thou art also of them.	
			They said therefore unto him, Art not thou also one of His disciples?
72 And again he denied with an oath, I do not know the Man.	70 And he denied it again.	And Peter said Man, I am not.	He denied it, and said, I am not.

COMMENTARY ON ST. JOHN'S GOSPEL. 381

THIRD DENIAL.

St. Matthew xxvi.	St. Mark xiv.	St. Luke xxii.	St. John xviii.
73 And after a while came unto him they that stood by, and said to Peter, Surely thou also art one of them; for thy speech bewrayeth thee.	And a little after, they that stood by said again to Peter, Surely thou art one of them: for thou art a Galilæan, and thy speech agreeth thereto.	59 And about the space of one hour after another confidently affirmed, saying, Of a truth this fellow also was with Him: for he is a Galilæan.	
			26 One of the servants of the High Priest, being his kinsman whose ear Peter cut off, saith, Did not I see thee in the garden with Him?
74 Then began he to curse and to swear, saying, I know not the Man,	71 But he began to curse and to swear,[1] saying, I know not this Man of whom ye speak.	60 And Peter said Man, I know not what thou sayest.	27 Peter then denied again:
And immediately	72 And the second time	And immediately while he yet spake,	and immediately
the cock crew.	the cock crew.	the cock crew. And the Lord turned and looked upon Peter.	the cock crew.
75 And Peter remembered the word of Jesus, which said unto him, Before the cock crow,	and Peter called to mind the word that Jesus said unto him, Before the cock crow twice,	And Peter remembered the word of the Lord, How He had said unto him, Before the crow,	
thou shalt deny Me thrice. And	thou shalt deny Me thrice. And when he thought thereon	thou shalt deny Me thrice.	
he went out and wept bitterly.	he wept.	62 And Peter went out, and wept bitterly.	

28 (Then led they Jesus) from Caiaphas unto (the hall of judgment), and it was early : and they themselves went

---

[1] To curse and to swear (ἀναθεματίζειν καὶ ὀμνύειν).—" These people are fearfully profane. Everybody curses and swears when in a passion. No people that I have ever known can compare with these Orientals for profaneness in the use of the names and attributes of God. The evil habit seems inveterate and universal. When Peter, therefore, began to curse and to swear on that dismal night of temptation, we are not to suppose it was something foreign to his former habits. He merely relapsed, under high excitement, into what, as a sailor and a fisherman, he had been accustomed to all his life. The people now use the very same sort of oaths that are mentioned and condemned by our Lord. They swear by the head, by their life, by heaven, and by the Temple, or what is in its place, the Church. The forms of cursing and swearing, however, are almost infinite, and fall on the pained ear all day long."—Thomson's *The Land and the Book*, p. 191.

382   COMMENTARY ON ST. JOHN'S GOSPEL.

not into (the judgment hall), (lest they should be defiled) : but that they might eat the Passover.[1]

(Margin, Pilate's house.)
(Alf. They lead Jesus therefore—the palace of the governor—the palace—that they might not be defiled.)

To enter the house of a Gentile, and consequently of an idolator, would cause defilement to a Jew for the rest of the day, and would disable him from partaking in the rites of his religion for the whole of that day. The Jewish officers, with probably a part of the Council, bring Jesus up to the gates of Pilate's house, the prætorium, but decline to enter it, "lest they should be defiled ; but that they might eat the Passover" (' ἵνα φάγωσι τὸ πάσχα). This was early on the morning of Friday, the 15th, but Jesus and His disciples had already eaten the Paschal lamb on the evening before, that is, on Thursday, the 14th. How was this ?

Two explanations of this have been offered. One is that the Jewish high priest and Council had been so intent on their one object, the death of Jesus, that they had neglected to kill and eat the

---

[1] But that they might eat the Passover (ἀλλ' ἵνα φάγωσι τὸ πάσχα).—"I. We have already shown (ii. 353) that the eating of the Paschal Lamb was never upon any occasion whatever transferred from the evening of the fourteenth day drawing to the close of it : no, not by reason of the Sabbath, or any uncleanness that had happened to the congregations, so that there needs little argument to assure us that the Jews eat the Lamb at the same time wherein Christ did. Only let me add this : Suppose they had entered Pilate's house, and had defiled themselves by entering the house of a heathen, yet might not that defilement come under the predicament of טְבוּל יוֹם? If so, then they might wash themselves in the evening and be clean enough to eat the Paschal Lamb, if it had been to have been eaten on that evening, but they had eaten it the evening before.

"II. Τὸ Πάσχα. The Passover, therefore, here doth not signify the Paschal Lamb, but the Paschal Chagigah, of which we will remark two or three things.

"1. Deut. xvi. 2, 'Thou shalt sacrifice the Passover unto the Lord thy God, of the flock and the herd.' Where R. Solomon, the flocks are meant of the lambs and the kids; the herd of the Chagigah. And R. Bechar in loc. The flocks are for the due of the Passover; the herd for the sacrifices of the Chagigah. So also R.

Nachman. The herd for the celebration of the Chagigah ; the flock for the Passover ; the oxen for the Chagigah.
"2. The Chagigah was for joy and mirth, according to that in Deut. xvi. 14 : ' And thou shalt rejoice in the feast,' &c. Hence the sacrifices that were prepared for that use are called sacrifices of Peace, or Eucharistic offerings, sacrifices of joy and mirth.
"3. The proper time of bringing the Chagigah was the fifteenth day of the month. They eat and drank and rejoiced and were bound to bring their sacrifices of Chagigah on the fifteenth day, that is, the first day of the feast.
"III. It was the fifteenth day of the month when the Fathers of the Council refused to enter into the Prætorium lest they should be defiled ; for they would eat the Passover, that is, the Chagigah.
"1. The Evangelist expresseth it, after the common way of speaking, when he calls it the Passover.
"2. The Elders of the Sanhedrin prepare and oblige themselves to eat the Chagigah [the Passover] on that day, because the next day was the Sabbath : and the Chagigah must not make void the Sabbath.
The Chagigah was not to be brought upon the Sabbath day, as also not in case of uncleanness."—Lightfoot ii., 610.

Paschal lamb at the proper time, the evening before. Their time had been spent first in arranging how to apprehend Jesus, and then by a lengthened and elaborate examination of Him to discover some ground, on which to prefer a civil charge against Him before Pilate, a charge of endangering the peace of the country and the safety of the Roman Government.

The other explanation is that the expression "that they might eat the Passover" does not refer to the Paschal lamb, which the Jews had already eaten and at the very time during which Jesus and the Twelve were eating the Paschal Supper in the Upper-Room. By eating the Passover here it is suggested that St. John means, either "that they might go on keeping the Passover," or that they might partake of the extra sacrifices which were offered during the seven days of unleavened bread, as, for instance, the Chagigah or festival sacrifices, which were usual at all festivals, and especially at the Passover.

Great as was the hypocritical scrupulosity of the Jews, it is difficult to believe that they could carry it so far as to change the day for eating the Paschal lamb, the very sin of Jeroboam, and then scruple to enter Pilate's house, lest they should be defiled, and so prevented from eating it on a day on which it was not appointed to be eaten.

29 (Pilate then) went out unto them [and said], What accusation bring ye against This Man?
[S. V. And saith.]
(Alf. Pilate therefore.)

30 They answered and said unto him, If He were not a malefactor, we would not have delivered Him up unto thee.

31 [(Then said Pilate)] unto them, (Take ye him), [and judge him according] to your law. (The Jews therefore said) unto him, It is not lawful for us to put any man to death.
[A. But Pilate said: S. And judge according.]
(Alf. Pilate therefore said—Take Him yourselves—The Jews said.)

32 That the saying of Jesus might be fulfilled, [which He spake,] signifying (what death) He should die.
[S. Omits, which He spake.]
(Alf. What manner of death.)

The Jews deliver Jesus up to Pilate. When he requires to know the charge which they bring against Him, they reply in general terms that He is a malefactor, a breaker of the laws of the country, and as such they request Pilate to proceed against Him according to law. Pilate who as yet did not understand that they intended the death of Jesus, and not wishing to be merely the executioner of their decrees, offers them the choice of judging and punishing Jesus according to their own laws. This the Jews decline on the ground that death was the punishment which Jesus had deserved, and that it was not lawful for them to put any man to death. Some have thought that they meant, that it was not lawful for them to put any man to death at such a high festival as the Passover. But the most probable interpretation is, that as a conquered nation, the Romans had withdrawn from them the right of capital punishment, and had reserved it for the Roman Governor alone.

Evidently the Jews had their own reasons for declining to take Jesus and judge Him according to their own laws, even if they might inflict on Him the punishment of death, of which according to their laws, as they said, He was guilty. Perhaps they might wish to avoid the odium, which the death of Jesus might bring on them from the people, who were at all times fickle, and who had often shown considerable favour towards Jesus, and who might look upon His death, if inflicted by the Jewish high-priest, &c., as the result of their private envy and malice. They might especially wish to avoid the appearance of severity at such a festival of mercy as the Passover. If Pilate put Jesus to death, it would be on a more public charge, and by a more ignominious death. If they accepted Pilate's offer and judged Him according to their own law, the charge against Him must be one of blasphemy, and His death would be by stoning (Levit. xxiv. 16), and the act would be that of the Jewish Sanhedrin alone. But if Pilate put Jesus to death, it must be on the ground of being a breaker of the law, a disturber of the peace of the country, a common criminal, His death would be by crucifixion, and the deed would be sanctioned by the authority of the whole Roman empire.

St. John has nowhere recorded that Jesus exactly said that He should be crucified, which St. Matthew does (xx. 18); but he has spoken of Him as using an equivalent expression with reference to His Death. (xii. 32, 33.)

33 (Then Pilate) entered into (the judgment hall) again, and called Jesus, and said unto Him, Art Thou the King of the Jews?

(Alf. Pilate therefore—the palace.)

Pilate had come to the gate of the palace to the chief priests and his party to receive their charge against Jesus. This charge had no relation whatever to blasphemy, of which alone they professed after their examination to have found Him guilty. They were quite aware that Pilate would pay no attention to such a charge. They therefore say, "We found this fellow perverting the nation, and forbidding to give tribute to Cæsar, saying, that He Himself is Christ a King."

(St. Luke xxiii. 2.) 1. He was perverting the nation; 2. He was forbidding to give tribute to Cæsar; 3. He was setting Himself up as King of the Jews. Here were three distinct charges, in every one of which Pilate as the Governor of Judæa had a direct interest. A new Pretender to the throne of Judæa! This was of itself sufficient to arouse the prejudice of Pilate. Having heard this accusation, he returns to his prisoner in the palace, and said unto Him, Art Thou the King of the Jews?

34 Jesus answered [him, Sayest thou (this thing)] of thyself, or did others tell it thee (of Me)?

[V. A. Omit him—S. Hast thou said this thing?]
(Alf. This—concerning Me.)

As Governor of Judæa and therefore as the representative of Cæsar its king, it was part of Pilate's duty to keep a ready ear to any claims that might be made to the sovereignty, and to put them down at once. Probably the object, that Jesus had in this question, was to force on Pilate's mind, that He had made no such claim, at least in the sense in which the Jews represented it.

35 Pilate answered, Am I a Jew? Thine Own nation [and the chief priests] (have delivered Thee) unto me: what hast Thou done?

[S. And the chief priest.]
(Alf. Delivered Thee.)

36 Jesus answered, My kingdom is not of this world: if My kingdom were of this world, [(then would My] servants fight,) that I should not be delivered to the Jews: but now is My kingdom not from hence.

[S. Then would also My.]
(Alf. My servants would fight.)

37 Pilate therefore said unto Him, Art thou a King then? Jesus answered, (Thou sayest that I am a King), [To this end] (was I born), and for this cause (came I) into the world, that I should bear witness unto the truth. Every one that is of the truth heareth My voice.

[A. To this end also.]
(Alf. Thou sayest: for I am a King—have I been born—am I come.)

Having drawn his attention to the fact, that Pilate had himself

2 c

no ground for believing that He laid claim to Cæsar's kingdom, but that this was a mere calumny of the Jews, Jesus answers his question, and admits that He is a King, and then points out the nature of the kingdom of which He is King—not one to interfere with the claims of Cæsar. He takes no notice of the surprise and scorn which Pilate had thrown into his question, Art Thou a King then ? Thou a King! (οὐκοῦν βασιλεὺς εἶ σύ;)

Of the four Evangelists St. John alone relates the full answer of Jesus to Pilate's question, "Art Thou the King of the Jews?" The other three content themselves with giving only the latter part of His answer, "Thou sayest," that is, I am, as thou sayest, the King of the Jews. Jesus meant that He was the King of the Jews, inasmuch as He was the Messiah, but He laid no claim to be king in the sense in which Cæsar or Herod was king. But the latter was the sense in which the Jews invidiously represented His claim to Pilate.

The truth to which Jesus came to bear witness was (1) The knowledge of the One True God, the Father, the Son, and the Holy Ghost, as opposed to the false gods of the heathen ; (2) It was the Incarnation, that Jesus, the Son of God, the Word, was made Flesh, was born of a Virgin in order to redeem man; (3) That true happiness consists not in the possession of the riches and pleasures of the body, but in an ever-increasing likeness to God; and that perfect happiness consists in the beatific Vision, or in the Vision of God which will transform man into His Own likeness.

To be of the truth here means much the same as to be of God. Jesus had probably a double object in saying, " Every one that is of the truth heareth My voice," partly to show the iniquity of the Jewish rulers, and partly to induce Pilate to act uprightly in his office as Judge. The Jewish high-priest, Scribes, and Pharisees were not of the truth. Their object was not the honour or the worship of God, but the gratification of their own selfish desires. Wealth, bodily pleasure, honour, or position in the world, was what they sought, how could they believe in Him, who came to bear witness unto the Truth?

38 Pilate saith unto Him, What is truth ? And when he had said this, he went out again unto the Jews, and saith unto them, (I find in Him no fault at all.)
(Alf. I find no fault in Him.)

39 But ye have a custom, that I should release unto you one at the Passover: will ye therefore that I release unto you the King of the Jews?

40 (Then cried they [all] again), saying, Not this Man, but Barabbas. Now Barabbas was a robber.[1]

[S. V. Omit all.]
(Alf. Then they all cried out again.)

Pilate was quite indifferent to the truth. He asked the question, What is truth? but he had no interest in it. He cared not to learn how it was that Jesus should claim to be a king, but that His kingdom was not of this world.

St. John omits many of the circumstances connected with the trial

---

[1] A Robber. — "These two words κλέπτης, and λῃστής occur together John x. 18, but do not constitute there or elsewhere a tautology, or mere rhetorical amplification. Both appropriate what is not theirs, but the κλέπτης by fraud and in secret (Matt. xxiv. 43; John xii. 6); the λῃστής by violence and openly (2 Cor. xi. 26): the one is the thief and steals; the other is the robber and plunders, as his name from λῄς or λεία (as our own robber from Raub, booty) sufficiently declares. They are severally the 'fur' and the 'tatio' of the Latin: fures insidianter et occultâ fraude decipiunt = latrones audacter aliena diripiunt (Jerome, in Osee. 7, 1.)

"Our Translators have always rendered κλέπτης by thief; they ought, with a like consistency, to have rendered λῃστής by robber; but it also they have oftener rendered as thief, effacing thus the distinction between the two. We cannot charge them with that carelessness here, of which those would be guilty who now should do the same. Passages out of number in our Elizabethan literature attest that in their day 'thief' and 'robber' had not those distinct meanings which since they have acquired. Thus Falstaff and his company, who, with open violence, rob the king's treasure on the king's highway, are 'thieves' throughout Shakespeare's Henry IV. Still one must regret that in several places in our Version we do not find 'robbers' rather than thieves. Thus at Matt. xxi. 13 we read: 'My house shall be called the house of prayer, but ye have made it a den of *thieves*:' but it is 'robbers' and not 'thieves' that have dens or caves; and it is rightly 'den of robbers' at Jer. vii. 11, whence this quotation is drawn. Again Matt. xxvi. 55: 'Are ye come out as against a *thief* with swords and staves for to take Me?' but it would be against some bold and violent robber that a party armed with swords and clubs would issue forth, not against a lurking thief. The poor traveller in the parable (Luke x. 30) fell not among 'thieves' but among 'robbers,' bloody and violent men, as their treatment of him plainly declared.

"No passage has suffered so seriously as this from this confounding of 'thief' and 'robber' as Luke xxiii. 39-43. The whole anterior moral condition of him whom we call the penitent *thief* is probably much obscured for us by the associations which naturally cling to this name. The two malefactors crucified with Jesus, the one obdurate, the other penitent, in all likelihood had belonged both to the band of Barabbas, who for murder and insurrection had been cast *with his fellow insurgents* into prison. (Mark xv. 7.) He too was himself a λῃστής (John xviii. 40), and yet no common malefactor, on the contrary 'a notable prisoner' (δέσμιος ἐπίσημος, (Matt. xxvii. 16). Now, considering the wild enthusiasm of the Jewish population on his behalf, and combining this with the fact that he was in prison for an unsuccessful insurrection; keeping in mind too the condition of the Jews at this period, with false Christs, false deliverers, every day starting up, we can hardly doubt that Barabbas was one of those fierce and stormy zealots who were evermore raising anew the standard of resistance against the Roman domination; flattering and feeding the insane hopes of their countrymen that they should yet break the Roman yoke from off their necks. These men, when hard pressed, would betake themselves to the mountains, and thence would levy petty war against their oppressors, living by plunder—if possible, by that of their enemies, if not, by that of any within their reach.

"And yet of stamp and character how different would many of these men, these of Jesus before Pilate, which the other Evangelists relate, such as the repeated accusations of Jesus by the chief-priests and elders, to which He gave no answer, which are recorded by St. Matthew xxvii. 12-14: such as the sending to Herod, and second proclamation of His innocence by Pilate, which is recorded by St. Luke xxiii. 5-16. St. John omits all this and goes on to relate—and that in a condensed form—in the 39th and 40th verses Pilate's attempt to release Jesus, and the opposition made to it by the rulers and by the crowd that had by this time collected at the gates of Pilate's palace.

At the Roman Lectisternium it was usual to grant an acquittal to prisoners. (Livy v. 13.) It is not now known, whether the custom of releasing one at the Passover was introduced among them, by the Roman Governors as a means of conciliating the Jews, or whether it was an old Jewish custom. There is scarcely sufficient reason to lead us to conclude that, the practice of releasing a prisoner was confined to the Feast of the Passover. Doubtless the corresponding expression used by the other three Evangelists, and as given in the English Authorised Version, "that feast" (Matt. xxvii. 15; Mark xv. 6), "the feast" (Luke xxiii. 17), would convey this impression. But it has been pointed out, that neither of these expressions is an accurate rendering of the original, but that they both, and especially the former, limit the meaning far too much. The correct translation of κατὰ ἑορτὴν is "at festival-time" or "at every feast," that is, at every feast which the Jews as a nation were accustomed to observe.

---

maintainers of a last protest against a foreign domination, probably be from the mean and cowardly purloiner, whom we call the 'thief.' The bands of these λησταί, numbering in their ranks some of the worst, would probably include also some that were originally of the noblest spirits of the nation—even though they had miserably mistaken the task which their time demanded, and had sought to work out by the wrath of man the righteousness of God. Such a one we may well imagine this penitent λῃστής to have been. Should there be any truth in this view of his former condition—and certainly it would go far to explain his sudden conversion—it is altogether obscured by the name of 'thief' which we have given him; nor can it under any circumstances be doubtful that he would be more accurately called ' the penitent robber.'"—Archbishop Trench on *Synonyms of New Testament*, p. 153.

INTRODUCTORY NOTE TO CHAPTER XIX.

THOSE who love to linger on our Saviour's Passion and on the several instruments of His Passion, will not think the following extracts too long.

The Crown of Thorns.—" We encamped about a mile to the south of Jericho, and stayed there all that day : there was a small wood to the east of us, where I saw the Zoccum tree ; the bark of it is like that of the holly, and has very strong thorns, and the leaf is something like that of the Barbary tree : it has a green nut : the skin or flesh over it is thin, and the nut is ribbed, and has a thick shell, and a very small kernel : they grind the whole, and press an oil out of it, as they do out of olives, and call it a balsam. But I take it to be the Myrobalanum mentioned by Josephus (De bell. Jud. iv. 8), as growing about Jericho : especially as it answers very well to this fruit described by Pliny as the produce of that part of Arabia, which was between Judæa and Egypt. Some think that Christ was crowned with this thorn."—Pocoke's *Travels*, ii. 82.

" Of other plants growing in the vale of Jericho, we noticed the Nebk, the most abundant thorn in the Holy Land, and which, it is commonly thought, was that of which the crown of thorns of our Saviour was made. Hasselquist's (*Voyage and Travels*, Eng. Trans. p. 288) says, ' In all probability this is the tree which afforded the crown of thorns put on the Head of Christ : it grows very common in the East.' This plant was very fit for the purpose, for it has many small and sharp spines, which are well adapted to give pain. The crown might be easily made of these soft round, and pliant branches : and what in my opinion seems to be the greatest proof, is, that the leaves much resemble those of ivy, as they are of a very deep green. Perhaps the enemies of Christ would have a plant somewhat resembling that with which emperors and generals were used to be crowned, that there might be calumny even in the punishment."—Wilson's *Lands of the Bible*, ii. 11.

" The thorn bushes, which during the summer and autumn had been so dark and bare, were clothed with delicate green sprays of finely-serrated leaves, which almost hid the sharp, cruel-looking thorns. They were sprinkled with little round buds ; when they opened, they threw out silky tufts of crimson, crowned with golden-coloured powder. The seed vessel is round, and divided into four quarters : at first it is almost white, but gradually becomes pink: and at the apex there is a little green tuft, in the shape of a Greek cross. When the seed is quite ripe, it is about half-an-inch in diameter, and of a very shining red colour. I had been told it was of this thorn that the wreath was made which once crowned the Head of Christ. It may be so: and I have never seen a plant of which so beautiful, and at the same time so cruel a crown could be composed. This thorn is the Poterium spinosum.

"About Easter it is seen in all its beauty, the leaves glossy and full-grown, the fruit or seed-vessels brilliantly red, like drops of blood, and the thorns sharper and stronger than at any other time. No plant or bush is so common on the hills of Judæa, Galilee, and Carmel as this."—Rogers' *Domestic Life in Palestine*, p. 170.

"An Arab brought us some dhom apples, the fruit of the nûbk, or Spina Christi. They were much withered and presented the appearance of a small dried crab-apple. It had a stone like the cherry; but the stone was larger, and there was less fruit on it in proportion to its size. It was sub-acid, and to us quite palateable."—Lynch's *Expedition to the Dead Sea*, p. 286.

"The nûbk or lotus tree, the Spina Christi of Hasselquist, called by the Arabs the dhom tree, has small dark-green, oval-shaped, ivy-like leaves. Clustering thick and irregularly upon the crooked branches, are sharp thorns, half an inch in length. The smaller branches are very pliant, which in common with the ivy-like appearance of the leaves, sustains the legend that of them was made the mock crown of the Redeemer. Its fruit, resembling a withered crab-apple is sub-acid, and of a pleasant flavour."—*Idem*, p. 290.

CHAPTER XIX.

1 Christ is scourged, crowned with thorns, and beaten; 4 Pilate is desirous to release Him; but, being overcome with the outrage of the Jews, he delivered Him to be crucified; 23 They cast lots for His garments; 26 He commendeth His mother to John; 28 He dieth; 31 His side is pierced; 38 He is buried by Joseph and Nicodemus.

1 Then Pilate therefore took Jesus and scourged Him.

We learn from St. Luke that the object which Pilate had in view in thus scourging Jesus, whom he believed to be innocent, was to excite their compassion for Him, that after such a severe punishment they might be satisfied, and allow Him to depart. " Pilate, therefore, willing to release Jesus, spake again to them. But they cried, saying, Crucify Him, crucify Him. And he saith unto them the third time, Why, what evil hath He done? I have found no cause of death in Him: I will therefore chastise Him and let Him go." (xxiii. 20-22.)

Such being Pilate's object, he would make the scourging as severe as possible, in order to render Jesus more an object for their compassion. Scourging was a Roman punishment, and where the punishment was intended to be severe, the whip which was used was a dreadful instrument (horribile flagellum, Horace calls it), knotted with bones or heavy indented circles of bronze, or terminated by hooks, in which case it was aptly denominated a scorpion. The infliction of punishment with it upon the naked back of the sufferer (Juv. l. c.) was sometimes fatal." (Hor. Sat. i. 2, 41.)[1]

2 And the soldiers platted a crown of thorns, and put it on His head, and (they put on Him a purple robe).[2]

(Alf. They clothed Him with a purple robe.)

---

[1] Smith's Classical Dict., Article "Flagrum."

[2] A crown of thorns (στέφανον ἐξ ἀκανθῶν.)—After showing that διάδημα is the word always used for a kingly or imperial crown, and στέφανος for a conqueror's, Archbishop Trench goes on to say: "The only occasion on which στέφανος might seem to be used of a kingly crown is Matt. xxvii. 29, with its parallels in the other Gospels, where the wearing of a crown of thorns (στέφανος ἀκάνθινος) and placing it on the Saviour's head, is evidently a part of that blasphemous caricature of royalty which the Roman soldiers would fain compel him to enact. But woven of such materials as it was, probably of the juncus marinus, or of the lycium spinosum, it is evident that διάδημα could not be applied to it: and the word, therefore, which was fittest in respect of the material whereof it was composed, takes place of that which

3 [(And said)], Hail, King of the Jews! and they smote Him with their hands.

[S. V. And came to Him and said.]
(Alf. And they kept coming unto Him and saying.)

The Sinaitic and Vatican MSS. say that the soldiers came unto Him and said, which, as a repeated act, has been well translated, kept coming unto Him and saying. They repeated their mock homage unto Him from time to time.

Besides the purple robe and the crown of thorns St. Matthew says they added another emblem of mock royalty. They put a reed into his right hand, and bowed the knee before Him, and mocked Him, saying, Hail, King of the Jews! And they spit upon Him, and took the reed, and smote Him on the head. (xxvii. 29, 30.)

4 [(Pilate therefore went forth] again), and saith unto them, Behold I bring Him forth to you, that ye may know that I find no fault [in Him.]

[S. Pilate went forth: V. A. And Pilate went forth: S. Omits, In Him.]
(Alf. And Pilate went forth again.)

5 (Then came Jesus forth), wearing the crown of thorns, and the purple robe. (And Pilate saith) unto them, Behold the Man!

(Alf. Jesus, therefore, came forth—and he saith.)

Pilate still continues his efforts, to engage the sympathies of the Jews in behalf of Jesus, and to excite their pity for Him. He brings Him forth to them pale and mangled, and reduced as He was by the

---

would have been the fittest in respect of the purpose for which it was intended."—Archbishop Trench on *Synonyms of New Testament*, p. 75.

A purple robe (ἱμάτιον πορφυροῦν.)— "The purple robe with which our Lord was arrayed in scorn by the mockers in Pilate's judgment-hall is called by St. Matthew (xxvii. 28, 31) χλαμύς, and we should not fail to observe the fitness of the word. Χλαμύς so constantly signifies a garment of dignity and office, that χλαμύδα περιτιθέναι was a proverbial phrase for assuming a magistracy. This might be a *civil* magistracy; but χλαμύς, like 'paludamentum' (which, and not 'sagum,' is its nearest Latin equivalent), far more commonly expresses the robe with which military officers, captains, commanders, or

imperators, would be clothed (2 Macc. xii. 35): and the employment of χλαμύς in the record of the Passion leaves little doubt that these profane mockers obtained, as it would have been so easy for them in the prætorium to obtain, the cast-off cloke of some high Roman officer, and with this arrayed the sacred Person of the Lord. We recognise a certain confirmation of this supposition in the epithet κόκκινος which St. Matthew gives it. It was 'scarlet,' the colour worn by Roman officers of rank. That the other Evangelists describe it as 'purple' (Mark. xv. 17; John xix. 2) does not affect this statement; for the purple of antiquity was a colour almost or altogether indefinite."—Archbishop Trench on *Synonyms of New Testament*, p. 177.

scourging, and still clothed in the purple robe and with the crown of thorns, and said unto them, Behold the Man! See what mockery, what degradation He has undergone! See to what a condition of weakness and suffering He has been reduced!

6 When the Chief Priests therefore (and officers) saw Him, they cried out, [saying,] [Crucify Him, crucify Him]: [Pilate] saith unto them (Take ye Him), and crucify Him: for I find no fault in Him.[1]

[S. Omits, Saying: S. A. Crucify, crucify Him: S. And Pilate.]
(Alf. And the officers—Take Him yourselves.)

Instead of being melted to pity, by Pilate's appeal to them to behold the condition to which Jesus had already been reduced by the punishment which he had inflicted on Him, instead of being filled with shame and remorse, the Jews clamour more earnestly than ever for His death, and the more Pilate asserted the innocence of Jesus the more they cry out for His death, and for His death by the most ignominious and the most cruel of all means. Crucifixion was not one of their national modes of inflicting death. They clamoured for it on this occasion, simply because it contained a higher degree of refinement in cruelty and in indignity than any mode of death which they, as a nation, were accustomed to use. In punishing Jesus by crucifixion on the plea that He was guilty of blasphemy, even of the highest form of blasphemy, they were themselves breaking the very law, which they pretended was their warrant for putting Him to death. God had appointed death as the punishment of blasphemy; but it was death by stoning, not by crucifixion. (Levit. xxiv. 16.)

Pilate's offer to the Jews, "Take Him yourselves and crucify Him," was the effect, partly of the message which his wife sent unto Him, "Have thou nothing to do with that Just Man" (Matt. xxvii. 19), and partly of his own conviction of His innocence. So certain was he of this, that he challenged the Jews to say what evil He had done. (Matt. xxvii. 3.) St. John relates that Pilate said three different times "I find no fault in Him." And St. Matthew says that he called Him "a Just Man." (xxvii. 24.)

---

[1] When the chief priests therefore and officers (οἱ ἀρχιερεῖς καὶ οἱ ὑπηρέται.)— "The high priests and the attendants (belonging to them)—the high priests and their attendants."—Winer's *Grammar of New Testament*, p. 140.

"Crucifixion was in use among the Egyptians (Gen. xl. 19), the Carthaginians, the Persians (Esth. vii. 10), the Assyrians, Scythians, Indians, Germans, and from the earliest times among the Greeks and Romans. Whether this mode of execution was known to the ancient Jews is a matter of dispute. Probably the Jews borrowed it from the Romans. It was unanimously considered the most horrible form of death. Among the Romans also the degradation was a part of the infliction, and the punishment if applied to freemen was only used in the case of the vilest criminals."—Smith's *Bible Dictionary.*

7 The Jews answered [him], We have a law, [(and by our law)] He ought to die, because He made Himself the Son of God.

[S. Omits, him : S. V. And by the law.]
(Alf. And by the law.)

8 When Pilate, therefore, heard (that saying) he was the more afraid:
(Alf. This saying.)

9 And went ([again] into the judgment hall), and saith unto Jesus, Whence art thou? But Jesus gave him no answer.

[S. Omits, Again.]
(Alf. Into the palace again.)

From his examination of Jesus Pilate would doubtless have been convinced already that He was no ordinary Man. His wife's message would have increased that conviction; and when the Jews accuse Him of saying that He is the Son of God, Pilate began to have] a fear, that He might take vengeance on him for abusing his office of Judge, and delivering Him up to death at the very time that he declared he had found no fault in Him, and that He was a Just Man. To Pilate, who was a heathen, the expression "the Son of God" would convey a very different meaning from that which it conveyed to the Jews. They meant by it the Son of the One living and true God, who made heaven and earth. He meant by it the son of Jupiter, or the son of Hercules, or of any other who ranked amongst the heathen as supernatural beings, who had power to inflict punishment on man for their supposed wrongs.
If Jesus was such a being, Pilate was conscious that he had given Him just ground for offence. But to his question, "Whence art thou?" Jesus returned him no answer.

When the false witnesses perverted His sayings and accused Him before Caiaphas, Jesus answered nothing. (Matt. xxvi. 62, &c.) When the chief priests and elders accused Him before Pilate, He answered nothing. (Matt. xxvii. 12.) Here again He answered nothing, when Pilate, in reference to the charge of the Jews, that He made Himself "the Son of God," said unto Him, Whence art Thou? that is not, from what country art Thou, but what is Thy origin? from which of the gods art Thou sprung? In each of these cases the silence of Jesus shows the want of truth in the accusation, and in the question, at least, as Pilate understood it.

10 ([Then] saith Pilate) unto Him, Speakest Thou not

unto me? knowest Thou not [(that I have power to crucify Thee, and have power to release Thee)]?

[S. A. Omits, Then: S. V. A. That I have power to release Thee, and have power to crucify Thee.]
(Alf. Pilate, therefore, saith—that I have power to release Thee, and have power to crucify Thee.)

11 Jesus [answered] [Thou couldest have] no power at all against Me, except it were given Thee from above: (therefore) he that delivered Me unto thee hath the greater sin.[1]

[S. V. Answered him: S. A. Thou hast no power.]
(Alf. Thou wouldest have—for this cause.)

Pilate would have no power over Jesus unless it were specially given him from above—that is, by the Father, both because Jesus was innocent, and therefore could not lawfully be condemned to death by Pilate, and also because Jesus had the power to deliver Himself. But the Godhead willed that He should die, and by His Death purchase the Redemption of mankind. For this purpose, in order to bring this about, He permitted Pilate to acquiesce in the unjust accusation of the Jews, and perform their will. But in doing this Pilate exercised a power to which he had no lawful right, and which he would not have exercised, had it not been for the urgency of the Jews. Those, therefore, who forced Pilate, as it were, to adopt this course, were guilty of a greater sin than he was in yielding to their wishes.

The sin of the Jews was that of rejecting the Son of God. Pilate's sin in this matter was condemning an innocent man to death, from motives of state policy, from a desire to keep fair with the Jews, who were his subjects. The office of the chief Priests, Scribes, and Elders was to examine the claims of Jesus to be the Son of God. With the clearest evidence to prove His claim, they had rejected Him and had delivered Him up to death as a malefactor, and by acting on Pilate's fears they compelled him, even against his own judgment, to execute their decree.

12 (And from thenceforth) Pilate sought to release Him: [but the Jews cried out, saying], If thou let this Man go, thou art not Cæsar's friend: (whosoever maketh himself a king) speaketh against Cæsar.

[S. But the Jews said.]
(Alf. Upon this—every one that maketh himself a king.)

---

[1] Thou couldst have no power, &c. —"Pluperfect in the conditional clause, and Imperfect in the principal: οὐκ εἶχες ἐξουσίαν οὐδεμίαν κατ' ἐμοῦ, εἰ μὴ ἦν σοι δεδομένον ἄνωθεν, thou couldest not have had ... if it had not been given to thee." —Winer's *Grammar of New Testament*, p. 321.

Anxious as he was to defend Jesus, because he knew Him to be innocent, fearful as he was of future vengeance from Him as evidently being some supernatural Person, Pilate was still more fearful of the charge of not being well affected to the reigning Emperor Tiberias Cæsar. He therefore relinquished his desire to defend the innocent in his fear to offend the suspicious ; lest through the accusations of the Jews he should incur the displeasure of Cæsar, who was intolerant of all lukewarm devotion to his cause and person.

13 When Pilate therefore heard [(that saying)], he brought Jesus forth, and sat down (in) the judgment seat in (a place that is called) the Pavement, [but] (in the Hebrew), Gabbatha.[1]

[S. V. A. These sayings : S. A. Omit, but.]
(Alf. These words—upon—a place called—in Hebrew.)

Harassed by these conflicting feelings and by the shouts which he had just heard, Pilate no longer offered any resistance to the wishes of the people, but brought Jesus out from the Palace, and sat down himself on the bema or customary seat of justice. This seat was placed on a part that was paved with tiles of divers patterns, and raised above the surrounding ground, in order that when he sat there to administer justice, he might be the better seen and heard by the people around him. Its Hebrew name expresses, that the place on which the bema was set was elevated above the rest, and its Greek name that it was paved with stones or tiles. It is said that Julius Cæsar always carried with him both the bema and also tiles on which to place the bema.

14 (And it was the preparation of the Passover),[2] [and]

---

[1] The Pavement, but in the Hebrew, Gabbatha (Λιθόστρωτον, Ἑβραϊστὶ δὲ Γαββαθᾶ).—" The specification of the place where Pilate gave judgment as the (tesselated) ' Pavement,' called in the Hebrew (from its being upon the rising ground) ' Gabbatha,' (and therefore, we may add, from its having a Hebrew name, a fixed spot, and not the portable mosaic work which the Roman generals sometimes carried about with them,) has been urged in favour of the view that Pilate's residence was not in Herod's palace, but in the tower of Antonia : because Josephus tells us that the whole of the temple hill, on part of which the tower of Antonia stood, was covered with this tesselated pavement. There seems, however, to be direct evidence for the statement that the procurators of Judæa occupied the palace of Herod when in Jerusalem : and it would hardly be likely that, supposing the whole of the hill to be covered with mosaic, a particular portion of it should be singled out to bear the name. The space in front of Herod's palace may have been laid down with mosaic : or it is possible, as Dr. Wieseler supposes, that there may have been a permanent and not portable *suggestum* (=' Gabbatha ') so decorated. In any case we cannot but notice the accuracy of St. John's description."—Sanday's *Historical Character of the Fourth Gospel*, p. 249.

[2] The preparation — the preparation of the Passover—the preparation, that is, the day before the Sabbath. " You will ask, whether any day going before the Sabbath was called Parasceve, the preparation. Among the Hebrews indeed it is commonly

(about the sixth hour): and he saith unto the Jews, Behold your King!

[S. V. A. Omit, and.]
(Alf. Now it was the preparation of the Passover. It was about the sixth hour, when.)

Two interpretations have been given to this expression, the preparation of the Passover. Some suppose that it means the preparation or day for making ready for the celebration of the Passover. The Paschal lamb they were to kill on the same evening on which they were to eat it, that is on the fourteenth day. (Exod. xii.) Others think that it means the day for making preparation for the Sabbath, for preparing the food which they should require on the next day, which would be the Sabbath in the Passover week. This appears to be much the more probable opinion.

The first day of unleavened bread would be from Thursday evening at sunset to Friday evening. The Sabbath, which fell within the week of the Passover would be from Friday evening to Saturday evening. This Sabbath was more solemn than the other Sabbaths, it was a "high day," because it occurred in the Passover week. Every Sabbath had its day of preparation, or making ready the necessary food, but especially this the most solemn Sabbath during the whole year. The expression the preparation, or day of preparation is used by all the four Evangelists, and from a comparison of the several places in which it occurs, little doubt will be left on the mind, that the only day of preparation mentioned in the Gospels is the preparation for the Sabbath, that is, the day before the Sabbath. This year it would be the first day of unleavened bread, from Thursday evening to Friday evening.

The only objections to this are that it is called by St. John the preparation of the Passover, and that the first day of unleavened bread is a holy convocation to the Lord. But the work forbidden on this day is servile work, not preparation of food. (Levit. xxiii. 7; Exod. xii. 16.)

---

said The eve of the Sabbath. But whence is it called the preparation? Either that they prepared themselves for the Sabbath, or rather, that they prepared provisions to be eaten on the Sabbath."

After many quotations from Maimonides and other Jewish writers, Lightfoot concludes: "The preparation, or the preparation of the Passover, denotes not either the preparation of the Paschal Lamb, nor the preparation of the people to eat the Lamb; but the preparation of meats to to be eaten in the Passover week. Nor in this place, if it be applied to the Sabbath, doth it denote any other thing than the preparation of food for the Sabbath now approaching. So that that day, wherein Christ was crucified, was a double preparation in the double sense alleged, namely, the whole day, but especially from the third hour, was the preparation of the Passover, or of the whole week following; and the evening of the day was the preparation of the Sabbath following on the morrow."—Lightfoot, ii. 358.

"παρασκευὴ τοῦ πάσχα does not mean the day of preparation for the Passover, but the preparation day (Friday) of the Passover week."—Winer's *Grammar of New Testament*, p. 202.

St. Matthew xxvii.	St. Mark xv.	St. Luke xxiii.	St. John xix.
			14 And it was the preparation of the Passover (παρασκευὴ τοῦ πάσχα) and about the sixth hour: and He saith unto the Jews, Behold your King!
			31 The Jews therefore, because it was the the preparation (παρασκευὴ), that the bodies should not remain upon the Cross on the Sabbath-day, for that Sabbath-day was an high day, besought Pilate, &c.
		53 And he took It down, and wrapped It in linen, and laid It in a sepulchre, that was hewn in stone, wherein never man before was laid.	42 There
	42 And now, when the even was come, because it was the preparation, that is, (παρασκευὴ ὅ ἐστι) the day before the Sabbath (προσάββατον).	54 And that day was the preparation (καὶ ἡμερα ἦν παρασ- κευὴ) and the Sabbath drew on (καὶ σάββατον ἐπέ- φωσκε).	laid they Jesus therefore because of (διὰ) the Jews' preparation day: (τὴν παρασκευήν τῶν Ἰουδαίων)
62 Now the next day that followed the day of the preparation (μετὰ τὴν παρασκευὴν) the chief priests and the scribes came together unto Pilate, &c.			for the sepulchre was nigh at hand.

From an inspection of these various passages it will be seen that St. John uses the expression the preparation or the preparation day, three different times, always meaning by it the same day. Once he calls it "the preparation of the Passover," which taken by itself might mean the preparation for the Passover, the day before the first day of unleavened bread. Twice he makes use of it in such close connection with the Sabbath, that it must mean the day of preparation for the Sabbath, that is, the day before the Sabbath. St. Matthew, St. Mark, and St. Luke each uses the phrase the preparation, or the day of preparation, once, and means by it the preparation for the Sabbath. The clear inference from this is, that whichever of these three expressions the Evangelists use "the preparation," "the day of preparation," or "the preparation of the Passover," they mean the preparation for the Sabbath which fell in the Passover week.

A comparison of all the passages in which the Crucifixion is related, shows in what the Evangelists agree, and in what they differ from each other.

St. Matthew xxvii.	St. Mark xv.	St. Luke xxiii.	St. John xix.
	25 And it was the third hour, (ὥρα τρίτη)		14 And it was the preparation of the Passover, and about the sixth hour: (ὥρα δὲ ὡσεὶ ἕκτη) and He saith unto the Jews, Behold your King . . . . 16 Then delivered he Him therefore unto them to be crucified.
	and they crucified Him.		
45 Now from the sixth hour there was darkness over all the land (ἐπὶ πᾶσαν τὴν γῆν) unto the ninth hour (ἕως ὥρας ἐνάτης).	33 And when the sixth hour was come, there was darkness over the whole land (ἐφ' ὅλην τὴν γῆν) until the ninth hour (ἕως ὥρας ἐνάτης).	44 And it was about the sixth hour, and there was a darkness over all the earth (ἐφ ὅλην τὴν γῆν) until the ninth hour (ἕως ὥρας ἐνάτης) 45 And the sun was darkened.	

All the four Evangelists agree as to the day on which the Crucifixion took place. It was the preparation—the day of preparation—the preparation of the Passover—the Jews' preparation day. Three of the Evangelists, St. Matthew, St. Mark, and St. Luke, state that there was darkness over the land from the sixth hour to the ninth hour. The only apparent discrepancy in the account of the Crucifixion is that given by St. Mark and St. John. St. Mark says, "It was the third hour and they crucified Him," while St. John says it was "about the sixth hour; and he (Pilate) saith unto the Jews, Behold your King!" and then delivered Him up to be crucified. The difficulty of reconciling these two statements was recognised in very early times.

Cornelius à Lapide enumerates seven different ways, in which it had been attempted before his time to reconcile the accounts of St. Mark and St. John. One method was, as it is still, to suppose that there is an error in one of the MSS. either in that of St. Mark or of St. John. But neither the Sinaitic, Vatican, nor Alexandrian MS. lends any assistance towards a solution of the difficulty by a difference of reading here.

The only solution proposed in modern times, which was unknown to the Fathers and Commentators before the Reformation, is, that St. John is here using a different notation from that used by the rest of the Evangelists, and that he reckons the hours from mid-day or midnight like ourselves. This is said to have been an Asiatic mode of computing time, and is the interpretation followed by Bishop Wordsworth in his Greek Testament, but rejected by Dean Alford.

St. Matthew, St. Mark, and St. Luke, as all admit, reckon the time by the method in common use among the Romans, which begins to count the hours from sunrise, or from about six o'clock in the morning. Adopting these two different notations of time, Pilate, as stated by St. John, would deliver Jesus up to the Jews "about" six o'clock in the morning. The interval between six and nine would be consumed by the mockery of the soldiers, by the changing of His robe, and leading Him to Calvary, &c.; at nine o'clock, the third hour of St. Mark, He would be crucified; from twelve o'clock to three, that is from the sixth hour to the ninth hour, as related by St. Matthew, St. Mark, and St. Luke, darkness would prevail over the earth.

Even though this method were a perfect solution of the difficulties, and reconciled all the apparent discrepancies, there would still be one objection to it, which would appear great to all, and to many insuperable. St. John nowhere in any part of his writings gives the slightest intimation, that he is using a notation different from that which the other Evangelists use. According to the received opinion St. John knew the narrative which the others had written, what they had said, and what they had left unsaid, and he wrote to supply what was lacking in their accounts, and especially to give a fuller relation of our Saviour's discourses. Is it then probable that he would introduce into the relation of the same events, a mode of reckoning the same hours totally different from theirs, and not give some intimation of this?

Another interpretation, which has the advantage of being old, is, that St. John is here using the same mode of reckoning the time which the other Evangelists use, but that St. Mark and St. John are not stating the time, at which the Crucifixion took place, from the same point of view.

St. John does not say, it was the sixth hour when Pilate brought Jesus forth and delivered Him up to the Jews to be crucified, but *about* the sixth hour. This general statement of time may therefore be received with the limitations, which the other Evangelists introduce into the narrative. St. Matthew and St. Mark say that from the sixth hour there was darkness over all the land until the ninth hour, and St. Luke from about the sixth hour. St. John does not refer to the darkness. From his use of the term (ὡσεί) *about*, it is plain that he is not intending an exact definition of the time in which these events took place. All that he may have meant to say, and all that his words really imply, is that Jesus was delivered up to the Jews to be crucified about the sixth hour, that is, before the darkness came over the earth.

St. Mark's language may fairly be interpreted more strictly, because he does not himself, by the use of the word (ὡσεί) about, introduce any latitude into his statement of the time. The Crucifixion might therefore *begin* at the third hour. But in the strict and literal use of words, Jesus would not be crucified either at the third or sixth hour. For the Crucifixion was a work of considerable time, probably of several hours. A part of it might be at the third hour, or a part of it at the sixth hour, but the whole Crucifixion would extend over considerably more time than the striking of a clock. The Crucifixion was not one act but a series of acts. Thus the period from nine o'clock to twelve would probably not be at all too long for the whole series of injustice, mockeries, and cruelties which we gather up into the one word "The Crucifixion." It may be therefore that St. Mark is describing the Crucifixion at its commencement, that it began at the third hour or nine o'clock in the morning, and that St. John is relating its completion, that all this was done somewhere about the sixth hour or twelve o'clock, that is, before the darkness came on.

This then is the state of the case. All the four Evangelists mention the day in which the Crucifixion took place, and there is no variation except in the use of four different designations of the day, but all referring to one and the same day. Three of them state the hour when the darkness came over the earth, and the length of time during which it lasted, and they agree together perfectly. The only point, we must not say, in which the Evangelists do not agree, nor in which we cannot satisfactorily account for their apparent divergence from each other, but in which, perhaps, we may fail to prove to unbelieving critics that they are in perfect accord, is, as to the hour of the Crucifixion mentioned by St. Mark and St. John. But there is nothing whatever in this apparent disagreement to cause distress or doubt to the most sensitive soul, who believes in the truth of the Christian Revelation. The best way, perhaps, is to admit that we have not now sufficient data, to enable us to dovetail together two relations of the Crucifixion, which happened eighteen hundred years ago, so perfectly as to account for one hour or so in the three, and, therefore, that we are unable to convince an unwilling mind, that St. Mark and St. John are in perfect agreement.

15 [(But they cried out)], Away with Him, away with Him, crucify Him. Pilate saith unto them, Shall I crucify your King ? The chief priests answered, We have no king but Cæsar.

[S. But they said: V. Therefore they cried out.]
(Alf. They cried out therefore.)

Pilate probably uttered these words to annoy the chief priests. He felt conscious that, by their appeal to his fears, they had beaten him in his attempt to release Jesus. He had made several efforts, and had only at last yielded to their threat of calling him disloyal, disloyal to Cæsar. This had still left in his mind a degree of bitterness towards the chief priests, which he shows in several ways.

16 Then delivered he Him therefore unto them to be crucified. And they took Jesus, and led Him away.

17 [And He bearing His Cross] went forth (into a place) called the place of a skull, which is called (in the Hebrew) Golgotha.[1]

[S.V. And He bearing the Cross by Himself.]
(Alf. Unto the place—in Hebrew.)

The other three Evangelists relate that, as they came out, they found a man of Cyrene, Simon by name, whom they compelled to bear the Cross after Jesus. St. John omits this incident, and only relates that Jesus left the city carrying His own Cross. The probability is, that Jesus was treated in all respects like a criminal, and that at first He carried His own Cross, and that being exhausted by the weight of the Cross, and by the treatment which He had received, His strength failed Him, and that then they laid hold of a chance passer-by to carry it for Him. This was done not with the object of relieving Jesus, but that they might the more speedily arrive at the place of Crucifixion.

The strength of human nature, even of His Human nature, unbroken as it was by sinful indulgence, could no longer sustain the weight of suffering, which Jesus had endured in Soul and Body since the preceding evening. When he had left the Upper Room with His disciples, He crossed over the brook Cedron to the Garden of Gethsemane. Here followed His prayer and Agony. After a time, He was seized by the soldiers and conducted to the house of Annas, from thence to that of Caiphas, from thence to Pilate, from thence to Herod, and from Him back again to Pilate. In each of these places, He had endured from the soldiers and servants every species of indignity and suffering, that malice and cruelty could devise. In order to excite the compassion of the Jews, and so to procure His release, Pilate scourges Him, and then exhibits Him to the people as one who had suffered all that human nature could endure short of taking His life. In one form of suffering or another the whole night had been passed, and now in the morning, probably between nine and twelve, He is led out of the city towards Calvary, bearing His own Cross.

Some have supposed that Simon of Cyrene, on the north coast of

---

[1] Golgotha.—"The ground on this side of the north road being rough, a place of gardens and graves, and for that reason shunned by all builders except lepers, beggars, and the poorest class of Jews. The gate opening from the city, into this quarter was called Genath, the garden gate. Almond trees grew in such profusion that the pool of Hezekiah, lying close by, had come to be known as the Almond Pool. On Gareb outside the garden gate, a monument had been erected to the high priest John. A few paces from this structure, Joseph of Arimathea, a noble Jew, a member of the Sanhedrin, had bought a bit of garden, with a wall of uncovered rock, in which he had hewn for himself a sepulchral vault. Outside Joseph's garden stood a mound called Golgotha, Skull Place, the Tyburn of Jerusalem, on which thieves, assassins, pirates, heretics, traitors, teachers of falsehood, men the most odious in Jewish eyes, were put to a shameful and cruel death, being nailed by the hands and feet to a wooden cross, and left in the burning sun to die."—Dixon's *Holy Land*, ii. 31.

Africa, must have been either a slave or a person of some low degree, otherwise they would not have impressed him into their service for an office so ignoble, as to carry the Cross for Jesus, condemned as a criminal to the most ignominious death they knew. St. Mark (xv. 21) speaks of his sons as men who were well known to those, for whom he wrote his Gospel, in fact, as so well known that he indicates who Simon was, by speaking of him as the father of Alexander and Rufus. An explanation of this is to be found in the tradition which represents Simon and his family, as soon after this converted to the Christian Faith. He, who in a literal sense, had followed Jesus and borne His Cross, afterwards in another and a higher sense, follows Him and bears His Cross after Him. When St. Paul, in his Epistle to the Romans, (xvi. 13) says, "Salute Rufus chosen in the Lord, and his mother and mine," it has generally been supposed that this was the son of Simon of Cyrene, and the Rufus mentioned by St. Mark. Some have also supposed that this Simon is the same Simon that was called Niger in the Acts (xiii. 1) : and with whom is associated a fellow-countryman, Lucius of Cyrene. Simon and Simeon are only two forms of the same name. Simon Peter was also called Simeon (Acts xv. 14).

Commentators have given various explanations of the origin of the name of Calvary, or place of a skull, or the place called a skull (Calvaria). (Luke xxiii. 33.) Some have supposed that it might be from the conical shape of the place not unlike a skull or smooth mound; but this is scarcely borne out by the fact. Others have thought that the place had its name from an old tradition, that here the skull of Adam was buried. The most probable account of the origin of this name is that this was the place of execution for common criminals, just as Tyburn once was in London. The very name and character of the place, in which the Saviour of mankind was crucified, was selected with the view of adding another mark of infamy to His death.

St. Luke (xxiii. 27), alone of the Evangelists relates that as He went to Calvary a great company of people and of women followed, which also bewailed and lamented Him, and that He turned and bade them weep not for Him, but for themselves and their children, and that He then foretold the miseries which should shortly befall their country. If such suffering was inflicted on Him "the green tree," ever affording shade and comfort and blessing to all, ever bringing forth the fruits of righteousness, what would be done in the case of the Jews, "the dry tree," never yielding fruit, or promise of fruit, never affording shelter or comfort to the distressed, good for nothing but to be burned?

That Calvary was nigh to the city but not within it is clear. Such a place in the city would of itself have been a great defilement to it. Jesus "went forth" out from the city to it. "Jesus suffered without the gate." (Heb. xiii. 12.) The man who was stoned for breaking the Sabbath was by the express command of God stoned "without the camp." (Numb. xv. 35.)

18 Where they crucified Him and (two other) with Him, on either side one, and Jesus in the midst.

(Alf. Two others.)

St. Matthew xxvii.	St. Mark xv.	St. Luke xxiii.	St. John xix.
			17 And He bearing His Cross went forth
33 And when they were come unto a place called Golgotha, that is, to say, a place of a skull,	22 And they bring Him unto the place Golgotha, which is, being interpreted, The place of a skull.	33 And when they were come to the place, which is called Calvary,	into a place called the place of a skull, which is called in the Hebrew Golgotha:
8 They gave Him vinegar to drink mingled with gall: and when He had tasted thereof, He would not drink.	23 And they gave Him to drink wine mingled with myrrh: but He received it not.		
		there they crucified Him, and the malefactors, one on the right hand, and the other on the left.	18 where they crucified Him, and two other with Him, on either side one, and Jesus in the midst.

Archbishop Trench has shown that the term *thieves* is a very unfortunate translation of the Greek word λῇσται which is applied to these two men by St. Matt. (xxvii. 38), St. Mark (xv. 27), and that they probably belonged to the robber-band which was led by Barabbas. We know from contemporary history, that many of the bands of Palestine had their origin in fair resistance to aggression, either on their own rights or on those of their country, and though these men might degenerate afterwards in their aim and habits from their first beginning, there would still be room left in their hearts for the exercise of many noble qualities, which would at once have been extinguished by a daily course of petty thieving. In one of these robbers there needed but the presence of the Righteous to draw from him a corresponding desire.

The ground on which the Jews clamoured for the death of Jesus was that He had spoken blasphemy; but their object in crucifying Him along with these two robbers, was to mislead the people and to identify Him with them, to represent Him to the spectators as guilty of similar crimes with theirs, and in short as one of their very band.

19 (And) Pilate wrote a title, and put it on the Cross. (And the writing was), Jesus of Nazareth, the King of the Jews.

(Alf. Moreover—And there was written.)

20 This title then read many of the Jews: (for) the place where Jesus was crucified was nigh to the city: and it was written [in Hebrew, and Greek, and Latin].
[S. V. In Hebrew and Latin and Greek.]
(Alf. Because—in Hebrew, and in Greek, and in Latin.)

21 (Then) said the chief priests of the Jews to Pilate, Write not, The King of the Jews: but that He said, I am (King) of the Jews.
(Alf. Therefore—the King.)

22 Pilate answered, What I have written I have written.

The title was written in three languages for the convenience of the large mixed population, that would then be present in Jerusalem for the celebration of the Passover. It was written in Hebrew, but not the Hebrew in which the Old Testament was written. That had not been in use since their seventy years' captivity in Babylon, but in the Aramaic or the Hebrew, which they spoke when they returned from the Captivity, and which was still used by the common people of Palestine. In Greek, for those Jews who, either from their residence at Alexandria, or from their intercourse with foreigners, had learned and used the Greek language, and read the Septuagint. In Latin, for the Romans and those connected with the government of Cæsar. The Latin language was in general use wherever the Roman conquests extended.

The chief Priests object to the title which Pilate had written. He had unconsciously recorded his testimony that Jesus was the King of the Jews, not that He only claimed, or pretended to be, their King. They at once see the difference between this, and remonstrate with Pilate, and wished it to be prominently stated in the title that Jesus pretended to be the King of the Jews, not that He was the King of the Jews. This Pilate resisted, and gave as his reason that what he had written he had written correctly, and did not intend to alter.

All the four Evangelists differ in their report of what this sentence was. The substance of it is the same in all of them; but the wording of it is different in all.

The following is the title, as given by each of the four Evangelists:—

St. Matthew xxvii. 87.	St. Mark xv. 26.	St. Luke xxiii. 38.	St. John xix. 19.
This is		This is	
Jesus			Jesus of Nazareth,
The King of the Jews.	The King of the Jews.	The King of the Jews. [S. V. The King of the Jews is This.]	The King of the Jews.

23 (Then the soldiers), [when they had crucified Jesus], took his garments and made four parts, to every soldier a part: [and also His coat]: now the coat was without seam, (woven) from the top throughout.

[S. Which had crucified Jesus: S. Omits, and also his coat.]
(Margin, Wrought.)
(Alf. The soldiers therefore.)

24 They said therefore (among themselves), Let us not rend it, but cast lots for it, whose it shall be: that the Scripture might be fulfilled [which saith], They parted (My raiment (τὰ ἱμάτια)) among them, and for My vesture (τὸν ἱματισμόν) they did cast lots. These things, therefore, the soldiers did.[1]

[S. V. Omit, Which saith.]
(Alf. One to another—My garments.)

St. Matthew xxvii.	St. Mark xv.	St. Luke xxiii.	St. John xix.
35 And they crucified Him, and parted His garments (τὰ ἱμάτια),	24 And when they had crucified Him, they parted His garments (τὰ ἱμάτια),	34 And they parted His raiment (τὰ ἱμάτια),	23 Then the soldiers, when they had crucified Jesus, took His garments (τὰ ἱμάτια), and made four parts, to every soldier a part: and also His coat (τὸν χιτῶνα): now the coat was without seam, woven from the top throughout.
casting lots:	casting lots upon them, what every man should take.	and cast lots.	24 They said therefore among themselves, Let us not rend it, but cast lots for it, whose it shall be: that the scripture might be fulfilled, which saith,
that it might be fulfilled which was spoken by the prophet, They parted My garments among them, and upon My vesture did they cast lots.			They parted My raiment (τὰ ἱμάτια) among them, and for My vesture (τὸν ἱματισμόν) they did cast lots. These things therefore the soldiers did.

[1] "My vesture. Ἱματισμός, a word of comparatively late introduction into the Greek language, is seldom, if ever, used, except of garments more or less splendid, stately, costly. It is the 'vesture'—this word expressing it well (cf. Gen. xli. 42; Ps. cii. 26; Rev. xix. 13, English Version)—of kings, thus of Solomon in all his glory (1 Kings, x. v.; is associated with gold and silver as part of a precious spoil (Exod. iii. 22; xii. 35): is found linked with such epithets as ἔνδοξος (Luke vii. 25), ποικίλος (Ezek. xvi.

We gather from St. Luke (xxiii. 34) that it was before they parted His garments that Jesus cried, "Father, forgive them, for they know not what they do." There were four soldiers and a centurion, and they divided His outer garments (ἱμάτια) into four parts, and cast lots for his inner close-fitting vesture (χιτών, or ἱματισμός). It has been thought, and with great probability, that this vesture was the work of the Blessed Virgin herself. As has been beautifully observed, it had that of cost and beauty about it which made even the rude soldiers unwilling to rend, and so to destroy it. The prophecy which all this fulfilled, and which the Evangelist transcribes, is a verbatim quotation from Ps. xxii. 18, as rendered by the Septuagint.

25 Now there stood by the Cross of Jesus His Mother, and His Mother's sister (Mary, the wife of Cleophas,) and Mary Magdalene.[1]

(Margin. Cleopas.)
(Alf. Mary, the [wife] of Cleopas.)

St. Luke merely states in general that the women that followed Him from Galilee, stood afar off, beholding these things (xxii. 49), without giving the names of any. The other three Evangelists mention several by name :—

St. Matthew xxvii. 56.	St. Mark xv. 40.	St. John xix. 25.
Mary Magdalene and Mary the mother of James and Joses, and the mother of Zebedee's children.	Mary Magdalene and Mary the mother of James the less and of Joses, and Salome.	His Mother, and His Mother's sister, Mary the wife of Cleophas, and Mary Magdalene.

If we compare St. Matthew and St. Mark together, without regard to the various reading afforded by the Sinaitic MS. on this verse of St. Matthew, as it is not in its original perfect state, it will appear that Salome was Zebedee's wife.

Anciently it was thought that Mary, the wife of Cleophas, was His mother's sister," mentioned by St. John. Of late years this has

---

18), διάχρυσος (Ps. xliv 10), πολυτηλής (1 Tim. ii. 9): is applied to our Lord's χιτών (Matt. xxvii 35 ; John xix. 24) which was ἄρραφος, and had that of cost and beauty about it which made even the rude soldiers unwilling to rend, and so to destroy it." — Archbishop Trench on *Synonyms of New Testament*, p. 176.

[1] **Mary the wife of Cleophas or Clopas**

(Μαρία ἡ τοῦ Κλωπᾶ).—"The precise meaning is, among the women called Mary, the (particular one) of Clopas—the wife of Clopas. The Article is not used where the annexed Genitive is not intended to convey any precise distinction, as, Luke vi. 16, Ἰούδαν Ἰακώβου; Acts i. 13, Ἰάκωβος Ἀλφαίου."—Winer's *Grammar of New Testament*, p. 148.

been questioned, and with some show of reason. St. Matthew and St. Mark both name three women who are present, without reckoning the Blessed Virgin. If then, in agreement with the other two Evangelists St. John intends to mention three women as present besides the Virgin Mary, he must mean two distinct women by "His Mother's sister" and "Mary, the wife of Cleophas." This would leave Mary, the wife of Cleophas, as the mother of James and Joses, and Salome, the wife of Zebedee, as the sister of the Blessed Virgin. St. John does not mention Salome by name, and it is thought that he may have extended the same habit of reticence to his mother, which he uses with respect to himself. For Salome being the wife of Zebedee would be the mother of St. John. If Zebedee's wife was the sister of the Blessed Virgin, it may have been from her near relationship to His Mother that she requested for her two sons that they might sit, the one on His right hand, and the other on His left in His kingdom. (Matt. xx. 20.)

26 [(When Jesus therefore saw] His Mother and the disciple standing by, whom He loved, He saith) unto His Mother, Woman, behold thy son!

[S. Now, when Jesus saw.]
(Alf. Jesus, therefore, seeing His Mother, &c.—saith.)

27 (Then saith He) to the disciple, Behold thy mother! And from that hour (that disciple) took her unto his own home.

(Alf. And then saith He—the disciple.)

Among the crowd assembled to witness the Crucifixion of Jesus, the Virgin Mary was probably the only one, who at all realized anything like the real nature of the Mystery, that was being transacted. She had long been used to keep the various parts of the Mystery of Redemption, and ponder them in her heart, as they gradually unfolded themselves before her. She above all women had found favour with God, and she had been chosen as the instrument for working out man's salvation. Great had been her personal holiness, and wonderful had been the privilege, with which she had been blessed. Now, as she stood before the Cross, a sword was to pierce through her heart. She had a trial to bear, such as had never fallen to the lot of woman before. She had to behold her Son and her God crucified before her eyes, and by the very men whose salvation He was thereby purchasing.

The actions of our Saviour, so far as we understand them, are so full of deep significance that it is impossible for man to fix any limits to them, and to say that they mean no more than this or that. It would be presumptuous to say, that when Jesus gave to His Mother a son in St. John, and to St. John a mother in the Blessed Virgin, that He meant no more than that the disciple was henceforth to provide a home for His Mother. It is probable that this action is also part of the Great Mystery. In the fulness of His meaning He might refer partly to the hour, of which He had spoken at the marriage in Cana (ii. 4), and that He now acknowledges her claims on Him for the supply of the necessaries of this life, as a Mother from her Son. Jesus commits His Mother, the most exalted of women, to the care of the most saintly of men, to St. John, the beloved disciple. This is the meaning which lies on the surface. What more His words may mean it is impossible for man, unless aided by the Holy Spirit, to discover. The only glimpse, which we have of the Blessed Virgin after the Resurrection, is not in the retired home of the individual Apostle, but in the midst of the assembled Church. (Acts i. 14.)

The fact that Jesus did not commit His mother to the care of Joseph, her husband, and therefore her natural guardian, has generally been considered a proof that Joseph was not now living. No mention is made of his death in the New Testament.

28 After this, Jesus knowing that all things were now (accomplished) that the Scripture might be (fulfilled), saith, I thirst.[1]

(Alf. Finished—accomplished.)

St. John says, "after this," without stating how long after: but it must have been three hours after. For Jesus committed His Mother to the care of the beloved disciple at the beginning of the Crucifixion, before the darkness came on; and He cried, "I thirst," almost at the end. The Psalmist, speaking in the person of Jesus, had said, hundreds of years before, "They gave Me also gall for My meat; and in My thirst they gave Me vinegar to drink." (Ps. lxix. 21.)

His thirst would be produced by want of food, by loss of blood from the scourging, and from the Crucifixion, and from exhaustion and excess of pain produced by hanging so long on the Cross. Great was the thirst which He endured in the Body from the Crucifixion; but how great must have been His thirst for the salvation of souls which led to the Crucifixion!

29 [Now] there was set a vessel full of vinegar, and

---

[1] That the Scripture might be fulfilled (ἵνα τελειωθῇ ἡ γραφή.)—"ἵνα here means *in order that*, whether with Luther, we join ἵνα τελειωθῇ to πάντα ἤδη τετέλεσται (so also Mayer), or, with Lücke and de Wette, to λέγει following. In the latter case ἵνα denotes a purpose attributed by John to Jesus."—Winer's *Grammar of New Testament*, p. 480.

[they filled a spunge with vinegar,] (and put it upon hyssop,) and put it to His mouth.

[V. A. Omits, Now : S. Therefore they put a spunge full of vinegar upon hyssop.] (Alf. And fixed it upon hyssop.)

30 When Jesus, therefore, had received the vinegar : He said, It is finished : and He bowed His head and gave up the ghost.

St. Matthew xxvii.	St. Mark xv.	St. Luke xxiii.	St. John xix.
			29 Now there was set a vessel full of vinegar:
48 And straightway one of them ran, and took a spunge, and filled it with vinegar, and put it on a reed, and gave Him to drink.	36 And one ran and filled a spunge full of vinegar, and put it on a reed, and gave Him to drink,		and they filled a spunge with vinegar and put it up on hyssop, and put it to His mouth.
49 The rest said, Let be, let us see whether Elias will come to save Him.	saying, Let alone; let us see whether Elias will come to take Him down.		
			30 When Jesus therefore had received the vinegar, He said. It is finished:
		45 And the veil of the Temple was rent in the midst.	
50 Jesus, when He had cried again with a loud voice,	37 And Jesus cried, with a loud voice,	46 And when Jesus had cried with a loud voice, He said, Father, Into Thy hands I commend My spirit: and having said thus,	
yielded up the ghost.	and gave up the ghost.	He gave up the ghost.	And He bowed His head, and gave up the ghost,

It was customary among the Romans, to give wine to persons suffering excruciating torture, to give them strength to go through the punishment. Either in derision of Jesus, or with a view to increase His suffering, or from some other motive, the soldiers gave Jesus vinegar instead of wine. St. John says that they placed a spunge filled with vinegar on hyssop (ὑσσώπῳ), St. Matthew and St. Mark say that they put it on a reed (καλάμῳ). Considerable difference of opinion exists as to which is the hyssop of Scripture. Clusius, the Dutch botanist, says that the common hyssop was a low bushy plant; but that the cultivated or garden hyssop of Palestine had a stalk a foot and a half high. One Evangelist, describing this with reference to its stalk, might call it a reed, and another, referring to its head, might speak of it as hyssop. Or, the reed and the hyssop may have been two different things bound together, the hyssop with its cup-shaped head to hold the spunge, and the reed to raise it to His lips. This may have been the reed, which they put into His right hand as a mock emblem of His kingly dignity, and with which they smote Him on the head. (Matt. xxvii. 29, 30.)

It is finished. The work appointed for Him to do is finished, the sufferings ordained for the Incarnate God to endure, the types and shadows of the Law, the prophecies of the Old Testament respecting the Passion are all finished, it only remains for His Human Soul to depart from His Body. Few words which have been uttered with reference to the history of man, contain in them such a depth of meaning as this, "It is finished. τετέλεσται. Then He bowed the head and gave up the ghost," as his own voluntary act, and at the time of the evening sacrifice.

While on the Cross Jesus spake seven times. These are not all recorded by the same Evangelist. St. Luke relates the I. and II., St. John the III., St. Matthew and St. Mark the IV., St. John the V. and VI., and St. Luke the VII.

ST. MATTHEW xxvii.	ST. MARK xv.	ST. LUKE xxiii.	ST. JOHN xix.
		I. Father, forgive them, for they know not what they do (34).	
		II. Verily, I say unto thee, To-day shalt thou be with Me in Paradise (43).	
			III. Woman, behold thy son; ... Behold thy Mother (26).
IV. Eli, Eli, lama Sabachthani (46).	IV. Eloi, Eloi, lama Sabachthani ? (34).		
			V. I thirst (28).
			VI. It is finished (30).
		VII. Father, into Thy hands I commend My Spirit (46).	

31 The Jews therefore (because) it was the preparation, that the bodies (should not) remain upon the Cross on the Sabbath day (for that Sabbath day was an high day) besought Pilate that their legs might be broken, and that they might be taken away.
(Alf. Since—might not.)

---

¹ That their legs might be broken (ἵνα κατεαγῶσιν αὐτῶν τὰ σκέλη.)—"Ordinarily, as every one knows, the Copula agrees in number, and the Predicate in number and gender, with the Subject; but the Predicate, if it consist of a substantive, may have a different gender and number from the Subject. It is only when prominence is to be given to the plurality and distinct existence of the Subject that the Predicate is put in the Plural. Ἵνα κατεαγῶσιν αὐτῶν (of the three persons crucified) τὰ σκέλη. Previously ἵνα μὴ μείνῃ τὰ σώματα is used."—Winer's *Grammar of New Testament*, p. 536.

32 (Then came the soldiers), and brake the legs of the first, and of the other which was crucified with Him.

(Alf. So the soldiers came.)

33 [But when they came to Jesus (and saw that He was dead already, they brake not)] His legs:

[S. But when they came to Jesus they found that He was dead already, and brake not.]

(Alf. And when they saw that He was dead already they brake not.)

The Jews give, as the reason for their desire to hasten the death of Jesus and the malefactors, their fear of polluting the approaching Sabbath by allowing the bodies to remain on the cross contrary to the law of Moses. (Deut. xxi. 21, 22.) It was now past three o'clock, and at sunset the Sabbath would commence, and that Sabbath was an high day. It was hallowed on two counts; first because it was the first day of unleavened bread, a holy convocation to the Lord (Exod. xii. 16); and secondly, because it was the seventh day, the usual Sabbath. This was the reason which they allege. But mixed with this there may have been some fear, some misgiving as to the enormity of the deed which they had just accomplished. Fearful, supernatural events had taken place during the last three hours. From the sixth to the ninth hour, from twelve o'clock until three, darkness had been spread over the whole earth, the sun was darkened, and the veil of the Temple was rent in twain from the top to the bottom, and the earth did quake, and the rocks rent, &c. All this may have awakened their conscience, and caused them to see how their conduct was condemned, or they may have feared lest the people should think so, lest the people, at all times fickle in their attachment, should turn against them as the authors of the deed, which had called forth such signal marks of displeasure from God.

Their legs would be broken by blows from some heavy instrument, either of wood or iron. This causing excess of pain and loss of blood would have the effect of hastening their end. The Death of Jesus before the others was the natural effect of the sufferings which He had endured, in Soul and Body, of the exhaustion of all the powers of nature: it was pre-ordained to fulfil the types and prophecies respecting Him in the Old Testament dispensation, and to prevent this very breaking of His legs, and so the imperfection and disfigurement of His Body after the Resurrection.

34 (But) one of the soldiers with a spear pierced His side, and forthwith (came there) out blood and water.

(Alf. Nevertheless—there came.)

35 And he that saw it (bare record), (and his record) is true: and he knoweth that he saith true, [that ye (might believe.)]

[S. A. That ye also might believe.]
(Alf. Hath borne witness—and his witness—may believe.)

The piercing of His side with a spear might not be from wanton cruelty on the part of the soldier, but in the proper fulfilment of his duty, to convince himself that Jesus was dead, and to prove to others, that though they had not broken his legs, they had taken sufficient precaution to ascertain that He was dead, before they removed His Body from the Cross.

The flow of blood and water from His side, after life had departed, was contrary to the laws of nature, which would have obtained in the case of an ordinary dead body. From known experiments we are driven to believe, either that this was a result natural to our Saviour's Body and to His only, or else that it was miraculously produced.

The Church, from the very earliest times, has looked upon this flowing of blood and water from the side of Jesus, as containing in it a fulness of meaning: as indicating the means through which man's salvation is wrought—water and blood, and that through the Incarnation, flowing from the Divine Body of the Son of God. In early times too writers gave this as one reason among others, why they always celebrated the Eucharist with the mixed chalice of wine and water, as a memorial of the water and blood which flowed from the pierced side of Jesus, and as a symbol that our salvation is through the Word made Flesh, and through His Death on the Cross. Few subjects afforded greater scope for instruction and illustration among the early Fathers of the Church than this.

Tradition records that the spear entered the right side of Jesus, and extended to the left through the heart, with a view of destroying the last remains of life, if He had not already laid down His life. This made the fifth wound in His Body—two in the hands, and two in the feet, and one in the side.

The person, who bears witness to the truth of the fact, that water and blood flowed from the pierced side of Jesus, is the Evangelist St. John himself, and on no subject does He give a more deliberate and a more distinct testimony, than He does to the truth of this, the testimony of an eye-witness, and of an eye-witness who has no doubt of the truth of what He says.

36 For these things (were done), that the scripture (should be) fulfilled, A bone of Him shall not be broken.

(Alf. Came to pass—might be.)

37 And again, another Scripture saith, They shall look on Him whom they pierced.[1]

In the passage from which the first quotation is taken, it is not expressed in the same way as it is given here. There it is part of the command which God gave to the children of Israel respecting the way in which they were to eat the Paschal lamb. "In one house shall it be eaten: thou shalt not carry forth ought of the flesh abroad out of the house: neither shall ye break a bone thereof." (Exod. xii. 46.)

According to the usage of Scripture the application of the same language to the Paschal Lamb and to Jesus, would so far identify them together, as to make the one a type or prophetic figure of the other. As the blood of the Paschal lamb sprinkled on the door-posts preserved the children of Israel, from the destroying angel and from the death of the body, so the Blood of Jesus poured out upon the Cross preserves the true Israel from the death of the soul.

In the second quotation which St. John says was fulfilled in Jesus and in the piercing of His side, the prophet Zechariah, who is speaking in the person of Jesus, says, "They shall look upon Me whom they have pierced." (Zech. xii. 10.) This was fulfilled when the Centurion, probably the very man who with his spear had pierced His side, "glorified God, saying, Certainly this was a righteous Man," and when "all the people that came together to that sight, beholding the things which were done, smote their breasts and returned." (St. Luke xxiii. 47, 48.) But probably the fulfilment, which the Evangelist meant, will be at the Day of Judgment. To this he again alludes in his book of the Revelation: "Behold, He cometh with clouds: and every eye shall see Him, and they also which pierced Him: and all kindreds of the earth shall wail because of Him." (i. 7.) Not only as nations and kindreds shall they look upon Him, but also as individuals, not only he who pierced Him with the spear, but also they who have pierced Him by their sins.

38 (And after this) Joseph of Arimathea,[2] being a disciple

---

[1] **Date of the Crucifixion.**—"Browne, in his *Ordo Sæculorum*, shows astronomically that in A.D. 29 the Paschal full moon fell on a Friday — Friday 18th March; and adopts this as the date of the Crucifixion. . . . It is satisfactory to remember that this year agrees with the constant tradition of the first five centuries (based doubtless on the *Acts of Pilate* before that document was corrupted), that Christ suffered in March in the consulship of the Gemini, A.D. 29."—Canon Norris's *Key to the Gospel Narrative*, p. 189.

[2] **Arimathæa.**—"A tradition as early as the sixth century makes Neby Samwîl the Ramah, or Ramathaim-Zophim, of the Old Testament the birth-place, residence, and burial place of Samuel. But a comparison of the statements made in Scripture with the topography of the country shows this tradition to be incorrect. When Saul was in search of his father's asses he visited Samuel at Ramah. On his departure for Gibeah, his native city, the prophet anointed him king, and described his way home as leading ' by Rachel's

of Jesus, (but secretly) for fear of the Jews, besought Pilate that he might take away the Body of Jesus : and Pilate gave him leave. He came therefore (and took the Body of Jesus.)

[S. They came therefore and took Him: V. took His Body.]
(Alf. And after these things—though in secret—and took away His Body.)

Arimathæa was early identified with Ramah the birth-place of Samuel. This is mentioned seven times at least in the Old Testament, and in the Septuagint it is rendered Armathaim or Armathaim Sepha. Its exact position has not been as yet ascertained.

Joseph though a native of Arimathæa seems to have been now living at Jerusalem. St. Matthew calls Joseph a rich man, who was also himself Jesus' disciple (xxvii. 57). St. Mark calls him an honourable counsellor (εὐσχήμων βουλευτής) which also waited for the kingdom of God (xv. 43). St. Luke says he was a counsellor : a good man and a just. (The same had not consented to the counsel and deed of them :) he was of Arimathæa a city of the Jews : who also himself waited for the kingdom of God. (xxiii. 50, 51) : and St. John, that he was a disciple of Jesus, but secretly, for fear of the Jews. From all this it is plain that Joseph was a member of the Sanhedrin, and that he had either absented himself from the assembly at which it was determined to put Jesus to death, or that he had voted against it.

Isaiah had already foretold that His rest should be glorious (xi. 10) ; and the Evangelist goes on to relate how this came to pass : how Joseph,

---

sepulchre on the border of Benjamin.' (1 Sam. x. 2.) Gibeah was situated on Tuleil el Fûl, only two and a half miles east from this spot; and Rachel's sepulchre is well known to be nearly seven miles south. Hence every step Saul would have taken from Neby Samwîl towards Rachel's sepulchre would have led him farther away from Gibeah".— *Handbook on Palestine*, p, 217.

"Within the last few centuries a monkish tradition has identified Ramleh with Ramathaim-Zophim, or Ramah of Samuel, and with the Arimathæa of the New Testament. For this, however, there is no evidence. The names have no analogy —Ramleh signifying 'sandy' and Ramah a 'hill.'. . . . In history there is no mention of Ramleh earlier than the ninth century, and Abulfeda states that it was founded in the earlier part of the eighth century by the Kalif Suleimân, after he had destroyed Ludd. The same fact is recorded by William of Tyre and others.— Ibid. p. 263.

Discussing the site of Arimathæa, Robinson sums up thus: "All this serves to show first, that Arimathæa was not Rentbieh which lies directly on the road between Antipatris and Lydda ; and, secondly, that it probably did lie somewhere between Lydda and Nobe, now Beit Nûba, a mile north east of Yâlo. Perhaps it is not too much to hope that the ancient site of Arimathæa may hereafter be discovered somewhere in that region, which, as yet, has not been fully discovered."—Robinson's *Later Researches*, p. 142.

Dean Stanley says the position of Ramah "is the most complicated and disputed problem of sacred topography. It is almost the only instance in which the text of the Scriptural narrative (1 Sam. ix. 1 ; x. 10) seems to be at variance with the existing localities."

"He enumerates eight different places, all of which have been thought to be the ancient Arimathæa and specifies the nature of their respective claims."—*Sinai and Palestine*, p. 224.

an honourable counsellor and a rich man, went in boldly unto Pilate and begged to be allowed to bury the Body of Jesus, not as a criminal but as a man of distinction, as a prophet of God. Either Pilate could not refuse a man of Joseph's character, and in the position in which he was, or he was willing to make some amends for the weakness and injustice, which he had shown in yielding to the pressure of the Jews, and condemning to death one he had himself pronounced to be a just man, and in whom there was no fault. St. John omits to record Pilate's surprise that Jesus was already dead, but simply says that Pilate gave him leave and that then he took away the Body of Jesus.

39 (And there came also Nicodemus) [which at the first came to Jesus by night,] (And brought) a mixture of myrrh and aloes, about an hundred pound weight.[1]

[V. A. Which at the first came to Him by night.]
(Alf. And there came Nicodemus also—to Him—bringing.)

40 Then took they [the Body of Jesus], and wound it in

---

[1] "Myrrh is a vegetable product of the gum resin kind, sent to us in loose granules from the size of a pepper corn to that of a walnut, of a reddish brown colour, with more or less of an admixture of yellow; its taste is bitter and acrid, with a peculiar aromatic flavour, but very nauseous; its smell is strong, but not disagreeable; it is brought from Ethopia, but the tree which produces it is wholly unknown. Our myrrh is the very drug known by the ancients under the same name; internally applied it is a powerful resolvent, and externally applied it is discutient and vulnerary."—Johnson's *Dictionary*, ed. 1765.

"Myrrh was used for embalming. (Herod. ii. 86.) Various conjectures have been made as to the real nature of the substance denoted by the Hebrew môr, and much doubt has existed as to the countries in which it is produced. According to the testimony of Herodotus (iii. 107), &c., the tree which produces myrrh grows in Arabia. Forstâl mentions two myrrh-producing trees, Amyris Kaláf and Amyris Kafal, as occurring near Haes in Arabia Felix. The myrrh-tree which Ehrenberg and Hemprich found on the borders of Arabia Felix, and that which Mr. Johnson saw in Abyssinia are believed to be identical; the tree is Balsamodrendron myrrha, 'a low thorny ragged-looking tree, with bright trifoliate leaves;' it is probably the Murr of Abu 'l Fadli, of which he says,

murr is the Arabic name of a thorny tree like an acacia, from which flows a white liquid, which thickens and becomes a gum."—Smith's *Biblical Dictionary*.

"Aloes.—A precious wood used in the east for perfumers, of which the best sort is of higher price than gold, and was the most valuable present given by the King of Siam, in 1686, to the King of France. It is called Tambac, and is the heart or innermost part of the aloe tree, the next part of which is called Calembac, which is sometimes imported into Europe, and though of inferior value to the Tambac, is much esteemed; the part next the bark is termed by the Portuguese Tao d'Aquila, or eagle wood; but some account the eagle wood not the outer part of the Tambac, but another species. Our knowledge of this wood is yet very imperfect."—Johnson's *Dictionary*.

"It is usually identified with the Aquilaria agallochum, a tree which supplies the agallochum or aloes-wood of commerce, much valued in India on account of its aromatic qualities for purposes of fumigation and for incense. This tree grows to the height of 120 feet, being twelve feet in girth. It is however uncertain whether the Ahâlim or Ahâlôth is in reality the aloes-wood of commerce; it is quite possible that some kind of odoriferous cedar may be the tree denoted by these terms."—Smith's *Biblical Dictionary*.

linen clothes with the spices, as the manner of the Jews [is to bury.]
[A. The Body of God: S. Was to bury.]
(Alf. They took therefore—as is the manner.)

St. Matthew xxvii.	St. Mark xv.	St. Luke xxiii.	St. John xix.
57 When the even was come,	42 And now when the even was come, because it was the preparation, that is, the day before the Sabbath,	50 And, behold, there was a man	38 And after this
there came a rich man of Arimathæa, namcd Joseph,	43 Joseph of Arimathæa, an honourable counsellor,	named Joseph, a counsellor: and he was a good man, and a just: (the same had not consented to the counsel and deed of them:) he was of Arimathæa, a city of the Jews:	Joseph of Arimathæa,
who also himself was Jesus' disciple:	which also waited for the kingdom of God,	who also himself waited for the kingdom of God.	being a disciple of Jesus, but secretly for fear of the Jews,
58 he went to Pilate and begged the Body of Jesus.	came and went in boldly unto Pilate and craved the Body of Jesus,	52 This man went unto Pilate, and begged the Body of Jesus.	besought Pilate that he might take away the Body of Jesus:
	44 And Pilate marvelled if He were already dead; and calling unto him the centurion, he asked him whether He had been any while dead?		
	45 And when he knew it of the centurion,		
Then Pilate commanded the Body to be delivered	he gave the Body to Joseph.		and Pilate gave him leave. He came therefore and took the Body of Jesus, and there came also Nicodemus, which at the first came to Jesus by night, and brought a mixture of myrrh and aloes, about an hundred pound weight.
59 And when Joseph had taken the Body, he wrapped It in a clean linen cloth.	46 And he bought fine linen and took Him down, and wrapped Him in the linen.	53 And he took It down, and wrapped It in linen.	40 Then took they the Body of Jesus, and wound It in linen clothes with the spices, as the manner of the Jews is to bury.

St. John is the only one of the four Evangelists who mentions Nicodemus. He alone relates that Nicodemus first came to Jesus by night to receive instruction from Him, (iii.), that he afterwards defended Him against the Pharisees in the Council, and that now he brought the necessary spices, and assisted Joseph in the pious office of wrapping the Body of Jesus in linen clothes with the spices, and laying It in the tomb. . From the expression which St. John uses, it would appear that Nicodemus paid more than one visit to Jesus, though that alone is recorded, "Nicodemus, which at the first came to Jesus by night."

Some Commentators have thought, that they brought a hundred pound weight of myrrh and aloes, as a proof of their liberality and affection for Jesus, and of their determination that there should be no deficiency, not that all this was required. This may or may not have been the case, nothing is stated either way. The quantity appears large, though it may not have been too much for the manner in which the Jews buried, and when they wished to pay the highest possible honour. The Jews derived their burial customs from the Egyptians, who were well known to have been lavish in the use of spices in embalming their dead.

41 Now in the place where He was crucified there was a garden: and in the garden a new sepulchre, wherein was never man yet laid.

42 (There laid they Jesus therefore, because of the Jews' preparation day: for the sepulchre was nigh at hand.)

(Alf. There therefore by reason of the Jews' preparation day, because the sepulchre was nigh at hand, they laid Jesus.)

It was past three o'clock before Jesus yielded up His Spirit. At sunset would begin the Sabbath, on which no burial could take place. Whatever arrangements respecting the burial of Jesus had to be made, must be before the Sabbath began, or left undone until it was over. Some time would have elapsed, while Joseph had gone to Pilate to beg the Body of Jesus, and while Pilate made the inquiries as to whether Jesus was already dead, which he thought it necessary to make. There was, therefore, no time to remove His Body to a more distant burial place. In the place where He was crucified, there was a garden: and in the garden a new sepulchre wherein was man never yet laid. There therefore by reason of the Jews' preparation day, because the sepulchre was nigh at hand, they laid Jesus.

St. Matthew alone relates that a great stone was rolled to the door of the sepulchre, that at the request of the Jews Pilate granted a guard to watch the sepulchre, that the sepulchre was made sure, the stone sealed, and the guard set.

The Body of Jesus was laid in a garden and in a new tomb. But it was laid there not from choice but from convenience. St. John does not say that it was chosen, because it was a rich man's tomb, or because it was a new tomb, or because it was in a garden, but because the time was short and this tomb was conveniently near.

INTRODUCTORY NOTE TO CHAPTER XX.

Sepulchres.—"There were more *common* and more *noble* Sepulchres. The *common* were in public burying places, as it is with us; but they were without the city. And through that place was no current of water to be made, through it was no public way to be, cattle were not to feed there, nor wood to be gathered from thence.

"The more *noble* Sepulchres were hewn out in some rock, in their own ground, with no little charge and art. You have the form of them described in these words:

"'He that selleth his neighbour a place of burial, and he that takes of his neighbour a place of burial, let him make the inner parts of the Cave four cubits, and six cubits: and let him open within it eight sepulchres.' They were not wont, say the Glosses, to bury men of the same family here and there, scatteringly, and by themselves, but altogether in one Cave: where if any one sells his neighbour a place of burial, he sells him room for two Caves, or hollows on both sides, and a floor in the middle.

"The tradition goes on. 'Three sepulchres are on this side, and three on that, and two near them. And those sepulchres are four cubits long, seven high, and six broad.'

"To those that entered into the sepulchral Cave, and carried the bier, there was first a floor where they stood and set down the bier, in order to their letting it down into the sepulchre: on this and the other side there was a Cave or a hollowed place, deeper than the floor by four cubits, into which they let down the corpse, divers coffins being there prepared for divers corpses. R. Simeon saith, 'The hollow of the cave consists of six cubits and eight cubits, and it opens thirteen sepulchres within it, four on this side and four on that, and three before them, and one on the right hand of the door, and another on the left. And the floor within the entrance into the Cave consists of a square, according to the dimensions of the bier, and of them that bear it, and from it open two Caves, one on this side, another on that.' R. Simeon saith, 'Four at the four sides of it.' Rabban Simeon ben Gamaliel saith, 'The whole is made according to the condition of the ground.'

"From these things now spoken you may more plainly understand many matters, which are related of the Sepulchre of our Saviour.

"Mark xvi. 5. The women entering into the Sepulchre saw a young man sitting on the right 'side:' in the very floor immediately after the entrance into the Sepulchre.

"Luke xxiv. 3. 'Going in they found not His Body,' &c. verse 5. 'While they bowed down their faces to the earth,' verse 12. 'Peter ran to the sepulchre, and when he had stooped down, he saw the linen clothes.' That is, the women and Peter after them, standing in the floor bow down their faces, and look downward into the place, where the sepulchres themselves were, which, as we said before, was four cubits deeper than the floor.

"John xx. 5. 'The disciple whom Jesus loved, came first to the Sepulchre; and when he had stooped down (standing on the floor, that he might look into the burying place) saw the linen clothes lie: yet went he not in. But Peter went in,' &c.; that is, from the floor he went down into the cave itself, where the rows of the graves were (in which nevertheless no corpses had been as yet laid, besides the Body of Jesus:) thither also after Peter, John goes down.

"And verse 2. 'But Mary weeping stood at the sepulchre without: and while she wept she stooped down to the sepulchre, and saw two angels in white sitting, one at the head and another at the feet, where the Body of Christ had lain.'

"She stood at the sepulchre without: that is, within the Cave on the floor, but without that deeper Cave, where the very graves were, or the very places for the bodies: bowing herself to look down thither, she saw two angels at the head and foot of that coffin, wherein the Body of Christ had been laid."—Lightfoot, ii. 89.

(422)

CHAPTER XX.

1. *Mary cometh to the Sepulchre; 8 So do Peter and John, ignorant of the Resurrection; 11 Jesus appeareth to Mary Magdalene; 19 And to His Disciples; 24 The incredulity, and confession of Thomas; 30 The Scripture is sufficient to salvation.*

1 (The first day of the week) cometh Mary Magdalene early, (when it was yet dark), unto the sepulchre, and seeth the stone, taken away [from the sepulchre.][1]

[S. From the door of the sepulchre.]
(Alf. Now on the first day of the week—while it was yet dark.]

---

[1] Mejdel, Magdala.—"One hour's ride along the shore brings us to this wretched hamlet, now the only inhabited spot in the plain of Gennesaret. In riding along, the wonderful richness of the soil strikes us. Nowhere else have we encountered such thistles, such grass, and such weeds —and such grain on the few spots cultivated. Josephus described Gennesaret eighteen centuries ago as an earthly Paradise, where the choicest fruits grew luxuriantly, and eternal spring reigned. His words were not much exaggerated; for now, though more a wilderness than a paradise, none can fail to remark its fertility. The shore is lined with a wide border of oleander: behind this come tangled thickets of the lote-tree: and here and there are little groups of dwarf palm. The voice of the turtle is heard on every side, and quails spring up from our feet at almost every step.

"Mejdel contains about twenty huts, and the ruins of a tower of modern date. Between the village and the shore are foundations and heaps of rubbish. Yet the name of this hamlet has been incorporated into every language of Christendom. It was the birth-place of Mary Magdalene, out of whom Jesus 'had cast seven devils,' and to whom He appeared immediately after His Resurrection. The name and sight of the village will call up that solemn scene related in John xx. 11-18."—*Handbook to Palestine*, p. 408.

"But the most sacred region of the lake—shall we not say of the world?—is the little plain of Gennesareth, which has been already mentioned, on the western shore. Few scenes have undergone a greater change. Of all the numerous towns and villages in what must have been the most thickly-peopled district of Palestine, one only remains. A collection of a few hovels stands at the south-eastern corner of the plain—its name hardly altered from the ancient Magdala or Migdol—so called, probably, from a watch-tower, of which ruins appear to remain, that guarded the entrance to the plain. Through its connection with her whom the long opinion of the Church identified with the penitent sinner, the name of that ancient tower has now been incorporated into all the languages of Europe. A large solitary thorn-tree stands beside it. Its situation, otherwise unmarked, is dignified by the high limestone rock which overhangs it on the south-west, perforated with caves, recalling, by a curious, though doubtless unintentional coincidence, the scene of Correggio's celebrated picture."—*Stanley's Sinai and Palestine*, p. 382.

St. Mark had related that "a stone" was rolled unto the door of the sepulchre, and St. Matthew that "a great stone" was rolled to the door of the sepulchre, and that the stone was sealed and a guard set. Neither St. Luke nor St. John mentions the stone until they relate, how that the women found it rolled away from the door of the sepulchre.

By comparing St. John's account with that given by the other three Evangelists, we shall be the better able to see the time at which they first went to the sepulchre, their object in going, as well as who the individuals were who went.

St. Matthew xxviii.	St. Mark xvi.	St. Luke xxiv.	St. John xx.
	1 And when the Sabbath was past, Mary Magdalene, and Mary the Mother of James and Salome, had bought sweet spices, that they might come and anoint Him.		
1 In the end of the Sabbath, as it began to dawn toward the first day of the week came Mary Magdalene and the other Mary to see the sepulchre.	2 And very early in the morning the first day of the week, they came unto the sepulchre at the rising of the sun.	1 Now upon the first day of the week, very early in the morning, they came unto the sepulchre, bringing the spices which they had prepared, and certain others with them.	1 The first day of the week cometh Mary Magdalene early, when it was yet dark, unto the sepulchre.

St. John names only Mary Magdalene, probably because she was conspicuous among the rest by her zeal and ardour. She evidently is the leader of the party.

The object of these women in going to the sepulchre was not to see if Jesus were risen. That was a thought, which had never crossed their minds. They went, in the abundance of their love and reverence, to anoint His Body with sweet spices. When alive they had loved and revered Him with an unbounded affection, and now that He was dead, they went to perform for Him the offices of love and affection, in the way that was most congenial to the Jewish mind. As soon as it was possible to purchase the spices, that is, after sunset on the day of the Sabbath, Mary Magdalene, Mary the mother of James the less, and Salome had gone into the city for that purpose, and had then carried the spices to the sepulchre, while it was yet dark. It was dark though it had become morning. They had no motive in waiting for the morning. It was night when they left to go and buy the spices, but the sun had risen or the morning hours had begun, before they reached the place of burial.

The same women had bought the spices, as were before mentioned beholding Him on the Cross, with the exception of the Blessed Virgin.

She is not now with them. She went not with them to anoint His Body, for she probably alone of all the party knew, that He would not be there, that He would have risen. Doubtless in retirement she pondered on the completion of the Mystery. We may reverently assume, that this was in some way vouchsafed to her by some personal communication, and not only through the report of the women and the disciples. Many have believed, that Jesus had first of all appeared to His Mother privately, though this is nowhere recorded in Scripture. But this would not be contrary to analogy, it would rather be in perfect keeping with the way, in which the Mystery of the Incarnation had been revealed to mankind.

St. John here omits many particulars, that are related by the other Evangelists, such as the earthquake, the descent of the angel of the Lord from heaven, the rolling away of the stone from the door of the sepulchre, and the angel's message unto the women.

2 Then she runneth, and cometh to Simon Peter, and to the other disciple, whom Jesus loved, and saith unto them, They have taken away the Lord out of the sepulchre, and we know not where they have laid Him.[1]

Either the women did not understand the angel's words that Jesus was risen, or they did not believe them. For Mary repeats to the disciples their first impression, They have taken away the Lord out of the sepulchre, and we know not where they have laid Him. St. John named only Mary as going to the sepulchre, but her words show that others were with her. The expression "we know not" shows that she is speaking for herself and her companions, in fact as the leader of the party.

3 Peter therefore went forth, and (that other disciple), [(and came to the sepulchre.)]

[S. Omits, and came to the sepulchre.]
(Alf. The other disciple—and they went toward the sepulchre.)

---

[1] And cometh to Simon Peter, and to the other disciple (ἔρχεται πρὸς Σίμωνα Πέτρον καὶ πρὸς τὸν ἄλλον μαθητὴν). "When two or more substantives, governed by one and the same preposition, and directly joined together by a copula, follow each other, the preposition is most naturally repeated, if the substantives in question denote things conceived to be distinct and independent. Bengel's conclusion from the repetition of the preposition here is that the two disciples were not in the same place, non una fuisse utrumque discipulum."— Winer's Grammar of New Testament, p. 439.

[2] And the other disciple did outrun Peter (καὶ ὁ ἄλλος μαθητὴς προέδραμεν τάχιον τοῦ Πέτρου.) "He ran on before, faster than Peter (closer specification)."— Winer's Grammar of New Testament, p. 627.

4 [(So) they ran both together : and the other disciple did outrun Peter,] and came first to the sepulchre.

[S. And they ran both together, but the other did outrun Peter : A. but the other.] (Alf. And.)

As the younger and more active of the two, St. John reaches the sepulchre first, but does not enter it until his companion had come up, perhaps from a feeling of modesty, and out of deference to St. Peter as his senior in age, and superior in position among the Apostles ; or it may be that he was seized with a sudden feeling of fearful reverence towards the Dead.

5 (And he stooping down, and looking in, saw) the linen clothes lying : yet went he not in.

(Alf. And stooping down, and looking in, he seeth.)

6 [Then cometh Simon Peter] following him, and went into the sepulchre (and seeth the linen clothes lie.)

[S. V. Then cometh also Simon Peter.]
(Alf. And beholdeth the linen clothes lying.)

7 And the napkin, that was (about His head,) not lying with the linen clothes, but wrapped together in a place by itself.

(Alf. On His head.)

The positions of the several pieces of linen, with which His Body was wrapped, St. John relates more minutely than the other Evangelists, for he alone is recording here, what he saw with his own eyes. He had noted them carefully, as they were the first things to strike his attention. They were to him so many indications of His Resurrection. They first prepared St. John to believe that Jesus might have risen. This belief—first produced by the sight of the sepulchre—was afterwards confirmed by other evidence which could not be gainsaid.

One thing, that drew St. John's special attention to the linen, lying as it was, wrapped in two separate places in the sepulchre, was the knowledge that when a dead body was wrapped in linen with spices, myrrh, aloes, &c. the linen had a tendency to adhere to the body. The myrrh was of a gummy, glutinous nature, and would make it extremely difficult to remove the linen from the Body. St. John himself—and he alone of the four Evangelists—had related that they wound the Body of Jesus in linen clothes with the spices (xix. 40). Had any one wished to remove the Body, to stay to unwrap the clothes was only adding to the risk of detection. But this had been the work of one who was deliberate and careful in doing, what he had done. There were no marks of hurry, no signs of haste from fear of discovery.

8 (Then went in also that other disciple), which came first to the sepulchre, and he saw and believed.

(Alf. Then went in therefore the other disciple also.)

9 [For as yet they knew not] the Scripture, that He must rise again from the dead.

[S. For as yet he knew not.]

Many Commentators[1] both ancient and modern have thought that the Evangelist meant to say here, that in consequence of what he saw in the sepulchre, he believed the words which Mary Magdalene had said unto them, namely that they had removed the Body of Jesus from the sepulchre. But it is far more in accordance with the context, that what he believed was, that Jesus had risen from the dead. For the first time the truth flashed upon his mind, that this was what Jesus Himself taught them. As yet, up to this time, he had not known, he had not understood the Scripture, that He must rise again from the dead. He had heard the words before, but without giving them any particular meaning, or at least any literal meaning, only such as was figurative. But now the appearance of the sepulchre, with its linen so carefully wrapped up and laid in different places, brought to his recollection the words of Jesus Himself, and forced on his mind the fact of the Resurrection. It was the Scripture, that he must rise again from the dead, which produced in St. John the conviction that Jesus had risen again; but it was what he saw in the sepulchre that brought the Scripture to his recollection, and prepared him to receive this conviction.

St. Peter had the same evidence, but he did not as yet believe that Jesus was risen from the dead. Perhaps there was in his very nature a backwardness to receive a new truth, except on the fullest proofs. It is true that he had formerly been the first to confess that Jesus was the Christ, the Son of the Living God. (Matt. xvi. 16); that in a moment of impetuous zeal he had attempted to defend his Master at the risk of his own life (John xviii. 10). But the gentle, loving temperament of the youthful St. John may have been more receptive of the great Mysteries of the Incarnation.

10 (Then) the disciples went away again unto their own home.

(Alf. So.)

---

[1] For the ancient commentators see Cornelius à Lapide, and for the modern see Dean Alford *in loco.*

The two disciples depart unto their own home; John believing that Jesus had risen, and Peter wondering, at a loss how to account for appearances. Mary remains rooted to the spot by love to her Lord, and by grief because they had removed, as she thought, His Body, and she knew not where they had laid Him.

11 [But Mary stood without at the sepulchre] weeping: and as she wept, she stooped down, and looked into the sepulchre,

[S. But Mary stood in the sepulchre: A. Omits without.]

12 And (seeth) [two] angels in white sitting, (the one) at the head, and the other at the feet, where the Body of Jesus had lain.

[S. Omits, two.]
(Alf. Beholdeth—one.)

13 [And] they say unto her, Woman, why weepest thou? [She saith] unto them, Because they have taken away my Lord, and I know not where they have laid Him.

[S. Omits, and: V. And she saith.]

What St. John had seen in the sepulchre had prepared him for a belief in the Resurrection of Jesus. What Mary sees was doubtless intended to prepare her for the appearance of Jesus Himself. The angels, their clothing in white, their posture sitting, the very place in which they sat, one at the head and the other at the feet, are all signs of His Resurrection, and of His Resurrection as perfect as He was when alive.

St. John does not relate the reply and the message of the angel to Mary, which the other Evangelists do, but he goes on to relate the appearance of Jesus to her.

14 [(And)when she had thus said,) she turned herself back, and saw Jesus standing, and knew not that it was Jesus.

[S. V. A. Omit, And.]
(Alf. And having thus said.)

15 Jesus saith unto her, Woman, Why weepest thou? Whom seekest thou? [She, supposing] (Him to be the gardener), saith unto Him, Sir, if thou (have borne) Him hence, tell me where thou hast laid him, and I will take Him away.

[S. Now she supposing.]
(Alf. That it was the gardener—hast borne.)

Jesus approached Mary from behind, and some suppose that the reason why she turned herself was, because she saw the angels assume an attitude of reverential worship, as if to some one behind her. Others have supposed that she turned, merely because she heard the sound of advancing footsteps.

It may be that Jesus appeared to Mary Magdalene first, in consequence of the excessive love which she bore towards Him, but that her eyes were holden so that she could not at first recognise Him, as the effect of her disbelief in the words of the angel, which said that He was alive, as well as a gentle rebuke for it. In his question, why weepest thou? Jesus intimates that there is need of faith, not of tears. There is no need to weep for Him, who is risen, and who is declared by the angels to be risen. She took Him for the gardener, just as the two disciples, going to Emmaus a little later on the same day, supposed that He was a stranger. (Luke xxiv. 13.)

16 Jesus saith unto her, Mary. [She turned herself, and saith unto Him,] Rabboni: which is to say, Master.

[S. But she turned herself: S. V. And saith unto Him in Hebrew.]

17 Jesus saith unto her, Touch Me not; for I am not yet ascended [to My Father]: [but go to My brethren] and say unto them, I ascend unto My Father and your Father: (and to My God and your God.)

[S. V. To the Father: S. but (A. omits) go to the brethren: S. Behold, I ascend.] (Alf. And My God, and your God.)

Mary would seem to have turned from Jesus towards the angels again, as if seeking from them some explanation of the circumstances, when she heard the sound of her own name uttered by the voice of Jesus, and with all the sweetness and graciousness with which He had been accustomed to address her. Like the Shunamite woman of old (2 Kings iv. 27), she fell on her knees and caught hold of the feet of Jesus, and began to indulge in her feelings of ecstatic delight, in this act of worship towards Him, and calling Him Rabboni, a term intended to convey the highest honour and most enduring love.

The difficulty of explaining the words $\mu\dot{\eta}$ $\mu o \upsilon$ $\ddot{a}\pi\tau o \upsilon$ rendered "Touch Me not," especially in the connection in which they stand, may be inferred from the number of interpretations that have been given to them. Cornelius à Lapide gives no less than five different interpretations of this passage. The explanation which he himself prefers, and which is the one advocated in this Commentary, found little favour with many of the ancient annotators, and not much more with many in modern times.

We may fairly conclude, that what Jesus forbade to Mary was not any touching of His Body whatever, but the touching him under certain conditions; either because there was a deficiency of love and reverence, or of faith and appreciation of His Divine nature, or because her adoration of Him from its length and rapture was unsuited to the present time, and to the commission with which He now entrusted her, namely, of announcing His Resurrection to the rest of His disciples. We may infer this, because He almost immediately grants this privilege to a number of women, which number probably included Mary Magdalene herself. "And as they (the women) went to tell His disciples, behold, Jesus met them, saying, All hail. And they came and held Him by the feet (ἐκράτησαν αὐτοῦ τοὺς πόδας) and worshipped Him. (Matt. xxviii. 9.) The very same day, in the evening, Jesus Himself invited His assembled disciples "to handle" Him (ψηλαφήσατέ με.) (Luke xxiv. 39.) A week after this He invited Thomas to thrust His hand into His side. (John xx. 27.) All this took place before Jesus had ascended unto the Father. Evidently then the fact, that He had not ascended unto the Father, could scarcely be given as a reason, why Mary Magdalene should not touch Him, since it did not prevent the others from touching Him. Neither can we believe that Jesus allowed this privilege to Thomas accompanied with the words, "Be not faithless, but believing," and that He refused it to Mary Magdalene, who had shown to Him at least equal faith and far more love than Thomas.

It could not be that Mary, when she was about to touch Him, was deficient in love or reverence, or in faith and appreciation of His Divine nature. We are apt to believe that she exceeded all the rest in love to Jesus, and that it was for this very reason, that He appeared to her first after His Resurrection. Her faith in the angel's words may have been defective, but as soon as she recognised Jesus Himself, there was no lack of faith, no lack of love or reverence towards Him.

Some explanation must be sought for more consistent with the context. This will probably be found in the meaning of the expression μή μου ἅπτου itself, which is imperfectly rendered, "Touch Me not." The literal meaning of these words is much more nearly represented by the English, "Cling to Me not," or "Cease to cling to Me, or to clasp Me." In this sense γούνων ἅπτεσθαι is not at all uncommon in classic Greek. Thus in Homer the herald who conducts Priam to the camp of the Greeks, seeing a stranger of whose intentions he was uncertain, asks Priam whether they should turn the horses and fly, or

γούνων ἀψάμενοι λιτανεύσομεν, αἴ κ' ἐλεήσῃ. (Book xxiv. 357.)

"Say, with the horses shall we fly at once,
Or *clasp his knees*, and for his mercy sue."
—Lord Derby's *Translation*.

When, therefore, Jesus said to Mary Magdalene,[1] μή μου ἅπτου "Touch Me not, for I am not yet ascended to My Father; but go to My brethren, and say unto them, I ascend unto My Father and your Father; and to My God and your God," it is probable that He did not forbid her to touch Him, but that He bade her not now to linger to worship and adore Him, not now to stay and pour out her affection for Him by kissing and embracing His feet, but to go and announce His Resurrection to His brethren, adding, that as He had not ascended to His Father, other opportunities would be afforded her of thus showing her love and devotion to Him, but that her present duty was to bring the tidings of His Resurrection and appearing to His brethren.

According to this interpretation our Saviour's words, "For I am not yet ascended unto My Father," do not imply that she should be allowed to worship Him by touching Him in any sense *after* He had ascended unto His Father, but that she should still have the opportunity of thus worshipping Him *before* He ascended unto His Father.

In the words "My Father and your Father" Jesus draws a marked distinction between God as His Father, and as their Father. God is His Father by nature, He is their Father by adoption and grace. In the words "My Father and your Father, My God and your God," He may also intend to remind them of His twofold nature, and may thus speak of God as His Father with reference to His Divine nature, and as His God with reference to His Human nature. Surprised and almost perplexed at His Resurrection, an event which they had so little expected, it may have been necessary to teach and remind them in every possible form, that He was "Perfect God and Perfect Man." He may also have said this to them and have called them His brethren, to remove from them the feeling of fear and of shame at their desertion of Him, and to remind them that though He had risen again, He was the same loving Master to them that He was before His Crucifixion.

18 Mary Magdalene (came and told) the disciples that she had seen the Lord, and that He had (spoken) these things unto her.

(Alf. Cometh and bringeth tidings to the disciples—said.)

By comparing the accounts which the Four Evangelists give of the Resurrection we shall see, that on the day of the Resurrection Jesus appeared five times, and that St. John records only two of these, the first and the last.

---

[1] Kypke, an oriental scholar of the last century, paraphrases the expression, μή μου ἅπτου thus, "desine Me jam adorare."—Quoted in *Grinfield's Greek Testament*.

St. Matthew xxviii.	St. Mark xvi.	St. Luke xxiv.	St. John xx.
	I. (9) Now when Jesus was risen early the first day of the week He appeared first to Mary Magdalene.[1] [S. V. omit all these verses from 9 to 20].		I. (1-18) The first day of the week cometh Mary Magdalene early, when it was yet dark. . . . . Jesus saith unto her, Mary. She turned herself, &c.
II. (1-10) In the end of the Sabbath, as it began to dawn toward the first day of the week. . . . . Jesus met them, saying, All hail! And they came and held Him by the feet, and worshipped Him, &c.			
		III. (34) Saying, The Lord is risen indeed, and hath appeared to Simon.	
	IV. (12) After that He appeared in another form unto two of them, as they walked, and went into the country.	IV. (13) And, behold, two of them went that same day to a village called Emmaus, ... 30 And it came to pass, as He sat at meat with them, He took bread and blessed It, and brake and gave to them. 31 And their eyes were opened, and they knew Him, &c.	
	V. (14) Afterward He appeared unto the eleven, as they sat at meat, &c. (Or, this may refer to His appearance after eight days, when Thomas was present).	V. (36-48) And as they thus spake, Jesus Himself stood in the midst of them, and saith unto them, Peace be unto you.	V. (19-23) Then the same day, at evening, being the first day of the week, when the doors were shut, where the disciples were assembled, for fear of the Jews, came Jesus and stood in the midst, and saith unto them, Peace be unto you.

Mary Magdalene and her companions, amongst whom were Mary, the mother of James the less, and Salome, came first to the sepulchre early in the morning, bringing with them the spices to anoint His Body. They find the stone rolled away from the door of the sepulchre. When they had seen the angels and heard their words, that Jesus was risen again, they return to the city to tell this to Peter and John, who immediately run to the sepulchre, the women also following them.

---

[1] **The last twelve verses of St. Mark's Gospel.**—Mr. Burgon in a learned treatise, a very marvel for patient investigation, has swept away the doubts and suspicions, which for the last fifty years had been cast on the closing verses of St. Mark so liberally, that these verses had almost come to be looked upon, as an acknowledged addition to the Gospel.

Peter and John enter the sepulchre and then go away again unto their own home. The women also set out to return home with the exception of Mary Magdalene, who still lingers about the garden, weeping, when Jesus appears to her and bids her carry the tidings of His Resurrection to His brethren. Mary then follows her companions in the direction of the city, and what wonder that, in her joy and delight at the thoughts of the message which she had to communicate to the disciples, she should overtake her companions who had left the sepulchre sad and disappointed, because they had not found the Body of Jesus. "And as they (the women) went to tell His disciples Jesus met them, saying, All hail. And they came and held Him by the feet and worshipped Him." His next appearance was unto Simon. (Luke xxiv. 34.) This is not circumstantially related by any of the Evangelists. Then He appeared unto the two disciples as they went to a village called Emmaus,[1] which was from Jerusalem

---

[1] Emmaus or Nicopolis.—"About one mile to the north-east of Látiôn, in full view, is the small village of Ammâs, situated on the western declivity of a low hill. . . . . This is the site of Emmaus or Nicopolis, situated at the foot of the mountains, and according to the *Jerusalem Itinerary*, twenty-two Roman miles from Jerusalem, and ten from Lydda.

"It is somewhat remarkable that from the third to the thirteenth century, the opinion was universal among Christian writers that this city was that Emmaus to which the two disciples were going from Jerusalem when our Lord appeared to them on the day of His Resurrection. But the express statement of the Evangelist, and the whole circumstances of the narrative, appear to make this impossible. Luke states that Emmaus was distant from Jerusalem 'threescore furlongs' [Sinaitic MS. has a hundred and threescore furlongs]. Nicopolis is *a hundred and sixty*. Besides, the two disciples, having come from Jerusalem to Emmaus in part of a day, returned there the same evening after Christ had revealed Himself to them. If this be Emmaus, they must have walked that day a distance of *forty miles*. (Luke xxiv. 13-35)."—*Handbook to Palestine*, p. 271.

These and other objections to Nicopolis being the Emmaus of the Evangelist Dr. Robinson ably answers as follows:—

"There can be no doubt, that in the earliest period of which we have any record, after the apostolic age, the opinion prevailed in the Church, that Nicopolis (as it was then called) was the scene of that narrative. Both Eusebius and Jerome, in the fourth century, are explicit on this point: the one a leading bishop and historian, the other a scholar and translator of the Scriptures. Indeed they seem to have known of no other interpretation; nor is there any trace of any other in any ancient writer. The same opinion continued general down through succeeding ages until the commencement of the fourteenth century: when slight traces began to appear of the later idea, which fixed an Emmaus at Kubeibeh : a transfer of which there is no earlier vestige, and for which there is no possible ground, except to find an Emmaus at about sixty stadia from the Holy City.

"Thus, for thirteen centuries did the interpretation current in the whole Church regard the Emmaus of the New Testament as identical with Nicopolis. This was not the voice of mere tradition, but the well-considered judgment of men of learning and critical skill, resident in the country, acquainted with the places in question, and occupied in investigating and describing the Scriptural topography of the Holy Land."

He then goes on to answer the objections. Two of these are raised from Josephus, and the correctness of his text. The third refers to St. Luke's reading of "threescore furlongs," which is answered by the reading of MSS. of as great antiquity and authority as the present Greek Text of the English Version, as for instance, the reading of the Sinaitic MS., "one hundred and threescore furlongs." The fourth he answers thus: "The distance of Nicopolis from Jerusalem is too great, it is said, to admit of the return of the two disciples the same evening so as to meet the assembled Apostles. This, how-about threescore furlongs, or, according to the Sinaitic MS., about one hundred and threescore furlongs. His last appearance on this day which the Evangelists record was in the evening, when His disciples were assembled together.

19 (Then the same day at evening, being the first day of the week, when the doors were shut,) where the disciples were [assembled] for fear of the Jews, came Jesus and stood in the midst, and saith [unto them], Peace be unto you.

[S. V. A. Omit, assembled : S. Omits, unto them.]

(Alf. When it was evening, therefore, on that same day, being the first day of the week, the doors being shut.)

They feared the Jews, because they had incurred their hatred and suspicion as disciples of Jesus. The Evangelist mentions the closed doors, to indicate the different nature of His Presence among them from what it was formerly. Before His Crucifixion He had gone in and out among them, as they themselves had done, except on one or two special occasions, when He had displayed His Divine power. Then His Body was apparently subject to the same laws as their own. It is also probable, that in His intercourse with them His Resurrection Body was subject to the same laws, as all bodies will be after the Resurrection. Material objects were no hindrance to His Presence. The doors

---

ever, would depend, not so much upon the distance as upon the time when they set off. They "rose up the same hour" (Luke xxiv. 32), and naturally returned in haste to make known their glad tidings, although with all their haste they could not well have traversed the distance in less than five hours. It was not yet evening when they arrived at Emmaus, and if they set off to return even as late as six o'clock, which at that season would be about sunset, they might reach the city by eleven o'clock. The Apostles were assembled, and the doors were shut, ' for fear of the Jews:' they had indeed partaken of an evening meal, but this had already been long ended, for Jesus afterwards inquires if they have any food. It was evidently late. There is nothing, therefore, impossible or improbable in the supposition that the two had hastened back a long distance, late at night, perhaps with much bodily effort, to declare to their brethren the wonderful things of which they had been witnesses. A like amount of travel, on an extraordinary occasion, would be nothing strange even at the present day.

The case then may be thus presented:

On the one hand, the reading of good MSS. gives the distance of Emmaus from Jerusalem at one hundred and sixty stadia, at which point there was a place called Emmaus, which still exists as the village Amwâs: and all this is further supported by the critical judgment of learned men residing in the country near the time, as also by the unbroken tradition of the first thirteen centuries. On the other hand there is the current reading of sixty stadia in most of the present MSS., written out of Palestine : supported only by a doubtful reading of Josephus : but with no place existing either now or at the end of the third century to which this specification can be referred. So far as it regards the New Testament, it is a question between two various readings : one, now the current one in MSS. and editions, but with no other valid support; the other, supported in like manner by MSS., as also by facts, by the judgment of early scholars and by early and unbroken tradition. After long and repeated consideration, I am disposed to acquiesce in the judgment of Eusebius and Jerome."

—Robinson's *Later Researches*, p. 147.

were shut, but He came and stood in the midst. He saith unto them, "Peace be unto you," probably to allay all fear of His anger at their conduct during His trial, and to quiet all the alarm which they naturally felt at His unexpected Presence, and at the unusual mode of His Presence among them. He communicates to them all the blessings conveyed in the word "Peace."

20 And when He had so said, He shewed unto them (His hands and His side). (Then were the disciples glad), when they saw the Lord.

(Alf. Both His hands and His side—The disciples therefore were glad.)

This, taken in connection with His own words before His Crucifixion, and with the words of the prophets of the Old Testament, must have been sufficient to convince the most unbelieving that He was the Messiah, the Son of God.

Both St. Mark and St. Luke relate this appearance of Jesus, and mention several particulars which St. John omits, and omit some which St. John records. St. Luke says that, besides showing them His hands and His side, He bade them "handle" Him (ψηλαφήσατέ με), and that He condescended to prove to them, by an argument as perfect as a syllogism, that He is not a spirit, but their risen Lord; and to show that there could not possibly be any illusion in the matter, He asked them for meat, and took a piece of a broiled fish, and of an honeycomb, and did eat it before them. This St. John omits, and goes on to relate the commission which Jesus now gave them.

21 [(Then said Jesus)] to them again, Peace be unto you : (as My Father) hath sent Me, [even so send I you.]

[S. Then said He : even so will I send you.]
(Alf. So then Jesus said—as the Father.)

The word (καθὼς) here translated "as" must imply partly an equality and partly a likeness or similarity. The power and authority of the sender was equal. As the Father had sent Him, so He the Son sent them. The power and authority of those who were sent must be similar. He had descended from the Father to form a kingdom on earth, and He was now about to return to the Father, and He gives them a commission to regulate and to govern this kingdom, to be the channels of His favour to the citizens of this kingdom. He sends them, too, with the same object as He Himself had been sent, the salvation of man. Though Himself ascended to the Father, He would refuse to His kingdom no blessing, which He had conferred on them during His Ministry on earth. In fact it was still His Ministry, but carried on through them as His agents; He it was, who conferred all the blessings, all the graces in His kingdom; the Apostles were to be the channels, through whom He should communicate these to the various individuals and nations. He then goes on to impart to them grace to carry on this Ministry, and to inform them in what it should consist.

22 And when He had said this, He breathed on them, and saith unto them, Receive ye the (Holy Ghost.)
(Alf. Holy Spirit.)

23 Whose soever sins ye remit, [they are remitted unto them]: (and) whose soever sins ye retain, they are retained.
[S. It shall be remitted unto them.]
(Alf. Omits, and.)

The things pertaining to the kingdom of God (Acts i. 3) was the great subject of our Saviour's instruction to the Apostles, during His forty days' intercourse with them after the Resurrection. The kingdom of God would continue for all time, the Apostles would remain to guide and direct its affairs but a small portion of that time. There must be a succession of men to take their place. His own words point out how this was to be done, "As My Father hath sent Me, even so send I you." This is the Church's warrant for her doctrine of Apostolical Succession. As the Father had sent Him and had given Him authority to send them, so He sent them with authority to send others. To none but the Apostles did Jesus ever say, "As My Father sent Me, even so send I you." The way too, in which He sent them, was to be the way in which they were to send others. He breathed on them, and thus showed, that the gift which He imparted to them was not an innate power, but one which He delegated to them, and by external means, and one which He, through their means, would delegate to others also.

By this act of breathing on them, Jesus conveys to His Apostles power to forgive sins, and power to retain sins. No form of words could more clearly express this. Before His Crucifixion He had given them power to cast out devils, and to heal all manner of sickness, and they had found by experience that His words were not a dead letter, but an actual conveyance to them of a supernatural power. That power chiefly concerned the bodies of men, this their souls. He now assigns them an office in His kingdom different from any, which He had before given them, namely, that of forgiving sins. He had given them by a formal ceremonial act the Holy Spirit, to enable them to convey pardon to the penitent sinner.

To explain the words of Jesus, as merely conferring on the Apostles a power of great or even of extraordinary discernment, is but trifling with His words, an evasion not an explanation of His meaning. He here gives them a commission not to discern the state of a man's heart, and then to declare what is the case already, but to convey a gift which will affect the future condition of his heart. When the Apostles said, "I absolve thee," the effect produced would no more depend on their discernment, than when they said, "I baptize thee." In each case the effect produced would depend on the repentance and faith of the penitent, and on the gift which God through His minister vouchsafed to bestow. What that gift is He here declares.

During the last evening which Jesus had spent with His disciples, He had said unto them, "He that hath been bathed needeth not save to wash his feet, but is clean every whit" (xiii. 10), that is, he that hath been washed in the waters of baptism does not again require a thorough purification of his nature, but only a cleansing from the stains, which he daily contracts in his walk through this world. Jesus here confers on His Apostles the qualification necessary for this cleansing.

Whatever Jesus gives here, He gives to all, who were present, equally. No one is singled out from the rest.

St. John relates only part of our Saviour's commission to His Apostles on this occasion. St. Mark and St. Luke give the rest.

24 But Thomas, one of the twelve, called Didymus, [was not with them when Jesus came.]

[S. Was not with them. When therefore Jesus came, the other disciples said unto him.]

25 The other disciples therefore said unto him, We have seen the Lord. But he said unto them, (Except I shall see) in His hands the print of the nails, and put my finger into the print of the nails, (and thrust) my hand into His side, I will not believe.

[S. And put my finger into His hand: A. And put my finger into the place of the nails.]

(Alf. Except I see—and put.)

The absence of Thomas has been variously accounted for. On the night of the Passion all the disciples forsook Him and fled. During the Sabbath they would probably rest in their several places of concealment. On the first day of the week they had returned one by one, it may be, from their place of refuge, and had assembled together in the Upper Room, where they had spent the last evening with Jesus. Thomas may not have returned until now.

St. Luke rather seems to imply (xxiv. 33) that, when the two disciples returned from Emmaus to relate how Jesus had appeared to them, Thomas was there. Or he may use the words "the eleven" as synonymous with "the Apostles." But however this may be, it is plain, that differences of opinion strongly expressed arose among the disciples, respecting the Resurrection of Jesus. They had regarded the report, which the women had brought as to the state of the sepulchre, as idle tales (λῆρος), mere foolish talk, nonsense, and they believed them not. Some have supposed that when Thomas heard the account, which the two disciples who had just returned from Emmaus gave, as to the way in which Jesus had appeared unto them, that he left the apartment in indignation at their credulity. This quite tallies with his conduct and his words afterwards. He refuses to credit the report of the other ten disciples, that Jesus had appeared to them. He cares nothing for their testimony, circumstantial and positive as it is, and declares that he will believe nothing short of his own sight, and his own touch. His unbelief amounted almost to unreasoning obstinacy, nor is this lessened by time and reflection. At the end of eight days he is still in the same opinion. From his words it is plain, that Thomas thought that the other disciples had been deceived, and that an apparition or phantom representing Jesus had appeared to them, and that Jesus Himself had not appeared truly, and in His Body, as they saw Him on the Cross.

26 And after eight days again [His disciples] were within, and Thomas with them, (then came Jesus), the doors being shut, and stood in the midst, and said, Peace be unto you.

[S. The disciples.]
(Alf. Jesus cometh.)

27 (Then saith He) to Thomas, Reach hither thy finger, and behold My hands: and reach hither thy hand, and (thrust) it into My side: and be not faithless, but believing.

(Alf. And then He saith—put.)

28 [And] Thomas answered and said unto Him, My Lord and My God.

[S. V. Omit, And.]
(Alf. Omits, And.)

Different opinions have been held as to whether St. John meant to say, that Thomas did put his finger into the print of the nails and thrust his hand into His side, or not. The more general opinion in ancient times was that he did. Nor is the Evangelist's language such as to imply, that Thomas believed on less evidence than he demanded.

Our Saviour's words to Thomas proved to him, that He knew the secret thoughts of the heart. The root of his unbelief in the Resurrection of Jesus, was the want of a sufficiently strong belief that He was God. The words of Jesus, His appearance, and probably Thomas's own act all convince him, that there is no deception of the senses, that He whom he beheld before him was the risen Jesus, God and Man— his Lord and his God.

The incredulity of Thomas was one more proof to the Church of the truth of the Resurrection, but it was not a blessing to himself. He was blessed in believing on such evidence as was afforded him, but they, who believed on less evidence, were more blessed. This may include the Apostle, or it may refer entirely to those who should afterwards believe on the testimony of the Apostles and Evangelists.

29 [Jesus saith] unto him, [(Thomas)], because thou hast seen Me, [thou hast believed]: blessed are they [that have not seen], and [yet] have believed.[1]

[S. But Jesus said: S. V. A. Omit Thomas : S. Thou hast also believed—S. That have not seen Me: A. Omits, yet.]
(Alf. Omits Thomas.)

30 (And) many other signs truly did Jesus in the presence [of His disciples], which are not written in this book.

[V. A. Of the disciples.]
(Alf. Omits, And.)

31 But these are written, that ye (might believe) that Jesus is the Christ, the Son of God: [and] that believing ye (might have) [life] (through His name).

[S. Omits, and: S. Everlasting life.]
(Alf. May believe—may have—in His name.)

Some suppose that St. John here means to say, that he has omitted many signs, which Jesus did all through His Ministry, and therefore before the unbelieving multitude, as well as before His disciples. Others again think that he refers only to signs, which Jesus wrought after His Resurrection, and during His forty days' intercourse with His disciples, and therefore in the presence of those only who believed on Him.

The Evangelist here declares the object with which he wrote his

---

[1] Because thou hast seen Me, thou hast believed (ὅτι ἑώρακάς με πεπίστευκας). "The Perfect is used for the Present only in as far as such Perfect denotes an action or state whose commencement and occa- sion were completed in time past, as in John xx: 29, where the origin of his (still existing faith) is indicated."—Winer's *Grammar of New Testament*, p. 288.

Gospel, which he expresses in much the same terms as he had at the beginning, namely, the salvation of man, that they might believe in Jesus: that He is the Saviour of the world, that He is the Christ, the Messiah spoken of by the prophets, that He is God, the second Person in the Holy Trinity, and that to all who believe on Him and obey His commands He bestows life, the life of grace here, and the life of glory hereafter.

Had no other chapter been added, this would have been a sufficiently formal close of his Gospel.

INTRODUCTORY NOTE TO CHAPTER XXI.

Tiberias.—" Now Herod the tetrarch, who was in great favour with Tiberius, built a city of the same name with him, and called it Tiberias. He built it in the best part of Galilee, at the lake of Gennesareth. There are warm baths at a little distance from it, in a village named Emmaus. Strangers came and inhabited this city : a great number of the inhabitants were Galilæans also : and many were [necessitated by Herod to come thither out of the country belonging to him, and were by force compelled to be its inhabitants—some of them were persons of condition. He also admitted poor people, such as those that were collected from all parts, to dwell in it. Nay, some of them were not quite freemen, and these he was a benefactor to, and made them free in great numbers, but obliged them not to forsake the city, by building them very good houses at his own expense, and by giving them land also : for he was sensible, that to make this place a habitation was to transgress the Jewish ancient laws, because many sepulchres were to be here taken away, in order to make room for the city Tiberias : whereas our law pronounces that such inhabitants are unclean for seven days."—Josephus *Antiq.*, xviii. 2, 3 ; Whiston's *Translation.*

" Tiberias was built by Herod the tetrarch in honour of Tiberius, and that in a common burying place, or in a place where many sepulchres had been. Hence it was, that the founder was fain to use all manner of persuasion, enticements, and liberality to invite inhabitants. The very delightful situation of the place seemed to put him on to wrestle with such a difficulty and inconvenience, rather than not to enjoy so pleasant a soil and seat. For on this side the sea washing upon it, on that side within a little way Jordan gliding by it, on the other side the hot baths of Chammath, and on another the most fruitful country Gennesaret adjacent, did every way begirt this city, when it was built, with pleasure and delight.

" It did every day increase in splendour, and became at last the chief city, not only of Galilee, but of the whole land of Israel. It obtained this honour by reason of the University translated thither by Rabbi Judah, and there continued for many ages. It was ennobled by thirteen synagogues, among which the ancient Scrongian synagogue was one. It was famous also for the Sanhedrin sitting there, for the

Talmudic Mishna, perhaps collected here by R. Judah, and for the Jerusalem Talmud, written there for certain."—Lightfoot, ii. 72.

" When the decree went out against the life of John the Baptist the tyrant's court was at Tiberias."—*Idem*, 196.

" Tiberias, in Arabic Tabaréyeh, lies directly upon the shore, at a point where the heights retire a little, leaving a narrow steep, not exactly of plain, but of undulating land, nearly two miles in length along the lake. Back of this the mountain ridge rises steeply. The town is situated near the northern end of this track in the form of a narrow parallelogram, about half a mile long: surrounded towards the land by a thick wall once not far from twenty feet high, with towers at regular intervals. Towards the sea the city is open. The castle is an irregular mass of buildings at the north-west corner. The walls of the town were thrown down by the earthquake of January 1st, 1837. . . . The castle also suffered greatly. Very many of the houses were destroyed: indeed few remained without injury.

" Tiberias and Safed are the two holy cities of the modern Jews in ancient Galilee, like Jerusalem and Hebron in Judæa. In A.D. 1759, October 30th, Tiberias was in like manner laid waste by a similar earthquake. Mariti, who visited it soon after, describes it as utterly in ruins, and says that several buildings were swallowed up."— Robinson's *Biblical Researches*, iii. 254.

" Tiberias west of the lake, nearly facing Gerasa, and about four miles south of Magdala. Antipas Herod was building a new city to outshine Julias, built by his brother Philip: which city he proposed to call Tiberias, and make the usual residence of his court. His plan was laid at the base of a steep hill, around the waters of a hot spring, among the ruins of a nameless town and the graves of a forgotten race. A great builder, like all the princes of his line, Antipas could now indulge his taste for temples, palaces, and public baths, conceived in a Roman spirit and executed on a Roman scale, while flattering that capricious master who might any day send him to die as his brother was dying in a distant land. The new city grew apace. A castle crowned the hill. High walls ran down from the heights into the sea. Streets and temples covered the low ground which lay between these walls. A gorgeous palace rose high above the rest of these public works: a palace for the prince and court, having a roof of gold, from which circumstance it came to be known as the golden house. A port was formed: a pier thrown out: a water-gate built: and a fleet of war ships and pleasure boats danced on the sparkling wave. Towers protected, and gates adorned a city which Antipas dedicated to his master, inscribed on his coins, and made the capital of his province, the residence of his court.

" This city was waxing great and famous. When the first stones were being laid near the sea, St. John was a little child playing on the beach at Capernaum with his father's nets; yet so swift was its growth, so wide its fame, that before he composed his Gospel, Tiberias had given its name to the waters on which it stood, like Geneva to Lake Leman, and Lucerne to that of the four cantons. When St. Matthew wrote his Gospel, the city was still young, and a Jew of Galilee might speak of Gennesareth: forty or fifty years later, a man who was born on its shores and had fished in its waters, spoke of the lake most familiarly by its Roman name."—Dixon's *Holy Land*, ii. 99.

CHAPTER XXI.

1 *Christ appearing again to His disciples was known to them by the great draught of fishes;* 12 *He dineth with them;* 15 *Earnestly commandeth Peter to feed His lambs and sheep;* 18 *Foretelleth him of his death;* 22 *Rebuketh his curiosity touching John;* 25 *The conclusion.*

A QUESTION has been raised in modern times respecting the genuineness of this chapter. This has not arisen from any ground which the chapter itself furnishes, but solely from the ending of the previous chapter, which from the very wording of it, as it is said, must have been intended by the Evangelist as a formal close of his Gospel.

The chapter is found in all the MSS. and Versions, and the internal evidence in favour of its genuiness is unquestionable. A further question has also been raised, was this chapter written and published by St. John at the same time as the rest of the Gospel, or at some later period? Both these opinions have been held, and it is impossible to decide which is the most correct.

Bishop Wordsworth in his Commentary on the Greek Testament has gone very fully into the genuineness of this chapter. He has examined both its relation to the MSS. and Versions, and also the internal evidence of the chapter itself. His conclusion is, that it was written by St. John, and published at the same time as the rest of the Gospel. Dean Alford has an equally strong conviction, that the chapter was written by St. John, but that it was written and published by him at some later period, as an appendix to his Gospel, probably to correct the misconception which began to prevail in the Church, respecting our Saviour's words to himself, to the effect that he should never die.

1 After these things (Jesus[1] shewed Himself) again to the disciples at the sea of Tiberias, (and on this wise shewed He Himself.)

(Alf. He manifested Himself—and He manifested Himself on this wise.)

This manifestation of Himself Jesus made in Galilee, where the angel had announced through the women to His disciples, that He would meet them. (Matt. xxviii. 7.) To Thomas this was the second time that He manifested Himself, to the other disciples it was the

---

[1] See note on Chap. i. 29.

third. After His resurrection His Body was not subject to the same conditions as before. Before His Resurrection He was visible at all times, except when He specially willed it otherwise; after His Resurrection He was not visible, unless He specially willed it.

2 There were together Simon Peter, and Thomas called Didymus, and Nathanael of Cana in Galilee, [and the sons of] Zebedee, and two other of His disciples.

[S. And the sons of.]

3 Simon Peter saith unto them, I go a fishing. They say unto him, We also go with thee. [They went forth,] and entered into (a ship) [immediately]: and that night they caught nothing.[1]

[S. Therefore they went forth: A. And they went forth: S. V. Omit, immediately.]
(Alf. The ship.)

As the Apostles were poor, and their trade of fishing an unobjectionable calling, they naturally return to it, to procure for themselves the necessaries of life. This was before the descent of the Holy Spirit, after which they were called upon, to give themselves entirely up to the preaching of the Gospel. After that it is never again said that the Apostles returned to their fishing.

---

[1] Fish in the Lake.—"The Sea of Galilee now, as in the days of our Saviour, is well stocked with various species of fish, some of excellent flavour. One species often appears in dense masses which blacken the surface of the water, the individual fish being packed so closely together that on one occasion a single shot from a revolver killed three. These shoals were most frequently seen near the shore of Gennesareth: perhaps not far from the place where the disciples let down their net into the sea, and inclosed a great multitude of fishes: and their net brake."—*Recovery of Jerusalem*, p. 341.

"The place soon asserted its right to the name Bethsaida by the exceeding abundance of the fish we saw tumbling in the water. The hot springs flowing in here over these rocks, and a little farther on in larger volume over a clean brown sand, warm all the ambient shallows for a hundred feet from shore, and, as much vegetable matter is brought down by the springs, and probably also insects which have fallen in, all these dainties are half cooked when they enter the lake. Evidently the fish agree to dine on these hot joints, and therefore in a large semicircle they crowd the water by myriads round the warm river mouth. Their backs are above the surface, as they bask or tumble and jostle crowded in the water. They gambol and splash, and the calm sea, fringed by a reeking crowd of vapour, has beyond this belt of living fish a long row of cormorants feeding on the half-boiled fish as the fish have fed on insects underdone. White gulls poise in flocks behind the grebes or cormorants, and beyond these again ducks bustle about on the water or whirl in the air. The whole is a most curious scene, and probably it has been thus from day to day for many thousand years. I paddled along the curved line of fishes' backs and flashing tails. Some leaped into the air, others struck my boat or paddle. Dense shoals moved in brigades as if by concert or command.—MacGregor's *Jordan*, p. 345.

COMMENTARY ON ST. JOHN'S GOSPEL. 445

4 But (when the morning) was [now] come, Jesus stood on the shore: (but) the disciples knew not that it was Jesus.

[S. Omits, now.]
(Alf. When morning—howbeit.)

5 Then (Jesus saith) unto them, (Children), have ye (any meat)? They answered Him, No.

(Margin, Sirs.)
(Alf. Jesus therefore saith—any fish.)

6 [And] He said unto them, Cast the net on the right side of the ship, and ye shall find. [They cast therefore and now they were not able] to draw it for the multitude of (fishes.)

[S. Omits, And: S. And they cast, and were no longer able.]
(Alf. The fishes.)

Jesus did not reveal Himself to them by His form, but by the miracle which He works, which miracle is probably intended to shadow out to them an outline of their future occupation: of their fishing for men, of their failure when relying on human skill and on industry alone, of their success when acting in dependence on the commands, and on the power of Jesus.

The word (παιδία) here translated children also expresses the relation, which a servant bears to his employer, and it has been thought that when Jesus asked the question, Have ye any fish, that He did so rather in the manner of one who asked to purchase from them. But He asked the question not with a view to buy, but to draw from them the confession of their own want of success.

7 Therefore that disciple whom Jesus loved saith unto Peter, It is the Lord. (Now when Simon Peter heard) that it was the Lord, he girt his fisher's coat unto him, (for he was naked), and (did cast) himself into the sea.[1]

(Alf. Simon Peter then, hearing—cast.)

---

[1] He girt his fisher's coat unto him for he was naked (τον ἐπενδύτην διεζώσατο· ἦν γὰρ γυμνός). Ἱμάτιον in its more restricted sense is used of the large upper garment, so large that a man would sometimes sleep in it (Exod. xxii, 26): the cloke as distinguished from χιτών, or close-fitting inner vest: and thus περιβάλλειν ἱμάτιον, but ἐνδύειν χιτῶνα. Ἱμάτιον and χιτών as the upper and the under garment, occur constantly together. (Acts ix. 39: Matt. v. 40: Luke vi. 29: John xix. 23.) Thus at Matt. v. 40, our Lord instructs His disciples 'If any man will sue thee at the law, and take away thy *coat* (χιτῶνα), let him have thy *cloke* (ἱμάτιον) also.' Here the spoiler is presumed to begin with the less costly, the under garment, from which he proceeds to the more costly, or upper: and the process of spo-

8 And the other disciples came (in a little ship) for they were not far from land, (but as it were two hundred cubits), dragging the net with fishes.

(Alf. In the boat—but about two hundred cubits off.)

As at the sepulchre it was not St. Peter, who was the first to perceive the Mysteries of the Incarnation, but St. John, so it was here. It was St. John who said unto Peter, It is the Lord. Probably there was something in the nature of the loving St. John, something more assimilated to Jesus Himself, that peculiarly fitted him to understand the revelation which He made of Himself. Peter, with his eager, ardent nature, was busied about the fish they had taken, and knew not that it was Jesus who addressed them. But when once he knew that it was Jesus, he could not wait till the boat reached the shore, near as it was, but threw on his upper tunic, and rushed through the sea to go to Him. Peter was toiling not absolutely naked, but bared to his inner vest. Out of reverence to Jesus he put on his upper or over tunic (τὸν ἐπενδύτην διεζώσατο.) Reckoning the cubit at eighteen inches would give 100 yards for the distance of the boat from the shore, when Peter cast himself into the sea.

9 As soon then (as they were come to land), (they saw) a fire of coals there, (and fish laid thereon), and bread.

(Alf. As they went on shore—they see—and fish lying thereon.)

10 Jesus saith unto them, Bring of the fish which ye have now caught.

11 [(Simon Peter] went up), and drew the net to land full of great fishes, an hundred and fifty and three:

---

liation being a legal one, there is nothing unnatural in such a sequence; but at Luke vi. 29, the order is reversed: 'Him that taketh away thy cloke (ἱμάτιον) forbid not to take away thy coat (χιτῶνα) also.' As the whole context plainly shows, the Lord is here contemplating an act of violent outrage: and therefore the cloke or upper garment, as that which would be the first seized, is also the first named. One was said to be γυμνός, who had laid aside his ἱμάτιον, and was only in his χιτών: not 'naked' as our translators have it (John xxi. 7), which suggests an unseemliness that certainly did not exist, but stripped for toil. It is naturally his ἱμάτιον which Joseph leaves in the hands of his temptress (Gen. xxxix. 12): while at Jude 23 χιτῶν has its fitness."—Archbishop Trench on *Synonyms of New Testament*, p. 175.

"All (five fishermen) wore the same kind of dress, a cloak or scarf (the 'fisher's coat'), and below it a short kilt. When a man had only this latter garment on, he was said to be 'naked.' This explains the expression used when Peter went into the sea to go to Christ—he girt his short loose dress about him with his Zummar (girdle)."—MacGregor's *Jordan*, p. 369.

and for all there were so many, (yet was not the net broken.)

[S. V. Therefore Simon Peter.]
(Alf. Simon Peter went aboard—the net was not rent.)

In this narration there are three separate events, all of a miraculous nature—the draught of fishes, the preserving the nets from breaking, which as St. John implies, in the natural course of things would have taken place, and the fire of coals with the fish laid thereon. The Evangelist does not say, in so many words, that Jesus created this fire of coals and the fish laid thereon for the occasion, but his whole narrative leads us to that conclusion.

It is probable that Jesus bade them bring of the fish which they had caught, partly that they might see the number which they had caught, and might thus recognise the greatness of the miracle, and partly that there might be sufficient to serve as a meal for them all. Many have concluded, from the careful way in which St. John records the exact number of the fish that were taken, a hundred and fifty and three, that some symbolical meaning was conveyed by this number. But the explanations hitherto given appear to recommend themselves, by their ingenuity rather than by their naturalness.

12 Jesus saith unto them, Come and dine. (And) none of the disciples durst ask Him, Who art Thou? knowing that it was the Lord.[1]

(Alf. Now.)

13 Jesus [then] cometh, and taketh (bread), and giveth them and (fish) likewise.[2]

[S.V. Omit, then.]
(Alf. Omits, then—the bread—the fish.)

14 [(This is now] the third time that Jesus shewed Himself) [to His disciples], after that He was risen from the dead.

[S. And this is now! S.V.A. To the disciples.]
(Alf. This third time now was Jesus manifested.)

" [1] Throughout all Greece, the natives seldom take any food before eleven o'clock, at which hour they have ἄριστον, which we translate dinner; then about eight or nine in the evening, they have δεῖπνον or supper, which is the chief meal. This explains the invitation of Our Lord to the disciples on the Lake of Galilee, Jesus saith unto them, 'Come and dine' (Δεῦτε ἀριστήσατε), that is, come and partake of the morning meal."—*Mission to the Jews from Scotland*, p. 342.

[2] Jesus then cometh, and taketh bread, and giveth them (ἔρχεται Ἰησοῦς καὶ λαμβανει τὸν ἄρτον καὶ δίδωσιν αὐτοῖς). "Every separate act of the wonderful occurrence is designedly specified, and, as it were, placed before the eyes."— Winer's *Grammar of New Testament*, p. 629.

They had been fishing all night without success. After they had taken the great draught of fishes, Jesus invites them to come and take their morning-meal (ἀριστήσατε). The ἄριστον was the morning meal, breakfast, usually taken at sun-rise.

Jesus taketh "the bread and the fish" (τὸν ἄρτον καὶ τὸ ὀψάριον) that is the bread and the fish, which they had seen lying on the coals of fire. He Himself probably partook of the fish which they had caught, in order to give them another proof of the truth and reality of His Resurrection Body. This is the second time that the Evangelists relate, that Jesus did eat before them, the third time that He appeared to the Apostles assembled together, which St. John here means, and the seventh time that He appeared at all after His Resurrection.

15 So when they had dined, Jesus saith to Simon Peter, Simon [son of Jonas], lovest thou Me more than these? He saith unto Him, Yea, Lord: Thou knowest that I love Thee. He saith unto him, Feed My lambs.[1]

[V. Son of John: S. Omits, son of Jonas.]

[1] Lovest thou me? "We have not, I believe, in any case attempted to discriminate between these two words, ἀγαπᾶς and φιλέω, in our English Version. It would not have been easy, perhaps not possible, to do it: and yet there is often a difference between them, one very well worthy to have been noted, if this had lain within the compass of our language: and which makes the two words to stand very much in the same relation to one another as 'diligo' and 'amo' in Latin. . . . . . Ernesti has successfully seized the law of their several uses, when he says: *Diligere* magis ad judicium, *amare* vero ad intimum animi sensum pertinet.' So that in fact Cicero in the following passage (Ep. Jam. xiii. 47) 'Ut scires illum a me non *diligi* solum, verum etiam *amari* is saying,—'I do not *esteem* the man merely, but I *love* him,' there is something of the passionate warmth of affection in the feeling with which I regard him.

"But from this it will follow, that while a friend may desire rather 'amari' than diligi by his friend, yet there are aspects in which the 'diligi' is a higher thing than the 'amari,' the ἀγαπᾶσθαι than the φιλεῖσθαι. The first expresses a more reasoning attachment, of choice and selection (diligere=deligere) from seeing in the object, upon whom it is bestowed, that which is worthy of regard; or else from a sense that such was fit and due toward the person so regarded, as being a benefactor, or the like: while the second without being necessarily an unreasoning attachment, does yet oftentimes give less account of itself to itself: is more instinctive, is more of the feelings, implies more passion.

"Out of this which has been said it may be explained, that while men are continually bidden ἀγαπᾶν τὸν Θεόν (Matt. xxii. 37; Luke x. 27: 1 Cor. viii. 3); and good men are declared to do so (Rom. viii. 28: 1 Pet. i. 8: 1 John iv. 21), the φιλεῖν τὸν Θεόν is commanded to them never. The Father, indeed, both ἀγαπᾶ τὸν υἱόν (John iii. 35): and also φιλεῖ τὸν υἱόν (John v. 20.)

"In almost all these passages of the New Testament the Vulgate, by the help of 'diligo' and 'amo,' has preserved and marked the distinction, which in each case we have been compelled to let go. It is especially to be regretted that at John xxi. 15-17, we have not been able to retain it, for the alternations are singularly instructive, and if we would draw the whole meaning of the passage forth, must not escape us unnoticed. On one occasion of that threefold 'Lovest thou Me?' which the risen Lord addresses to Peter, He asks him first, ἀγαπᾷς με; at this moment, when all the pulses in the heart of the now penitent apostle are beating with an earnest affection towards his Lord, this word on that Lord's lips sounds too cold: not sufficiently expressing the warmth of his personal affection towards

COMMENTARY ON ST. JOHN'S GOSPEL. 449

16 He saith to him again [the second time], Simon, [son of Jonas], lovest thou Me? He saith unto Him, [Yea], Lord; Thou knowest that I love Thee: He saith unto him, (Feed My sheep.)
[S. Omits, the second time: S. V. Son of John: S. Omits, Yea.]
(Alf. Keep My sheep.)

17 He saith unto him the third time, Simon, [son of Jonas], lovest thou Me? [Peter was grieved] because He said unto him the third time, [Lovest thou Me? And he said unto Him], Lord, Thou knowest all things; thou knowest [that I love Thee. Jesus saith] unto him, Feed My sheep.[1]
[S. V. Son of John: S. Now Peter was grieved: S. And lovest thou Me? And he saith unto Him: A. He (omits, And) saith unto him: V. Omits unto him: S. That I love Thee. And He saith.]

I. Jesus saith to Simon Peter, Simon, son of Jonas, lovest thou (ἀγαπᾷς) Me more than these?	he saith unto Him, Yea, Lord, Thou knowest that I love (φιλῶ) Thee.	He saith unto him, Feed (βόσκε) My lambs (τὰ ἀρνία μου).
II. He saith unto him again the second time, Simon, son of Jonas, lovest thou (ἀγαπᾷς) Me?	he saith unto Him, Yea, Lord, Thou knowest that I love (φιλῶ) Thee.	He saith unto him, Feed (ποίμαινε) My sheep (τὰ πρόβατά μου).
III. He saith unto him the third time, Simon, son of Jonas, lovest thou (φιλεῖς) Me?	Peter was grieved because He said unto him the third time, lovest thou (φιλεῖς) Me? And he said to Him, Lord, Thou knowest all things. Thou knowest that I love (φιλῶ) Thee.	Jesus saith unto him, Feed (βόσκε) My sheep (τὰ πρόβατά μου).

Him. Besides the question itself, which grieves and hurts Peter (ver. 17), there is an additional pang in the form which the question takes, sounding as though it were intended to put him at a comparative distance from his Lord, and to keep him there; or at least as not permitting him to approach so near to Him as he fain would be. He therefore in his answer substitutes for it the word of a more personal love φιλῶ σε (ver. 15). When Christ repeats the question in exactly the same words, Peter in his reply again substitutes his φιλῶ for the ἀγαπᾷς of his Lord (ver. 16). And now at length he has conquered:

for when the third time his Master puts the question to him, He does it—not any more with ἀγαπᾷς but φιλεῖς—with the word which Peter feels will express, even as it alone will express, all that is in his heart. The question, grievous anyhow, as seeming to imply a doubt in his love, is not any longer made more grievous still by the peculiar shape which it assumes. All this subtle and delicate play of feeling, disappears perforce, where the narration in the words used is incapable of being reproduced.'—Archbishop Trench, *Synonyms of New Testament*, p. 89.

[1] Feed My sheep.—" While βόσκεις

2 G

From a careful examination and comparison of our Saviour's three questions, and of St. Peter's answer to each of these questions, and of our Saviour's three separate charges to Peter, we shall be able to ascertain, what are the different shades of meaning in the words which they use, and thus to see what is the force implied in each question, and in each answer, and in each charge.

Jesus asks His first two questions "Lovest Thou Me," by ἀγαπᾶς,

and ποιμαίνειν are both often employed in a figurative and spiritual sense in the Old Testament (1 Chron. xi. 2 ; Ezek. xxxiv. 3 ; Ps. lxxviii. 72 ; Jer. xxiii. 2), and ποιμαίνειν in the New : the only occasions in the latter, on which βόσκειν is so used, are John xxi. 15, 17. There our Lord, giving to St. Peter that thrice-repeated commission to feed His 'lambs' (ver. 15), His 'sheep' (ver. 16), and again His 'sheep' (ver. 17), uses first βόσκε, then secondly, ποιμαῖνε, returning to βόσκε at the last. This return, on the third and last repetition of the charge, to the word employed on the first, has been a strong argument with some for an absolute identity in the meaning of the words. They have urged with some show of reason, that Christ could not have had *progressive aspects* of the pastoral work in His intention here, else He would not have come back in the end to the βόσκε, with which He began. Yet I cannot ascribe to accident the variation of the words, any more than the changes, in the same verses, from ἀγαπᾷν to φιλεῖν, from ἀρνία to πρόβατα. It is true that our Version, rendering βόσκε and ποίμαινε alike by 'Feed' as the Vulgate by 'Pasce,' has not attempted to follow the changes of the original text, nor do I perceive any resources of languages by which either our own Version or the Latin could have helped themselves here. The German, by aid of 'weiden' (=βόσκειν) and 'hüten' (=ποιμαίνειν), might have done it. De Wette, however, has 'weiden' throughout.

"The distinction, notwithstanding, is very far from fanciful. βόσκω, the Latin 'pasco,' is simply to feed: but ποιμαίνω involves much more : the whole office of the shepherd, the guiding, guarding, folding of the flock, as well as the finding of nourishment for it. Thus Lampe: Hoc symbolum totum regimen ecclesiasticum comprehendit: and Bengel, βόσκειν est pars τοῦ ποιμαίνειν. The wider reach and larger meaning of ποιμαίνειν makes itself felt at Rev. ii. 27 ; xix. 15, where at once we are conscious how impossible it would be to substitute βόσκειν.

"There is a fitness in the shepherd's work for the setting forth of the highest ministeries of men for the weal of the fellows, out of which the name, shepherds of their people, has been continually transferred to those who are, or should be, the faithful guides and guardians of others committed to their charge. Thus kings in Homer are ποιμένες λαῶν : nay more, in Scripture God Himself is a Shepherd (Is. xl. 11 ; Ezek. xxxiv. 11-31 ; Ps. xxiii.), and God manifest in the flesh avouches Himself as ὁ ποιμὴν ὁ καλός (John x. 11) : He is ἀρχιποιμήν (1 Peter v. 4): ὁ μέγας ποιμὴν τῶν προβάτων (Heb. xiii. 20) : as such fulfilling the prophecy of Micah, v. 4.

"But it may very naturally be asked, if ποιμαίνειν be thus so much the more significant and comprehensive word, and if on this account the ποίμαινε was added to the βόσκε in the Lord's latest instruction to His Apostle, how account for His going back to βόσκε again, and concluding thus, not as we should expect with the stronger, but with the weaker admonition? In Dean Stanley's *Sermons and Essays on the Apostolical Age*, p. 138, the answer is given. The lesson, in fact, which we learn from this is a most important one, and one which the Church, and all that bear rule in the Church, have need diligently to lay to heart: this namely, that whatever else of discipline and rule may be superadded thereto, still, the feeding of the flock, the finding for them of spiritual nourishment is the first and the last: nothing else will supply the room of this, nor may be allowed to put this out of that foremost place which by right it should occupy. How often, in a false ecclesiastical system, the preaching of the Word loses its pre-eminence : the βόσκειν falls into the background, is swallowed up in the ποιμαίνειν, which presently becomes no true ποιμαίνειν, because it is not a βόσκειν as well, but such a shepherding rather as God's Word by the prophet Ezekiel has denounced (xxxiv. 2, &c. ; cf. Zech. xi. 15-17 ; Matt. xxii.)."—Archbishop Trench on *Synonyms of New Testament*, p. 81.

Peter expresses his answer to both these, "Thou knowest that I love Thee," by φιλῶ. Jesus then takes up Peter's word, and asks His third question, "Lovest Thou Me," by φιλεῖς. To which Peter again replies as before, "Thou knowest that I love Thee," by φιλῶ.

It has been shown, (see note) that the word which Peter chose to express his answer to the question, "Lovest Thou Me," implied a stronger degree of personal affection than was contained in the word, which Jesus had Himself used, to convey His question the first and second time; and that when Peter continued to use the stronger form of expressing his love, that Jesus Himself asked His question the third time with the stronger word, and that Peter then replied as before.

In His first charge to Peter, "Feed My lambs," and in His last charge, "Feed My sheep," Jesus uses the word βόσκειν, and in His second charge, "Feed or keep My sheep," He uses the word ποιμαίνειν. The difference between these two words is, that the first implies to feed, in the sense of supplying with food, with spiritual nourishment, and the second to tend or keep, to guard and guide and protect, it may be, by a human system of discipline.

In His first charge Jesus says to Peter, "Feed my lambs," τὰ ἀρνία μου) and in the second and third, Keep and Feed My sheep (τὰ πρόβατά μου). In the first charge He bids Peter feed His "lambs," the newly-born, the tender in the faith, little children in Christ; in the second and third He bids him feed His "sheep," the more advanced in the faith, the young men, the fathers in Christ.

Jesus had changed Simon's name into Cephas or Peter (John i. 42), as a mark of honour, as the name by which he was to be known among the Apostles. But after He had Himself changed his name, He twice calls him Simon Bar-jona, or Simon son of Jonas; once on this occasion, probably to remind him of the natural weakness of his flesh and blood, without the sustaining power of God, and once before, when He tells him that flesh and blood had not revealed to him that Jesus was the Christ, the Son of the Living God. (Matt. xvi. 17.)

Before His Crucifixion Peter had said unto Jesus, "Though all men shall be offended because of Thee, yet will I never be offended." (Matt. xxvi. 33.) But now he was humbled at the recollection of his repeated denial of Him, and when He said unto him, "Simon, son of Jonas, Lovest Thou Me, more than these?" taught by past experience Peter is cautious and modest. He answers for himself and for his own love to Jesus, in the strongest form that language afforded him, but he says nothing of his love for Him as compared with that of the other disciples.

Peter was grieved because Jesus said unto him the third time, "Lovest thou Me." Perhaps it was, that he thought that He even yet feared for his constancy, or that he feared for it himself. His own weakness was an event never to be forgotten. A tradition, consistent enough with the probabilities of the case, records that the cock crowing, or the time of the cock crowing, always brought his denial of Jesus to his recollection.

Jesus does not put these questions or give these charges to the other Apostles, but only to St. Peter. Was it that he did this to Peter, because he alone had denied Him, and that He thus wished to reinstate him in his former position among the Apostles, and for each separate denial of Him, to give Peter an opportunity of declaring the depth of his affection, and of receiving from Him the personal assurance of His entire forgiveness, or at least an equivalent for this? Many have thought that this is the meaning of our Saviour's words to him.

Others have held that Jesus did not merely assure Peter of his pardon for his past denial, but that He also invested him with a degree of pre-eminence or primacy among the Apostles, or even of supremacy over the rest of his brethren; that he constituted Peter, and in Peter his successors, the centre and source of all ecclesiastical authority. But this is one of those doctrines or opinions which, as history shows, have flourished most at the greatest distance from the time of the persons to whom they relate. In writers of the ages immediately succeeding the Apostolic, a few traces may perhaps be found of the primacy of St. Peter, but none of the supremacy. This doctrine unknown in the earliest ages was gradually developed, as it was required to support the authority of those, who were called the succesors of St. Peter.

At the same time it is impossible to avoid the impression, that this chapter is little more than a record of the sayings and doings, either of Peter himself, or of Jesus to him. It is Peter, who first proposed to go a fishing: Peter, to whom John communicates his belief that it is the Lord: Peter, who in his eagerness to reach the Lord, casts himself into the sea: Peter, who drew the net to land: Peter, to whom Jesus three times addressed the question, "Lovest thou Me?" and to whom He as often committed the office of feeding His lambs or His sheep: it is Peter, whose death by crucifixion Jesus foretells, and it is Peter, who inquires of Jesus what would be the lot of St. John.

18 Verily, verily, I say unto thee, When thou wast young, thou girdedst thyself, and walkedst whither thou wouldest: but when (thou shalt be) old, thou shalt stretch forth [thy hands, and another shall gird thee, and (carry) thee whither thou wouldest not.]

[S. Thy hand, and others shall gird thee—and do to thee what thou willest not.]
(Alf. Thou art—shall carry.)

19 This spake He, signifying (by what death) he should

glorify God. And when he had spoken this, He saith unto him, Follow Me.

(Alf. By what manner of death.)

From our Saviour's words we may gather that at this time Peter was not young, nor yet old, but rather in the prime of life, and that his crucifixion would take place many years hence, when he was old. When he was old, another should gird him and carry him whither he would not, that is, to crucifixion, from which, however much in spirit he might wish to glorify God by martyrdom, there would still be a natural shrinking, through the weakness of the flesh.

All early writers agree that St. Peter was put to death by crucifixion in the reign of Nero, who reigned from A.D. 55 to 69—much about the same time that St. Paul also suffered. An early tradition says that at his own request he was crucified with his head downwards, as being unworthy of such an honour as crucifixion in the same way, in which his Lord and Master was crucified.

Some suppose that, when Jesus said to Peter "Follow thou Me," He meant him to imitate Him, to follow Him in his life by a zealous discharge of the pastoral office, and in his death by a willing martyrdom. Others think that in addition to this Jesus rose up, and that Peter followed, and that he thus expressed by his act what He had commanded in words. The latter explanation seems more in harmony with the following verse.

20 [(Then)] Peter, turning about, seeth the disciple, whom Jesus loved [following]; which also leaned on His breast (at supper), [and said,] Lord, which is he that betrayeth Thee?

[V. A. Omit, Then: S. Omits, following: S. And saith unto Him.]
(Alf. Omits, Then—at the supper.)

21 (Peter seeing) him saith to Jesus, Lord, and what shall this man do?

(Alf. Peter therefore seeing.)

22 Jesus saith unto him, If I will that he tarry till I come, what is that to thee? (follow thou Me.)

(Alf. Do thou follow Me.)

23 (Then went this saying) abroad among the brethren, that that disciple (should not die): (yet) Jesus saith not unto him, (He shall not die): but if I will that he tarry till I come, [what is that to thee]?

[S. Omits, what is that to thee.]
(Alf. This saying therefore went—was not to die—and yet—that he was not to die.)

It would seem that, when Jesus said to Peter "Follow thou Me," He rose up and that Peter followed, and that John and the other disciples began to follow at a little distance, and that then Peter seeing John asked the question, And what shall this man do? The Evangelist does not explain what Jesus meant by the words, "Till I come." His object was to give a true statement of the words, which Jesus used on this occasion, which had been incorrectly reported among the brethren, and which had thus given rise to a belief, that St. John would never die. There is no reason to suppose that he agreed with the current rumour respecting himself.

The two principal explanations, that have been given of our Saviour's words, "Till I come," are 1. Till He comes in the Day of Judgment. 2. Till He came to punish the Jewish nation for their rejection of Him the Messiah, by the destruction of Jerusalem, by the overthrow of their Temple, their worship, and of their very existence as a nation. This latter interpretation has been followed by many commentators, both ancient and modern.[1] But whatever may be the

---

[1] For the ancient Commentators who held this opinion see Cornelius à Lapide, and for the modern, Dean Alford. The following long extract from Lightfoot contains a full explanation of this and similar expressions in this sense:—

"'Till I come,' that is, till I come to destroy the city and nation of the Jews. As to this kind of phrase take a few instances.

"Our Saviour saith (Matt. xvi. 28), 'There be some standing here which shall not taste of death, till they see the Son of Man coming in His Kingdom.' Which must not be understood of His coming to the last judgment: for there was not one standing there that could live till that time:' nor ought it to be understood of His Resurrection, as some would have it, for probably not only some, but in a manner all that stood there, lived till that time. His coming, therefore, in this place, must be understood of His coming to take vengeance against those enemies of His, which would not have Him to rule over them. Luke xix. 12, 27."

He then goes on to show: 1. That the destruction of Jerusalem and the whole Jewish state is described as if the whole frame of this world were to be dissolved; 2. That the times immediately preceding this ruin are called the last days and the last times; 3. That the times and state of things immediately following the destruction of Jerusalem are called a New Creation, New Heavens, and a New Earth; 4. That the day, the time, and the manner of the execution of this vengeance upon this people are called, the day of the Lord, the day of Christ, His coming in the Clouds, in His Glory, in His Kingdom.

"I. The destruction of Jerusalem and the whole Jewish state is described as if the whole frame of this world were to be dissolved. Nor is this strange, when God destroyed His habitation and city, places once so dear to Him, with so direful and sad an overthrow. His own people whom He accounted of as much or more than the whole world beside, by so dreadful and amazing plagues. Matt. xxiv. 29, 30: 'The Sun shall be darkened,' &c. 'Then shall appear the sign of the Son of Man,' &c., which yet are said to fall out within that generation, ver. 24. 2 Pet. iii. 10: 'The heavens shall pass away with a great noise, and the elements shall melt with fervent heat,' &c. Compare with this Deut. xxxii. 2; Heb. xii. 26; and observe that by elements are understood the Mosaic elements; Gal. iv. 9, Coloss. ii. 20, and you will not doubt that St. Peter speaks only of the conflagration of Jerusalem, the destruction of the nation, and the abolishing the dispensation of Moses.

"Rev. vi. 12, 14: 'The Sun became black as sackcloth of hair,' &c., 'and the heavens departed as a scroll when it is rolled together,' &c. Where, if we take notice of the foregoing plagues, by which, according to the most frequent threatenings, He destroyed that people, viz., the sword, ver. 4, famine, ver. 5, 6, and the plague, ver. 8. Withal comparing those words, 'They say to the mountains fall on us and cover us,' with Luke xxiii. 30, it

COMMENTARY ON ST. JOHN'S GOSPEL. 455

meaning of these words " Till I come," we know that as a matter of
fact, St. John did survive the destruction of Jerusalem, the dispersion
of the Jewish nation, and the cessation of the Jewish worship, and
that St. Peter did not. Several dates have been fixed on for St. John's
death. One of the earliest of these is A.D. 101. This would be in
the ninety-third year of his age, and in the sixty-eighth from the
Crucifixion of Jesus. It is generally believed that St. John was the

will sufficiently appear that by those phrases is understood the dreadful judgment and overthrow of that nation and city. With these also agrees that of Jer. iv., from ver. 22 to 28, and clearly enough explains this phrase. To this appertain those and other such expressions as we meet with: 1 Cor x. 11, 'On us the ends of the world are come;' and 1 Pet. iv. 7, 'The end of all things is at hand.'

" II. With reference to this, and under this notion, the times immediately preceding this ruin are called the last days and the last times, that is, the last times of the Jewish city, nation, and economy. This manner of speaking frequently occurs, which let our St. John himself interpret. 1 John ii. 13: 'There are many Antichrists, whereby we know it is the last time;' and that this nation is upon the very verge of destruction, whenas it hath already arrived at the utmost pitch of infidelity, apostasy, and wickedness.

" III. With the same reference it is, that the times and state of things immediately following the destruction of Jerusalem are called a New Creation, New heavens, and a New earth. Isai. lxv. 17 : ' Behold I create a New heaven and a New earth.' When should that be? Read the whole chapter and you will find the Jews rejected and cut off, and from that time is that New Creation of the Evangelical world among the Gentiles.

" Compare 2 Cor. v. 17, and Rev. xxi. 1, 2, where, the old Jerusalem being cut off and destroyed, a new one succeeds, and new heavens and a new earth are created.

" 2 Peter iii. 13: 'We, according to His promise, look for new heavens and a new earth.' The heavens and the earth of the Jewish Church and Commonwealth must be all on fire, and the Mosaic elements burnt up: but we, according to the promise made to us by Isaiah the prophet, when all these are consumed, look for the new creation of the Evangelical state.

" IV. The day, the time, and the man-

ner of the execution of this vengeance upon this people, are called ' the day of the Lord,' ' the day of Christ,' His coming in the clouds ' in His glory,' ' in His kingdom.' Nor is this without reason, for from hence doth this form and mode of speaking take its rise.

" Christ had not as yet appeared but in a state of humility, contemned, blasphemed, and at length murdered by the Jews: His Gospel rejected, laughed at, and trampled under foot: His followers pursued with extreme hatred, persecution, and death itself. At length, therefore, He displays Himself in His glory, His kingdom, and power, and calls for those cruel enemies of His, that they may be slain before Him.

" Acts ii. 20 : ' Before that great and notable day of the Lord come.' Let us take notice how St. Peter applies this prophecy of Joel to those very times, and it will be clear enough, without any commentary, what that ' day of the Lord is.'

" 2 Thess. ii. 2 : ' As if the day of Christ was at hand,' &c. To this also do those passages belong. Heb. x. 37: ' Yet a little while, and He that shall come, will come.' James v. 9: ' Behold the Judge is at the door.' Rev. i. 7: ' He cometh in the clouds ;' and xxii. 12: ' Behold I come quickly ;' with many other passages of that nature, all which must be understood of Christ's coming in judgment and vengeance against that wicked nation. And in this very sense must the word now before us be taken and no otherwise, ' I will that he tarry till I come.' For thy part, Peter, thou shalt suffer death by thy countrymen the Jews: but as for him, I will that he shall tarry till I come and avenge Myself upon this generation : and if I will so, what is that to thee ? The story that is told of both these Apostles confirms this exposition : for it is taken for granted by all, that St. Peter had his crown of martyrdom before Jerusalem fell, and St. John survived the ruins of it."—Lightfoot, ii. 625.

youngest of the Apostles, and that he was the only survivor among them, at the overthrow of Jerusalem by Vespasian, A.D. 70.

24 This is the disciple [which testifieth] of these things, and wrote these things; and we know that his testimony is true.

[V. Which also testifieth.]

25 [And there are also many other things which Jesus did, the which, if they should be written every one, I suppose that even the world itself could not contain the books that should be written. [Amen.[1]]

[S.* Omits, this verse: V. A. Omit, Amen.]
(Alf. Moreover there are many other things—omits Amen.)

St. John closes his Gospel with a distinct and formal declaration of the truth of what he had written, as the testimony of an eye and ear witness. On the truth of these things he states his character for honesty and capacity. In the expression "we know that his testimony is true," he implies that there are others associated with him, whose belief in their truth is as strong as his own. Either they were a few who remained of those, who lived during our Saviour's Ministry, or they had gained this conviction from St. John.

To express the small number that he had recorded, but a very small number of the acts and miracles of Jesus, in comparison with the immense number which He wrought, the Evangelist uses an expression which seems almost to amount to exaggeration. What he means to say is that no language can express the number and the greatness of the works, which Jesus wrought while upon earth.

---

[1] And there are also many other things, &c.—"No extant manuscript favours the omission of ver. 25, although the hyperbole it contains caused it to be suspected by some, as we learn from the Scholia to Codd. 36, 237 and others. But it is quoted without the least misgiving by a long array of Patristic writers from Origen (who alleges it five times over), and Pamphilus downwards; and it is exactly in St. John's simple manner to assert broadly that which cannot be true to the letter, leaving its necessary limitation to the common sense of the reader."—Scrivener's *Introduction to Collation of Sinaitic MS.*, lix.

[INDEX

INDEX OF AUTHORS QUOTED IN THE NOTES.

Alford's, Dean, Greek Testament (sixth ed., 1868), p. 374, &c.

Beaufort's (Lady Strangford) Travels in Syria (1861), p. 61, 291.
Burgon, Rev. J. W., On the last Twelve Verses of St. Mark (1871), p. 11, 25, 187, 207, 238.

Carnarvon, Earl of, Druses of the Lebanon (2nd ed., 1860), p. 84.
Cornelius, à Lapide, Commentary on Holy Scripture, 17th cent. (Paris, 1864), 53, &c.

Dixon's, Hepworth, Travels in the Holy Land (1865), p. 3, 22, 41, 57, 60, 76, 86, 114, 155, 181, 208, 241, 243, 245, 261, 267, 270, 338, 401, 442.

Early Travels in Palestine (Bohn's ed., 1848), p. 141, 142.
Eothen (Tauchnitz ed.), p. 60.

Gladstone, Right Hon. W. E., Studies on Homer (1856), p. 12, 49.
——————————, Juventus Mundi (1869), p. 12, 352.

Irby and Mangles, Travels in the Holy Land (1844), p. 257, 292.

Johnson's, Dr. S., Dictionary with Quotations (1767), p. 270, 416.
Josephus' Antiquities, &c., p. 365, 440.

Lightfoot's, Dr. John, Works, 2 vols. (1684), p. 10, 11, 13, 14, 17, 19, 21, 23, 24, 29, 30, 31, 32, 34, 37, 44, 50, 57, 62, 65, 66, 72, 87, 89, 90, 95, 101, 109, 110, 111, 115, 116, 121, 122, 126, 161, 173, 175, 176, 187, 188, 211, 213, 214, 218, 235, 263, 367, 382, 397, 420, 441, 455.
Lightfoot, Dr. J. B., On Revision of the New Testament (1871), p. 95, 125, 135, 169, 178, 187, 206, 219, 232, 276, 305, 311, 315.
Lindsay's, Lord, Letters on the Holy Land (1839), p. 34, 43, 60, 249.
Lynch's, Lieut. W. F., Expedition to the Jordan and the Dead Sea (2nd ed., 1850), p. 22, 390.

Macleod's, Dr., Eastward, p. 1.
Macgregor's, Capt., Rob Roy on the Jordan (1869), p. 2, 7, 60, 129, 132, 136, 144, 446.
Macmillan, Rev., Treatise on the True Vine (1871), p. 120, 154, 276, 326, 328.
Middleton, Bishop T. F., On the Greek Article (new ed., 1833), p. 10, 69, 95, 98, 176, 188, 269, 295, 301, 343, 368, 374.
Mission to the Jews from Scotland (1839), p. 35, 214, 228, 298, 367, 447.
Mitford's History of Greece (8 vols., 1835), p. 270.

Norris, Canon, Key to the Narrative of the Four Gospels (new ed., 1871), p. 260, 414.

Origen's Works (Migne's ed., 1857), p. 25.

Pococke's, Bishop Rich. (1745), Travels in the East, p. 26, 43, 82, 84, 142, 143, 257, 389.

Porter, Rev. J. L., Giant Cities of Bashan (1867), p. 35.
——————————— Handbook to Palestine, Murray's (new ed., 1868), p. 4, 7, 236, 258, 264, 414, 422, 432.
——————————— Five Years in Damascus (1870), p. 225.

INDEX OF AUTHORS QUOTED IN THE NOTES.

Recovery of Jerusalem, Wilson, Warren, &c. (1871), p. 1, 2, 6, 30, 41, 42, 61, 77, 82. 106, 107, 110, 131, 143, 155, 214, 336, 444.

Robinson's, Dr. Ed., Biblical Researches in Palestine (1841), p. 82, 83, 87, 113, 291.
———————————— Later Researches (1856), p. 59, 74, 81, 228, 257, 415, 433.

Rogers, Miss, Domestic Life in Palestine (1862), p. 260, 291, 376, 390.

Sandays, Mr., Authorship and Historical Character of the Fourth Gospel (1872), p. 260, 304, 324, 367, 368, 396.

Scrivener's, Rev. F. H., Introduction to Criticism of the New Testament (1861), p. 19, 32, 111, 176, 187.
———————————— Collation of Sinaitic MS. (2nd ed., 1867), p. 19, 456.

Smith's Concise Dictionary of the Bible (2nd ed., 1871), p. 276, 321, 416.

Stanley's, Dean, Sinai and Palestine (3rd ed., 1856), p. 1, 2, 34, 191, 258, 264, 415, 422.

Thomson's, Dr. W. M., The Land and the Book (1863), p. 84, 226, 3 81.

Thrupp's Ancient Jerusalem, p. 367.

Trench, Archbishop, Authorised Version, p. 69, 88, 96, 221, 232, 272.
———————————— Synonyms of the New Testament (new ed., 1865), p. 13, 18, 22, 78, 102, 116, 122, 124, 172, 185, 262, 284, 297, 328, 340, 346, 368, 376, 387, 391, 393, 406, 446, 449, 450.

Williams's, Dr. G., Holy City (2nd ed., 1849), p. 364.

Wilson's Lands of the Bible (1847), p. 225, 389.

Winer's, Dr. G. B., Grammar of New Testament Diction, translated (sixth ed., 1866), p. 14, 15, 27, 56, 68, 79, 88, 92, 93, 97, 110, 112, 119, 121, 133, 138, 151, 164, 165, 167, 172, 173, 178, 179, 180, 181, 193, 196, 197, 200, 202, 207, 212, 215, 219, 220, 221, 223, 233, 238, 239, 240, 249, 250, 251, 261, 262, 270, 273, 281, 294, 295, 296, 301, 306, 307, 314, 316, 317, 323, 324, 329, 330, 333, 350, 355, 357, 360, 371, 373, 393, 395, 397, 407, 409, 411, 424, 438.

Wordsworth, Bishop Chr. (4th ed., 1863), p. 374, &c.

(459)

INDEX TO THE NOTES.

Advent, preparation for, p. 12.
Adulteræ pericope, accounted for, 186; explained, 188.
Advocate a better word than Comforter for παράκλητος, 311.
Αἰτέω and ἐρωτάω distinguished, 346.
Angel at the pool of Bethesda, quoted by Tertullian, 111.
Ἄν, when omitted, 221.
Ἀνακείμενος and ἀναπεσών distinguished, 305.
Anointed ἀλείψασα (xi. 2) refers to the former anointing (Luke vii.), 244.
Aorist does not express what is wont to be done, 197; Aorist Participle never employed as a Future, 244; only in appearance used as Future, 307, 330; Aorist in condition, imperfect in conclusion, 333; does not stand for a Perfect, 355.
Article, the, wrongly translated that, 178.
Ἀρχὴν τὴν, means, throughout, altogether, 196.
Αὐτὰ referring to a singular that has gone before, 320.

Baptism, place of Christ's, 25.
Bath, meaning of, 298.
Βασιλικὸς, how translated, 101.
Baskets when carried by the Jews and why, 136.
Βαστάζειν, 272.
Beds, 113.
Before ἔμπροσθεν an adverb of place not of time in John i. 15; wrongly translated by the Vulgate, 17.
Βεβληκότος, 294.
Bethany a more ancient reading than Bethabara in John i. 28, 25.
Bethesda, Pool of, 106; meaning of the word, 110; an angel at the pool quoted by Tertullian, 111.
Bethlehem, Jews believed that Christ would first appear here, a full grown man, 170.

Branch, κλῆμα and κλάδος distinguished, 328; branches of Palm-trees, βαΐα and κλῆμα distinguished, 276.
Brethren of Jesus, 43.
Burial, manner of, 260.

Caiaphas and the Council, 261.
Cake, Passover, 291.
Cana, whether Kefr Kana or Khurbet Kana, description of, 43.
Capernaum, place of Christ's abode, 30; meaning of the word, 50; description and modern site, 155.
Cedron, the brook, reading, meaning, 367.
Church lessons account for the omission of passages in MSS., 207.
Christ when used as a Proper name, 218.
Clay forbidden to be put on the eyes on the Sabbath-day, 213.
Cold of Jerusalem, 376.
Conditional clauses with εἰ, 323.
Culture, natural, in relation to supernatural, 352.
Crown, the, of thorns, 389.
Crown, διάδημα and στέφανος distinguished, 391.
Crucifixion in use among several nations, 393.
Cursing and swearing, a common habit among Orientals, 381.

Dealings, they have no, συγχρῶνται, meaning of, 89.
Δευτερόπρωτον Σάββατον, &c., 109.
Dedication feast of, what feast is meant, 235.
Departure from the Upper Room begun but delayed, 324.
Drawing, vessel for, ἄντλημα hauritorium, 90.

INDEX TO THE NOTES.

Drag, draw, σύρειν and ἑλκύειν distinguished, 284.
Dinner (ἄριστον) what time, 447.
Distance off, temporal and local, 251.
Dispersed the, among the Gentiles, among the Babylonians, and among the Greeks, 173.
Δοῦλος and θεράπων distinguished, 376.
Druses, origin of, 84.

Eat to, Christ's Flesh, expressed by two Greek verbs φάγω and τρώγω, 154.
Εἰ μή and εἰ οὐ distinguished, 240.
Εἶναι and γίνεσθαι distinguished, 206.
Effectual, redundant (James v. 16), 249.
Ἐκ with a Genitive not equivalent to a Genitive, 270.
Ἕκαστος with Plural verb, 350.
Ἐλέγχειν and ἐπιτιμᾶν distinguished, 30.
Ἐξένευσε (conveyed Himself away, John v. 13), how derived, 114.
Emmaus the ancient Nicopolis, 432.
Ἐν and διά distinguished, 357.
Ephraim, the same place as Ophrah, 264.
Evil, various meanings of, 121.
Examination of Jesus, 374.
Excommunication, different kinds of, 218.

Feast, gathering for, 266.
Feast-day, first day of the festival, week, 57.
Falsehood, father of, 202.
Feed to, βόσκειν and ποιμαίνειν distinguished, 449.
Fig-tree as a shade, 35.
Fish in Lake of Tiberias, 444.
Fold (ποίμνη) wrongly translated flock, 232.
For (ἀντί) meaning of, in grace for grace, 17.
Ford, Jesus safe at the Jordan-ford, 241.
Fountain of the Apostles, 250.
Fruitfulness, the end intended, 328.

Galilee, territorial divisions, character, chief towns, 2, 3; liable from its position to become lax, and to imitate Gentiles, 34; inhabited by a mixed population, 181.
Gates of Jerusalem, open and closed, 110.

Γάρ, inferential particle in a question, 178; causal particle, 230.
Genitive case, its meaning, 121.
Given (διδόμενον) not found in the Greek, (John vii. 39), 176.
Glory of the Son, 15.
"Go about" (ζητεῖτε) wrongly translated, 160.
God, occurs in New Testament more than 1300 times, never in the sense of a superior or inferior God, 10; His Name the same as Himself, 14.
"God" not "Son" in John i. 18 in some MSS., 19.

Hebrew tongue, in the, meaning of, 110.
Hereafter ἀπαρτί, 87.
High-priest, capriciously changed, 368.
Homer's works in relation to the Old Testament, 12.
Hosanna, 276.
Hour the, the appointed time, 281.
Houses in Palestine, 80.

Imperative mood not the same as the Future, 56; two connected by καί, 181; not simply permissive, 306.
Imperfect not to be translated by a Pluperfect, 116.
Ἱμάτιον and χιτών distinguished, 445.
Indicative Present, force of, 261.
Infants, Jewish notion respecting infants sinning, 211.
Inferential Particle γάρ in a question, 178.
Interpolations, as John and Jesus, in Scripture how explained, 25, 32.
Interpreted words, added by the Evangelist, 31.

Jacob's Well, description of, 81.
Jerusalem, its history, 5; general character, elevation, extent, walls, 6, 7; gradually became more Grecian in its architecture, 57; distance from Nazareth, 86.
Jerusalem, destruction of, an emblem of the end of the world, 454.
Jewish parties, 208.
Jews, the, mean Sanhedrin, 19, 116.
John Baptist bears witness not by one act, but by his whole ministry, 16, 25.
Johannean words, 326.

INDEX TO THE NOTES. 461

Jona, a common name among the Jews, 31.
Jordan, derivation of the name, its general character, length, &c., 59.
Journey from Jerusalem to the Jordan, 241.
Jude or Judas, 321.
Judæa, extent, government, mountains, barrenness, 3, 4.

Κλῆμα and κλάδος distinguished, 328.
Κλῆμα and βαΐα distinguished, 276.

Lake of Tiberias, names, character, size, 129; description of a storm on, 131; its navy, 132; Fish in it, 444.
Λαλιά and λόγος distinguished, 201.
Lazarus, 267.
Λαμπάς, λύχνος, and φανός distinguished, 368.
Light, lamp, not sufficiently distinguished in our Version, 124.
Love to, ἀγαπᾶν, and φιλεῖν distinguished, 448.
Λούω and νίπτειν distinguished, 297.

Meals, Eastern customs at, 296.
Mejdel or Magdala, 422.
Μή (μήτι) used when a negative answer is expected, 97, 172.
Μή and οὐ distinguished, 180; also, εἰ μή and εἰ οὐ, 240.
Miracle, Test of, 49.

Nathanael, spelt Nethaneel, an Old Testament name; while Philip, Andrew, and Nicodemus are of Greek origin, probably an Apostle, 33.
Nazareth, a beautiful description of it, comparing it in situation to a rose, 34; distance from Jerusalem, 86.
Negative, particle, wrong translation of, 96.
Negations, two or more produce one, 329.
Nicodemus came to Jesus that night, 62.
Nicopolis the same as Emmaus, 432.
Nouns plural with singular meaning, 14.

Officers, 172.
On (ἐπί) the well, 88.
Οὖν, meaning of, 200.
Οὗτος and ἐκεῖνος distinguished, 179.
Other, the, disciple, 374.

Palestine, character, extent, elevation, atmosphere, territorial division, 1, 2.
Παρά, after λαμβάνειν, distinguished from ἀπό, 233.
Παράκλητος, better translated Advocate than Comforter, 311.
Πᾶς with ἀλήθεια, 343.
Πᾶσαν appropriately placed (John v. 22) 119.
Palm-trees, the, meaning of the Article here, 276.
Passover, in the expression that they might eat the Passover (John xviii. 28), refers to the chagigah, not to the Paschal Lamb, 382.
Passover cake, 392.
Pavement, the, where it was, 396.
Pence, three hundred, 271.
Penny, inadequate expression of its value, 135.
Pericope adulteræ accounted for, 186; explained, 188.
Perception, verbs of, 200.
Perfect, when used for the Present, 438.
Pharisees used for Sanhedrin, 20.
Ποίμνη flock, wrongly translated fold, 232.
Pool of Siloam, 107, 214.
Present active particle expresses continuous action of faith, 119.
Present tense used to denote what is just about to take place, 239; only in appearance used for future, 314.
Preparation, the, 397.
Prophet, not any particular one foretold in Deut. xviii. 15, but a succession, 20.
Πρός, repeated before two substantives, 424.
Pronoun αὐτός used for emphasis, 371.
Purple robe, 392.

Rabbi, when first used, 29.
Reprove, to, and convince or convict, distinguished, 340.

Sabbath, first second-day (δευτερόπρωτον), 109; how observed in the Temple, 114.
Samaria, extent, chief towns, 3.
Samaritans, origin of, 83.
Sanhedrin, 208.
Sea of Galilee. (See Lake.)

Search the Scriptures (ἐρευνᾶτε τὰς γραφὰς), whether an Indicative or Imperative, 126.
Sepulchres, common form of, Christ's Sepulchre, 420.
Signs and wonders (τέρας, σημεῖον, &c.), distinguished, 101.
Siloam, Pool of, 107, 214.
Sheep, their habits, numbers in Palestine, 225.
Sheep-fold, low door into, 228.
Servant (δοῦλος, and minister (θεράπων), distinguished, 376.
Solomon's Porch, 236.
Spikenard, 270.
Spirit and truth, in (ἐν πνεύματι καὶ ἀληθείᾳ), 93.
Σπεῖρα ἡ, meaning of, 368.
Συνήχθη ὁ Ἰησοῦς, 368.
Σύρειν and ἑλκύειν, distinguished, 284.
Sychar, description of, 86.
Synagogue, number in Jerusalem, 336; White Synagogue in Capernaum, 336; put out of the Synagogue, 338.
Standeth (ἕστηκεν), or hath stood, 24.

Tabernacles, feast of, 161, 175, 191.
Talmudic traditions explanatory of Christ's words, 122.
Temple ἱερόν and ναός distinguished, 184.
Temple, Herod's, description of, 39.
Temples, the three, dates of, description of, 39.
Tombs in Palestine, 257.
Thieves and robbers (κλέπτης and λῃστής), distinguished, 387.
Thorns, the crown of, 389.
Tiberias, 440.
Τετήρηκεν, meaning of perfect tense, 273.
Three hundred pence, 271.
True saying, how with the article, and how without it, 98.

True, saidst true differs from saidst truly 92.
Thus ὄντως, meaning of, 86.
Truth, opposed not to what is false, but to what is imperfect and shadowy, 18.

Verses, differently divided, 11, 121, 324.
Verse 25, ch. xxi.; no authority for omission, 456.
Various readings caused by the commencement of a Church lectionary, 237.
Verily, a peculiar use by the Jews, 36 why doubled by St. John, 64.
Voice, Word, how distinguished, applied to the Baptist and to Christ, 21.

Wash to, λούω and νίπτειν distinguished, 297.
Water-supply of Jerusalem, 106.
Way, the, Christ Himself, wrongly translated this way, that way, 315.
Well, Jacob's, description of, 81.
Wells, mode of drawing water from, 82.
Woman, whether the disciples marvelled because Christ talked with a woman or with this particular woman, 95.
Wilderness of Judæa, its character, 22.
Withered, 111.
Word, not pronounced but substantial, common title for Son of God in Chaldee Paraphrast, 10.
World, its material and ethical meanings 13.

ὤν, peculiar use of, 219.

INDEX TO THE COMMENTARY.

Abraham's seed, meaning of, illustrated by events in his own household, p. 199.
Abraham's seed (σπέρμα) and Abraham's children (τέκνα) distinguished, 200.
Across, meaning of, as applied to the Lake of Galilee, 133.
Adricomius gives up the traditionary site of the feeding of 5000, followed by Reland and others, 143.
Against, probably a more appropriate rendering of ἐπὶ than upon, 258.
Amen, St. John always doubles it, 65.
Andrew, 280.
Annas had great influence, as ex-high-priest Sagan, father-in-law of Caiaphas, or as head of a Jewish party, 373.
Anointings of Jesus, how many, &c., 245.
Antichrists, said to have been sixty in number, 128.
Apostolical Succession, the Church's warrant for, 435.
Appearance of Jesus on the Resurrection-Day, 432.
Arculf's testimony as to the traditionary site of feeding the 5000, 141.
Arimathœa, Joseph of, 288, 415.
Ascension of the Human body into heaven a great Mystery, 314.
Avarice and treason to Christ intimately connected, 277.

Baptism, Christ's, how different from John's, 24, 73.
Bartholomew, same person as Nathanael, 33.
Believing a person and believing in a person, distinguished, 289.
Bethany, an older reading in John i. 28 than Bethabara, 25.
Bethesda, pool of, used for washing not animals but men, 111; the clause respecting the angel troubling the pool not found in certain MSS., but quoted by Tertullian, 112.
Bethphage, early tradition respecting its situation, 277.

Bethsaida situated on the west side of the Lake, 141.

Caiaphas, Joseph, high priest during Christ's Ministry, 373; his prophecy, 263.
Calendar for the Passover week, 268.
Calls with a loud voice to Lazarus, Jesus, why, 260.
Cana, our doubt as to its site does not affect the truth of the Gospel narrative, 43; distant from Capernaum, twenty-five miles, 103.
Christ used as a Proper name not until after His Resurrection, 355.
Come, in expression till I come, meanings assigned to, 454.
Communion with God through His Church, 227.
Crucifixion spoken of as an exaltation, 198; St. Mark and St. John's account of it, how reconciled, 399.

Day, My, meaning of, as applied to Abraham, 207.
Day, the, used of Jesus continuing with them, 212.
Death, not lawful for the Jews to put any man to, 384.
Dedication, feast of, 235.
Devil, his personality, a liar, &c., 202.
Didymus, meaning of, 250.
Door, the, into the sheepfold, Jesus 229.
Dread, Jesus not saved from, 282.

'Ενεβριμήσατο He groaned, meaning of, 255.
'Εσμεν used to express plurality of Persons, ἓν unity of substance (John x. 30), 238.
Ephraim, 264.

Eucharist, institution of, not recorded by St. John, where in his narrative it should come in, 303.
Examination of Jesus, two different opinions about it, 373.

Faith in His power required by Jesus before healing, 253.
Feed, βόσκε and ποίμαινε distinguished, 451.
Feet used as symbolic of the affections of the soul, 300.
Fifty years, time when the Levites were superannuated, 206.
Fulfilled, that the Scripture may be, 359.

Genuineness of chapter xxi. shown, 443.
Glory of God, 356.
Glorification of God, 308, 354.
God, used in two senses, 239; how He comes to a man, &c., 321.
Grace not given by Moses, 17.
Groaned He, ἐνεβριμήσατο, 255.

Hallel, the, what, when used, 366.
Harvest began at the Passover, 98.
Holy Spirit, office of, 341.
Hour, the tenth, 30; the sixth, 88; the seventh, 103.
Human nature of Jesus, subject to weakness, but kept free from sin, 324.

Incarnation, the, basis of the Christian Religion, and first battle-field in the Church, 9; how explained by the Catholic Church, 15; the cause of man's unbelief in the Incarnation, 71; those chosen as instruments in the Incarnation already eminent for their devout lives, 152; a right belief in the Incarnation necessary for salvation, 354.
Increase by death, 281.
Isaiah saw a representation of the Trinity, 287.
Iscariot, meaning of, 160.

John Baptist, how before Jesus and after Him, 17; mission of the Pharisees to John, 20; how not Elias, 22; his baptism compared with Christ's, 24; gives testimony to Jesus, 16, 18, 25; how did not know Jesus before His Baptism, 27; duration of his ministry, scene of it, 74; checks the jealousy of his disciples towards Jesus, 75.
John the Evangelist said to calculate time differently from the other Evangelists, 30, 88, 103, 399; never speaks of himself by name, 31; always doubles the Amen, 65; omits all the transactions of Christ's second year, 134; records no events of the first half of Christ's last year, 163; enters more fully than the other Evangelists into the Mystery of the Incarnation, 305; "to whom I shall give a sop," &c., spoken to John privately, 306; gives only one of the four reasons why Peter should put up his sword, 371; more receptive of the Mysteries of the Incarnation than Peter, 426; the only survivor of the Apostles at the destruction of Jerusalem, what is said to be the date of his Gospel, 455.
Judas Iscariot, 275; his feet supposed to have been washed first, 296; why chosen, not in ignorance, 302; present at the Paschal Supper, the washing of the feet, and the institution of the Eucharist, 306; sop given to Judas a mark of good will, 306.

Lazarus of Bethany, a rich man, &c., 245.
Lovest thou, φιλεῖς and ἀγαπᾶς distinguished, 450.
Law, the, compared with the kingdom of heaven, 18, 49; its ceremonial washings did not cleanse the heart, 68.
Life everlasting, meaning of, 79, 120, 151, 204, &c.; Jesus the source of life through eating His Flesh and drinking His Blood, 153, 156.
Life, Jesus lays down His life voluntarily, 233; used by Jesus partly of the body and partly of the soul, 252.
Lifted up understood of Crucifixion, 285.
Light used virtually of Jesus, and also personally, 12; difference between a light and the light, 12, 289.

Manna, the, contrasted with the true Bread, 149.
Mary, Blessed Virgin, meaning of Christ's words to her, "Woman, what have I to

do with thee?" 45; did not go with the other women to the tomb on the morning of the Resurrection, and why, 424; where next seen, 409.
Mary Magdalene and Mary of Bethany, were they the same, 245.
Merciful applied to the Father, 358.
Miracles, Christ's, their completeness usually shown, 113, 137; Jesus wrought the same miracles which it was foretold God would work, 125; why He prayed before His miracles, 136; traditionary site of the miracle of feeding the 5000 altered by Adricomius, though exposed by Cornelius à Lapide, followed by Reland and most modern Commentators, 143; do not necessarily carry conviction with them, 287.
Myrrh, large quantity of, 418; its nature and effect on the linen, 425.

Naked, in what sense Peter was, 446.
Nathanael, the same person as Bartholomew, 33; how an Israelite indeed, 36.
Nard Pistic, 271.
Nazareth, why objected to, 35; though generally included under the term Galilee, once used in contradistinction to it, 100.
New-birth, description of, 14, 65.
Nicodemus, his character, position, member of the Jewish Sanhedrin, 62; the effect of his conversation with Jesus on him, 72, 288; only mentioned by St. John, 418.
Night, the, used of Jesus' departure from them, 221.
Nobleman's son, not the centurion's son, 103.

Other, the, disciple, 375,
'Ορφανούς explained, 320.
Over, over the sea, meaning of, 145.

Palace of the high priest, 375.
Paneas, name changed to Cæsarea, 145.
Paschal Supper, St. John's account not easy to reconcile with the other accounts, 293.
Passover, St. John mentions three by name, the other Evangelists only one, 51; many things observed in the perpetual Passover, that were not in the Egyptian Passover, 53; the principal Feast of the Jews, 108; Jesus at Jerusalem at the third Passover, 164; meaning of the word Passover in the expression "but that they might eat the Passover" (xviii. 28), 382.
Petra, meaning of, applied to Peter, 32.
Peter, when he struck with the sword, 372; his three denials of Jesus where, 379; his primacy, 452.
Πέραν and its compounds, how used as applied to the Lake of Galilee, 133.
Philip, called to be Christ's disciple, 32; why appealed to before the miracle of multiplying the bread, 135, 280.
Pistic, Nard, 271.
Pococke, Bishop, testimony to the traditionary site of feeding the 5000, 142.
Porter of the Sheep-fold, the Holy Spirit, 230.
Prayer, Jesus the medium of all, 348.
Prays, Jesus, to the Father, not from lack of power, 259, 353.
Priests, high, frequently changed by the Roman Governors, 262.
Preparation, the, 397.
Presence, difference of Christ's, before the Resurrection and after, 444.
Prisoners, customary to release, at all the feasts, 388.

Resurrection of the unjust as well as the just, 122.
Resurrection not new to Martha, known to the Maccabees, 252; of Jesus supposed to have been privately revealed to Blessed Virgin Mary, 424.
Rock or Rocky, how applied to Peter, 32.
Routes, two, from Galilee to Jerusalem, 166.

Sabbath, law of, gave place to the law of Circumcision, 170.
Sœwulf's testimony to the traditionary site of feeding the 5000, 142.
Samaria, practice of the Galilæans to go through, on their way to Jerusalem for the feasts, 86.
Samaritan, Jesus called, 203.
Sanctification, 360.
Scourging a frightful punishment, 391.
Serpent, brazen, a type of the crucified God Incarnate, 70.

2 H

See to, and to show, how used with reference to the Father and the Son, 118.
Sheep of the fold, 230; other sheep, 234.
Shepherd of the fold, Jesus, 230.
Simon the leper, 269.
Sons of God, how made, 14.
Son, the, and the Father, One, 117, 118, 123; Son of Man will judge, 119.
Son of God, how understood by Pilate, 394.
Sop given to Judas a mark of goodwill, 306.
Sychar or Shechem, 87, 92.

Tabernacles, feast of, not celebrated in the Temple, 167; Reference to its ceremonies, 174.
Temple, what it includes, 53; in what part the market was held, 54; the three Temples, 56.
Testimony of the Baptist, 16, 18, 25; its admissibility in evidence, 194.
Tests, Jesus gives two, by which to know His doctrine, 168.
Tenth hour, 30.
Thirst, applied to the soul, 176.
Thomas, called Didymus, why called both; his zeal for Jesus, 250; his hardness of belief, 436; whether he did put his hand into His side, 437.
Time, St. John said to calculate it differently from the other Evangelists, 30, 88, 103, 399.
Tombs, form of Lazarus's, 258.
Thunder, a voice came to Jesus like, 283.
Τέκνια, how to be understood, 309.
"Touch me not," an imperfect rendering of μή μου ἅπτου, its meaning, 428.
Treasury, the most public place in the Temple, 195.

Unbelief of the Jews had a moral origin, 334.
Union between the Father and the Son, not adequately represented by the relation between a human father and his son, 316, 323; best expressed in the Athanasian Creed, 323.

Vine, Jesus the True, His Apostles branches, 327; why the vine was selected to illustrate the union between Jesus and His Apostles, 328.
Virgin Mary, not with the women on the morning of the Resurrection, why, 424; Jesus may have appeared to her privately, 424.

Washings, ceremonial, of the Law, did not convey the Holy Spirit, 68.
Washed in the Bath; its meaning, 299.
Washing of the feet not instead of the institution of the Eucharist, 304.
Water, symbolical of the Holy Spirit, 89, 91, 177.
Wine, quantity of, made from the water at the marriage feast, 48.
Word, the, Second Person in the Godhead, 10; author of all life, natural and moral, 11.
World, unbelievers, 341, 345, 350.

Zacharias, tradition respecting murder of, 207.

www.ingramcontent.com/pod-product-compliance
Lightning Source LLC
Chambersburg PA
CBHW021426300426
44114CB00010B/675